펼쳐 보면 느껴집니다

단 한 줄도 배움의 공백이 생기지 않도록
문장 한 줄마다 20년이 넘는
해커스의 영어교육 노하우를 담았음을

덮고 나면 확신합니다

수많은 선생님의 목소리와
정확한 출제 데이터 분석으로 꽉 찬
교재 한 권이면 충분함을

해커스북 ^{중·고등}
HackersBook.com

해커스
중학영어듣기
모의고사 24회가
특별한 이유!

최신 경향과 출제 패턴을 반영한 문제로 실전 대비!

1
최신 출제경향을
그대로 반영한
**양질의
실전 모의고사**

2
듣기 능력을 한 단계
업그레이드해주는
**만점 도전
고난도 모의고사**

3
시험에 매번 나오는
기출 유형을 익히는
**14개
대표 기출문제**

해커스 중학영어듣기 모의고사 24회

Level 1   Level 2   Level 3

다양한 버전의 음성으로 편리한 학습!

4

수준별로 속도를
선택해서 듣는
**기본 속도/1.2배속/
1.5배속 MP3**

5

복습이 간편해지는
**딕테이션 MP3/
문항별 MP3**

6

모든 음성 버전을
한 손에 쏙!
**문제 음성 듣기
QR코드**

해커스 중학영어듣기 모의고사 시리즈를 검토해주신 선생님들

경기
김하윤	프라임EM보습학원
이미림	다능학원
장윤진	골든클래스아카데미
조은혜	이든영수학원
최유리	제이엠학원
최희정	SJ클쌤영어

광주
박지수	JC에듀영어수학학원
조성영	이지스터디학원

대전
신주희	파써블영어학원

부산
정호경	A+단과학원

서울
이계윤	씨앤씨(목동) 학원
이지안	제임스영어
편영우	자이언학원

전북
김효성	연세입시학원

충남
성승민	SDH어학원 불당캠퍼스

해커스 어학연구소 자문위원단 3기

강원
박정선	잉글리쉬클럽
최현주	최쌤영어

경기
강민정	YLP김진성열정어학원
강상훈	평촌RTS학원
강지인	강지인영어학원
권계미	A&T+ 영어
김미아	김쌤영어학원
김설화	업라이트잉글리쉬
김성재	스윗스터디학원
김세훈	모두의학원
김수아	더스터디(The STUDY)
김영아	백송고등학교
김유경	벨트어학원
김유경	포시즌스어학원
김유동	이스턴영어학원
김지숙	위디벨럽학원
김지현	이지프레임영어학원
김해빈	해빛영어학원
김현지	지앤비영어학원
박가영	한민고등학교
박영서	스윗스터디학원
박은별	더킹영수학원
박재홍	록키어학원
성승민	SDH어학원 불당캠퍼스
신소연	Ashley English
오귀연	루나영어학원
유신애	에듀포커스학원
윤소정	ILP이화어학원
이동진	이룸학원
이상미	버밍엄영어교습소
이연경	명품M비욘드수학영어학원
이은수	광주세종학원
이지혜	리케이온
이진희	이엠원영수학원
이충기	영어나무
이효명	갈매리드앤톡영어독서학원
임한글	Apsun앞선영어학원
장광명	엠케이영어학원
전상호	평촌이지어학원
정선영	코어플러스영어학원
정준	고양외국어고등학교
조연아	카이트학원
채기림	고려대학교EIE영어학원
최지영	다른영어학원
최한나	석사영수전문
최희정	SJ클쌤영어학원
현지환	모두의학원
홍태경	공감국어영어전문학원

경남
강다원	더(the)오르다영어학원
라승희	아이작잉글리쉬
박주언	유니크학원
배송현	두잇영어교습소
안윤서	어썸영어학원
임진희	어썸영어학원

경북
권현민	삼성영어석적우방교실
김으뜸	EIE영어학원 옥계캠퍼스
배세왕	비케이영수전문고등관학원
유영선	아이비티어학원

광주
김유희	김유희영어학원
서희연	SDL영어수학학원
오진우	SLT어학원수학원
정영철	정영철영어전문학원
최경옥	봉선중학교

대구
권익재	제이슨영어
김명일	독학인학원
김보곤	베스트영어
김연정	달서고등학교
김혜란	김혜란영어학원
문애주	프렌즈입시학원
박정근	공부의힘pnk학원
박희옥	열공열강영어수학학원
신동기	신통외국어학원
위영선	위영선영어학원
윤창원	공터영어학원 상인센터
이승현	학문당입시학원
이주현	이주현영어학원
이헌욱	이헌욱영어학원
장준현	장쌤독해종결영어학원
최윤정	최강영어학원

대전
곽선영	위드유학원
김지운	더포스둔산학원
박미현	라시움영어대동학원
박세리	EM101학원

부산
김건희	레지나잉글리쉬 영어학원
김미나	위드중고등영어학원
박수진	정모클영어국어학원
박수진	지니잉글리쉬
박인숙	리더스영어전문학원
옥지윤	더센텀영어학원
윤진희	위니드영어전문교습소
이종혁	진수학원
정혜인	엠티엔영어학원
조정래	알파카의영어농장
주태양	솔라영어학원

서울
Erica Sull	하버드브레인영어학원
강고은	케이앤학원
강신아	교우학원
공현미	이은재어학원
권영진	경동고등학교
김나영	프라임클래스영어학원
김달수	대일외국어고등학교
김대니	채움학원
김문영	창문여자고등학교
김정은	강북뉴스터디학원
김혜경	대동세무고등학교
남혜원	함영원입시전문학원
노시은	케이앤학원
박선정	강북세일학원
박수진	이은재어학원
박지수	이플러스영수학원
서승희	함영원입시전문학원
양세희	양세희수능영어학원
우정용	제임스영어앤드학원
이박원	이박원어학원
이승혜	스텔라영어
이정욱	이은재어학원
이지연	중계케이트영어학원
임예찬	학습컨설턴트
장지희	고려대학교사범대학부속고등학교
정미라	미라정영어학원
조민규	조민규영어
채가희	대성세그루영수학원

울산
김기태	그라티아어학원
이민주	로이아카데미
홍영민	더이안영어전문학원

인천
강재민	스터디위드제이쌤
고현순	정상학원
권효진	Genie's English
김솔	전문과외
김정아	밀턴영어학원
서상천	최정서학원
이윤주	트리플a
최예영	영웅아카데미

전남
강희진	강희진영어학원
김두환	해남맨체스터영수학원
송승연	송승연영수학원
윤세광	비상구영어학원

전북
김길자	맨투맨학원
김미영	링크영어학원
김효성	연세입시학원
노빈나	노빈나영어전문학원
라성남	하포드어학원
박재훈	위니드수학지앤비영어학원
박향숙	STA영어전문학원
서종원	서종원영어학원
이상훈	나는학원
장지원	링컨더글라스학원
지근영	한솔영어수학학원
최성령	연세입시학원
최혜영	이든영어수학학원

제주
김랑	KLS어학원
박자은	KLS어학원

충남
김예지	더배움프라임영수학원
김철홍	청경학원
노태겸	최상위학원

충북
라은경	이화윤스영어교습소
신유정	비타민영어클리닉학원

영어듣기 만점을 위한 **완벽한 실전 대비서**

해커스
중학영어듣기
모의고사 24회

LEVEL
3

해커스 어학연구소

목차

기출 유형 분석

실전 모의고사

고난도 모의고사

• **정답 및 해설** [책 속의 책]

책의 구성과 특징

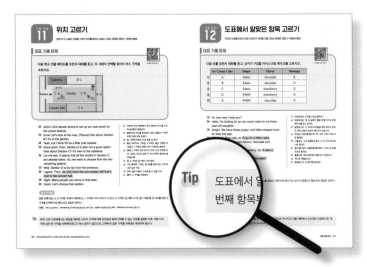

기출 유형 분석

<전국 16개 시·도교육청 공동 주관 영어듣기능력 평가>에 꼭 나오는 문제 유형을 철저히 분석했습니다. 14개 대표 기출 문제를 풀어보며 듣기 시험 전략을 적용해볼 수 있습니다.

유형별 빈출 오답 포인트나 자주 출제되는 단어, 표현 등 유용한 정보를 Tip에서 추가로 익힐 수 있습니다.

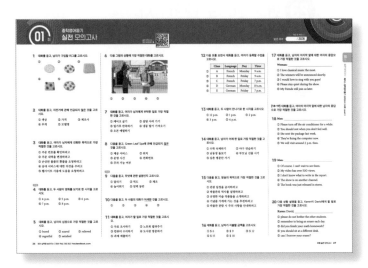

실전 모의고사 20회

실제 시험과 유형 및 출제 순서, 난이도가 동일한 20회분의 실전 모의고사 문제를 풀어보며 문제 풀이 능력을 향상시키고 듣기 실력을 쌓을 수 있습니다.

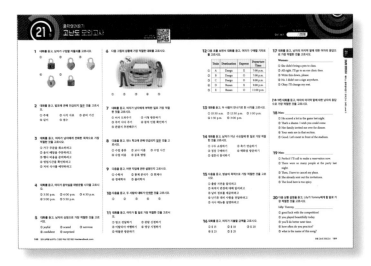

고난도 모의고사 4회

실제 시험보다 길이가 더 길고 어려운 표현이 쓰인 4회분의 고난도 모의고사를 풀어보며 실제 시험에서 어려운 문제가 나와도 흔들리지 않고 고득점을 받을 수 있도록 완벽히 대비할 수 있습니다.

Dictation

매회 문제 풀이 후 Dictation을 하며 정답 단서를 스스로 확인하고, 잘 못 들었던 부분도 다시 들으며 복습할 수 있습니다.

연음 등 잘 들리지 않는 발음과 빈출 표현을 **적중! Tip**에서 짚어보며 듣기 기본기를 확실히 다질 수 있습니다.

정답 및 해설

정답을 결정하는 단서와 자세한 해설을 통해 스스로 오답의 이유를 찾으며 다시 틀리지 않도록 확실하게 복습할 수 있습니다.

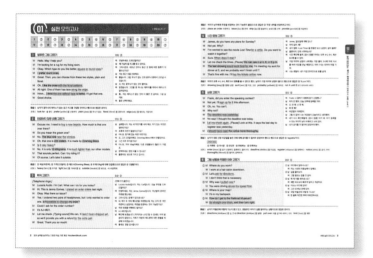

다양한 버전의 MP3

다양한 버전의 MP3를 이용해 학습 목적과 수준에 맞게 효과적으로 학습할 수 있습니다.

- 기출과 동일한 속도의 **기본 속도 MP3**
- 듣기 실력 향상을 위한 **1.2배속 / 1.5배속 MP3**
- 틀린 문제만 골라 다시 들으며 복습하는 **문항별 MP3**
- 대화문만 들으며 Dictation 하는 **딕테이션 MP3**

MP3 스트리밍 QR코드

매회 모의고사와 Dictation에 있는 QR코드로 간편하게 음성을 이용할 수 있습니다.
HackersBook.com에서 MP3 파일 다운로드도 가능합니다.

시험 소개

■ <전국 16개 시·도교육청 공동 주관 영어듣기능력평가>란?

<전국 16개 시·도교육청 공동 주관 영어듣기능력평가>는 **매년 4월과 9월, 총 두 차례**에 걸쳐 전국 16개 시·도교육청 주관 하에 시행되는 시험입니다.
학교에 따라 영어 내신 수행평가 점수에 5%~20%까지 반영되므로 실제 시험과 비슷한 모의고사를 풀어보면서 대비해두는 것이 좋습니다.

■ 문제 출제 패턴

매회 **총 20문제가 출제**되며, 시험에 나오는 문제 유형이 정해져 있고, 출제 순서도 매회 크게 달라지지 않는답니다.
최근에는 각 문제 유형이 아래와 같은 순서로 자주 출제되고 있습니다.

제1회 전국 16개 시·도교육청 공동 주관 영어듣기능력평가(중3)

1. 알맞은 그림 고르기	**11.** 할 일 고르기
2. 언급하지 않은 내용 고르기	**12.** 도표에서 알맞은 항목 고르기 출제율 43%
3. 목적 고르기	위치 고르기 출제율 43%
4. 시간 정보 고르기	시간 정보 고르기 출제율 14%
5. 심정 고르기 출제율 57%	**13.** 시간 정보 고르기 출제율 86%
장소 고르기 출제율 29%	위치 고르기 출제율 14%
그림 상황에 적절한 대화 고르기 출제율 14%	**14.** 한 일 고르기
6. 그림 상황에 적절한 대화 고르기 출제율 86%	**15.** 목적 고르기
장소 고르기 출제율 14%	**16.** 금액 정보 고르기
7. 부탁·요청한 일 고르기	**17.** 적절한 응답 고르기
8. 언급하지 않은 내용 고르기	**18.** 적절한 응답 고르기
9. 화제 고르기	**19.** 적절한 응답 고르기
10. 어색한 대화 고르기	**20.** 상황에 적절한 말 고르기

듣기 문제 풀이 Tip

듣기 문제를 풀 때에 어떤 문제 유형이든 빠짐없이 적용할 수 있는 두 가지 Tip이 있습니다. 어려운 문제도 수월하게 풀 수 있는 방법이니 기억해두고, 듣기 문제를 풀 때 꼭 실천하세요.

1 문제와 보기를 꼼꼼히 읽습니다.

음성이 나오기 전에 문제와 보기를 꼼꼼히 읽어두면 어떤 내용이 나올지 미리 파악할 수 있고, 대화에서 여자와 남자 중 어떤 사람의 말을 더 주의 깊게 들어야 할지 확인할 수 있습니다. 문제 음성이 끝나면 문제를 푸는 시간이 주어지므로, 음성이 끝나면 바로 정답을 체크하고, 남은 시간 동안 다음 문제와 보기를 확인해두면 좋습니다.

[문제지]

9 대화를 듣고, 여자가 대화 직후에 할 일로 가장 적절한 것을 고르시오.

① 기념품 사러 가기   ② 범퍼카 타러 가기

③ 퍼레이드 구경하기   ④ 핫도그 먹으러 가기

⑤ 안내데스크 방문하기

이 대화를 마치고 나서 여자가 할 일에 대해 언급하겠구나. 보기에 나온 단어를 말하는지 잘 들어보자.

2 음성은 끝까지 주의 깊게 듣습니다.

음성에서 여러 가지 선택지를 언급하다가 마지막 부분에서야 결정적인 정답 단서가 나오는 경우도 있으니 음성이 끝날 때까지 잘 듣고 정답을 고릅니다. 대화의 앞부분이나 일부 단어만 듣고 섣불리 정답을 판단하는 것은 좋지 않습니다.

[음성]

M Wow! The bumper cars were really fun.

W Yeah. It was so exciting.

M Where do you want to go next?

W Well... I feel a little hungry now.

M **Then why don't we have some hotdogs?**

W **Sounds good.** Let's go get some.

남자가 핫도그를 먹자고 제안했는데 여자가 좋다고 했으니 ④번이 정답! '범퍼카'에 속을 뻔 했지만 끝까지 잘 들었어!

기출 유형 분석

기출 유형 01 알맞은 그림 고르기

비슷한 그림들 중 대화에서 묘사한 특징과 일치하는 그림을 고르는 문제로, 매회 1문항씩 출제

대표 기출 문제

대화를 듣고, 여자가 구입할 쿠션을 고르시오.

▲ 음성 바로 듣기

① ② ③ ④ ⑤

M Hello, ma'am. What can I do for you?	남 안녕하세요, 손님. 무엇을 도와드릴까요?
W Hi, I'd like to buy a cushion.	여 안녕하세요, 쿠션을 사고 싶은데요.
M All right. These are the ones we have. There are square- and heart-shaped ones.	남 그러시군요. 이것들이 저희가 가지고 있는 것들입니다. 네모난 모양과 하트 모양의 것들이죠.
W Oh, I like these heart-shaped ones. I'll get one of them.	여 오, 저는 하트 모양이 좋네요. 그것들 중 하나로 살게요.
M Okay. And there are two styles, plain and striped.	남 알겠습니다. 그러면 무늬가 없는 것과 줄무늬의 두 가지 스타일이 있습니다.
W Well, I prefer a striped one.	여 음, 저는 줄무늬를 더 좋아해요.
M All right. One of them has the word "LOVE" on it.	남 그렇군요. 그것들 중 하나에는 'LOVE'라는 글자가 쓰여 있어요.
W I prefer the one without it. I'll take this one.	여 없는 게 더 좋네요. 이걸로 할게요.
M Okay.	남 알겠습니다.

정답 및 해설

여자가 하트 모양의 쿠션이 좋다고 했고, 줄무늬가 있으며 글자는 없는 것을 더 좋아한다고 했으므로 정답은 ④이다.

어휘 prefer [prifə́ːr] 통 좋아하다, 선호하다

Tip 알맞은 그림 고르기 문제에서는 사물의 모양, 무늬, 장식을 묘사하기 위해 특정한 어휘가 자주 쓰이므로 이를 미리 익혀둔다. 또한 각각의 특징을 한 번에 묘사하지 않고 여러 차례로 나눠서 설명할 수 있으므로 끝까지 주의 깊게 듣는다.

• round 둥근	• square 네모난	• heart-shaped 하트 모양의	• plain 무늬가 없는
• dot 물방울무늬	• stripe 줄무늬	• ribbon 리본	• pocket 주머니
• handle 손잡이	• wheel 바퀴	• zipper 지퍼	• button 단추

기출 유형 02
언급하지 않은 내용 고르기

담화나 대화에서 언급하지 않은 내용을 고르는 문제로, 매회 2문항씩 출제

대표 기출 문제

▲ 음성 바로 듣기

대화를 듣고, World Food Festival에 관해 언급되지 <u>않은</u> 것을 고르시오.

① 개최 시기 ② 행사 장소 ③ 프로그램
④ 참가비   ⑤ 기념품

W Honey, look at this poster about the World Food Festival.
M Oh, that's an annual festival held in early May, right?
W Yes. This year, it'll be held at the Seoul Grand Hotel. So, we can go.
M Great. Will there be special programs for kids?
W Oh, here it says there's a cooking program.
M Cool. Our kids would love it.
W Yeah. And tickets are only 8 dollars each if we get them by next weekend.
M Okay! Let's buy them today!

여 여보, World Food Festival에 관한 여기 포스터 좀 봐.
남 오, 그건 5월 초에 열리는 연례 축제잖아, 맞지?
여 응. 올해는 서울 그랜드 호텔에서 열릴 거야. 그러니까 우리도 갈 수 있어.
남 좋아. 아이들을 위한 특별한 프로그램들도 있을까?
여 오, 여기 요리 프로그램이 있다고 쓰여 있어.
남 멋진데. 우리 아이들이 좋아할 거야.
여 그러게. 그리고 티켓은 우리가 다음 주까지 산다면 한 장에 겨우 8달러야.
남 알겠어! 오늘 티켓을 사자!

정답 및 해설

① 개최 시기(5월 초), ② 행사 장소(서울 그랜드 호텔), ③ 프로그램(요리 프로그램), ④ 참가비(한 장에 8달러)에 대해 순서대로 언급한 반면, 기념품에 대해서는 언급하지 않았으므로 정답은 ⑤이다.

어휘 annual [ǽnjuəl] 형 연례의 hold [hould] 통 열다, 개최하다; 잡다

Tip 언급하지 않은 내용 고르기 문제에서는 일반적으로 선택지의 순서대로 내용을 언급하므로, ①부터 차례대로 언급되었는지 확인하며 듣는다.

목적 고르기

방송의 목적이나 대화 속 화자가 전화한 목적을 고르는 문제로, 매회 2문항씩 출제

대표 기출 문제

▲ 음성 바로 듣기

다음을 듣고, 방송의 목적으로 가장 적절한 것을 고르시오.

① 학교 규칙을 설명하려고
② 학생회 가입을 홍보하려고
③ 행사 장소 변경을 공지하려고
④ 행사 참여 방법을 안내하려고
⑤ 감사 표현의 중요성을 강조하려고

M Good afternoon! This is Matthew from the student council. This Friday is Friendship Day. There will be a special event. To take part in it, write a thank-you or apology letter to a friend. Then, come to the student council office before lunch. You can pick up a rose there to give your friend with the letter. Thank you very much.

남 안녕하세요! 저는 학생회의 Matthew입니다. 이번 주 금요일은 우정의 날입니다. 특별한 행사가 있을 예정입니다. 행사에 참여하려면, 친구에게 감사 편지나 사과 편지를 쓰세요. 그리고 나서 점심 시간 전까지 학생회실로 오세요. 그곳에서 편지와 함께 친구에게 줄 장미를 가져갈 수 있습니다. 정말 감사합니다.

정답 및 해설

이번 주 금요일에 있을 우정의 날 행사에 참여하기 위한 방법을 설명하고 있으므로 정답은 ④이다.

어휘 **student council** 학생회, 학생 위원회 **friendship** [fréndʃip] 圐 우정 **take part in** ~에 참여하다 **apology** [əpάlədʒi] 圐 사과

Tip 목적 고르기 문제에서는 한 번에 목적을 다 밝히지 않고 여러 차례로 나눠서 설명하거나 간접적으로 목적을 드러낼 수 있으므로, 방송이나 대화의 전체적인 맥락을 파악하며 듣는다.

기출 유형 04 시간/금액 정보 고르기

문제에서 물어본 시간이나 금액을 대화 속에서 파악하여 고르는 문제로, 시간 정보는 매회 2문항씩, 금액 정보는 1문항씩 출제

대표 기출 문제

▲ 음성 바로 듣기

대화를 듣고, 두 사람이 만나기로 한 시각을 고르시오.

① 1 p.m.   ② 2 p.m.   ③ 3 p.m.

④ 4 p.m.   ⑤ 5 p.m.

W Good afternoon, Mr. Kim. Do you have a minute?
M Sure. What is it?
W Would you be able to give me feedback on my essay?
M Sure. But I'm on my way to a teachers' meeting. Can you come back at 3 p.m. tomorrow?
W I'm afraid I have an after-school class then. Are you free at 5 p.m.?
M Let me see. *[Pause]* I'm meeting with another student then. Can you come at 4 p.m.?
W Yes. Thank you. I'll see you then.

여 안녕하세요, 김 선생님. 시간 괜찮으신가요?
남 물론이지. 왜 그러니?
여 제 에세이에 대해 피드백을 주실 수 있으실까요?
남 물론이지. 그런데 내가 교무 회의에 가는 길이란다. 내일 오후 3시에 다시 올 수 있겠니?
여 유감스럽지만 제가 그때는 방과 후 수업이 있어요. 오후 5시에는 한가하신가요?
남 어디 보자. *[잠시 멈춤]* 그때는 다른 학생과 만날 거란다. 오후 4시에 와 주겠니?
여 네. 감사합니다. 그때 뵐게요.

정답 및 해설

마지막에 남자가 오후 4시에 만날 것을 제안하자 여자가 그러겠다고 했으므로 정답은 ④이다.

앞서 제안된 오후 3시, 오후 5시는 둘 다 여자의 방과 후 수업과 남자의 학생 면담으로 인해 거절되었으므로 ③이나 ⑤를 고르지 않도록 주의한다.

어휘 feedback [fíːdbæk] 몡 피드백, 의견   after-school class 방과 후 수업

Tip 시간 정보 고르기 문제에서는 두 사람이 만날 시각 외에도 출발 시각, 시작 시각, 예약 시각, 만날 요일, 방문 날짜 등을 물어볼 수 있다.

기출 유형 05 심정/장소 고르기

대화 속 화자의 심정이나, 대화가 이루어지는 장소를 고르는 문제로, 둘 중 한 유형으로 매회 1문항씩 출제

대표 기출 문제

대화를 듣고, 남자의 심정으로 가장 적절한 것을 고르시오.

▲ 음성 바로 듣기

① bored   ② excited   ③ jealous

④ regretful   ⑤ surprised

W Tom, what's wrong?
M I wasted too much money buying unnecessary things again.
W Oh, you did! You told me you weren't going to do that again.
M I know, but I always end up spending much more than I plan.
W Did you spend all the money that you had saved for your trip?
M Yes... I should not have spent so much money.

여 Tom, 무슨 일이야?
남 난 또다시 쓸데없는 물건을 사는 데 돈을 너무 많이 썼어.
여 오, 그랬구나! 나한테 다시는 안 그러겠다고 말했었잖아.
남 맞아, 그런데 난 항상 내가 계획한 것보다 결국 더 많이 쓰게 돼.
여 여행을 위해 모아뒀던 돈을 전부 써버린 거야?
남 응... 그렇게 돈을 많이 쓰지 말았어야 했는데.

정답 및 해설

남자가 돈을 너무 많이 써버린 것에 대해 후회하고 있으므로 정답은 ④이다.

선택지 해석   ① 지루한   ② 신난   ③ 질투하는   ④ 후회하는   ⑤ 놀란

어휘   unnecessary [ʌnnésəseri] 형 쓸데없는, 불필요한   end up 결국 ~하게 되다

Tip   심정 고르기 문제에서는 사람의 감정을 나타내는 어휘나 표현이 자주 쓰이므로 이를 미리 익혀둔다.

- can't wait 기대되다
- surprised 놀란
- grateful 고마운
- satisfied 만족한
- relieved 안도한
- scared 무서운
- concerned 걱정스러운
- jealous 질투하는
- disappointed 실망한
- regretful 후회하는
- should have p.p. ~했어야 했는데 (하지 않았다)

기출 유형 06

그림 상황에 적절한 대화 고르기

주어진 그림 속 상황에 적절한 대화를 고르는 문제로, 매회 1문항씩 출제

대표 기출 문제

▲ 음성 바로 듣기

다음 그림의 상황에 가장 적절한 대화를 고르시오.

① ② ③ ④ ⑤

① **M** Good morning, how may I help you?
   W I'd like to order a pizza.
② **M** Can you put those books in the correct place?
   W Sure. I'll do that right away.
③ **M** Would you like to exchange the items or get a refund?
   W I'd like to return them.
④ **M** These bags are so heavy.
   W Let me help you carry them.
⑤ **M** Here's your order. Have a nice day.
   W Thank you. You too.

① 남 좋은 아침입니다, 무엇을 도와드릴까요?
   여 피자를 주문하고 싶어요.
② 남 저 책들을 올바른 장소에 꽂아 줄래?
   여 물론이지. 지금 바로 할게.
③ 남 물건을 교환하시겠습니까, 아니면 환불을 받으시겠습니까?
   여 전 환불받고 싶어요.
④ 남 이 가방들은 너무 무거워.
   여 내가 그것들을 나르는 걸 도와줄게.
⑤ 남 여기 주문하신 것 나왔습니다. 좋은 하루 보내세요.
   여 감사합니다. 당신도요.

정답 및 해설

음식점에서 점원이 주문받은 음료를 손님에게 전달하고 있는 상황이므로 정답은 ⑤이다.

어휘 exchange [ikstʃéindʒ] 통 교환하다 get a refund 환불받다

Tip 그림 상황에 적절한 대화 고르기 문제에서 그림에 팻말이나 말풍선이 있을 경우, 이는 대화의 장소나 상황을 빠르게 파악하도록 돕는 단서가 된다. 또한 선택지가 짧은 대화로 이루어져 있으므로 대화를 놓치지 않도록 집중하며 듣는다.

부탁·요청한 일 고르기

대화 속 화자가 부탁·요청한 일을 고르는 문제로, 매회 1문항씩 출제

▌대표 기출 문제

▲ 음성 바로 듣기

대화를 듣고, 여자가 남자에게 부탁한 일로 가장 적절한 것을 고르시오.

① 요리하기 ② 세탁하기 ③ 설거지하기

④ 옷장 정리하기 ⑤ 화장실 청소하기

M	Hey. What are you doing?
W	I'm cooking for Mom and Dad because it's Parents' Day.
M	They'll like that. I want to do something too.
W	Well, I'm also planning on doing the laundry and cleaning the bathroom. Would you like to do one of those things?
M	Yeah. Which should I do?
W	Can you do the laundry while I clean the bathroom?
M	Sure. Of course.

남 누나. 뭐 하고 있어?
여 어버이날이라서 엄마와 아빠를 위해 요리하는 중
　이야.
남 부모님이 좋아하시겠다. 나도 뭔가를 하고 싶어.
여 음, 나는 빨래랑 화장실 청소도 할 예정이야. 이 중
　에서 하나 할래?
남 그래. 어떤 걸 해야 할까?
여 내가 화장실 청소하는 동안에 빨래를 해 줄래?
남 물론. 당연하지.

> **정답 및 해설**

마지막에 여자가 남자에게 빨래를 해 달라고 부탁했으므로 정답은 ②이다.

어휘 do the laundry 빨래하다, 세탁하다

Tip 부탁·요청한 일 고르기 문제에서는 대화 마지막에 조동사 can이나 could를 써서 부탁하거나 요청하는 경우가 많으므로, 해당 표현이 나오면 주의 깊게 듣는다.

· **Can** you please order our meals first? 우리 식사 먼저 주문해 줄래?
· **Can** you buy me some medicine? 내게 약을 좀 사다 줄래?
· **Could** you go get the charger from the bedroom? 침실에서 충전기를 가져다줄래?
· **Could** you choose the clothes for the play? 연극 의상을 골라 줄래?

화제 고르기

담화에서 설명하는 대상이 무엇인지 고르는 문제로, 매회 각 1문항씩 출제

대표 기출 문제

▲ 음성 바로 듣기

다음을 듣고, 무엇에 관한 설명인지 고르시오.

① 골프 ② 축구 ③ 배구
④ 농구 ⑤ 발야구

M This is a team sport. It's one of the most popular sports in the world. Two teams play together. They usually play on a big grass field. Players pass a ball to each other by kicking it. Most of them can't touch the ball with their hands. Among the 11 players on a team, only one player can touch the ball with their hands. To score, players kick or head the ball into a large net.

남 이것은 단체 운동입니다. 이것은 세계에서 가장 인기 있는 운동 중 하나입니다. 두 팀이 함께 경기합니다. 그들은 보통 넓은 잔디밭 위에서 경기합니다. 선수들은 공을 차서 서로에게 패스합니다. 그들 중 대부분은 공을 손으로 만져서는 안 됩니다. 한 팀의 11명의 선수 중에서, 오직 한 선수만이 손으로 공을 만질 수 있습니다. 득점하기 위해, 선수들은 공을 큰 그물망 안으로 차거나 헤딩합니다.

정답 및 해설

이것(This)을 하는 선수들이 공을 차서 패스하고, 득점을 위해 그물망 안으로 공을 차거나 헤딩한다고 했으므로 정답은 ②이다.

어휘 kick [kik] 통 차다 net [net] 명 그물망, 네트

Tip 화제 고르기 문제에서 설명하는 대상은 운동, 음식, 물건, 직업, 장소, 동물, 교통수단 등과 같이 다양하다. 하지만 담화 초반에 모든 선택지에 적용되는 공통적인 특징이 언급되고 나서, 그 이후에 정답에 대한 구체적인 단서가 나오는 흐름은 동일하다. 따라서 담화에서 언급한 특징 모두에 해당하는 것이 무엇인지 파악하며 듣는다.

대표 기출 문제

▲ 음성 바로 듣기

다음을 듣고, 두 사람의 대화가 <u>어색한</u> 것을 고르시오.

①　　　②　　　③　　　④　　　⑤

① **M**　What's your favorite type of tea?
　W　They sell different kinds of tea.
② **M**　How long does it take to get to Busan?
　W　It takes about three hours by train.
③ **M**　I can't wait to see my best friend this weekend.
　W　You must be happy to see her.
④ **M**　Can we meet at 10 o'clock?
　W　I'm afraid I can't. I have a swimming lesson.
⑤ **M**　I can't believe I failed the test.
　W　Cheer up! You'll do much better next time.

① 남　네가 가장 좋아하는 차 종류는 뭐야?
　여　그들은 다양한 종류의 차를 팔아.
② 남　부산 가는 데 얼마나 오래 걸려?
　여　기차로 세 시간 정도 걸려.
③ 남　이번 주말에 내 절친을 만나는 게 너무 기대돼.
　여　그녀를 만나게 돼서 분명 행복하겠어.
④ 남　우리 10시에 만날 수 있을까?
　여　유감이지만 안 돼. 나 수영 수업이 있어.
⑤ 남　내가 시험을 망쳤다니 믿을 수 없어.
　여　힘내! 다음에는 훨씬 더 잘할 거야.

[정답 및 해설]

남자가 여자에게 가장 좋아하는 차의 종류를 물었으므로, 여자는 구체적인 차의 종류를 답해야 한다. 그러나 여자가 그들은 다양한 종류의 차를 팔고 있다는 어색한 대답을 했으므로 정답은 ①이다.

[어휘]　fail [feil] 통 망치다; 실패하다　**cheer up** 힘내다, 기운 내다

Tip　어색한 대화 고르기 문제에서는 짧은 대화로 이루어진 선택지가 연달아서 나오므로 집중력을 잃으면 대화를 놓치기 쉽다. ①부터 차례대로 O, X 표시를 하며 듣도록 한다.

기출 유형 10 할 일/한 일 고르기

대화 속 화자가 할 일 또는 한 일을 고르는 문제로, 매회 각 1문항씩 출제

대표 기출 문제

▲ 음성 바로 듣기

대화를 듣고, 여자가 할 일로 가장 적절한 것을 고르시오.

① 텐트 설치하기　　　　　　② 고기 구입하기
③ 여행 가방 챙기기　　　　　④ 캠핑장 예약하기
⑤ 캠핑 의자 대여하기

M	Honey, I'm so excited to go camping tomorrow.
W	Me too. Have you packed the tent and sleeping bags?
M	Yes, I did.
W	Excellent. What about the camping chairs and table?
M	I put them in the car already.
W	Good. We still have to get the most important thing we need, the meat for the barbecue!
M	Right. Let's go shopping for the meat.
W	I'll do it myself now. You've done a lot already.
M	Okay. Thanks.

남　여보, 난 내일 캠핑 가는 게 너무 기대돼.
여　나도 그래. 텐트랑 침낭은 챙겼지?
남　응, 챙겼어.
여　훌륭해. 캠핑 의자와 탁자는?
남　차에 이미 실어뒀지.
여　좋아. 우린 아직 우리에게 필요한 가장 중요한 걸 사야 해, 바로 바비큐용 고기 말이야!
남　맞아. 고기 사러 가자.
여　그건 이제 나 혼자서 할게. 당신은 이미 너무 많은 걸 했어.
남　알겠어. 고마워.

정답 및 해설

마지막에 남자가 여자에게 고기를 사러 가자고 제안하자, 여자가 그것은 자신이 혼자서 하겠다고 했으므로 정답은 ②이다.

[어휘] sleeping bag 침낭　meat [miːt] 명 고기

Tip 할 일 고르기 문제에서는 대화 마지막에 조동사 will 또는 be going to(~할 것이다)를 써서 할 일을 말하거나, 제안하는 표현을 이용하여 할 일을 언급하는 경우가 많으므로, 해당 표현이 나오면 주의 깊게 듣는다.

- **I will** cook for her this evening. 난 오늘 저녁에 그녀에게 요리해 줄 거야.
- **I'm going to** return the science book. 난 과학책을 반납하러 갈 거야.
- **Why don't you** ask her? 그녀에게 물어보는 게 어때?

기출 유형 11 위치 고르기

대화 속 두 사람이 선택할 구역의 위치를 배치도 상에서 고르는 문제로, 매회 0~1문항씩 출제

대표 기출 문제

▲ 음성 바로 듣기

다음 학교 건물 배치도를 보면서 대화를 듣고, 두 사람이 선택할 동아리 부스 구역을 고르시오.

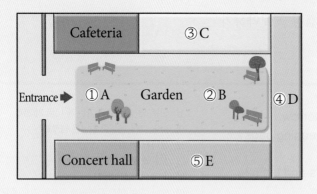

	내용
M	Jimin! Let's decide where to set up our club booth for the school festival.
W	Sure! Let's look at the map. *[Pause]* How about Section B? It's in the garden.
M	Yeah, but I think it'll be a little cold outside.
W	Good point. Then, Section A is also not a good option. How about Section C? It's next to the cafeteria.
M	Let me see. It seems that all the booths in Section C are already taken. So, we have to choose from the two remaining options.
W	Well, Section D is too far from the entrance.
M	I agree. Then, we only have the one section left that's next to the concert hall.
W	Right. Many people can come to that area.
M	Good. Let's choose that section.

남 지민아! 학교 축제에서 우리 동아리 부스를 어디에 설치할지 정해보자.
여 물론이야! 지도를 살펴보자. *[잠시 멈춤]* B 구역은 어때? 정원 안에 있잖아.
남 응, 그런데 야외는 조금 추울 것 같아.
여 좋은 지적이야. 그러면, A 구역도 좋은 선택은 아니겠다. C 구역은 어때? 거긴 구내식당 옆이야.
남 글쎄. C 구역의 모든 부스가 이미 다 찬 것처럼 보여. 그래서, 우리는 남은 두 가지 선택지 중에서 골라야만 해.
여 음, D 구역은 입구에서 너무 멀어.
남 나도 동의해. 그러면, 콘서트홀 옆에 있는 구역 하나만 남은 거네.
여 맞아. 많은 사람이 그곳에 올 수 있을 거야.
남 좋아. 그 구역을 선택하자.

정답 및 해설

정원 안에 있는 A, B 구역은 추워서 제외하고, C 구역은 이미 자리가 다 찼고, D 구역은 입구에서 너무 멀기 때문에, 콘서트홀 옆인 E 구역을 선택하기로 했으므로 정답은 ⑤이다.

어휘 set up 설치하다 remaining [riméiniŋ] ⑧ 남은, 남아 있는 option [ápʃən] ⑲ 선택지 entrance [éntrəns] ⑲ 입구

Tip 위치 고르기 문제에서는 정답을 제외한 나머지 구역에 대해 장단점과 함께 선택할 수 없는 이유를 설명한 이후, 대화 마지막에 남은 한 구역을 선택해야겠다고 하는 경우가 많으므로, 선택하지 않은 구역을 차례대로 제외하며 듣는다.

기출 유형 **12**

도표에서 알맞은 항목 고르기

주어진 도표를 보면서 대화 속 화자가 선택할 것을 고르는 문제로, 매회 0~1문항씩 출제

▎ 대표 기출 문제

▲ 음성 바로 듣기

다음 표를 보면서 대화를 듣고, 남자가 구입할 아이스크림 케이크를 고르시오.

	Ice Cream Cake	Shape	Flavor	Message
①	A	kitten	chocolate	X
②	B	kitten	chocolate	O
③	C	kitten	strawberry	X
④	D	puppy	strawberry	O
⑤	E	puppy	chocolate	X

W Hi, how may I help you?
M Hello, I'm looking for an ice cream cake for my three-year-old daughter.
W Alright. We have these puppy- and kitten-shaped ones for kids that age.
M She really likes cats, so I'll go for a kitten cake.
W Okay. They come in two flavors, chocolate and strawberry.
M She prefers chocolate to strawberry. So I'll take a chocolate one.
W Sure. Do you want a message on the cake?
M No, thanks.
W Okay. I'll get that ready for you.

여 안녕하세요, 무엇을 도와드릴까요?
남 안녕하세요, 제 세 살배기 딸을 위해 아이스크림 케이크를 찾고 있어요.
여 알겠습니다. 그 나이의 아이들을 위한 강아지 모양과 새끼 고양이 모양의 케이크가 있답니다.
남 제 딸은 고양이를 좋아하니까, 새끼 고양이 케이크로 할게요.
여 그렇군요. 그건 초콜릿과 딸기, 이 두 가지 맛으로 나와 있어요.
남 딸이 딸기보다 초콜릿을 좋아해요. 그러니까 초콜릿으로 할게요.
여 물론이죠. 케이크에 메시지를 남기시겠어요?
남 아니요, 괜찮습니다.
여 알겠습니다. 곧 준비해드릴게요.

정답 및 해설

남자가 새끼 고양이 모양에 초콜릿 맛의 아이스크림 케이크를 골랐고, 케이크에 메시지는 남기지 않겠다고 했으므로 정답은 ①이다.

어휘 flavor [fléivər] 명 맛, 풍미

Tip 도표에서 알맞은 항목 고르기 문제에서는 보통 세 가지 항목이 조건으로 주어지고 이를 대화에서 순서대로 언급하므로, 첫 번째 항목부터 차례대로 어떤 것을 선택했는지 표시하며 듣는다.

기출 유형 분석 **21**

적절한 응답 고르기

대화의 흐름상 마지막 말에 이어질 가장 적절한 응답을 고르는 문제로, 매회 3문항씩 출제

대표 기출 문제

▲ 음성 바로 듣기

대화를 듣고, 여자의 마지막 말에 대한 남자의 응답으로 가장 적절한 것을 고르시오.

Man: _____

① Sure. I'll see you on Friday.

② Okay. I'll be there at that time.

③ I'm sorry. You can't join that club.

④ Yes. I'm interested in the music club.

⑤ No. The library is not open on Wednesday.

W Ryan, this article says teenagers don't read many books these days.

M That's not surprising. I tried reading more books earlier this year, but I couldn't do it.

W I've been able to read more since I joined a book club a couple of months ago.

M Really?

W Yeah. It makes reading books fun because you get to share your feelings about them with others.

M Sounds interesting! I'd like to join.

W Everyone is welcome to join. We meet every Wednesday at 3 p.m. in the library.

M _____

여 Ryan, 이 기사에 십 대들이 요즘에 책을 많이 읽지 않는다고 쓰여 있어.

남 놀랄 일도 아냐. 나도 올해 초에 책을 더 많이 읽으려고 해봤는데, 못 했어.

여 난 몇 달 전 독서 동아리에 가입한 이후로 더 많이 읽을 수 있게 됐어.

남 정말?

여 응. 네가 책에 대해 느낀 점을 다른 사람들과 나눌 수 있게 되니까 동아리가 책 읽는 걸 재미있게 해줘.

남 흥미로울 것 같은걸! 나도 가입하고 싶어.

여 누구나 가입하면 환영이지. 우리는 매주 수요일 오후 3시에 도서관에서 모여.

남 _____

정답 및 해설

남자가 독서 동아리에 가입하고 싶다고 하자, 여자가 회원들이 매주 수요일 오후 3시에 도서관에서 모인다고 했으므로 정답은 ②이다. ①은 금요일에 보자는 말이므로, 수요일마다 모인다는 마지막 말에 대한 응답이 될 수 없다.

선택지 해석
① 물론이지. 금요일에 보자.
② 알겠어. 그때 거기로 갈게.
③ 미안. 넌 동아리에 가입할 수 없어.
④ 응. 난 음악 동아리에 관심이 있어.
⑤ 아니. 도서관은 수요일에는 열지 않아.

어휘 article [ɑ́ːrtikl] 몡 기사 teenager [tíːnèidʒər] 몡 십 대 share [ʃɛər] 동 나누다, 공유하다

Tip 적절한 응답 고르기 문제에서는 대화의 마지막 말을 놓치지 않도록 끝까지 집중하며 듣는다. 특히 마지막 말이 평서문일 경우, 마지막 말 외에도 대화의 전체적인 상황까지 고려하여 질문에 적절한 응답을 고른다.

기출 유형

14 상황에 적절한 말 고르기

담화 속 인물이 주어진 상황에서 하기에 적절한 말을 고르는 문제로, 매회 1문항씩 출제

대표 기출 문제

▲ 음성 바로 듣기

다음 상황 설명을 듣고, Mark가 Ms. Olivia에게 할 말로 가장 적절한 것을 고르시오.

Mark: Ms. Olivia, _____

① could you turn off the air conditioner for a while?

② I'm worried that it's too noisy in the library.

③ when did you clean the air conditioner?

④ is it okay to copy this science book?

⑤ I think the air conditioner is broken.

M Mark is a middle school student. Today, he's studying in the school library for his English test. Ms. Olivia, the librarian, turns on the air conditioner because it's too hot. After a few hours, Mark feels really cold. So, he would like to ask Ms. Olivia if she could stop the air conditioner for a short time. In this situation, what would Mark most likely say to Ms. Olivia?

Mark Ms. Olivia, _____

남 Mark는 중학생입니다. 오늘 그는 학교 도서관에서 영어 시험공부를 하고 있습니다. 사서인 Olivia 선생님은 날이 너무 더워서 에어컨을 켭니다. 몇 시간 후, Mark는 몹시 춥다고 느낍니다. 그래서 그는 Olivia 선생님에게 그녀가 잠깐 동안 에어컨을 멈춰줄 수 있는지 묻고 싶습니다. 이러한 상황에서, Mark가 Olivia 선생님에게 가장 할 것 같은 말은 무엇입니까?

Mark Olivia 선생님, _____

정답 및 해설

Mark가 Olivia 선생님에게 잠깐 동안 에어컨을 멈춰줄 수 있는지 묻고 싶다고 했으므로 정답은 ①이다.

선택지 해석
① 잠깐 에어컨을 꺼주실 수 있을까요?
② 도서관이 너무 시끄러워서 걱정이에요.
③ 언제 에어컨을 청소하셨나요?
④ 이 과학책을 복사해도 괜찮나요?
⑤ 에어컨이 고장 난 것 같아요.

어휘 air conditioner 에어컨 noisy [nɔ́izi] 혱 시끄러운 broken [bróukən] 혱 고장 난

Tip 상황에 적절한 말 고르기 문제에서는 담화 속 인물이 상대방에게 묻고 싶거나 부탁하고 싶은 말을 고르도록 출제되는 경우가 많다. 이때 ask if(~인지 묻다), ask A to B(A에게 B해달라고 부탁하다), tell A to B(A에게 B해달라고 말하다)와 같은 표현을 주로 사용하므로, 해당 표현이 나오면 주의 깊게 듣는다.

· Susie would like to **ask if** he is the owner of the wallet. Susie는 그가 지갑의 주인인지 묻고 싶습니다.
· Brian wants to **ask** her **to** take a picture again. Brian은 그녀에게 사진을 다시 찍어달라고 부탁하고 싶습니다.
· Crystal decides to **tell** him not **to** be late again. Crystal은 그에게 다시는 늦지 말라고 말하기로 결심합니다.

www.HackersBook.com

실전
모의고사

01~20회 실전 모의고사

1 대화를 듣고, 남자가 구입할 러그를 고르시오.

2 대화를 듣고, 자전거에 관해 언급되지 <u>않은</u> 것을 고르시오.

① 색상　　　② 가격　　　③ 제조사
④ 무게　　　⑤ 모델명

3 대화를 듣고, 여자가 남자에게 전화한 목적으로 가장 적절한 것을 고르시오.

① 주문 번호를 확인하려고
② 주문 내역을 변경하려고
③ 손상된 물품의 환불을 요청하려고
④ 응대 서비스에 대한 의견을 주려고
⑤ 웹사이트 사용에 도움을 요청하려고

고난도
4 대화를 듣고, 두 사람이 영화를 보기로 한 시각을 고르시오.

① 4 p.m.　　　② 5 p.m.　　　③ 6 p.m.
④ 7 p.m.　　　⑤ 8 p.m.

5 대화를 듣고, 남자의 심정으로 가장 적절한 것을 고르시오.

① bored　　　② scared　　　③ relieved
④ regretful　　　⑤ satisfied

6 다음 그림의 상황에 가장 적절한 대화를 고르시오.

① 　　　② 　　　③ 　　　④ 　　　⑤

7 대화를 듣고, 여자가 남자에게 부탁한 일로 가장 적절한 것을 고르시오.

① 케이크 굽기　　　② 설탕 사러 가기
③ 밀가루 반죽하기　　　④ 냉동 딸기 가져오기
⑤ 오븐 예열하기

8 다음을 듣고, Green Leaf Spa에 관해 언급되지 <u>않은</u> 것을 고르시오.

① 제공 서비스　　　② 위치
③ 운영 시간　　　④ 전화번호
⑤ 주차 가능 여부

고난도
9 다음을 듣고, 무엇에 관한 설명인지 고르시오.

① 달리기　　　② 역도　　　③ 체조
④ 높이뛰기　　　⑤ 암벽 등반

10 다음을 듣고, 두 사람의 대화가 <u>어색한</u> 것을 고르시오.

① 　　　② 　　　③ 　　　④ 　　　⑤

11 대화를 듣고, 여자가 할 일로 가장 적절한 것을 고르시오.

① 자료 조사하기　　　② 노트북 빌려주기
③ 컴퓨터 수리하기　　　④ 도서관 방문하기
⑤ 과제 제출하기

12 다음 표를 보면서 대화를 듣고, 여자가 등록할 수업을 고르시오.

	Class	Language	Day	Time
①	A	French	Monday	9 a.m.
②	B	French	Friday	9 a.m.
③	C	French	Friday	7 p.m.
④	D	German	Monday	10 a.m.
⑤	E	German	Friday	7 p.m.

13 대화를 듣고, 두 사람이 만나기로 한 시각을 고르시오.

① 12 p.m.   ② 1 p.m.   ③ 2 p.m.

④ 3 p.m.   ⑤ 4 p.m.

14 대화를 듣고, 남자가 어제 한 일로 가장 적절한 것을 고르시오.

① 수학 숙제하기   ② 야구 연습하기

③ 남동생 돌보기   ④ 부모님 선물 사기

⑤ 삼촌 병문안 가기

15 다음을 듣고, 방송의 목적으로 가장 적절한 것을 고르시오.

① 관광 일정을 공지하려고

② 박물관의 역사를 설명하려고

③ 유명한 미술 작품들을 소개하려고

④ 기념품 가게에 가는 것을 추천하려고

⑤ 박물관 관람 시 주의 사항을 안내하려고

16 대화를 듣고, 남자가 지불할 금액을 고르시오.

① $ 6   ② $ 9   ③ $ 12

④ $ 15   ⑤ $ 18

17 대화를 듣고, 남자의 마지막 말에 대한 여자의 응답으로 가장 적절한 것을 고르시오.

Woman: _____

① I love classical music the most.

② The winners will be announced shortly.

③ I would love to sing with you guys!

④ Please stay quiet during the show.

⑤ My friends will join us later.

[18-19] 대화를 듣고, 여자의 마지막 말에 대한 남자의 응답으로 가장 적절한 것을 고르시오.

18 Man: _____

① Please turn off the air conditioner for a while.

② You should rest when you don't feel well.

③ She sent the package last week.

④ They're fixing the computer now.

⑤ We will visit around 2 p.m. then.

19 Man: _____

① Of course. I can't wait to see them.

② My video has over 500 views.

③ I don't know what to write in the report.

④ The show is on another channel.

⑤ The book was just released in stores.

20 다음 상황 설명을 듣고, Karen이 David에게 할 말로 가장 적절한 것을 고르시오.

Karen: David, _____

① please do not bother the other students.

② remember to bring an eraser each day.

③ did you finish your math homework?

④ you should sit at a different desk.

⑤ can I borrow your eraser?

이회 중학영어듣기 실전 모의고사 Dictation 음성을 들으며 빈칸에 알맞은 단어를 채우시오.

1 | 알맞은 그림 고르기

대화를 듣고, 남자가 구입할 러그를 고르시오.

① ② ③

④ ⑤

W Hello. May I help you?
M I'm looking for a rug for my living room.
W Okay. Which type do you like better, _____ _____ _____ _____?
M I prefer round ones.
W Great. Then, you can choose from these two styles, plain and floral.
M Oh, I like the ones _____ _____ _____ _____.
W All right. One of them has lace _____ _____ _____.
M Hmm... I think _____ _____ _____ _____ is better. I'll get that one.
W Good choice.

2 | 언급하지 않은 내용 고르기

대화를 듣고, 자전거에 관해 언급되지 않은 것을 고르시오.

① 색상　② 가격　③ 제조사
④ 무게　⑤ 모델명

🎯 적중! Tip It is
[잇 이즈]보다는 [이리즈]로 들린다. [t]가 모음 사이에서 발음될 때는 약화되어 [r]에 가깝게 발음되기 때문이다.

M Excuse me. I need to _____ _____ _____ _____. How much is that one over there?
W Do you mean the green one?
M No. The blue one _____ _____ _____.
W Oh, that one is 225 dollars. It is made by Downing Bikes.
M _____ _____ _____ _____?
W No. It is only 10 kilograms. It is _____ _____ _____ our other models.
M That sounds perfect. Can I try riding it?
W Of course. Let's take it outside.

3 | 목적 고르기

대화를 듣고, 여자가 남자에게 전화한 목적으로 가장 적절한 것을 고르시오.

① 주문 번호를 확인하려고
② 주문 내역을 변경하려고
③ 손상된 물품의 환불을 요청하려고
④ 응대 서비스에 대한 의견을 주려고
⑤ 웹사이트 사용에 도움을 요청하려고

[Telephone rings.]
M Lucaria Audio. I'm Carl. What can I do for you today?
W Hi. This is Jenna Gomez. I _____ _____ _____ _____ last night.
M Okay. Was there an issue?
W Yes. I ordered two pairs of headphones, but I only wanted to order one. Is it _____ _____ _____ my order?
M Could I ask for the order number?
W It's AJ-4821.
M Let me check. [Typing sound] We can. It _____ _____ _____ _____, so we'll provide you with a refund _____ _____ _____.
W Great. Thank you so much!

4 | 시간 정보 고르기 [고난도]

대화를 듣고, 두 사람이 영화를 보기로 한 시각을 고르시오.

① 4 p.m.　② 5 p.m.　③ 6 p.m.

④ 7 p.m.　⑤ 8 p.m.

W James, do you have any plans for Sunday?

M Not yet. Why?

W I've wanted to see the movie *Lost Time* _____ _____ _____. Do you want to watch it together?

M Sure. _____ _____ _____ _____ ?

W Let me check the times. *[Pause]* We can see it at 4, 6, or 8 p.m.

M The last showing _____ _____ _____ _____ me. I'm meeting my aunt for dinner at 5, and we probably won't finish until 7.

W That's fine with me. I'll _____ _____ _____ _____ now.

5 | 심정 고르기

대화를 듣고, 남자의 심정으로 가장 적절한 것을 고르시오.

① bored　② scared　③ relieved

④ regretful　⑤ satisfied

> 🎯 적중! Tip　**No way!**
>
> 어떠한 상황이 믿기지 않음을 나타낼 때 사용되는 표현으로 '그럴 리가 없다, 말도 안 된다'라는 의미이다.
>
> · No way. It's impossible.
>   말도 안 돼. 그건 불가능해.

W Frank, did you enter the speaking contest?

M Not yet. I'll _____ _____ _____ _____ this afternoon.

W Oh, no. You can't.

M Why not?

W _____ _____ _____ _____.

M No way! I thought the deadline was today.

W _____ _____ _____ _____. *[Pause]* Look at this. It says the last day to register was yesterday.

M I _____ _____ _____ the notice more thoroughly.

6 | 그림 상황에 적절한 대화 고르기

다음 그림의 상황에 가장 적절한 대화를 고르시오.

①　②　③　④　⑤

① M Where do you work?

　 W I work at a hair salon downtown.

② M Let's _____ _____ _____.

　 W I don't think that is necessary.

③ M Why was I _____ _____ ?

　 W You were driving _____ _____ _____.

④ M Where is your map?

　 W It's in my backpack.

⑤ M How do I get to the National Museum?

　 W _____ _____ _____ _____, and then turn right.

대화를 듣고, 여자가 남자에게 부탁한 일로 가장 적절한 것을 고르시오.

① 케이크 굽기　　② 설탕 사러 가기
③ 밀가루 반죽하기　④ 냉동 딸기 가져오기
⑤ 오븐 예열하기

M What are you looking for, Mom?
W I can't find the flour _____ _____.
M Isn't it next to _____ _____ _____ _____?
W I thought so, but it isn't here.
M That's strange. *[Pause]* Oh, I forgot I put it _____ _____ _____ _____ last time I baked a cake.
W I see. Now, could you get _____ _____ _____?
M No problem.

다음을 듣고, Green Leaf Spa에 관해 언급되지 <u>않은</u> 것을 고르시오.

① 제공 서비스　　② 위치
③ 운영 시간　　　④ 전화번호
⑤ 주차 가능 여부

W Do you need to take a break from daily life? If so, you should visit Green Leaf Spa. We _____ _____ _____, such as massages and beauty treatments. All staff members _____ _____. We are located at 128 Center Avenue. Our hours are Monday to Saturday from 8 a.m. to 9 p.m. Call us at 555-9282 to _____ _____ _____. We hope to see you soon!

다음을 듣고, 무엇에 관한 설명인지 고르시오.

① 달리기　　② 역도　　③ 체조
④ 높이뛰기　⑤ 암벽 등반

W This is a sport that doesn't require a player to _____ _____ _____ _____. Players try to set a better record. They run fast and then _____ _____ _____ _____ a very high bar. The bar is raised when players jump over it. When a player hits the bar three times, they _____ _____ _____. To win, a player must leap _____ _____ _____ _____ of the other players.

다음을 듣고, 두 사람의 대화가 <u>어색한</u> 것을 고르시오.

①　②　③　④　⑤

🎯 적중! Tip did **y**ou
[디드 유]보다는 [디쥬]로 들린다. [d]로 끝나는 단어 뒤에 y-로 시작하는 단어가 이어지면 두 소리가 연결되어 [쥬]로 발음되기 때문이다.

① W What time did you go to bed last night?
　 M I _____ _____ _____ at 8 a.m.
② W Do you want to go to the hockey game next week?
　 M Sure! Let me buy the tickets.
③ W Can I use your smartphone?
　 M Yes. _____ _____ _____.
④ W Where did you find that scarf?
　 M It was _____ _____ _____ _____ my closet.
⑤ W Wow. That dance class was really exciting.
　 M I know. _____ _____ _____.

11 | 할 일 고르기

대화를 듣고, 여자가 할 일로 가장 적절한 것을 고르시오.

① 자료 조사하기　　② 노트북 빌려주기
③ 컴퓨터 수리하기　④ 도서관 방문하기
⑤ 과제 제출하기

> 🎯 적중! Tip　**need to**
> [니드 투]보다는 [니투]로 들린다. [d]와 [t]처럼 발음할 때 혀의 위치가 비슷한 자음이 나란히 나오면 앞 단어의 끝 자음이 탈락되기 때문이다.
> · spen**d t**ime [스펜타임]　· fron**t d**esk [프론데스크]

W What are you doing, Sehun?

M I'm trying to ＿＿＿＿＿ ＿＿＿＿＿, but it's so slow.

W Why don't you use your laptop instead?

M It's broken right now. I need to ＿＿＿＿＿ ＿＿＿＿＿.

W I understand. Do you have an urgent assignment to do?

M Yes. I need to ＿＿＿＿＿ for an essay.

W Then, I'll ＿＿＿＿＿ ＿＿＿＿＿ for today. You can use it for your research.

M That's ＿＿＿＿＿ ＿＿＿＿＿.

12 | 도표에서 알맞은 항목 고르기

다음 표를 보면서 대화를 듣고, 여자가 등록할 수업을 고르시오.

	Class	Language	Day	Time
①	A	French	Monday	9 a.m.
②	B	French	Friday	9 a.m.
③	C	French	Friday	7 p.m.
④	D	German	Monday	10 a.m.
⑤	E	German	Friday	7 p.m.

M Hi. What can I do for you today?

W Hello. I want to ＿＿＿＿＿ ＿＿＿＿＿.

M Okay. Here's our class schedule. Currently, we only have French and German classes.

W I'd like to study French ＿＿＿＿＿ ＿＿＿＿＿ ＿＿＿＿＿.

M Great. We have French on Mondays and Fridays.

W Hmm... I ＿＿＿＿＿ ＿＿＿＿＿ ＿＿＿＿＿ every Monday morning, so I can't take one then.

M Then, you can choose from the other two classes.

W I'll ＿＿＿＿＿ ＿＿＿＿＿ ＿＿＿＿＿.

13 | 시간 정보 고르기

대화를 듣고, 두 사람이 만나기로 한 시각을 고르시오.

① 12 p.m.　② 1 p.m.　③ 2 p.m.
④ 3 p.m.　⑤ 4 p.m.

M Hey, Katie. I'm going to the park tomorrow afternoon ＿＿＿＿＿ ＿＿＿＿＿ ＿＿＿＿＿ of the flowers. Do you want to come?

W Sure. When do you want to go?

M I want to get there by 3 p.m.

W Okay. Why don't we play badminton there together too? It'll ＿＿＿＿＿ ＿＿＿＿＿ ＿＿＿＿＿ for working out.

M I'd love to. Then, when should we meet?

W Is 2 o'clock okay?

M We will ＿＿＿＿＿ ＿＿＿＿＿ ＿＿＿＿＿. How about 1?

W That works for me.

14 | 한 일 고르기

대화를 듣고, 남자가 어제 한 일로 가장 적절한 것을 고르시오.

① 수학 숙제하기 ② 야구 연습하기
③ 남동생 돌보기 ④ 부모님 선물 사기
⑤ 삼촌 병문안 가기

W Why didn't you go to baseball practice yesterday, Brad?
M Unfortunately, I was _____ _____ _____.
W Really? What were you doing?
M Well, my parents visited my uncle in the hospital.
W I see. Did you go with them?
M No. I had to _____ _____ _____ _____ at home while they were at the hospital.
W What did you do with him?
M _____ _____, _____. He had lots of homework to do that day.

15 | 목적 고르기

다음을 듣고, 방송의 목적으로 가장 적절한 것을 고르시오.

① 관광 일정을 공지하려고
② 박물관의 역사를 설명하려고
③ 유명한 미술 작품들을 소개하려고
④ 기념품 가게에 가는 것을 추천하려고
⑤ 박물관 관람 시 주의 사항을 안내하려고

W Hi, everyone. Welcome to the Moss Museum of Fine Art. I'd like to _____ _____ _____ _____ before our tour begins. First, no food or drink is allowed. I will have to _____ _____ _____ if you bring any into the exhibit areas. Secondly, you may not take any photographs or videos. Just _____ _____ while you are here. Lastly, do not touch any of _____ _____ _____. Now please follow me into the east wing.

16 | 금액 정보 고르기

대화를 듣고, 남자가 지불할 금액을 고르시오.

① $ 6   ② $ 9   ③ $ 12
④ $ 15   ⑤ $ 18

🎯 적중! Tip one of
[원 오브]보다는 [워너브]로 들린다. 앞에 나온 단어의 끝 자음과 뒤에 나온 단어의 첫 모음이 연음되기 때문이다.
· have a [해버] · take out [테이카웃]

W Hello. Can I help you with anything?
M Hi. I need some new notebooks for school. Do you _____ _____ _____?
W This is one of our most popular notebooks, and it's just four dollars.
M That's perfect. I'll _____ _____ _____ _____.
W If you want some pens too, these are three dollars each. Are you _____ _____ _____?
M That's okay. I'll just take the notebooks for now.
W Okay. You can pay over here.

17 | 적절한 응답 고르기

대화를 듣고, 남자의 마지막 말에 대한 여자의 응답으로 가장 적절한 것을 고르시오.

Woman: _____

① I love classical music the most.
② The winners will be announced shortly.
③ I would love to sing with you guys!
④ Please stay quiet during the show.
⑤ My friends will join us later.

M Your performance _____ _____ _____ _____ was amazing, Sohee!
W Thanks. I practiced a lot.
M What kind of songs do you usually sing?
W _____ _____ _____ _____. I want to be in a famous band one day.
M Really? I'm actually in a band now.
W Wow! I didn't know that. Who do you play with?
M I play with Jaehong and Bohyun. You should _____ _____ _____.

18 | 적절한 응답 고르기

대화를 듣고, 여자의 마지막 말에 대한 남자의 응답으로 가장 적절한 것을 고르시오.

Man: _____

① Please turn off the air conditioner for a while.
② You should rest when you don't feel well.
③ She sent the package last week.
④ They're fixing the computer now.
⑤ We will visit around 2 p.m. then.

[Cellphone rings.]
W Hello?
M Hi. This is Global Technology Store. Is this Jiwon Kim?
W Yes, that's me.
M _____ _____ _____ your new air conditioner. It was going to _____ _____ _____ at 3 p.m.
W That's right. Is there a problem?
M Well, a few of _____ _____ _____ _____, so we can't make all of our deliveries. Is it okay if our team comes tomorrow instead?
W Oh, sure. But I _____ _____ _____ in the morning, so please come in the afternoon.

19 | 적절한 응답 고르기

대화를 듣고, 여자의 마지막 말에 대한 남자의 응답으로 가장 적절한 것을 고르시오.

Man: _____

① Of course. I can't wait to see them.
② My video has over 500 views.
③ I don't know what to write in the report.
④ The show is on another channel.
⑤ The book was just released in stores.

M Heather, what are you writing down?
W Oh, I'm just _____ _____ _____ for video ideas.
M I didn't know you made videos.
W I don't yet, but I want to _____ _____ _____ _____.
M What will your videos be about?
W I'm trying to decide between _____ _____ _____ or recording my daily life.
M I think the book idea is great. You know so much about books.
W Really? Would you _____ _____ _____?

> 🎯 적중! Tip **I'm trying to ~.**
> 어떤 일을 집중해서 하고 있거나 노력해서 하고 있음을 나타낼 때 사용되는 표현으로, to 다음에는 동사원형이 온다.
> · I'm trying to study English.
>   난 영어를 공부하려 하는 중이야.

20 | 상황에 적절한 말 고르기

다음 상황 설명을 듣고, Karen이 David에게 할 말로 가장 적절한 것을 고르시오.

Karen: David, _____

① please do not bother the other students.
② remember to bring an eraser each day.
③ did you finish your math homework?
④ you should sit at a different desk.
⑤ can I borrow your eraser?

W David and Karen are in the same math class. David often _____ _____ _____ an eraser to class. As he sits next to Karen, he _____ _____ _____ _____. The first time this happened, Karen did not mind. But now it is starting to bother her. She wants to tell David to always _____ _____ _____ _____ _____. In this situation, what would Karen most likely say to David?

실전 모의고사
음성 바로 듣기 ▶

1 대화를 듣고, 여자가 구입할 여행 가방을 고르시오.

2 대화를 듣고, 음악 앱에 관해 언급되지 <u>않은</u> 것을 고르시오.

① 이름   ② 구독료   ③ 특징
④ 음질   ⑤ 할인 정보

3 대화를 듣고, 남자가 여자에게 전화한 목적으로 가장 적절한 것을 고르시오.

① 숙제를 물어보려고
② 교과서를 빌리려고
③ 약속 장소를 변경하려고
④ 저녁 식사에 초대하려고
⑤ 수업 준비물을 알아보려고

4 대화를 듣고, 여자가 봉사활동을 하러 갈 시각을 고르시오.

① 9:00 a.m.   ② 10:30 a.m.   ③ 11:30 a.m.
④ 12:30 p.m.   ⑤ 2:00 p.m.

5 대화를 듣고, 여자의 심정으로 가장 적절한 것을 고르시오.

① shy   ② annoyed   ③ relieved
④ surprised   ⑤ regretful

고난도
6 다음 그림의 상황에 가장 적절한 대화를 고르시오.

①   ②   ③   ④   ⑤

7 대화를 듣고, 여자가 남자에게 부탁한 일로 가장 적절한 것을 고르시오.

① 회의 자료 찾기   ② 아침 준비하기
③ 차 열쇠 건네주기   ④ 커피 사 오기
⑤ 회사 데려다주기

8 다음을 듣고, Morris Elementary School Talent Show에 관해 언급되지 <u>않은</u> 것을 고르시오.

① 진행자   ② 공연 길이   ③ 참가 자격
④ 상품 종류   ⑤ 심사위원 수

9 다음을 듣고, 무엇에 관한 설명인지 고르시오.

① 송편   ② 김밥   ③ 만두
④ 햄버거   ⑤ 고로케

10 다음을 듣고, 두 사람의 대화가 <u>어색한</u> 것을 고르시오.

①   ②   ③   ④   ⑤

11 대화를 듣고, 남자가 대화 직후에 할 일로 가장 적절한 것을 고르시오.

① 쇼핑몰 가기   ② 문자 보내기
③ 학용품 사기   ④ 옷 구매하기
⑤ 음식 포장하기

12 다음 영화관 좌석 배치도를 보면서 대화를 듣고, 두 사람이 선택할 구역을 고르시오.

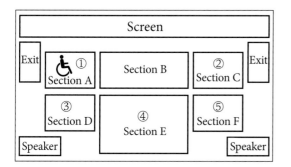

고난도

13 대화를 듣고, 두 사람이 만나기로 한 시각을 고르시오.

① 5 p.m.　　② 6 p.m.　　③ 7 p.m.

④ 8 p.m.　　⑤ 9 p.m.

14 대화를 듣고, 여자가 어제 한 일로 가장 적절한 것을 고르시오.

① 보트 타기　　　② 바다낚시 가기

③ 일광욕하기　　　④ 여행 가방 싸기

⑤ 모래성 쌓기

15 다음을 듣고, 방송의 목적으로 가장 적절한 것을 고르시오.

① 새로운 가게를 홍보하려고

② 지역 행사를 설명하려고

③ 멤버십 가입을 추천하려고

④ 운영 시간을 알리려고

⑤ 할인 정보를 안내하려고

16 대화를 듣고, 남자가 지불할 금액을 고르시오.

① $ 20　　　② $ 30　　　③ $ 40

④ $ 50　　　⑤ $ 60

17 대화를 듣고, 여자의 마지막 말에 대한 남자의 응답으로 가장 적절한 것을 고르시오.

Man: _____

① Okay. I'll show up early next time.

② She grows all kinds of fruits.

③ That's right! She'd love some of them.

④ There are more activities on the farm.

⑤ Let's change this basket for a smaller one.

[18-19] 대화를 듣고, 남자의 마지막 말에 대한 여자의 응답으로 가장 적절한 것을 고르시오.

고난도

18 Woman: _____

① We just sold out of that product.

② When will I receive the money?

③ She sent me the email yesterday.

④ I accidentally lost my receipt.

⑤ Your couch should be delivered tomorrow.

19 Woman: _____

① Let me know your phone number.

② Yes. We'll have steak and vegetables.

③ I'm so sorry about the delay.

④ I practiced dancing every day this week.

⑤ Of course. Here you go.

20 다음 상황 설명을 듣고, Martin이 가게 직원에게 할 말로 가장 적절한 것을 고르시오.

Martin: _____

① How much are these shoes?

② I usually run around five kilometers.

③ Do you have these in a smaller size?

④ Well, the shoes are too tight for me.

⑤ These blue ones are my style.

02회 중학영어듣기 실전 모의고사 Dictation 음성을 들으며 빈칸에 알맞은 단어를 채우시오.

1 | 알맞은 그림 고르기

대화를 듣고, 여자가 구입할 여행 가방을 고르시오.

① ② ③
④ ⑤

M Hello, do you need help?

W Yes. I'm looking for a suitcase _____ _____ _____ to France.

M All right. Would you like a suitcase with two wheels or four?

W I'd prefer a four-wheeled suitcase. It _____ _____ _____ _____.

M Okay. We have ones with prints and ones without them. They are all very trendy. You can choose any of these.

W I like simple things, so the ones _____ _____ _____ would be better.

M Good choice! Now, do you need one with a front pocket?

W Yes. That would be more convenient. So, I'll take the one _____ _____ _____ _____.

M Okay. I hope you have a wonderful trip.

2 | 언급하지 않은 내용 고르기

대화를 듣고, 음악 앱에 관해 언급되지 않은 것을 고르시오.

① 이름 ② 구독료 ③ 특징
④ 음질 ⑤ 할인 정보

W Do you use a music app, Ken?

M I do. I _____ _____ _____ on CloudR.

W What do you think of it?

M First of all, CloudR has more songs than other apps. And it _____ _____ that I would like _____ _____ my song lists.

W But isn't it a little expensive?

M It is 15 dollars per month. But it offers a discount with _____ _____ _____ credit cards.

W I only pay five dollars for the app I use.

M Well, that's _____ _____.

W Maybe I don't need to use CloudR then.

3 | 목적 고르기

대화를 듣고, 남자가 여자에게 전화한 목적으로 가장 적절한 것을 고르시오.

① 숙제를 물어보려고
② 교과서를 빌리려고
③ 약속 장소를 변경하려고
④ 저녁 식사에 초대하려고
⑤ 수업 준비물을 알아보려고

[Cellphone rings.]

W Hello, Brett.

M Hi, Kyla. Are you _____ _____ _____ _____?

W No. What do you need?

M I forgot my English textbook at school. I can't do my homework without it.

W Oh, do you want to _____ _____ _____?

M _____ _____ _____ _____, actually.

W Okay. Can you come pick it up now?

M What about after dinner? I could _____ _____ around 8.

W That's fine. I'll see you then.

4 | 시간 정보 고르기

대화를 듣고, 여자가 봉사활동을 하러 갈 시각을 고르시오.

① 9:00 a.m. ② 10:30 a.m. ③ 11:30 a.m.
④ 12:30 p.m. ⑤ 2:00 p.m.

🎯 적중! Tip **h**our

[아워]로 발음된다. 단어의 맨 처음에 쓰인 [h]는 묵음인 경우가 있다.

· **h**onor [아너] · **h**onest [어니스트]

W Hello. I'd like to do some volunteer work here this Saturday.
M We have a few programs. What time are you free?
W I'd like to _____ _____ _____ _____.
M We have a reading program at 9. Volunteers read to our patients during breakfast.
W That's a little early. Are there _____ _____ _____?
M We also have a game time _____ _____ 10:30.
W What time does that end?
M It lasts for an hour, so you'd be done by 11:30.
W That's perfect. I'll _____ _____ _____ then.

5 | 심정 고르기

대화를 듣고, 여자의 심정으로 가장 적절한 것을 고르시오.

① shy ② annoyed ③ relieved
④ surprised ⑤ regretful

M Is everyone enjoying my magic show so far?
W Yes. It's fantastic!
M For my next trick, I need a helper. _____ _____ _____?
W I'd love to!
M Thank you. Please _____ _____ to the stage.
W Alright. *[Pause]* What should I do for you?
M Please _____ _____ this magic hat.
W There's nothing inside the hat.
M _____ _____ _____. But now there's a rabbit inside it.
W Wow, amazing! I _____ _____ _____!

고난도
6 | 그림 상황에 적절한 대화 고르기

다음 그림의 상황에 가장 적절한 대화를 고르시오.

① ② ③ ④ ⑤

① M _____ _____ _____ is interesting.
   W What is it about?
② M Can I see your library card?
   W I _____ _____ _____ it.
③ M How long can I borrow books for?
   W Two weeks.
④ M What are you doing?
   W _____ _____ for my history test.
⑤ M What are you watching?
   W It's _____ _____ about gorillas.

7 | 부탁·요청한 일 고르기

대화를 듣고, 여자가 남자에게 부탁한 일로 가장 적절한 것을 고르시오.

① 회의 자료 찾기 ② 아침 준비하기
③ 차 열쇠 건네주기 ④ 커피 사 오기
⑤ 회사 데려다주기

🎯 적중! Tip mee**t**ing

[미팅]보다는 [미링]으로 들린다. [t]가 모음 사이에서 발음될 때는 약화되어 [r]에 가깝게 발음되기 때문이다.

· no**t**ice [노리스] · bo**tt**om [바럼]

W Why are you _____ _____ _____, Honey?
M I have a big meeting at work today, so I want to prepare for it.
W Do you want some breakfast? We have eggs and bacon.
M Sure. And do we have _____ _____ _____?
W Let me check. *[Pause]* Oh, no. We don't.
M I can go to the store _____ _____ _____.
W No. You _____ _____ and prepare for your meeting. I will go. Could you just _____ _____ the car keys on the table?
M Of course.

8 | 언급하지 않은 내용 고르기

다음을 듣고, Morris Elementary School Talent Show에 관해 언급되지 않은 것을 고르시오.

① 진행자   ② 공연 길이   ③ 참가 자격
④ 상품 종류   ⑤ 심사위원 수

M Welcome to the Morris Elementary School Talent Show. I am Principal Jim Williams, and I will _____ _____ _____ of the competition. Before we begin today, I want to explain the contest. Each student will have five minutes _____ _____. Four teachers will be the judges. The student _____ _____ _____ _____ from the judges will win. The prize for the winner is _____ _____ _____. I hope all of you enjoy the show today.

9 | 화제 고르기

다음을 듣고, 무엇에 관한 설명인지 고르시오.

① 송편   ② 김밥   ③ 만두
④ 햄버거   ⑤ 고로케

M This is enjoyed in various ways by people all over the world. It can be a snack, _____ _____ _____, or a meal. It is especially popular in Asia. To make it, you take flour and make some dough. Next, you make _____ _____ _____ _____ _____. Then, you put some filling inside. Popular things _____ _____ _____ are meat and vegetables. After you close the piece of dough, you boil it, fry it, or _____ _____.

10 | 어색한 대화 고르기

다음을 듣고, 두 사람의 대화가 <u>어색한</u> 것을 고르시오.

①   ②   ③   ④   ⑤

🎯 적중! Tip **want to**

[원트 투]보다는 [원투]로 들린다. 발음이 같은 자음이 나란히 나오면 앞 단어의 끝 자음이 탈락되기 때문이다.

① **M** Do you want to have the lesson in the morning or the afternoon?
   W _____ _____ is okay with me.
② **M** Excuse me. Where is the pool?
   W It's _____ _____ _____. I'll show you where it is.
③ **M** I saw that a new gardening store opened.
   W Oh, let's go there. We need some _____ _____ _____.
④ **M** It's too cold in here. Let's turn on the heater.
   W I think I _____ _____ _____ too.
⑤ **M** I'd like to speak with the manager.
   W I'm the manager. How can I help you?

11 | 할 일 고르기

대화를 듣고, 남자가 대화 직후에 할 일로 가장 적절한 것을 고르시오.

① 쇼핑몰 가기   ② 문자 보내기
③ 학용품 사기   ④ 옷 구매하기
⑤ 음식 포장하기

[Cellphone rings.]
M _____ _____, Wendy?
W Hi, James. What are you doing right now?
M I'm shopping at the mall. Why?
W Really? I need to _____ _____ _____. Can I join you?
M Sure. When can you come?
W I'll be there in 30 minutes.
M Okay. I'll _____ _____ _____ while I wait for you.
W Alright. I'll _____ _____ when I arrive.

12 | 위치 고르기

다음 영화관 좌석 배치도를 보면서 대화를 듣고, 두 사람이 선택할 구역을 고르시오.

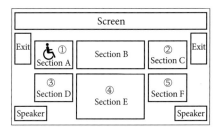

```
              Screen
Exit  ①  ⑴                    ②      Exit
    Section A   Section B    Section C
         ③                    ⑤
       Section D      ④    Section F
                  Section E
    Speaker                      Speaker
```

W Jack, should we get tickets for the movie tonight?

M Yeah, let's _____ _____. Where do you usually sit in a theater?

W I always sit _____ _____ _____ _____. I usually go to the restroom in the middle of the movie.

M One section is _____ _____ _____, so we can't sit there. Also, I like sitting near the speakers.

W It's okay to sit _____ _____ _____ this time.

M Thanks. It seems like Section D's already full. We can choose between E and F.

W How about the one _____ _____ _____ _____ and the exit?

M Great.

13 | 시간 정보 고르기

고난도

대화를 듣고, 두 사람이 만나기로 한 시각을 고르시오.

① 5 p.m.   ② 6 p.m.   ③ 7 p.m.
④ 8 p.m.   ⑤ 9 p.m.

> 🎯 적중! Tip   What are you up to ~?
> 무엇을 할 예정인지 또는 무엇을 하는 중인지 물을 때 사용되는 표현으로, to 다음에는 시간을 나타내는 말이 온다.
> · What are you up to tomorrow?
>   내일 뭐 할 거야?

[Cellphone rings.]

M Hi, Jenny. What are you up to this Friday?

W I'm going to _____ _____ _____ at the Coleman Gallery on that evening. Do you want to come?

M Well, _____ _____ _____ meet another friend at 9 p.m.

W We could go before then. I was _____ _____ _____ to the gallery around 5.

M I don't finish work until 6.

W Then, what about 7? We'll be done by 8 at the latest. So, you'll still have time to get to _____ _____ _____.

M Perfect. And how about coming with me after the exhibit? I'm sure my friend would love to meet you.

W Sure. I'd love _____ _____ _____.

14 | 한 일 고르기

대화를 듣고, 여자가 어제 한 일로 가장 적절한 것을 고르시오.

① 보트 타기   ② 바다낚시 가기
③ 일광욕하기   ④ 여행 가방 싸기
⑤ 모래성 쌓기

> 🎯 적중! Tip   li**tt**le
> [리틀]보다는 [리를]로 들린다. [t]가 모음과 단어 끝의 -le 사이에 있으면 약화되어 [r]에 가깝게 발음되기 때문이다.
> · ba**tt**le [배를]   · se**tt**le [새를]

M Mia, are you okay? Your face is a little red.

W Yeah. _____ _____ I was in the sun all day.

M What did you do?

W My family went to the beach for a week.

M Did you forget to _____ _____?

W I was so careful all week. But then we went on _____ _____ yesterday, and I forgot a hat and sunscreen.

M Oh, no. I hope _____ _____ _____ _____ soon.

W Thank you.

다음을 듣고, 방송의 목적으로 가장 적절한 것을 고르시오.

① 새로운 가게를 홍보하려고
② 지역 행사를 설명하려고
③ 멤버십 가입을 추천하려고
④ 운영 시간을 알리려고
⑤ 할인 정보를 안내하려고

M Good evening, customers. We hope you are finding everything you need at Nature's Market. Since it is the end of the day, we have _____ _____ _____ currently on sale. Our broccoli and cucumbers are _____ _____ 50% off right now. In addition, a few of our baked goods are also being sold at _____ _____ _____. Please pick up these products before we close to _____ _____ _____ these discounts. Happy shopping!

대화를 듣고, 남자가 지불할 금액을 고르시오.

① $ 20   ② $ 30   ③ $ 40
④ $ 50   ⑤ $ 60

W Welcome to Johnson City Aquarium. What can I _____ _____ _____?

M Hi. I'd like to buy two tickets. How much are they?

W A general ticket is 20 dollars, but a ticket for _____ _____ _____ is 30 dollars.

M Two tickets for the guided experience, please.

W Okay, then _____ _____ is 60 dollars.

M Can I use this discount coupon?

W Let me check. [Pause] Yes. You can _____ _____ _____ _____.

M Great. I'll pay with cash then.

대화를 듣고, 여자의 마지막 말에 대한 남자의 응답으로 가장 적절한 것을 고르시오.

Man: _____

① Okay. I'll show up early next time.
② She grows all kinds of fruits.
③ That's right! She'd love some of them.
④ There are more activities on the farm.
⑤ Let's change this basket for a smaller one.

W I'm sorry for being late. The bus took so long.

M That's okay. It's _____ _____ _____ here.

W Yes. But it is beautiful here. It's so nice being outside of the city.

M Right. It's so green here.

W I'm also _____ _____ _____ picking apples. How many apples can we pick?

M _____ _____ _____ this basket can hold.

W Great! We should _____ _____ to our teacher next week. She loves apples.

고난도

18 | 적절한 응답 고르기

대화를 듣고, 남자의 마지막 말에 대한 여자의 응답으로 가장 적절한 것을 고르시오.

Woman: _____

① We just sold out of that product.
② When will I receive the money?
③ She sent me the email yesterday.
④ I accidentally lost my receipt.
⑤ Your couch should be delivered tomorrow.

🎯 적중! Tip   Hold on.

전화 통화에서 상대방에게 전화를 끊지 말고 기다려달라고 말할 때 사용되는 표현이다.

· Please hold on a second.
  잠시만 기다려 주세요.

[Telephone rings.]

M Home Décor Warehouse. How can I help you?

W Hi. I want to check on _____ _____ _____ _____ _____.

M Alright. Can you tell me _____ _____ _____?

W I'm looking at the email with the purchase details, but I can't find the order number.

M It should be _____ _____ _____ of the email.

W Okay. Hold on. [Pause] It's G4BIWI.

M Got it. Thanks. So, _____ _____ _____ _____ about the refund?

19 | 적절한 응답 고르기

대화를 듣고, 남자의 마지막 말에 대한 여자의 응답으로 가장 적절한 것을 고르시오.

Woman: _____

① Let me know your phone number.
② Yes. We'll have steak and vegetables.
③ I'm so sorry about the delay.
④ I practiced dancing every day this week.
⑤ Of course. Here you go.

W Are you going to _____ _____ _____ _____ _____ tonight, Jaemin?

M Yes. I'll be there. It's at 5 o'clock, isn't it?

W Actually, it starts two hours later today.

M Oh, that's _____ _____. What about dinner?

W It's okay _____ _____ _____ _____ _____. We can eat and then practice.

M I need to tell my parents then. We usually have dinner together.

W You should _____ _____ _____.

M [Pause] I don't have my phone. I left it at home this morning. Can I _____ _____?

20 | 상황에 적절한 말 고르기

다음 상황 설명을 듣고, Martin이 가게 직원에게 할 말로 가장 적절한 것을 고르시오.

Martin: _____

① How much are these shoes?
② I usually run around five kilometers.
③ Do you have these in a smaller size?
④ Well, the shoes are too tight for me.
⑤ These blue ones are my style.

M Martin needs some new running shoes, so he visits _____ _____ _____ to look at some. He _____ _____ lots of shoes until he finally finds a pair that he likes. They are blue and very comfortable. However, they are _____ _____ _____ _____. So, Martin wants to ask the store employee for _____ _____ _____. In this situation, what would Martin most likely say to the store employee?

1 대화를 듣고, 여자가 구입할 치마를 고르시오.

① ② ③

④ ⑤

고난도
2 대화를 듣고, 작문 과제에 관해 언급되지 않은 것을 고르시오.

① 주제 　　② 요구 분량 　　③ 실제 제출일
④ 양식 　　⑤ 마감 기한

3 대화를 듣고, 남자가 여자에게 전화한 목적으로 가장 적절한 것을 고르시오.

① 새로운 식자재를 주문하려고
② 식당을 예약하려고
③ 배송 상태를 확인하려고
④ 도로 상황을 안내하려고
⑤ 배달 지연을 알리려고

4 대화를 듣고, 어머니가 아들을 데리러 갈 시각을 고르시오.

① 2:00 p.m. 　　② 2:30 p.m. 　　③ 3:00 p.m.
④ 3:30 p.m. 　　⑤ 4:00 p.m.

5 대화를 듣고, 두 사람이 대화하는 장소로 가장 적절한 곳을 고르시오.

① 문구점 　　　　　② 자동차 정비소
③ 슈퍼마켓 　　　　④ 옷 가게
⑤ 세탁소

6 다음 그림의 상황에 가장 적절한 대화를 고르시오.

① 　　② 　　③ 　　④ 　　⑤

7 대화를 듣고, 여자가 남자에게 부탁한 일로 가장 적절한 것을 고르시오.

① 방충제 뿌리기 　　　② 담요 준비하기
③ 텐트 설치하기 　　　④ 자외선 차단제 꺼내기
⑤ 스피커 챙기기

8 다음을 듣고, 도서 박람회에 관해 언급되지 않은 것을 고르시오.

① 장소 　　② 날짜 　　③ 지불 방법
④ 웹사이트 　　⑤ 기념품

9 다음을 듣고, 어떤 직업에 관한 설명인지 고르시오.

① 비평가 　　② 지휘자 　　③ 큐레이터
④ 합창단원 　　⑤ 피아니스트

10 다음을 듣고, 두 사람의 대화가 어색한 것을 고르시오.

① 　　② 　　③ 　　④ 　　⑤

11 대화를 듣고, 여자가 할 일로 가장 적절한 것을 고르시오.

① 피자 주문하기 　　　② 케이크 굽기
③ 파티장 꾸미기 　　　④ 풍선 구매하기
⑤ 가구 옮기기

고난도
12 다음 행사장 배치도를 보면서 대화를 듣고, 두 사람이 선택할 부스 구역을 고르시오.

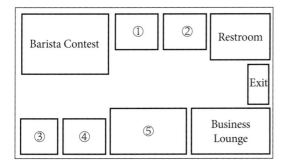

13 대화를 듣고, 여자가 탑승하려는 비행기의 출발 시각을 고르시오.

① 7 a.m.　　② 11 a.m.　　③ 12 p.m.
④ 4 p.m.　　⑤ 8 p.m.

14 대화를 듣고, 여자가 어제 한 일로 가장 적절한 것을 고르시오.

① 축구 경기하기　　② 집 청소하기
③ TV 시리즈 보기　　④ 음악 감상하기
⑤ 온라인 강의 듣기

15 다음을 듣고, 방송의 목적으로 가장 적절한 것을 고르시오.

① 새로운 놀이 기구를 소개하려고
② 라디오 프로그램을 광고하려고
③ 팬 미팅 시간 변경을 공지하려고
④ 무료 티켓 얻는 방법을 설명하려고
⑤ 사연 신청 방법을 안내하려고

16 대화를 듣고, 남자가 지불할 금액을 고르시오.

① $ 15　　② $ 20　　③ $ 25
④ $ 30　　⑤ $ 35

17 대화를 듣고, 남자의 마지막 말에 대한 여자의 응답으로 가장 적절한 것을 고르시오.

Woman: _____

① There was a car accident down the road.
② I'd love to look around the traditional village.
③ You should visit the website to purchase tickets.
④ I wore a hanbok last time I traveled there.
⑤ It'll take four hours to get there by bus.

[18-19] 대화를 듣고, 여자의 마지막 말에 대한 남자의 응답으로 가장 적절한 것을 고르시오.

18 Man: _____

① My dog is fed twice per day.
② I'm bored because my friends are busy.
③ Okay. I'll try to have fun by myself.
④ You're right. I'll go by the pet store.
⑤ Let's go for a walk since it's so nice outside.

19 Man: _____

① I prefer romance to horror.
② Great. I've wanted to go there for a while.
③ I will order the drink now.
④ You just go down this street, and then turn left.
⑤ Thanks, but I already feel full.

20 다음 상황 설명을 듣고, Peter가 종업원에게 할 말로 가장 적절한 것을 고르시오.

Peter: _____

① I'd like a piece of cheesecake.
② What dishes do you recommend?
③ I'll bring you the menu right away.
④ Could you show me the dessert list, please?
⑤ We need a table for four.

03회 중학영어듣기 실전 모의고사 Dictation 음성을 들으며 빈칸에 알맞은 단어를 채우시오.

1 | 알맞은 그림 고르기

대화를 듣고, 여자가 구입할 치마를 고르시오.

① ② ③
④ ⑤

M Welcome to Women's Clothing. May I help you find something?
W Yes. I'm looking for a new skirt for this summer.
M I see. Do you want _____ _____ _____ of skirt?
W I need a longer one that _____ _____ _____.
M Okay. How about this jean skirt? We just got it.
W Hmm... No. The material _____ _____ _____.
M Alright. Then, you can choose from these linen ones. They come in several colors and patterns.
W I like the one _____ _____ _____ on it. It makes me feel like _____ _____ _____.
M Great choice! It is really comfortable and popular.

고난도
2 | 언급하지 않은 내용 고르기

대화를 듣고, 작문 과제에 관해 언급되지 않은 것을 고르시오.

① 주제   ② 요구 분량   ③ 실제 제출일
④ 양식   ⑤ 마감 기한

W Todd, thank you for coming.
M Sure, Ms. Sanchez. Do you want to talk about _____ _____ _____ ?
W Yes. You did a good job. But there were some problems.
M I see.
W First off, _____ _____ _____ _____. I asked for a four-page essay, but yours has seven pages.
M Okay. I'll be _____ _____ _____ _____ next time.
W Good. You should also turn in your essay on time. It was _____ _____. But you handed it in _____ _____ _____, didn't you?
M Yes. I'm sorry about that.

3 | 목적 고르기

대화를 듣고, 남자가 여자에게 전화한 목적으로 가장 적절한 것을 고르시오.

① 새로운 식자재를 주문하려고
② 식당을 예약하려고
③ 배송 상태를 확인하려고
④ 도로 상황을 안내하려고
⑤ 배달 지연을 알리려고

🎯 적중! Tip You've reached ~.
전화 통화에서 수신자가 전화를 받으며 자신이 누구인지 말해줄 때 사용되는 표현으로, reached 다음에는 전화를 받는 측의 이름이 온다.
· You've reached Dr. Kim's office.
  김 박사님 사무실로 전화 주셨습니다.

[Telephone rings.]
W You've reached Anderson Grill. This is Amanda speaking.
M Hi, Amanda. I'm Jake from Vernon Food Supplies. I'm _____ _____ _____ _____.
W Oh, is there a problem?
M There is. Due to the poor road conditions, we can't _____ _____ _____ this afternoon.
W I see. When will our supplies arrive then?
M We will deliver everything by 10 a.m. tomorrow. We _____ _____ _____ _____ _____. My apologies.
W Okay. Well, thanks for _____ _____ _____.

4 | 시간 정보 고르기

대화를 듣고, 어머니가 아들을 데리러 갈 시각을 고르시오.

① 2:00 p.m. ② 2:30 p.m. ③ 3:00 p.m.
④ 3:30 p.m. ⑤ 4:00 p.m.

> 🎯 적중! Tip Could you
>
> [쿠드 유]보다는 [쿠쥬]로 들린다. [d]로 끝나는 단어 뒤에 y-로 시작하는 단어가 이어지면 두 소리가 연결되어 [쥬]로 발음되기 때문이다.

[Cellphone rings.]

M Hi, Mom. Can I _____ _____ _____ ?
W Of course. What is it?
M Could you pick me up from the department store this afternoon?
W Sure. When will _____ _____ _____ ?
M By 2. But I want to play arcade games afterward. Can you come at 3?
W I'll be busy until 3:30. Would 4 be too late to _____ _____ _____ ?
M No. _____ _____. I'll wait for you at the main entrance.

5 | 장소 고르기

대화를 듣고, 두 사람이 대화하는 장소로 가장 적절한 곳을 고르시오.

① 문구점   ② 자동차 정비소
③ 슈퍼마켓   ④ 옷 가게
⑤ 세탁소

W How can I help you?
M Can you clean these shirts? I _____ _____ _____ on them.
W I think so. How many do you have _____ _____ ?
M There are five here.
W Okay. Is there _____ _____ _____ _____ ?
M I also have this pair of pants. They need to be cleaned too.
W Alright. Your clothes _____ _____ _____ in two days.
M Thank you.

6 | 그림 상황에 적절한 대화 고르기

다음 그림의 상황에 가장 적절한 대화를 고르시오.

① ② ③ ④ ⑤

① **W** Can I make an appointment on Saturday?
   M I'm sorry. We're _____ _____.
② **W** How long will I have to wear this?
   M Your arm _____ _____, but it will be two more weeks.
③ **W** I'm here to see Dr. Robinson.
   M Please _____ _____ _____ _____ here.
④ **W** My arm is _____ _____.
   M I think you should do some stretches.
⑤ **W** You need to start eating _____ _____.
   M Okay. I'll stop eating junk food.

7 | 부탁·요청한 일 고르기

대화를 듣고, 여자가 남자에게 부탁한 일로 가장 적절한 것을 고르시오.

① 방충제 뿌리기   ② 담요 준비하기
③ 텐트 설치하기   ④ 자외선 차단제 꺼내기
⑤ 스피커 챙기기

> 🎯 적중! Tip what about
>
> [왓 어바웃]보다는 [와러바웃]으로 들린다. [t]가 모음 사이에서 발음될 때는 약화되어 [r]에 가깝게 발음되기 때문이다.

[Cellphone rings.]

M What's up, Mina?
W Hey. I'm about five minutes away from your house.
M Perfect. _____ _____ _____ _____ my bag.
W Did you pack bug spray and sunscreen for the hike?
M Yes. I also packed some extra blankets. It _____ _____ _____ in the tent.
W Good idea. We have everything then.
M Oh, what about music? Did you _____ _____ _____ ?
W I totally forgot. Can you _____ _____ instead?
M Yes. I'll get it now.

다음을 듣고, 도서 박람회에 관해 언급되지 않은 것을 고르시오.

① 장소   ② 날짜   ③ 지불 방법
④ 웹사이트   ⑤ 기념품

🎯 적중! Tip   fair

'요금'이라는 의미의 명사 fare의 발음도 [페어]로 비슷하다. 이러한 동음이의어는 문맥 속에서 뜻을 파악하는 것이 중요하다.

W Hi, class. There will be _____ _____ _____ _____ next month. It'll be held for three days from February 20th. We will accept _____ _____ _____ _____ for book purchases at the fair. You can also order books before the event through the book fair website at bookfair20.com. Also, everyone will be _____ _____ _____ as a gift.

다음을 듣고, 어떤 직업에 관한 설명인지 고르시오.

① 비평가   ② 지휘자   ③ 큐레이터
④ 합창단원   ⑤ 피아니스트

W People who have this job _____ _____ _____ _____ or a choir. When a group of musicians or singers perform, they _____ _____ _____. They move around their hands or a stick made of wood to help people play or sing _____ _____ _____ _____. To have this job, you need to know a lot about music.

다음을 듣고, 두 사람의 대화가 어색한 것을 고르시오.

①   ②   ③   ④   ⑤

① M I saw a great movie last night.
   W Oh, yeah? _____ _____ _____ of the movie?
② M The math test was so hard.
   W Don't worry. You'll get a good score!
③ M How much did _____ _____ _____ _____?
   W They will play this song at the concert.
④ M Do you like drinking coffee?
   W Yes. I drink two cups a day.
⑤ M What do you think about _____ _____?
   W I think _____ _____.

대화를 듣고, 여자가 할 일로 가장 적절한 것을 고르시오.

① 피자 주문하기   ② 케이크 굽기
③ 파티장 꾸미기   ④ 풍선 구매하기
⑤ 가구 옮기기

M How are the plans for Aaron's surprise party going?
W Well, we still need food and _____ _____.
M Balloons would look good for decorations.
W Yes. But I don't know _____ _____ _____ them.
M I'll buy them at a store later. Can you _____ _____ _____?
W Thank you. I ordered a cake, but I need to get food for dinner.
M Why don't you just _____ _____ _____?
W Okay, I will. I can do that now.

고난도

12 | 위치 고르기

다음 행사장 배치도를 보면서 대화를 듣고, 두 사람이 선택할 부스 구역을 고르시오.

| Barista Contest | ① | ② | Restroom |
| ③ | ④ | ⑤ | Business Lounge |

Exit

M Ms. Evans, should I book a booth for the coffee expo?

W Yes, please. Do you have the map?

M Yes. Where should we set up our booth?

W Somewhere _____ _____ _____ _____. It smelled so bad last year.

M Okay. How about this one?

W Hmm... I think it's better to have our booth _____ _____ _____ _____ _____. We can watch the other people compete too.

M Sure. Do we need a large booth this year?

W _____ _____ _____ _____. Let's get a smaller one.

M Okay. We have two choices left.

W Let's _____ _____ _____ _____ the Business Lounge.

M No problem.

13 | 시간 정보 고르기

대화를 듣고, 여자가 탑승하려는 비행기의 출발 시각을 고르시오.

① 7 a.m.　　② 11 a.m.　　③ 12 p.m.
④ 4 p.m.　　⑤ 8 p.m.

[Telephone rings.]

M This is the Express Air customer service center. What can I do for you?

W I'd like to _____ _____ _____.

M Could you tell me your name and booking number?

W My name is Louis White, and my booking number is 94848.

M Okay, Ms. White. I see _____ _____ _____ _____ a flight to Oakland on June 14th. It leaves at 4 p.m.

W That's right. I'd like to arrive before 12 p.m. on the same day.

M Let me see. [Typing sound] Then, _____ _____ _____ _____ the flight that leaves at 7 a.m. and arrives at 11 a.m. _____ _____ _____ _____?

W Yes. Thanks.

14 | 한 일 고르기

대화를 듣고, 여자가 어제 한 일로 가장 적절한 것을 고르시오.

① 축구 경기하기　　② 집 청소하기
③ TV 시리즈 보기　　④ 음악 감상하기
⑤ 온라인 강의 듣기

적중! Tip That's a pity.
실망스러운 일이나 안 좋은 일에 대해 유감이나 동정을 나타낼 때 사용되는 표현이다.

M Emma, how was your weekend? Didn't you have a soccer game?

W Actually, _____ _____ _____, so we couldn't play.

M That's a pity. Why was it canceled?

W _____ _____ _____ _____ _____ because of the rain.

M It did rain a lot. So, what did you do instead?

W I just _____ _____ _____ _____ at home yesterday.

M That sounds relaxing.

W Yes. I enjoyed not being so busy.

15 | 목적 고르기

15 | 목적 고르기

다음을 듣고, 방송의 목적으로 가장 적절한 것을 고르시오.

① 새로운 놀이 기구를 소개하려고
② 라디오 프로그램을 광고하려고
③ 팬 미팅 시간 변경을 공지하려고
④ 무료 티켓 얻는 방법을 설명하려고
⑤ 사연 신청 방법을 안내하려고

W Listeners, don't miss your chance to go to Adventure World! Throughout the next hour, we'll be giving away free tickets to the theme park. To _____ _____ _____, call in to make a song request in the next hour. Seven callers will be picked to join DJ Max on air. And if you can _____ _____ _____ _____ about your favorite band, you'll win four all-day passes for Adventure World. So, stay tuned, and _____ _____ _____ _____ at 555-3257.

16 | 금액 정보 고르기

대화를 듣고, 남자가 지불할 금액을 고르시오.

① $ 15　　② $ 20　　③ $ 25
④ $ 30　　⑤ $ 35

W Welcome to Quality Candles. How may I help you?
M I'd like to _____ _____ _____ for my friend. Which one do you recommend?
W Our most popular candle is the one that smells like lavender. _____ _____ _____ is 15 dollars, and a large one is 20 dollars.
M Okay. I'll take a medium-sized lavender candle.
W If you buy a large one, you will get a set of small candles _____ _____.
M Really? Then, I'll _____ _____ _____ _____ instead.
W Excellent idea.

17 | 적절한 응답 고르기

대화를 듣고, 남자의 마지막 말에 대한 여자의 응답으로 가장 적절한 것을 고르시오.

Woman: _____

① There was a car accident down the road.
② I'd love to look around the traditional village.
③ You should visit the website to purchase tickets.
④ I wore a hanbok last time I traveled there.
⑤ It'll take four hours to get there by bus.

M The holiday is coming up. Do you have any plans?
W I might go to Jeonju, but _____ _____ _____ _____.
M Yeah. It can be pretty bad if you take a bus. Have you looked at train tickets?
W Yes. But they're _____ _____ _____. I think a bus is my only option.
M You can leave really early in the morning. The traffic might be better.
W That's true. I hope it _____ _____ _____ _____.
M I'm sure you'll have a lot of fun. What do you _____ _____ _____ there?

18 | 적절한 응답 고르기

대화를 듣고, 여자의 마지막 말에 대한 남자의 응답으로 가장 적절한 것을 고르시오.

Man: _____

① My dog is fed twice per day.

② I'm bored because my friends are busy.

③ Okay. I'll try to have fun by myself.

④ You're right. I'll go by the pet store.

⑤ Let's go for a walk since it's so nice outside.

> 🎯 적중! Tip **walk**
>
> [웍]으로 발음된다. -k 앞에 오는 [l]은 묵음이다.
> · talk [톡] · chalk [촉]

W Hey, Mingyu. Is this your dog? It's so cute.

M Yes! I'm just _____ _____ _____ _____ _____ around the neighborhood.

W How often do you walk him?

M I take him outside twice a day, but he _____ _____ _____.

W Does he have any toys?

M Yes. But they're very old, so he doesn't like to play with them.

W You _____ _____ _____ more toys. Then, he won't get bored easily.

19 | 적절한 응답 고르기

대화를 듣고, 여자의 마지막 말에 대한 남자의 응답으로 가장 적절한 것을 고르시오.

Man: _____

① I prefer romance to horror.

② Great. I've wanted to go there for a while.

③ I will order the drink now.

④ You just go down this street, and then turn left.

⑤ Thanks, but I already feel full.

W What time does _____ _____ _____, Jungwon?

M It starts at 2 p.m.

W Really? It's only 11 a.m. now. We have a lot of time before it begins.

M I know. What should we do?

W Well, we can _____ _____ _____ in the park. It's a beautiful day.

M Why don't we get some drinks first? We can _____ _____ _____ to the park.

W Sure. What do you want to drink?

M I'd like a smoothie or juice.

W Let's _____ _____ _____ _____ down the street then.

20 | 상황에 적절한 말 고르기

다음 상황 설명을 듣고, Peter가 종업원에게 할 말로 가장 적절한 것을 고르시오.

Peter: _____

① I'd like a piece of cheesecake.

② What dishes do you recommend?

③ I'll bring you the menu right away.

④ Could you show me the dessert list, please?

⑤ We need a table for four.

W Peter is at a restaurant with some of his friends. They order lots of food and _____ _____ _____ _____. However, Peter is still hungry and wants to order a dessert. He doesn't remember _____ _____ _____, and there is no menu at his table. So, he decides to ask the server if he can _____ _____ _____ _____. In this situation, what would Peter most likely say to the server?

04 회 실전 모의고사

실전 모의고사
음성 바로 듣기 ▶

1 대화를 듣고, 여자가 구입할 이어폰 케이스를 고르시오.

① 　② 　③

④ 　⑤

2 대화를 듣고, 비디오 게임에 관해 언급되지 <u>않은</u> 것을 고르시오.

① 이름　　② 가격　　③ 제조사
④ 발매일　⑤ 난이도

3 대화를 듣고, 남자가 여자에게 전화한 목적으로 가장 적절한 것을 고르시오.

① 매장 운영 시간을 확인하려고
② 애견 호텔에 대해 문의하려고
③ 미용 작업이 완료되었음을 알리려고
④ 서비스 지연에 대해 안내하려고
⑤ 제품에 대해 항의하려고

4 대화를 듣고, 남자가 선택한 수영 수업의 시작 시각을 고르시오.

① 9 a.m.　　② 10 a.m.　　③ 11 a.m.
④ 12 p.m.　⑤ 1 p.m.

5 대화를 듣고, 남자의 심정으로 가장 적절한 것을 고르시오.

① joyful　　② grateful　　③ relaxed
④ concerned　⑤ surprised

6 다음 그림의 상황에 가장 적절한 대화를 고르시오.

① 　② 　③ 　④ 　⑤

7 대화를 듣고, 여자가 남자에게 부탁한 일로 가장 적절한 것을 고르시오.

① 시 제목 붙이기　　② 대회 추천서 쓰기
③ 작품 검토하기　　④ 과제 제출일 늦추기
⑤ 볼펜 가져오기

8 다음을 듣고, Drama Festival에 관해 언급되지 <u>않은</u> 것을 고르시오.

① 주최자　　② 연극 개수　　③ 개최 장소
④ 행사 기간　⑤ 배우 이름

9 다음을 듣고, 어떤 장소에 관한 설명인지 고르시오.

① 박물관　　② 전망대　　③ 수족관
④ 식물원　　⑤ 놀이공원

10 다음을 듣고, 두 사람의 대화가 어색한 것을 고르시오.

① 　② 　③ 　④ 　⑤

11 대화를 듣고, 남자가 할 일로 가장 적절한 것을 고르시오.

① 식탁 구매하기　　② 식당에 전화하기
③ 샌드위치 주문하기　④ 요리 재료 확인하기
⑤ 강가에서 산책하기

12 다음 표를 보면서 대화를 듣고, 두 사람이 구입할 노트북을 고르시오.

	Laptop	Screen	Color	Price
①	A	14 inch	White	$ 850
②	B	15 inch	White	$ 900
③	C	14 inch	Black	$ 900
④	D	15 inch	Black	$ 950
⑤	E	17 inch	Black	$ 1,500

고난도
13 대화를 듣고, 여자가 에어컨을 설치 받기로 한 날짜를 고르시오.

① 6월 17일　　② 6월 19일　　③ 6월 20일

④ 6월 22일　　⑤ 6월 24일

14 대화를 듣고, 여자가 지난 일요일에 한 일로 가장 적절한 것을 고르시오.

① 피아노 연습하기　　② 집안일 하기

③ 음악 과제 하기　　④ 농장 일 돕기

⑤ 할머니 병문안 가기

15 다음을 듣고, 방송의 목적으로 가장 적절한 것을 고르시오.

① 지역 체육 행사를 홍보하려고

② 반려동물 등록 방법을 알리려고

③ 정원 관리 방법을 설명하려고

④ 새로운 워터 파크를 소개하려고

⑤ 공원 이용 시 주의 사항을 안내하려고

16 대화를 듣고, 남자가 지불할 금액을 고르시오.

① $ 30　　② $ 60　　③ $ 90

④ $ 120　　⑤ $ 150

17 대화를 듣고, 남자의 마지막 말에 대한 여자의 응답으로 가장 적절한 것을 고르시오.

Woman: _____

① It's on the second floor of the mall.

② She turns 15 tomorrow.

③ I keep my diary locked in a drawer.

④ Can I borrow a pencil, please?

⑤ Don't open your gifts yet.

[18-19] 대화를 듣고, 여자의 마지막 말에 대한 남자의 응답으로 가장 적절한 것을 고르시오.

고난도
18 Man: _____

① That's the last peach.

② Sorry, but you're not allowed.

③ Sure. I'll give it to you later.

④ Thank you for helping our staff.

⑤ I don't see your name on the list.

19 Man: _____

① He trained for over six months.

② Sure. I'll go buy some drinks.

③ Yes. He'll be here soon.

④ Don't worry. I already got some.

⑤ I go for a run every morning.

20 다음 상황 설명을 듣고, Angela가 경찰관에게 할 말로 가장 적절한 것을 고르시오.

Angela: Excuse me, _____

① how late does the subway run?

② what time does this store open?

③ I want to buy a ticket for the exhibition.

④ how do I get to the museum from here?

⑤ where is the closest subway station?

04회 중학영어듣기 실전 모의고사 Dictation 음성을 들으며 빈칸에 알맞은 단어를 채우시오.

1 | 알맞은 그림 고르기

대화를 듣고, 여자가 구입할 이어폰 케이스를 고르시오.

① ② ③
④ ⑤

M Welcome. What can I do for you?

W I lost my earphone case, so I need to buy one.

M Alright. Our cases have many unique designs _____ _____ _____ _____. The dinosaur-shaped one is the most popular.

W Oh, it _____ _____ _____ _____ _____ _____. That had a dinosaur on it. But this time, I want to try something new.

M Then, how about this cupcake-shaped one?

W Wow, that is cute. The chocolate cupcake _____ _____.

M Good. And we can _____ _____ _____ on it if you want.

W Thanks, but that's okay.

2 | 언급하지 않은 내용 고르기

대화를 듣고, 비디오 게임에 관해 언급되지 않은 것을 고르시오.

① 이름　　② 가격　　③ 제조사
④ 발매일　　⑤ 난이도

🎯 적중! Tip vi**d**eo

[비디오]보다는 [비리오]로 들린다. [d]가 모음 사이에서 발음될 때는 약화되어 [r]에 가깝게 발음되기 때문이다.
· bo**d**y [바리]　· we**dd**ing [웨링]

W What are you doing, Brad?

M I'm playing a new video game. It _____ _____ on May 10th.

W What's it called?

M _____ _____ _____ Space Attack. You fly a spaceship and fight aliens.

W _____ _____ made it?

M Bright Star Media. It is that company's first game.

W Is it _____ _____ _____?

M No. It's very easy, actually.

W Maybe I will buy it then. It sounds fun.

3 | 목적 고르기

대화를 듣고, 남자가 여자에게 전화한 목적으로 가장 적절한 것을 고르시오.

① 매장 운영 시간을 확인하려고
② 애견 호텔에 대해 문의하려고
③ 미용 작업이 완료되었음을 알리려고
④ 서비스 지연에 대해 안내하려고
⑤ 제품에 대해 항의하려고

[Cellphone rings.]

M Hello, is this Jenny Barnes?

W Yes, that's me.

M This is Grant from Pampered Pets. I'm _____ _____ _____ _____, Rex.

W Is everything okay?

M Of course. I am _____ _____ _____ _____ his hair, so he is ready for pickup.

W Oh, I see. But I'm at an appointment right now. Can I _____ _____ _____ _____?

M Yes. What time can you get him?

W I should be done around 3 p.m., so I can get there by 3:30.

M That's fine. _____ _____ at 5 p.m.

W Great. Thank you for letting me know.

4 | 시간 정보 고르기

대화를 듣고, 남자가 선택한 수영 수업의 시작 시각을 고르시오.

① 9 a.m.　　② 10 a.m.　　③ 11 a.m.
④ 12 p.m.　　⑤ 1 p.m.

M Mom, can I take _____ _____ _____ on Saturdays at the pool downtown?

W Sure. What time does the lesson start?

M I'd like to join the lesson _____ _____ _____ _____. It begins at 10 a.m. and lasts for one hour.

W Oh, no. I have to _____ _____ _____ _____ soccer practice at 9 a.m. on Saturdays.

M What time does her practice end?

W It doesn't end until 11 a.m.

M In that case, there is _____ _____ that starts at 1 p.m.

W Okay. _____ _____ _____ that one.

5 | 심정 고르기

대화를 듣고, 남자의 심정으로 가장 적절한 것을 고르시오.

① joyful　　② grateful　　③ relaxed
④ concerned　　⑤ surprised

🎯 적중! Tip　I'm not feeling good.
몸이 아프거나 컨디션이 좋지 않음을 나타낼 때 사용되는 표현이다.

W Brandon, are you okay?

M I'm not feeling good.

W Did you see a doctor?

M Yes. The doctor suggested that I _____ _____ _____. So, I'm waiting for the results.

W When will you get the results?

M Sometime next week. I'm afraid I have _____ _____ _____.

W Don't worry. I'm sure everything will be fine.

M But I can't _____ _____ _____ _____ the worst.

6 | 그림 상황에 적절한 대화 고르기

다음 그림의 상황에 가장 적절한 대화를 고르시오.

① W Do you _____ _____ _____ ?
　 M No. I'm not very hungry.
② W Are you almost done with your homework?
　 M It will take 30 more minutes.
③ W That will be 12 dollars and 50 cents, please.
　 M _____ _____ _____.
④ W Why don't we take a taxi to the theater?
　 M _____ _____ _____ _____.
⑤ W Where is the nearest bus stop?
　 M There's one over there.

7 | 부탁·요청한 일 고르기

대화를 듣고, 여자가 남자에게 부탁한 일로 가장 적절한 것을 고르시오.

① 시 제목 붙이기　　② 대회 추천서 쓰기
③ 작품 검토하기　　④ 과제 제출일 늦추기
⑤ 볼펜 가져오기

M _____ _____ _____ _____, Erica.

W Thank you, Mr. Park.

M Do you write often?

W I try to write every day.

M That's great. You could _____ _____ _____ one day.

W I hope so. Could you _____ _____ _____ of my poems? I'd love to hear your opinions.

M _____ _____ _____ _____ at any time.

다음을 듣고, Drama Festival에 관해 언급되지 **않은** 것을 고르시오.

① 주최자　② 연극 개수　③ 개최 장소
④ 행사 기간　⑤ 배우 이름

W Good morning, students. I _____ _____ _____ _____ you about the Drama Festival. Mr. Ferris, the club advisor, and his drama club _____ _____ _____ _____ this year. There will be four short plays. They will be performed in _____ _____ _____. The festival will _____ _____ two days, beginning on April 15th. I hope that all of you will attend. And please _____ _____ _____ your friends and family members!

다음을 듣고, 어떤 장소에 관한 설명인지 고르시오.

① 박물관　② 전망대　③ 수족관
④ 식물원　⑤ 놀이공원

M People can enjoy nature at this place. This place has _____ _____ with plants from all over the world. During the spring, many people visit this place _____ _____ _____ _____. The workers at this place can teach you about _____ _____ _____ there. Sometimes this place hosts fun events, but its main purpose is to _____, _____, _____ _____ diverse plants.

다음을 듣고, 두 사람의 대화가 **어색한** 것을 고르시오.

①　　②　　③　　④　　⑤

> 🎯 적중! Tip tol**d y**ou
>
> [톨드 유]보다는 [톨쥬]로 들린다. [d]로 끝나는 단어 뒤에 y-로 시작하는 단어가 이어지면 두 소리가 연결되어 [쥬]로 발음되기 때문이다.
> · woul**d y**ou [우쥬] · di**d y**ou [디쥬]

① W My face really _____ _____.
　 M I told you to wear a hat.
② W Did you paint this beautiful picture?
　 M _____ _____ _____ is 10 dollars.
③ W Does this bus go to the Bradford?
　 M It does. It takes about 15 minutes.
④ W _____ _____ _____ _____ _____ burgers for lunch?
　 M Sure. I'm hungry.
⑤ W I have a question to ask you.
　 M _____ _____. What is it?

대화를 듣고, 남자가 할 일로 가장 적절한 것을 고르시오.

① 식탁 구매하기　② 식당에 전화하기
③ 샌드위치 주문하기　④ 요리 재료 확인하기
⑤ 강가에서 산책하기

M It's finally warm outside.
W I know! Last week was really cold.
M Let's eat at that _____ _____ _____ by the river today. They have outside tables, so we can _____ _____ _____.
W Yes. Their food looks delicious, but isn't it always busy? Can we even get a table?
M I'll call them and _____ _____ _____ now.
W That'll be great.

12 | 도표에서 알맞은 항목 고르기

다음 표를 보면서 대화를 듣고, 두 사람이 구입할 노트북을 고르시오.

	Laptop	Screen	Color	Price
①	A	14 inch	White	$ 850
②	B	15 inch	White	$ 900
③	C	14 inch	Black	$ 900
④	D	15 inch	Black	$ 950
⑤	E	17 inch	Black	$ 1,500

M Honey, I'm going to _____ _____ _____ now.

W Oh, okay. Are you going to get one with a 17-inch screen?

M No. It is _____ _____.

W I see. Well, a 15-inch screen should be _____ _____.

M Do you think I should get a white or a black one?

W Look. The black ones are more expensive than the white ones. I think you should get _____ _____ _____.

M I agree. I'll order it now.

고난도

13 | 시간 정보 고르기

대화를 듣고, 여자가 에어컨을 설치 받기로 한 날짜를 고르시오.

① 6월 17일　　② 6월 19일　　③ 6월 20일
④ 6월 22일　　⑤ 6월 24일

🎯 적중! Tip　I'm calling about ~.

전화 통화에서 전화를 건 용건을 밝힐 때 사용되는 표현으로, about 다음에는 용건을 설명하는 명사구가 온다.

· I'm calling about your recent order.
　최근에 주문하신 것 때문에 전화 드렸습니다.

[Telephone rings.]

W Hello?

M Hello, this is Grayson Electronics. I'm calling about the air conditioner you ordered last week.

W Oh, is there _____ _____ _____ _____ _____?

M No. It's just that orders are piled up, so the delivery and installation date _____ _____ _____ a bit.

W That's fine. When can I get it installed then?

M _____ _____ _____ would be June 19th.

W Let me see. [Pause] I'll be on a holiday during that week. What about _____ _____ _____ _____?

M You can choose between the 22nd and 24th.

W The 24th sounds okay.

M Perfect.

---

14 | 한 일 고르기

대화를 듣고, 여자가 지난 일요일에 한 일로 가장 적절한 것을 고르시오.

① 피아노 연습하기　　② 집안일 하기
③ 음악 과제 하기　　④ 농장 일 돕기
⑤ 할머니 병문안 가기

M Did you finish your music project, Nora?

W No, _____ _____. I'm doing it now.

M Oh, you usually finish your projects so early. What happened?

W My family decided to _____ _____ _____ in the countryside last Sunday. We were there all day.

M What did you do there?

W We helped them _____ _____ _____. It was hard work, but we enjoyed _____ _____ _____.

M That sounds like a nice day.

다음을 듣고, 방송의 목적으로 가장 적절한 것을 고르시오.

① 지역 체육 행사를 홍보하려고
② 반려동물 등록 방법을 알리려고
③ 정원 관리 방법을 설명하려고
④ 새로운 워터 파크를 소개하려고
⑤ 공원 이용 시 주의 사항을 안내하려고

> 🎯 적중! Tip **Lastly**
>
> [래스틀리]보다는 [래쓸리]로 들린다. [t]와 [l]처럼 발음할 때 혀의 위치가 비슷한 자음이 나란히 나오면 앞 발음이 탈락되기 때문이다.
> · shor**tly** [숄을리] · la**tely** [레잇을리]

M Good afternoon, everyone. We hope you all are enjoying your time at Riverside Park. Here are _____ _____ _____ _____ the park. Please _____ _____ _____ you throw all of your trash away before leaving the area. Also, you must _____ _____ _____ your pets if you bring them. Lastly, be careful not to walk on the flowers in the park, and _____ _____ _____ instead. Thank you for your time.

대화를 듣고, 남자가 지불할 금액을 고르시오.

① $ 30   ② $ 60   ③ $ 90
④ $ 120   ⑤ $ 150

W Welcome to Travel Car Rentals. How may I help you?
M Hello. I need to _____ _____ _____. How much is it?
W _____ _____ _____ is 30 dollars per day. How long will you use the car?
M I will use it for three days.
W Then, your total is 90 dollars.
M Okay. And how much is this booklet about _____ _____ _____? It looks very interesting.
W That's actually free. You can take it.
M Great. I'll _____ _____ _____ _____ then.

대화를 듣고, 남자의 마지막 말에 대한 여자의 응답으로 가장 적절한 것을 고르시오.

Woman: _____

① It's on the second floor of the mall.
② She turns 15 tomorrow.
③ I keep my diary locked in a drawer.
④ Can I borrow a pencil, please?
⑤ Don't open your gifts yet.

W David, have you bought your present for Maria?
M No, I haven't. I think I _____ _____ _____ _____ one. I can't decide on a gift.
W I went to Arts and Crafts Central in the mall. There are _____ _____ _____ _____ _____. It's a good place to look.
M Arts and Crafts Central?
W Yes. I think Maria wants a new pencil case, and the store has many.
M That sounds perfect then. Where can I _____ _____ _____?

18 | 적절한 응답 고르기 [고난도]

대화를 듣고, 여자의 마지막 말에 대한 남자의 응답으로 가장 적절한 것을 고르시오.

Man: _____

① That's the last peach.
② Sorry, but you're not allowed.
③ Sure. I'll give it to you later.
④ Thank you for helping our staff.
⑤ I don't see your name on the list.

> 🎯 적중! Tip   I would love to ~.
> 어떤 일을 하고 싶음을 강조하여 나타낼 때 사용되는 표현으로, to 다음에는 동사원형이 온다.
> · I would love to visit Korea.
>   난 한국을 방문하고 싶어.

M Sunhee, are you _____ _____ _____?
W I would love to volunteer. I used to help out at the children's hospital.
M Well, a local orchard will _____ _____ _____ _____ _____ to people who need food.
W _____ _____ _____ _____ _____!
M But the orchard needs help with picking them. Do you want to go with me?
W Sure. Where can I get the sign-up form?
M I'm _____ _____ _____ to get one now.
W Oh, I have to change clothes for P.E. class. Can you _____ _____ for me?

19 | 적절한 응답 고르기

대화를 듣고, 여자의 마지막 말에 대한 남자의 응답으로 가장 적절한 것을 고르시오.

Man: _____

① He trained for over six months.
② Sure. I'll go buy some drinks.
③ Yes. He'll be here soon.
④ Don't worry. I already got some.
⑤ I go for a run every morning.

[Cellphone rings.]
M Hi, Tabby.
W Hey. Did Justin _____ _____ _____ _____?
M No. But he should finish soon.
W Okay. Where are you now? I will _____ _____ _____ _____ _____.
M I'm at the finish line. I have a big sign with his name on it.
W That's great! I'm so _____ _____ _____ for doing this race.
M Yeah. I think he'll be happy to see us _____ _____ _____.
W Should I _____ _____ _____ or water for him? I can go to the store quickly.

20 | 상황에 적절한 말 고르기

다음 상황 설명을 듣고, Angela가 경찰관에게 할 말로 가장 적절한 것을 고르시오.

Angela: Excuse me, _____

① how late does the subway run?
② what time does this store open?
③ I want to buy a ticket for the exhibition.
④ how do I get to the museum from here?
⑤ where is the closest subway station?

M Angela is visiting New York for a holiday. She _____ _____ _____ the Museum of Modern Art. She wants to take the subway there, but she cannot _____ _____ _____. Luckily, she sees a police officer standing in front of a store. She decides to _____ _____ _____ _____ to the nearest subway station. In this situation, what would Angela most likely say to the police officer?

1 대화를 듣고, 여자가 구입할 부채를 고르시오.

2 대화를 듣고, 청바지에 관해 언급되지 <u>않은</u> 것을 고르시오.

① 색상　　　② 사이즈　　　③ 가격
④ 디자인　　　⑤ 제조사 번호

고난도
3 대화를 듣고, 남자가 여자에게 전화한 목적으로 가장 적절한 것을 고르시오.

① 비행기 표 환불을 요청하려고
② 비행시간을 변경하려고
③ 약속 장소를 확인하려고
④ 회의 시간을 변경하려고
⑤ 데리러 올 것을 부탁하려고

4 대화를 듣고, 두 사람이 선택한 미술 강좌의 시작 시각을 고르시오.

① 10 a.m.　　　② 11 a.m.　　　③ 12 p.m.
④ 2 p.m.　　　⑤ 4 p.m.

5 대화를 듣고, 여자의 심정으로 가장 적절한 것을 고르시오.

① fearful　　　② angry　　　③ grateful
④ relaxed　　　⑤ frustrated

6 다음 그림의 상황에 가장 적절한 대화를 고르시오.

①　　②　　③　　④　　⑤

7 대화를 듣고, 여자가 남자에게 부탁한 일로 가장 적절한 것을 고르시오.

① 필기 도와주기　　　② 배구공 정리하기
③ 가방 들어주기　　　④ 병원 데려다주기
⑤ 붕대 감아주기

고난도
8 다음을 듣고, 현장 학습에 관해 언급되지 <u>않은</u> 것을 고르시오.

① 날짜　　　② 참가 대상　　　③ 목적
④ 복장　　　⑤ 필요 서류

9 다음을 듣고, 어떤 직업에 관한 설명인지 고르시오.

① 약사　　　② 수의사　　　③ 치과의사
④ 구조대원　　　⑤ 사회복지사

10 다음을 듣고, 두 사람의 대화가 <u>어색한</u> 것을 고르시오.

①　　②　　③　　④　　⑤

11 대화를 듣고, 여자가 할 일로 가장 적절한 것을 고르시오.

① 동아리 가입하기　　　② 과제 제출하기
③ 선생님 찾아뵙기　　　④ 과학 실험하기
⑤ 친구 병문안 가기

12 다음 야영장 배치도를 보면서 대화를 듣고, 두 사람이 선택할 캠핑 위치를 고르시오.

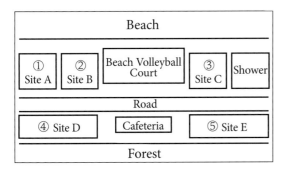

13 대화를 듣고, 여자가 개인 운동 강습을 받을 날짜를 고르시오.

① 4월 5일   ② 4월 6일   ③ 4월 7일
④ 4월 8일   ⑤ 4월 9일

14 대화를 듣고, 여자가 어제 한 일로 가장 적절한 것을 고르시오.

① 레시피 검색하기   ② 국어 공부하기
③ 파티 준비하기   ④ 식당 방문하기
⑤ 파스타 요리하기

15 다음을 듣고, 방송의 목적으로 가장 적절한 것을 고르시오.

① 음악가들을 소개하려고
② 특별 공연을 홍보하려고
③ 공연장 예절을 안내하려고
④ 공연 영상 시청 방법을 설명하려고
⑤ 오케스트라 가입 절차를 안내하려고

16 대화를 듣고, 남자가 지불할 금액을 고르시오.

① $ 5   ② $ 15   ③ $ 25
④ $ 35   ⑤ $ 45

17 대화를 듣고, 남자의 마지막 말에 대한 여자의 응답으로 가장 적절한 것을 고르시오.

Woman: _____

① Yes. We had a good time.
② That's a great plan. Thanks!
③ I found it yesterday.
④ They're serving ice cream today.
⑤ Sorry, my meeting took a long time.

18 대화를 듣고, 여자의 마지막 말에 대한 남자의 응답으로 가장 적절한 것을 고르시오.

Man: _____

① Yes. We climbed it quickly.
② I leave for my vacation tomorrow.
③ Our hotel is just up that hill over there.
④ No. The ones you're wearing are fine.
⑤ Did you forget your swimsuit?

19 대화를 듣고, 남자의 마지막 말에 대한 여자의 응답으로 가장 적절한 것을 고르시오.

Woman: _____

① Our commute is about two hours.
② Let me introduce you to my sister.
③ I am happy to finish the book report.
④ They took the subway instead of the bus.
⑤ Alright. I'll drop by at 6:30 then.

20 다음 상황 설명을 듣고, Phil이 Olivia에게 할 말로 가장 적절한 것을 고르시오.

Phil: Olivia, _____

① I need to go to a doctor soon.
② what do you want to do after the movie?
③ let's meet at the theater at 11.
④ I'm afraid we can't get tickets.
⑤ can we see the movie another time?

05회 중학영어듣기 실전 모의고사 Dictation 음성을 들으며 빈칸에 알맞은 단어를 채우시오.

1 | 알맞은 그림 고르기

대화를 듣고, 여자가 구입할 부채를 고르시오.

① ② ③

④ ⑤

M Hey, Mijin. How about buying one of _____ _____ _____ _____ for your friend Emily?
W I like that idea! The paintings on them all look beautiful.
M Oh, I like this fan with a picture of two birds.
W Well, Emily _____ _____ _____ _____.
M Then, this one has a picture of _____ _____ _____ _____. Emily will like it.
W Perfect. And I also like that it has the word "KOREA" on it. I'll take this one.

2 | 언급하지 않은 내용 고르기

대화를 듣고, 청바지에 관해 언급되지 <u>않은</u> 것을 고르시오.

① 색상   ② 사이즈   ③ 가격
④ 디자인   ⑤ 제조사 번호

W I finally got the jeans I ordered on the Internet.
M What color are they?
W They're _____ _____.
M Oh, they look a bit big for you.
W Let me check. [Pause] Oh, no! They sent me _____ _____ _____.
M You need to exchange them for the correct size.
W And these also _____ _____ _____. This isn't the design I ordered.
M Look here. You can call 555-3251 to _____ _____ _____.
W I think I should call.

고난도
3 | 목적 고르기

대화를 듣고, 남자가 여자에게 전화한 목적으로 가장 적절한 것을 고르시오.

① 비행기 표 환불을 요청하려고
② 비행시간을 변경하려고
③ 약속 장소를 확인하려고
④ 회의 시간을 변경하려고
⑤ 데리러 올 것을 부탁하려고

[Cellphone rings.]
W Hi, Terry. How are you?
M Hey, Jane. _____ _____ _____ _____ by four hours.
W Oh, I'm sorry to hear it.
M Yeah. Now I _____ _____ _____ Chicago until 2 a.m.
W That's so late!
M I know. I'm really sorry, but could you _____ _____ _____ at the airport then?
W Of course. I'll come and get you.
M Thank you so much. I _____ _____ _____.

4 | 시간 정보 고르기

대화를 듣고, 두 사람이 선택한 미술 강좌의 시작 시각을 고르시오.

① 10 a.m.　② 11 a.m.　③ 12 p.m.
④ 2 p.m.　⑤ 4 p.m.

🎯 적중! Tip　I wonder if ~.

궁금한 점을 묻고 싶을 때 사용되는 표현이다. 다양한 시제로 사용할 수 있다.

· I'm wondering if you can come with me.
　네가 나랑 같이 갈 수 있을지 궁금해.

[Cellphone rings.]

M Hi, Anne.

W Hello, Samuel. What's up?

M I just saw that the Brentwood Community Center _____ _____ _____ _____ on Saturday. I was wondering if you'd like to attend one with me.

W That sounds interesting. Umm... What time do you want to go?

M I was thinking of going to the one that begins at 10 a.m. It lasts for two hours.

W I don't know. I usually _____ _____ _____ _____ _____ on Saturday mornings. I don't finish until 11.

M Then, what about in the afternoon? There is one that _____ _____ 2 to 4 p.m.

W Great. Let's _____ _____ _____ .

5 | 심정 고르기

대화를 듣고, 여자의 심정으로 가장 적절한 것을 고르시오.

① fearful　② angry　③ grateful
④ relaxed　⑤ frustrated

🎯 적중! Tip　how to

[하우 투]보다는 [하우르]로 들린다. [t]가 모음 사이에서 발음될 때는 약화되어 [r]에 가깝게 발음되고, to와 같은 기능어는 약하게 발음되기 때문이다.

M Rachel, are you studying?

W Yes. I'm busy working on my math homework, Andy.

M Mom made apple juice for you. How about _____ _____ _____ ?

W Sounds great. But I got stuck on this problem. I don't know how to solve it.

M Then, I can help you. I'm _____ _____ math.

W Really? But do you have time? I don't want to bother you.

M It's no problem. I can always _____ _____ _____ _____ .

W You're so kind. I really _____ _____ .

6 | 그림 상황에 적절한 대화 고르기

다음 그림의 상황에 가장 적절한 대화를 고르시오.

①　②　③　④　⑤

① M Did you remember to _____ _____ _____ ?

　W Of course I did.

② M Don't _____ _____ _____ !

　W I have it right here.

③ M I'm glad the rain finally stopped.

　W Me too. I didn't want to _____ _____ .

④ M Is this your house? It's very nice.

　W Actually, I live in the one _____ _____ _____ .

⑤ M Why did you come home so early?

　W I wasn't _____ _____ .

대화를 듣고, 여자가 남자에게 부탁한 일로 가장 적절한 것을 고르시오.

① 필기 도와주기　　② 배구공 정리하기
③ 가방 들어주기　　④ 병원 데려다주기
⑤ 붕대 감아주기

M What's wrong with your arm, Hyomin?
W I hurt it _____ _____ _____ yesterday.
M Oh, no. When will your arm be better?
W I have to _____ _____ _____ for two weeks.
M Can you write during class?
W I tried, but it is difficult. Could you _____ _____ _____
_____ today?
M Sure. Don't worry about it.

다음을 듣고, 현장 학습에 관해 언급되지 않은 것을 고르시오.

① 날짜　　② 참가 대상　　③ 목적
④ 복장　　⑤ 필요 서류

M Hi, students. This is Henry Mann, the German teacher. The school is
holding _____ _____ _____ _____ next month on
Saturday, November 5th. We will be visiting the annual Pumpkin
Festival. Anyone from the first and second grades can attend if
interested. You'll _____ _____ _____ _____ signed by
your parents. Also, don't forget to _____ _____ _____
since it will be a little cold in the pumpkin field. I hope you can come
join us.

다음을 듣고, 어떤 직업에 관한 설명인지 고르시오.

① 약사　　② 수의사　　③ 치과의사
④ 구조대원　　⑤ 사회복지사

M People who have this job help the sick. They ask customers _____
_____ _____ and recommend different medications to help
them feel better. They also prepare and _____ _____
_____ _____ _____ after they see a doctor. You need to
give them a doctor's note to get certain medicine. To do this job, you
must _____ _____ _____.

다음을 듣고, 두 사람의 대화가 어색한 것을 고르시오.

①　　②　　③　　④　　⑤

🎯 적중! Tip　drink coffee

[드링크 커피]보다는 [드링커피]로 들린다. 발음이 같은 자음이 나란히 나오면 앞 단어의 끝 자음이 탈락되기 때문이다.
· help for [헬포]　· this store [디스토어]

① W Are you going to the school play tonight?
M Yes. I think it's going to be interesting.
② W Is it okay to drink coffee here?
M No. Not _____ _____ _____.
③ W I love the red painting in the living room.
M Oh, I _____ _____ _____ everywhere.
④ W How's the weather outside?
M It's perfect right now.
⑤ W What did you do today? You look happy.
M I _____ _____ _____ _____ at school.

11 | 할 일 고르기

대화를 듣고, 여자가 할 일로 가장 적절한 것을 고르시오.

① 동아리 가입하기　② 과제 제출하기
③ 선생님 찾아뵙기　④ 과학 실험하기
⑤ 친구 병문안 가기

🎯 적중! Tip　I'm looking forward to ~.
어떤 일을 몹시 기대하고 있음을 나타낼 때 사용되는 표현으로, to 다음에는 (동)명사가 온다.
· I'm looking forward to the movie.
  그 영화 너무 기대하고 있어.

W　Where are you going, Richard?
M　Hey, Katie. I'm going to see Mr. Brown.
W　I'll ＿＿＿＿ ＿＿＿＿ ＿＿＿＿. Why are you seeing Mr. Brown?
M　I need to talk to him ＿＿＿＿ ＿＿＿＿ ＿＿＿＿. Do you need to see him too?
W　No. But the sign-up sheet for the art club is next to his room.
M　Are you going to ＿＿＿＿ ＿＿＿＿ ＿＿＿＿ the club?
W　Yes. 🎯 I'm looking forward to it.

12 | 위치 고르기

다음 야영장 배치도를 보면서 대화를 듣고, 두 사람이 선택할 캠핑 위치를 고르시오.

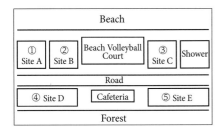

W　Honey, let's make ＿＿＿＿ ＿＿＿＿ ＿＿＿＿ ＿＿＿＿
＿＿＿＿ for the weekend.
M　Are we camping at the same campground as last time?
W　Yeah. But I want to stay at a different site. There were too many bugs.
M　I think it was because of the forest. Let's stay at one ＿＿＿＿
＿＿＿＿ ＿＿＿＿ this time.
W　Okay. How about Site A?
M　But I want to watch people ＿＿＿＿ ＿＿＿＿ ＿＿＿＿. It looked so fun.
W　Then, we have two options.
M　Why don't we choose the one ＿＿＿＿ ＿＿＿＿ ＿＿＿＿
＿＿＿＿? It'll be much more convenient.
W　Sure. I'll book that site.

13 | 시간 정보 고르기

대화를 듣고, 여자가 개인 운동 강습을 받을 날짜를 고르시오.

① 4월 5일　② 4월 6일　③ 4월 7일
④ 4월 8일　⑤ 4월 9일

[Cellphone rings.]
M　Hello. This is Ben Nicholas at Spring Gym.
W　Hi, this is Kelly Johnson. I'd like to change my appointment for ＿＿＿＿ ＿＿＿＿ this week.
M　Okay. ＿＿＿＿ ＿＿＿＿ ＿＿＿＿ was April 5th, right?
W　No. It was April 7th. But I ＿＿＿＿ ＿＿＿＿ ＿＿＿＿ ＿＿＿＿
＿＿＿＿ because of a family trip.
M　When do you want to ＿＿＿＿ ＿＿＿＿ ＿＿＿＿ ＿＿＿＿?
W　Can I change it to the 6th?
M　Sorry, but our gym will be closed that day. How about the 8th?
W　Yeah. I think I ＿＿＿＿ ＿＿＿＿ ＿＿＿＿ that day.
M　Alright. I'll put it in my schedule.
W　Thank you.

대화를 듣고, 여자가 어제 한 일로 가장 적절한 것을 고르시오.

① 레시피 검색하기
② 국어 공부하기
③ 파티 준비하기
④ 식당 방문하기
⑤ 파스타 요리하기

🎯 적중! Tip **try**

[트라이]보다는 [츄라이]로 들린다. tr-로 시작하는 단어에서 [t]는 [츄]에 가깝게 발음되기 때문이다.

· **tr**ouble [츄러블]   · **tr**ain [츄레인]

M Do you like pasta, Chloe?
W Yes. It's _____ _____ _____. Why?
M There's a new pasta restaurant that opened around the corner. The food _____ _____.
W I saw it. It does look nice.
M Do you want to eat there this afternoon? I'd like to try it.
W Actually, I _____ _____ yesterday, so I already have some at home.
M I see. We can go another time then.

다음을 듣고, 방송의 목적으로 가장 적절한 것을 고르시오.

① 음악가들을 소개하려고
② 특별 공연을 홍보하려고
③ 공연장 예절을 안내하려고
④ 공연 영상 시청 방법을 설명하려고
⑤ 오케스트라 가입 절차를 안내하려고

M Thanks for coming everyone. Before the St. Louis Orchestra takes the stage, I want to _____ _____ _____ for audience members. Firstly, we ask that everyone _____ _____ during the performance. _____ _____ _____ by loudly talking. Second, eating and drinking is _____ _____. Lastly, you are not allowed to make any recordings for the concert. Anyone recording a video will be _____ _____ _____. Thanks for listening.

대화를 듣고, 남자가 지불할 금액을 고르시오.

① $ 5
② $ 15
③ $ 25
④ $ 35
⑤ $ 45

W Hello. How may I help you?
M I'd like to _____ _____ _____ to Finland. How much would it be?
W It's five dollars per kilogram. Please put the package _____ _____ _____.
M Sure. *[Beeping sound]* It's seven kilograms.
W Then, it's 35 dollars in total.
M Okay. I need some more tape for my package. Do I need to _____ _____ for some?
W No. _____ _____. You can find it over there.
M Thank you.

대화를 듣고, 남자의 마지막 말에 대한 여자의 응답으로 가장 적절한 것을 고르시오.

Woman: _____

① Yes. We had a good time.
② That's a great plan. Thanks!
③ I found it yesterday.
④ They're serving ice cream today.
⑤ Sorry, my meeting took a long time.

M How was your day, Grace?
W It was _____ _____ _____, Dad.
M What happened?
W I lost one of my earphones, and I also forgot my lunch.
M Oh, no. I'm sorry you had a bad day. Why don't we do something fun tonight _____ _____ _____ _____?
W Okay. What should we do?
M Let's get some ice cream. We can bring it home and _____ _____ _____.

18 | 적절한 응답 고르기

대화를 듣고, 여자의 마지막 말에 대한 남자의 응답으로 가장 적절한 것을 고르시오.

Man: _____

① Yes. We climbed it quickly.

② I leave for my vacation tomorrow.

③ Our hotel is just up that hill over there.

④ No. The ones you're wearing are fine.

⑤ Did you forget your swimsuit?

> 🎯 적중! Tip **aroun**d **the**
> [어라운드 더]보다는 [어라운더]로 들린다. 비슷하게 발음되는 자음이 나란히 나오면 앞 단어의 끝 자음이 탈락되기 때문이다.

M Honey, I'm so happy to be on vacation. What should we do at the lake today?

W Let's go _____ _____ _____. Then, we can enjoy the nice view of the hills around the lake.

M That sounds fun, but the water is a little cold right now.

W Oh, you're probably right.

M Why don't we _____ _____ _____ around the lake? We can stop at a café somewhere too.

W _____ _____ _____? I didn't bring any hiking shoes.

19 | 적절한 응답 고르기

대화를 듣고, 남자의 마지막 말에 대한 여자의 응답으로 가장 적절한 것을 고르시오.

Woman: _____

① Our commute is about two hours.

② Let me introduce you to my sister.

③ I am happy to finish the book report.

④ They took the subway instead of the bus.

⑤ Alright. I'll drop by at 6:30 then.

[Cellphone rings.]

M What's up, Jessica?

W Hi, Edward. Did you ever _____ _____ _____ _____, *Endless Smile*?

M I finished it last week. Why?

W Can I borrow it? I want to read it on the subway. After my move, it _____ _____ to get to school.

M Sure. But please return it _____ _____ _____ _____. My sister wants to read it too.

W No problem. Can I come and pick it up today?

M Yes. You can _____ _____ _____ after 6.

20 | 상황에 적절한 말 고르기

다음 상황 설명을 듣고, Phil이 Olivia에게 할 말로 가장 적절한 것을 고르시오.

Phil: Olivia, _____

① I need to go to a doctor soon.

② what do you want to do after the movie?

③ let's meet at the theater at 11.

④ I'm afraid we can't get tickets.

⑤ can we see the movie another time?

M The other day, Phil _____ _____ with his friend Olivia. They were going to watch _____ _____ _____ _____ together on Saturday. However, Phil woke up that morning _____ _____ _____. Phil would like to ask Olivia if they can see the movie _____ _____ _____. In this situation, what would Phil most likely say to Olivia?

1 대화를 듣고, 남자가 만든 응원봉을 고르시오.

2 대화를 듣고, 배낭에 관해 언급되지 <u>않은</u> 것을 고르시오.

① 소재   ② 색상   ③ 가격
④ 크기   ⑤ 추가 구성품

3 대화를 듣고, 여자가 남자에게 전화한 목적으로 가장 적절한 것을 고르시오.

① 검사 결과를 전달하려고
② 진료를 예약하려고
③ 예약 시간을 변경하려고
④ 병원 위치를 알려주려고
⑤ 새로운 치료 방법을 홍보하려고

4 대화를 듣고, 남자가 탑승하려는 비행기의 출발 시각을 고르시오.

① 1 p.m.   ② 2 p.m.   ③ 3 p.m.
④ 4 p.m.   ⑤ 5 p.m.

5 다음 그림의 상황에 가장 적절한 대화를 고르시오.

①   ②   ③   ④   ⑤

6 대화를 듣고, 두 사람이 대화하는 장소로 가장 적절한 곳을 고르시오.

① 과학실   ② 국립공원   ③ 스키장
④ 미술관   ⑤ 도서관

7 대화를 듣고, 여자가 남자에게 부탁한 일로 가장 적절한 것을 고르시오.

① 컴퓨터 고치기
② 영화 티켓 예매하기
③ 택시 부르기
④ 자녀의 옷 갈아입히기
⑤ 자녀에게 출발한다고 알리기

_{고난도}
8 다음을 듣고, 리모델링에 관해 언급되지 <u>않은</u> 것을 고르시오.

① 목적   ② 담당자   ③ 소요 기간
④ 시작 일자   ⑤ 보상 방법

9 다음을 듣고, 무엇에 관한 설명인지 고르시오.

① 반지   ② 골무   ③ 고무장갑
④ 오븐 장갑   ⑤ 손목 보호대

10 다음을 듣고, 두 사람의 대화가 <u>어색한</u> 것을 고르시오.

①   ②   ③   ④   ⑤

11 대화를 듣고, 여자가 할 일로 가장 적절한 것을 고르시오.

① 샤워하기   ② 자전거 타기
③ 얼음물 가져오기   ④ 선풍기 틀기
⑤ 소파 옮기기

12 대화를 듣고, 두 사람이 만나기로 한 시각을 고르시오.

① 11 a.m.　　② 12 p.m.　　③ 2 p.m.

④ 5 p.m.　　⑤ 6 p.m.

13 다음 스터디 카페 배치도를 보면서 대화를 듣고, 두 사람이 선택할 스터디룸을 고르시오.

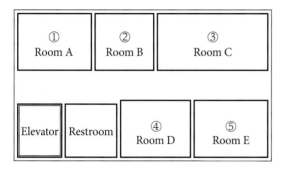

14 대화를 듣고, 여자가 지난 금요일에 한 일로 가장 적절한 것을 고르시오.

① 재킷 수선하기　　② 디자인 수업 듣기

③ 물건 반품하기　　④ 통장 개설하기

⑤ 시장 방문하기

15 다음을 듣고, 방송의 목적으로 가장 적절한 것을 고르시오.

① 경기 결과를 보도하려고

② 도로 폐쇄를 공지하려고

③ 마라톤 신청 방법을 설명하려고

④ 행사장으로 오는 길을 안내하려고

⑤ 새로운 버스 노선을 소개하려고

고난도

16 대화를 듣고, 여자가 지불할 금액을 고르시오.

① $ 15　　② $ 25　　③ $ 35

④ $ 45　　⑤ $ 55

17 대화를 듣고, 남자의 마지막 말에 대한 여자의 응답으로 가장 적절한 것을 고르시오.

Woman: _____

① That's so helpful. I appreciate it.

② Let's move on to the next article.

③ Really? You're already finished?

④ Sorry. I don't know the answer.

⑤ My sister's name is Rachel.

18 대화를 듣고, 여자의 마지막 말에 대한 남자의 응답으로 가장 적절한 것을 고르시오.

Man: _____

① No. The notebook is inside the drawer.

② We're doing an experiment in class today.

③ Yeah. The blue and the pink one.

④ I forgot to bring my science homework.

⑤ You can sit in that desk over there.

19 대화를 듣고, 남자의 마지막 말에 대한 여자의 응답으로 가장 적절한 것을 고르시오.

Woman: _____

① I already ate, so I'm not hungry.

② This is the line to get inside.

③ You take the line two and then the line one.

④ That's perfect! Let's go there then.

⑤ Our reservation is for 7 p.m.

20 다음 상황 설명을 듣고, Kelly가 남자에게 할 말로 가장 적절한 것을 고르시오.

Kelly: _____

① Would you take a picture of us, please?

② Smile for the camera!

③ Why don't we go to lunch after this?

④ Thank you so much for coming.

⑤ Congratulations on your graduation.

06회 중학영어듣기 실전 모의고사 Dictation 음성을 들으며 빈칸에 알맞은 단어를 채우시오.

1 | 알맞은 그림 고르기

대화를 듣고, 남자가 만든 응원봉을 고르시오.

① ② ③
④ ⑤

W Mark, are you ready? It's time to _____ _____ _____ _____.

M Wait, Mom. I need to get my light-up cheer stick.

W Oh, what's that?

M I made this to _____ _____ Jane. I want her to win the quiz show.

W Your sister will love it! How did you make it?

M It was simple. First, I wrote the words "GO JANE" on a piece of black paper, and then cut it into _____ _____ _____.

W Then, you _____ _____ to a yellow LED stick.

M Yes.

2 | 언급하지 않은 내용 고르기

대화를 듣고, 배낭에 관해 언급되지 않은 것을 고르시오.

① 소재 ② 색상 ③ 가격
④ 크기 ⑤ 추가 구성품

🎯 적중! Tip clim**b**ing

[클라이밍]으로 발음된다. m- 뒤에 오면서 단어의 맨 마지막에 쓰인 [b]는 묵음이다.

· bom**b** [밤] · lam**b** [램]

M Welcome to the Trek Store. How can I help you?

W I need to buy _____ _____ _____. I enjoy climbing on the weekends.

M _____ _____ _____ is popular with climbers.

W What _____ _____ _____ _____?

M Leather and nylon.

W How much does it cost?

M It is _____ _____ _____ 65 dollars.

W That is a little expensive.

M Well, it _____ _____ _____ _____ _____ and a water bottle.

W Hmm... In that case, I'll take it.

3 | 목적 고르기

대화를 듣고, 여자가 남자에게 전화한 목적으로 가장 적절한 것을 고르시오.

① 검사 결과를 전달하려고
② 진료를 예약하려고
③ 예약 시간을 변경하려고
④ 병원 위치를 알려주려고
⑤ 새로운 치료 방법을 홍보하려고

[Cellphone rings.]

M Hello?

W Hi, _____ _____ _____ _____ Jacob Simmons?

M That's me.

W This is Carol from Dr. Kim's office. _____ _____ _____ your dental appointment.

M Sure. What is it?

W Dr. Kim is going to be out of the office on Saturday, so we have to _____ _____ _____.

M Okay. When can I come in?

W You can see him on Thursday at 4 p.m. or Friday at 2 p.m.

M I'll come on Thursday.

4 | 시간 정보 고르기

대화를 듣고, 남자가 탑승하려는 비행기의 출발 시각을 고르시오.

① 1 p.m.　　② 2 p.m.　　③ 3 p.m.
④ 4 p.m.　　⑤ 5 p.m.

[Telephone rings.]
W World Connections Airlines. How may I help you?
M Hello. My flight from London to Boston was just canceled, so I need to _____ _____ _____ _____.
W Alright. Let me see. *[Typing sound]* Do you want _____ _____ _____?
M My last ticket was for business class.
W Well, there's a flight that leaves at 2 p.m. with business-class seats.
M I won't _____ _____ _____ to make that flight.
W What about 4? There is only economy class left for that flight.
M _____ _____ _____ _____.
W Okay. I'll book your ticket now then.

5 | 그림 상황에 적절한 대화 고르기

다음 그림의 상황에 가장 적절한 대화를 고르시오.

①　②　③　④　⑤

① M Could you _____ _____ _____ for me?
　W Sure. I'll do it in a minute.
② M Where should I put this?
　W _____ _____ _____, please.
③ M Did you order some new bedding?
　W Yes. It _____ _____ _____ this week.
④ M Did we _____ _____ _____ _____?
　W I got a letter from Mr. Dave.
⑤ M Why are you washing your sneakers?
　W I _____ _____ a puddle earlier.

6 | 장소 고르기

대화를 듣고, 두 사람이 대화하는 장소로 가장 적절한 곳을 고르시오.

① 과학실　　② 국립공원　　③ 스키장
④ 미술관　　⑤ 도서관

🎯 적중! Tip　**art**ist
[알티스트]보다는 [아리스트]로 들린다. [rt]가 모음 사이에서 발음될 때는 약화되어 [r]에 가깝게 발음되기 때문이다.

M Do you like this painting, Bora?
W Yes. The beach in it is beautiful _____ _____ _____.
M I love this painting of the mountains too. The artist is very talented.
W Do you prefer _____ _____ _____?
M Yes. I like them because I like being in nature.
W Right. But I prefer the _____ _____ _____ _____.
M Oh, really? Do you like history?
W Yes. It's my favorite subject. I find _____ _____ _____ _____ _____ so interesting.

7 | 부탁·요청한 일 고르기

대화를 듣고, 여자가 남자에게 부탁한 일로 가장 적절한 것을 고르시오.

① 컴퓨터 고치기
② 영화 티켓 예매하기
③ 택시 부르기
④ 자녀의 옷 갈아입히기
⑤ 자녀에게 출발한다고 알리기

W Honey, where are the kids?
M _____ _____ _____ on the computer.
W Are they _____ _____ _____? The movie starts at 6 p.m.
M Yes, they are ready. So, I don't think we have to hurry.
W Actually, the traffic looks bad. We _____ _____ _____.
M Okay. Should I tell the kids that we are leaving now?
W I'll do it. Can you just _____ _____ _____?
M Yes. I'll do that now.

8 | 언급하지 않은 내용 고르기

다음을 듣고, 리모델링에 관해 언급되지 <u>않은</u> 것을 고르시오.

① 목적　　② 담당자　　③ 소요 기간
④ 시작 일자　　⑤ 보상 방법

🎯 적중! Tip **months**

[먼뜨스]보다는 [먼쓰]로 들린다. 자음 3개가 연속해서 나오면 중간 자음은 발음되지 않기 때문이다.

· than**k**s [땡쓰]　· em**p**ty [엠티]

W This is an announcement for members of Health First Gym. We want to _____ _____ _____ _____ _____ _____, so we've decided to remodel our facility. _____ _____ _____ will take three months, and it will begin on September 1st. We understand that this will _____ _____ _____, so we will give all members a 30% discount on their fees during this time. When the construction is finished, we will have new fitness rooms for classes and upgraded machines. _____ _____ _____, and thank you for your support.

9 | 화제 고르기

다음을 듣고, 무엇에 관한 설명인지 고르시오.

① 반지　　② 골무　　③ 고무장갑
④ 오븐 장갑　　⑤ 손목 보호대

W This is something you wear on your hands. You need this when you _____ _____ _____ in the kitchen. It's usually made of _____ _____ and comes in various colors and patterns. You simply put your hand inside of it to use it. Then, you can _____ _____ _____ _____ hot dishes with your covered hand. Without this, you can _____ _____ _____ badly.

10 | 어색한 대화 고르기

다음을 듣고, 두 사람의 대화가 <u>어색한</u> 것을 고르시오.

①　　②　　③　　④　　⑤

① **M** Did you do anything fun last weekend?
　　W Yes. I went skiing with some friends.
② **M** Do you want to _____ _____ _____ or some chicken?
　　W Dinner isn't ready.
③ **M** Where do you usually _____ _____ _____ _____?
　　W I go to Sally's Salon.
④ **M** How can I help you?
　　W Where is _____ _____ _____ _____?
⑤ **M** Here is the tool I borrowed.
　　W Thank you for returning it so quickly!

11 | 할 일 고르기

대화를 듣고, 여자가 할 일로 가장 적절한 것을 고르시오.

① 샤워하기　　② 자전거 타기
③ 얼음물 가져오기　　④ 선풍기 틀기
⑤ 소파 옮기기

M _____ _____ _____ was hard, Honey.
W I agree. I'm so tired.
M Do you want to _____ _____ _____ and relax?
W Yes. But it's a little hot in here.
M I just showered, but I'm _____ _____ from the workout.
W I'll _____ _____ _____ then.
M Good. I'll get us two cups of iced water.

12 | 시간 정보 고르기

대화를 듣고, 두 사람이 만나기로 한 시각을 고르시오.

① 11 a.m.　　② 12 p.m.　　③ 2 p.m.
④ 5 p.m.　　⑤ 6 p.m.

🎯 적중! Tip　That works for me.
약속 시간, 제안 사항 등이 나에게 괜찮다고 말할 때 사용되는 표현으로, 특히 약속을 잡을 때 많이 사용된다.

W Jake, do you want to have lunch this Friday?
M Okay. _____ _____ _____ _____ _____ to meet?
W How about 12? We can go to that Chinese restaurant downtown.
M Actually, I have _____ _____ _____ at 11 a.m., and it will take longer than an hour. What about meeting at 2?
W That's _____ _____ _____ for me. I'll need to eat before then.
M Then, why don't we just _____ _____ _____ ?
W Yeah. That's a good idea. Is 6 okay?
M That works for me. See you then.

13 | 위치 고르기

다음 스터디 카페 배치도를 보면서 대화를 듣고, 두 사람이 선택할 스터디룸을 고르시오.

① Room A	② Room B	③ Room C

Elevator	Restroom	④ Room D	⑤ Room E

M Sarah, did you book a study room for our group project?
W Not yet. I just found this new study café. It looks quiet.
M Oh, that's nice. Let's _____ _____ there.
W How about Room C? _____ _____ _____ .
M There are only four of us, so we don't need a room that big.
W Okay. How about Room A or Room D?
M I don't want to book those rooms because they are close to _____
_____ _____ _____ _____ .
W I agree with you. Then, we have two options left.
M I think the one _____ _____ _____ would be quiet.
W Let's choose that one then.

14 | 한 일 고르기

대화를 듣고, 여자가 지난 금요일에 한 일로 가장 적절한 것을 고르시오.

① 재킷 수선하기　　② 디자인 수업 듣기
③ 물건 반품하기　　④ 통장 개설하기
⑤ 시장 방문하기

M That's a cool jacket, Zoe.
W Thank you. It was made by a local designer.
M Where did you find it?
W I _____ _____ _____ _____ on Friday and saw it.
There are so many nice clothes there.
M Are they expensive?
W _____ _____ _____ . But this jacket is a little big for me, so I will _____ _____ _____ _____ later today.
M Maybe I will go to the market too. I need _____ _____
_____ .
W You should.

06회 실전 모의고사 해커스 중학영어듣기 모의고사 24회 Level 3

15 | 목적 고르기

다음을 듣고, 방송의 목적으로 가장 적절한 것을 고르시오.

① 경기 결과를 보도하려고
② 도로 폐쇄를 공지하려고
③ 마라톤 신청 방법을 설명하려고
④ 행사장으로 오는 길을 안내하려고
⑤ 새로운 버스 노선을 소개하려고

W This is Vanessa Watkins at *BBS News*. This morning, _____ _____ _____ was held. It was a hot day, but thousands of people ran in the race. In _____ _____ _____, Benson Turner won for the third year in a row with a time of two hours and four minutes. Gina Jenkins _____ _____ _____ _____. She finished in two hours and 30 minutes. We congratulate both winners and everyone else _____ _____ today.

16 | 금액 정보 고르기

대화를 듣고, 여자가 지불할 금액을 고르시오.

① $ 15   ② $ 25   ③ $ 35
④ $ 45   ⑤ $ 55

🎯 적중! Tip   That's a great deal.
가격이 저렴하거나 거래 조건이 좋다는 것을 말할 때 사용되는 표현이다.

M Hi. How may I help you?
W I'm interested in _____ _____ _____ _____ for beginners. How much is it?
M If you take the class _____ _____ _____, it's 35 dollars. But you can also take the class three times a week _____ _____ _____ _____.
W How much is _____ _____ _____?
M You have to pay 10 dollars more.
W That's a great deal. Can I _____ _____ _____ three classes per week then, please?
M Of course. If you enjoy it, you can sign up for more classes afterward.
W Thank you.

17 | 적절한 응답 고르기

대화를 듣고, 남자의 마지막 말에 대한 여자의 응답으로 가장 적절한 것을 고르시오.

Woman: _____

① That's so helpful. I appreciate it.
② Let's move on to the next article.
③ Really? You're already finished?
④ Sorry. I don't know the answer.
⑤ My sister's name is Rachel.

M We need to _____ _____ _____ for the school newspaper, Hanna.
W I agree. We should work on it this weekend.
M We have so much to do, so let's meet before then.
W I'm sorry, but I'm _____ _____ _____ my sister every night this week. My parents will work late.
M Oh, so you can't go anywhere?
W No. She's _____ _____ _____ _____ home alone.
M That's fine. If you want, I can _____ _____ _____ _____ and we can work there.

18 | 적절한 응답 고르기

대화를 듣고, 여자의 마지막 말에 대한 남자의 응답으로 가장 적절한 것을 고르시오.

Man: _____

① No. The notebook is inside the drawer.
② We're doing an experiment in class today.
③ Yeah. The blue and the pink one.
④ I forgot to bring my science homework.
⑤ You can sit in that desk over there.

> 🎯 적중! Tip **st_udying**
> [스터딩]보다는 [스떠딩]으로 들린다. [s] 뒤에 [t] 발음이 오면 된소리로 발음되기 때문이다.
> · st_ory [스또리]   · st_ick [스띡]

[Cellphone rings.]
W Hello?
M Mom, can you bring _____ _____ _____ to David's house?
W Oh, did you forget it?
M Yes. I left it at home and brought my math homework instead. But we _____ _____ _____ _____ today.
W I see. I'll bring it over now then. Do you need anything else?
M Actually, can you also _____ _____ _____? I want them for studying.
W Sure. Do you want the ones _____ _____ _____?

19 | 적절한 응답 고르기

대화를 듣고, 남자의 마지막 말에 대한 여자의 응답으로 가장 적절한 것을 고르시오.

Woman: _____

① I already ate, so I'm not hungry.
② This is the line to get inside.
③ You take the line two and then the line one.
④ That's perfect! Let's go there then.
⑤ Our reservation is for 7 p.m.

M Are you ready for the concert tonight, Minji?
W _____ _____ _____. Are we meeting outside of the stadium at 6?
M Maybe we should _____ _____ _____ _____ _____ before the show. What do you think?
W That's a great idea. Where should we eat?
M There aren't a lot of places _____ _____ _____, so we can go somewhere at the next subway stop.
W Yeah. That area has lots of restaurants.
M And I know _____ _____ _____ _____ around there.

20 | 상황에 적절한 말 고르기

다음 상황 설명을 듣고, Kelly가 남자에게 할 말로 가장 적절한 것을 고르시오.

Kelly: _____

① Would you take a picture of us, please?
② Smile for the camera!
③ Why don't we go to lunch after this?
④ Thank you so much for coming.
⑤ Congratulations on your graduation.

W Kelly is at _____ _____ _____ _____. She is happy because her entire family came to the event to congratulate her. Kelly _____ _____ _____ to remember this day. So, she decides to ask a man standing next to her family _____ _____ _____. In this situation, what would Kelly most likely say to the man?

1 대화를 듣고, 남자가 구입할 수면 안대를 고르시오.

①   ②   ③

④   ⑤

2 대화를 듣고, The Latest Show에 관해 언급되지 <u>않은</u> 것을 고르시오.

① 진행자   ② 방영 시간   ③ 초대 손님
④ 길이   ⑤ 수상 기록

고난도
3 대화를 듣고, 남자가 여자에게 전화한 목적으로 가장 적절한 것을 고르시오.

① 고객 설문조사를 실시하려고
② 파손된 제품의 교환을 요청하려고
③ 주문 정보를 확인하려고
④ 환불 규정을 확인하려고
⑤ 전자 제품 할인율을 문의하려고

4 대화를 듣고, 남자가 미용실을 예약한 시각을 고르시오.

① 8 a.m.   ② 9 a.m.   ③ 10 a.m.
④ 11 a.m.   ⑤ 12 p.m.

5 대화를 듣고, 두 사람이 대화하는 장소로 가장 적절한 곳을 고르시오.

① 우체국   ② 시청   ③ 지하철역
④ 극장   ⑤ 공항

6 다음 그림의 상황에 가장 적절한 대화를 고르시오.

①   ②   ③   ④   ⑤

7 대화를 듣고, 여자가 남자에게 부탁한 일로 가장 적절한 것을 고르시오.

① 과제 검토하기   ② 역사 알려주기
③ 필기 보여주기   ④ 자료 빌려주기
⑤ 이메일 발송하기

8 다음을 듣고, Oakhill Art Gallery에 관해 언급되지 <u>않은</u> 것을 고르시오.

① 소유자   ② 개관 연도   ③ 전시품 종류
④ 운영 시간   ⑤ 입장료

9 다음을 듣고, 무엇에 관한 설명인지 고르시오.

① 비커   ② 온도계   ③ 현미경
④ 플라스크   ⑤ 망원경

10 다음을 듣고, 두 사람의 대화가 <u>어색한</u> 것을 고르시오.

①   ②   ③   ④   ⑤

11 대화를 듣고, 여자가 할 일로 가장 적절한 것을 고르시오.

① 휴대폰 맡기기   ② 디자인 고르기
③ 벽화 그리기   ④ 케이스 교체하기
⑤ 가방 구매하기

12 다음 표를 보면서 대화를 듣고, 여자가 앉을 좌석을 고르시오.

	Way	Class	Seat
①	one-way	Economy	aisle
②	round-trip	Economy	window
③	one-way	Economy	window
④	round-trip	Business	aisle
⑤	one-way	Business	window

고난도
13 대화를 듣고, 두 사람이 비료를 사러 갈 날짜를 고르시오.

① April 19th ② April 20th ③ April 21st

④ April 22nd ⑤ April 23rd

14 대화를 듣고, 남자가 어제 한 일로 가장 적절한 것을 고르시오.

① 책 주문하기 ② 독후감 쓰기
③ 추리소설 읽기 ④ 영화 감상하기
⑤ 도서관 방문하기

15 다음을 듣고, 방송의 목적으로 가장 적절한 것을 고르시오.

① 스트레스의 주요 원인을 설명하려고
② 더 좋은 성적을 내기 위한 습관을 추천하려고
③ 시험 일정의 변경 사항을 공지하려고
④ 충분한 수면 시간의 중요성을 강조하려고
⑤ 시험 기간에 건강하게 지낼 방법을 알려주려고

16 대화를 듣고, 여자가 지불할 금액을 고르시오.

① $ 2 ② $ 4 ③ $ 6
④ $ 8 ⑤ $ 10

17 대화를 듣고, 여자의 마지막 말에 대한 남자의 응답으로 가장 적절한 것을 고르시오.

Man: _____

① I forgot to bring sunscreen.
② You look great in this picture.
③ Sure. Make sure to tell me which one you picked.
④ Thank you for sharing these beautiful photos.
⑤ There's something wrong with the camera.

18 대화를 듣고, 남자의 마지막 말에 대한 여자의 응답으로 가장 적절한 것을 고르시오.

Woman: _____

① I'll try to arrive as soon as possible.
② I'm not sure if the bus goes to the zoo.
③ Don't blame me. It's not my fault.
④ It's generous of her to forgive my being late.
⑤ I'll keep my fingers crossed!

19 대화를 듣고, 여자의 마지막 말에 대한 남자의 응답으로 가장 적절한 것을 고르시오.

Man: _____

① I can help you with the assignment.
② He didn't answer the phone.
③ I will be 15 years old tomorrow.
④ That's okay. He teaches all levels.
⑤ You'll play well in the match.

20 다음 상황 설명을 듣고, Jane이 남자에게 할 말로 가장 적절한 것을 고르시오.

Jane: Excuse me, _____

① can you close the curtains?
② how long is this train ride?
③ I need to get off because this is my stop.
④ can you turn your music down?
⑤ this song is by a K-pop artist, right?

07회 중학영어듣기 실전 모의고사 Dictation 음성을 들으며 빈칸에 알맞은 단어를 채우시오.

1 | 알맞은 그림 고르기

대화를 듣고, 남자가 구입할 수면 안대를 고르시오.

① ② ③

④ ⑤

W Good afternoon. How can I help you?
M I'm _____ _____ _____ _____ for my son.
W How about this one _____ _____ _____ on it?
M It's not bad, but it's not his style.
W Alright. Then, how about _____ _____ _____? You can choose from a chick, raccoon, or fox face.
M My son will like _____ _____ _____ _____. I'll take that one.
W Good choice.

2 | 언급하지 않은 내용 고르기

대화를 듣고, The Latest Show에 관해 언급되지 않은 것을 고르시오.

① 진행자   ② 방영 시간   ③ 초대 손님
④ 길이   ⑤ 수상 기록

W Dirk, did you see *The Latest Show* last night?
M You mean _____ _____ _____ _____ Jeremy Wilson, right? I missed it.
W Oh, why?
M I don't know when the show _____ _____.
W It's on TV at 9 o'clock every Saturday. I'm _____ _____ _____ _____ _____. They had a special guest yesterday.
M I know! Wasn't Hojun Shin on it _____ _____ his new movie?
W Yeah. He was so funny that I _____ _____ _____ _____ 60 minutes.
M I guess I'll have to watch it on the Internet later.

고난도
3 | 목적 고르기

대화를 듣고, 남자가 여자에게 전화한 목적으로 가장 적절한 것을 고르시오.

① 고객 설문조사를 실시하려고
② 파손된 제품의 교환을 요청하려고
③ 주문 정보를 확인하려고
④ 환불 규정을 확인하려고
⑤ 전자 제품 할인율을 문의하려고

[Telephone rings.]
W Good morning. Four-Star Electronics customer service.
M Hi. I'd like to know about _____ _____ _____ _____.
W Are you having a problem with one of our products?
M I'm not happy with my new headphones. _____ _____ _____ isn't that great.
W Well, if you've had them for less than 15 days, you can return them _____ _____ _____.
M I've only had them for four days.
W Then, you'll just need to mail them to us in the original packaging. _____ _____ _____ _____ _____, however, we cannot accept them.
M Got it. Thanks for the explanation.

4 | 시간 정보 고르기

대화를 듣고, 남자가 미용실을 예약한 시각을 고르시오.

① 8 a.m.　② 9 a.m.　③ 10 a.m.
④ 11 a.m.　⑤ 12 p.m.

M Excuse me. I'd like to make an appointment to _____ _____ _____.

W Okay. When do you want to come in?

M Tomorrow morning _____ _____ _____ for me.

W Of course. We usually open at 11 in the morning.

M Hmm... _____ _____ _____ _____ an interview at 10. I want to look nice in the interview.

W Then, I can open _____ _____ _____. How about 9?

M Thank you so much. That would be best.

5 | 장소 고르기

대화를 듣고, 두 사람이 대화하는 장소로 가장 적절한 곳을 고르시오.

① 우체국　② 시청　③ 지하철역
④ 극장　⑤ 공항

🎯 적중! Tip　check again

[체크 어게인]보다는 [체커게인]으로 들린다. 앞에 나온 단어의 끝 자음과 뒤에 나온 단어의 첫 모음이 연음되기 때문이다.
· pass away [패서웨이]　· sold out [솔다웃]

W I'm _____ _____ _____ _____ _____.

M Me too. And I can't believe we got _____ _____ _____!

W Yes. There are some very famous actors in this play, so I was afraid I wouldn't _____ _____ _____.

M The story also sounds very exciting.

W Yeah. I read some good reviews of this play in a magazine.

M I'm _____ _____ _____ _____ it. By the way, did you silence your phone? It _____ _____!

W I think so, but I'll check again.

6 | 그림 상황에 적절한 대화 고르기

다음 그림의 상황에 가장 적절한 대화를 고르시오.

① ② ③ ④ ⑤

① W How did you hurt yourself?
　M I _____ _____ _____ _____.
② W I'd like to buy some flowers, please.
　M What kind do you want?
③ W Can I ride my bike in this park?
　M No. _____ _____ _____.
④ W You should wear a cap in the pool.
　M You're right. I'll _____ _____ _____ now.
⑤ W Is that a new bike?
　M Yes. I _____ _____ _____.

7 | 부탁·요청한 일 고르기

대화를 듣고, 여자가 남자에게 부탁한 일로 가장 적절한 것을 고르시오.

① 과제 검토하기　② 역사 알려주기
③ 필기 보여주기　④ 자료 빌려주기
⑤ 이메일 발송하기

🎯 적중! Tip　Do you mind ~?

상대방에게 무언가를 요청하거나 양해를 구할 때 사용되는 표현으로 '~해 줄래?, ~해도 괜찮을까?'라는 의미이다. 이때 mind 다음에는 동명사가 온다.
· Do you mind closing the door?
　문 좀 닫아 줄래?

[Cellphone rings.]

M What's up, Hayley?

W Hey. I'm a little worried about _____ _____ _____.

M Did you finish it?

W I did, but I _____ _____ _____ about it.

M How can I help?

W You're just so good at history. Do you mind _____ _____ _____?

M Of course. Just email it to me.

다음을 듣고, Oakhill Art Gallery에 관해 언급되지 않은 것을 고르시오.

① 소유자　　② 개관 연도　　③ 전시품 종류
④ 운영 시간　　⑤ 입장료

W Welcome to the Oakhill Art Gallery. Before the tour begins, I will tell you about our gallery, which ＿＿＿＿＿ ＿＿＿＿＿ Peter Williams. He opened this gallery in 1983 to ＿＿＿＿ ＿＿＿＿ ＿＿＿＿. Many of the exhibits include ＿＿＿＿ ＿＿＿＿ ＿＿＿＿. The gallery is open from 10 a.m. to 11 p.m., Monday to Saturday. However, we sometimes ＿＿＿＿ ＿＿＿＿ on Sundays for special events. Now, let's start the tour.

다음을 듣고, 무엇에 관한 설명인지 고르시오.

① 비커　　② 온도계　　③ 현미경
④ 플라스크　　⑤ 망원경

M This is a very useful experiment tool for scientists. People use this device to ＿＿＿＿ ＿＿＿＿ ＿＿＿＿ by looking through the lens. It ＿＿＿＿ ＿＿＿＿ ＿＿＿＿ ＿＿＿＿, so it is easy to study them. Many people learn to use this device in school, and it is used everyday ＿＿＿＿ ＿＿＿＿ around the world.

다음을 듣고, 두 사람의 대화가 <u>어색한</u> 것을 고르시오.

①　　②　　③　　④　　⑤

🎯 적중! Tip　I bet ~.

어떤 상황에 대한 확신을 나타낼 때 사용되는 표현으로 '틀림없이 ~이다'라는 의미이다.

· I bet you'll like it.
　틀림없이 넌 그걸 좋아할 거야.

① W Do you think you can fix my computer?
　M I bet I can. Let me try.
② W Is it ＿＿＿＿ ＿＿＿＿?
　M No. I wore my snow boots.
③ W Can you ＿＿＿＿ ＿＿＿＿ ＿＿＿＿ for me?
　M Of course. I'd be happy to.
④ W Is it ＿＿＿＿ ＿＿＿＿ ＿＿＿＿ ＿＿＿＿?
　M Here, please. I'm too hungry to wait until I get home.
⑤ W Let's go for a hike this afternoon.
　M I have ＿＿＿＿ ＿＿＿＿ ＿＿＿＿ at 2 p.m.

대화를 듣고, 여자가 할 일로 가장 적절한 것을 고르시오.

① 휴대폰 맡기기　　② 디자인 고르기
③ 벽화 그리기　　④ 케이스 교체하기
⑤ 가방 구매하기

M Hi. Do you need help?
W Yes. I'm looking for ＿＿＿＿ ＿＿＿＿ ＿＿＿＿ ＿＿＿＿.
M What kind of design do you want?
W I don't want ＿＿＿＿ ＿＿＿＿ ＿＿＿＿ ＿＿＿＿. I just want it to be one color.
M Here are some phone cases in ＿＿＿＿ ＿＿＿＿ ＿＿＿＿.
W I like the purple one. Can I buy it, please?
M Sure. I'll get you a bag for it.
W No need. I'll ＿＿＿＿ ＿＿＿＿ ＿＿＿＿ on my phone now.

12 | 도표에서 알맞은 항목 고르기

다음 표를 보면서 대화를 듣고, 여자가 앉을 좌석을 고르시오.

	Way	Class	Seat
①	one-way	Economy	aisle
②	round-trip	Economy	window
③	one-way	Economy	window
④	round-trip	Business	aisle
⑤	one-way	Business	window

M What can I do for you?

W Hi. I'd like to reserve a ticket to New York on May 14th, please.

M Would you like a one-way ticket or _____ _____ _____?

W One-way, please.

M Let's see. There are _____ _____ _____ the 8 a.m. flight. However, the business-class section is full.

W I'm _____ _____ _____.

M Which do you prefer, a window seat or _____ _____ _____?

W A window seat please. I like _____ _____ _____ while flying.

13 | 시간 정보 고르기

대화를 듣고, 두 사람이 비료를 사러 갈 날짜를 고르시오.

① April 19th   ② April 20th   ③ April 21st
④ April 22nd   ⑤ April 23rd

W Honey, have you looked in _____ _____ _____?

M No. Why?

W I think some of the trees are withering.

M Oh, I thought they _____ _____ _____.

W No. So, I think we should _____ _____ _____. Are you free on Thursday?

M Isn't that April 19th? Did you forget about Jenny's school concert? I don't think we'll have time to _____ _____ _____ _____ _____ that day.

W You're right. I completely forgot. What about the 22nd?

M But that's Sunday. The store will be closed then. Let's _____ _____ _____.

W That sounds perfect. We can spread the fertilizer on Sunday.

14 | 한 일 고르기

대화를 듣고, 남자가 어제 한 일로 가장 적절한 것을 고르시오.

① 책 주문하기   ② 독후감 쓰기
③ 추리소설 읽기   ④ 영화 감상하기
⑤ 도서관 방문하기

🎯 적중! Tip exci**t**ed

[익사이티드]보다는 [익사이리드]로 들린다. [t]가 모음 사이에서 발음될 때는 약화되어 [r]에 가깝게 발음되기 때문이다.

· la**t**er [레이러] · pre**tt**y [프리리]

W I have some good news, Daejun.

M What is it?

W I just _____ _____ *The Secret Crime*, so you can finally borrow the book.

M Oh, thank you. But I don't _____ _____ _____.

W Really? You said you were excited to read it.

M I am, but I _____ _____ _____ online yesterday.

W But why?

M It's a long book, and I didn't want to _____ _____ _____ _____ _____ it. But you read it so quickly.

W Yes. I couldn't _____ _____ _____ _____ _____.

다음을 듣고, 방송의 목적으로 가장 적절한 것을 고르시오.

① 스트레스의 주요 원인을 설명하려고
② 더 좋은 성적을 내기 위한 습관을 추천하려고
③ 시험 일정의 변경 사항을 공지하려고
④ 충분한 수면 시간의 중요성을 강조하려고
⑤ 시험 기간에 건강하게 지낼 방법을 알려주려고

🎯 적중! Tip **bo_d_y**
[바디]보다는 [바리]로 들린다. [d]가 모음 사이에서 발음될 때는 약화되어 [r]에 가깝게 발음되기 때문이다.

W Hello, students. This is your principal, Ms. Greer. I hope _____ _____ _____ _____. I know this can be a stressful time of year, so I want to share some ways to _____ _____ _____ during this time. First, please remember to get enough sleep. Your body and brain _____ _____ _____ to work hard. Everyone should also take a 20-minute break every hour or so while studying. Lastly, eat _____ _____ _____ such as fruit and vegetables. Good luck!

대화를 듣고, 여자가 지불할 금액을 고르시오.

① $ 2　　② $ 4　　③ $ 6
④ $ 8　　⑤ $ 10

M Hello. Are you _____ _____ _____?
W Yes. I'd like a chocolate donut, please.
M That will be four dollars. But if you pay two dollars more, you can _____ _____ _____ _____ _____.
W Oh, that's great. I'll pay two dollars more then.
M Okay. Would you like any other donuts? We have _____ _____ _____.
W Thanks, but I'm okay.
M Alright. Will you eat this here?
W Yes, I'll _____ _____ _____.

대화를 듣고, 여자의 마지막 말에 대한 남자의 응답으로 가장 적절한 것을 고르시오.

Man: _____

① I forgot to bring sunscreen.
② You look great in this picture.
③ Sure. Make sure to tell me which one you picked.
④ Thank you for sharing these beautiful photos.
⑤ There's something wrong with the camera.

W _____ _____ _____ _____ last weekend, Woobin?
M It was beautiful! The sky was clear, and it was very warm.
W Did you _____ _____ _____?
M Sure. I have some here on my phone.
W Wow! _____ _____ _____. You're so good at photography.
M Thanks. I love to take photographs of nature.
W Can you _____ _____ _____ _____ _____? I want to make one of them the background image on my phone.

18 | 적절한 응답 고르기

대화를 듣고, 남자의 마지막 말에 대한 여자의 응답으로 가장 적절한 것을 고르시오.

Woman: _____

① I'll try to arrive as soon as possible.

② I'm not sure if the bus goes to the zoo.

③ Don't blame me. It's not my fault.

④ It's generous of her to forgive my being late.

⑤ I'll keep my fingers crossed!

> 🎯 적중! Tip That's a relief.
> 안도감을 나타낼 때 사용되는 표현으로 '다행이다'라는 의미이다.

[Cellphone rings.]

M Hi, Molly. I don't see you. _____ _____ _____ we leave for our field trip soon?

W I know, Mr. Jones. But I just _____ _____ _____. I will be late.

M Can you ask your parents _____ _____ _____?

W They are both at work now.

M I see. Well, some other students will also be late. So, Ms. Baker _____ _____ _____ _____ to the zoo later.

W That's a relief. And I'm sorry for being late.

M That's okay, but please _____ _____.

19 | 적절한 응답 고르기

대화를 듣고, 여자의 마지막 말에 대한 남자의 응답으로 가장 적절한 것을 고르시오.

Man: _____

① I can help you with the assignment.

② He didn't answer the phone.

③ I will be 15 years old tomorrow.

④ That's okay. He teaches all levels.

⑤ You'll play well in the match.

W Do you want to study together tonight, Daniel?

M I'm sorry, but I can't. I have to go to _____ _____ _____.

W I didn't know you played tennis. When did you start playing?

M I started lessons when I was nine. I play _____ _____ _____ _____ _____.

W You must be good then. I want to play tennis too.

M Do you want _____ _____ _____ _____? He really helped me get better.

W Sure. But I am only at _____ _____ _____.

20 | 상황에 적절한 말 고르기

다음 상황 설명을 듣고, Jane이 남자에게 할 말로 가장 적절한 것을 고르시오.

Jane: Excuse me, _____

① can you close the curtains?

② how long is this train ride?

③ I need to get off because this is my stop.

④ can you turn your music down?

⑤ this song is by a K-pop artist, right?

W Jane is riding on the train. She is on the way to _____ _____ _____ in the countryside. She is trying to read her book, but the man next to her is _____ _____ _____ _____. Jane is not enjoying her ride because of this. So, she wants to ask the man to _____ _____ _____ of his music. In this situation, what would Jane most likely say to the man?

1 대화를 듣고, 남자가 구입할 헬멧을 고르시오.

①   ②   ③

④   ⑤

2 대화를 듣고, 여자가 남자에게 부탁한 일로 가장 적절한 것을 고르시오.

① 크레파스 가져오기   ② 컵 받침 뜨기
③ 현수막 주문하기   ④ 포스터 붙이기
⑤ 동아리 이름 정하기

3 다음 그림의 상황에 가장 적절한 대화를 고르시오.

①   ②   ③   ④   ⑤

4 대화를 듣고, 두 사람이 예약한 시티투어버스의 출발 시각을 고르시오.

① 10 a.m.   ② 11 a.m.   ③ 2 p.m.
④ 4 p.m.   ⑤ 5 p.m.

5 대화를 듣고, 작품에 관해 언급되지 않은 것을 고르시오.

① 작품명   ② 사용된 색
③ 작가의 출신 국가   ④ 작품 시리즈 수
⑤ 작품 제작 연도

6 대화를 듣고, 두 사람이 대화하는 장소로 가장 적절한 곳을 고르시오.

① 도서관   ② 가방 가게   ③ 공연장
④ 편의점   ⑤ 공항

7 다음을 듣고, 두 사람의 대화가 <u>어색한</u> 것을 고르시오.

①   ②   ③   ④   ⑤

8 대화를 듣고, 여자가 남자에게 부탁한 일로 가장 적절한 것을 고르시오.

① 택배 찾아오기   ② 새해 인사 보내기
③ 우표 사 오기   ④ 엽서 골라주기
⑤ 동물원 티켓 사기

9 다음을 듣고, 무엇에 관한 안내 방송인지 고르시오.

① 문화재 취급법   ② 박물관 운영 시간
③ 사진 수업 등록   ④ 새 전시회 개관
⑤ 박물관 주의 사항

고난도
10 대화를 듣고, 여자가 지불할 금액을 고르시오.

① $ 10   ② $ 15   ③ $ 20
④ $ 25   ⑤ $ 30

11 대화를 듣고, 남자가 할 일로 가장 적절한 것을 고르시오.

① 화분 구매하기   ② 나무 운반하기
③ 도움 요청하기   ④ 택시비 지불하기
⑤ 사무실 꾸미기

12 다음을 듣고, 기부 행사에 관해 언급되지 <u>않은</u> 것을 고르시오.

① 행사 날짜　　② 행사 장소　　③ 기부 품목
④ 기부 목적　　⑤ 신청 방법

고난도
13 다음 표를 보면서 대화를 듣고, 두 사람이 대여할 자전거를 고르시오.

	Bike	Number of seats	Color	Price (per hour)
①	A	1	Purple	$ 4
②	B	1	Purple	$ 5
③	C	2	Purple	$ 6
④	D	1	Pink	$ 4
⑤	E	2	Pink	$ 5

14 다음을 듣고, 무엇에 관한 설명인지 고르시오.

① 개미　　　　② 사슴벌레　　　③ 거미
④ 달팽이　　　⑤ 나비

15 대화를 듣고, 여자가 할 일로 가장 적절한 것을 고르시오.

① 부엌 청소하기　　　② TV 시청하기
③ 냉장고 비우기　　　④ 옷장 정리하기
⑤ 음악 재생하기

16 대화를 듣고, 두 사람이 선택한 요리 수업의 시작 시각을 고르시오.

① 1 p.m.　　　② 2 p.m.　　　③ 3 p.m.
④ 4 p.m.　　　⑤ 5 p.m.

17 대화를 듣고, 남자의 마지막 말에 대한 여자의 응답으로 가장 적절한 것을 고르시오.

Woman: _____

① I can fix your chair. It's easy.
② The manager isn't here right now.
③ You can get a refund or exchange the item.
④ We need some nails and a hammer.
⑤ Okay. I will come back to the store this afternoon.

18 대화를 듣고, 여자의 마지막 말에 대한 남자의 응답으로 가장 적절한 것을 고르시오.

Man: _____

① My cat acts very funny sometimes.
② Please do not record any videos.
③ We ought to feed our hamster.
④ I'll give you the link instead.
⑤ Sure. I also love watching comedy films.

19 대화를 듣고, 남자의 마지막 말에 대한 여자의 응답으로 가장 적절한 것을 고르시오.

Woman: _____

① I went to Italy last summer.
② Yes. I'll pay the bill now.
③ She can't eat spicy food.
④ The tomato salad will be good.
⑤ I am allergic to mushrooms.

20 다음 상황 설명을 듣고, Isaac이 Rachel에게 할 말로 가장 적절한 것을 고르시오.

Isaac: Rachel, _____

① I already have plans today.
② why don't we meet at 3?
③ what part do you want to take?
④ can you bring a science textbook?
⑤ where do you want to meet on Saturday?

08회 중학영어듣기 실전 모의고사 Dictation 음성을 들으며 빈칸에 알맞은 단어를 채우시오.

1 | 알맞은 그림 고르기

대화를 듣고, 남자가 구입할 헬멧을 고르시오.

① ② ③

④ ⑤

M Hello, I'm here to buy a helmet.
W You're in the right place. Do you want ones _____ _____?
M No. I don't need them.
W Then, what do you think of this one with four holes _____ _____ _____? It's light but strong.
M Sorry, but I don't like the word "FAST" on it. Do you have the same model _____ _____ _____?
W Sure. It comes in black or blue.
M That's good. I'll take _____ _____ _____.
W Okay.

2 | 부탁·요청한 일 고르기

대화를 듣고, 여자가 남자에게 부탁한 일로 가장 적절한 것을 고르시오.

① 크레파스 가져오기　② 컵 받침 뜨기
③ 현수막 주문하기　④ 포스터 붙이기
⑤ 동아리 이름 정하기

🎯 적중! Tip　Would you
[우드 유]보다는 [우쥬]로 들린다. [d]로 끝나는 단어 뒤에 y-로 시작하는 단어가 이어지면 두 소리가 연결되어 [쥬]로 발음되기 때문이다.

W I'd like to start _____ _____ _____, Mike. Would you like to help me?
M That's a good idea. But how do we start one?
W Well, we can _____ _____ and put them around the school. If _____ _____ _____ _____, they can tell us.
M Okay. Should we make posters this weekend?
W Yes. We can meet at my house.
M What should I bring?
W Can you _____ _____ _____? I will buy the poster paper.
M Sounds good.

3 | 그림 상황에 적절한 대화 고르기

다음 그림의 상황에 가장 적절한 대화를 고르시오.

① ② ③ ④ ⑤

① W Could you turn down the TV?
　M Sorry. _____ _____ _____ it was too loud.
② W I don't see _____ _____ _____.
　M Let's go to another restaurant.
③ W How much were the concert tickets?
　M They were 50 dollars each.
④ W _____ _____ _____ long?
　M I just started taking lessons.
⑤ W The song _____ _____ is my favorite.
　M It's very nice.

4 | 시간 정보 고르기

대화를 듣고, 두 사람이 예약한 시티투어버스의 출발 시각을 고르시오.

① 10 a.m. ② 11 a.m. ③ 2 p.m.
④ 4 p.m. ⑤ 5 p.m.

> 🎯 적중! Tip had better
> 어떤 일을 하자는 제안이나 강한 충고를 나타낼 때 사용되는 표현으로 '~하는 게 좋겠다, 낫겠다'라는 의미이다. 이때 had better(='d better) 다음에는 동사원형이 온다.
> · You'd better wake up early.
> 넌 일찍 일어나는 게 좋겠어.

M What's the matter, Suyeon?

W I'm enjoying our family trip, but my feet hurt, Dad. I _____ _____ _____.

M Then, we'd better take a city tour bus tomorrow. I got this pamphlet for a city tour.

W That sounds fun. Why don't we leave at 10 a.m.?

M _____ _____ _____ _____ leaves at 11. But your mom wants to try the hotel buffet for lunch. I think we should leave at 2.

W What time will we get back?

M The tour lasts for _____ _____ _____ _____, so we should return to our hotel by 5.

W That sounds great. _____ _____ _____ on the 2 p.m. bus then.

5 | 언급하지 않은 내용 고르기

대화를 듣고, 작품에 관해 언급되지 <u>않은</u> 것을 고르시오.

① 작품명 ② 사용된 색
③ 작가의 출신 국가 ④ 작품 시리즈 수
⑤ 작품 제작 연도

M Hyojoo, what is that painting you're looking at?

W This is a painting by Claude Monet. _____ _____ *Houses of Parliament, Sunset.*

M Oh, I've heard about Monet. He is _____ _____ _____, right?

W That's right. This is one of my favorite pieces by him.

M _____ _____ _____ _____ _____ in the sky are beautiful.

W I know, right? It's part of a series. He painted the same place at different times of day.

M _____ _____ _____ _____ _____ ?

W Monet painted this one in 1903.

6 | 장소 고르기

대화를 듣고, 두 사람이 대화하는 장소로 가장 적절한 곳을 고르시오.

① 도서관 ② 가방 가게 ③ 공연장
④ 편의점 ⑤ 공항

> 🎯 적중! Tip neither
> 미국식으로는 [니더]로 발음되고, 영국식으로는 [나이더]로 발음된다.

W Josh, they just _____ _____ _____. Our flight leaves at 5 p.m. now.

M Oh, I really didn't expect the delay.

W Yeah. Me neither. We _____ _____ _____ _____ the plane an hour ago.

M We have so much time before the flight. What will we do?

W Why don't we get some coffee and snacks _____ _____ _____ ?

M But we have all of our luggage here. It will be hard to carry around.

W Then, one of us can wait here _____ _____ _____.

M Okay. I'll go get the drinks and snacks then.

다음을 듣고, 두 사람의 대화가 <u>어색한</u> 것을 고르시오.

① ② ③ ④ ⑤

🎯 **적중! Tip** Would you like to leave a message?

부재중인 사람을 대신해서 전화를 받았을 때, 전할 말이 있는지 상대방에게 물어보기 위해 사용되는 표현이다.

① W Aren't you late for your violin lesson?

　　M I still _____ .

② W Jerry's not here. Would you like to leave a message?

　　M No. I'll _____ _____ later.

③ W When did you take this amazing picture of a rainbow?

　　M I took it while I was walking in the park.

④ W _____ _____ _____ _____ a movie?

　　M I finished reading it a few hours ago.

⑤ W That will be 10 dollars and 92 cents.

　　M Here's _____ _____ _____ .

대화를 듣고, 여자가 남자에게 부탁한 일로 가장 적절한 것을 고르시오.

① 택배 찾아오기　　② 새해 인사 보내기
③ 우표 사 오기　　④ 엽서 골라주기
⑤ 동물원 티켓 사기

[Cellphone rings.]

W Could you _____ _____ _____ , Justin?

M Sure, Alice. What's up?

W You are at the post office, right?

M Yes. I'm _____ _____ to send my package.

W Then, can you buy me some of _____ _____ _____

　　_____ ? They're sold only during this week.

M Sure. But there are a lot of different ones here. _____ _____ do

　　you want?

W Can you get me the Lunar New Year ones? They have a tiger on them.

　　I just _____ _____ _____ .

M No problem. I'll get some now.

다음을 듣고, 무엇에 관한 안내 방송인지 고르시오.

① 문화재 취급법　　② 박물관 운영 시간
③ 사진 수업 등록　　④ 새 전시회 개관
⑤ 박물관 주의 사항

W Attention, please. I'm Maria, your museum tour guide. Let me tell you

　　_____ _____ _____ _____ for your visit to the

　　museum today. First, please do not _____ _____ _____

　　the artworks in the exhibits. Second, do not touch any of the items on

　　display, and _____ _____ _____ _____ from them.

　　Third, running is not allowed in the museum at any time. We thank

　　you for your cooperation and hope you enjoy your time here.

대화를 듣고, 여자가 지불할 금액을 고르시오.

① $ 10　　② $ 15　　③ $ 20
④ $ 25　　⑤ $ 30

M Can I help you _____ _____ ?

W Yes. I'm looking for a scarf.

M _____ _____ _____ are the brown and gray ones. They are

　　10 dollars each.

W I'll _____ _____ _____ _____ , please.

M Okay. Do you need anything else?

W Well, I'd also like a winter hat. Do you have any that match this scarf?

M We do. The hat is 15 dollars.

W Then, I'll _____ _____ _____ too.

M Great. Here you are.

11 | 할 일 고르기

대화를 듣고, 남자가 할 일로 가장 적절한 것을 고르시오.

① 화분 구매하기　　② 나무 운반하기
③ 도움 요청하기　　④ 택시비 지불하기
⑤ 사무실 꾸미기

M Hello. Do you need help with anything?
W I'm looking for ＿＿＿ ＿＿＿ ＿＿＿ for my office.
M We have many options here. ＿＿＿ ＿＿＿ do you want it to be?
W I have a small office, so ＿＿＿ ＿＿＿ ＿＿＿ ＿＿＿ .
M What about this one? It's a good size.
W That's perfect! I'll take that one.
M Okay. You can pay now, and then I'll ＿＿＿ ＿＿＿ ＿＿＿ ＿＿＿ ＿＿＿ for you.
W Thank you for your help.

12 | 언급하지 않은 내용 고르기

다음을 듣고, 기부 행사에 관해 언급되지 않은 것을 고르시오.

① 행사 날짜　　② 행사 장소　　③ 기부 품목
④ 기부 목적　　⑤ 신청 방법

M Hello, residents in Ashton Apartments. This is George Hallow from the Ashton Apartments Committee. ＿＿＿ ＿＿＿ ＿＿＿ ＿＿＿ that we'll be holding our annual food donation event on July 17th. It'll be held at our community center on the second floor. You can donate ＿＿＿ ＿＿＿ ＿＿＿ ＿＿＿ at this event. It will be donated to the local senior home to ＿＿＿ ＿＿＿ . Please call 555-3251 if you have any questions.

고난도
13 | 도표에서 알맞은 항목 고르기

다음 표를 보면서 대화를 듣고, 두 사람이 대여할 자전거를 고르시오.

	Bike	Number of seats	Color	Price (per hour)
①	A	1	Purple	$ 4
②	B	1	Purple	$ 5
③	C	2	Purple	$ 6
④	D	1	Pink	$ 4
⑤	E	2	Pink	$ 5

W Dad, they rent bikes here. Can we rent one?
M You don't know ＿＿＿ ＿＿＿ ＿＿＿ ＿＿＿ ＿＿＿ .
W Yeah. But they have bikes for two people.
M Why don't I teach you instead? Let's get one ＿＿＿ ＿＿＿ ＿＿＿ .
W Okay. I think the pink one is ＿＿＿ ＿＿＿ ＿＿＿ . It is too small.
M There are still two other options.
W The more expensive one looks too big for me though.
M I think so. You won't need that.
W I agree. I'll ＿＿＿ ＿＿＿ ＿＿＿ ＿＿＿ . I'm so excited!

14 | 화제 고르기

다음을 듣고, 무엇에 관한 설명인지 고르시오.

① 개미　　② 사슴벌레　　③ 거미
④ 달팽이　　⑤ 나비

M Many people think this animal is ＿＿＿ ＿＿＿ , but it is not, actually. This animal is found all over the world. It has eight legs. It can bite you, but it is ＿＿＿ ＿＿＿ ＿＿＿ . This animal is famous for ＿＿＿ ＿＿＿ . It makes them with silk and uses them ＿＿＿ ＿＿＿ ＿＿＿ . Many people are scared of this animal, but some have one as a pet.

15 | 할 일 고르기

대화를 듣고, 여자가 할 일로 가장 적절한 것을 고르시오.

① 부엌 청소하기 ② TV 시청하기
③ 냉장고 비우기 ④ 옷장 정리하기
⑤ 음악 재생하기

> **적중! Tip should**
> [슈드]로 발음된다. -d 앞에 오는 [l]은 묵음이다.
> · could [쿠드] · would [우드]

M Honey, what should we do today?
W The house is _____ _____. We should clean.
M Yes. We are so busy during the week.
W I know. But we can _____ _____ _____ _____
  together now.
M That's true. I will clean the kitchen first then.
W I'll _____ _____ _____ first. Could you play some music?
M Yes. I'll put some on.

16 | 시간 정보 고르기

대화를 듣고, 두 사람이 선택한 요리 수업의 시작 시각을 고르시오.

① 1 p.m. ② 2 p.m. ③ 3 p.m.
④ 4 p.m. ⑤ 5 p.m.

W James, do you want to take _____ _____ _____ with me?
M Sounds interesting! Where can we take it?
W _____ _____ _____ offers cooking classes on weekends.
M Cool. I _____ _____ _____ on Saturdays.
W What time can you go?
M Is there a class that starts at 3 or 4 p.m.? I _____ _____
  _____ _____ take a morning class.
W Let me check. [Pause] No. But there is one that starts at 1.
M The 1 p.m. class is fine. I'm really _____ _____ _____ this.
  It will be a lot of fun.

17 | 적절한 응답 고르기

대화를 듣고, 남자의 마지막 말에 대한 여자의 응답으로 가장 적절한 것을 고르시오.

Woman: _____

① I can fix your chair. It's easy.
② The manager isn't here right now.
③ You can get a refund or exchange the item.
④ We need some nails and a hammer.
⑤ Okay. I will come back to the store this
   afternoon.

[Telephone rings.]
M This is Richard from Furniture World. How may I help you?
W I just got home after _____ _____ _____ from your store.
M Okay. Is there a problem with your purchase?
W Yes. I opened the package with the chair parts, and one of _____
  _____ _____ _____.
M I apologize for that. You can _____ _____ _____ today if
  you want.
W Do I need to bring anything else?
M Just bring all of the parts and _____ _____.

18 | 적절한 응답 고르기

대화를 듣고, 여자의 마지막 말에 대한 남자의 응답으로 가장 적절한 것을 고르시오.

Man: _____

① My cat acts very funny sometimes.
② Please do not record any videos.
③ We ought to feed our hamster.
④ I'll give you the link instead.
⑤ Sure. I also love watching comedy films.

W What are you laughing at, Hajun?
M It's a video of a cat that _____ _____ _____ _____.
W Oh, can I see?
M Sure. Let me restart it.
W *[Pause]* That's so funny! Do you know _____ _____ _____ _____?
M Yes. I like to watch them in my free time.
W Are there any videos with hamsters in them? They're _____ _____ _____.
M Yes, I know a great one with _____ _____ _____ _____.
W Please _____ _____ _____ _____. I'd love to watch it.

19 | 적절한 응답 고르기

대화를 듣고, 남자의 마지막 말에 대한 여자의 응답으로 가장 적절한 것을 고르시오.

Woman: _____

① I went to Italy last summer.
② Yes. I'll pay the bill now.
③ She can't eat spicy food.
④ The tomato salad will be good.
⑤ I am allergic to mushrooms.

🎯 적중! Tip **ch**ef
[쉐프]로 발음된다. 프랑스어에서 유래한 단어는 [ch]를 [쉬]로 발음한다.
· para**ch**ute [패러슈트] · ma**ch**ine [머쉰]

M Welcome to A Taste of Rome. How may I help you?
W Can you _____ _____ _____ for me?
M Our spaghetti is very popular.
W I'll have an order of that then, please.
M Do you mind _____ _____ _____ in the sauce?
W That's fine. I just don't want _____ _____ with it.
M I will tell the chef. Also, please let me know _____ _____ _____ you would like.

20 | 상황에 적절한 말 고르기

다음 상황 설명을 듣고, Isaac이 Rachel에게 할 말로 가장 적절한 것을 고르시오.

Isaac: Rachel, _____

① I already have plans today.
② why don't we meet at 3?
③ what part do you want to take?
④ can you bring a science textbook?
⑤ where do you want to meet on Saturday?

M Isaac and Rachel have to do _____ _____ _____ together. Because it is _____ _____ _____, they need to work on the project soon. Isaac wants to meet Rachel on Saturday to work on it. They decide to meet in the afternoon, but they don't _____ _____ _____. Isaac wants to ask Rachel about _____ _____ _____. In this situation, what would Isaac most likely say to Rachel?

실전 모의고사
음성 바로 듣기 ▶

1 대화를 듣고, 여자가 만든 식탁보를 고르시오.

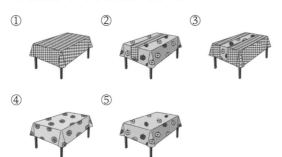

① ② ③ ④ ⑤

2 대화를 듣고, 여자가 남자에게 부탁한 일로 가장 적절한 것을 고르시오.

① 주차장 알아보기 ② 입장권 구매하기
③ 음료 주문하기 ④ 자전거 대여하기
⑤ 식당 예약하기

3 다음 그림의 상황에 가장 적절한 대화를 고르시오.

① ② ③ ④ ⑤

4 대화를 듣고, 남자가 수업을 듣기로 한 요일을 고르시오.

① 월요일 ② 수요일 ③ 금요일
④ 토요일 ⑤ 일요일

5 대화를 듣고, 여행 가방에 관해 언급되지 않은 것을 고르시오.

① 소재 ② 제조사 ③ 가격
④ 크기 ⑤ 색상

6 대화를 듣고, 두 사람이 대화하는 장소로 가장 적절한 곳을 고르시오.

① 경찰서 ② 영화관 ③ 레스토랑
④ 야구장 ⑤ 연주회장

7 다음을 듣고, 두 사람의 대화가 어색한 것을 고르시오.

① ② ③ ④ ⑤

8 대화를 듣고, 남자가 여자에게 부탁한 일로 가장 적절한 것을 고르시오.

① 빨래 개기 ② 설거지하기
③ 숙제 도와주기 ④ 부엌 청소하기
⑤ 놀이공원 데려가기

9 다음을 듣고, 무엇에 관한 안내 방송인지 고르시오.

① 찬반 토론 주제 ② 학교생활 규칙
③ 도서관 이용 방법 ④ 휴대폰 약관 변경
⑤ 학습용 앱 출시

고난도
10 대화를 듣고, 여자가 지불할 금액을 고르시오.

① $ 10 ② $ 20 ③ $ 30
④ $ 40 ⑤ $ 50

11 대화를 듣고, 남자가 할 일로 가장 적절한 것을 고르시오.

① 응원 팻말 만들기 ② 자동차 게임 하기
③ 마라톤 참가하기 ④ 신청서 제출하기
⑤ 달리기 연습하기

고난도

12 다음을 듣고, 크루즈 여행에 관해 언급되지 <u>않은</u> 것을 고르시오.

① 여행 기간　② 관광 비용　③ 활동
④ 부대시설　⑤ 정박 장소

13 대화를 듣고, 두 사람이 앉을 자리를 고르시오.

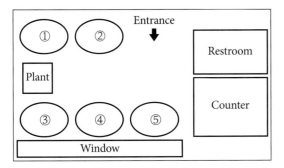

14 다음을 듣고, 무엇에 관한 설명인지 고르시오.

① 배구　② 피구　③ 농구
④ 럭비　⑤ 축구

15 대화를 듣고, 여자가 할 일로 가장 적절한 것을 고르시오.

① 그릇 만들기　② 할머니 댁 가기
③ 택배 보내기　④ 소포 확인하기
⑤ 우표 구매하기

16 대화를 듣고, 두 사람이 축제에 참여할 날짜를 고르시오.

① 9월 15일　② 9월 16일　③ 9월 17일
④ 9월 19일　⑤ 9월 20일

17 대화를 듣고, 여자의 마지막 말에 대한 남자의 응답으로 가장 적절한 것을 고르시오.

Man: _____

① I need to report a missing item.
② Thank you. I'll see you soon.
③ The living room is down the hall.
④ Let me give you directions to my house.
⑤ Good. I'd like to help you make some juice.

[18-19] 대화를 듣고, 남자의 마지막 말에 대한 여자의 응답으로 가장 적절한 것을 고르시오.

18 **Woman:** _____

① Yes. I turned it in yesterday.
② People didn't believe his story.
③ It was good, but I didn't like the ending.
④ That'll help. I need ideas.
⑤ I can speak English fluently.

19 **Woman:** _____

① Thank you for helping me pack my things.
② I will come and visit you soon.
③ You're not allowed to take photos here.
④ You can return the gift with the receipt.
⑤ Okay. I'll go to the store today then.

20 다음 상황 설명을 듣고, George가 호텔 직원에게 할 말로 가장 적절한 것을 고르시오.

George: _____

① Where is the nearest subway station?
② I'd like to book a tour for tomorrow.
③ Could you recommend a traditional restaurant for me?
④ What kind of food service do you provide?
⑤ Your luggage will be delivered shortly.

09회 중학영어듣기 실전 모의고사 Dictation 음성을 들으며 빈칸에 알맞은 단어를 채우시오.

---

1 | 알맞은 그림 고르기

대화를 듣고, 여자가 만든 식탁보를 고르시오.

① ② ③

④ ⑤

M Yeri, did you _____ _____ _____ in the kitchen? It looks handmade.

W Yes, Dad. I made it in an after-school program.

M Great! You used two different kinds of fabric. They go well together.

W Thanks. At first, I thought of making it with _____ _____ _____ only, but it would look plain.

M I see. _____ _____ _____ _____ the apple-patterned cloth in the middle.

W That's right. _____ _____ _____ makes our kitchen look brighter.

M You're right.

---

2 | 부탁·요청한 일 고르기

대화를 듣고, 여자가 남자에게 부탁한 일로 가장 적절한 것을 고르시오.

① 주차장 알아보기　　② 입장권 구매하기
③ 음료 주문하기　　④ 자전거 대여하기
⑤ 식당 예약하기

> 🎯 적중! Tip　next to
> [넥스트 투]보다는 [넥스투]로 들린다. 발음이 같은 자음이 나란히 나오면 앞 단어의 끝 자음이 탈락되기 때문이다.
> · last time [래스타임]　· had dinner [해디너]

[Cellphone rings.]

W Are you at the park, Darling?

M Yes. _____ _____ _____ on a bench.

W Okay. I'm almost there.

M What do you want to do after you arrive? We can go to dinner.

W It's a little early. _____ _____ _____ _____ before dinner.

M There are _____ _____ _____ at a gallery next to the park. We could go look at them.

W That sounds fun. Can you go ahead and _____ _____?

M Okay. See you at the gallery then.

---

3 | 그림 상황에 적절한 대화 고르기

다음 그림의 상황에 가장 적절한 대화를 고르시오.

① ② ③ ④ ⑤

① M Where are the T-shirts?
　 W They are _____ _____ _____.
② M Which tie is better?
　 W The green one _____ _____ _____ you.
③ M When does the store open?
　 W In about an hour.
④ M I'd like to _____ _____ _____.
　 W Do you have the receipt?
⑤ M I don't think it is _____ _____ _____.
　 W I agree. Try on a larger one.

4 | 시간 정보 고르기

대화를 듣고, 남자가 수업을 듣기로 한 요일을 고르시오.

① 월요일   ② 수요일   ③ 금요일
④ 토요일   ⑤ 일요일

[Telephone rings.]

W   Hello, Global Language School. What can I do for you?

M   Hi, I'd like to _____ _____ _____ _____ _____.

W   We have a popular French class on Wednesday mornings. Would that _____ _____ _____?

M   I can't come on Wednesdays. I have _____ _____ _____ _____ on that day. Do you have classes on Saturdays too?

W   We do, but they are all full right now. What about Sunday?

M   I _____ _____ _____.

W   Great. I'll take your information and sign you up.

M   Thank you for the help.

5 | 언급하지 않은 내용 고르기

대화를 듣고, 여행 가방에 관해 언급되지 <u>않은</u> 것을 고르시오.

① 소재   ② 제조사   ③ 가격
④ 크기   ⑤ 색상

🎯 적중! Tip I'll

[아일]보다는 [아을]로 들린다. 조동사 will의 축약형은 앞에 나오는 주어와 연결해서 약하게 발음되기 때문이다.

M   Can I help you find anything?

W   Yes. I want to buy a new suitcase.

M   _____ _____ _____ is popular.

W   I saw that on your website. It is made by Glide Luggage, right?

M   Yes. It is on sale right now for 125 dollars.

W   Is it _____ _____ _____?

M   That's right. So, it is very light. In fact, it only weighs three kilograms.

W   It seems perfect. I'll take it.

M   Okay. I'll carry it _____ _____ _____ _____ for you.

6 | 장소 고르기

대화를 듣고, 두 사람이 대화하는 장소로 가장 적절한 곳을 고르시오.

① 경찰서   ② 영화관   ③ 레스토랑
④ 야구장   ⑤ 연주회장

W   Oh, no. There are _____ _____ _____ _____ left for *The Police Officer.*

M   Really?

W   Yes. The 7 p.m. show only has seats _____ _____ _____ _____.

M   What about the 7:30 p.m. show?

W   Let me check. *[Pause]* There are still some good seats.

M   Alright, then let's get two seats in the middle row. We can buy some popcorn and wait a little longer _____ _____ _____.

W   Good idea. I'll buy the tickets while you get the popcorn.

M   Sure. I'll go to _____ _____ _____ now.

다음을 듣고, 두 사람의 대화가 <u>어색한</u> 것을 고르시오.

① ② ③ ④ ⑤

① W What did you eat for lunch?
　 M I _____ _____ _____ with Fred.
② W Did you bring an umbrella?
　 M No. But it's _____ _____ _____ _____ today.
③ W Where did you get these muffins?
　 M I bought them at the bakery on Main Street.
④ W _____ _____ _____ do you want?
　 M It smells really fresh.
⑤ W Do you need a plastic bag?
　 M No, thank you. I _____ _____ _____.

대화를 듣고, 남자가 여자에게 부탁한 일로 가장 적절한 것을 고르시오.

① 빨래 개기　　　　② 설거지하기
③ 숙제 도와주기　　④ 부엌 청소하기
⑤ 놀이공원 데려가기

W Let's go to _____ _____ _____ today, Dad.
M I don't know. The house is very messy, and you have homework.
W We can do everything after we come back home.
M No. We will be too tired afterward.
W Then, why don't we _____ _____ _____ _____? After we finish them, we can visit the park.
M _____ _____ _____. But what about your homework?
W _____ _____ I will do it tomorrow morning.
M Alright. Then, can you begin _____ _____ _____ _____ _____?
W Of course!

다음을 듣고, 무엇에 관한 안내 방송인지 고르시오.

① 찬반 토론 주제　　② 학교생활 규칙
③ 도서관 이용 방법　④ 휴대폰 약관 변경
⑤ 학습용 앱 출시

W Can I _____ _____ _____? I'm Ms. Andrews, principal of the Clay Middle School. Before we begin the semester, I want to go over a couple of _____ _____ _____ _____. First, all students must wear their school uniform. Second, cellphones _____ _____ _____ during class unless there are special instructions from the teacher. Lastly, any kind of _____ _____ will not be tolerated. Thank you for listening, and have a great day.

대화를 듣고, 여자가 지불할 금액을 고르시오.

① $ 10　　② $ 20　　③ $ 30
④ $ 40　　⑤ $ 50

M Welcome to Neighborhood Flower Shop. Can I help you?
W Hello. I'd like to buy some flowers for my friend. _____ _____ _____ _____?
M Our yellow roses are gorgeous today. Five of them cost 10 dollars.
W I'll take 10 yellow roses then.
M Great choice. _____ _____ _____ _____ _____?
W Umm... A vase for the flowers would also be nice.
M This one here is 10 dollars. It would look beautiful with the flowers.
W Okay. I'll _____ _____ _____ too.

11 | 할 일 고르기

대화를 듣고, 남자가 할 일로 가장 적절한 것을 고르시오.

① 응원 팻말 만들기 ② 자동차 게임 하기
③ 마라톤 참가하기 ④ 신청서 제출하기
⑤ 달리기 연습하기

W Minjun, I will run in _____ _____ _____ next month.
M That's amazing!
W Thanks. Now I need to start preparing for it.
M What are you going to do?
W I _____ _____ _____ six kilometers every day.
M Wow. I'm sure you'll _____ _____ in the race.
W I hope so. My parents are coming to watch. You should too.
M Of course. I'll _____ _____ _____ _____
   while I cheer.
W That's so nice of you.

고난도

12 | 언급하지 않은 내용 고르기

다음을 듣고, 크루즈 여행에 관해 언급되지 <u>않은</u> 것을 고르시오.

① 여행 기간 ② 관광 비용 ③ 활동
④ 부대시설 ⑤ 정박 장소

🎯 적중! Tip live
live는 형용사로 쓰일 때는 [라이브]로, 동사로 쓰일 때는 [리브]로 발음된다.

M Good afternoon, everyone. We offer _____ _____ _____
   during our five-day cruise. Throughout the day, we offer several
   _____ _____ _____. Every night after dinner, there will be
   live music from our band. So, come join us on the dance floor. Also,
   our ship features three pools, a roller-skating rink, and _____
   _____ _____. The ship _____ _____ _____
   San Juan, Puerto Rico and in Cozumel, Mexico. Welcome aboard,
   everyone!

---

13 | 위치 고르기

대화를 듣고, 두 사람이 앉을 자리를 고르시오.

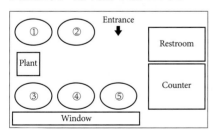

🎯 적중! Tip counter
[카운터]보다는 [카우널]로 들린다. 모음 사이에서 [n] 뒤에 오는 [t] 발음은 약화되어 거의 들리지 않기 때문이다.
· plenty [플레니] · fantasy [패너시]

W Where do you want to sit, Chris?
M How about the table _____ _____ _____?
W Wouldn't it be too noisy? And the restroom is a bit close.
M You're right. I think it's better to sit _____ _____
   _____.
W Yeah. I like watching people passing by.
M I want to _____ _____ _____ the counter.
   People will be walking around.
W I agree. Let's take the table _____ _____ _____ then.
M Great. Why don't you go sit down? I'll order the coffee.

다음을 듣고, 무엇에 관한 설명인지 고르시오.

① 배구　　② 피구　　③ 농구
④ 럭비　　⑤ 축구

M This is a team sport. There are two teams and they stand in a big square. The square has _____ _____ _____ _____ _____ _____ .
One team stands on one side and the other team stands on the other.
Players _____ _____ _____ at each other. If the ball _____ _____ _____ , the player is out. But if a player _____ _____ _____ , the player can keep playing. The goal is to _____ _____ _____ .

대화를 듣고, 여자가 할 일로 가장 적절한 것을 고르시오.

① 그릇 만들기　　② 할머니 댁 가기
③ 택배 보내기　　④ 소포 확인하기
⑤ 우표 구매하기

M Mom, I made _____ _____ for Grandma.
W Oh, Doyoon, it's so beautiful! I love the color.
M Thank you. I want to _____ _____ _____ _____ soon.
W Well, we'll visit her next month.
M _____ _____ _____ _____ to her in a package? Then, she can get it sooner.
W Okay. I'll _____ _____ _____ this week.

대화를 듣고, 두 사람이 축제에 참여할 날짜를 고르시오.

① 9월 15일　　② 9월 16일　　③ 9월 17일
④ 9월 19일　　⑤ 9월 20일

W Brian, do you know when the Apple Festival starts this year?
M I think it starts around September 20th.
W Let's _____ _____ _____ .
M Oh, it starts on September 15th this year. That's early.
W I want to _____ _____ _____ this year. I missed it last year.
M The festival's held for three days, and the parade runs every day.
W _____ _____ _____ go on the 17th then? They always have fireworks _____ _____ _____ _____ of the festival.
M That's a good idea.

대화를 듣고, 여자의 마지막 말에 대한 남자의 응답으로 가장 적절한 것을 고르시오.

Man: _____

① I need to report a missing item.
② Thank you. I'll see you soon.
③ The living room is down the hall.
④ Let me give you directions to my house.
⑤ Good. I'd like to help you make some juice.

[Cellphone rings.]
M Hello?
W Hi, Jin. I'm _____ _____ _____ . I will be at your house soon.
M Great! Do you know where it is?
W It's on Park Street, right?
M Yes. It's the white house close to _____ _____ _____ .
W Got it. Do you want me to bring anything to your house?
M Actually, can you buy some juice? I _____ _____ _____ orange juice.
W Yes. I'll _____ _____ _____ _____ before I come.

18 | 적절한 응답 고르기

대화를 듣고, 남자의 마지막 말에 대한 여자의 응답으로 가장 적절한 것을 고르시오.

Woman: _____

① Yes. I turned it in yesterday.
② People didn't believe his story.
③ It was good, but I didn't like the ending.
④ That'll help. I need ideas.
⑤ I can speak English fluently.

🎯 적중! Tip I wish ~.
바람이나 소원을 나타낼 때 사용되는 표현으로 '~라면 좋을 텐데'라는 의미이다.
· I wish I could dance well.
  춤을 잘 출 수 있으면 좋을 텐데.

M Have you _____ _____ _____ for English class, Haneul?
W Not yet. I don't know _____ _____ _____ _____.
M Well, the assignment is due soon. You should think of something fast.
W I know. What did you write about?
M My story is about a person _____ _____ _____ in time.
W That's so interesting! How did you _____ _____ _____ that?
M I write lots of stories in my free time. I picked my favorite one.
W I wish I were more creative.
M I can help you _____ _____ _____ _____.

19 | 적절한 응답 고르기

대화를 듣고, 남자의 마지막 말에 대한 여자의 응답으로 가장 적절한 것을 고르시오.

Woman: _____

① Thank you for helping me pack my things.
② I will come and visit you soon.
③ You're not allowed to take photos here.
④ You can return the gift with the receipt.
⑤ Okay. I'll go to the store today then.

🎯 적중! Tip I can't believe ~.
어떤 상황에 대한 놀람 또는 믿기지 않음을 나타낼 때 사용되는 표현이다.
· I can't believe our graduation is next week.
  우리 졸업이 다음 주라는 게 믿기지 않아.

M I can't believe that Cindy _____ _____.
W Yeah. She's a great friend.
M We should give her something to show her that _____ _____ _____ _____.
W Okay. What about making her a memory book? We can add some of our photographs together.
M She'd love that. I have lots of pictures of us.
W Great! Can you print them? I will _____ _____ _____ _____.
M Yeah. We can meet this weekend to _____ _____ _____ _____.

20 | 상황에 적절한 말 고르기

다음 상황 설명을 듣고, George가 호텔 직원에게 할 말로 가장 적절한 것을 고르시오.

George: _____

① Where is the nearest subway station?
② I'd like to book a tour for tomorrow.
③ Could you recommend a traditional restaurant for me?
④ What kind of food service do you provide?
⑤ Your luggage will be delivered shortly.

W George is a tourist in Spain. After a long day of _____ _____ _____, George returns to his hotel for some rest. Eventually, _____ _____ _____. He wants to eat at a nice traditional restaurant. So, he would like to ask the hotel employee if she knows a good place _____ _____ _____. In this situation, what would George most likely say to the hotel employee?

1 대화를 듣고, 남자가 구입할 주방 저울을 고르시오.

① ② ③ ④ ⑤

2 대화를 듣고, 여자가 남자에게 전화한 목적으로 가장 적절한 것을 고르시오.

① 연극 티켓 구매 방법을 설명하려고
② 학교 동아리 가입에 대해 문의하려고
③ 행사에 참여할 것을 촉구하려고
④ 행사가 취소된 이유를 안내하려고
⑤ 연습 시간이 변경됐음을 알려주려고

3 다음 그림의 상황에 가장 적절한 대화를 고르시오.

① ② ③ ④ ⑤

4 대화를 듣고, 남자가 스터디룸을 빌리기로 한 요일을 고르시오.

① 화요일 ② 수요일 ③ 목요일
④ 금요일 ⑤ 토요일

5 다음을 듣고, Grandview Amusement Park에 관해 언급되지 않은 것을 고르시오.

① 위치 ② 입장료 ③ 기구 종류
④ 식당 유무 ⑤ 특별 공연

6 대화를 듣고, 두 사람의 관계로 가장 적절한 것을 고르시오.

① 극장 직원 — 관객 ② 승무원 — 승객
③ 바리스타 — 손님 ④ 배우 — 매니저
⑤ 택시 운전사 — 손님

7 다음을 듣고, 두 사람의 대화가 <u>어색한</u> 것을 고르시오.

① ② ③ ④ ⑤

8 대화를 듣고, 여자가 남자에게 부탁한 일로 가장 적절한 것을 고르시오.

① 저녁상 차리기 ② 생선 손질하기
③ 정육점 들르기 ④ 우유 사 오기
⑤ 치킨 포장해오기

9 대화를 듣고, 남자의 마지막 말에 담긴 의도로 가장 적절한 것을 고르시오.

① 불만 ② 요청 ③ 격려
④ 제안 ⑤ 후회

10 대화를 듣고, 남자가 지불할 금액을 고르시오.

① $ 5 ② $ 10 ③ $ 15
④ $ 20 ⑤ $ 25

11 대화를 듣고, 여자가 대화 직후에 할 일로 가장 적절한 것을 고르시오.

① 휴식 취하기 ② 스케이트보드 타기
③ 상처 치료하기 ④ 진통제 복용하기
⑤ 약국 방문하기

12 다음을 듣고, 직업의 날에 관해 언급되지 <u>않은</u> 것을 고르시오.

① 행사 진행 순서　　② 초빙 연사 수

③ 행사 목적　　④ 행사 장소

⑤ 준비 사항

고난도
13 다음 표를 보면서 대화를 듣고, 두 사람이 선택할 수업을 고르시오.

	Class	Day	Instructor	Time
①	A	Mon/Fri	Mr. Dorsey	10 a.m.
②	B	Tue/Thu	Mr. Dorsey	9 a.m.
③	C	Wed	Mr. Jones	9 a.m.
④	D	Wed	Mr. Jones	10 a.m.
⑤	E	Tue/Thu	Mr. Jones	10 a.m.

14 다음을 듣고, 무엇에 관한 설명인지 고르시오.

① 기차　　② 지하철　　③ 모노레일

④ 케이블카　　⑤ 에스컬레이터

15 대화를 듣고, 여자가 할 일로 가장 적절한 것을 고르시오.

① 샐러드 만들기　　② 소금 가져다주기

③ 스테이크 주문하기　　④ 음료수 따라주기

⑤ 계산서 건네주기

고난도
16 대화를 듣고, 여자가 구입할 물건을 고르시오.

① candle　　② plate　　③ cushion

④ mug　　⑤ fork

17 대화를 듣고, 여자의 마지막 말에 대한 남자의 응답으로 가장 적절한 것을 고르시오.

Man: _____

① It's too crowded. We'll come back later.

② I'm so glad we are finished now.

③ Thank you for your attention today.

④ No. We are not done yet.

⑤ Excellent. Let's get started.

[18-19] 대화를 듣고, 남자의 마지막 말에 대한 여자의 응답으로 가장 적절한 것을 고르시오.

18 Woman: _____

① The interview went well.

② He taught me acting skills.

③ Okay. Let's change the channel.

④ I bet you'll like it.

⑤ I didn't know you prefer fantasy shows.

19 Woman: _____

① All right. We can wait for a bus there.

② There is no entrance fee.

③ This zip line is so high up. I'm terrified.

④ Please, drive a little faster. I'm in a hurry.

⑤ The sign says it's over there.

20 다음 상황 설명을 듣고, Lisa가 가게 점원에게 할 말로 가장 적절한 것을 고르시오.

Lisa: _____

① I dropped it while I tried on the dress.

② Can I use your phone for a moment?

③ I'm sorry, but I think I left my phone here.

④ I'd like a cup of cappuccino.

⑤ Does this come in a smaller size?

10회 중학영어듣기 실전 모의고사 Dictation 음성을 들으며 빈칸에 알맞은 단어를 채우시오.

1 | 알맞은 그림 고르기

대화를 듣고, 남자가 구입할 주방 저울을 고르시오.

① ② ③

④ ⑤

W Do you need any help?
M Yes. I'm looking for _____ _____ _____.
W We have digital and mechanical ones. Which do you prefer?
M I want _____ _____ _____.
W Alright. How about _____? It can measure up to five kilograms.
M That's good. But it doesn't have _____ _____ _____.
W Yeah. When you put things on it, it _____ _____ _____.
M Wow, amazing! I'll take that one.

2 | 목적 고르기

대화를 듣고, 여자가 남자에게 전화한 목적으로 가장 적절한 것을 고르시오.

① 연극 티켓 구매 방법을 설명하려고
② 학교 동아리 가입에 대해 문의하려고
③ 행사에 참여할 것을 촉구하려고
④ 행사가 취소된 이유를 안내하려고
⑤ 연습 시간이 변경됐음을 알려주려고

[Cellphone rings.]
M Hello.
W Hey, Greg. This is Amanda _____ _____ _____.
M Hi, Amanda. What's going on?
W It's _____ _____ _____ for the play we are going to perform next week.
M Has it been canceled?
W No, that's not it. We are going to _____ _____ _____ _____ than planned. So, be there at 4 p.m.
M Okay. Why was _____ _____ _____?
W Another club is using the room until 3:30.

3 | 그림 상황에 적절한 대화 고르기

다음 그림의 상황에 가장 적절한 대화를 고르시오.

① ② ③ ④ ⑤

① W Excuse me, this seat is _____ _____ _____.
　 M Oh, sorry. I didn't notice it.
② W When does the bus arrive?
　 M In about 20 minutes.
③ W Would you like me to _____ _____ _____?
　 M Yes, please. I feel a little cold.
④ W _____ _____ _____ _____ _____ here?
　 M For about nine years now.
⑤ W There are many people in the station.
　 M _____ _____ it's the weekend.

10회

실전 모의고사 해커스 중학영어듣기 모의고사 24회 Level 3

4 | 시간 정보 고르기

대화를 듣고, 남자가 스터디룸을 빌리기로 한 요일을 고르시오.

① 화요일   ② 수요일   ③ 목요일
④ 금요일   ⑤ 토요일

[Phone rings.]

W Hello, this is the university library help desk.
M Hi, I'd like to _____ _____ _____ _____.
W You can use the study rooms from Monday to Saturday.
M How long can I reserve a room for?
W You can make a reservation for up to five hours.
M _____ _____ _____ _____ rent too?
W Yes. But computers are unavailable on the weekends.
M Okay. I'll make a reservation for a room _____ _____ _____ _____ then.
W Sure.

5 | 언급하지 않은 내용 고르기

다음을 듣고, Grandview Amusement Park에 관해 언급되지 <u>않은</u> 것을 고르시오.

① 위치   ② 입장료   ③ 기구 종류
④ 식당 유무   ⑤ 특별 공연

> 🎯 적중! Tip **Be sure to ~.**
> 어떤 일을 꼭 해야 한다고 조언하거나 경고할 때 사용되는 표현으로, to 다음에는 동사원형이 온다.
> · Be sure to take your umbrella.
>   우산을 꼭 챙겨.

M Are you looking to have fun with your family? Visit the Grandview Amusement Park. Our park _____ _____ _____ Central City Plaza. The entrance fee is 15 dollars for children and 25 dollars _____ _____. This includes 10 ride tickets. Be sure to try our famous roller coaster or our amazing Ferris wheel. If you get hungry, there are _____ _____ _____ and restaurants on our grounds. So, visit us soon to enjoy all of the fun experiences.

6 | 관계 고르기

대화를 듣고, 두 사람의 관계로 가장 적절한 것을 고르시오.

① 극장 직원 — 관객   ② 승무원 — 승객
③ 바리스타 — 손님   ④ 배우 — 매니저
⑤ 택시 운전사 — 손님

M Excuse me, but you should use your headphones while _____ _____ _____ _____ _____ _____.
W Oh, really?
M Yes. The noise can make _____ _____ _____ uncomfortable.
W Got it. Just to check, can I drink my coffee on the train?
M That's fine. Drinks are allowed _____ _____ _____.
W Good. Also, I want to change seats. Is that okay?
M Yes. But if a person _____ _____ the train with a ticket for that seat, you _____ _____ _____ _____.

7 | 어색한 대화 고르기

다음을 듣고, 두 사람의 대화가 <u>어색한</u> 것을 고르시오.

①   ②   ③   ④   ⑤

> 🎯 적중! Tip **mi**ss **s**chool
> [미스 스쿨]보다는 [미스쿨]로 들린다. 발음이 같은 자음이 나란히 나오면 앞 단어의 끝 자음이 탈락되기 때문이다.
> · thi**s s**carf [디스칼프] · drin**k c**offee [드링커피]

① **W** Did you _____ _____ _____ _____ yesterday?
  M Of course, I'll make some now.
② **W** Do you need me to give you a ride?
  M No. I'll take the subway.
③ **W** Do you like _____ _____?
  M I think it's the best one in the museum.
④ **W** _____ _____ _____ _____ at this bakery?
  M Well, the garlic bread is the most popular thing here.
⑤ **W** Why did you miss school yesterday?
  M I had _____ _____ _____.

대화를 듣고, 여자가 남자에게 부탁한 일로 가장 적절한 것을 고르시오.

① 저녁상 차리기　　② 생선 손질하기
③ 정육점 들르기　　④ 우유 사 오기
⑤ 치킨 포장해오기

🎯 적중! Tip　Do you want me to ~?
상대방에게 무언가를 제안하며 의향을 물을 때 사용되는 표현으로 '제가 ~할까요, 내가 ~해줄까?'라는 의미이다. 이때 to 다음에는 동사원형이 온다.
· Do you want me to turn on the TV?
　제가 TV 켤까요?

[Cellphone rings.]
W Where are you, Dad?
M I'm _____ _____ _____ _____. I just left work.
W Do you want me to start cooking dinner?
M We don't have any food. I'll _____ _____ the supermarket now.
W What will you get?
M We can eat _____ _____ _____. Which sounds better?
W Chicken sounds delicious. But can you also _____ _____ _____? We just ran out.
M Yes, I'll get some.

대화를 듣고, 남자의 마지막 말에 담긴 의도로 가장 적절한 것을 고르시오.

① 불만　　② 요청　　③ 격려
④ 제안　　⑤ 후회

M Are you okay? _____ _____ _____.
W Yeah. I'm worried about my final exam for biology class.
M Is that tomorrow?
W Yeah. And the exam is worth 50% of my grade.
M There's _____ _____ _____ _____. We can review the material together tonight.
W Thanks. But _____ _____ _____ if that will be enough.
M You're a great student. And you _____ _____ all semester. You'll be fine.

대화를 듣고, 남자가 지불할 금액을 고르시오.

① $ 5　　② $ 10　　③ $ 15
④ $ 20　　⑤ $ 25

W Welcome to Best Haircuts. How may I help you?
M Hello. How much is a haircut?
W It is 15 dollars.
M Okay. I'd _____ _____ _____ then, please.
W Great. Do you want me to _____ _____ _____ your hair too?
M How much is _____ _____ _____?
W It is another five dollars.
M Sure. I'll _____ _____ _____ _____.
W Okay. Then, please follow me.

대화를 듣고, 여자가 대화 직후에 할 일로 가장 적절한 것을 고르시오.

① 휴식 취하기　　② 스케이트보드 타기
③ 상처 치료하기　　④ 진통제 복용하기
⑤ 약국 방문하기

🎯 적중! Tip　wrong
[뤙]으로 발음된다. -r 앞에 오면서 단어의 맨 처음에 쓰인 [w]는 묵음이다.
· wrist [리스트]　· wrap [랩]

W What's wrong, Nick?
M I _____ _____ of my skateboard, and now my leg hurts.
W Let me see. *[Pause]* Oh, you have _____ _____ _____.
M Yeah. It's _____ _____ _____. I should clean it.
W You'll also need some bandages.
M Is there _____ _____ _____ _____?
W Yes. _____ _____ _____. You stay here and rest.
M Thank you so much.

12 | 언급하지 않은 내용 고르기

다음을 듣고, 직업의 날에 관해 언급되지 <u>않은</u> 것을 고르시오.

① 행사 진행 순서 ② 초빙 연사 수
③ 행사 목적 ④ 행사 장소
⑤ 준비 사항

W Good afternoon, class. Tomorrow is career day. You will learn about _____ _____ _____. Then, we will have three special guest speakers. They are a doctor, _____ _____, _____ _____ _____. They are all parents of students here at Parker Middle School. They will visit our classroom and _____ _____ _____ for us. For homework, I _____ _____ _____ _____ three questions for each speaker.

고난도
13 | 도표에서 알맞은 항목 고르기

다음 표를 보면서 대화를 듣고, 두 사람이 선택할 수업을 고르시오.

	Class	Day	Instructor	Time
①	A	Mon/Fri	Mr. Dorsey	10 a.m.
②	B	Tue/Thu	Mr. Dorsey	9 a.m.
③	C	Wed	Mr. Jones	9 a.m.
④	D	Wed	Mr. Jones	10 a.m.
⑤	E	Tue/Thu	Mr. Jones	10 a.m.

🎯 적중! Tip **Why not?**
상대방의 의견이나 제안에 동의할 때 쓰는 표현이다. '왜 안 되겠어?'라는 뉘앙스로 즉, '물론 좋지, 당연하지'라는 의미이다.

W Sam, what _____ _____ _____ there?
M It's a schedule for taekwondo classes. I'm going to take one this summer.
W Can I take it with you?
M Why not? I _____ _____ _____ _____ to take though.
W I go swimming _____ _____ _____ _____.
M There are three options we can choose then.
W Do you know which taekwondo instructor is the best?
M _____ _____ _____ Mr. Jones.
W Then, let's take this class.
M Isn't it too early?
W There isn't any class _____ _____ _____.

14 | 화제 고르기

다음을 듣고, 무엇에 관한 설명인지 고르시오.

① 기차 ② 지하철 ③ 모노레일
④ 케이블카 ⑤ 에스컬레이터

W This vehicle moves passengers or things up to higher places. It carries people in cabins that _____ _____ _____ _____. The wires move with a motor, so the cabins _____ _____ _____ _____ high places like mountains. Usually, a small group of passengers can board this and _____ _____ _____ on their way to the top.

대화를 듣고, 여자가 할 일로 가장 적절한 것을 고르시오.

① 샐러드 만들기   ② 소금 가져다주기
③ 스테이크 주문하기   ④ 음료수 따라주기
⑤ 계산서 건네주기

🎯 적중! Tip wa**s y**our

[워즈 유얼]보다는 [워쥬얼]로 들린다. [z]로 끝나는 단어 뒤에 y-로 시작하는 단어가 이어지면 두 소리가 연결되어 [쥬]로 발음되기 때문이다.

W _____ _____ _____ _____ with a side of mashed potatoes, sir.
M Thank you.
W How was your salad?
M It was very fresh. I am _____ _____ _____ so far.
W Great. Do you need anything else?
M Can I _____ _____ _____, please?
W Of course. I'll get that right away. _____ _____ _____ _____ some more water?
M That would be great.

대화를 듣고, 여자가 구입할 물건을 고르시오.

① candle   ② plate   ③ cushion
④ mug   ⑤ fork

M Do we _____ _____ _____ _____ for Yuna's housewarming party tonight?
W Maybe we should get her _____ _____ _____ for her new house.
M What about some coffee mugs or new plates?
W She _____ _____ _____ _____ of those. We could get her some cushions for her couch instead?
M Hmm... But they might not _____ _____ _____ _____.
W That's true. I'll just _____ _____ _____ _____ then. I can go to the store quickly now.
M That's a good idea.

대화를 듣고, 여자의 마지막 말에 대한 남자의 응답으로 가장 적절한 것을 고르시오.

Man: _____

① It's too crowded. We'll come back later.
② I'm so glad we are finished now.
③ Thank you for your attention today.
④ No. We are not done yet.
⑤ Excellent. Let's get started.

W I'm excited to be partners with you for this project, Alex.
M Yes. I think we _____ _____ _____ _____.
W I agree. How should we _____ _____ _____ between us?
M Well, we have to make a slide show and _____ _____ _____.
W I get nervous _____ _____ _____ _____. Can you give the presentation?
M That's fine. You can make the slide show.
W Cool. I brought my laptop, so we can _____ _____ _____ now.

18 | 적절한 응답 고르기

대화를 듣고, 남자의 마지막 말에 대한 여자의 응답으로 가장 적절한 것을 고르시오.

Woman: _____

① The interview went well.
② He taught me acting skills.
③ Okay. Let's change the channel.
④ I bet you'll like it.
⑤ I didn't know you prefer fantasy shows.

🎯 적중! Tip **wee**k**end**
[위크엔드]보다는 [위껜드]로 들린다. 강세가 없는 [k]는 된소리로 발음되기 때문이다.

M How was your weekend, Wendy?
W I met _____ _____ _____, so it was amazing!
M Who is your favorite celebrity?
W His name is Robert Stan. He was so nice, and he _____ _____ _____ _____.
M I don't know him. What is he _____ _____?
W He's the main character in that television show, *After Dark*.
M Is that _____ _____ _____ about vampires?
W Yes. I highly recommend it.
M I usually _____ _____ _____, but I will watch it later.

19 | 적절한 응답 고르기

대화를 듣고, 남자의 마지막 말에 대한 여자의 응답으로 가장 적절한 것을 고르시오.

Woman: _____

① All right. We can wait for a bus there.
② There is no entrance fee.
③ This zip line is so high up. I'm terrified.
④ Please, drive a little faster. I'm in a hurry.
⑤ The sign says it's over there.

W What are you reading, Dad?
M I just got a message. Our zip line experience was canceled. The company needs to _____ _____ _____ on it today.
W Oh, no. What should we do instead?
M Why don't we look around the city today? There are _____ _____ _____ _____ _____ here.
W Where would you like to go?
M The traditional market looks interesting, and there's a palace. We have enough time to see _____ _____ _____.
W Should we take the bus?
M A cab is easier. Let's _____ _____ _____ _____.

20 | 상황에 적절한 말 고르기

다음 상황 설명을 듣고, Lisa가 가게 점원에게 할 말로 가장 적절한 것을 고르시오.

Lisa: _____

① I dropped it while I tried on the dress.
② Can I use your phone for a moment?
③ I'm sorry, but I think I left my phone here.
④ I'd like a cup of cappuccino.
⑤ Does this come in a smaller size?

M Lisa _____ _____ _____ some new clothes at a store. Then, she left to meet her friend for a coffee. She realized at the café her phone _____ _____, so she returned to the store. Lisa wants to tell the store's clerk that she _____ _____ _____ there. In this situation, what would Lisa most likely say to the store's clerk?

1 대화를 듣고, 여자가 구입할 사무실 서랍장을 고르시오.

① ② ③ ④ ⑤

2 대화를 듣고, 청소 로봇에 관해 언급되지 <u>않은</u> 것을 고르시오.

① 기능　　　② 충전 방식　　③ 출시일
④ 가격　　　⑤ 할인 정보

고난도
3 대화를 듣고, 여자가 남자에게 전화한 목적으로 가장 적절한 것을 고르시오.

① 꽃을 주문하려고
② 선인장 품종을 확인하려고
③ 물 주는 법을 문의하려고
④ 환불을 요청하려고
⑤ 꽃꽂이 수업 시간을 확인하려고

4 대화를 듣고, 남자가 여자의 집에 방문할 시각을 고르시오.

① 11 a.m.　　② 12 p.m.　　③ 1 p.m.
④ 3 p.m.　　⑤ 5 p.m.

5 대화를 듣고, 여자의 심정으로 가장 적절한 것을 고르시오.

① upset　　　② proud　　③ peaceful
④ ashamed　　⑤ depressed

6 다음 그림의 상황에 가장 적절한 대화를 고르시오.

① ② ③ ④ ⑤

7 대화를 듣고, 여자가 남자에게 부탁한 일로 가장 적절한 것을 고르시오.

① 호텔 예약하기　　　② 스테이크 요리하기
③ 수영장 입장권 사기　④ 휴대폰 장점 설명하기
⑤ 생일 파티 준비하기

고난도
8 다음을 듣고, 프로그램에 관해 언급되지 <u>않은</u> 것을 고르시오.

① 이름　　　② 진행 시간　　③ 진행 절차
④ 목적　　　⑤ 제한 사항

9 다음을 듣고, 무엇에 관한 설명인지 고르시오.

① 이어폰　　　② 마이크　　③ 녹음기
④ 확성기　　　⑤ 소음 측정기

10 다음을 듣고, 두 사람의 대화가 <u>어색한</u> 것을 고르시오.

① ② ③ ④ ⑤

11 대화를 듣고, 남자가 할 일로 가장 적절한 것을 고르시오.

① 초대장 만들기　　　② 안과 방문하기
③ 상품 수령하기　　　④ 대회 개최하기
⑤ 해적 옷 입기

고난도

12 다음 서점 배치도를 보면서 대화를 듣고, 여자가 찾아갈 구역을 고르시오.

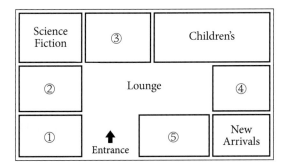

Science Fiction	③	Children's
②	Lounge	④
①	Entrance	⑤	New Arrivals

13 대화를 듣고, 두 사람이 만나기로 한 시각을 고르시오.

① 8 a.m. ② 9 a.m. ③ 10 a.m.
④ 11 a.m. ⑤ 12 p.m.

14 대화를 듣고, 여자가 지난 겨울 방학에 한 일로 가장 적절한 것을 고르시오.

① 스키 타기 ② 배낭 여행하기
③ 서핑 수업 듣기 ④ 얼음낚시 체험하기
⑤ 영어 캠프 참가하기

15 다음을 듣고, 방송의 목적으로 가장 적절한 것을 고르시오.

① 개인 정보 보호 방법을 설명하려고
② 전자 제품 할인 정보를 공유하려고
③ 기술 혁신의 중요성을 강조하려고
④ 새로운 소프트웨어 프로그램을 홍보하려고
⑤ 비밀번호 변경 시기를 안내하려고

16 대화를 듣고, 여자가 지불할 금액을 고르시오.

① $ 5 ② $ 7 ③ $ 14
④ $ 16 ⑤ $ 18

17 대화를 듣고, 여자의 마지막 말에 대한 남자의 응답으로 가장 적절한 것을 고르시오.

Man: _____

① No problem. I promise I will.
② No. I don't like carrots.
③ Sorry, but the lunch is still not ready.
④ Sure. I'll take my laptop to the repair shop.
⑤ Yes. The homework is due tomorrow.

[18-19] 대화를 듣고, 남자의 마지막 말에 대한 여자의 응답으로 가장 적절한 것을 고르시오.

18 Woman: _____

① I'm sorry. I can't fix these headphones.
② You're so nice. I'll return the favor.
③ Please visit our website for more information.
④ I can't find my wallet anywhere.
⑤ No, thanks. I already ordered new ones.

19 Woman: _____

① You can buy an umbrella in the convenience store.
② Please wear a cap in the pool.
③ Many artists participated in the exhibit.
④ Its main theme is the Second World War.
⑤ We are learning about that in history class right now.

20 다음 상황 설명을 듣고, Aria가 남자에게 할 말로 가장 적절한 것을 고르시오.

Aria: Excuse me, _____

① would you like to change seats with me?
② do you know why the flight is delayed?
③ I think you are in my seat.
④ I need to take a taxi to the airport.
⑤ do you mind opening the window?

11회 중학영어듣기 실전 모의고사 Dictation 음성을 들으며 빈칸에 알맞은 단어를 채우시오.

1 | 알맞은 그림 고르기

대화를 듣고, 여자가 구입할 사무실 서랍장을 고르시오.

① ② ③
④ ⑤

M Welcome to Modern Furniture. Can I help you with something?
W Hello. I _____ _____ _____ for my office.
M Alright. _____ _____ _____ do you want in the cabinet? We have cabinets with either three or five drawers.
W I _____ _____ _____ _____ many items in the cabinet. So, I'd like a three-drawer one.
M Okay. Then, how about this one _____ _____?
W Yeah. That looks good. The wheels would be convenient when I need to move it.
M Right. Now, do you need one with or without handles?
W Hmm... The one _____ _____ _____ _____ _____. I'll take it.
M Great choice! Please let me know the delivery address.

2 | 언급하지 않은 내용 고르기

대화를 듣고, 청소 로봇에 관해 언급되지 <u>않은</u> 것을 고르시오.

① 기능   ② 충전 방식   ③ 출시일
④ 가격   ⑤ 할인 정보

🎯 적중! Tip **art**icle
[알티클]보다는 [아리클]로 들린다. [rt]가 모음 사이에서 발음될 때는 약화되어 [r]에 가깝게 발음되기 때문이다.
· par**t**y [파리] · for**t**y [포리]

M What are you reading, Amy?
W It's an article about a new cleaning robot.
M Oh, that sounds interesting. How is it different from older ones?
W It can _____ _____ _____ with a mop.
M Oh, really? It's not a vacuum cleaner?
W No. And it _____ _____ _____ the charger when the battery's low.
M Cool! But isn't it expensive?
W No. It's only 160 dollars. It's _____ _____ _____ _____.
M Maybe I should get one.
W Make sure to buy it soon. You can get _____ _____ _____ _____ until March 13th.

3 | 목적 고르기

고난도

대화를 듣고, 여자가 남자에게 전화한 목적으로 가장 적절한 것을 고르시오.

① 꽃을 주문하려고
② 선인장 품종을 확인하려고
③ 물 주는 법을 문의하려고
④ 환불을 요청하려고
⑤ 꽃꽂이 수업 시간을 확인하려고

[Telephone rings.]
M Hello. Erikson Flower Shop.
W Hi. I _____ _____ _____ _____ from your shop a few days ago, and I wanted to _____ _____ _____ about it.
M Oh, hi. You bought the one with little flowers, didn't you?
W Yeah, that's right. _____ _____ do I have to water it again?
M Once a month. But do not soak the soil. A cactus can easily die _____ _____ _____ _____ _____.
W Okay. Thank you.
M No problem.

4 | 시간 정보 고르기

대화를 듣고, 남자가 여자의 집에 방문할 시각을 고르시오.

① 11 a.m.　② 12 p.m.　③ 1 p.m.
④ 3 p.m.　⑤ 5 p.m.

🎯 적중! Tip　Can you give me a hand?
상대방에게 도움을 요청할 때 사용되는 표현이다.

M　Sally, did you finish _____ _____ _____ for Christmas?
W　Not yet. Can you give me a hand?
M　No problem. _____ _____ _____ this Sunday.
W　Great. Could you come to my house at 11 a.m.?
M　I have to go to church. I should be finished by 1 p.m.
W　_____ _____ _____ _____ at 3? We'll be done around
　　5, and then I'll _____ _____ _____ _____ .
M　Okay. See you then.

5 | 심정 고르기

대화를 듣고, 여자의 심정으로 가장 적절한 것을 고르시오.

① upset　② proud　③ peaceful
④ ashamed　⑤ depressed

🎯 적중! Tip　last night
[래스트 나잇]보다는 [래스나잇]으로 들린다. 자음 3개가 연속해서 나오면 중간 자음은 발음되지 않기 때문이다.

M　Hi, Cathy. How are you doing?
W　I'm fine, thanks. Did you see the ice hockey game last night?
M　Of course. It was _____ _____ _____ between the United
　　States and Canada.
W　Then, you saw the moment the player _____ _____
　　_____ , right?
M　Sure. David Wood did it! He's an amazing player.
W　Actually, that's my brother.
M　Wow! Now I understand why you _____ _____ _____ .
W　Yeah. I'm so happy that he _____ _____ in the game.

6 | 그림 상황에 적절한 대화 고르기

다음 그림의 상황에 가장 적절한 대화를 고르시오.

①　②　③　④　⑤

① M　I don't see _____ _____ _____ .
　　W　There is one over there!
② M　Thank you for buying me tea.
　　W　_____ _____ _____ _____ .
③ M　Do you need a receipt?
　　W　No. That won't be necessary.
④ M　How is your food?
　　W　It's _____ _____ _____ , actually.
⑤ M　Are you _____ _____ _____ ?
　　W　Yes. I'll have a hamburger, please.

7 | 부탁·요청한 일 고르기

대화를 듣고, 여자가 남자에게 부탁한 일로 가장 적절한 것을 고르시오.

① 호텔 예약하기　② 스테이크 요리하기
③ 수영장 입장권 사기　④ 휴대폰 장점 설명하기
⑤ 생일 파티 준비하기

W　What did you do _____ _____ _____ , Max?
M　I stayed in a nice hotel with my parents.
W　That sounds lovely.
M　Yeah. We had fun at the pool and ate lots of steak.
W　Did you _____ _____ _____ ?
M　Actually, my parents got me this smartphone.
W　Wow! I really want that phone. Can you tell me what _____
　　_____ _____ are?
M　Sure. It takes great photographs. I _____ _____ _____ .

8 │ 언급하지 않은 내용 고르기

다음을 듣고, 프로그램에 관해 언급되지 <u>않은</u> 것을 고르시오.

① 이름   ② 진행 시간   ③ 진행 절차
④ 목적   ⑤ 제한 사항

M This is an announcement for supporters of The Friendly Dog Shelter. From this Tuesday, we will start _____ _____ _____ _____ Walk and Play. Every Tuesday and Thursday from 12 to 5 p.m., people will have the chance to _____ _____ _____ _____ our shelter dogs. Our goal is to socialize our dogs and introduce them to _____ _____ _____. Everyone must apply to take part beforehand on our website, www.friendlydog.com. Children under 12 are not _____ _____ _____. As always, thank you for your help.

9 │ 화제 고르기

다음을 듣고, 무엇에 관한 설명인지 고르시오.

① 이어폰   ② 마이크   ③ 녹음기
④ 확성기   ⑤ 소음 측정기

M This is a device used in places like concert halls and auditoriums. It usually has _____ _____ _____ with a circular part at the top of it. People speak into the circular part to _____ _____ _____ _____. For example, people speak into this so that a large audience can hear them. They just press a button _____ _____ _____ _____. With this, people can also record their voices.

10 │ 어색한 대화 고르기

다음을 듣고, 두 사람의 대화가 <u>어색한</u> 것을 고르시오.

①   ②   ③   ④   ⑤

🎯 적중! Tip   **receipt**

[리시트]로 발음된다. 단어 중간에 쓰인 [p]는 묵음인 경우가 있다.
· ras**p**berry [래즈베리] · cu**p**board [커벌드]

① **W** What did you do in art class today?
   M Our teacher showed us _____ _____ _____ birds.
② **W** Hi. Can I _____ _____ _____ _____ I bought last week?
   M Yes. Just give me the receipt, please.
③ **W** How long will you stay at the hotel?
   M I will be there for two nights.
④ **W** Hi. Can you send someone to _____ _____ _____ ?
   M Sure. Please describe the details.
⑤ **W** What time will you _____ _____ after school?
   M We met in the morning.

11 │ 할 일 고르기

대화를 듣고, 남자가 할 일로 가장 적절한 것을 고르시오.

① 초대장 만들기   ② 안과 방문하기
③ 상품 수령하기   ④ 대회 개최하기
⑤ 해적 옷 입기

M _____ _____ _____ _____ Anna's costume party?
W Yes, I am.
M I'm very excited. _____ _____ for the person with the best costume.
W I still don't know which costume to wear.
M Did you look at costumes online?
W Yes. But I want to just make one at home. What will you dress up as?
M I'll wear _____ _____ _____. I have a fake bird and an eye patch.
W That will look great.
M Yes. I _____ _____ _____ the costume contest.

고난도

12 | 위치 고르기

다음 서점 배치도를 보면서 대화를 듣고, 여자가 찾아 갈 구역을 고르시오.

Science Fiction	③	Children's
②	Lounge	④
①	↑ Entrance	⑤	New Arrivals

M Welcome to Tote's Bookstore. How can I help you?

W I'm looking for a novel. Could you tell me _____ _____ _____ _____ ?

M It's between the science fiction and children's sections.

W Thank you. *[Pause]* Could you _____ _____ _____ _____ ? I don't see it at the mystery's section.

M What's the title of the book?

W It's *Into the Shadows*.

M Oh! You can find it at the best-seller section.

W Where's that section?

M It's _____ _____ _____ _____ and the children's section.

W Thanks again.

13 | 시간 정보 고르기

대화를 듣고, 두 사람이 만나기로 한 시각을 고르시오.

① 8 a.m.   ② 9 a.m.   ③ 10 a.m.
④ 11 a.m.   ⑤ 12 p.m.

W Do you want to go with me to the shopping mall this weekend, Charlie?

M Yeah. I need to _____ _____ _____ _____ . When do you want to go?

W Can you meet at 9 a.m. on Sunday?

M Oh, I don't know. _____ _____ _____ . How about 11 instead?

W Well, my favorite store opens before that, and I want to _____ _____ _____ .

M Then, is _____ _____ _____ ?

W That should be fine. I'll meet you there then.

14 | 한 일 고르기

대화를 듣고, 여자가 지난 겨울 방학에 한 일로 가장 적절한 것을 고르시오.

① 스키 타기   ② 배낭 여행하기
③ 서핑 수업 듣기   ④ 얼음낚시 체험하기
⑤ 영어 캠프 참가하기

🎯 적중! Tip  spend the

[스펜드 더]보다는 [스펜더]로 들린다. 비슷하게 발음되는 자음이 나란히 나오면 앞 단어의 끝 자음이 탈락되기 때문이다.

M I didn't see you during the winter vacation, Caroline. Did you go skiing?

W No, I didn't. _____ _____ _____ for the vacation.

M Really? Where were you?

W I was _____ _____ , so it was really hot outside. We stayed with my dad's family.

M That's amazing. What did you do there?

W I _____ _____ _____ . It was a great way to spend the vacation.

M You _____ _____ _____ a lot of fun.

W I did. I hope to go back.

다음을 듣고, 방송의 목적으로 가장 적절한 것을 고르시오.

① 개인 정보 보호 방법을 설명하려고
② 전자 제품 할인 정보를 공유하려고
③ 기술 혁신의 중요성을 강조하려고
④ 새로운 소프트웨어 프로그램을 홍보하려고
⑤ 비밀번호 변경 시기를 안내하려고

W Good afternoon, listeners. This is Lora Willis with tips for dealing with modern technology. Today, I want to talk about _____ _____ _____ _____. Just follow a few simple rules, and you'll _____ _____ _____ _____. You won't need any special software for this. First, make sure to _____ _____ _____ often. Once a month should be fine. Secondly, use different passwords for every site. Finally, don't ever _____ _____ _____ _____ with others. I hope you follow these tips to protect your personal data.

대화를 듣고, 여자가 지불할 금액을 고르시오.

① $ 5   ② $ 7   ③ $ 14
④ $ 16   ⑤ $ 18

M Hello, and welcome to The Travel Gift Shop. How may I help you?
W I'd like to _____ _____ _____ for my friends. How much are they?
M These hand-painted postcards are _____ _____ _____, and the photograph postcards are five dollars each.
W I love the hand-painted ones.
M Okay. If you buy two, then we will _____ _____ _____ _____ _____ for free.
W That's amazing! I'll take two hand-painted postcards.
M Great. I'll help you pay at the counter.

대화를 듣고, 여자의 마지막 말에 대한 남자의 응답으로 가장 적절한 것을 고르시오.

Man: _____

① No problem. I promise I will.
② No. I don't like carrots.
③ Sorry, but the lunch is still not ready.
④ Sure. I'll take my laptop to the repair shop.
⑤ Yes. The homework is due tomorrow.

W Your dad is almost _____ _____ _____, Tom.
M Great! I'm so hungry. What did he make?
W He made noodles with vegetables.
M That sounds delicious. But _____ _____ _____ in my room?
W Why? Are you busy?
M I need to _____ _____ _____. It's taking a long time.
W Alright. You can eat your lunch in your room then.
M Also, can I _____ _____ _____? Mine is so slow.
W Yes. But _____ _____ _____ it.

18 | 적절한 응답 고르기

대화를 듣고, 남자의 마지막 말에 대한 여자의 응답으로 가장 적절한 것을 고르시오.

Woman: _____

① I'm sorry. I can't fix these headphones.
② You're so nice. I'll return the favor.
③ Please visit our website for more information.
④ I can't find my wallet anywhere.
⑤ No, thanks. I already ordered new ones.

W What are you looking at, Dahoon?
M I found _____ _____ _____ over here. Do you like them?
W Wow, those are the ones _____ _____ _____ .
M I think these are _____ _____ _____ _____ .
W You should buy them then. I'll get them later.
M But didn't your headphones break?
W Yes. They _____ _____ _____ last week.
M Then, you should have them. I will _____ _____ _____ _____ online.

19 | 적절한 응답 고르기

대화를 듣고, 남자의 마지막 말에 대한 여자의 응답으로 가장 적절한 것을 고르시오.

Woman: _____

① You can buy an umbrella in the convenience store.
② Please wear a cap in the pool.
③ Many artists participated in the exhibit.
④ Its main theme is the Second World War.
⑤ We are learning about that in history class right now.

> 🎯 적중! Tip   That's a shame.
> 실망스러운 일이나 안 좋은 일에 대해 유감이나 동정을 나타낼 때 사용되는 표현이다.

W _____ _____ _____ we can swim tomorrow, Richard.
M Oh, why not?
W The weather report says that _____ _____ _____ a lot.
M Really? That's a shame. I was excited to go to the outdoor pool.
W Me too. But we can do something else.
M Do you have any ideas?
W _____ _____ _____ _____ at the history museum. It just opened.
M That might be interesting. _____ _____ _____ _____ ?

20 | 상황에 적절한 말 고르기

다음 상황 설명을 듣고, Aria가 남자에게 할 말로 가장 적절한 것을 고르시오.

Aria: Excuse me, _____

① would you like to change seats with me?
② do you know why the flight is delayed?
③ I think you are in my seat.
④ I need to take a taxi to the airport.
⑤ do you mind opening the window?

M Aria is leaving for her trip to Mexico. When it is time for her to _____ _____ _____ , she notices that a man is sitting in her seat. Aria _____ _____ _____ _____ so that she could enjoy the view during the flight. So, she wants to tell the man that he is _____ _____ _____ _____ . In this situation, what would Aria most likely say to the man?

1 대화를 듣고, 여자가 구입할 이불을 고르시오.

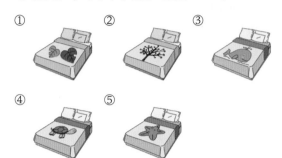

① ② ③
④ ⑤

2 대화를 듣고, 학교 미술 숙제에 관해 언급되지 <u>않은</u> 것을 고르시오.

① 추가 재료 ② 색상 개수 ③ 그림 대상
④ 크기 ⑤ 마감일

3 대화를 듣고, 남자가 여자에게 전화한 목적으로 가장 적절한 것을 고르시오.

① 주문 수량을 변경하려고
② 배송 주소를 확인하려고
③ 영업시간을 문의하려고
④ 오배송 문제를 해결하려고
⑤ 환불을 요청하려고

4 대화를 듣고, 남자가 탑승하려는 버스의 출발 시각을 고르시오.

① 1 p.m. ② 2 p.m. ③ 3 p.m.
④ 4 p.m. ⑤ 5 p.m.

5 대화를 듣고, 남자의 심정으로 가장 적절한 것을 고르시오.

① excited ② relaxed ③ jealous
④ sorrowful ⑤ disappointed

6 다음 그림의 상황에 가장 적절한 대화를 고르시오.

① ② ③ ④ ⑤

7 대화를 듣고, 남자가 여자에게 부탁한 일로 가장 적절한 것을 고르시오.

① 비행기표 예매하기
② 여행 가방 싸기
③ 여권 신청하기
④ 투어 프로그램 검색하기
⑤ 머무를 호텔 찾아보기

고난도
8 다음을 듣고, Fairview Library에 관해 언급되지 <u>않은</u> 것을 고르시오.

① 공사 기간 ② 개관 시기 ③ 층수
④ 이용 자격 ⑤ 시설

고난도
9 다음을 듣고, 어떤 장소에 관한 설명인지 고르시오.

① 법원 ② 은행 ③ 시청
④ 국회 ⑤ 경찰서

10 다음을 듣고, 두 사람의 대화가 <u>어색한</u> 것을 고르시오.

① ② ③ ④ ⑤

11 대화를 듣고, 남자가 대화 직후에 할 일로 가장 적절한 것을 고르시오.

① 유니폼 빨기 ② 세탁기 청소하기
③ 빨래 널기 ④ 소풍 준비하기
⑤ 배구 경기 보기

12 다음 표를 보면서 대화를 듣고, 남자가 주문한 음료를 고르시오.

	Drink	Size	Syrup
①	black coffee	small	X
②	black coffee	large	O
③	black coffee	large	X
④	green tea	small	O
⑤	green tea	large	X

13 대화를 듣고, 여자가 에어컨을 수리받기로 한 날짜를 고르시오.

① 7월 3일　　② 7월 4일　　③ 7월 6일
④ 7월 7일　　⑤ 7월 9일

14 대화를 듣고, 여자가 어제 한 일로 가장 적절한 것을 고르시오.

① 택배 보내기　　② 축하 편지 쓰기
③ 과자 구입하기　　④ 태국 음식 만들기
⑤ 생일 파티 참석하기

15 다음을 듣고, 방송의 목적으로 가장 적절한 것을 고르시오.

① 웹사이트 보수 시간을 공지하려고
② 새로운 온라인 기능을 소개하려고
③ 은행 앱 출시를 홍보하려고
④ 은행 사이트 가입 절차를 설명하려고
⑤ 올바른 금융 습관에 대해 조언하려고

16 대화를 듣고, 여자가 지불할 금액을 고르시오.

① $ 10　　② $ 15　　③ $ 20
④ $ 25　　⑤ $ 30

17 대화를 듣고, 남자의 마지막 말에 대한 여자의 응답으로 가장 적절한 것을 고르시오.

Woman: _____

① Great job! You played so well.
② Be careful so you don't get hurt.
③ Always look before crossing the street.
④ I will come with you then.
⑤ Let me explain the symptoms.

18 대화를 듣고, 여자의 마지막 말에 대한 남자의 응답으로 가장 적절한 것을 고르시오.

Man: _____

① I used the service of a moving company.
② It's around the corner over there.
③ I'm making potato soup tonight.
④ Then, let me take you to the city hall instead.
⑤ The big supermarket sells lots of items.

19 대화를 듣고, 남자의 마지막 말에 대한 여자의 응답으로 가장 적절한 것을 고르시오.

Woman: _____

① I will wear this necklace with my dress.
② Of course. Just give me a few minutes.
③ Actually, we already started opening the presents.
④ Thank you for the beautiful flowers.
⑤ Yeah. It's our fifth anniversary.

20 다음 상황 설명을 듣고, Mollie가 Ben에게 할 말로 가장 적절한 것을 고르시오.

Mollie: Ben, _____

① you'd better go to bed early and focus in class.
② what games do you usually play?
③ is it okay to copy your notes again?
④ please wake me up before the history class begins.
⑤ I can't understand your handwriting.

12회 중학영어듣기 실전 모의고사 Dictation 음성을 들으며 빈칸에 알맞은 단어를 채우시오.

1 | 알맞은 그림 고르기

대화를 듣고, 여자가 구입할 이불을 고르시오.

① ② ③

④ ⑤

W Hi. I heard your store has lots of fashionable bed covers.
M It was nice of you to come here. _____ _____ _____ _____ do you need?
W I need one for a queen-size bed.
M Then, you can _____ _____ _____. How about this one with a leaf pattern?
W It _____ _____, but could you show me some other designs?
M No problem. We also have these designs with _____ _____ _____. The whale, turtle, and starfish are all popular.
W Oh, I like the one with _____ _____ _____ _____. I'll take it.

2 | 언급하지 않은 내용 고르기

대화를 듣고, 학교 미술 숙제에 관해 언급되지 않은 것을 고르시오.

① 추가 재료   ② 색상 개수   ③ 그림 대상
④ 크기   ⑤ 마감일

🎯 적중! Tip   pain**t** brush
[페인트 브러시]보다는 [페인브러시]로 들린다. 자음 3개가 연속해서 나오면 중간 자음은 발음되지 않기 때문이다.

W Brian, do you need _____ _____ _____ _____ for your school art project?
M Yeah. I need some green and brown paint. Also, I need another paint brush.
W _____ _____ _____ _____?
M I have to make a painting with only four colors. I'm going to _____ _____ _____.
W Oh, that's interesting. And when is it due?
M _____ _____.
W Then, let's go to the art supply store now.
M Sure!

3 | 목적 고르기

대화를 듣고, 남자가 여자에게 전화한 목적으로 가장 적절한 것을 고르시오.

① 주문 수량을 변경하려고
② 배송 주소를 확인하려고
③ 영업시간을 문의하려고
④ 오배송 문제를 해결하려고
⑤ 환불을 요청하려고

[Telephone rings.]
W Hello, Best Fit Clothing Store. How can I help you?
M Hi. I just received some shirts from your shop in the mail, but they are _____ _____ _____ _____ _____.
W I apologize for that. Would you _____ _____ _____?
M No. I still want the other shirts.
W Okay. You can _____ _____ _____ to us for free. Then, we will send you the new shirts.
M _____ _____ will that process take?
W It should only _____ _____ _____.
M That's fine then.

4 | 시간 정보 고르기

대화를 듣고, 남자가 탑승하려는 버스의 출발 시각을 고르시오.

① 1 p.m.　②2 p.m.　③ 3 p.m.
④ 4 p.m.　⑤ 5 p.m.

M Has the bus for Preston left already?

W Yes. It _____ _____ 1 p.m. You missed it by 30 minutes.

M I see. Is there another one at 2?

W _____, _____. But there is one at 3 p.m.

M I _____ _____ _____ in Preston at 5. Will I get there in time?

W I think so. You _____ _____ _____ at 4 p.m.

M I'll get the ticket for the 3 p.m. bus then.

W Okay. That will be 15 dollars.

5 | 심정 고르기

대화를 듣고, 남자의 심정으로 가장 적절한 것을 고르시오.

① excited　② relaxed　③ jealous
④ sorrowful　⑤ disappointed

적중! Tip I'm walking on air.
몹시 기분이 좋음을 나타낼 때 사용되는 표현이다.

W Jake, you're _____ _____ _____ _____ today.

M Yeah. You know I sent my song to my favorite singer.

W Did you get an answer from him?

M Yes. He said he wants to _____ _____ _____ on his next album.

W Congratulations! I'm _____ _____ _____ _____.

M It's like I'm walking on air.

W You must feel great.

M Yeah. I _____ _____ _____.

6 | 그림 상황에 적절한 대화 고르기

다음 그림의 상황에 가장 적절한 대화를 고르시오.

①　②　③　④　⑤

① W Did you _____ _____ _____?
　M Yeah. I booked a table for two.
② W _____ _____ _____ _____ from here?
　M It's about a 10-minute drive.
③ W What's the weather like?
　M It's _____ _____ _____.
④ W Do you want to go for a swim?
　M No. I want to _____ _____ _____ _____.
⑤ W Is there a problem?
　M Yeah. The umbrella's broken.

7 | 부탁·요청한 일 고르기

대화를 듣고, 남자가 여자에게 부탁한 일로 가장 적절한 것을 고르시오.

① 비행기표 예매하기
② 여행 가방 싸기
③ 여권 신청하기
④ 투어 프로그램 검색하기
⑤ 머무를 호텔 찾아보기

M Alright. We're going to Paris, Honey! I just booked the flights.

W I'm so excited! _____ _____ _____ _____ _____ for the trip?

M We leave on March 13th and _____ _____ _____ March 27th.

W Excellent. We have a lot to do before then.

M Yes. I'll _____ _____ _____ _____ and activities.

W Good thinking. There will be so many options to choose from.

M Can you _____ _____ _____? We should reserve a room soon.

W I'll start looking now.

8 | 언급하지 않은 내용 고르기

다음을 듣고, Fairview Library에 관해 언급되지 않은 것을 고르시오.

① 공사 기간 　② 개관 시기 　③ 층수
④ 이용 자격 　⑤ 시설

> 🎯 적중! Tip **lit**erature
>
> [리터러철]보다는 [리러러철]로 들린다. [t]가 모음 사이에서 발음될 때는 약화되어 [r]에 가깝게 발음되기 때문이다.

M Good afternoon. We are here to celebrate the completion of the new library. At this location, we started building the Fairview Library 12 months ago. It will _____ _____ _____, at the beginning of the new year. The new five-story building will _____ _____ _____ _____ and thousands of books. There will also _____ _____ _____ _____ _____ _____ and a children's literature collection. The library will also have a café with a beautiful garden where visitors can _____ _____ _____ from time to time. Thank you for making this possible, everyone.

9 | 화제 고르기

다음을 듣고, 어떤 장소에 관한 설명인지 고르시오.

① 법원 　② 은행 　③ 시청
④ 국회 　⑤ 경찰서

W This is a public place of government. Many kinds of decisions _____ _____ _____ are made in this place. _____ _____ _____ work here. People go to this place to _____ _____ _____ with other people in trials. When a person _____ _____ _____, they visit this place to learn about their punishment.

10 | 어색한 대화 고르기

다음을 듣고, 두 사람의 대화가 어색한 것을 고르시오.

①　②　③　④　⑤

> 🎯 적중! Tip **pr**es**e**nt
>
> present는 명사나 형용사로 쓰일 때는 [프레즌트]로, 동사로 쓰일 때는 [프리젠트]로 발음된다.

① M Is Monday a national holiday?
　W No. That's next Tuesday.
② M Will you try this and _____ _____ _____ _____ okay?
　W Wow, this sauce is delicious!
③ M We _____ _____ _____ at 11 a.m. What happened?
　W My train leaves at 2 in the afternoon.
④ M That blue hat looks really _____ _____ _____!
　W Thanks. My brother gave it to me as a birthday present.
⑤ M Can I help you find something?
　W I _____ _____ _____ the *Harry Potter* series.

11 | 할 일 고르기

대화를 듣고, 남자가 대화 직후에 할 일로 가장 적절한 것을 고르시오.

① 유니폼 빨기 　② 세탁기 청소하기
③ 빨래 널기 　④ 소풍 준비하기
⑤ 배구 경기 보기

W Do you see my volleyball uniform anywhere, Dad?
M No. Did you look _____ _____ _____?
W Yes. I looked everywhere in my room. It's not there.
M Let me _____ _____ _____ _____ _____. *[Pause]* Oh, it's in here, but it's dirty.
W Oh, no. I have a game tomorrow.
M I'll _____ _____ _____, and it might have time to dry.
W Can we _____ _____ _____ after it's washed? It will dry faster in the sun.
M Good idea.

12 | 도표에서 알맞은 항목 고르기

다음 표를 보면서 대화를 듣고, 남자가 주문한 음료를 고르시오.

	Drink	Size	Syrup
①	black coffee	small	X
②	black coffee	large	O
③	black coffee	large	X
④	green tea	small	O
⑤	green tea	large	X

W May I ＿＿＿＿ ＿＿＿＿ ＿＿＿＿ ?
M Yes, please. I'd like a latte.
W Sorry, sir. We're ＿＿＿＿ ＿＿＿＿ ＿＿＿＿ right now, so you can order a black coffee or green tea.
M Then, I'll have a black coffee.
W Do you want a small or large one?
M ＿＿＿＿ ＿＿＿＿ ＿＿＿＿ , please.
W Sure. Do you want ＿＿＿＿ ＿＿＿＿ ＿＿＿＿ ＿＿＿＿ ?
M No, thanks.
W The total is four dollars.

13 | 시간 정보 고르기

대화를 듣고, 여자가 에어컨을 수리받기로 한 날짜를 고르시오.

① 7월 3일   ② 7월 4일   ③ 7월 6일
④ 7월 7일   ⑤ 7월 9일

🎯 적중! Tip **sche**dule
미국식으로는 [스케쥴]로 발음되고, 영국식으로는 [쉐쥴]로 발음된다.

[Telephone rings.]
W Hello?
M Hello. This is Brandon Miller from Apex Repair Shop.
W Oh, I've ＿＿＿＿ ＿＿＿＿ ＿＿＿＿ ＿＿＿＿ to call.
M Yes. I called to schedule the visit to fix your air conditioner.
W ＿＿＿＿ ＿＿＿＿ ＿＿＿＿ you can come?
M It would be July 4th. Next Tuesday.
W I ＿＿＿＿ ＿＿＿＿ ＿＿＿＿ that day. How about July 6th?
M Yeah. That ＿＿＿＿ ＿＿＿＿ ＿＿＿＿ .
W Good. What time will you visit?
M Does 10 a.m. sound okay to you?
W Sure. I'll see you then!

14 | 한 일 고르기

대화를 듣고, 여자가 어제 한 일로 가장 적절한 것을 고르시오.

① 택배 보내기   ② 축하 편지 쓰기
③ 과자 구입하기   ④ 태국 음식 만들기
⑤ 생일 파티 참석하기

M What are you doing after school today, Sofia?
W I will go to the post office ＿＿＿＿ ＿＿＿＿ ＿＿＿＿ .
M What package?
W It's a gift for ＿＿＿＿ ＿＿＿＿ ＿＿＿＿ ＿＿＿＿ . It's for her birthday.
M That's nice of you.
W Yes. She loves the snacks from here, so I ＿＿＿＿ ＿＿＿＿ ＿＿＿＿ yesterday. I will send them to her in the package.
M Will they get there on her birthday?
W I hope so. Her birthday is ＿＿＿＿ ＿＿＿＿ .

15 | 목적 고르기

다음을 듣고, 방송의 목적으로 가장 적절한 것을 고르시오.

① 웹사이트 보수 시간을 공지하려고
② 새로운 온라인 기능을 소개하려고
③ 은행 앱 출시를 홍보하려고
④ 은행 사이트 가입 절차를 설명하려고
⑤ 올바른 금융 습관에 대해 조언하려고

🎯 적중! Tip representative

[레프리젠터티브]보다는 [레프리제너디브]로 들린다. 모음 사이에서 [n] 뒤에 오는 [t] 발음은 약화되어 거의 들리지 않기 때문이다.

W Hello, loyal customers. This is Hannah Godwin, the founder of Bada Bank. Are you tired of _____ _____ _____ _____ for help with banking? Well, now you don't have to. Bada Bank will now _____ _____ _____ _____ for people online. Simply enter your name in the chat, and you _____ _____ _____ _____ a representative online. We hope you _____ _____ _____ _____. Thank you.

16 | 금액 정보 고르기

대화를 듣고, 여자가 지불할 금액을 고르시오.

① $ 10   ② $ 15   ③ $ 20
④ $ 25   ⑤ $ 30

M Hello. How may I help you?
W Hi. I'd like to buy _____ _____ _____ _____ at 6 p.m. How much are they?
M _____ _____ _____ is 15 dollars, and a ticket for a child _____ _____ _____ _____ is 10 dollars.
W One adult and one child, please.
M Okay. Your total is 25 dollars.
W I have a five-dollar discount coupon. Can I use it?
M I'm sorry, but you _____ _____ _____ for this performance.
W That's okay. Here's my credit card.

17 | 적절한 응답 고르기

대화를 듣고, 남자의 마지막 말에 대한 여자의 응답으로 가장 적절한 것을 고르시오.

Woman: _____

① Great job! You played so well.
② Be careful so you don't get hurt.
③ Always look before crossing the street.
④ I will come with you then.
⑤ Let me explain the symptoms.

W Did you see Namjun at the soccer game yesterday?
M No. He couldn't _____ _____ _____ _____.
W Why not?
M He was _____ _____ _____ _____ the other day.
W Oh, no! Is he okay?
M He _____ _____ _____, but it wasn't serious.
W That's a relief. We should go see him soon.
M Yes. He's resting at home right now. I _____ _____ _____ _____ after school today.

18 | 적절한 응답 고르기

대화를 듣고, 여자의 마지막 말에 대한 남자의 응답으로 가장 적절한 것을 고르시오.

Man: _____

① I used the service of a moving company.

② It's around the corner over there.

③ I'm making potato soup tonight.

④ Then, let me take you to the city hall instead.

⑤ The big supermarket sells lots of items.

> 🎯 적중! Tip   Don't mention it.
> 감사하다는 말에 답할 때 사용되는 표현으로 '별말씀을요, 천만에요'라는 의미이다.

M   You _____ _____ . Can I help you find something?

W   Oh, yes. I want to go to the city hall.

M   It's just _____ _____ _____ on the right.

W   Thank you for your help. I just moved here, so I don't know the area well.

M   Don't mention it. Do you need _____ _____ _____ ?

W   Actually, I also need to go to a supermarket. Do you know _____ _____ _____ ?

M   There are two near here. There is a big one and a small one.

W   I just need to buy one ingredient. Can you tell me _____ _____ _____ _____ _____ ?

19 | 적절한 응답 고르기

대화를 듣고, 남자의 마지막 말에 대한 여자의 응답으로 가장 적절한 것을 고르시오.

Woman: _____

① I will wear this necklace with my dress.

② Of course. Just give me a few minutes.

③ Actually, we already started opening the presents.

④ Thank you for the beautiful flowers.

⑤ Yeah. It's our fifth anniversary.

W   Welcome to Finest Jewelry. How can I help you?

M   I want to _____ _____ _____ _____ _____ for our wedding anniversary.

W   All of our most popular necklaces are over here. Do you like any of these?

M   These are all very big. She _____ _____ _____ _____ .

W   I have this one here too. It's new to the store.

M   That's perfect. _____ _____ _____ _____ _____ , please?

W   Yes. I'll prepare it for you now.

M   Can you _____ _____ _____ ? I want the package to look nice.

20 | 상황에 적절한 말 고르기

다음 상황 설명을 듣고, Mollie가 Ben에게 할 말로 가장 적절한 것을 고르시오.

Mollie: Ben, _____

① you'd better go to bed early and focus in class.

② what games do you usually play?

③ is it okay to copy your notes again?

④ please wake me up before the history class begins.

⑤ I can't understand your handwriting.

W   Mollie sits next to Ben in history class. Ben _____ _____ _____ while the teacher is talking. He doesn't take notes when this happens, and he asks Mollie for hers. Ben sometimes tells Mollie that he is tired because he _____ _____ _____ playing games. Mollie thinks that Ben should take his own notes. So, she wants to tell him that he should _____ _____ _____ so that he can _____ _____ _____ _____ . In this situation, what would Mollie most likely say to Ben?

1 대화를 듣고, 여자가 구입할 조끼를 고르시오.

①   ②   ③

④   ⑤

고난도
2 대화를 듣고, Ocean Adventure에 관해 언급되지 않은 것을 고르시오.

① 장르   ② 주연 배우   ③ 상영 시각
④ 길이   ⑤ 상영 장소

3 대화를 듣고, 남자가 여자에게 전화한 목적으로 가장 적절한 것을 고르시오.

① 미리 메뉴를 주문하려고
② 주소를 확인하려고
③ 메뉴에 대해 문의하려고
④ 예약을 확인하려고
⑤ 영업시간 변경을 안내하려고

4 대화를 듣고, 여자의 밴드 연습이 시작될 시각을 고르시오.

① 10:00 a.m.   ② 11:00 a.m.   ③ 1:30 p.m.
④ 2:30 p.m.   ⑤ 3:30 p.m.

5 대화를 듣고, 두 사람이 대화하는 장소로 가장 적절한 곳을 고르시오.

① 치과   ② 옷가게   ③ 제과점
④ 농구 경기장   ⑤ 빙수 전문점

6 다음 그림의 상황에 가장 적절한 대화를 고르시오.

①   ②   ③   ④   ⑤

7 대화를 듣고, 남자가 여자에게 부탁한 일로 가장 적절한 것을 고르시오.

① 퀴즈 정답 알려주기   ② 목도리 가져다주기
③ 양말 찾아주기   ④ 시계 알람 맞추기
⑤ 학교 데려다주기

8 다음을 듣고, 자전거에 관해 언급되지 않은 것을 고르시오.

① 발매일   ② 성능   ③ 색상
④ 무게   ⑤ 판매 장소

9 다음을 듣고, 어떤 직업에 관한 설명인지 고르시오.

① 농부   ② 목수   ③ 정원사
④ 정비사   ⑤ 건축가

10 다음을 듣고, 두 사람의 대화가 어색한 것을 고르시오.

①   ②   ③   ④   ⑤

11 대화를 듣고, 여자가 할 일로 가장 적절한 것을 고르시오.

① 강의 추천하기   ② 도서 빌려주기
③ 선생님께 연락하기   ④ 중국어책 읽기
⑤ 수업 복습하기

12 다음 공원 배치도를 보면서 대화를 듣고, 두 사람이 선택할 구역을 고르시오.

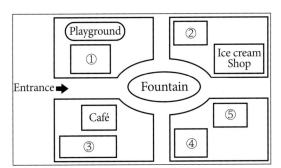

13 대화를 듣고, 두 사람이 만나기로 한 시각을 고르시오.

① 9 a.m.　　② 11 a.m.　　③ 2 p.m.

④ 3 p.m.　　⑤ 5 p.m.

14 대화를 듣고, 여자가 여름 캠프에서 한 일로 가장 적절한 것을 고르시오.

① 등산하기　　　　② 수영 배우기

③ 승마 연습하기　　④ 토마토 키우기

⑤ 해수욕장 놀러 가기

15 다음을 듣고, 방송의 목적으로 가장 적절한 것을 고르시오.

① 숙제 제출 일자를 공지하려고

② 글쓰기 방식에 대해 조언하려고

③ 신간 소설을 소개하려고

④ 작문 대회 참가를 안내하려고

⑤ 독서 동아리 가입을 홍보하려고

고난도
16 대화를 듣고, 여자가 지불할 금액을 고르시오.

① $ 10　　② $ 20　　③ $ 30

④ $ 40　　⑤ $ 50

17 대화를 듣고, 여자의 마지막 말에 대한 남자의 응답으로 가장 적절한 것을 고르시오.

Man: _____

① You're to blame. You dropped my phone.

② Here. You can use mine.

③ This charger isn't working.

④ Did he call you back?

⑤ Let me look inside my bag.

[18-19] 대화를 듣고, 남자의 마지막 말에 대한 여자의 응답으로 가장 적절한 것을 고르시오.

18　Woman: _____

① I want to paint this room green.

② Your pizza is being delivered now.

③ Okay. I'll be there then.

④ You need a designer to decorate the new house.

⑤ The poster shop is on the second floor.

19　Woman: _____

① Pardon me? I can't understand you.

② I hope you can go there one day.

③ The mail will be sent this afternoon.

④ We've never met each other before.

⑤ Good luck with your trip!

20 다음 상황 설명을 듣고, Mr. Bryant가 Sarah에게 할 말로 가장 적절한 것을 고르시오.

Mr. Bryant: Sarah, _____

① I apologize for hurting your feelings.

② our next game is this weekend.

③ you need to say sorry to your teammates.

④ welcome to the team.

⑤ you shouldn't be late to practice again.

13회 중학영어듣기 실전 모의고사 Dictation 음성을 들으며 빈칸에 알맞은 단어를 채우시오.

1 | 알맞은 그림 고르기

대화를 듣고, 여자가 구입할 조끼를 고르시오.

① ② ③
④ ⑤

> 🎯 적중! Tip **buttons**
> [버튼즈]보다는 [벋은즈]로 들린다. [n] 앞에 오는 [t] 발음
> 은 약화되어 거의 들리지 않기 때문이다.
> · kit**t**en [킷은] · ea**t**en [잇은]

M How may I help you?
W I'd like to buy a padded vest.
M Okay. Do you have _____ _____ _____ _____ ?
W I want one that _____ _____ _____ _____
_____ .
M Then, would you like a vest with buttons or a zipper?
W I guess one with a zipper would _____ _____ _____
_____ .
M Got it. You can choose from these two. One has a hood, and the other
doesn't.
W I like the one with a hood. It _____ _____ _____
_____ than the one without a hood.
M That's true. Covering the head is good for staying warm.

고난도

2 | 언급하지 않은 내용 고르기

대화를 듣고, Ocean Adventure에 관해 언급되지 않
은 것을 고르시오.

① 장르   ② 주연 배우   ③ 상영 시각
④ 길이   ⑤ 상영 장소

W Do you want to see a movie tonight?
M Which one?
W What about *Ocean Adventure*?
M I haven't _____ _____ _____ _____ .
W Yeah, that's because it's an independent documentary movie.
M That sounds interesting. _____ _____ _____ _____ ?
W Brett Williams has _____ _____ _____ .
M What time does it start?
W We can watch it at 7 tonight.
M Is it playing at the Odeon Theater?
W Yeah. That's _____ _____ _____ .
M Okay. Let's go watch it.

3 | 목적 고르기

대화를 듣고, 남자가 여자에게 전화한 목적으로 가장
적절한 것을 고르시오.

① 미리 메뉴를 주문하려고
② 주소를 확인하려고
③ 메뉴에 대해 문의하려고
④ 예약을 확인하려고
⑤ 영업시간 변경을 안내하려고

[Cellphone rings.]
W Hello?
M Hi. This is Tom from Taste of Home Restaurant.
W Oh, is this _____ _____ ?
M That's right. Do you still _____ _____ _____ at 7 p.m.?
W Yes, I do.
M I called to double-check your reservation since you made it _____
_____ _____ _____ .
W I see. I made it so early because it's my _____ _____ _____
_____ _____ .
M Thank you for letting us know. We will prepare a free dessert for you
then.

4 | 시간 정보 고르기

대화를 듣고, 여자의 밴드 연습이 시작될 시각을 고르시오.

① 10:00 a.m. ② 11:00 a.m. ③ 1:30 p.m.
④ 2:30 p.m. ⑤ 3:30 p.m.

🎯 적중! Tip Do you have a minute?
상대방에게 간단한 대화를 요청할 때 사용되는 표현으로 '잠시 시간 있으세요?'라는 의미이다.

W Do you have a minute, Mr. Davidson?
M Sure, Wendy. What do you need?
W It's about _____ _____ _____ _____ on Thursday. I'm worried because I have band practice that day.
M We'll _____ _____ _____ _____ at 10 in the morning. Is that a problem for you?
W No. I was just wondering what time _____ _____ _____ _____.
M Well, our bus will leave at 1:30, so we will arrive back at the school around 2:30.
W Oh, great. My band practice starts at 3:30. I don't have to be _____ _____ _____ _____.

5 | 장소 고르기

대화를 듣고, 두 사람이 대화하는 장소로 가장 적절한 곳을 고르시오.

① 치과 ② 옷가게 ③ 제과점
④ 농구 경기장 ⑤ 빙수 전문점

M Hello. Would you like to try a chocolate chip cookie?
W No, thank you. I am here _____ _____ _____ _____ for my friend's birthday.
M Okay. What kind of cake do you want?
W _____ _____ _____ _____ _____ with vanilla icing.
M What size do you want, a small, medium, or large?
W I want a large cake, please. Also, can you _____ _____ _____ to the cake? My friend loves basketball.
M Of course. _____ _____ _____ _____ _____ on Thursday.

6 | 그림 상황에 적절한 대화 고르기

다음 그림의 상황에 가장 적절한 대화를 고르시오.

① ② ③ ④ ⑤

① M What would you like to drink?
   W Coffee, please.
② M Oh, no! I _____ _____ _____.
   W It's okay. Let me get you some tissue.
③ M Who _____ _____ _____?
   W I did. I'm so sorry.
④ M Would you like to _____ _____ _____ _____?
   W Yes, please. It's so hot today.
⑤ M Whose notebook is that?
   W I think it is Brent's.

대화를 듣고, 남자가 여자에게 부탁한 일로 가장 적절한 것을 고르시오.

① 퀴즈 정답 알려주기   ② 목도리 가져다주기
③ 양말 찾아주기   ④ 시계 알람 맞추기
⑤ 학교 데려다주기

W Yoonsu, hurry up! _____ _____ _____ for school.
M I'm sorry, Mom. I woke up late this morning.
W Why? Didn't you hear your alarm clock?
M I _____ _____ _____ _____ because I was tired. I studied for a quiz all night.
W Well, you will miss the bus. I will just _____ _____ _____ _____.
M Okay. Can you _____ _____ _____ from the closet? I will pack my book bag.
W Sure. But we need to leave in five minutes.

다음을 듣고, 자전거에 관해 언급되지 <u>않은</u> 것을 고르시오.

① 발매일   ② 성능   ③ 색상
④ 무게   ⑤ 판매 장소

M The Voyager electric bicycle will change the way you ride. Its electric motor will _____ _____ _____ _____ _____ or carry heavy loads. Plus, it is not only useful _____ _____ _____ _____. It is available in many different colors. And, _____ _____ _____ _____ _____, it's light. It only weighs 15 kilograms. The Voyager electric bike will be _____ _____ _____ _____ and in stores around the country. What are you waiting for? Start your voyage today.

다음을 듣고, 어떤 직업에 관한 설명인지 고르시오.

① 농부   ② 목수   ③ 정원사
④ 정비사   ⑤ 건축가

W People who have this job _____ _____ _____ and lots of tools. When a person needs _____ _____ _____ _____ _____ for their home, they can make it. They can also help build _____ _____ _____ _____. To have this job, you need to learn about _____ _____ _____ _____ and the tools to cut and shape wood.

다음을 듣고, 두 사람의 대화가 <u>어색한</u> 것을 고르시오.

①   ②   ③   ④   ⑤

🎯 적중! Tip She's so
[쉬즈 쏘]보다는 [쉬쏘]로 들린다. 비슷하게 발음되는 자음이 나란히 나오면 앞 단어의 끝 자음이 탈락되기 때문이다.

① W Are you almost _____ _____ _____? We have to leave soon.
    M Give me five minutes.
② W Is there anything I can help you with?
    M Of course. _____ _____ _____ a snack.
③ W Aren't you feeling a little cold?
    M I am. I think I'll _____ _____ _____ _____.
④ W Is this your new cat? She's so cute.
    M Thank you. Her name is Shadow.
⑤ W I don't like this drama. Let's _____ _____ _____.
    M But I want to finish watching it.

11 | 할 일 고르기

대화를 듣고, 여자가 할 일로 가장 적절한 것을 고르시오.

① 강의 추천하기　② 도서 빌려주기
③ 선생님께 연락하기　④ 중국어책 읽기
⑤ 수업 복습하기

W Do you know ＿＿＿＿ ＿＿＿＿ ＿＿＿＿, Edward?
M Yes. I know some Chinese.
W Really? I want to speak Chinese.
M You have to study a lot, but ＿＿＿＿ ＿＿＿＿ ＿＿＿＿ it.
W I want to learn it because I want to be a diplomat one day.
M I can give you some of my old books for studying it. But ＿＿＿＿ ＿＿＿＿ ＿＿＿＿ ＿＿＿＿ ＿＿＿＿ is with a teacher.
W Yeah. I'll contact one soon. Do you ＿＿＿＿ ＿＿＿＿ ＿＿＿＿?
M Yes. I have a few.

12 | 위치 고르기

다음 공원 배치도를 보면서 대화를 듣고, 두 사람이 선택할 구역을 고르시오.

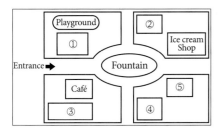

Playground ①
②
Ice cream Shop
Entrance → Fountain
Café ③
⑤
④

🎯 적중! Tip　Why **don't** we
[와이 돈트 위]보다는 [와이런위]로 들린다. [d]가 모음 사이에서 발음될 때는 약화되어 [r]에 가깝게 발음되며, -nt로 끝나는 단어에서 마지막 [t] 발음은 약화되어 거의 들리지 않기 때문이다.

M Honey, where are the kids?
W They are on the slide at the playground.
M I see. Do you want to go to the café?
W I brought a picnic mat. Why don't we ＿＿＿＿ ＿＿＿＿ ＿＿＿＿?
M Sure. How about over there?
W I think we should sit where we can ＿＿＿＿ ＿＿＿＿ ＿＿＿＿ ＿＿＿＿ the kids.
M Yeah, I agree. How about near the entrance?
W It's ＿＿＿＿ ＿＿＿＿ ＿＿＿＿. Why don't we go over there?
M Oh, nice. And it's right next to the ice cream shop. I'll go get some if you ＿＿＿＿ ＿＿＿＿ ＿＿＿＿.

13 | 시간 정보 고르기

대화를 듣고, 두 사람이 만나기로 한 시각을 고르시오.

① 9 a.m.　② 11 a.m.　③ 2 p.m.
④ 3 p.m.　⑤ 5 p.m.

M Beth, let's study ＿＿＿＿ ＿＿＿＿ ＿＿＿＿ ＿＿＿＿ together in the library on Sunday.
W Okay. What time do you want to meet?
M Is 9 a.m. too early?
W Yeah. I ＿＿＿＿ ＿＿＿＿ ＿＿＿＿ ＿＿＿＿ on the weekends. How about at 2 p.m. instead?
M Actually, I have to ＿＿＿＿ ＿＿＿＿ ＿＿＿＿ ＿＿＿＿ ＿＿＿＿ between 3 and 5 on that day. My parents will go out.
W Oh, I am going to my grandparent's house for dinner that evening. Maybe we should ＿＿＿＿ ＿＿＿＿ ＿＿＿＿ ＿＿＿＿ after all.
M How about 11 a.m.?
W That's fine. I will see you then.

14 | 한 일 고르기

대화를 듣고, 여자가 여름 캠프에서 한 일로 가장 적절한 것을 고르시오.

① 등산하기
② 수영 배우기
③ 승마 연습하기
④ 토마토 키우기
⑤ 해수욕장 놀러 가기

M How was summer camp, Sojin?

W It was great! I didn't want to go home _____ _____ _____.

M Don't you usually ride horses there?

W Yes. But this year I wanted to _____ _____ _____ _____, so I chose hiking. I hiked up many mountains _____ _____ _____.

M Will you continue to hike in the future?

W Yes. It's _____ _____ _____. I'll go on the weekends now.

M I hope I can join you on a hike sometime.

15 | 목적 고르기

다음을 듣고, 방송의 목적으로 가장 적절한 것을 고르시오.

① 숙제 제출 일자를 공지하려고
② 글쓰기 방식에 대해 조언하려고
③ 신간 소설을 소개하려고
④ 작문 대회 참가를 안내하려고
⑤ 독서 동아리 가입을 홍보하려고

M Good morning, everyone. I _____ _____ _____ _____ about the school essay contest. The deadline to submit a personal essay is May 1st. Your essay should be _____ _____ _____ _____. You should explain why it is your favorite and _____ _____ _____ _____ _____ _____. The essay should be 500 to 1,000 words long. The judges will not read your essay if it is too long or too short. The top three essay writers _____ _____ _____. Thank you for listening.

고난도
16 | 금액 정보 고르기

대화를 듣고, 여자가 지불할 금액을 고르시오.

① $ 10
② $ 20
③ $ 30
④ $ 40
⑤ $ 50

🎯 적중! Tip **Are you interested in ~?**
상대방의 관심에 대해 물을 때 사용되는 표현으로, in 다음에는 (동)명사가 온다.
· Are you interested in playing soccer?
  축구 하는 데 관심 있으세요?

M Hello. Are you interested in a boat tour?

W Yes. _____ _____ _____ _____ for the Midday Boat Tour. How much is it?

M The tickets are 15 dollars each, but you can enjoy _____ _____ _____ _____ if you pay more.

W How much is the lunch?

M It's 10 dollars per person. Would you like to _____ _____?

W Hmm... Okay. Please add the meal for two people.

M Great. I'll _____ _____ _____ now then.

17 | 적절한 응답 고르기

대화를 듣고, 여자의 마지막 말에 대한 남자의 응답으로 가장 적절한 것을 고르시오.

Man: _____

① You're to blame. You dropped my phone.
② Here. You can use mine.
③ This charger isn't working.
④ Did he call you back?
⑤ Let me look inside my bag.

M Excuse me. You dropped your phone.

W Oh, thank you. Where was it?

M It was on the floor over there. It _____ _____ _____ your bag.

W Thank you for bringing it to me.

M _____ _____ _____.

W [Pause] Oh, no. _____ _____ _____.

M It probably broke during the fall. Can you still use it?

W I don't think so. It's pretty damaged. But I need to _____ _____ _____.

18 | 적절한 응답 고르기

대화를 듣고, 남자의 마지막 말에 대한 여자의 응답으로 가장 적절한 것을 고르시오.

Woman: _____

① I want to paint this room green.
② Your pizza is being delivered now.
③ Okay. I'll be there then.
④ You need a designer to decorate the new house.
⑤ The poster shop is on the second floor.

> 🎯 적중! Tip **treat you**
> [트릿 유]보다는 [트리츄]로 들린다. [t]로 끝나는 단어 뒤에 y-로 시작하는 단어가 이어지면 두 소리가 연결되어 [츄]로 발음되기 때문이다.

W Did you just move in to a new house, Chris?
M Yes. My parents _____ _____ _____.
W Do you like it?
M I do. It _____ _____ _____ _____. Plus, my room is really big.
W Did you already decorate it?
M No. I have some posters and pictures, but I didn't _____ _____ _____ _____ _____ yet.
W I can help you. I love to decorate.
M Sure. You can _____ _____ _____ _____. I'll treat you to pizza after doing it.

19 | 적절한 응답 고르기

대화를 듣고, 남자의 마지막 말에 대한 여자의 응답으로 가장 적절한 것을 고르시오.

Woman: _____

① Pardon me? I can't understand you.
② I hope you can go there one day.
③ The mail will be sent this afternoon.
④ We've never met each other before.
⑤ Good luck with your trip!

W Who are you _____ _____ _____ _____, Carl?
M This is a letter for my friend in Spain. His name is Lucas.
W Wow! _____ _____ _____ _____ him?
M We started to write letters to each other through school.
W Through school?
M Yes. Everyone in my school has to write a letter to a student _____ _____ _____.
W That's so cool! But why did you pick someone from Spain?
M I _____ _____ _____ _____ in the future. It's my dream.

20 | 상황에 적절한 말 고르기

다음 상황 설명을 듣고, Mr. Bryant가 Sarah에게 할 말로 가장 적절한 것을 고르시오.

Mr. Bryant: Sarah, _____

① I apologize for hurting your feelings.
② our next game is this weekend.
③ you need to say sorry to your teammates.
④ welcome to the team.
⑤ you shouldn't be late to practice again.

W Mr. Bryant is a high school soccer coach. One day after school, he is helping his team practice. A girl on the team named Sarah _____ _____ _____ _____ to her teammates because she wants to _____ _____ _____. Mr. Bryant decides to tell Sarah to _____ _____ _____ _____ after practice. In this situation, what would Mr. Bryant most likely say to Sarah?

1 대화를 듣고, 여자가 구입할 엽서를 고르시오.

①
PISA

②
VENICE

③
ROME

④
ROME

⑤
VATICAN

2 대화를 듣고, 작문 과제에 관해 언급되지 <u>않은</u> 것을 고르시오.

① 제목　　　② 장르　　　③ 배경
④ 등장인물　⑤ 예상 분량

3 대화를 듣고, 남자가 여자에게 전화한 목적으로 가장 적절한 것을 고르시오.

① 늦는 이유를 알리려고
② 약속 시간을 확인하려고
③ 같이 공부할 것을 제안하려고
④ 시험 날짜를 물어보려고
⑤ 도서관 폐관 시간을 물어보려고

4 대화를 듣고, 남자가 탑승하려는 여객선의 출발 시각을 고르시오.

① 8 a.m.　　② 9 a.m.　　③ 10 a.m.
④ 11 a.m.　　⑤ 12 p.m.

고난도
5 대화를 듣고, 남자의 심정으로 가장 적절한 것을 고르시오.

① lonely　　② annoyed　　③ pleased
④ thankful　⑤ concerned

6 다음 그림의 상황에 가장 적절한 대화를 고르시오.

①　　②　　③　　④　　⑤

7 대화를 듣고, 여자가 남자에게 부탁한 일로 가장 적절한 것을 고르시오.

① 꽃 사 오기　　　② 행사 진행하기
③ 케이크 찾아오기　④ 선물 정리하기
⑤ 작별 인사 전하기

고난도
8 다음을 듣고, 행사에 관해 언급되지 <u>않은</u> 것을 고르시오.

① 제목　　　② 요일　　　③ 장소
④ 참가비　　⑤ 활동

9 다음을 듣고, 어떤 직업에 관한 설명인지 고르시오.

① 시인　　　　　② 편집자
③ 영업사원　　　④ 일러스트레이터
⑤ 카피라이터

10 다음을 듣고, 두 사람의 대화가 <u>어색한</u> 것을 고르시오.

①　　②　　③　　④　　⑤

11 대화를 듣고, 여자가 대화 직후에 할 일로 가장 적절한 것을 고르시오.

① 커피 만들기　　② 길 알려주기
③ 걷기 운동하기　④ 버스 정류장 찾기
⑤ 주문 줄 서기

12 다음 회의실 배치도를 보면서 대화를 듣고, 두 사람이 사용할 회의실을 고르시오.

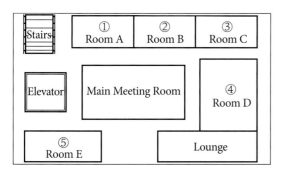

13 대화를 듣고, 여자가 식당에 방문할 날짜를 고르시오.

① July 5th ② July 6th ③ July 7th
④ July 12th ⑤ July 13th

14 대화를 듣고, 여자가 어제 한 일로 가장 적절한 것을 고르시오.

① 병원 가기 ② 티켓 예매하기
③ 집 꾸미기 ④ 놀이공원 가기
⑤ 체온계 주문하기

15 다음을 듣고, 방송의 목적으로 가장 적절한 것을 고르시오.

① 수리로 인한 정전을 공지하려고
② 전기 절약 방법을 설명하려고
③ 엘리베이터 안전 수칙을 안내하려고
④ 입주민을 위한 행사를 홍보하려고
⑤ 아파트의 새 시설을 소개하려고

16 대화를 듣고, 여자가 지불할 금액을 고르시오.

① $ 5 ② $ 10 ③ $ 15
④ $ 20 ⑤ $ 25

17 대화를 듣고, 여자의 마지막 말에 대한 남자의 응답으로 가장 적절한 것을 고르시오.

Man: _____

① I'll make sure to wake you up.
② We should arrive at the campsite in 10 minutes.
③ Why don't we turn on the radio before sleeping?
④ Me too. I'm tired after the long drive here.
⑤ I don't like to take naps during the day.

18 대화를 듣고, 남자의 마지막 말에 대한 여자의 응답으로 가장 적절한 것을 고르시오.

Woman: _____

① Set the alarm at 6 a.m.
② Yes. They are in the refrigerator.
③ All right. Take a good care of him.
④ No. There's no sugar left.
⑤ Why not? Let's buy some grapes for your dad.

19 대화를 듣고, 여자의 마지막 말에 대한 남자의 응답으로 가장 적절한 것을 고르시오.

Man: _____

① I want to buy this bag with a scarf around its handle.
② Where is the lost and found center?
③ You should pack warm clothes.
④ I'm sorry, but this table is reserved.
⑤ I'll do that while you check your bag again.

20 다음 상황 설명을 듣고, Dean이 Ms. Garcia에게 할 말로 가장 적절한 것을 고르시오.

Dean: Ms. Garcia, _____

① are you on your way to the hospital?
② what does this word mean?
③ please turn off your phone during class.
④ I'm afraid I need to stop the lesson now.
⑤ can we reschedule the lesson?

14회 중학영어듣기 실전 모의고사 Dictation 음성을 들으며 빈칸에 알맞은 단어를 채우시오.

1 | 알맞은 그림 고르기

대화를 듣고, 여자가 구입할 엽서를 고르시오.

① PISA
② VENICE
③ ROME
④ ROME
⑤ VATICAN

M Hello. May I help you?

W Yes. I'm looking for a souvenir postcard to remember _____ _____ _____ _____.

M How about this one with an image of Venice?

W Well, _____ _____ _____ Rome and Pisa during this trip.

M I see. Then, _____ _____ _____ _____ _____ this one with a picture of the Leaning Tower of Pisa.

W Oh, that's perfect. The tower was _____ _____. I also like the postcard has the word "PISA" on it.

2 | 언급하지 않은 내용 고르기

대화를 듣고, 작문 과제에 관해 언급되지 않은 것을 고르시오.

① 제목   ② 장르   ③ 배경
④ 등장인물   ⑤ 예상 분량

M What are you writing, Jisun?

W This is my story _____ _____ _____.

M Oh, I didn't start mine yet. What is yours about?

W It's _____ _____ _____ _____. It's set in space.

M That sounds interesting. What are _____ _____ _____ _____?

W The main character is a woman named Johanna. She's _____ _____. And there's a really evil villain.

M You wrote a lot. How _____ _____ _____ _____?

W Right now, it's eight pages, but I will add two more.

M That's great! I should start mine soon.

3 | 목적 고르기

대화를 듣고, 남자가 여자에게 전화한 목적으로 가장 적절한 것을 고르시오.

① 늦는 이유를 알리려고
② 약속 시간을 확인하려고
③ 같이 공부할 것을 제안하려고
④ 시험 날짜를 물어보려고
⑤ 도서관 폐관 시간을 물어보려고

⊙ 적중! Tip   rea**d**y

[레디]보다는 [레리]로 들린다. [d]가 모음 사이에서 발음될 때는 약화되어 [r]에 가깝게 발음되기 때문이다.

[Cellphone rings.]

W Hi, Dave.

M Hi, Mindy. What are you doing this afternoon?

W I _____ _____ _____ _____ yet. Why?

M Are you ready for the math test on Monday?

W Not really. I _____ _____ _____ _____ for it today or tomorrow.

M Why don't we _____ _____ _____? We could go to the library at 2 p.m.

W That sounds like a good plan. I will see if Jenna _____ _____ _____ as well.

M Great! I'll meet you by the main entrance.

4 | 시간 정보 고르기

대화를 듣고, 남자가 탑승하려는 여객선의 출발 시각을 고르시오.

① 8 a.m.   ② 9 a.m.   ③ 10 a.m.
④ 11 a.m.   ⑤ 12 p.m.

W Hi. Do you need a ticket?
M Yes. I'd like to _____ _____ _____ for a ferry to Devon Island.
W When would you like to go?
M I'd like to _____ _____ _____ .
W There's a ferry at 10 a.m. But there are _____ _____ _____ _____ on that boat, so you would have to stand.
M How long is the ferry ride?
W It is about two hours long.
M That's too long to stand. What about _____ _____ _____ _____ ?
W There's one that leaves at 11 a.m., and _____ _____ _____ _____ .
M Okay. I'll buy a ticket for that ferry then.

고난도
5 | 심정 고르기

대화를 듣고, 남자의 심정으로 가장 적절한 것을 고르시오.

① lonely   ② annoyed   ③ pleased
④ thankful   ⑤ concerned

 적중! Tip   Don't get worked up.
화를 내고 있는 상대방에게 '속상하지 마, 흥분하지 마'라는 의미로 사용되는 표현이다.

W Henry, what's the problem?
M I _____ _____ _____ with my sister.
W Oh, what happened?
M I _____ _____ when I think about it.
W Don't get worked up, and tell me the story.
M She _____ _____ on my favorite T-shirt! I can't stand her anymore.
W Calm down. I guess she didn't _____ _____ _____ _____ .
M I think she did. My sister _____ _____ _____ .

6 | 그림 상황에 적절한 대화 고르기

다음 그림의 상황에 가장 적절한 대화를 고르시오.

① ② ③ ④ ⑤

① W I thought you _____ _____ _____ ?
   M At 9, actually.
② W This is my favorite exhibit.
   M It is _____ _____ .
③ W The line is very long.
   M _____ _____ _____ to buy tickets.
④ W Did you enjoy the guided tour?
   M I found it a little boring.
⑤ W _____ _____ _____ _____ _____ ?
   M The science one.

7 | 부탁·요청한 일 고르기

대화를 듣고, 여자가 남자에게 부탁한 일로 가장 적절한 것을 고르시오.

① 꽃 사 오기　　　② 행사 진행하기
③ 케이크 찾아오기　④ 선물 정리하기
⑤ 작별 인사 전하기

[Cellphone rings.]

M What's up, Daphne?

W Hey, Chulho. Did you ＿＿＿ ＿＿＿ ＿＿＿ ＿＿＿?

M What's tomorrow?

W It's Ms. Kang's ＿＿＿ ＿＿＿ ＿＿＿!

M Oh, no! I forgot about that.

W You still have time to buy a card.

M I'll ＿＿＿ ＿＿＿ ＿＿＿ ＿＿＿ now. Do I need to do anything else?

W Can you ＿＿＿ ＿＿＿ ＿＿＿ ＿＿＿ I ordered? The bakery is on your way.

M Okay, I will.

고난도

8 | 언급하지 않은 내용 고르기

다음을 듣고, 행사에 관해 언급되지 <u>않은</u> 것을 고르시오.

① 제목　　② 요일　　③ 장소
④ 참가비　⑤ 활동

M Good afternoon, community members. I am Jack Richards from the city council. This is an announcement about ＿＿＿ ＿＿＿ ＿＿＿ ＿＿＿, Music in the Park. We will hold a concert on ＿＿＿ ＿＿＿ ＿＿＿ of every month in Central Park to showcase different types of musicians and bands. The event ＿＿＿ ＿＿＿ from 3 to 6 p.m. There will be food and activities such as ＿＿＿ ＿＿＿ ＿＿＿ ＿＿＿. All families are welcome and ＿＿＿ ＿＿＿ ＿＿＿ ＿＿＿ picnic blankets and chairs. Please come and enjoy some live music with us!

---

9 | 화제 고르기

다음을 듣고, 어떤 직업에 관한 설명인지 고르시오.

① 시인　　　　② 편집자
③ 영업사원　　④ 일러스트레이터
⑤ 카피라이터

M People who have this job try to ＿＿＿ ＿＿＿ ＿＿＿ ＿＿＿. They choose the words to describe items and make ＿＿＿ ＿＿＿ ＿＿＿ ＿＿＿. They also check the sentences on a company's website for errors. When there is a mistake in an advertisement, ＿＿＿ ＿＿＿ ＿＿＿. To do this job, you need to ＿＿＿ ＿＿＿ and good at writing.

---

10 | 어색한 대화 고르기

다음을 듣고, 두 사람의 대화가 <u>어색한</u> 것을 고르시오.

①　　②　　③　　④　　⑤

① W I think you are a great singer.
　 M Thank you. I ＿＿＿ ＿＿＿ ＿＿＿.

② W I'd like to mail a package to New Zealand.
　 M I'm sorry, but ＿＿＿ ＿＿＿ ＿＿＿ are fully booked.

③ W What time will you get home tonight?
　 M I will ＿＿＿ ＿＿＿ ＿＿＿ because I have a swimming lesson.

④ W Do you want to get some popcorn before the movie?
　 M Yeah. Let's get soda too.

⑤ W Have you ever been to Brazil?
　 M No. ＿＿＿ ＿＿＿ ＿＿＿ ＿＿＿ South America.

11 | 할 일 고르기

대화를 듣고, 여자가 대화 직후에 할 일로 가장 적절한 것을 고르시오.

① 커피 만들기　　　② 길 알려주기
③ 걷기 운동하기　　④ 버스 정류장 찾기
⑤ 주문 줄 서기

[Cellphone rings.]

W Jinsu, _____ _____ _____ _____?

M I'm walking to the café now.

W Did you miss the bus?

M No. I got lost, but I can _____ _____ _____ now.

W There are many people waiting to order coffee, so I'll _____ _____ _____ now.

M Thank you. I'll be there _____ _____ _____ _____.

W See you soon.

12 | 위치 고르기

다음 회의실 배치도를 보면서 대화를 듣고, 두 사람이 사용할 회의실을 고르시오.

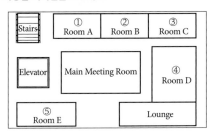

M Kate, which room are we going to use for the meeting on Thursday?

W I was thinking about the room _____ _____ _____ _____. It's spacious and has a large window.

M But isn't it _____ _____ _____ _____ the lounge? People chat a lot there.

W You're right. Hmm... What about Room A?

M Mr. Jenkins _____ _____ A and C for interviews.

W We have two options left. Oh! Aren't they done remodeling _____ _____ _____?

M I think so. And I think that one would be a perfect size.

W Let's _____ _____ _____ _____.

13 | 시간 정보 고르기

대화를 듣고, 여자가 식당에 방문할 날짜를 고르시오.

① July 5th　　② July 6th　　③ July 7th
④ July 12th　　⑤ July 13th

🎯 적중! Tip　Is it possible ~ ?
어떤 일을 하는 것이 가능한지 물을 때 사용되는 표현이다.
· Is it possible to book a table for tonight?
　오늘 밤 자리를 예약하는 게 가능한가요?

[Telephone rings.]

M Hello, Susie's Grill. How may I help you?

W Hi, I'd like to _____ _____ _____ for July 6th.

M I'm sorry, but we don't take reservations on Saturdays.

W Can I make a reservation for Friday then?

M _____ _____ _____ will there be?

W It'll be a group of eight.

M We're currently fully booked for tables _____ _____ _____ six on the 5th.

W Is it possible on the 12th, a week after that?

M Yes. Would you like a table for eight _____ _____ _____?

W That would be great.

대화를 듣고, 여자가 어제 한 일로 가장 적절한 것을 고르시오.

① 병원 가기　　　　② 티켓 예매하기
③ 집 꾸미기　　　　④ 놀이공원 가기
⑤ 체온계 주문하기

M Did you make it to the amusement park's grand opening last Saturday, Eva?
W No, I didn't. I _____ _____ _____ _____.
M Oh, no. What were you sick with?
W I had a fever, so I _____ _____ _____ _____
_____.
M I'm sorry you missed it.
W It's okay. I _____ _____ _____ yesterday so that I can go this weekend instead.
M That's great! _____ _____ _____ _____ _____?
W Of course.

다음을 듣고, 방송의 목적으로 가장 적절한 것을 고르시오.

① 수리로 인한 정전을 공지하려고
② 전기 절약 방법을 설명하려고
③ 엘리베이터 안전 수칙을 안내하려고
④ 입주민을 위한 행사를 홍보하려고
⑤ 아파트의 새 시설을 소개하려고

M Good morning, residents of Ocean Shores Apartments. This is an announcement about _____ _____ in the building. From 3 p.m. to 6 p.m. today, the building will _____ _____ _____ while a problem is fixed. We apologize for this inconvenience and hope that it _____ _____ _____ _____ _____ too seriously. Thank you.

대화를 듣고, 여자가 지불할 금액을 고르시오.

① $ 5　　　② $ 10　　　③ $ 15
④ $ 20　　　⑤ $ 25

M Hello. How may I help you?
W Hi. My friend and I want to _____ _____ _____ _____. How much would that be?
M It's five dollars per hour. How long will you play tennis?
W Around three hours.
M Then, it's 15 dollars in total.
W We also _____ _____ _____. Do we need to pay for those?
M The balls _____ _____ _____ _____. There are baskets of them here.
W Thank you. I'll _____ _____ _____.

대화를 듣고, 여자의 마지막 말에 대한 남자의 응답으로 가장 적절한 것을 고르시오.

Man: _____

① I'll make sure to wake you up.
② We should arrive at the campsite in 10 minutes.
③ Why don't we turn on the radio before sleeping?
④ Me too. I'm tired after the long drive here.
⑤ I don't like to take naps during the day.

M This is a beautiful campsite.
W I know! Thank you for _____ _____ _____, Honey.
M Of course. I'm excited to sit by the fire tonight.
W Me too. Are there _____ _____ _____ _____ _____ the campsite?
M We need to _____ _____ _____ _____ _____.
W Alright. Anything else?
M We should not make a lot of noise after 9 p.m.
W That's fine. I will probably _____ _____ _____ _____ tonight.

18 | 적절한 응답 고르기

대화를 듣고, 남자의 마지막 말에 대한 여자의 응답으로 가장 적절한 것을 고르시오.

Woman: _____

① Set the alarm at 6 a.m.
② Yes. They are in the refrigerator.
③ All right. Take a good care of him.
④ No. There's no sugar left.
⑤ Why not? Let's buy some grapes for your dad.

M Can I go to Steven's house, Mom?
W I don't know... You need to _____ _____ _____ _____ for school.
M But I won't stay late, and I have already finished all of my homework.
W What will you do there?
M We want to _____ _____ _____ _____ _____ he bought.
W I guess that's fine. But be home before 9.
M Okay. Can I take _____ _____ _____ _____ to share with him?

19 | 적절한 응답 고르기

대화를 듣고, 여자의 마지막 말에 대한 남자의 응답으로 가장 적절한 것을 고르시오.

Man: _____

① I want to buy this bag with a scarf around its handle.
② Where is the lost and found center?
③ You should pack warm clothes.
④ I'm sorry, but this table is reserved.
⑤ I'll do that while you check your bag again.

M What's wrong, Sumi?
W I _____ _____ _____ _____ anywhere.
M It's not in your bag?
W No. It might be _____ _____ _____.
M Maybe you left it on your chair.
W I think I did. Should I go back for it tomorrow?
M We _____ _____ _____ _____ from there now. We can get off at the next stop and go back to find it.
W Okay. But let's _____ _____ _____ _____. Maybe they found it already.

🎯 적중! Tip **get off**
[겟 오프]보다는 [게러프]로 들린다. [t]가 모음 사이에서 발음될 때는 약화되어 [r]에 가깝게 발음되기 때문이다.

20 | 상황에 적절한 말 고르기

다음 상황 설명을 듣고, Dean이 Ms. Garcia에게 할 말로 가장 적절한 것을 고르시오.

Dean: Ms. Garcia, _____

① are you on your way to the hospital?
② what does this word mean?
③ please turn off your phone during class.
④ I'm afraid I need to stop the lesson now.
⑤ can we reschedule the lesson?

W Dean is at a Spanish lesson. His teacher is Ms. Garcia. She _____ _____ _____ today. Dean is doing very well in the lesson, but suddenly he _____ _____ _____ from his mom. His grandfather is sick, so Dean _____ _____ _____ _____. Dean would like to tell Ms. Garcia that he needs to _____ _____ _____ _____. In this situation, what would Dean most likely say to Ms. Garcia?

🎯 적중! Tip **this situation**
[디스 시츄에이션]보다는 [디시츄에이션]으로 들린다. 발음이 같은 자음이 나란히 나오면 앞 단어의 끝 자음이 탈락되기 때문이다.

1 대화를 듣고, 남자가 만든 쿠키를 고르시오.

① ② ③

④ ⑤

2 대화를 듣고, Billy's Restaurant에 관해 언급되지 않은 것을 고르시오.

① 식당 규모 　② 배달료 　③ 메뉴
④ 할인 여부 　⑤ 휴무일

3 대화를 듣고, 여자가 남자에게 전화한 목적으로 가장 적절한 것을 고르시오.

① 요금 지불 방식을 문의하려고
② 문제 사항을 확인하려고
③ 고객센터 위치를 알려주려고
④ 배송 예정 시간을 안내하려고
⑤ 새로운 가전제품을 홍보하려고

4 대화를 듣고, 남자가 운동화를 사러 올 시각을 고르시오.

① 10 a.m. 　② 11 a.m. 　③ 12 p.m.
④ 1 p.m. 　⑤ 6 p.m.

5 다음 그림의 상황에 가장 적절한 대화를 고르시오.

① 　② 　③ 　④ 　⑤

6 대화를 듣고, 두 사람이 대화하는 장소로 가장 적절한 곳을 고르시오.

① 과수원 　② 식료품점 　③ 야영장
④ 제과점 　⑤ 목장

7 대화를 듣고, 남자가 여자에게 부탁한 일로 가장 적절한 것을 고르시오.

① 체육복 챙기기 　② 생수 사 오기
③ 농구공 가져오기 　④ 자전거 대여하기
⑤ 친구들 부르기

고난도
8 다음을 듣고, 잡지에 관해 언급되지 않은 것을 고르시오.

① 이름 　② 가격 　③ 발매일
④ 구매 방법 　⑤ 수익금 용도

9 다음을 듣고, 무엇에 관한 설명인지 고르시오.

① 씨름 　② 펜싱 　③ 양궁
④ 복싱 　⑤ 태권도

10 다음을 듣고, 두 사람의 대화가 어색한 것을 고르시오.

① 　② 　③ 　④ 　⑤

11 대화를 듣고, 남자가 할 일로 가장 적절한 것을 고르시오.

① 여행 계획 짜기 　② 자동차 빌리기
③ 공원 산책하기 　④ 배드민턴 채 사기
⑤ 버스표 예매하기

12 대화를 듣고, 남자가 작가 사인회에 참석할 시각을 고르시오.

① 5:00 p.m. ② 5:30 p.m. ③ 6:00 p.m.
④ 6:30 p.m. ⑤ 7:30 p.m.

13 다음 공연장 좌석 배치도를 보면서 대화를 듣고, 두 사람이 선택할 구역을 고르시오.

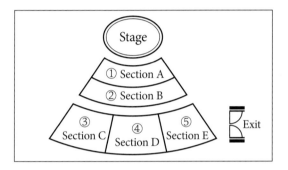

14 대화를 듣고, 남자가 어제 한 일로 가장 적절한 것을 고르시오.

① 방 페인트칠하기   ② 가구 구입하기
③ 기념식 참석하기   ④ 축하 편지 쓰기
⑤ 파티 준비하기

15 다음을 듣고, 방송의 목적으로 가장 적절한 것을 고르시오.

① 행사 참여를 독려하려고
② 행사 날짜 변경을 공지하려고
③ 학생회장 선거 일정을 공지하려고
④ 올바른 재활용 방법을 설명하려고
⑤ 에너지 절약의 중요성을 강조하려고

16 대화를 듣고, 남자가 지불할 금액을 고르시오.

① $ 32   ② $ 35   ③ $ 38
④ $ 41   ⑤ $ 44

17 대화를 듣고, 남자의 마지막 말에 대한 여자의 응답으로 가장 적절한 것을 고르시오.

Woman: _____

① Good. I'll bring you some popcorn and drink.
② Yes. I'll do that right now.
③ I recommend visiting the jellyfish zone first.
④ Okay. I won't forget to fill up the car with gas.
⑤ My schedule is full today, sorry.

18 대화를 듣고, 여자의 마지막 말에 대한 남자의 응답으로 가장 적절한 것을 고르시오.

Man: _____

① The store opens at 8 a.m.
② The shirt is sold out. I'm sorry.
③ A staff member will help you shortly.
④ Of course. The store is called Unique Style.
⑤ How about looking up the word online?

19 대화를 듣고, 남자의 마지막 말에 대한 여자의 응답으로 가장 적절한 것을 고르시오.

Woman: _____

① The view up here is beautiful.
② The doctor wants me to stay home.
③ You can have one of my snacks.
④ I ordered some French fries.
⑤ Please get me a bottle of water from the store.

고난도

20 다음 상황 설명을 듣고, Emma가 Max에게 할 말로 가장 적절한 것을 고르시오.

Emma: Max, _____

① can you lend me your laptop charger?
② we should finish our homework quickly.
③ I think it is too noisy when we type.
④ what is the website called?
⑤ could you help me search for information?

15회 중학영어듣기 실전 모의고사 Dictation 음성을 들으며 빈칸에 알맞은 단어를 채우시오.

1 | 알맞은 그림 고르기

대화를 듣고, 남자가 만든 쿠키를 고르시오.

① ② ③
④ ⑤

W Tim, _____ _____ _____ in this kitchen. What is it?
M I baked some cookies, Sally. Now, they're finished.
W Wow, you _____ _____ _____ _____ Halloween!
M Yeah. I'll take them to school tomorrow.
W Pumpkin-shaped cookies are perfect for Halloween. You even _____ _____ _____ _____! Great job!
M Thanks. I think I'll make ghost-shaped cookies _____ _____.
W Good idea.

2 | 언급하지 않은 내용 고르기

대화를 듣고, Billy's Restaurant에 관해 언급되지 않은 것을 고르시오.

① 식당 규모 ② 배달료 ③ 메뉴
④ 할인 여부 ⑤ 휴무일

🎯 적중! Tip sandwiches
[샌위치]로 발음된다. 모음 사이에서 [n] 뒤에 오는 [d] 발음은 약화되어 거의 들리지 않기 때문이다.

W Scott, do you remember _____ _____ _____ is from Billy's Restaurant?
M Yeah. It's five dollars. Why?
W I was thinking of ordering from there. Would you recommend it for lunch?
M Yes. They have _____ _____ _____ _____.
W Great. I wanted to get a salad.
M The sandwiches are good too. One of them _____ _____ _____ _____ _____ for six dollars.
W That's nice. Do they open on weekends too?
M Sadly, no. They're _____ _____ _____.

3 | 목적 고르기

대화를 듣고, 여자가 남자에게 전화한 목적으로 가장 적절한 것을 고르시오.

① 요금 지불 방식을 문의하려고
② 문제 사항을 확인하려고
③ 고객센터 위치를 알려주려고
④ 배송 예정 시간을 안내하려고
⑤ 새로운 가전제품을 홍보하려고

[Cellphone rings.]
W Hi. This is Morales Electronics. We received your message about _____ _____ _____.
M Yes. I left a message.
W We wanted to _____ _____ _____ _____. Can you describe the problem you're experiencing?
M My washing machine _____ _____ _____. I don't know why.
W I can send someone to check your washing machine.
M That would be great.
W Okay. Our technician can _____ _____ _____ _____. Will you be home around 10?
M Yes. That's perfect.
W All right. I'll _____ _____ _____ for then.

4 | 시간 정보 고르기

대화를 듣고, 남자가 운동화를 사러 올 시각을 고르시오.

① 10 a.m.   ② 11 a.m.   ③ 12 p.m.
④ 1 p.m.   ⑤ 6 p.m.

🎯 적중! Tip   Pardon me.

낯선 사람에게 정중하게 말을 걸 때 사용되는 표현으로 '실례합니다'라는 의미이다.

M Pardon me, but I can't find the new sneakers from Gonza anywhere in the store.

W They _____ _____ _____ . But we already ordered more, and they will arrive tomorrow.

M _____ _____ _____ _____ _____ exactly?

W They will get here at 10 a.m. But the shoes probably won't _____ _____ _____ until 11.

M I was thinking of dropping by around 6 p.m. Is that too late?

W Hmm... You might _____ _____ _____ _____ . Those sneakers are very popular.

M I see. Well, I have a lunch break from 11:30 to 1:00, so I will come _____ _____ . Thanks.

5 | 그림 상황에 적절한 대화 고르기

다음 그림의 상황에 가장 적절한 대화를 고르시오.

①   ②   ③   ④   ⑤

① **W** Could you please _____ _____ _____ ?
   M Sure. I'd be happy to.
② **W** How much is this camera?
   M It's on sale for 145 dollars.
③ **W** _____ _____ _____ _____ _____ ?
   M Why don't you get the one with a statue on it?
④ **W** Where should we _____ _____ _____ ?
   M How about in the living room?
⑤ **W** I like your hat.
   M Thanks. I _____ _____ _____ _____ _____ .

6 | 장소 고르기

대화를 듣고, 두 사람이 대화하는 장소로 가장 적절한 곳을 고르시오.

① 과수원   ② 식료품점   ③ 야영장
④ 제과점   ⑤ 목장

W What did Mom tell us to buy, Rick?

M She said that we need some carrots, onions, and beef.

W Alright. I'll go _____ _____ _____ , and you go get the meat.

M Where is the meat? I don't see it in this section.

W I think it's _____ _____ _____ _____ . We can look for it together after I get the vegetables.

M Okay. Do you think _____ _____ _____ _____ _____ ?

W Yeah. I'll grab one now.

실전 모의고사 해커스 중학영어듣기 모의고사 24회 Level 3 | 15회

대화를 듣고, 남자가 여자에게 부탁한 일로 가장 적절한 것을 고르시오.

① 체육복 챙기기　　② 생수 사 오기
③ 농구공 가져오기　④ 자전거 대여하기
⑤ 친구들 부르기

[Cellphone rings.]
M　Where are you, Nara? I'm already at the basketball court.
W　I'm so sorry, but I arrived home from school late.
M　Then, _____ _____ _____ _____ here?
W　I will change my clothes and ride my bicycle there. I should arrive in 20 minutes.
M　That's fine. I'll buy _____ _____ water and wait.
W　Is it crowded there? If so, I'd like to play with other people.
M　Sure. Oh, can you _____ _____ _____? Mine is really old.
W　Yes. I will bring mine.

다음을 듣고, 잡지에 관해 언급되지 <u>않은</u> 것을 고르시오.

① 이름　　② 가격　　③ 발매일
④ 구매 방법　⑤ 수익금 용도

W　Greetings, fellow students. This is Amy Logan, editor of the school's literary magazine, *Creative Flow*. I'd like to announce that _____ _____ _____ _____ the 2022 edition of our magazine. You can order one on our school's website www.DublinSchool.com, or you can purchase one _____ _____ _____ _____ _____, Ms. Green. The magazine costs five dollars, and all the profits will be donated to _____ _____ _____ _____.
Thank you for your support.

다음을 듣고, 무엇에 관한 설명인지 고르시오.

① 씨름　　② 펜싱　　③ 양궁
④ 복싱　　⑤ 태권도

> 🎯 적중! Tip　**sp**ort
> [스포트]보다는 [스뽈트]로 들린다. [s] 뒤에 [p] 발음이 오면 된소리로 발음되기 때문이다.
> · **sp**ell [스뻴]　· **sp**eak [스삐크]

W　This is a martial sport. Two people _____ _____ _____ _____ in a fight. To score points, a player needs _____ _____ _____ the other player on the body or head. The players all _____ _____ _____ with colored belts. These belts show the rank of the player. The players must also wear a lot of _____ _____ _____. It was started in Korea, but now it's enjoyed all over the world.

다음을 듣고, 두 사람의 대화가 <u>어색한</u> 것을 고르시오.
①　　②　　③　　④　　⑤

①　W　Which sticker do you like best?
　　M　I like the one with the bear.
②　W　What's wrong? You _____ _____ _____.
　　M　I exercised a lot yesterday, and now my body's sore.
③　W　Did you cook this soup? It's delicious!
　　M　Actually, I _____ _____ _____ _____ down the street.
④　W　Would you like to _____ _____ _____?
　　M　That café sells different kinds of tea and coffee.
⑤　W　That was _____ _____ _____!
　　M　Yeah. I think we ran 10 kilometers.

11 | 할 일 고르기

대화를 듣고, 남자가 할 일로 가장 적절한 것을 고르시오.

① 여행 계획 짜기 ② 자동차 빌리기
③ 공원 산책하기 ④ 배드민턴 채 사기
⑤ 버스표 예매하기

[Cellphone rings.]
W What's up, Joonwoo?
M Hey. What _____ _____ _____ this Saturday?
W I might go to the park and play badminton. Why?
M Do you want to take _____ _____ _____ to the beach?
W Oh, that would be lovely. But how will we get there?
M We can take a bus there. I'll _____ _____ _____.
W Great. I can't wait.

12 | 시간 정보 고르기

대화를 듣고, 남자가 작가 사인회에 참석할 시각을 고르시오.

① 5:00 p.m. ② 5:30 p.m. ③ 6:00 p.m.
④ 6:30 p.m. ⑤ 7:30 p.m.

M Excuse me. Can I _____ _____ _____?
W Sure. What is it?
M I heard Janice Walker will sign _____ _____ _____ _____ at this bookstore tomorrow.
W That's right. She will be here at 5 p.m.
M I'd love to meet her. But I have to work until 6. Would _____ _____ _____ if I came here at 6:30?
W That will be fine. Ms. Walker will _____ _____ 7:30.
M Wonderful. Thank you.

13 | 위치 고르기

다음 공연장 좌석 배치도를 보면서 대화를 듣고, 두 사람이 선택할 구역을 고르시오.

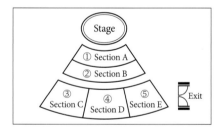

M Erica, let's get tickets for the musical.
W Where do you want to sit?
M I want to _____ _____ _____ _____. But I think those seats are a bit expensive.
W Yeah. They are 200 dollars. How about in the middle?
M I think that section _____ _____ _____. There are only three sections left then.
W Is there _____ _____ _____ among the three?
M Let me see. *[Pause]* No. They are all 100 dollars.
W Well, then I'd like to sit _____ _____ _____.
M Okay.

14 | 한 일 고르기

대화를 듣고, 남자가 어제 한 일로 가장 적절한 것을 고르시오.

① 방 페인트칠하기 ② 가구 구입하기
③ 기념식 참석하기 ④ 축하 편지 쓰기
⑤ 파티 준비하기

🎯 적중! Tip
[리데코레이팅]보다는 [리데코레이링]으로 들린다. [t]가 모음 사이에서 발음될 때는 약화되어 [r]에 가깝게 발음되기 때문이다.

M What are you doing this Friday, Subin?
W I don't have any plans. Why?
M I will _____ _____ _____ at my house, and I'd love for you to come.
W That sounds nice. What are we celebrating?
M I finally finished redecorating my house. I _____ _____ _____ _____ yesterday, and the new furniture will be delivered tomorrow.
W That's great news. I know _____ _____ _____ _____ for a long time.
M Yes. I can't wait for you to see it.

다음을 듣고, 방송의 목적으로 가장 적절한 것을 고르시오.

① 행사 참여를 독려하려고
② 행사 날짜 변경을 공지하려고
③ 학생회장 선거 일정을 공지하려고
④ 올바른 재활용 방법을 설명하려고
⑤ 에너지 절약의 중요성을 강조하려고

M Good morning! This is Peter from the student council. Next Wednesday, our school will be holding Eco Day. I'd like to _____ _____ _____ _____ this event. There will be information booths about various environmental issues. For example, you can learn _____ _____ _____ _____ and recycle properly. Anyone who wants to set up a booth should visit the student council's website. You _____ _____ _____ _____ about the event there. I hope many of you participate. Thanks!

대화를 듣고, 남자가 지불할 금액을 고르시오.

① $ 32   ② $ 35   ③ $ 38
④ $ 41   ⑤ $ 44

> 🎯 적중! Tip **I'd**
> [아이드]보다는 [아인]으로 들린다. 조동사 would의 축약형은 앞에 나오는 주어와 연결해서 약하게 발음되기 때문이다.

W Hi. How may I help you?
M I'm checking out of my room, and I'd like to _____ _____ _____ for room service.
W Alright, let me see. *[Typing sound]* Were you in Room 402?
M That's correct.
W Your dinner was 35 dollars last night. Did you have _____ _____ _____ _____ ?
M Yes. I had a bottle of soda.
W Okay. It's three dollars for the soda and 35 dollars _____ _____ _____ then.
M Thanks. Here's my credit card.

대화를 듣고, 남자의 마지막 말에 대한 여자의 응답으로 가장 적절한 것을 고르시오.

Woman: _____

① Good. I'll bring you some popcorn and drink.
② Yes. I'll do that right now.
③ I recommend visiting the jellyfish zone first.
④ Okay. I won't forget to fill up the car with gas.
⑤ My schedule is full today, sorry.

M Who was on the phone, Jaemin?
W It was my friend, Andy. I'm sorry _____ _____ _____ _____ the movie.
M I don't mind. Is everything okay?
W Oh, yes. We just made plans to go to the aquarium next week.
M Remember that _____ _____ _____ Aunt Mijung on Thursday for the holiday.
W Oh, _____ _____ _____ . What time are we leaving?
M We're leaving the house around 7 a.m. _____ _____ _____ in your calendar so you don't forget.

18 | 적절한 응답 고르기

대화를 듣고, 여자의 마지막 말에 대한 남자의 응답으로 가장 적절한 것을 고르시오.

Man: _____

① The store opens at 8 a.m.
② The shirt is sold out. I'm sorry.
③ A staff member will help you shortly.
④ Of course. The store is called Unique Style.
⑤ How about looking up the word online?

> 🎯 적중! Tip **It's my first time ~.**
>
> 어떤 일이 처음 하는 경험임을 나타낼 때 사용되는 표현으로 '처음으로 ~하다, ~하는 것은 처음이다'라는 의미이다. 이때 first time 다음에는 동명사나 to부정사가 온다.
>
> · It's my first time eating turkey.
>   처음으로 칠면조를 먹는 거야.

W I love your shirt, Tom.
M Thanks. It's my first time _____ _____.
W The color is so unique. Where did you get it?
M I actually _____ _____ _____ _____ _____ in New York.
W Oh, that's a shame. I want to buy one too.
M They _____ _____ _____ _____. It's a big store.
W Can you tell me the name of the store? I'll _____ _____ _____.

19 | 적절한 응답 고르기

대화를 듣고, 남자의 마지막 말에 대한 여자의 응답으로 가장 적절한 것을 고르시오.

Woman: _____

① The view up here is beautiful.
② The doctor wants me to stay home.
③ You can have one of my snacks.
④ I ordered some French fries.
⑤ Please get me a bottle of water from the store.

W Are you okay, Woomin?
M No. _____ _____ _____.
W Did you drink some water?
M Actually, I _____ _____ _____ _____ _____ earlier in the hike.
W Have some of mine then. And let's sit down for a while.
M _____ _____ _____ the top of the mountain?
W We are really close, but you need to take a break before we hike again.
M Oh, I _____ _____ _____ something too.

고난도

20 | 상황에 적절한 말 고르기

다음 상황 설명을 듣고, Emma가 Max에게 할 말로 가장 적절한 것을 고르시오.

Emma: Max, _____

① can you lend me your laptop charger?
② we should finish our homework quickly.
③ I think it is too noisy when we type.
④ what is the website called?
⑤ could you help me search for information?

M Emma and her friend Max are in the library. They _____ _____ _____ _____ on their laptops. Emma still needs to do some research online, but her laptop is _____ _____ _____. Unfortunately, she forgot to bring a charger. So, she wants to ask Max if _____ _____ _____ his charger. In this situation, what would Emma most likely say to Max?

1 대화를 듣고, 남자가 구입할 액자를 고르시오.

①   ②   ③

④   ⑤

2 대화를 듣고, Happy Pillow에 관해 언급되지 <u>않은</u> 것을 고르시오.

① 기능　　② 색상　　③ 무늬
④ 가격　　⑤ 크기

3 대화를 듣고, 여자가 남자에게 전화한 목적으로 가장 적절한 것을 고르시오.

① 어학연수 비용을 확인하려고
② 수업 등록 방법을 문의하려고
③ 웹사이트 오류에 대해 항의하려고
④ 수업 준비물을 알아보려고
⑤ 다른 수업으로 변경하려고

4 대화를 듣고, 두 사람이 테니스를 치기로 한 시각을 고르시오.

① 1 p.m.　　② 2 p.m.　　③ 3 p.m.
④ 4 p.m.　　⑤ 5 p.m.

5 대화를 듣고, 두 사람이 대화하는 장소로 가장 적절한 곳을 고르시오.

① 안과　　② 안경원　　③ 동물 병원
④ 약국　　⑤ 호텔

6 다음 그림의 상황에 가장 적절한 대화를 고르시오.

①　　②　　③　　④　　⑤

7 대화를 듣고, 남자가 여자에게 부탁한 일로 가장 적절한 것을 고르시오.

① 보충 자료 주기　　② 수영 연습 감독하기
③ 시험 범위 알려주기　④ 수영복 사다 주기
⑤ 외출 허가서 써주기

8 다음을 듣고, 연극에 관해 언급되지 <u>않은</u> 것을 고르시오.

① 공연 회차　　　② 감독 이름
③ 출연진 수　　　④ 연극의 길이
⑤ 다과 제공 여부

9 다음을 듣고, 무엇에 관한 설명인지 고르시오.

① 사과　　② 망고　　③ 바나나
④ 아보카도　　⑤ 파인애플

10 다음을 듣고, 두 사람의 대화가 <u>어색한</u> 것을 고르시오.

①　　②　　③　　④　　⑤

11 대화를 듣고, 여자가 할 일로 가장 적절한 것을 고르시오.

① 단편 영화 고르기　　② 아이스크림 사기
③ 최신 음악 듣기　　　④ 담요 가져오기
⑤ 코미디 공연 보기

12 다음 표를 보면서 대화를 듣고, 두 사람이 관람할 전시회를 고르시오.

	Exhibit	Type	Place	Audio tour
①	A	Art	Soho Museum	X
②	B	History	Soho Museum	O
③	C	Art	Lake Plaza	O
④	D	Art	Lake Plaza	X
⑤	E	History	Lake Plaza	X

13 대화를 듣고, 두 사람이 캠핑을 가기로 한 날짜를 고르시오.

① 5월 4일 ② 5월 5일 ③ 5월 6일
④ 5월 7일 ⑤ 5월 8일

14 대화를 듣고, 남자가 어제 한 일로 가장 적절한 것을 고르시오.

① 컴퓨터 조립하기 ② 욕실 청소하기
③ 편지 답장 쓰기 ④ 친구와 수다 떨기
⑤ 휴대폰 수리 맡기기

15 다음을 듣고, 방송의 목적으로 가장 적절한 것을 고르시오.

① 여름철 열차 단축 운행을 공지하려고
② 대중교통 이용 예절을 알려주려고
③ 새로운 지하철 노선을 홍보하려고
④ 민원 문자 보내는 방법을 설명하려고
⑤ 지하철 냉방 운영 지침을 안내하려고

16 대화를 듣고, 여자가 지불할 금액을 고르시오.

① $ 10 ② $ 15 ③ $ 20
④ $ 25 ⑤ $ 30

17 대화를 듣고, 여자의 마지막 말에 대한 남자의 응답으로 가장 적절한 것을 고르시오.

Man: _____

① I don't know the name of that planet.
② The show is called *Space Travels*.
③ I can't see anything because it's too dark.
④ I'll meet you there then.
⑤ It was a good chance to observe stars.

[18-19] 대화를 듣고, 남자의 마지막 말에 대한 여자의 응답으로 가장 적절한 것을 고르시오.

18 **Woman:** _____

① Sure. Let's take a photograph that you can use.
② Thank you. I just got your message.
③ Try turning your face to the right.
④ This case doesn't fit my phone.
⑤ Then, you can give stars to this app here.

고난도
19 **Woman:** _____

① The title of the video is *Sing Along*.
② I'll write it down for you so you can look it up later.
③ Please don't make any recordings during the show.
④ Yes. Of course I will dance with you.
⑤ The comment you left was so thoughtful.

20 다음 상황 설명을 듣고, Elizabeth가 미용사에게 할 말로 가장 적절한 것을 고르시오.

Elizabeth: _____

① The water is too hot.
② Can you cut my hair shorter, please?
③ I'm sorry, but I don't like the color.
④ Do you have a comb?
⑤ Your hair looks beautiful.

16회 Dictation

16회 중학영어듣기 실전 모의고사 Dictation 음성을 들으며 빈칸에 알맞은 단어를 채우시오.

1 | 알맞은 그림 고르기

대화를 듣고, 남자가 구입할 액자를 고르시오.

① ② ③
④ ⑤

W Hello. What can I do for you?
M I'd like to _____ _____ _____ _____ for my family photo.
W Is there _____ _____ _____ you would like?
M I'd like to have one that my five-year-old daughter would like.
W All right. We have these animal-shaped ones. _____ _____ _____ _____ an elephant, rabbit, or hedgehog.
M They all look good. But my daughter _____ _____ _____ _____. I'll take it.
W Great choice. I'm sure she'll be glad to get it.

2 | 언급하지 않은 내용 고르기

대화를 듣고, Happy Pillow에 관해 언급되지 않은 것을 고르시오.

① 기능 ② 색상 ③ 무늬
④ 가격 ⑤ 크기

> 🎯 적중! Tip than**ks a** lot
> [땡크스 어 랏]보다는 [땡써랏]으로 들린다. 자음 3개가 연속해서 나오면 중간 자음은 발음되지 않고, 앞에 나온 단어의 끝 자음과 뒤에 나온 단어의 첫 모음이 연음되기 때문이다.

M Hey, Amy. Have you ever tried a Happy Pillow before?
W Yes. I use one every night. Why?
M I'm _____ _____ _____ _____ for my mom.
W Great idea. They're famous for _____ _____ _____.
M Then, it'll be perfect for my mom because she doesn't sleep well nowadays.
W Yeah, she'll love it. You can choose from _____ _____ _____ online. All the designs look nice, but _____ _____ _____ _____ is my favorite.
M Good to know. Can you tell me how much it is?
W Of course. It's only nine dollars.
M I see. _____ _____ _____ _____ a large size?
W Yes. There are many different sizes you can choose from.
M Okay, thanks a lot.

3 | 목적 고르기

대화를 듣고, 여자가 남자에게 전화한 목적으로 가장 적절한 것을 고르시오.

① 어학연수 비용을 확인하려고
② 수업 등록 방법을 문의하려고
③ 웹사이트 오류에 대해 항의하려고
④ 수업 준비물을 알아보려고
⑤ 다른 수업으로 변경하려고

[Telephone rings.]
M Good afternoon. You've reached the Danton Language School.
W Hi. A friend told me that you have _____ _____ _____ _____.
M That's right. Classes are held on Tuesday and Thursday evenings, and _____ _____ _____ one hour.
W Great. I'd like to _____ _____ _____ _____. How do I do that?
M Just go to our website. You will see _____ _____ _____ _____ for courses on the main page.
W Got it. Can I pay for it online as well?
M Of course. And if you have any problems, _____ _____ _____ me back.
W I appreciate your help.

4 | 시간 정보 고르기

대화를 듣고, 두 사람이 테니스를 치기로 한 시각을 고르시오.

① 1 p.m.　　② 2 p.m.　　③ 3 p.m.
④ 4 p.m.　　⑤ 5 p.m.

W Dad, do you want to play tennis this afternoon?
M Sure. I have to go to the supermarket right now, but _____ _____ _____ _____ by 1 p.m.
W Why don't we go to the tennis court at 4?
M _____ _____ _____ _____? We could start at 2.
W My favorite TV show is on from 2 to 3. I really _____ _____ _____ _____.
M Oh, then 4 is fine. But we'll just _____ _____ _____ _____ we are done by 5.
W No problem! I think an hour will be _____ _____ _____ _____ tennis.

5 | 장소 고르기

대화를 듣고, 두 사람이 대화하는 장소로 가장 적절한 곳을 고르시오.

① 안과　　② 안경원　　③ 동물 병원
④ 약국　　⑤ 호텔

M Good morning. Are you feeling okay today?
W I think so, but _____ _____ _____ a little.
M That's normal for now. _____ _____ _____ _____?
W They are fine. Did the surgery go well?
M Yes, it did. _____ _____ _____ _____ soon.
W So, when can I leave?
M You need to stay here _____ _____ _____ for some tests. After that, we will give you some medicine, and you can go home.

6 | 그림 상황에 적절한 대화 고르기

다음 그림의 상황에 가장 적절한 대화를 고르시오.

①　②　③　④　⑤

① W Let's go home.
　 M Good idea. I'm a little tired.
② W This is _____ _____ _____ _____.
　 M Maybe you should get a membership.
③ W Why don't we play some badminton?
　 M _____ _____ _____ this soccer game on TV.
④ W What's the score?
　 M _____ _____ _____ three points.
⑤ W Is the pharmacy open today?
　 M No. It is _____ _____ _____.

7 | 부탁·요청한 일 고르기

대화를 듣고, 남자가 여자에게 부탁한 일로 가장 적절한 것을 고르시오.

① 보충 자료 주기　　② 수영 연습 감독하기
③ 시험 범위 알려주기　　④ 수영복 사다 주기
⑤ 외출 허가서 써주기

W Can I talk to you, Jake?
M Sure, Ms. Reed. What's going on?
W _____ _____ _____ _____ on your last test. Is there something wrong?
M No. I'm just so busy lately. _____ _____ _____ _____ a lot of time.
W Well, remember that school is important too.
M I know. Can you give me _____ _____ _____ _____?
W Sure. Stop by after class to pick them up.

🎯 적중! Tip important too

[임포턴트 투]보다는 [임포은투]로 들린다. 자음 사이에 오는 [t] 발음은 약화되어 거의 들리지 않고, 발음이 같은 자음이 나란히 나오면 앞 단어의 끝 자음이 탈락되기 때문이다.

8 | 언급하지 않은 내용 고르기

다음을 듣고, 연극에 관해 언급되지 않은 것을 고르시오.

① 공연 회차
② 감독 이름
③ 출연진 수
④ 연극의 길이
⑤ 다과 제공 여부

W Good evening, everyone. Thank you for coming to our play tonight. I'm _____ _____ _____ _____ , Kendra Young. This is the 14th play by our drama club since 2002. I want to thank the student-actors. _____ _____ _____ _____ _____ worked so hard on this play. After the performance, don't leave right away. _____ _____ _____ _____ outside the auditorium. Also, you'll _____ _____ _____ _____ with our cast members.

9 | 화제 고르기

다음을 듣고, 무엇에 관한 설명인지 고르시오.

① 사과
② 망고
③ 바나나
④ 아보카도
⑤ 파인애플

W This is one of _____ _____ _____ _____ _____ . This is a very common fruit, so you can buy it _____ _____ _____ . You can eat this for breakfast or as a healthy snack between meals. It is long and has _____ _____ _____ _____ . To eat it, you must remove its peel and _____ _____ _____ _____ inside. Then, you can enjoy its sweet taste. When this fruit becomes too old to eat, it _____ _____ _____ _____ .

10 | 어색한 대화 고르기

다음을 듣고, 두 사람의 대화가 <u>어색한</u> 것을 고르시오.

①   ②   ③   ④   ⑤

🎯 적중! Tip **What do you think of ~?**

어떤 대상에 대한 상대방의 의견을 물을 때 사용되는 표현으로, of 다음에는 (동)명사가 온다.

· What do you think of this painting?
  이 그림에 대해 어떻게 생각해?

① W What do you think of your new phone?
   M I like it because it's _____ _____ _____ my old one.
② W Which one is your house?
   M That one _____ _____ _____ _____ _____ is mine.
③ W Can you help me? I can't open this bottle.
   M _____ _____ _____ _____ for you.
④ W What size shirt do you usually wear?
   M I like the ones _____ _____ _____ _____ .
⑤ W How was your presentation about polar bears?
   M I was _____ _____ _____ _____ , but I think I did well.

11 | 할 일 고르기

대화를 듣고, 여자가 할 일로 가장 적절한 것을 고르시오.

① 단편 영화 고르기
② 아이스크림 사기
③ 최신 음악 듣기
④ 담요 가져오기
⑤ 코미디 공연 보기

🎯 적중! Tip **pic<u>k</u> up**

[픽 업]보다는 [피껍]으로 들린다. 앞에 나온 단어의 끝 자음과 뒤에 나온 단어의 첫 모음이 연음되고, 이때 강세가 없는 [k]는 된소리로 발음되기 때문이다.

[Cellphone rings.]
W Hey, Carson.
M Hi. Are you _____ _____ _____ _____ tonight?
W Yes. Did you _____ _____ _____ _____ ?
M Not yet. There are two new films that were just released. One is a comedy, and the other is a drama.
W _____ _____ _____ .
M Okay. And how about you pick up something to eat on your way here?
W Sure. I'll _____ _____ _____ _____ .
M Perfect. I can't wait for our movie night!

12 | 도표에서 알맞은 항목 고르기

다음 표를 보면서 대화를 듣고, 두 사람이 관람할 전시회를 고르시오.

	Exhibit	Type	Place	Audio tour
①	A	Art	Soho Museum	X
②	B	History	Soho Museum	O
③	C	Art	Lake Plaza	O
④	D	Art	Lake Plaza	X
⑤	E	History	Lake Plaza	X

W Larry, you need to choose which exhibition you want to go to tomorrow.

M Okay. _____ are there?

W You can choose between _____ _____ _____ _____ exhibition.

M History sounds boring. Let's go to an art exhibition.

W Sure. I want to go to the one at the Lake Plaza so that we can _____ _____ _____.

M Is there an audio tour for the exhibit? Those are _____ _____ _____.

W Sadly, there isn't. But we can get a brochure.

M That will do.

13 | 시간 정보 고르기

대화를 듣고, 두 사람이 캠핑을 가기로 한 날짜를 고르시오.

① 5월 4일　　② 5월 5일　　③ 5월 6일
④ 5월 7일　　⑤ 5월 8일

M Did you say you _____ _____ _____ _____, Jamie?

W Yeah. I already borrowed the equipment from my brother.

M Oh, really? Well, let's choose a campground. This one _____ _____ _____ _____ _____ looks nice.

W I've seen that place before. _____ _____ _____ _____ on May 5th? It's a national holiday.

M No, I don't think so. But it seems that we can reserve a site on the 4th or 7th.

W Isn't May 4th a Wednesday? I have a yoga class that day.

M _____ _____ _____ _____?

W I can, but I don't want to. Let's go on the 7th.

M Sure. I'll _____ _____ _____ now.

14 | 한 일 고르기

대화를 듣고, 남자가 어제 한 일로 가장 적절한 것을 고르시오.

① 컴퓨터 조립하기　　② 욕실 청소하기
③ 편지 답장 쓰기　　④ 친구와 수다 떨기
⑤ 휴대폰 수리 맡기기

W Tim, I messaged you on Tuesday but _____ _____ _____.

M I'm sorry. What was your message about?

W Don't worry about it. I just wanted to _____ _____ _____ with you. By the way, why didn't you see my message?

M I _____ _____ _____ in the sink, so it stopped working.

W Oh, no. Did you take it to the repair shop?

M Yes. I just _____ _____ _____ yesterday.

W I'm glad it's fixed now.

15 | 목적 고르기

다음을 듣고, 방송의 목적으로 가장 적절한 것을 고르시오.

① 여름철 열차 단축 운행을 공지하려고
② 대중교통 이용 예절을 알려주려고
③ 새로운 지하철 노선을 홍보하려고
④ 민원 문자 보내는 방법을 설명하려고
⑤ 지하철 냉방 운영 지침을 안내하려고

W Good morning, passengers. Please note the following information. As the weather gets warmer, we will be _____ _____ _____ _____ on the subway more often. If you _____ _____ _____ _____, please text us at 8877. Make sure the message includes your subway car number and whether it is too hot or too cold. In addition, passengers who are _____ _____ _____ _____ should ride in the first six cars of the train. It will be _____ _____ _____ _____ than in the others. Thank you for listening, and I hope you enjoy your ride today!

16 | 금액 정보 고르기

대화를 듣고, 여자가 지불할 금액을 고르시오.

① $ 10   ② $ 15   ③ $ 20
④ $ 25   ⑤ $ 30

M How may I help you?
W I'd like to _____ _____ _____ for a birthday party. How much will it be?
M It'll be 20 dollars, but you can _____ _____ _____ _____ with it for an extra fee.
W How much will that be?
M It'll be 10 dollars. Do you want the additions?
W Okay. But can I _____ _____ _____ _____?
M Yes, you can. That will take five dollars off.
W Great. I'll _____ _____ _____ _____ then.

17 | 적절한 응답 고르기

대화를 듣고, 여자의 마지막 말에 대한 남자의 응답으로 가장 적절한 것을 고르시오.

Man: _____

① I don't know the name of that planet.
② The show is called *Space Travels*.
③ I can't see anything because it's too dark.
④ I'll meet you there then.
⑤ It was a good chance to observe stars.

적중! Tip Experts

[엑스펄츠]로 발음된다. [ex]는 [엑스], [이그즈], [익스] 중 하나로 발음된다.

· **ex**am [이그잼]   · **ex**treme [익스트림]

W What are you doing tonight, Minjae?
M I don't _____ _____ _____. Why?
W There's a lecture on stars. Do you want to come with me?
M A lecture on stars?
W Yes. Experts will _____ _____ _____ _____ to us, and they will teach us about them.
M I'd be _____ _____ _____. I'm very interested in space. What time does it start?
W It begins at 7 in the park downtown.

18 | 적절한 응답 고르기

대화를 듣고, 남자의 마지막 말에 대한 여자의 응답으로 가장 적절한 것을 고르시오.

Woman: _____

① Sure. Let's take a photograph that you can use.
② Thank you. I just got your message.
③ Try turning your face to the right.
④ This case doesn't fit my phone.
⑤ Then, you can give stars to this app here.

M You're glued to your phone. What are you playing with?
W A new picture app _____ _____ _____. Do you want to see it?
M What does it do?
W You can _____ _____ _____ you take on your phone. See? There are lots of _____ _____ _____.
M That's really cool. What photographs did you change with it?
W I added heart and flower stickers to this one of _____ _____ _____ _____. And I changed the colors in this one.
M It _____ _____ _____ now. Can I try changing one?

---

19 | 적절한 응답 고르기

대화를 듣고, 남자의 마지막 말에 대한 여자의 응답으로 가장 적절한 것을 고르시오.

Woman: _____

① The title of the video is *Sing Along*.
② I'll write it down for you so you can look it up later.
③ Please don't make any recordings during the show.
④ Yes. Of course I will dance with you.
⑤ The comment you left was so thoughtful.

> 🎯 적중! Tip I'm sure ~.
> 어떤 상황에 대한 확신을 나타낼 때 사용되는 표현으로 '꼭 ~라고 생각하다'라는 의미이다.
> · I'm sure you can do it.
>   네가 꼭 해낼 거라고 생각해.

M What are you doing, Jude?
W I'm planning my next dance video.
M I didn't know you made dance videos.
W I _____ _____ _____ _____, and then I dance to them. I like to post the videos online so _____ _____ _____ _____ them.
M Do you have lots of followers?
W Yes. But I don't care about followers. _____ _____ _____ _____.
M Good for you. I'm jealous of your hobby.
W I'm sure _____ _____ _____ _____.
M Maybe. I'd love to watch some of your videos. Please _____ _____ _____ _____ _____ your channel.

---

20 | 상황에 적절한 말 고르기

다음 상황 설명을 듣고, Elizabeth가 미용사에게 할 말로 가장 적절한 것을 고르시오.

Elizabeth: _____

① The water is too hot.
② Can you cut my hair shorter, please?
③ I'm sorry, but I don't like the color.
④ Do you have a comb?
⑤ Your hair looks beautiful.

M Elizabeth is at the hair salon to _____ _____ _____. The hairdresser washes and cuts her hair. Then, he _____ _____ _____ _____. Elizabeth likes her haircut, but she wants her hair _____ _____ _____. So, she decides to ask the hairdresser if he can cut _____ _____ _____ _____ _____. In this situation, what would Elizabeth most likely say to the hairdresser?

1 대화를 듣고, 남자가 구입할 포장지를 고르시오.

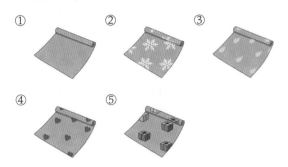

2 대화를 듣고, 남자가 여자에게 부탁한 일로 가장 적절한 것을 고르시오.

① 모래성 쌓기　　　② 여동생 찾아오기
③ 수영 가르쳐주기　④ 선크림 발라주기
⑤ 화상 연고 사 오기

3 다음 그림의 상황에 가장 적절한 대화를 고르시오.

① 　　② 　　③ 　　④ 　　⑤

4 대화를 듣고, 여자가 탑승하려는 기차의 출발 시각을 고르시오.

① 12 p.m.　　② 1 p.m.　　③ 2 p.m.
④ 3 p.m.　　⑤ 4 p.m.

5 대화를 듣고, 장기 자랑에 관해 언급되지 않은 것을 고르시오.

① 참가 자격　　② 공연 날짜　　③ 공연 장소
④ 신청 방법　　⑤ 신청 마감일

6 대화를 듣고, 두 사람이 대화하는 장소로 가장 적절한 곳을 고르시오.

① 카페　　　　② 교실　　　　③ 서점
④ 공원　　　　⑤ 도서관

7 다음을 듣고, 두 사람의 대화가 어색한 것을 고르시오.

① 　　② 　　③ 　　④ 　　⑤

고난도
8 대화를 듣고, 남자가 여자에게 부탁한 일로 가장 적절한 것을 고르시오.

① 학생회장으로 추천하기
② 학생회 담당 교사 맡기
③ 시험 일정 알려주기
④ 입후보 신청서 건네주기
⑤ 선거 공약 검토하기

9 다음을 듣고, 무엇에 관한 안내 방송인지 고르시오.

① 온라인 수업 개설　　② 수영장 나이 제한
③ 국립공원 안전 수칙　④ 여름 캠프 등록
⑤ 야외 활동 주의 사항

10 대화를 듣고, 여자가 지불할 금액을 고르시오.

① $ 5　　　　② $ 8　　　　③ $ 11
④ $ 14　　　⑤ $ 17

11 대화를 듣고, 여자가 대화 직후에 할 일로 가장 적절한 것을 고르시오.

① 이삿짐 풀기　　　② 의자 나르기
③ 상자 접기　　　　④ 형광등 교체하기
⑤ 방 살펴보기

고난도

12 다음을 듣고, 항공편에 관해 언급되지 <u>않은</u> 것을 고르시오.

① 목적지　　② 지연 사유　　③ 출발 시각
④ 탑승 순서　　⑤ 탑승구

13 다음 표를 보면서 대화를 듣고, 여자가 구입할 여행 가방을 고르시오.

	Bag	Color	Wheel	Price
①	A	Red	2	$ 150
②	B	Gray	4	$ 130
③	C	Gray	4	$ 150
④	D	White	2	$ 130
⑤	E	White	4	$ 150

14 다음을 듣고, 무엇에 관한 설명인지 고르시오.

① 건조기　　② 청소기　　③ 세탁기
④ 전자레인지　　⑤ 식기 세척기

15 대화를 듣고, 여자가 할 일로 가장 적절한 것을 고르시오.

① 지퍼 고치기　　② 쿠폰 발행하기
③ 눈 구경하기　　④ 옷 수선하기
⑤ 코트 구매하기

16 대화를 듣고, 여자가 카센터에 차를 맡기러 갈 시각을 고르시오.

① 10 a.m.　　② 11 a.m.　　③ 1 p.m.
④ 2 p.m.　　⑤ 3 p.m.

17 대화를 듣고, 여자의 마지막 말에 대한 남자의 응답으로 가장 적절한 것을 고르시오.

Man: _____

① I only see her during long holidays.
② Yes. It's just two blocks away.
③ She lives in Jeongseon.
④ I really love this painting.
⑤ Thanks! I'm glad you like this.

[18-19] 대화를 듣고, 남자의 마지막 말에 대한 여자의 응답으로 가장 적절한 것을 고르시오.

18 **Woman:** _____

① The movie comes out later this year.
② There is a break in the middle of the play.
③ No. I like having a big audience.
④ The auditions start on Tuesday.
⑤ Yes. I'm afraid of spiders.

19 **Woman:** _____

① Tommy is fine. He is seeing the dentist.
② I will take a shower before we go out.
③ The items on the shelf are all on sale.
④ The lesson begins at 6 p.m. Don't be late.
⑤ Alright. I'll see you at home later then.

20 다음 상황 설명을 듣고, Veronica가 경비원에게 할 말로 가장 적절한 것을 고르시오.

Veronica: Excuse me, _____

① where do I buy tickets?
② why isn't it open yet?
③ our gallery is closed after 9 p.m.
④ you have to wait in line.
⑤ when was this picture painted?

17회 중학영어듣기 실전 모의고사 Dictation 음성을 들으며 빈칸에 알맞은 단어를 채우시오.

1 | 알맞은 그림 고르기

대화를 듣고, 남자가 구입할 포장지를 고르시오.

① ② ③

④ ⑤

M Excuse me. Do you have _____ _____ _____ _____ ?

W Of course. These are the ones we have. They are all _____ _____ _____ _____ .

M I think a patterned paper would _____ _____ _____ my gift.

W I see. How about this one with hearts on it?

M It's pretty, but I'm worried it would _____ _____ _____ _____ .

W Okay. Then, how about this one with snowflakes on it?

M Oh, it looks nice. I'll buy it.

2 | 부탁·요청한 일 고르기

대화를 듣고, 남자가 여자에게 부탁한 일로 가장 적절한 것을 고르시오.

① 모래성 쌓기 ② 여동생 찾아오기
③ 수영 가르쳐주기 ④ 선크림 발라주기
⑤ 화상 연고 사 오기

W Are you _____ _____ _____ _____ at the beach, Danny?

M Yes, Mom! The water is _____ _____ _____ .

W I'm glad. Where is your sister?

M She's _____ _____ _____ down the beach.

W Okay. We'll stay here for another two hours and then go back to the hotel.

M Can you _____ _____ _____ _____ on my back then? I feel like it is burning a bit.

W Sure. We don't want you to get burned badly.

3 | 그림 상황에 적절한 대화 고르기

다음 그림의 상황에 가장 적절한 대화를 고르시오.

① ② ③ ④ ⑤

① M Do you have the key?
   W You just need to _____ _____ _____ .
② M Your garden looks beautiful.
   W _____ _____ _____ you to say that.
③ M Can I help you with something?
   W Yes. I can't _____ _____ _____ on this shelf.
④ M Do you want me to mail this letter for you?
   W No. I'll go to the post office later.
⑤ M Let me _____ _____ _____ for you.
   W Thanks for your help.

4 | 시간 정보 고르기

대화를 듣고, 여자가 탑승하려는 기차의 출발 시각을 고르시오.

① 12 p.m. ② 1 p.m. ③ 2 p.m.
④ 3 p.m. ⑤ 4 p.m.

[Telephone rings.]

M Thank you for calling Western Rail. How can I help you?

W I need to get to Seattle by 4 p.m. Could I _____ _____ _____ on the 3 p.m. train?

M Unfortunately, that one is fully booked. But there are still _____ _____ _____ the 12 p.m. train.

W That would get me to Seattle too early.

M Then, how about a 1 p.m. departure? You would arrive at 2.

W I guess _____ _____ _____.

M Okay. Could I get your name, please?

W It is Sarah Warren.

5 | 언급하지 않은 내용 고르기

대화를 듣고, 장기 자랑에 관해 언급되지 않은 것을 고르시오.

① 참가 자격 ② 공연 날짜 ③ 공연 장소
④ 신청 방법 ⑤ 신청 마감일

> 🎯 적중! Tip **How do we**
>
> [하우 두 위]보다는 [하루위]로 들린다. how를 빠르게 발음할 때는 [하우] 대신 [하]로 발음되고, [d]는 모음 사이에서 발음될 때는 약화되어 [r]에 가깝게 발음되기 때문이다.

M Mary, did you see the posters _____ _____ _____ _____?

W I did. Every student in the school can join, right?

M Yeah! Do you want to _____ _____ _____ _____?

W Sure, that sounds fun. When is the show happening?

M On April 7th.

W How do we sign up?

M _____ _____ _____ _____. The deadline is Thursday.

W Let's _____ _____ _____ _____.

6 | 장소 고르기

대화를 듣고, 두 사람이 대화하는 장소로 가장 적절한 곳을 고르시오.

① 카페 ② 교실 ③ 서점
④ 공원 ⑤ 도서관

> 🎯 적중! Tip **Here you go.**
>
> 상대방에게 무언가를 건네줄 때 사용되는 표현으로 '여기 있어요'라는 의미이다.

W Excuse me. I'd like to borrow this book, please.

M Alright. Can I _____ _____ _____ _____?

W Yes. Here you go.

M Let me _____ _____ _____. *[Pause]* Well, you have another book that you _____ _____ _____ _____.

W Really? Which one?

M It's *Flowers of Europe*. It was _____ _____ _____.

W Oh, no. I left that in class yesterday. I'll bring it back tomorrow.

7 | 어색한 대화 고르기

다음을 듣고, 두 사람의 대화가 어색한 것을 고르시오.

① ② ③ ④ ⑤

> 🎯 적중! Tip **water**
>
> [워털]보다는 [워럴]로 들린다. [t]가 모음 사이에서 발음될 때는 약화되어 [r]에 가깝게 발음되기 때문이다.

① **M** Did you see the soccer game last night?
  W Yeah. It was _____ _____ _____.
② **M** Can you water the flowers on the balcony this afternoon?
  W Sure. I'll _____ _____ _____.
③ **M** What time does the bank close today?
  W It closes at 5 o'clock.
④ **M** May I _____ _____ _____ please?
  W I'm here to buy a new phone.
⑤ **M** The bus will leave _____ _____ _____.
  W Let's run since I don't want to miss it.

8 | 부탁·요청한 일 고르기

대화를 듣고, 남자가 여자에게 부탁한 일로 가장 적절한 것을 고르시오.

① 학생회장으로 추천하기
② 학생회 담당 교사 맡기
③ 시험 일정 알려주기
④ 입후보 신청서 건네주기
⑤ 선거 공약 검토하기

M When is the _____ _____ _____ _____, Ms. Lewis?
W It will be next month. Why?
M I'm _____ _____ _____ _____ the election.
W Oh, you would do a good job.
M Really? _____ _____ _____ _____ would I have as school president?
W You would work with school council members _____ _____ _____ _____ students want.
M Then, I want to sign up to run. Can you give me the form?
W Of course. Please _____ _____ _____ _____.

9 | 주제 고르기

다음을 듣고, 무엇에 관한 안내 방송인지 고르시오.

① 온라인 수업 개설
② 수영장 나이 제한
③ 국립공원 안전 수칙
④ 여름 캠프 등록
⑤ 야외 활동 주의 사항

W Can I have your attention, please? This is an announcement from North Ridge National Park. I'm excited to _____ _____ _____ for our annual children's camp this summer. The camp will _____ _____ _____ June 1st to 8th at the park. Children aged 10 to 15 are _____ _____ _____ _____ for activities such as swimming, hiking, and archery at the camp. Parents can _____ _____ _____ _____ online from today. Thank you for listening, and enjoy the rest of your day.

10 | 금액 정보 고르기

대화를 듣고, 여자가 지불할 금액을 고르시오.

① $ 5   ② $ 8   ③ $ 11
④ $ 14   ⑤ $ 17

🎯 적중! Tip For here or to go?
식당에서 손님에게 음식을 매장에서 먹을지 아니면 포장해 갈지 물을 때 사용되는 표현이다.

M Hi. Can I _____ _____ _____?
W Yes. I'd like a peanut butter sandwich, please.
M That will be five dollars. Do you _____ _____ _____?
W How much are French fries and a drink?
M If you _____ _____ _____ _____, you can get French fries and a drink too.
W I'll take the sandwich, fries, and drink then.
M Great choice. ♂ For here or to go?
W To go, thank you.

11 | 할 일 고르기

대화를 듣고, 여자가 대화 직후에 할 일로 가장 적절한 것을 고르시오.

① 이삿짐 풀기
② 의자 나르기
③ 상자 접기
④ 형광등 교체하기
⑤ 방 살펴보기

M How do you like our new house, Lily?
W It has _____ _____ _____, Dad!
M I know. This room here will be the living room. And then our bedrooms are _____ _____ _____. Did you see them?
W Not yet!
M Well, you need to _____ _____ _____. There are two choices.
W I'll look at _____ _____ _____ now.
M Okay. When you are finished, come and _____ _____ _____.
W Of course.

12 | 언급하지 않은 내용 고르기

다음을 듣고, 항공편에 관해 언급되지 <u>않은</u> 것을 고르시오.

① 목적지   ② 지연 사유   ③ 출발 시각
④ 탑승 순서   ⑤ 탑승구

W Attention passengers, Ohio Airways Flight 221 to Daytona, Florida will be delayed. It will now _____ _____ at 11:05 p.m. The flight will still leave from the _____ _____ _____ : Gate 4C. Passengers with small children and _____ _____ _____ _____ will board first. Have your passport and ticket ready when you _____ _____ _____ . Our team will try to check them _____ _____ _____ _____ . We apologize for the inconvenience.

13 | 도표에서 알맞은 항목 고르기

다음 표를 보면서 대화를 듣고, 여자가 구입할 여행 가방을 고르시오.

	Bag	Color	Wheel	Price
①	A	Red	2	$ 150
②	B	Gray	4	$ 130
③	C	Gray	4	$ 150
④	D	White	2	$ 130
⑤	E	White	4	$ 150

M Hello. Are you looking for something?
W I need a new suitcase _____ _____ _____ _____ tomorrow.
M We have _____ _____ _____ _____ here. How about this red one?
W It looks nice. Do you have a red one _____ _____ _____ ?
M I'm sorry, but it's out of stock right now. We only have gray and white ones with four wheels.
W Can I see the gray ones then?
M Here you go.
W Hmm... _____ _____ _____ _____ ?
M This one is on sale, so it's 130 dollars. The other one is 150 dollars.
W I'll get _____ _____ _____ _____ .

14 | 화제 고르기

다음을 듣고, 무엇에 관한 설명인지 고르시오.

① 건조기   ② 청소기   ③ 세탁기
④ 전자레인지   ⑤ 식기 세척기

M This is _____ _____ _____ _____ when you do housework. It is usually large and square-shaped. With this, we can clean _____ _____ _____ _____ after we use them. We simply put them inside of the device and _____ _____ _____ _____ . Then, we press some buttons and wait for the device to clean our clothes. It usually makes a beeping sound _____ _____ _____ _____ with this.

대화를 듣고, 여자가 할 일로 가장 적절한 것을 고르시오.

① 지퍼 고치기   ② 쿠폰 발행하기
③ 눈 구경하기   ④ 옷 수선하기
⑤ 코트 구매하기

W It's _____ _____ _____ _____ with the snow.
M Why don't you zip up your coat? _____ _____ _____
_____ .
W The zipper is broken on my coat.
M Can you fix it?
W I'm not sure. It's _____ _____ _____ _____ .
M Why don't you buy a new one? The Westwood Department Store is
having a sale.
W Yeah. I'll _____ _____ _____ _____ .

대화를 듣고, 여자가 카센터에 차를 맡기러 갈 시각을 고르시오.

① 10 a.m.   ② 11 a.m.   ③ 1 p.m.
④ 2 p.m.   ⑤ 3 p.m.

[Telephone rings.]
M Eastgate Service Center. How can I help you today?
W Hi. My car is _____ _____ _____ _____ . I'd like to get
it checked.
M Okay. Which day is _____ _____ _____ to bring it in?
W Saturday at 10 or 11 a.m. would be best.
M Unfortunately, all our mechanics are busy then. _____ _____
_____ _____ at 1 in the afternoon?
W I have a doctor's appointment at that time. What about later that day?
I'm free any time after 2.
M _____ _____ _____ _____ is available at 3.
W That's fine.

대화를 듣고, 여자의 마지막 말에 대한 남자의 응답으로 가장 적절한 것을 고르시오.

Man: _____

① I only see her during long holidays.
② Yes. It's just two blocks away.
③ She lives in Jeongseon.
④ I really love this painting.
⑤ Thanks! I'm glad you like this.

🎯 적중! Tip gran**d**mother
[그랜드마덜]보다는 [그랜마덜]로 들린다. 자음 3개가 연속
해서 나오면 중간 자음은 발음되지 않기 때문이다.

M Who are you drawing, Jisun?
W I'm drawing my grandmother. This is a gift for her birthday.
M It's really good _____ _____ _____ . She'll love
it.
W I hope so. I want to show her _____ _____ _____
_____ .
M Do you see her often?
W Yes. She _____ _____ _____ to me, so I visit her at least
once a week.
M You are lucky. My grandmother lives in the countryside, so I _____
_____ _____ _____ .
W When do you _____ _____ _____ _____ ?

18 | 적절한 응답 고르기

대화를 듣고, 남자의 마지막 말에 대한 여자의 응답으로 가장 적절한 것을 고르시오.

Woman: _____

① The movie comes out later this year.
② There is a break in the middle of the play.
③ No. I like having a big audience.
④ The auditions start on Tuesday.
⑤ Yes. I'm afraid of spiders.

> 🎯 적중! Tip seven years old
> [세븐 이얼즈 올드]보다는 [세브니얼졸드]로 들린다. 앞에 나온 단어의 끝 자음과 뒤에 나온 단어의 첫 모음이 연음되기 때문이다.

M You were so great in the play today, Subin.
W Thank you! I _____ _____ _____ a lot.
M I can tell. Did you always love acting?
W Yes. _____ _____ _____ at seven years old.
M That's impressive.
W Well, I _____ _____ _____ a famous actress one day.
M Do you want to be in movies or in plays?
W I prefer plays. I love being on the stage.
M But _____ _____ _____ _____?

19 | 적절한 응답 고르기

대화를 듣고, 남자의 마지막 말에 대한 여자의 응답으로 가장 적절한 것을 고르시오.

Woman: _____

① Tommy is fine. He is seeing the dentist.
② I will take a shower before we go out.
③ The items on the shelf are all on sale.
④ The lesson begins at 6 p.m. Don't be late.
⑤ Alright. I'll see you at home later then.

[Cellphone rings.]
W Honey, what's up?
M Are you at home right now?
W No. I'm at the shop. We need some more shampoo.
M Can you also _____ _____ _____? We just _____ _____ _____ _____ too.
W Of course. There are also some bathrobes for sale _____ _____ _____ _____. Should I get a few?
M No. We don't need them. But could you _____ _____ _____ _____ to get some bread?
W Sure. I'll be home after I buy everything.
M Oh, and _____ _____ _____ _____ Tommy from piano class today. I have a late meeting.

20 | 상황에 적절한 말 고르기

다음 상황 설명을 듣고, Veronica가 경비원에게 할 말로 가장 적절한 것을 고르시오.

Veronica: Excuse me, _____

① where do I buy tickets?
② why isn't it open yet?
③ our gallery is closed after 9 p.m.
④ you have to wait in line.
⑤ when was this picture painted?

M Veronica is _____ _____ _____ _____. She goes to the art gallery for a new exhibit. But it is closed _____ _____ _____. Veronica is confused because the gallery usually opens at 9 a.m. She sees a security guard and _____ _____ _____ _____ the gallery is still closed. In this situation, what would Veronica most likely say to the security guard?

1 대화를 듣고, 여자가 만든 비누를 고르시오.

①   ②   ③

④   ⑤

2 대화를 듣고, 남자가 여자에게 부탁한 일로 가장 적절한 것을 고르시오.

① 체온 재기　　　② 구급차 부르기
③ 자녀 데려오기　　④ 감기약 사 오기
⑤ 얼음주머니 올리기

3 다음 그림의 상황에 가장 적절한 대화를 고르시오.

①　　②　　③　　④　　⑤

4 대화를 듣고, 두 사람이 만나기로 한 요일을 고르시오.

① 월요일　　② 수요일　　③ 목요일
④ 금요일　　⑤ 토요일

5 대화를 듣고, 카페에 관해 언급되지 않은 것을 고르시오.

① 이름　　② 위치　　③ 인기 음료
④ 영업시간　　⑤ 수상 이력

6 대화를 듣고, 두 사람이 대화하는 장소로 가장 적절한 곳을 고르시오.

① 전망대　　② 놀이공원　　③ 자동차 매장
④ 주스 가게　　⑤ 쇼핑몰

7 다음을 듣고, 두 사람의 대화가 어색한 것을 고르시오.

①　　②　　③　　④　　⑤

8 대화를 듣고, 남자가 여자에게 부탁한 일로 가장 적절한 것을 고르시오.

① 창문에 커튼 달기　　② 러그 교체하기
③ 가족사진 들고 있기　　④ 벽에 시계 걸기
⑤ 소파 침실로 옮기기

9 다음을 듣고, 무엇에 관한 안내 방송인지 고르시오.

① 학교 체육관 폐관　　② 경기 등록 방법
③ 농구 시간 변경　　④ 시민 회관 가는 길
⑤ 배구 연습 장소

10 대화를 듣고, 여자가 지불할 금액을 고르시오.

① $ 15　　② $ 25　　③ $ 35
④ $ 45　　⑤ $ 55

11 대화를 듣고, 남자가 할 일로 가장 적절한 것을 고르시오.

① 후기 작성하기　　② 소설책 읽기
③ 노트북 가져오기　　④ 기차표 예매하기
⑤ 영화 다운받기

고난도

12 다음을 듣고, VR 헤드셋에 관해 언급되지 <u>않은</u> 것을 고르시오.

① 제조 공장 위치　　② 제품 판매 시작일

③ 제품 가격　　　　④ 제품 무게

⑤ 배터리 지속 시간

13 다음 배치도를 보면서 대화를 듣고, 여자가 안내받은 곳을 고르시오.

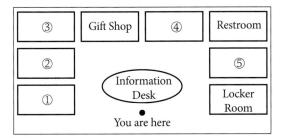

14 다음을 듣고, 무엇에 관한 설명인지 고르시오.

① 악어　　　② 하마　　　③ 펭귄

④ 거북이　　⑤ 도마뱀

15 대화를 듣고, 여자가 대화 직후에 할 일로 가장 적절한 것을 고르시오.

① 수학 문제 풀기　　② 공연장 찾아보기

③ 과제 제출하기　　④ 간식 준비하기

⑤ 가수 사인 받기

고난도

16 대화를 듣고, 여자가 비행기에 탑승하기로 한 날짜를 고르시오.

① 8월 8일　　② 8월 11일　　③ 8월 15일

④ 8월 17일　　⑤ 8월 18일

17 대화를 듣고, 여자의 마지막 말에 대한 남자의 응답으로 가장 적절한 것을 고르시오.

Man: _____

① You're right. I shouldn't be afraid.

② I want it to be shorter.

③ No. It doesn't look nice with my shoes.

④ This is my favorite fashion magazine.

⑤ Yeah. I also prefer blue to red.

[18-19] 대화를 듣고, 남자의 마지막 말에 대한 여자의 응답으로 가장 적절한 것을 고르시오.

18 **Woman:** _____

① It's a kind of cactus.

② Good idea. Let's plant the flowers here.

③ Thanks for holding my bag.

④ Right. I'll let it in the sunshine.

⑤ Okay. I'll take a good care of it.

19 **Woman:** _____

① How about going to the hospital?

② They are too sweet to eat. They make me ill.

③ That seems like a good idea.

④ Yes. He's in very good health for his age.

⑤ I recommend walking for exercise.

20 다음 상황 설명을 듣고, Yuri가 소년에게 할 말로 가장 적절한 것을 고르시오.

Yuri: _____

① The pool closes in 30 minutes.

② Please stop running next to the pool.

③ Could you put on a life jacket?

④ Are you here with one of your parents?

⑤ Thank you for explaining the safety rules.

18회 중학영어듣기 실전 모의고사 Dictation 음성을 들으며 빈칸에 알맞은 단어를 채우시오.

1 | 알맞은 그림 고르기

대화를 듣고, 여자가 만든 비누를 고르시오.

① ② ③

④ ⑤

M Mom, what's in the box?
W Handmade soap. As you know, I _____ _____ _____.
M Oh, please show me what you made.
W Okay. Here it is.
M It has _____ _____ _____ _____. *[Pause]* Wow, you
　 made watermelon soap! I didn't notice until I _____ _____
　 _____ _____.
W Yeah. I wanted the soap to be fun. _____ _____ _____
　 _____ _____ was the hardest part.
M You're skillful with your hands.

2 | 부탁·요청한 일 고르기

대화를 듣고, 남자가 여자에게 부탁한 일로 가장 적절
한 것을 고르시오.
① 체온 재기　　② 구급차 부르기
③ 자녀 데려오기　④ 감기약 사 오기
⑤ 얼음주머니 올리기

W Are you okay, Darling? You don't look well.
M _____ _____ _____ _____.
W Do you have a fever?
M Hold on, I'll _____ _____ _____. *[Pause]* Oh, yes. My
　 temperature is high.
W Well, you should rest then. _____ _____ _____ _____
　 _____?
M But I have to take the kids to school soon.
W Don't worry about that. I can do it. Do you need anything _____
　 _____ _____?
M Can you get some medicine? I think it would help.
W Sure. Now, go rest.

3 | 그림 상황에 적절한 대화 고르기

다음 그림의 상황에 가장 적절한 대화를 고르시오.

① ② ③ ④ ⑤

① M _____ _____ _____ a taxi?
　 W Let's walk, instead.
② M Where do you need to go?
　 W The Coleman Bank on Freedman street, please.
③ M _____ _____ _____ _____ to work.
　 W Don't mention it.
④ M I like your new car.
　 W I bought it last month.
⑤ M My order number is 8373.
　 W _____ _____ _____, please.

4 | 시간 정보 고르기

대화를 듣고, 두 사람이 만나기로 한 요일을 고르시오.

① 월요일   ② 수요일   ③ 목요일
④ 금요일   ⑤ 토요일

[Cellphone rings.]

M Hi, Lisa. _____ _____ _____ that new restaurant next to the park? It finally opened.

W Oh, really? We _____ _____ _____ _____!

M I think so too. Are you free for dinner on Thursday?

W Actually, I'm not. My book club meets on Thursday nights. How about Saturday?

M On Saturday I will _____ _____ _____ _____ _____ out of town. Is Friday good?

W I can _____ _____ _____. Let's try to go around 7.

M Alright. I'll _____ _____ _____ then.

5 | 언급하지 않은 내용 고르기

대화를 듣고, 카페에 관해 언급되지 <u>않은</u> 것을 고르시오.

① 이름   ② 위치   ③ 인기 음료
④ 영업시간   ⑤ 수상 이력

> 🎯 적중! Tip **friend**s
> [프렌드즈]보다는 [프렌즈]로 들린다. 자음 3개가 연속해서 나오면 중간 자음은 발음되지 않기 때문이다.

M Zoey, did you _____ _____ _____ last weekend?

W Yeah. I went to a special café with some friends. It's called Café Mer.

M Café Mer? Is that the one _____ _____ _____ _____?

W That's right. It's famous for its strawberry latte.

M Oh, _____ _____ _____.

W The shop won a big award recently too. It _____ _____ _____ in the city. You should really try it!

M I will.

6 | 장소 고르기

대화를 듣고, 두 사람이 대화하는 장소로 가장 적절한 곳을 고르시오.

① 전망대   ② 놀이공원   ③ 자동차 매장
④ 주스 가게   ⑤ 쇼핑몰

M Christine, that Ferris wheel was so fun!

W I know. The view _____ _____ _____ was amazing.

M What do you want to ride next?

W Well, I'm actually _____ _____ _____. Can we get some drinks?

M Sure. But after that, I really want to ride the roller coaster.

W _____ _____ _____ _____ _____ for it?

M The line isn't too long right now because it is _____ _____ _____ _____.

W Alright, let's buy drinks and go _____ _____ _____.

7 | 어색한 대화 고르기

다음을 듣고, 두 사람의 대화가 <u>어색한</u> 것을 고르시오.

①   ②   ③   ④   ⑤

> 🎯 적중! Tip I don't think so.
> 상대방의 말에 대해 이의를 제기할 때 사용되는 표현이다.

① **M** Why don't we take a break?
   W Sure. _____ _____ _____.

② **M** Do you want to come play soccer with us this weekend?
   W Yeah. I'd like _____ _____.

③ **M** Can I _____ _____ _____ _____?
   W I'm fine, thank you.

④ **M** It's so hot in the classroom!
   W I don't think so. It's just _____ _____ _____.

⑤ **M** Which color do you prefer, white or black?
   W I have _____ _____ _____ _____.

대화를 듣고, 남자가 여자에게 부탁한 일로 가장 적절한 것을 고르시오.

① 창문에 커튼 달기   ② 러그 교체하기
③ 가족사진 들고 있기   ④ 벽에 시계 걸기
⑤ 소파 침실로 옮기기

🎯 적중! Tip mi**dd**le

[미들]보다는 [미를]로 들린다. [d]가 모음과 단어 끝의 -le 사이에 있으면 약화되어 [r]에 가깝게 발음되기 때문이다.

W Honey, _____ _____ _____ _____ this room?
M Why don't we put the couch by the window?
W Okay. Then, we can put _____ _____ _____ in the middle of the room.
M What about our paintings and pictures?
W I'll hold up this first painting on the wall. Tell me _____ _____ _____.
M Hmm... It doesn't look nice with the room. Can you hold up _____ _____ _____ instead?
W Sure. Let me get it.

다음을 듣고, 무엇에 관한 안내 방송인지 고르시오.

① 학교 체육관 폐관   ② 경기 등록 방법
③ 농구 시간 변경   ④ 시민 회관 가는 길
⑤ 배구 연습 장소

M Attention, students. I'm Dave, the school's sports director. I'm sorry to announce that the school's gym will be _____ _____ _____ _____ from this Monday. The gym will be renovated. We are _____ _____ _____ and seating. School basketball and volleyball games will be held _____ _____ _____, and sports practices will _____ _____ _____ the local community center. We are _____ _____ _____ _____, and thank you for all your patience.

대화를 듣고, 여자가 지불할 금액을 고르시오.

① $ 15   ② $ 25   ③ $ 35
④ $ 45   ⑤ $ 55

🎯 적중! Tip re**c**ord

record는 명사로 쓰일 때는 [레컬드]로, 동사로 쓰일 때는 [리콜드]로 발음된다.

M Welcome to Every Song Music Store. How may I help you?
W I'd like to _____ _____ _____ _____.
M Let me see. [Beeping sound] Okay. It will be 25 dollars for the records. Did you want to _____ _____ _____?
W How much is _____ _____ _____ _____?
M It is 30 dollars.
W Great. I'll take it and the records.

대화를 듣고, 남자가 할 일로 가장 적절한 것을 고르시오.

① 후기 작성하기   ② 소설책 읽기
③ 노트북 가져오기   ④ 기차표 예매하기
⑤ 영화 다운받기

[Cellphone rings.]
W Hi, Jake. Is everything okay?
M Yes. I'm just _____ _____ _____ _____ _____ now.
W Oh, great. What time is our train again?
M It leaves at 6 p.m.
W I'll go to the station _____ _____ _____ then.
M It'll be a long train ride.
W _____ _____ _____ _____ your laptop? We can watch a movie together.
M Okay. I will. That will be fun.

고난도

12 | 언급하지 않은 내용 고르기

다음을 듣고, VR 헤드셋에 관해 언급되지 <u>않은</u> 것을 고르시오.

① 제조 공장 위치 ② 제품 판매 시작일
③ 제품 가격 ④ 제품 무게
⑤ 배터리 지속 시간

W Thank you for _____ _____ _____ _____. I'm Nora Burton, the CEO of Auden Technology. I'm pleased to announce our new VR headset. We are making it _____ _____ _____ here in Canada. The headset _____ _____ _____ to buy on June 11th. This product is special for a three main reasons. First, the headset is _____ _____ _____. Second, it is completely wireless. Finally, it works for five hours _____ _____ _____ _____. This means it has the best battery life on the market. Would you like to try it out?

13 | 위치 고르기

다음 배치도를 보면서 대화를 듣고, 여자가 안내받은 곳을 고르시오.

③	Gift Shop	④	Restroom
②			⑤
①	Information Desk		Locker Room

You are here

W Excuse me, sir. I _____ _____ _____ _____ _____ at the gift shop.
M When did you lose it?
W About an hour ago.
M _____ _____ _____ _____ to our desk. Why don't you check the lost and found?
W Could you tell me _____ _____ _____?
M Do you know where the restroom is?
W Yeah. Is it in the office between the restroom and the gift shop?
M No. It's in the office between the restroom _____ _____ _____ _____.
W Oh, I see. Thanks for the help.
M You're welcome. I _____ _____ _____ _____ _____.

14 | 화제 고르기

다음을 듣고, 무엇에 관한 설명인지 고르시오.

① 악어 ② 하마 ③ 펭귄
④ 거북이 ⑤ 도마뱀

W This is a land animal, but it _____ _____ _____ _____ in water. This animal lives in _____ _____ _____ _____. It has a huge head and _____ _____. It is usually a brown and pink color. This is _____ _____ _____ _____ _____ on the planet. It has big teeth, but it usually eats grass.

대화를 듣고, 여자가 대화 직후에 할 일로 가장 적절한 것을 고르시오.

① 수학 문제 풀기　　② 공연장 찾아보기
③ 과제 제출하기　　④ 간식 준비하기
⑤ 가수 사인 받기

W Are you ready for the concert, Charlie?
M Not yet, Mom. How much time do we have _____ _____ _____?
W We have about 30 minutes. Why?
M I'm trying to _____ _____ _____ _____ now, but they're so hard.
W Do you have _____ _____ _____ _____?
M Yes. And they are due tomorrow.
W Well, _____ _____ _____ _____ quickly. While you do that, I will make a snack for us.
M Okay. I'll do my best.

대화를 듣고, 여자가 비행기에 탑승하기로 한 날짜를 고르시오.

① 8월 8일　　② 8월 11일　　③ 8월 15일
④ 8월 17일　　⑤ 8월 18일

[Telephone rings.]
M Hi, Phantom Airline. How can I help you?
W Hi, I'd like to book a ticket to London. I want to go _____ _____ _____ _____ of August. The 8th, maybe?
M Let me check. [Pause] I'm sorry, but we're fully booked that week.
W Oh, no. What about _____ _____ _____ _____?
M We have seats on the 15th and 18th.
W I need to _____ _____ _____ on the 17th.
M Okay. You can _____ _____ _____ _____ that leaves in the morning or the afternoon on the 15th.
W I'll take the earlier flight.

대화를 듣고, 여자의 마지막 말에 대한 남자의 응답으로 가장 적절한 것을 고르시오.

Man: _____

① You're right. I shouldn't be afraid.
② I want it to be shorter.
③ No. It doesn't look nice with my shoes.
④ This is my favorite fashion magazine.
⑤ Yeah. I also prefer blue to red.

M I like your new hair style, Sua.
W Thanks. I just got my hair _____ _____ _____.
M What made you want blue hair?
W Well, it's my favorite color. And I was _____ _____ _____ _____ _____.
M I'm jealous of your overall style. It's so unique.
W Don't you like your style, too?
M I do, but I'm _____ _____ _____ some things. People might not like them.
W You should always wear _____ _____ _____ _____. Don't worry about other people.

18 | 적절한 응답 고르기

대화를 듣고, 남자의 마지막 말에 대한 여자의 응답으로 가장 적절한 것을 고르시오.

Woman: _____

① It's a kind of cactus.
② Good idea. Let's plant the flowers here.
③ Thanks for holding my bag.
④ Right. I'll let it in the sunshine.
⑤ Okay. I'll take a good care of it.

> 🎯 적중! Tip pu**t it**
> [풋 잇]보다는 [푸릿]으로 들린다. [t]가 모음 사이에서 발음될 때는 약화되어 [r]에 가깝게 발음되기 때문이다.

W What are you holding, Nick?
M _____ _____ _____ for you.
W Really? That's so nice!
M It's a small plant. I bought it _____ _____ _____ yesterday.
W Wow, I love it! I will put it _____ _____ _____.
M That's good because it needs lots of sunlight.
W This type of plant doesn't _____ _____ _____ _____ _____, right?
M Yes. You should only water it _____ _____ _____.

19 | 적절한 응답 고르기

대화를 듣고, 남자의 마지막 말에 대한 여자의 응답으로 가장 적절한 것을 고르시오.

Woman: _____

① How about going to the hospital?
② They are too sweet to eat. They make me ill.
③ That seems like a good idea.
④ Yes. He's in very good health for his age.
⑤ I recommend walking for exercise.

> 🎯 적중! Tip I'm aware of ~.
> 무언가를 알고 있음을 나타낼 때 사용되는 표현으로, of 다음에는 명사(구)가 온다.
> · I'm aware of all the changes.
>   나는 모든 변화를 알고 있어.

W Are you having another soda, Rob?
M Yes. This is _____ _____ _____.
W But you already drank two today.
M What's wrong with that?
W There's _____ _____ _____ _____ in soda. It's not good for your health _____ _____ _____ too many.
M I'm aware of that, but they're delicious.
W Even so, you _____ _____ _____ them.
M It's _____ _____ _____ so quickly. But I'll drink some sugarless soda instead for now.

20 | 상황에 적절한 말 고르기

다음 상황 설명을 듣고, Yuri가 소년에게 할 말로 가장 적절한 것을 고르시오.

Yuri: _____

① The pool closes in 30 minutes.
② Please stop running next to the pool.
③ Could you put on a life jacket?
④ Are you here with one of your parents?
⑤ Thank you for explaining the safety rules.

W Yuri is a lifeguard. She works _____ _____ _____ _____. One day, she is watching some kids play in the water. A boy _____ _____ _____ _____ along the side of the pool. This is _____ _____ _____ _____. He could fall because it's slippery. So, Yuri would like to tell him _____ _____ _____ next to the pool. In this situation, what would Yuri most likely say to the boy?

1 대화를 듣고, 남자가 구입할 스피커를 고르시오.

① 　② 　③

④ 　⑤

2 대화를 듣고, 여자가 남자에게 전화한 목적으로 가장 적절한 것을 고르시오.

① 약속 시간을 바꾸려고
② 병원 진료를 예약하려고
③ 주말 계획을 취소하려고
④ 식당 위치를 확인하려고
⑤ 점심 메뉴를 결정하려고

3 다음 그림의 상황에 가장 적절한 대화를 고르시오.

①　　②　　③　　④　　⑤

4 대화를 듣고, 남자가 차를 가지러 가기로 한 요일을 고르시오.

① 월요일　　② 화요일　　③ 수요일
④ 목요일　　⑤ 금요일

5 다음을 듣고, 연주회에 관해 언급되지 않은 것을 고르시오.

① 주최자　　② 연주곡　　③ 장소
④ 날짜　　⑤ 입장료

6 대화를 듣고, 두 사람의 관계로 가장 적절한 것을 고르시오.

① 시장 — 기자
② 환경운동가 — 학생
③ 경찰관 — 시민
④ 버스 운전사 — 승객
⑤ 쇼 진행자 — 방청객

7 다음을 듣고, 두 사람의 대화가 어색한 것을 고르시오.

①　　②　　③　　④　　⑤

8 대화를 듣고, 남자가 여자에게 부탁한 일로 가장 적절한 것을 고르시오.

① 장갑 뜨개질하기
② 눈사람 만들기
③ 세탁물 찾아오기
④ 옷장 조립하기
⑤ 세탁실 청소하기

9 대화를 듣고, 여자의 마지막 말에 담긴 의도로 가장 적절한 것을 고르시오.

① 거절　　② 위로　　③ 감사
④ 제안　　⑤ 칭찬

10 대화를 듣고, 남자가 지불할 금액을 고르시오.

① $ 15　　② $ 16　　③ $ 17
④ $ 18　　⑤ $ 19

11 대화를 듣고, 남자가 할 일로 가장 적절한 것을 고르시오.

① 케이크 만들기
② 쿠키 굽기
③ 시식회 참석하기
④ 요리법 검색하기
⑤ 과일잼 만들기

고난도

12 다음을 듣고, 버스 투어에 관해 언급되지 <u>않은</u> 것을 고르시오.

① 투어 장소　　　　② 가이드 이름
③ 하차 장소　　　　④ 환승 비용
⑤ 운영 시간

13 다음 표를 보면서 대화를 듣고, 남자가 구입할 꽃다발을 고르시오.

	Flower	Color	Ribbon
①	tulip	yellow	O
②	tulip	red	X
③	rose	red	X
④	rose	red	O
⑤	rose	yellow	O

14 다음을 듣고, 무엇에 관한 설명인지 고르시오.

① 독서대　　　② 북엔드　　　③ 북커버
④ 책갈피　　　⑤ 탁상 램프

15 대화를 듣고, 여자가 대화 직후에 할 일로 가장 적절한 것을 고르시오.

① 튜브 빌리기　　　　② 파도풀장 가기
③ 물놀이 기구 타기　　④ 남편 기다리기
⑤ 구명조끼 입기

16 대화를 듣고, 남자가 배울 악기를 고르시오.

① piano　　　② drum　　　③ flute
④ violin　　　⑤ guitar

17 대화를 듣고, 남자의 마지막 말에 대한 여자의 응답으로 가장 적절한 것을 고르시오.

Woman: _____

① The bus was canceled because of heavy snow.
② Yes. It takes over four hours to get there.
③ No. I don't have any sisters or brothers.
④ You are at the wrong stop.
⑤ I like to do short trips by train.

[18-19] 대화를 듣고, 여자의 마지막 말에 대한 남자의 응답으로 가장 적절한 것을 고르시오.

18 **Man:** _____

① Sure. Keeping a journal seems too hard.
② The topic is your dream job.
③ Right. Taking notes is a good habit.
④ I would love to do that.
⑤ My best friend's name is Tim.

고난도

19 **Man:** _____

① The time in Switzerland is 11 a.m.
② Please write a thank-you letter to them.
③ I'll try to video call them now.
④ I'll wrap this watch in a box.
⑤ We can't. Everything will be closed today.

20 다음 상황 설명을 듣고, Lucy가 직원에게 할 말로 가장 적절한 것을 고르시오.

Lucy: _____

① Can you repair my bike?
② Don't you need a bike helmet too?
③ Do you have this one in green?
④ Sorry, I'm going to be late this morning.
⑤ Luckily, this model comes in many different colors.

19회 중학영어듣기 실전 모의고사 Dictation 음성을 들으며 빈칸에 알맞은 단어를 채우시오.

1 | 알맞은 그림 고르기

대화를 듣고, 남자가 구입할 스피커를 고르시오.

① ② ③
④ ⑤

W Welcome to Best Electronics. May I help you?
M Yes. I need a wireless speaker.
W Then, I _____ _____ _____ _____. It even has a clock function.
M Well, I don't _____ _____ _____. Do you have any others?
W How about _____ _____ _____? It has a strap, so you can easily carry it anywhere.
M Sorry, but I don't like the brand logo on it. I see the round one _____ _____ _____ _____.
W Right. Do you want to buy this one?
M Yes. I'll take it.

2 | 목적 고르기

대화를 듣고, 여자가 남자에게 전화한 목적으로 가장 적절한 것을 고르시오.

① 약속 시간을 바꾸려고
② 병원 진료를 예약하려고
③ 주말 계획을 취소하려고
④ 식당 위치를 확인하려고
⑤ 점심 메뉴를 결정하려고

[Cellphone rings.]
M Hello, Nancy. Is everything okay?
W Hi, David. I'm so sorry, but we have to _____ _____ _____ _____ for today.
M What happened?
W I forgot about _____ _____ _____ _____. I have to be there at 12 o'clock.
M What time will it finish?
W It _____ _____ _____ _____ 1:30.
M That's no problem. We can just meet later then.
W _____ _____ _____.

3 | 그림 상황에 적절한 대화 고르기

다음 그림의 상황에 가장 적절한 대화를 고르시오.

① ② ③ ④ ⑤

① W Is there another bathroom?
  M There's one _____ _____ _____ _____. I'll show you.
② W What time does the museum tour start?
  M It begins in about 20 minutes.
③ W How much does a gym membership cost?
  M It's 100 dollars _____ _____.
④ W I'm looking for the Elderberry Library.
  M It's _____ _____ _____ _____.
⑤ W I need a new television _____ _____ _____ _____.
  M What about this model?

4 │ 시간 정보 고르기

대화를 듣고, 남자가 차를 가지러 가기로 한 요일을 고르시오.

① 월요일　　② 화요일　　③ 수요일
④ 목요일　　⑤ 금요일

> 🎯 적중! Tip　**I'm afraid ~.**
>
> 어떤 요청을 거절해야 하거나 기대에 못 미치는 소식을 전해야 하는 상황에서 정중하게 의사를 전달할 때 사용되는 표현이다.
>
> · I'm afraid I can't join you.
> 　미안하지만 너와 함께 못 갈 것 같아.

[Cellphone rings.]

W Hello, Mr. Richardson. I'm ＿＿＿＿＿＿＿ ＿＿＿＿＿＿＿. I am repairing it here at the Auto Repair Center.

M Is everything alright?

W Yes. Your car will be ready for pickup next week. What day would you like to ＿＿＿＿ ＿＿＿＿ ＿＿＿＿＿＿?

M Can I come on Monday?

W I'm afraid ＿＿＿＿ ＿＿＿＿ ＿＿＿＿ ＿＿＿＿ Mondays. How about Tuesday?

M I'm too busy on Tuesday. ＿＿＿＿ ＿＿＿＿ ＿＿＿＿?

W That's fine.

5 │ 언급하지 않은 내용 고르기

다음을 듣고, 연주회에 관해 언급되지 <u>않은</u> 것을 고르시오.

① 주최자　　② 연주곡　　③ 장소
④ 날짜　　　⑤ 입장료

W Hi, students. This is your music teacher, Ms. Torrance. I'm happy to tell you that a concert will be ＿＿＿＿ ＿＿＿＿ ＿＿＿＿ ＿＿＿＿. They will perform ＿＿＿＿ ＿＿＿＿ ＿＿＿＿ ＿＿＿＿ for a year, including some from the famous *Pirates of Caribbean* soundtrack. The concert will be at Danvers Auditorium on November 19th. Everyone is invited, so please ＿＿＿＿ ＿＿＿＿ ＿＿＿＿ ＿＿＿＿. Thank you.

고난도

6 │ 관계 고르기

대화를 듣고, 두 사람의 관계로 가장 적절한 것을 고르시오.

① 시장 — 기자　　　② 환경운동가 — 학생
③ 경찰관 — 시민　　④ 버스 운전사 — 승객
⑤ 쇼 진행자 — 방청객

> 🎯 적중! Tip　**support it**
>
> [서포트 잇]보다는 [서포릿]으로 들린다. [rt]가 모음 사이에서 발음될 때는 약화되어 [r]에 가깝게 발음되기 때문이다.

W This is Jessica Smith reporting for *Morning News*. I'm ＿＿＿＿＿ ＿＿＿＿ ＿＿＿＿ ＿＿＿＿ with David Kim.

M Thank you for inviting me.

W So, how do you feel ＿＿＿＿ ＿＿＿＿ ＿＿＿＿ ＿＿＿＿?

M I'm very excited and so thankful to all of the voters.

W What will you do first ＿＿＿＿ ＿＿＿＿ ＿＿＿＿ ＿＿＿＿ of the city?

M I will work hard to reduce our city's pollution.

W And what is your opinion on the plan ＿＿＿＿ ＿＿＿＿ ＿＿＿＿?

M I support it. I hope to see more buses and trains in the future.

7 │ 어색한 대화 고르기

다음을 듣고, 두 사람의 대화가 <u>어색한</u> 것을 고르시오.

①　　②　　③　　④　　⑤

① **M** You like that board game *Wizards and Wheels*, don't you?
　W Yes. It's really fun. Let's play it now.

② **M** Something is ＿＿＿＿ ＿＿＿＿ ＿＿＿＿ ＿＿＿＿.
　W I got that question wrong too.

③ **M** How ＿＿＿＿ ＿＿＿＿ ＿＿＿＿ ＿＿＿＿?
　W I do yoga once a week.

④ **M** Do you want me to ＿＿＿＿ ＿＿＿＿ ＿＿＿＿ ＿＿＿＿?
　W No. I want to read it now.

⑤ **M** May I ＿＿＿＿ ＿＿＿＿ ＿＿＿＿, ma'am?
　W Yes, please. I'd like a steak with French fries.

대화를 듣고, 남자가 여자에게 부탁한 일로 가장 적절한 것을 고르시오.

① 장갑 뜨개질하기　　② 눈사람 만들기
③ 세탁물 찾아오기　　④ 옷장 조립하기
⑤ 세탁실 청소하기

[Cellphone rings.]
W　Hi. What's going on, Honey?
M　Did you _____ _____ _____ this morning?
W　Hmm... No. Did you _____ _____ _____?
M　Yes. But they aren't there.
W　When did you wear them last?
M　A few days ago. I _____ _____ _____ with the kids.
W　Oh, they must be _____ _____ _____ _____.
M　Okay. Also, could you remember to pick up the dry cleaning tonight? We'll need our jackets tomorrow.
W　I will.

대화를 듣고, 여자의 마지막 말에 담긴 의도로 가장 적절한 것을 고르시오.

① 거절　　② 위로　　③ 감사
④ 제안　　⑤ 칭찬

M　How are you doing, Liz?
W　I'm busy. I have a lot of homework _____ _____ _____ _____.
M　Yeah? What are you working on?
W　I have to write two essays. One for my English class and _____ _____ _____ _____.
M　Let me know _____ _____ _____ _____. I could proofread your writing.
W　Thanks. That would really help.

대화를 듣고, 남자가 지불할 금액을 고르시오.

① $ 15　　② $ 16　　③ $ 17
④ $ 18　　⑤ $ 19

W　Hi. Did you _____ _____ _____ _____?
M　Yes. I'd like to buy _____ _____ _____.
W　Okay. Those are 15 dollars.
M　Oh, and what about these socks? I didn't see those before.
W　These socks are on sale, so it's only two dollars _____ _____ _____.
M　Can I get two packs of those too?
W　Of course. _____ _____ _____ _____ 19 dollars.
M　I have a three-dollar discount coupon. Is it okay to use it _____ _____ _____?
W　Yes. That will work.

11 | 할 일 고르기

대화를 듣고, 남자가 할 일로 가장 적절한 것을 고르시오.

① 케이크 만들기　② 쿠키 굽기
③ 시식회 참석하기　④ 요리법 검색하기
⑤ 과일잼 만들기

적중! Tip　It's my passion.
어떤 일에 대해 자신이 아주 좋아하는 일이라며, 열정적으로 하는 취미 활동임을 나타낼 때 사용되는 표현이다.

W _____ _____ _____ _____, Alan.
M Thank you. I made them yesterday.
W _____ _____ _____ _____ ?
M Yes. It's my passion. I love to bake, and I really want to _____ _____ _____ one day.
W Well, you always _____ _____ _____ . These cookies are so great.
M Next week, I'll bake a raspberry and lemon cake. It's _____ _____ _____ .
W Can I try it after it's finished?
M Of course!

고난도
12 | 언급하지 않은 내용 고르기

다음을 듣고, 버스 투어에 관해 언급되지 않은 것을 고르시오.

① 투어 장소　② 가이드 이름
③ 하차 장소　④ 환승 비용
⑤ 운영 시간

W Good morning, visitors. I'm Martha. I'll be your guide today on our bus tour. I will give you _____ _____ _____ _____ here in Madrid. _____ _____ _____ in the city will be the Prado Museum. Then, we'll head to Royal Palace of Madrid, _____ _____ _____ _____ . Remember, you can get off and spend time _____ _____ _____ . If you want to, _____ _____ _____ . You can get on the next bus for no extra charge.

---

13 | 도표에서 알맞은 항목 고르기

다음 표를 보면서 대화를 듣고, 남자가 구입할 꽃다발을 고르시오.

	Flower	Color	Ribbon
①	tulip	yellow	O
②	tulip	red	X
③	rose	red	X
④	rose	red	O
⑤	rose	yellow	O

M Hi. I'd like to get _____ _____ _____ _____ .
W Okay. What does she like?
M I'm not sure, but I know _____ _____ _____ _____ .
W How about these roses?
M They are beautiful. What are those yellow ones?
W They are roses too, but they are _____ _____ _____ _____ .
M Oh. Then, can I have 10 red ones?
W Would you like me to _____ _____ _____ _____ _____ ?
M Yes, please. How much is it?

---

14 | 화제 고르기

다음을 듣고, 무엇에 관한 설명인지 고르시오.

① 독서대　② 북엔드　③ 북커버
④ 책갈피　⑤ 탁상 램프

적중! Tip　helpful
[헬프풀]보다는 [헬풀]로 들린다. [p]와 [f]처럼 발음할 때 혀의 위치가 비슷한 자음이 나란히 나오면 그중 하나만 발음되기 때문이다.

W This is very helpful when you read books. It is usually long, flat, and _____ _____ _____ _____ . But it also comes in many different designs. It is _____ _____ _____ _____ between two pages. People use it to _____ _____ _____ in a book. With this, people _____ _____ _____ the pages of their books.

대화를 듣고, 여자가 대화 직후에 할 일로 가장 적절한 것을 고르시오.

① 튜브 빌리기   ② 파도풀장 가기
③ 물놀이 기구 타기   ④ 남편 기다리기
⑤ 구명조끼 입기

W How was the water slide, Geonu?
M It was fun! I _____ _____ _____ really fast.
W What will you ride next?
M There's another water ride, but _____ _____ _____ _____ to ride it.
W Well, your dad went to get _____ _____ _____ _____.
M Then, why don't you ride it with me, Mom?
W Sure. I'll _____ _____ _____ _____ now.
M Thanks, Mom.

대화를 듣고, 남자가 배울 악기를 고르시오.

① piano   ② drum   ③ flute
④ violin   ⑤ guitar

🎯 적중! Tip   lesson**s** **s**oon
[레슨즈 쑨]보다는 [레슨쑨]으로 들린다. 비슷하게 발음되는 자음이 나란히 나오면 앞 단어의 끝자음이 탈락되기 때문이다.

M What are your plans tonight, Lily?
W I'll go to my piano lesson. I have a class every Thursday evening.
M When did you _____ _____ _____ _____?
W I started to play the piano _____ _____ _____ _____.
M You must be good then.
W It helps me relax. But what about you? Do you _____ _____ _____?
M I _____ _____ _____ _____ _____, but now I want to play the guitar. I will start lessons soon.
W I _____ _____ _____ _____.

대화를 듣고, 남자의 마지막 말에 대한 여자의 응답으로 가장 적절한 것을 고르시오.

Woman: _____

① The bus was canceled because of heavy snow.
② Yes. It takes over four hours to get there.
③ No. I don't have any sisters or brothers.
④ You are at the wrong stop.
⑤ I like to do short trips by train.

W Excuse me. _____ _____ _____ _____?
M No, it isn't. You can sit here.
W Thank you. The other seats are full, and I don't want to stand _____ _____ _____.
M I understand. Where are you traveling to?
W I will go to Smithville to visit my family.
M _____ _____ _____ _____ is that?
W It's at the end of the train line.
M Oh, wow. It must be _____ _____ _____ then.

18 | 적절한 응답 고르기

대화를 듣고, 여자의 마지막 말에 대한 남자의 응답으로 가장 적절한 것을 고르시오.

Man: _____

① Sure. Keeping a journal seems too hard.
② The topic is your dream job.
③ Right. Taking notes is a good habit.
④ I would love to do that.
⑤ My best friend's name is Tim.

M What is that, Laura?
W It's my journal.
M Do you write in it every day?
W I try to _____ _____ _____ every day, but sometimes I forget.
M What _____ _____ _____ _____ _____?
W I write about school, relationships with friends, and my goals. It _____ _____ _____ and feelings.
M That sounds like a great idea. Maybe I will buy a journal so I can _____ _____ _____ _____ _____.
W Then, why don't we _____ _____ _____ _____ sometime?

고난도

19 | 적절한 응답 고르기

대화를 듣고, 여자의 마지막 말에 대한 남자의 응답으로 가장 적절한 것을 고르시오.

Man: _____

① The time in Switzerland is 11 a.m.
② Please write a thank-you letter to them.
③ I'll try to video call them now.
④ I'll wrap this watch in a box.
⑤ We can't. Everything will be closed today.

🎯 적중! Tip I can't wait to ~.
어떤 일을 몹시 기대하고 있음을 나타낼 때 사용되는 표현으로, to 다음에는 동사원형이 온다.
· I can't wait to go to the play.
  연극 보러 가는 것이 기대돼요.

M What are those, Mom?
W They're _____ _____ _____ _____ in Switzerland.
M Wow, _____ _____ _____ _____?
W I'm not sure. But they're probably presents for Christmas.
M That's nice of them. Can I open the packages now?
W Sure. Just be careful.
M *[Rustling sound]* They _____ _____ _____! I think this one is for me. It's so sophisticated.
W Oh, yes. It seems like _____ _____ _____ _____ _____.
M I will send pictures of it to my friends. I can't wait to wear it.
W First, _____ _____ _____. You need to say thank you.

20 | 상황에 적절한 말 고르기

다음 상황 설명을 듣고, Lucy가 직원에게 할 말로 가장 적절한 것을 고르시오.

Lucy: _____

① Can you repair my bike?
② Don't you need a bike helmet too?
③ Do you have this one in green?
④ Sorry, I'm going to be late this morning.
⑤ Luckily, this model comes in many different colors.

W Lucy _____ _____ _____ her bike to work. However, it's very old, so _____ _____ _____ _____ _____.
She goes to the bike store and _____ _____ _____ _____ _____. But it is black, and Lucy likes the color green.
So, she would like _____ _____ _____ _____ if the bike comes in green. In this situation, what would Lucy most likely say to the employee?

1 대화를 듣고, 두 사람이 구입할 장난감을 고르시오.

①   ②   ③

④   ⑤

2 대화를 듣고, 남자가 여자에게 전화한 목적으로 가장 적절한 것을 고르시오.

① 박물관 위치를 확인하려고
② 박물관 입장료를 문의하려고
③ 박물관이 문을 여는지 알아보려고
④ 박물관 소장품에 대해 물어보려고
⑤ 박물관 투어 일정을 정하려고

3 다음 그림의 상황에 가장 적절한 대화를 고르시오.

① ② ③ ④ ⑤

4 대화를 듣고, 두 사람이 만나기로 한 요일을 고르시오.

① 월요일 ② 수요일 ③ 금요일
④ 토요일 ⑤ 일요일

5 다음을 듣고, 행사에 관해 언급되지 <u>않은</u> 것을 고르시오.

① 목적 ② 시간 ③ 종료 일자
④ 장소 ⑤ 제공 물품

6 대화를 듣고, 두 사람의 관계로 가장 적절한 것을 고르시오.

① 감독 ─ 운동선수 ② 의사 ─ 환자
③ 약사 ─ 손님 ④ 수의사 ─ 견주
⑤ 교사 ─ 학부모

7 다음을 듣고, 두 사람의 대화가 <u>어색한</u> 것을 고르시오.

① ② ③ ④ ⑤

8 대화를 듣고, 남자가 여자에게 부탁한 일로 가장 적절한 것을 고르시오.

① 택시 부르기
② 일몰 사진 찍기
③ 강가 산책하기
④ 영화관 가는 길 알려주기
⑤ 전동 스쿠터 대여 방법 보여주기

9 대화를 듣고, 여자의 마지막 말에 담긴 의도로 가장 적절한 것을 고르시오.

① 제안 ② 충고 ③ 요청
④ 격려 ⑤ 거절

10 대화를 듣고, 여자가 지불할 금액을 고르시오.

① $ 20 ② $ 24 ③ $ 40
④ $ 44 ⑤ $ 60

11 대화를 듣고, 여자가 내일 할 일로 가장 적절한 것을 고르시오.

① 가족 모임 참여하기 ② 체조 수업 듣기
③ 스키 타러 가기 ④ 친구 집 방문하기
⑤ 경기 시청하기

고난도
12 다음을 듣고, 입학 설명회에 관해 언급되지 <u>않은</u> 것을 고르시오.

① 일시   ② 담당자   ③ 참가 방법

④ 설명 내용   ⑤ 준비물

고난도
13 다음 표를 보면서 대화를 듣고, 남자가 대여할 스터디 룸을 고르시오.

	Room	Time	Seating Capacity	Price (an hour)
①	A	9:00~10:00 a.m.	2	$ 6
②	B	9:00~11:00 a.m.	4	$ 8
③	C	9:30~11:30 a.m.	8	$ 12
④	D	1:00~2:00 p.m.	2	$ 5
⑤	E	1:00~3:00 p.m.	4	$ 8

14 다음을 듣고, 무엇에 관한 설명인지 고르시오.

① 볼링   ② 당구   ③ 탁구

④ 스쿼시   ⑤ 배드민턴

15 대화를 듣고, 남자가 대화 직후에 할 일로 가장 적절한 것을 고르시오.

① 멕시코 관광하기   ② 카메라 수리하기

③ 스쿠버 다이빙하기   ④ 사진 보여주기

⑤ 산행 준비하기

16 대화를 듣고, 여자가 탑승하려는 비행기의 출발 시각을 고르시오.

① 9 a.m.   ② 10 a.m.   ③ 11 a.m.

④ 12 p.m.   ⑤ 2 p.m.

17 대화를 듣고, 남자의 마지막 말에 대한 여자의 응답으로 가장 적절한 것을 고르시오.

Woman: _____

① These fruits are ready to pick.

② Okay. Just wait for me to pay for this.

③ No. My favorite flavor is vanilla.

④ The candle you lit smells so good.

⑤ You're not supposed to eat in here.

[18-19] 대화를 듣고, 여자의 마지막 말에 대한 남자의 응답으로 가장 적절한 것을 고르시오.

18 Man: _____

① The street is already wet.

② That shirt is too dirty.

③ I forgot my umbrella this morning.

④ Yes. But I'll do the laundry first.

⑤ Oh, no. We are missing one of our bags.

19 Man: _____

① I didn't get an invitation.

② Let me explain the rules of the game.

③ I ordered a hot dog with mustard.

④ The bakery sold out of cheesecake.

⑤ Sure. I'll make some almond cookies.

20 다음 상황 설명을 듣고, Chanho가 Linda에게 할 말로 가장 적절한 것을 고르시오.

Chanho: Linda, _____

① why don't we take the subway instead?

② can we buy some records after the concert?

③ please arrive early to the show.

④ we should have taken the subway.

⑤ let's check if there are still seats available.

20_회 Dictation

Dictation
음성 바로 듣기 ▶

20회 중학영어듣기 실전 모의고사 Dictation 음성을 들으며 빈칸에 알맞은 단어를 채우시오.

1 | 알맞은 그림 고르기

대화를 듣고, 두 사람이 구입할 장난감을 고르시오.

M Honey, what are we going to buy for our son this Children's Day?
W He is _____ _____ _____ _____ _____ . I suggest we buy one of these sets of toy blocks.
M Good! How about _____ _____ _____ ?
W Well, I think he'd prefer the castle toy.
M Do you mean the _____ _____ _____ _____ ?
W No. That one is too big. That one with _____ _____ _____ _____ is a good size, though.
M Oh, I see. Let's buy it.

2 | 목적 고르기

대화를 듣고, 남자가 여자에게 전화한 목적으로 가장 적절한 것을 고르시오.

① 박물관 위치를 확인하려고
② 박물관 입장료를 문의하려고
③ 박물관이 문을 여는지 알아보려고
④ 박물관 소장품에 대해 물어보려고
⑤ 박물관 투어 일정을 정하려고

[Telephone rings.]
W Thank you for calling the National Art Museum. How can I help you?
M Hi. I'm _____ _____ _____ the special exhibit of Egyptian art.
W Okay. We _____ _____ _____ _____ until June 15th.
M I saw that on your website. But I couldn't find any information _____ _____ _____ .
W Oh, it is eight dollars for students, and 10 dollars _____ _____ _____ _____ .
M Great. Do I need to show my student ID card to _____ _____ _____ ?
W That's right.
M Thank you.

3 | 그림 상황에 적절한 대화 고르기

다음 그림의 상황에 가장 적절한 대화를 고르시오.

① W We should give the dog a bath.
  M Yeah. He played _____ _____ _____ all day.
② W Who left these clothes on the floor?
  M Sorry. I'll _____ _____ _____ now.
③ W I fixed your printer.
  M Thank you so much!
④ W Why are you so dirty?
  M I was _____ _____ _____ _____ all morning.
⑤ W When will lunch be ready?
  M I'm _____ _____ _____ it.

① ② ③ ④ ⑤

4 │ 시간 정보 고르기

대화를 듣고, 두 사람이 만나기로 한 요일을 고르시오.

① 월요일　　② 수요일　　③ 금요일
④ 토요일　　⑤ 일요일

W Hi, David. Do you want to go to the Spring Music Festival this year?
M Of course! ＿＿＿ ＿＿＿ ＿＿＿ ?
W It starts on May 5th, and ＿＿＿ ＿＿＿ ＿＿＿ Sunday.
M Okay. Do you want to go on the Friday?
W I'll be at work ＿＿＿ ＿＿＿ ＿＿＿ ＿＿＿ . What about Sunday?
M I usually eat lunch with my parents.
W ＿＿＿ ＿＿＿ ＿＿＿ ＿＿＿ that week?
M I don't think so. Are you ＿＿＿ ＿＿＿ ＿＿＿ ?
W Fine. Let's go on that day.

5 │ 언급하지 않은 내용 고르기

다음을 듣고, 행사에 관해 언급되지 <u>않은</u> 것을 고르시오.

① 목적　　② 시간　　③ 종료 일자
④ 장소　　⑤ 제공 물품

M Hello, students. This is your student president, Andy Thomas. As some of you already know, we are starting ＿＿＿ ＿＿＿ ＿＿＿ ＿＿＿ called Snack Hour to allow students to take a break. Every day in the library's presentation room from 2 to 3 p.m., we will ＿＿＿ ＿＿＿ ＿＿＿ and iced tea for students. Please come, meet, and ＿＿＿ ＿＿＿ ＿＿＿ for a good break from studying. Maybe this is ＿＿＿ ＿＿＿ ＿＿＿ ＿＿＿ a new friend or study partner. We hope to see you soon!

6 │ 관계 고르기

대화를 듣고, 두 사람의 관계로 가장 적절한 것을 고르시오.

① 감독 — 운동선수　　② 의사 — 환자
③ 약사 — 손님　　④ 수의사 — 견주
⑤ 교사 — 학부모

🎯 적중! Tip　That's why ~.
어떤 일에 대한 이유를 나타낼 때 사용되는 표현으로 '그래서 ~하다, 그것이 ~한 이유이다'라는 의미이다.
· That's why he went to the doctor.
　그래서 그가 진찰을 받았던 거예요.

M Ms. Johns, I'm ＿＿＿ ＿＿＿ ＿＿＿ ＿＿＿ .
W So, ＿＿＿ ＿＿＿ ＿＿＿ ＿＿＿ ?
M He hurt his front right leg. That's why his behavior isn't normal.
W Maybe he got hurt at the park. He was ＿＿＿ ＿＿＿ ＿＿＿ .
M Well, he needs to ＿＿＿ ＿＿＿ ＿＿＿ . He shouldn't run for about a week.
W Okay. Is there anything else I should do?
M I will ＿＿＿ ＿＿＿ ＿＿＿ ＿＿＿ for him.

7 │ 어색한 대화 고르기

다음을 듣고, 두 사람의 대화가 <u>어색한</u> 것을 고르시오.

①　②　③　④　⑤

🎯 적중! Tip　hear**d th**at
[헐드 댓]보다는 [헐댓]으로 들린다. 비슷하게 발음되는 자음이 나란히 나오면 앞 단어의 끝 자음이 탈락되기 때문이다.

① W Excuse me. Can you give me directions to the post office?
　M No problem. Just ＿＿＿ ＿＿＿ ＿＿＿ .
② W This book is ＿＿＿ ＿＿＿ ＿＿＿ ＿＿＿ .
　M Don't worry. The train should be here in 30 minutes.
③ W What size shoes ＿＿＿ ＿＿＿ ＿＿＿ ?
　M My shoe size is 250 millimeters.
④ W ＿＿＿ ＿＿＿ ＿＿＿ me the salt?
　M Here you go.
⑤ W I heard that a new café ＿＿＿ ＿＿＿ Anderson Street.
　M Let's go there this Friday.

대화를 듣고, 남자가 여자에게 부탁한 일로 가장 적절한 것을 고르시오.

① 택시 부르기
② 일몰 사진 찍기
③ 강가 산책하기
④ 영화관 가는 길 알려주기
⑤ 전동 스쿠터 대여 방법 보여주기

M That was a nice movie.
W Yes, it was. _____ _____ _____ _____ now?
M Why don't we watch the sunset somewhere?
W Okay. There's _____ _____ _____ _____ the sunset near the river.
M Well, the sun is _____ _____ _____. How far is it?
W It's a little far. We can rent some of those electric scooters.
M Okay. But I don't know _____ _____ _____ _____.
  Can you show me how to do it?
W Sure. It's easy.

대화를 듣고, 여자의 마지막 말에 담긴 의도로 가장 적절한 것을 고르시오.

① 제안   ② 충고   ③ 요청
④ 격려   ⑤ 거절

🎯 적중! Tip | I see.
상대방의 말을 듣고 이해했음을 나타낼 때 사용되는 표현이다.

W Are you looking for something?
M Yeah. I can't find _____ _____ _____ anywhere.
W I see. Does your laptop _____ _____ _____ _____?
M No. It's completely out of power. And I need it to do some research.
W _____ _____ _____ do you have?
M It's an Orange Book 7.
W I have the same one. How about _____ _____ _____ _____?

대화를 듣고, 여자가 지불할 금액을 고르시오.

① $ 20   ② $ 24   ③ $ 40
④ $ 44   ⑤ $ 60

M Are you _____ _____ _____?
W Yes. I'd like to buy these two cups.
M Alright. _____ _____ _____ _____ 10 dollars. Do you also want to buy some of these plates? They're discounted right now.
W No, thank you. But can you _____ _____ _____?
M These over here are _____ _____ _____ _____.
  They're 12 dollars each.
W _____ _____ _____. I'll take two.
M Okay, so it's 20 dollars for the cups and 24 dollars for the bowls.
W Thank you. Here is my card.

대화를 듣고, 여자가 내일 할 일로 가장 적절한 것을 고르시오.

① 가족 모임 참여하기   ② 체조 수업 듣기
③ 스키 타러 가기   ④ 친구 집 방문하기
⑤ 경기 시청하기

[Cellphone rings.]
M Hey, Charlotte. What are you doing?
W I'm with my friend Helen, Dad.
M Do you need anything?
W Helen _____ _____ _____ _____ with her family tomorrow. Can I go?
M Oh, I'm so sorry, but you have _____ _____ _____ tomorrow.
W I forgot about that. We can _____ _____ _____ then.
M Okay. I'll see you at home soon.

고난도

12 | 언급하지 않은 내용 고르기

다음을 듣고, 입학 설명회에 관해 언급되지 <u>않은</u> 것을 고르시오.

① 일시　　② 담당자　　③ 참가 방법
④ 설명 내용　　⑤ 준비물

🎯 적중! Tip　visi**t o**ur

[비짓 아월]보다는 [비지라월]로 들린다. [t]가 모음 사이에서 발음될 때는 약화되어 [r]에 가깝게 발음되기 때문이다.

W Hello, students. My name is Sumin Lee, and I'm _____ _____ the online information sessions for the National Art School. As you know, _____ _____ _____ _____ next Tuesday at 10 a.m. If you want to participate, please visit our website. We will _____ _____ _____, curriculum guidelines, and more. I'll contact you if _____ _____ _____ _____. Thank you.

고난도

13 | 도표에서 알맞은 항목 고르기

다음 표를 보면서 대화를 듣고, 남자가 대여할 스터디룸을 고르시오.

	Room	Time	Seating Capacity	Price (an hour)
①	A	9:00~10:00 a.m.	2	$ 6
②	B	9:00~11:00 a.m.	4	$ 8
③	C	9:30~11:30 a.m.	8	$ 12
④	D	1:00~2:00 p.m.	2	$ 5
⑤	E	1:00~3:00 p.m.	4	$ 8

M Hi. I'd like to _____ _____ _____ _____ for tomorrow morning.
W How long will you use it?
M I need it for at least _____ _____ _____ _____. Maybe even longer.
W How many people will be using it?
M _____ _____ _____ _____.
W In that case, you have two options.
M How much is _____ _____ _____?
W It's 12 dollars an hour.
M That's too expensive. I'll _____ _____ _____ _____.
W Okay. Please write down your name and number here.

14 | 화제 고르기

다음을 듣고, 무엇에 관한 설명인지 고르시오.

① 볼링　　② 당구　　③ 탁구
④ 스쿼시　　⑤ 배드민턴

M This is an indoor sport. People of all ages can enjoy this sport. To play this game, people roll a heavy ball _____ _____ _____ _____. There are 10 pins _____ _____ _____ _____ _____ _____ at the end of the track. A player must _____ _____ _____ to score points. Players can play this sport on teams or _____ _____ _____ _____.

대화를 듣고, 남자가 대화 직후에 할 일로 가장 적절한 것을 고르시오.

① 멕시코 관광하기　　② 카메라 수리하기
③ 스쿠버 다이빙하기　④ 사진 보여주기
⑤ 산행 준비하기

W _____ _____ _____ _____ in Mexico, Junseo?
M It was fantastic. I didn't want to come home.
W What did you do?
M I went _____, _____, _____ _____ _____.
W Wow! Did you see any cool fish while scuba diving?
M Of course. I _____ _____ _____ with my camera.
W You can take your camera underwater?
M Yeah. I'll _____ _____ _____ _____ now.

대화를 듣고, 여자가 탑승하려는 비행기의 출발 시각을 고르시오.

① 9 a.m.　　② 10 a.m.　　③ 11 a.m.
④ 12 p.m.　　⑤ 2 p.m.

W Jiho, can you _____ _____ _____ _____ _____ to Jeju?
M Sure, Mom. Let me just get my laptop. *[Pause]* What time _____ _____ _____ _____ _____ tomorrow?
W The conference starts at 2 p.m. Is there a flight _____ _____ _____ _____ _____ at 12 p.m.?
M Hold on. *[Typing sound]* No. But there are seats on a flight that leaves at 10 a.m. and arrives at 11.
W That means I would have to be at the airport by 9. It's _____ _____ _____ _____ I planned, but I guess it's my only option.
M Okay. I'll _____ _____ _____ on the 10 a.m. flight.
W Thanks.

대화를 듣고, 남자의 마지막 말에 대한 여자의 응답으로 가장 적절한 것을 고르시오.

Woman: _____

① These fruits are ready to pick.
② Okay. Just wait for me to pay for this.
③ No. My favorite flavor is vanilla.
④ The candle you lit smells so good.
⑤ You're not supposed to eat in here.

> 🎯 적중! Tip　this store
>
> [디스 스토어]보다는 [디스토어]로 들린다. 발음이 같은 자음이 나란히 나오면 앞 단어의 끝 자음이 탈락되기 때문이다.
>
> · gas station [개스테이션]　· of view [오뷰]

M What are you looking for, Kelly?
W I'm _____ _____ _____ _____ _____. I can't decide on one.
M What do they smell like?
W This one _____ _____ _____, and this one smells like vanilla.
M I like vanilla more, but _____ _____ _____.
W I'll buy the vanilla one. Do you _____ _____ _____ this store?
M No. But do you want to get some macarons after this? The shop is _____ _____ _____ _____ _____.

18 | 적절한 응답 고르기

대화를 듣고, 여자의 마지막 말에 대한 남자의 응답으로 가장 적절한 것을 고르시오.

Man: _____

① The street is already wet.
② That shirt is too dirty.
③ I forgot my umbrella this morning.
④ Yes. But I'll do the laundry first.
⑤ Oh, no. We are missing one of our bags.

W Are you _____ _____ _____ _____, Logan?
M Not yet, Mom. I want to check the weather before I pack.
W It will _____ _____ _____ _____, so pack lots of pants and long sleeves.
M Do I have _____ _____ some of my clothes?
W Yes. But do it _____ _____ _____ _____. We leave early on Wednesday, and they'll need time to dry.
M Okay. I'll do that right now.
W Oh, and will you _____ _____ _____ pack? He might _____ _____ _____ with it.

19 | 적절한 응답 고르기

대화를 듣고, 여자의 마지막 말에 대한 남자의 응답으로 가장 적절한 것을 고르시오.

Man: _____

① I didn't get an invitation.
② Let me explain the rules of the game.
③ I ordered a hot dog with mustard.
④ The bakery sold out of cheesecake.
⑤ Sure. I'll make some almond cookies.

> 🎯 적중! Tip almost finished
> [얼모스트 피니쉬드]보다는 [얼모스피니쉬드]로 들린다. 자음 3개가 연속해서 나오면 중간 자음은 발음되지 않기 때문이다.

M Beth, are you _____ _____ _____ _____ for the end of the year?
W Yes! I'm _____ _____ _____ and food.
M Are you almost finished?
W Yes. I came up with lots of fun games. But I think _____ _____ _____ _____ _____.
M What food will there be?
W We will have hot dogs, but I need to find a dessert too.
M Well, I'm really _____ _____ _____ and love to make cookies. I could make some for the party.
W Really? I think _____ _____ _____ _____ _____.

20 | 상황에 적절한 말 고르기

다음 상황 설명을 듣고, Chanho가 Linda에게 할 말로 가장 적절한 것을 고르시오.

Chanho: Linda, _____

① why don't we take the subway instead?
② can we buy some records after the concert?
③ please arrive early to the show.
④ we should have taken the subway.
⑤ let's check if there are still seats available.

M Chanho is going to a concert with Linda. It starts at 7 p.m. Linda _____ _____ _____ _____ there. However, Chanho is worried that they would be late _____ _____ _____ _____ _____. He is very excited about the concert, so he doesn't want to be late. Therefore, he wants to ask Linda _____ _____ _____ instead. In this situation, what would Chanho most likely say to Linda?

www.HackersBook.com

고난도
모의고사

21~24회 고난도 모의고사

1 대화를 듣고, 남자가 구입할 자물쇠를 고르시오.

① ② ③

④ ⑤

2 대화를 듣고, 발표에 관해 언급되지 <u>않은</u> 것을 고르시오.

① 주제　　② 시각 자료　　③ 준비 기간
④ 길이　　⑤ 점수

3 대화를 듣고, 여자가 남자에게 전화한 목적으로 가장 적절한 것을 고르시오.

① 가구 주문을 취소하려고
② 음식 배달을 주문하려고
③ 행사 비용을 문의하려고
④ 영업시간을 확인하려고
⑤ 저녁 식사를 예약하려고

4 대화를 듣고, 여자가 음악실을 재방문할 시각을 고르시오.

① 3:30 p.m.　② 4:00 p.m.　③ 4:30 p.m.
④ 5:00 p.m.　⑤ 5:30 p.m.

5 대화를 듣고, 남자의 심정으로 가장 적절한 것을 고르시오.

① joyful　　② scared　　③ nervous
④ confident　⑤ surprised

6 다음 그림의 상황에 가장 적절한 대화를 고르시오.

①　　②　　③　　④　　⑤

7 대화를 듣고, 여자가 남자에게 부탁한 일로 가장 적절한 것을 고르시오.

① 이사 도와주기　　　② 시청 방문하기
③ 쿠키 사다 주기　　　④ 참석 인원 확인하기
⑤ 관광지 추천해주기

8 다음을 듣고, 댄스 학교에 관해 언급되지 <u>않은</u> 것을 고르시오.

① 수업 종류　② 교사 이름　③ 수업 시간
④ 수업 비용　⑤ 등록 방법

9 다음을 듣고, 어떤 직업에 관한 설명인지 고르시오.

① 수학자　　② 통계 분석가　③ 회계사
④ 경제학자　⑤ 물리학자

10 다음을 듣고, 두 사람의 대화가 <u>어색한</u> 것을 고르시오.

①　　②　　③　　④　　⑤

11 대화를 듣고, 여자가 할 일로 가장 적절한 것을 고르시오.

① 링크 전달하기　　　② 관람 신청하기
③ 이탈리아 여행하기　④ 영상 시청하기
⑤ 박물관 방문하기

12 다음 표를 보면서 대화를 듣고, 여자가 구매할 기차표를 고르시오.

	Train	Destination	Express	Departure Time
①	A	Daegu	X	7:00 p.m.
②	B	Daegu	O	7:00 p.m.
③	C	Daegu	O	9:00 p.m.
④	D	Busan	X	9:00 p.m.
⑤	E	Busan	O	11:00 p.m.

13 대화를 듣고, 두 사람이 만나기로 한 시각을 고르시오.

① 10:30 a.m. ② 12:30 p.m. ③ 1:00 p.m.
④ 1:30 p.m. ⑤ 3:00 p.m.

14 대화를 듣고, 남자가 지난 수요일에 한 일로 가장 적절한 것을 고르시오.

① 구두 쇼핑하기 ② 축가 연습하기
③ 정장 구매하기 ④ 백화점 방문하기
⑤ 결혼식 참석하기

15 다음을 듣고, 방송의 목적으로 가장 적절한 것을 고르시오.

① 출발 지연을 알리려고
② 목적지 변경에 대해 알리려고
③ 날씨 정보를 제공하려고
④ 난기류 대비 사항을 전달하려고
⑤ 식사 메뉴를 설명하려고

16 대화를 듣고, 여자가 지불할 금액을 고르시오.

① $ 15 ② $ 18 ③ $ 20
④ $ 23 ⑤ $ 25

17 대화를 듣고, 남자의 마지막 말에 대한 여자의 응답으로 가장 적절한 것을 고르시오.

Woman: _____

① She didn't bring a pen to class.
② All right. I'll go to an eye clinic then.
③ Write this down, please.
④ No. I didn't see a sign anywhere.
⑤ Okay. I'll change my seat.

[18-19] 대화를 듣고, 여자의 마지막 말에 대한 남자의 응답으로 가장 적절한 것을 고르시오.

18 Man: _____

① He scored a lot in the game last night.
② That's a shame. I wish you could come.
③ Her family invited me over for dinner.
④ Your seats are in that section.
⑤ Good. Let's meet in front of the stadium.

19 Man: _____

① Perfect! I'll call to make a reservation now.
② There were so many people at the party last night.
③ Then, I have to cancel my plans.
④ She already sent out the invitations.
⑤ The food here is too spicy.

20 다음 상황 설명을 듣고, Lily가 Tommy에게 할 말로 가장 적절한 것을 고르시오.

Lily: Tommy, _____

① good luck with the competition!
② you played beautifully today.
③ you'll do better next time.
④ how often do you practice?
⑤ what is the name of this song?

21회 중학영어듣기 고난도 모의고사 Dictation 음성을 들으며 빈칸에 알맞은 단어를 채우시오.

1 | 알맞은 그림 고르기

대화를 듣고, 남자가 구입할 자물쇠를 고르시오.

① ② ③

④ ⑤

W Hello. Do you need help?
M Yes. I'm looking for a lock.
W We have key locks and number locks. _____ _____ _____ _____ ?
M I think I would _____ _____ _____ . So, I'd better get a number lock.
W Okay. _____ _____ _____ _____ _____ a three-digit or a four-digit combination.
M I'd like a three-digit combination lock.
W Got it. Now, please _____ _____ _____ . You can choose between these two. We have square and heart ones.
M _____ _____ _____ is perfect. I'll take it.
W Good choice.

2 | 언급하지 않은 내용 고르기

대화를 듣고, 발표에 관해 언급되지 않은 것을 고르시오.

① 주제　　② 시각 자료　　③ 준비 기간
④ 길이　　⑤ 점수

🎯 적중! Tip **wh**ole

[호울]로 발음된다. 단어의 맨 처음에 쓰인 wh-에서 [w]나 [h] 중 하나는 묵음이다.
· **w**ho [후]　· **wh**y [와이]

W _____ _____ _____ _____ _____ , Carl! I learned so much about turtles.
M Thanks, Linda.
W _____ _____ _____ _____ were really helpful. I want to do something like that for my next speech.
M You should. Pictures _____ _____ _____ _____ _____ things.
W Did it _____ _____ _____ _____ _____ to prepare?
M Yes. I also practiced the whole presentation several times a day _____ _____ _____ .
W I see. Well, _____ _____ _____ that A+.
M Thanks for the compliment!

3 | 목적 고르기

대화를 듣고, 여자가 남자에게 전화한 목적으로 가장 적절한 것을 고르시오.

① 가구 주문을 취소하려고
② 음식 배달을 주문하려고
③ 행사 비용을 문의하려고
④ 영업시간을 확인하려고
⑤ 저녁 식사를 예약하려고

[Cellphone rings.]
M The Garden Restaurant. How may I help you?
W Hello. _____ _____ _____ _____ _____ two tonight at 8.
M I'm sorry, but we can't accept any more reservations. The restaurant _____ _____ _____ tonight.
W Oh, that's too bad.

M The holiday is very busy for us. We do _____ _____ _____ _____, though.

W No, thanks. I'm just looking for _____ _____ _____ _____ tonight.

M I understand. Have a good day.

W You too.

4 | 시간 정보 고르기

대화를 듣고, 여자가 음악실을 재방문할 시각을 고르시오.

① 3:30 p.m.   ② 4:00 p.m.   ③ 4:30 p.m.
④ 5:00 p.m.   ⑤ 5:30 p.m.

W Good morning, Mr. Wilkins. Do you _____ _____ ?

M Sorry, but I'm just going to _____ _____ _____ now.

W I wanted to ask _____ _____ _____ _____.

M Then, could you come back to the music room at 4 today?

W _____ _____ _____ will end at 5. Would 5:30 be okay?

M Sure. I'll be free after 5, so that will give us _____ _____ _____ _____ _____.

W Great. I'll see you then.

5 | 심정 고르기

대화를 듣고, 남자의 심정으로 가장 적절한 것을 고르시오.

① joyful   ② scared   ③ nervous
④ confident   ⑤ surprised

🎯 적중! Tip   How come?
어떤 상황에 대해 의아한 느낌을 담아 이유를 물을 때 사용되는 표현으로 '어째서?, 왜?'라는 의미이다.

W Martin, you're looking good today.

M Thanks. I have _____ _____ _____ this afternoon.

W Oh, you _____ _____ _____.

M Actually, I'm not that nervous.

W That's a bit surprising. ♂ How come?

M I _____ _____ _____ _____ at the company last summer.

W Wow. Lucky you! Then, the interview will _____ _____ _____.

M Yeah. Unless there's an unexpected problem, I'm sure I'll _____ _____ _____.

6 | 그림 상황에 적절한 대화 고르기

다음 그림의 상황에 가장 적절한 대화를 고르시오.

① ② ③ ④ ⑤

① W Do you think you can fix it?
   M No. We _____ _____ _____ _____ _____ _____.
② W Would you please _____ _____ _____ ?
   M Oh, okay. I almost forgot to do that.
③ W Take me to Main Street, please.
   M Sure. It'll take 20 minutes to get there.
④ W _____ _____ _____ _____ _____ ?
   M It's on the corner of this street.
⑤ W _____ _____ _____ _____ _____ today.
   M Maybe there was an accident.

대화를 듣고, 여자가 남자에게 부탁한 일로 가장 적절한 것을 고르시오.

① 이사 도와주기　　② 시청 방문하기
③ 쿠키 사다 주기　　④ 참석 인원 확인하기
⑤ 관광지 추천해주기

🎯 적중! Tip　How about ~?

어떤 일을 제안하거나 권유할 때 사용되는 표현으로 '~하는 게 어때?'라는 의미이다. 이때 about 다음에는 동명사가 온다.

· How about taking the bus?
  버스를 타는 게 어때?

W　Henry, are you going on the club trip to Centerville this weekend?
M　Yes. I'm so excited. Are you also going?
W　No, I can't. _____ _____ _____ to a new apartment on Saturday.
M　That's a pity. I wanted _____ _____ _____ _____ with you.
W　Actually, I went there last summer.
M　Really? Can you recommend any good places?
W　One of _____ _____ _____ there is peanut cookies. How about trying some?
M　Sounds good! _____ _____ _____ _____ _____ ?
W　There are stores by City Hall. If you go, could you _____ _____ _____ _____ ?
M　Of course.

다음을 듣고, 댄스 학교에 관해 언급되지 <u>않은</u> 것을 고르시오.

① 수업 종류　② 교사 이름　③ 수업 시간
④ 수업 비용　⑤ 등록 방법

W　Hello, customers. This is Lola from Blue Rhythm Dance School. I'm so happy to share that we will _____ _____ _____ _____ at our school _____ _____ _____ the tap, jazz, and ballroom dancing classes we already hold. The class's teacher is Emily Blake, _____ _____ _____ at the local ballet company. She will teach a ballet class _____ _____ _____ _____ at 7 p.m. and for higher levels on Tuesdays at 6 p.m. Please call us soon to sign up. We _____ _____ _____ _____ you there!

다음을 듣고, 어떤 직업에 관한 설명인지 고르시오.

① 수학자　　② 통계 분석가　③ 회계사
④ 경제학자　⑤ 물리학자

W　People who have this job have _____ _____ _____ _____ _____ . They help companies and people record the amounts of money they _____ _____ _____ . They also help people when they need to _____ _____ _____ _____ _____ . To do this job, you must pass a difficult exam and have good math skills.

다음을 듣고, 두 사람의 대화가 어색한 것을 고르시오.

①　②　③　④　⑤

① M　We _____ _____ _____ _____ _____ , right?
　 W　That sounds great.
② M　How often do you go to the gym?
　 W　I _____ _____ _____ _____ _____ .
③ M　Did you hear that the Joan's Furniture Store is closing?
　 W　I didn't. _____ _____ _____ .

④ **M** Do you want to go for a walk with me?

W No. I _____ _____ _____ _____ this homework.

⑤ **M** Wow. You have so many books in your room.

W Well, I _____ _____ _____ .

11 | 할 일 고르기

대화를 듣고, 여자가 할 일로 가장 적절한 것을 고르시오.

① 링크 전달하기 ② 관람 신청하기
③ 이탈리아 여행하기 ④ 영상 시청하기
⑤ 박물관 방문하기

M What video are you watching, Haeun?

W Oh, this is _____ _____ _____ .

M What's that?

W A tour guide in another part of the world _____ _____ _____ _____ _____ online.

M That's cool. So, you can see a famous place _____ _____ _____ _____ ?

W Exactly. I'll _____ _____ _____ _____ for the website. I'm taking a tour of an Italian museum right now.

M Thank you. I'd love to try it.

12 | 도표에서 알맞은 항목 고르기

다음 표를 보면서 대화를 듣고, 여자가 구매할 기차표를 고르시오.

	Train	Destination	Express	Departure Time
①	A	Daegu	X	7:00 p.m.
②	B	Daegu	O	7:00 p.m.
③	C	Daegu	O	9:00 p.m.
④	D	Busan	X	9:00 p.m.
⑤	E	Busan	O	11:00 p.m.

M May I help you?

W Yes, please. _____ _____ _____ _____ to Busan.

M There's a train at 9 p.m.

W Is it _____ _____ _____ ?

M No, ma'am. It'll take more than four hours to reach Busan.

W Oh, no. I have to get there _____ _____ _____ _____ _____ .

M Why don't you take the express train to Daegu and _____ _____ ?

W When does the train for Daegu leave?

M There's one at 7 p.m. and another at 9 p.m.

W I'll take _____ _____ _____ .

13 | 시간 정보 고르기

대화를 듣고, 두 사람이 만나기로 한 시각을 고르시오.

① 10:30 a.m. ② 12:30 p.m. ③ 1:00 p.m.
④ 1:30 p.m. ⑤ 3:00 p.m.

W Greg, would you like to go to the amusement park on Saturday?

M _____ _____ _____ . Should we meet at 3 p.m.?

W I'd prefer to _____ _____ _____ _____ . Can you come to the amusement park at 10:30 a.m.?

M I _____ _____ _____ _____ at 10.

W Oh, I see. Then, how about 1 p.m.?

M Do you want to eat something first? We _____ _____ _____ _____ at 12:30 and then enter the amusement park at around 1:30.

W Good idea.

14 | 한 일 고르기

대화를 듣고, 남자가 지난 수요일에 한 일로 가장 적절한 것을 고르시오.

① 구두 쇼핑하기　　② 축가 연습하기
③ 정장 구매하기　　④ 백화점 방문하기
⑤ 결혼식 참석하기

> **적중! Tip** we**dd**ing
>
> [웨딩]보다는 [웨링]으로 들린다. [d]가 모음 사이에서 발음될 때는 약화되어 [r]에 가깝게 발음되기 때문이다.

W _____ _____ _____ Rose's wedding, Michael?
M Of course. Are you?
W Yes. But I still _____ _____ _____ _____ _____
　 for it. I'm a little worried because the wedding is so soon.
M I _____ _____ _____ _____ last Wednesday, but I should buy
　 some new shoes.
W We can go to the mall together _____ _____ _____.
M Sure. When do you want to go?
W Maybe we should go tonight. I don't _____ _____ _____
　 _____ _____ the wedding.
M All right.

15 | 목적 고르기

다음을 듣고, 방송의 목적으로 가장 적절한 것을 고르시오.

① 출발 지연을 알리려고
② 목적지 변경에 대해 알리려고
③ 날씨 정보를 제공하려고
④ 난기류 대비 사항을 전달하려고
⑤ 식사 메뉴를 설명하려고

M Good evening, everyone. This is your captain speaking. I've turned on
　 the seatbelt sign. This is because we _____ _____ _____
　 _____ _____. We expect some turbulence in a few minutes. It
　 will be a little bumpy, so please _____ _____ _____
　 _____. Also, the meal service will be a little delayed. Dinner will
　 only be served when we _____ _____ _____ the storm.
　 Thanks in advance _____ _____ _____.

16 | 금액 정보 고르기

대화를 듣고, 여자가 지불할 금액을 고르시오.

① $ 15　　② $ 18　　③ $ 20
④ $ 23　　⑤ $ 25

> **적중! Tip** discoun**t** coupon
>
> [디스카운트 쿠폰]보다는 [디스카운쿠폰]으로 들린다. 자음 3개가 연속해서 나오면 중간 자음은 발음되지 않기 때문이다.

M Welcome to Delicious Chicken. How may I help you?
W _____ _____ _____ _____ the original fried chicken.
M That will be 15 dollars. _____ _____ _____ _____ soda and fries
　 as well?
W Sure. How much are those?
M Those are an extra five dollars. Your total is 20 dollars.
W Okay. Do _____ _____ _____ _____ _____ _____?
M We have cookies for three dollars.
W I'll have _____ _____ _____ _____ _____. Can I
　 use this discount coupon?
M Yes. It will _____ _____ _____ _____ of your total.
W Great.

17 | 적절한 응답 고르기

대화를 듣고, 남자의 마지막 말에 대한 여자의 응답으로 가장 적절한 것을 고르시오.

Woman: _____

① She didn't bring a pen to class.
② All right. I'll go to an eye clinic then.
③ Write this down, please.
④ No. I didn't see a sign anywhere.
⑤ Okay. I'll change my seat.

M What's wrong, Soyoung?
W I don't understand my math notes. _____ _____ _____.
M Let me see. [Pause] Oh, you didn't write everything down.
W I had to sit in the back of the class, so I _____ _____
　 _____ _____.
M You _____ _____ _____ _____. They can help you
　 see the board from far away.

W I know, but I heard they _____ _____ _____. So, I don't want to wear them.

M But glasses will help you in class. I suggest that you _____ _____ _____ _____ first.

18 | 적절한 응답 고르기

대화를 듣고, 여자의 마지막 말에 대한 남자의 응답으로 가장 적절한 것을 고르시오.

Man: _____

① He scored a lot in the game last night.
② That's a shame. I wish you could come.
③ Her family invited me over for dinner.
④ Your seats are in that section.
⑤ Good. Let's meet in front of the stadium.

W Hey, what happened? You look so happy.

M _____ _____ _____ _____ _____ to a basketball game!

W Wow, that's great! Which game _____ _____ _____ _____?

M I will watch the Eagles play the Dragons.

W _____ _____ _____. The Dragons are my favorite team.

M You can _____ _____ _____ if you want. It should be a great game.

W Really? That's so nice. When is it?

M It's on Friday night at 7.

W Oh, no! I _____ _____ my grandparents then.

19 | 적절한 응답 고르기

대화를 듣고, 여자의 마지막 말에 대한 남자의 응답으로 가장 적절한 것을 고르시오.

Man: _____

① Perfect! I'll call to make a reservation now.
② There were so many people at the party last night.
③ Then, I have to cancel my plans.
④ She already sent out the invitations.
⑤ The food here is too spicy.

W Are you doing anything this Sunday, Ben?

M It's Annie's birthday on Sunday, so I want to _____ _____ _____.

W Oh, I forgot about her birthday! Did she make any plans yet?

M No. But I plan _____ _____ _____ _____ _____ for her.

W Good idea. Can I help?

M Sure. But first, we need to _____ _____ _____ for the party.

W Annie _____ _____ _____. What about Tasty Pho?

20 | 상황에 적절한 말 고르기

다음 상황 설명을 듣고, Lily가 Tommy에게 할 말로 가장 적절한 것을 고르시오.

Lily: Tommy, _____

① good luck with the competition!
② you played beautifully today.
③ you'll do better next time.
④ how often do you practice?
⑤ what is the name of this song?

🎯 **적중! Tip** hi**s s**ong

[히즈 쏭]보다는 [히쏭]으로 들린다. 비슷하게 발음되는 자음이 나란히 나오면 앞 단어의 끝 자음이 탈락되기 때문이다.

W Lily is attending a piano competition. She is there to _____ _____ _____ _____ Tommy. When it is Tommy's _____ _____ _____, he plays his song perfectly. Soon after, the judges announce that he _____ _____ _____. Lily goes to give Tommy flowers and a card when the award ceremony is finished. She wants to tell him that he _____ _____ _____ _____. In this situation, what would Lily most likely say to Tommy?

1 대화를 듣고, 여자가 구입할 스케이트보드를 고르시오.

①   ②   ③

④   ⑤

2 대화를 듣고, 영화 Wonder-Man에 관해 언급되지 <u>않</u>은 것을 고르시오.

① 개봉일 ② 등장인물 ③ 배경
④ 결말 ⑤ 속편 여부

3 대화를 듣고, 여자가 남자에게 전화한 목적으로 가장 적절한 것을 고르시오.

① 통신 장비를 구입하려고
② 방문 일자를 정하려고
③ 제품 수리를 요청하려고
④ 사무실 임대를 문의하려고
⑤ 설치 비용을 안내하려고

4 대화를 듣고, 남자가 선택한 에어로빅 수업의 시작 시각을 고르시오.

① 12 p.m. ② 1 p.m. ③ 2 p.m.
④ 4 p.m. ⑤ 5 p.m.

5 대화를 듣고, 두 사람이 대화하는 장소로 가장 적절한 곳을 고르시오.

① 백화점 ② 공원 ③ 화장품 가게
④ 식당 ⑤ 우체국

6 다음 그림의 상황에 가장 적절한 대화를 고르시오.

① ② ③ ④ ⑤

7 대화를 듣고, 여자가 남자에게 부탁한 일로 가장 적절한 것을 고르시오.

① 추천서 작성하기 ② 신청서 출력하기
③ 진로 상담하기 ④ 여름 캠프 참석하기
⑤ 방학 계획 알려주기

8 다음을 듣고, 축제에 관해 언급되지 <u>않</u>은 것을 고르시오.

① 날짜 ② 시간 ③ 장소
④ 활동 ⑤ 대표국 수

9 다음을 듣고, 무엇에 관한 설명인지 고르시오.

① 자 ② 연필 ③ 가위
④ 형광펜 ⑤ 수정테이프

10 다음을 듣고, 두 사람의 대화가 <u>어색한</u> 것을 고르시오.

① ② ③ ④ ⑤

11 대화를 듣고, 남자가 대화 직후에 할 일로 가장 적절한 것을 고르시오.

① 컴퓨터 게임 하기 ② 강아지 산책시키기
③ 슈퍼마켓 가기 ④ 과학 숙제하기
⑤ 봉사 활동하기

12 다음 건물 배치도를 보면서 대화를 듣고, 두 사람이 선택할 호텔을 고르시오.

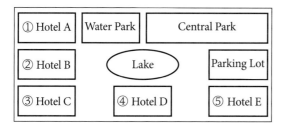

13 대화를 듣고, 두 사람이 뮤지컬을 관람할 날짜를 고르시오.

① 11월 18일   ② 11월 19일   ③ 11월 20일

④ 11월 21일   ⑤ 11월 22일

14 대화를 듣고, 여자가 어제 한 일로 가장 적절한 것을 고르시오.

① 쪽지 시험 준비하기   ② 볼링 치기

③ 연극 감상하기   ④ 친구와 쇼핑 가기

⑤ 감상평 전달하기

15 다음을 듣고, 방송의 목적으로 가장 적절한 것을 고르시오.

① 화재 시 대피 요령을 알리려고

② 나무 심기의 중요성을 강조하려고

③ 소방관의 업무에 대해 소개하려고

④ 화재 사고 예방법을 설명하려고

⑤ 신속한 화재 진압 방법을 안내하려고

16 대화를 듣고, 남자가 지불할 금액을 고르시오.

① $ 26   ② $ 36   ③ $ 46

④ $ 56   ⑤ $ 66

17 대화를 듣고, 여자의 마지막 말에 대한 남자의 응답으로 가장 적절한 것을 고르시오.

Man: _____

① The boat comes every 30 minutes.

② No. I didn't book it yet.

③ Then, I should wear a life jacket for safety.

④ Got it. I'll get there by 10:45 a.m.

⑤ The best time to visit is in June.

[18-19] 대화를 듣고, 남자의 마지막 말에 대한 여자의 응답으로 가장 적절한 것을 고르시오.

18 **Woman:** _____

① You can gain more muscle with exercise.

② I will pick up some food on my way home.

③ You can take this salad for your lunch.

④ That's great. I ought to eat healthier too.

⑤ Oh, that's why you added salt to the soup.

19 **Woman:** _____

① I need to buy a new charger.

② Watch out. You're driving too fast.

③ Okay. I will create a playlist.

④ My pleasure. Here is my phone.

⑤ We're sold out of that puzzle.

20 다음 상황 설명을 듣고, Nathan이 사서에게 할 말로 가장 적절한 것을 고르시오.

Nathan: _____

① You can read it after me.

② The science fiction books are located over here.

③ What is your favorite animal?

④ The books about animal health are checked out now.

⑤ Where is the animal section?

22회 중학영어듣기 고난도 모의고사 Dictation 음성을 들으며 빈칸에 알맞은 단어를 채우시오.

1 | 알맞은 그림 고르기

대화를 듣고, 여자가 구입할 스케이트보드를 고르시오.

① ② ③
④ ⑤

M Welcome. How may I help you?
W Hi, I'd like to buy my first skateboard.
M All right. We have _____ _____ _____ _____ _____.
W Actually, I _____ _____ _____ _____ _____ on it. What do you think? Would it be good for a beginner?
M Well, it's too narrow. I _____ _____ _____ _____. It will be safer and easier to balance on.
W I see. Then, could you show me wider ones with a similar print?
M Sure. How about these ones with _____ _____ _____?
W I prefer the one _____ _____ _____ "RUN" on it.
M Okay.

2 | 언급하지 않은 내용 고르기

대화를 듣고, 영화 Wonder-Man에 관해 언급되지 않은 것을 고르시오.

① 개봉일   ② 등장인물   ③ 배경·
④ 결말   ⑤ 속편 여부

M Did you see the new *Wonder-Man* movie?
W Yeah. I watched it on the day _____ _____ _____.
M Oh, yeah? I saw it on Wednesday too.
W _____ _____ _____ _____ _____ Thomas Moreland?
M He's great. I love _____ _____ _____, Dr. Perplexo too.
W I know. The atmosphere was terrifying. _____ _____ _____ _____ _____ was weird, though.
M Yeah. I didn't understand the ending at all.
W Maybe the next *Wonder-Man* movie will _____ _____.
M I hope so.

3 | 목적 고르기

대화를 듣고, 여자가 남자에게 전화한 목적으로 가장 적절한 것을 고르시오.

① 통신 장비를 구입하려고
② 방문 일자를 정하려고
③ 제품 수리를 요청하려고
④ 사무실 임대를 문의하려고
⑤ 설치 비용을 안내하려고

[Cellphone rings.]
M Hello. _____ _____ Rob.
W Hi, this is Tina from QualNet Cable. You _____ _____ _____ _____ yesterday.
M Right. _____ _____ _____ in the message, I need a Wi-Fi connection installed in my new office.
W Yes. We can _____ _____ _____ tomorrow.
M Great! What time will _____ _____ _____ _____?
W We'll send someone between the hours of 2 p.m. and 6 p.m.
M That will work. But please call me _____ _____ _____.

4 | 시간 정보 고르기

대화를 듣고, 남자가 선택한 에어로빅 수업의 시작 시각을 고르시오.

① 12 p.m.   ② 1 p.m.   ③ 2 p.m.
④ 4 p.m.   ⑤ 5 p.m.

W Welcome to the Power Fitness Center. How can I help you?
M I'd like to ＿＿＿＿ ＿＿＿＿ ＿＿＿＿ ＿＿＿＿ on Saturdays. Do you have one that starts at 3 p.m.?
W No, but there is one at 1. It ends at 2.
M I usually have lunch at 12, and I don't like to ＿＿＿＿ ＿＿＿＿ ＿＿＿＿ ＿＿＿＿ ＿＿＿＿.
W Then, what about 4? We have ＿＿＿＿ ＿＿＿＿ ＿＿＿＿ ＿＿＿＿.
M So, it ends at 5?
W That's right. It is one hour long.
M Okay. I'll ＿＿＿＿ ＿＿＿＿ ＿＿＿＿ that class.

5 | 장소 고르기

대화를 듣고, 두 사람이 대화하는 장소로 가장 적절한 곳을 고르시오.

① 백화점   ② 공원   ③ 화장품 가게
④ 식당   ⑤ 우체국

⊙ 적중! Tip send some

[센드 썸]보다는 [센썸]으로 들린다. 자음 3개가 연속해서 나오면 중간 자음은 발음되지 않기 때문이다.

W Hello. What can I do for you?
M I need to ＿＿＿＿ ＿＿＿＿ ＿＿＿＿ to Australia.
W Alright. What is in the package?
M I'd like to send some skin-care products like face masks to a friend.
W So, there's ＿＿＿＿ ＿＿＿＿ ＿＿＿＿?
M No. Those are the only items.
W Okay. Then, please fill out this form. You must ＿＿＿＿ ＿＿＿＿ ＿＿＿＿ ＿＿＿＿ so the package goes to the correct place.
M Got it. Also, I'd like to select ＿＿＿＿ ＿＿＿＿ ＿＿＿＿ ＿＿＿＿.
W Okay. Then, your package will ＿＿＿＿ ＿＿＿＿ ＿＿＿＿ ＿＿＿＿ in three days.

6 | 그림 상황에 적절한 대화 고르기

다음 그림의 상황에 가장 적절한 대화를 고르시오.

① ② ③ ④ ⑤

① M How long does it take to get to Mirae University?
　 W It takes 30 minutes on foot.
② M Could I ＿＿＿＿ ＿＿＿＿ ＿＿＿＿, please?
　 W Of course. Here you go.
③ M I believe you are ＿＿＿＿ ＿＿＿＿ ＿＿＿＿ ＿＿＿＿.
　 W Oh, sorry. I'll move.
④ M I hope ＿＿＿＿ ＿＿＿＿ ＿＿＿＿ ＿＿＿＿.
　 W It was a lot of fun.
⑤ M Is the pool open today?
　 W It is closed ＿＿＿＿ ＿＿＿＿ ＿＿＿＿.

대화를 듣고, 여자가 남자에게 부탁한 일로 가장 적절한 것을 고르시오.

① 추천서 작성하기   ② 신청서 출력하기
③ 진로 상담하기   ④ 여름 캠프 참석하기
⑤ 방학 계획 알려주기

W I'm sorry, Mr. Evans. Are you busy?
M Not at all. Do you need something?
W I want to go to _____ _____ _____ _____ this summer. I'm working on an application now.
M That's great! You _____ _____ science.
W Well, I need two recommendations for the application. It's _____ _____ _____ _____ .
M Who will you ask?
W _____ _____ _____ _____ for me? I'll get my science teacher from last year to write the other one.
M _____ _____ _____ write one for you.

다음을 듣고, 축제에 관해 언급되지 <u>않은</u> 것을 고르시오.

① 날짜   ② 시간   ③ 장소
④ 활동   ⑤ 대표국 수

W Hello, students. This is your principal, Ms. Foster. I'm excited to _____ _____ _____ _____ our school's annual culture festival. The event _____ _____ _____ on August 15th. It'll be held from 10 a.m. to 5 p.m. Each class will set up a booth and _____ _____ , _____ , _____ _____ representing a chosen country's culture. There will be over 10 countries represented at the event. Students will _____ _____ _____ _____ _____ and enjoying the rest of the festival. Parents and friends are also welcome to attend. We hope to see you there!

다음을 듣고, 무엇에 관한 설명인지 고르시오.

① 자   ② 연필   ③ 가위
④ 형광펜   ⑤ 수정테이프

W This is _____ _____ _____ _____ _____ _____ school supplies. It is _____ _____ _____ _____ _____ . It is long and thin, and it comes in many different bright colors. With this, we can color words on a paper to help them _____ _____ _____ other words. We can use it to emphasize important information. We simply remove its cap and _____ _____ _____ on words we want to color to use it.

다음을 듣고, 두 사람의 대화가 <u>어색한</u> 것을 고르시오.

①   ②   ③   ④   ⑤

🎯 **적중! Tip** Is it okay if ~?

상대방에게 어떤 일을 해도 되는지 허가 여부를 물을 때 사용되는 표현이다.

· Is it okay if I open the window?
  내가 창문을 열어도 괜찮을까?

① **M** Excuse me. Where is the restroom?
   W It's _____ _____ _____ _____ .
② **M** I _____ _____ _____ _____ _____ on my English test.
   W Nice. Congratulations!
③ **M** This soup is too spicy.
   W Really? It _____ _____ _____ _____ _____ .
④ **M** Is it okay if I use your calculator?
   W Sure. It's in my desk.
⑤ **M** Can you turn down the volume? The music is too loud.
   W Let me _____ _____ _____ for you.

11 | 할 일 고르기

대화를 듣고, 남자가 대화 직후에 할 일로 가장 적절한 것을 고르시오.

① 컴퓨터 게임 하기   ② 강아지 산책시키기
③ 슈퍼마켓 가기   ④ 과학 숙제하기
⑤ 봉사 활동하기

[Cellphone rings.]

M What's up, Mom?

W Hi, Joonwon. _____ _____ _____ _____?

M I'm playing some games. I just got home from school.

W Remember to _____ _____ _____ _____.
I don't want you to stay up late.

M Sure. By the way, where are you?

W I'm taking your brother to _____ _____ _____ now. Then,
I'll stop by the supermarket.

M You won't be home for a while then. Should I take the dog _____
_____ _____?

W Yes. That would be great.

M Okay. _____ _____ _____ now.

12 | 위치 고르기

다음 건물 배치도를 보면서 대화를 듣고, 두 사람이 선택할 호텔을 고르시오.

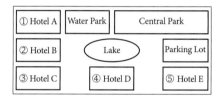

① Hotel A	Water Park	Central Park
② Hotel B	Lake	Parking Lot
③ Hotel C	④ Hotel D	⑤ Hotel E

M I'm so excited for our trip to LA!

W Me too. But we still _____ _____ _____ _____
_____ at a hotel.

M Originally, I wanted to stay at Hotel D. But _____ _____
_____ _____.

W It's because they have a beautiful view of the lake and Central Park.

M I know. I _____ _____ _____ _____ _____ of the
parking lot, though.

W Also, Hotel C _____ _____ _____ because other hotels are
blocking the view.

M In that case, we have two choices left.

W Let's stay at the hotel _____ _____ the water park.

M Yeah. I _____ _____ _____.

13 | 시간 정보 고르기

대화를 듣고, 두 사람이 뮤지컬을 관람할 날짜를 고르시오.

① 11월 18일   ② 11월 19일   ③ 11월 20일
④ 11월 21일   ⑤ 11월 22일

 적중! Tip visiting

[비지팅]보다는 [비지링]으로 들린다. [t]가 모음 사이에
서 발음될 때는 약화되어 [r]에 가깝게 발음되기 때문이다.

[Cellphone rings.]

M Hello?

W Hi, James. I just _____ _____ _____ for *Welcome to the
Nation*. Remember we talked about that musical last week?

M Oh, yeah! I remember _____ _____ _____ _____. I'd
love to see it soon. When does it premiere?

W Next week. I think _____ _____ _____ is on Wednesday.

M That'd be the 19th, right?

W Yeah. November 19th.

M I _____ _____ _____ _____ _____ then. My grandmother's
visiting our house on that day.

W Then, _____ _____ _____ _____ _____ _____? I want
to watch it before long.

M _____ _____ on that day. I'll book the tickets now.

대화를 듣고, 여자가 어제 한 일로 가장 적절한 것을 고르시오.

① 쪽지 시험 준비하기　② 볼링 치기
③ 연극 감상하기　　　④ 친구와 쇼핑 가기
⑤ 감상평 전달하기

> ⊙ 적중! Tip ha**ve** **f**un
>
> [해브 펀]보다는 [해펀]으로 들린다. [v]와 [f]처럼 발음할 때 혀의 위치가 비슷한 자음이 나란히 나오면 앞 단어의 끝 자음이 탈락되기 때문이다.
> · ha**ve f**orever [해포레버]
> · mo**ve f**orward [무포월드]

M　Sally, I heard you ＿＿＿＿＿ ＿＿＿＿＿ ＿＿＿＿＿ ＿＿＿＿＿ with Greg yesterday. How was it?

W　Actually, we didn't go.

M　Oh, no. What happened?

W　Greg was told his class ＿＿＿＿＿ ＿＿＿＿＿ ＿＿＿＿＿ ＿＿＿＿＿ today. So, we decided to go to a play this Sunday instead.

M　What did you do yesterday then?

W　I met another friend and ＿＿＿＿＿ ＿＿＿＿＿ ＿＿＿＿＿ ＿＿＿＿＿.

M　That sounds nice. Anyway, I hope you have fun this Sunday.

W　Thanks. I'll ＿＿＿＿＿ ＿＿＿＿＿ ＿＿＿＿＿ ＿＿＿＿＿ next week.

다음을 듣고, 방송의 목적으로 가장 적절한 것을 고르시오.

① 화재 시 대피 요령을 알리려고
② 나무 심기의 중요성을 강조하려고
③ 소방관의 업무에 대해 소개하려고
④ 화재 사고 예방법을 설명하려고
⑤ 신속한 화재 진압 방법을 안내하려고

M　Hello. This is Samuel Reddy from the Riverside Fire Station. I want to talk to you about ＿＿＿＿＿ ＿＿＿＿＿ ＿＿＿＿＿ ＿＿＿＿＿ that cause fires. Fires can start in many ways. At home, they often start in the kitchen. When cooking, never ＿＿＿＿＿ ＿＿＿＿＿ ＿＿＿＿＿ ＿＿＿＿＿ for long. Stay near the oven or stove, or check it often. Also, unplug ＿＿＿＿＿ ＿＿＿＿＿ ＿＿＿＿＿ when they are not in use. Leaking electricity can easily cause a fire. Lastly, store flammable objects properly. ＿＿＿＿＿ ＿＿＿＿＿ ＿＿＿＿＿ ＿＿＿＿＿ ＿＿＿＿＿, and you'll be much safer.

대화를 듣고, 남자가 지불할 금액을 고르시오.

① $ 26　　② $ 36　　③ $ 46
④ $ 56　　⑤ $ 66

W　Welcome to Home Goods Store. Do you need any help?

M　Hello, I'd like to buy this pillow. How much is it?

W　It's 13 dollars, but there's ＿＿＿＿＿ ＿＿＿＿＿ ＿＿＿＿＿ today. If you buy two, you can get one for free.

M　Three for 26 dollars? That's a good deal. I'll take ＿＿＿＿＿ ＿＿＿＿＿ ＿＿＿＿＿ then.

W　Great. Are you interested in anything else?

M　Actually, yes. ＿＿＿＿＿ ＿＿＿＿＿ ＿＿＿＿＿ ＿＿＿＿＿ too. How much is that one?

W　It's 20 dollars.

M　I'll ＿＿＿＿＿ ＿＿＿＿＿ ＿＿＿＿＿ ＿＿＿＿＿.

대화를 듣고, 여자의 마지막 말에 대한 남자의 응답으로 가장 적절한 것을 고르시오.

Man: ＿＿＿＿＿＿＿＿＿＿＿＿＿＿＿

① The boat comes every 30 minutes.
② No. I didn't book it yet.
③ Then, I should wear a life jacket for safety.
④ Got it. I'll get there by 10:45 a.m.
⑤ The best time to visit is in June.

[Cellphone rings.]

M　Hello?

W　Hi. This is Olivia from Amazing Boat Tours. I'm calling to ＿＿＿＿＿ ＿＿＿＿＿ ＿＿＿＿＿.

M　Oh, yes. The tour is tomorrow, right?

W　That's correct. You booked a tour for 11 a.m.

M　Excellent. ＿＿＿＿＿ ＿＿＿＿＿ ＿＿＿＿＿ ＿＿＿＿＿?

W It will be about two hours long. Please bring _____ _____ _____ _____ because it will be very sunny.

M What else do I need to do?

W _____ _____ _____ _____ _____ before boarding, so arrive at least 15 minutes early.

18 | 적절한 응답 고르기

대화를 듣고, 남자의 마지막 말에 대한 여자의 응답으로 가장 적절한 것을 고르시오.

Woman: _____

① You can gain more muscle with exercise.
② I will pick up some food on my way home.
③ You can take this salad for your lunch.
④ That's great. I ought to eat healthier too.
⑤ Oh, that's why you added salt to the soup.

> 🎯 적중! Tip I find myself ~.
> 자신의 근황이나 생각을 나타낼 때 사용되는 표현으로 '나는 ~하게 되다, 나는 최근 ~하다'라는 의미이다.
> · I find myself dreaming of becoming a singer.
>   난 가수가 되는 걸 꿈꾸게 됐어.

W Your lunch _____ _____ _____, Zach.

M Yeah. I'm _____ _____ _____ _____ nowadays.

W Why is that?

M I watched a documentary about fast food. It's really _____ _____ _____ _____.

W That's true. How has your diet changed then?

M I eat _____ _____ _____ _____, and I have fast food only on the weekend.

W Do you feel any difference?

M Actually, I _____ _____ _____ now. Also, I find myself liking less salty food.

19 | 적절한 응답 고르기

대화를 듣고, 남자의 마지막 말에 대한 여자의 응답으로 가장 적절한 것을 고르시오.

Woman: _____

① I need to buy a new charger.
② Watch out. You're driving too fast.
③ Okay. I will create a playlist.
④ My pleasure. Here is my phone.
⑤ We're sold out of that puzzle.

W When will we arrive, Dad?

M We need to drive for another two hours.

W But _____ _____ _____. This drive is so long.

M I know. But I must drive slowly in the snow.

W Can I _____ _____ _____? It's almost out of battery.

M Sure. Why don't you solve a crossword puzzle while it is charging?

W Okay. Can you also _____ _____ _____?

M My phone is connected to the speakers. _____ _____ _____.

20 | 상황에 적절한 말 고르기

다음 상황 설명을 듣고, Nathan이 사서에게 할 말로 가장 적절한 것을 고르시오.

Nathan: _____

① You can read it after me.
② The science fiction books are located over here.
③ What is your favorite animal?
④ The books about animal health are checked out now.
⑤ Where is the animal section?

> 🎯 적중! Tip book about
> [북 어바웃]보다는 [부커바웃]으로 들린다. 앞에 나온 단어의 끝 자음과 뒤에 나온 단어의 첫 모음이 연음되기 때문이다.

W Nathan wants to become a vet. So, he _____ _____ _____ _____ to find a book about animals. While he is there, Nathan sees _____ _____ _____ books on a variety of topics. However, he _____ _____ _____ books related to animals. He decides to ask the librarian where _____ _____ _____ _____. In this situation, what would Nathan most likely say to the librarian?

1 대화를 듣고, 남자가 만들 신발 가방을 고르시오.

① 　② 　③

④ 　⑤

2 대화를 듣고, 여자가 남자에게 부탁한 일로 가장 적절한 것을 고르시오.

① 우승 상품 준비하기　② 노인회관 방문하기
③ 바닷가 함께 가기　④ 보드게임 고르기
⑤ 체스 대회 감독하기

3 다음 그림의 상황에 가장 적절한 대화를 고르시오.

①　　②　　③　　④　　⑤

4 대화를 듣고, 박물관에서 두 사람이 함께 참가할 프로그램의 시작 시각을 고르시오.

① 9 a.m.　② 10 a.m.　③ 12 p.m.
④ 2 p.m.　⑤ 4 p.m.

5 대화를 듣고, 체육관에 관해 언급되지 않은 것을 고르시오.

① 회원권 종류　② 회원권 가격
③ 운동복 제공 여부　④ 운영 시간
⑤ 샤워 시설

6 대화를 듣고, 두 사람이 대화하는 장소로 가장 적절한 곳을 고르시오.

① 휴게소　② 호텔　③ 버스 터미널
④ 정비소　⑤ 카페

7 다음을 듣고, 두 사람의 대화가 어색한 것을 고르시오.

①　　②　　③　　④　　⑤

8 대화를 듣고, 여자가 남자에게 부탁한 일로 가장 적절한 것을 고르시오.

① 수학 시험 범위 알려주기
② 숙제 같이 하기
③ 학교생활 상담해주기
④ 자습서 추천해주기
⑤ 과외 선생님 연락처 알려주기

9 다음을 듣고, 무엇에 관한 안내 방송인지 고르시오.

① 주간 일기 예보　② 배달 지연 현황
③ 부두 위치 변경　④ 선박 관광 취소
⑤ 도로 공사 일정

10 대화를 듣고, 남자가 지불할 금액을 고르시오.

① $ 20　② $ 25　③ $ 30
④ $ 35　⑤ $ 40

11 대화를 듣고, 남자가 할 일로 가장 적절한 것을 고르시오.

① 엄마 선물 사기　② 식료품점 찾기
③ 식탁 정리하기　④ 무용 수업 듣기
⑤ 식재료 구매하기

12 다음을 듣고, 노트북에 관해 언급하지 <u>않은</u> 것을 고르시오.

① 모델명　　　② 무게　　　③ 보안 기능
④ 충전 시간　⑤ 메모리 사양

13 다음 표를 보면서 대화를 듣고, 두 사람이 관람할 영화를 고르시오.

	Movie	Genre	Actor	Time
①	A	Horror	Adam Surley	12:30 p.m.
②	B	Horror	James Collins	2:00 p.m.
③	C	Comedy	Adam Surley	12:30 p.m.
④	D	Comedy	James Collins	12:30 p.m.
⑤	E	Comedy	James Collins	2:00 p.m.

14 다음을 듣고, 무엇에 관한 설명인지 고르시오.

① 다이빙　　　② 자유형　　　③ 수구
④ 비치 발리볼　⑤ 수중발레

15 대화를 듣고, 남자가 할 일로 가장 적절한 것을 고르시오.

① 포스터 제작하기　　　② 실험 준비하기
③ 기후 전망 발표하기　　④ 빙하기 조사하기
⑤ 대본 작성하기

16 대화를 듣고, 여자가 예약한 공항 셔틀버스의 출발 시각을 고르시오.

① 6 a.m.　　② 7 a.m.　　③ 8 a.m.
④ 9 a.m.　　⑤ 11 a.m.

17 대화를 듣고, 남자의 마지막 말에 대한 여자의 응답으로 가장 적절한 것을 고르시오.

Woman: _____

① It's your turn to play the game.
② I'll let you know when I finish the starting level.
③ Both of my parents are from Seoul.
④ It's boring. I want to return my purchase.
⑤ Sure. Get your phone out so I can show you.

18 대화를 듣고, 여자의 마지막 말에 대한 남자의 응답으로 가장 적절한 것을 고르시오.

Man: _____

① The mop is in the closet.
② I appreciate your help.
③ This machine is taken right now.
④ I just sent you the money.
⑤ Please clean the lobby first.

19 대화를 듣고, 남자의 마지막 말에 대한 여자의 응답으로 가장 적절한 것을 고르시오.

Woman: _____

① You can see the mountains from the terrace.
② Take a picture of me beside this tree.
③ Okay. I'll take care of that now.
④ Can you tell me where the restroom is?
⑤ I'm sorry that I spilled my drink.

20 다음 상황 설명을 듣고, Ms. Brown이 Mark에게 할 말로 가장 적절한 것을 고르시오.

Ms. Brown: Mark, _____

① I'd like you to read this story I wrote.
② why don't you sign up for the competition?
③ who is your favorite author these days?
④ you should not be late for English class.
⑤ I'm impressed that you were the winner.

23회 중학영어듣기 고난도 모의고사 Dictation 음성을 들으며 빈칸에 알맞은 단어를 채우시오.

1 | 알맞은 그림 고르기

대화를 듣고, 남자가 만들 신발 가방을 고르시오.

① ② ③
④ ⑤

M Mom, do you know _____ _____ _____ a zipper to a bag?
W Sorry, but _____ _____ _____ _____ . Why do you ask?
M I'm trying to make a shoe bag to _____ _____ _____ _____ _____ .
W Wow! Did you make it all on your own?
M Yes. I was thinking of drawing a horse on it, but I changed my mind. I _____ _____ _____ on it and added these two handles.
W Awesome! But I don't think it needs a zipper. How about just _____ _____ _____ ?
M That's a good idea. Thanks.

2 | 부탁·요청한 일 고르기

대화를 듣고, 여자가 남자에게 부탁한 일로 가장 적절한 것을 고르시오.

① 우승 상품 준비하기 ② 노인회관 방문하기
③ 바닷가 함께 가기 ④ 보드게임 고르기
⑤ 체스 대회 감독하기

W Darling, do you want to go to the beach this weekend?
M Well, we _____ _____ _____ on Saturday.
W That's right. I completely forgot. We'll be at _____ _____ _____ , right?
M Yes. We'll oversee the board games activity time.
W Okay. I'll _____ _____ _____ _____ _____ to take.
M Should we also _____ _____ _____ for the winners?
W Sure. But I need a favor. I won't _____ _____ _____ _____ _____ them on Friday.
M No problem. I can visit the store before then.

3 | 그림 상황에 적절한 대화 고르기

다음 그림의 상황에 가장 적절한 대화를 고르시오.

① ② ③ ④ ⑤

① W Would you like to _____ _____ _____ _____ ?
　 M Let's do it tomorrow.
② W Pets _____ _____ _____ in the store.
　 M Oh, I didn't realize that.
③ W Can I _____ _____ _____ ?
　 M Sure. He's very friendly.
④ W _____ _____ _____ _____ here?
　 M I don't think it is allowed.
⑤ W I can't _____ _____ _____ .
　 M Did you check in the kitchen?

4 | 시간 정보 고르기

대화를 듣고, 박물관에서 두 사람이 함께 참가할 프로그램의 시작 시각을 고르시오.

① 9 a.m.　　② 10 a.m.　　③ 12 p.m.
④ 2 p.m.　　⑤ 4 p.m.

[Cellphone rings.]

W Hi, Mike. I think you're _____ _____, right?

M Yes. Science is my favorite subject. Why?

W The Museum of Science is _____ _____ _____ _____ during the holiday. Why don't we join one on Saturday?

M That sounds interesting. But could we do it in the morning? I will _____ _____ with Dave from 2 to 4 that afternoon.

W Sure. There are two programs in the morning. I like to join the program _____ _____ _____. It starts at 9.

M Well, _____ _____ _____ _____ the one about 3D printing that starts at 10 instead?

W No. _____ _____ _____ too. Let's go to it together.

5 | 언급하지 않은 내용 고르기

대화를 듣고, 체육관에 관해 언급되지 <u>않은</u> 것을 고르시오.

① 회원권 종류　　② 회원권 가격
③ 운동복 제공 여부　　④ 운영 시간
⑤ 샤워 시설

🎯 적중! Tip　Feel free to ~.

상대방이 부탁하거나 요청한 일을 기꺼이 허락해 줄 때 사용되는 표현으로 '부담 없이 ~하세요, 얼마든지 ~하세요'라는 의미이다. 이때 to 다음에는 동사원형이 온다.

· Feel free to call me.
　부담 없이 전화 주세요.

[Telephone rings.]

M Hero Gym. How can I help you?

W Hello. I _____ _____ _____ at your gym, so I want to ask some questions about the membership.

M Okay. Please feel free to ask.

W How long _____ _____ _____ _____ _____?

M We have memberships for three months, six months, and a year. They cost 150 dollars, 240 dollars, and 360 dollars.

W _____ _____ _____ _____? Are they provided?

M For newly registered members, gym clothes _____ _____ _____ _____ for three months.

W Are you open around 10 p.m. today?

M Yes. We're open 24 hours a day _____ _____ _____.

W Okay. Thank you!

6 | 장소 고르기

대화를 듣고, 두 사람이 대화하는 장소로 가장 적절한 곳을 고르시오.

① 휴게소　　② 호텔　　③ 버스 터미널
④ 정비소　　⑤ 카페

🎯 적중! Tip　walk around

[워크 어라운드]보다는 [워커라운드]로 들린다. 앞에 나온 단어의 끝 자음이 뒤에 나온 단어의 첫 모음이 연음되기 때문이다.

W I need to walk around after _____ _____ _____ _____ so long.

M Well, we will be here for a few minutes because I need to _____ _____ _____ _____.

W How much longer will we drive after this?

M Traffic is bad, so it will take another three hours to get to the hotel.

W I will _____ _____ _____ on the way back to the car. Do you want anything?

M I'd like some grilled potatoes and _____ _____ _____ _____, please.

W Alright.

7 | 어색한 대화 고르기

다음을 듣고, 두 사람의 대화가 <u>어색한</u> 것을 고르시오.

①   ②   ③   ④   ⑤

🎯 적중! Tip   rea**d th**e

[레드 더]보다는 [레더]로 들린다. read가 과거형이나 과거분사형으로 쓰일 때는 [레드]로 발음되고, 비슷하게 발음되는 자음이 나란히 나오면 앞 단어의 끝 자음이 탈락되기 때문이다.

① W   I love your sunglasses.
    M   Thanks. I _____ _____ yesterday.
② W   How do you like my new song?
    M   It _____ _____. I really like it.
③ W   Where did you _____ _____ _____ for bulgogi?
    M   I found it online.
④ W   Have you ever read the book *Amy in Madrid*?
    M   No. I've _____ _____ _____.
⑤ W   Do you have any plans for this weekend?
    M   I'm going _____ _____ _____ my friends.

8 | 부탁·요청한 일 고르기

대화를 듣고, 여자가 남자에게 부탁한 일로 가장 적절한 것을 고르시오.

① 수학 시험 범위 알려주기
② 숙제 같이 하기
③ 학교생활 상담해주기
④ 자습서 추천해주기
⑤ 과외 선생님 연락처 알려주기

M   Are you okay, Kelly? You _____ _____ _____.
W   I'm not doing well in my math class, so I'm stressed _____
    _____ _____.
M   Do you spend enough time on your homework?
W   I spend _____ _____ _____ _____
    _____, but it's always difficult for me to do.
M   Well, my math tutor is really helpful. I _____ _____ _____
    _____ a lot with him.
W   Will you _____ _____ _____ _____ _____? I
    could use some help.
M   Sure. I'll text you his information.

9 | 주제 고르기

다음을 듣고, 무엇에 관한 안내 방송인지 고르시오.

① 주간 일기 예보   ② 배달 지연 현황
③ 부두 위치 변경   ④ 선박 관광 취소
⑤ 도로 공사 일정

M   Attention, please. This is _____ _____ _____ TSI Tours.
I'm sorry to announce that today's glass-bottom boat tour _____
_____. Strong winds are expected, and this _____ _____
_____ _____ the fish and other marine life. It is
also dangerous because _____ _____ _____ _____
the boat may be overturned. You'll be able to _____ _____
_____ _____ or exchange your ticket for another time with no
charge. Again, I'd like to apologize for the inconvenience.

10 | 금액 정보 고르기

대화를 듣고, 남자가 지불할 금액을 고르시오.

① $ 20   ② $ 25   ③ $ 30
④ $ 35   ⑤ $ 40

W   Hello. _____ _____ _____ _____?
M   Yes. I'd like two tickets for the 5 p.m. train to New York.
W   The tickets are 20 dollars each. It's 40 dollars in total. Would you like to
    pay more for _____ _____ _____ _____?
M   _____ _____ _____ do I have to pay?
W   It would be an extra 10 dollars per person.

M No, thank you. I'll just get _____ _____ _____ _____.
But can I use this coupon too?

W Sure. With that coupon, you can get a five-dollar discount _____
_____ _____ _____.

M Excellent.

11 | 할 일 고르기

대화를 듣고, 남자가 할 일로 가장 적절한 것을 고르시
오.

① 엄마 선물 사기　②식료품점 찾기
③ 식탁 정리하기　④무용 수업 듣기
⑤ 식재료 구매하기

W Hey, Siwoo. What are you doing?

M _____ _____ _____ for my mom. What about you?

W I'm on my way to my modern dance class.

M I _____ _____ _____ _____.

W Yes. I take lessons three times a week.

M Does the lesson start soon?

W No. I _____ _____ _____ _____. Do you want me to
come to the store with you?

M Sure. I'm just going to _____ _____ _____ for dinner
tonight. My mom is busy at home.

W Okay. I'll _____ _____ _____ _____.

12 | 언급하지 않은 내용 고르기

다음을 듣고, 노트북에 관해 언급하지 <u>않은</u> 것을 고르
시오.

① 모델명　②무게　③ 보안 기능
④ 충전 시간　⑤메모리 사양

🎯 적중! Tip **ex**istence
[이그지스턴스]로 발음된다. [ex]는 [이그즈], [엑스], [익스]
중 하나로 발음된다.

W Hello, welcome to our showcase. I'll introduce you to _____
_____ _____ _____, the Air 20. This is the lightest laptop
in existence at only 920 grams. _____ _____ _____ makes
it easy to carry around. Moreover, after charging for 30 minutes, the
battery _____ _____ _____ 20 hours. As for the safety
features, you can log in _____ _____ _____ _____.
Please try the sample products at the front of the room, and _____
_____ _____ if you have any questions.

13 | 도표에서 알맞은 항목 고르기

다음 표를 보면서 대화를 듣고, 두 사람이 관람할 영화
를 고르시오.

	Movie	Genre	Actor	Time
①	A	Horror	Adam Surley	12:30 p.m.
②	B	Horror	James Collins	2:00 p.m.
③	C	Comedy	Adam Surley	12:30 p.m.
④	D	Comedy	James Collins	12:30 p.m.
⑤	E	Comedy	James Collins	2:00 p.m.

M Jess, which movie do you want to watch?

W How about _____ _____ _____ _____? Adam Surley
is my favorite actor.

M Sorry, but I really don't like horror movies.

W Oh, it's okay. Hmm... Why don't we _____ _____ _____?
I'd like _____ _____ _____.

M Sure. _____ _____ _____ James Collins?

W Yeah. His movies are always hilarious.

M Great. It's 11:50 a.m. now. Should we eat something before the movie?

W I _____ _____ _____ _____ _____, so I'm not that hungry.

M Me neither. Then, let's watch _____ _____ _____.

W Sure.

14 | 화제 고르기

다음을 듣고, 무엇에 관한 설명인지 고르시오.

① 다이빙　　② 자유형　　③ 수구
④ 비치 발리볼　　⑤ 수중발레

M This is a water sport. _____ _____ _____ in the summer Olympics. Team members _____ _____ to music. They move together, _____ _____ . Once the performance is finished, the team is evaluated. The judge gives the team a score _____ _____ _____ _____ the members moved together. The judge also considers how the performance _____ _____ _____ _____ . The team that receives the highest score is the winner of the competition.

15 | 할 일 고르기

대화를 듣고, 남자가 할 일로 가장 적절한 것을 고르시오.

① 포스터 제작하기　　② 실험 준비하기
③ 기후 전망 발표하기　　④ 빙하기 조사하기
⑤ 대본 작성하기

> 🎯 적중! Tip Wha**t** **e**lse
> [왓 앨스]보다는 [와랠스]로 들린다. [t]가 모음 사이에서 발음될 때는 약화되어 [r]에 가깝게 발음되기 때문이다.

W Our poster _____ _____ _____ looks perfect. This will be an amazing presentation.
M I agree, but we _____ _____ .
W What else do we need to do?
M We have to _____ _____ _____ .
W Well, you are _____ _____ _____ . How about I write the script, and then you present to the class?
M That's fine with me. I'll add _____ _____ _____ _____ _____ of the global climate at the end.

16 | 시간 정보 고르기

대화를 듣고, 여자가 예약한 공항 셔틀버스의 출발 시각을 고르시오.

① 6 a.m.　　② 7 a.m.　　③ 8 a.m.
④ 9 a.m.　　⑤ 11 a.m.

W Excuse me. Does this hotel offer a free airport shuttle? I _____ _____ _____ _____ _____ tomorrow morning.
M We do have one. What time does _____ _____ _____ ?
W It leaves at 11 a.m. But I need to be at the airport _____ _____ _____ _____ earlier.
M Then, can I book you on the 6 a.m. shuttle? You will get to the airport at 8.
W That's a little too early. Is there _____ _____ _____ at 7?
M Yes. And it arrives at the airport at 9.
W Perfect. Please _____ _____ _____ on that shuttle.
M No problem. I'll just need your name and room number, please.

17 | 적절한 응답 고르기

대화를 듣고, 남자의 마지막 말에 대한 여자의 응답으로 가장 적절한 것을 고르시오.

Woman: _____

① It's your turn to play the game.
② I'll let you know when I finish the starting level.
③ Both of my parents are from Seoul.
④ It's boring. I want to return my purchase.
⑤ Sure. Get your phone out so I can show you.

M What did you do last night, Jihyo?
W I _____ _____ with my parents and played that new phone game.
M The one you downloaded yesterday?
W Yes. I _____ _____ _____ to play it.
M What level are you on?

W I just got to level eight. But it _____ _____ _____

_____.

M Wow! _____ _____ _____. I also downloaded the game,
but I'm only on level three.

W Do you _____ _____ _____ _____ ?

M Yes. But I'm not doing so well on it right now. Can you help me

_____ _____ _____ _____ _____ ?

18 | 적절한 응답 고르기

대화를 듣고, 여자의 마지막 말에 대한 남자의 응답으로 가장 적절한 것을 고르시오.

Man: _____

① The mop is in the closet.
② I appreciate your help.
③ This machine is taken right now.
④ I just sent you the money.
⑤ Please clean the lobby first.

🎯 적중! Tip Could you put me through to ~?

전화 통화에서 다른 사람이 전화를 받았을 때 통화하길 원하는 사람을 바꿔 달라고 부탁하기 위해 사용되는 표현이다. 이때 to 다음에는 바꿔 달라고 할 사람의 이름이 온다.

[Telephone rings.]

W Hello?

M This is Cleaning Solutions. ♂Could you put me through to Mr. Jones?

W I'm sorry, but he's _____ _____ _____ _____ at the
moment.

M Can you _____ _____ _____ _____ then?

W Sure. What is it?

M Please tell him that our team _____ _____ _____
_____ _____ tomorrow. We will reduce the price for the
cleaning _____ _____ _____.

W Alright. I'll _____ _____
later.

19 | 적절한 응답 고르기

대화를 듣고, 남자의 마지막 말에 대한 여자의 응답으로 가장 적절한 것을 고르시오.

Woman: _____

① You can see the mountains from the terrace.
② Take a picture of me beside this tree.
③ Okay. I'll take care of that now.
④ Can you tell me where the restroom is?
⑤ I'm sorry that I spilled my drink.

M Is this table okay, Mina?

W Yes! _____ _____ _____ _____ _____. I really
like the terrace of this café.

M Me too. And sitting outside _____ _____ _____.

W Yeah. I prefer sitting outside over sitting inside.

M Do you want some tea? It looks like they have many kinds.

W Yeah. I will _____ _____ _____. But first I need to wash
my hands. Do you need _____ _____ _____ ?

M Actually, can you tell someone to _____ _____ _____
_____ by our table? It's a little cold.

20 | 상황에 적절한 말 고르기

다음 상황 설명을 듣고, Ms. Brown이 Mark에게 할 말로 가장 적절한 것을 고르시오.

Ms. Brown: Mark, _____

① I'd like you to read this story I wrote.
② why don't you sign up for the competition?
③ who is your favorite author these days?
④ you should not be late for English class.
⑤ I'm impressed that you were the winner.

M Ms. Brown is Mark's English teacher. She thinks that he is _____
_____ _____ _____. This is because _____ _____
_____ many imaginative and interesting stories for her class. In
fact, she feels that he has the potential to be _____ _____
_____ someday. So, she wants to suggest that he _____
_____ _____ _____ _____ for students. In this
situation, what would Ms. Brown most likely say to Mark?

1 대화를 듣고, 여자가 구입할 냉장고 자석을 고르시오.

①   ②   ③

④   ⑤

2 다음을 듣고, 스마트 화분에 관해 언급되지 <u>않은</u> 것을 고르시오.

① 회사명   ② 제품명   ③ 기능
④ 가격   ⑤ 이용 방법

3 대화를 듣고, 남자가 여자에게 전화한 목적으로 가장 적절한 것을 고르시오.

① 예약을 취소하려고
② 숙박 기간을 연장하려고
③ 위치를 물어보려고
④ 비용을 문의하려고
⑤ 방문 시간을 알리려고

4 대화를 듣고, 여자가 강당을 사용하기로 한 요일을 고르시오.

① 월요일   ② 화요일   ③ 수요일
④ 목요일   ⑤ 금요일

5 대화를 듣고, 여자의 심정으로 가장 적절한 것을 고르시오.

① scared   ② nervous   ③ relieved
④ satisfied   ⑤ frustrated

6 다음 그림의 상황에 가장 적절한 대화를 고르시오.

①   ②   ③   ④   ⑤

7 대화를 듣고, 남자가 여자에게 부탁한 일로 가장 적절한 것을 고르시오.

① 현재 위치 확인하기   ② 타이어 교체하기
③ 회사까지 태워주기   ④ 주유소 들르기
⑤ 정비사 부르기

8 다음을 듣고, 주스에 관해 언급되지 <u>않은</u> 것을 고르시오.

① 출시일   ② 제조사   ③ 재료
④ 가격   ⑤ 맛

9 다음을 듣고, 무엇에 관한 설명인지 고르시오.

① 마스크   ② 튜브   ③ 낙하산
④ 보안경   ⑤ 구명조끼

10 다음을 듣고, 두 사람의 대화가 <u>어색한</u> 것을 고르시오.

①   ②   ③   ④   ⑤

11 대화를 듣고, 여자가 할 일로 가장 적절한 것을 고르시오.

① 영화 티켓 구매하기   ② 버스 시간 확인하기
③ 포스터 구매하기   ④ 시사회 참석하기
⑤ 게임 레벨 올리기

12 다음 숙소 내부 배치도를 보면서 대화를 듣고, 여자가 잠을 잘 곳을 고르시오.

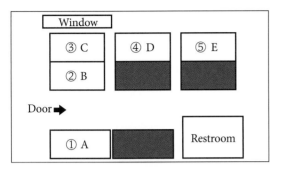

13 대화를 듣고, 남자가 박물관을 방문할 날짜를 고르시오.

① 2월 1일   ② 2월 8일   ③ 2월 15일
④ 2월 16일   ⑤ 2월 23일

14 대화를 듣고, 남자가 지난 연휴에 한 일로 가장 적절한 것을 고르시오.

① 호수 캠핑 가기   ② 도난 신고하기
③ 기차표 예매하기   ④ 가방 쇼핑하기
⑤ 신분증 신청하기

15 다음을 듣고, 방송의 목적으로 가장 적절한 것을 고르시오.

① 현장 학습 장소를 공지하려고
② 장기 자랑 우승자를 발표하려고
③ 수업 일정 변경을 알리려고
④ 안전 수칙을 설명하려고
⑤ 견학 준비 사항을 안내하려고

16 대화를 듣고, 남자가 지불할 금액을 고르시오.

① $ 10   ② $ 15   ③ $ 20
④ $ 25   ⑤ $ 30

17 대화를 듣고, 여자의 마지막 말에 대한 남자의 응답으로 가장 적절한 것을 고르시오.

Man: _____

① Yes. I want to hear your opinion on the topic.
② Let's take our cloth bags to the supermarket.
③ The trash can is over there.
④ Thanks. I can learn a lot about how to recycle.
⑤ The newspaper says we should reduce food waste.

[18-19] 대화를 듣고, 남자의 마지막 말에 대한 여자의 응답으로 가장 적절한 것을 고르시오.

18 Woman: _____

① Don't worry. We can rent them easily.
② Yeah. Riding a bike is good exercise.
③ I want to buy cherries for her.
④ No problem. The trail leads this way.
⑤ Alright. I'll lend you my transportation card.

19 Woman: _____

① I think the summer vacation is too short.
② My family will go fishing or swimming.
③ I'm looking forward to seeing Big Ben in London.
④ We're on our way to the airport now.
⑤ I would rather take a plane.

20 다음 상황 설명을 듣고, Mike가 접수원에게 할 말로 가장 적절한 것을 고르시오.

Mike: _____

① Please be careful not to fall.
② Can I please book an appointment for 5 p.m.?
③ Could you tell me when the hospital opens?
④ My ankle still hurts, so I want to get an X-ray this time.
⑤ Sorry, but the doctor is busy right now.

24회 중학영어듣기 고난도 모의고사 Dictation 음성을 들으며 빈칸에 알맞은 단어를 채우시오.

1 | 알맞은 그림 고르기

대화를 듣고, 여자가 구입할 냉장고 자석을 고르시오.

① ② ③ ④ ⑤

M What are you looking for, Emma?
W Hey. I want _____ _____ _____ for my mom. She likes to collect them.
M Then, _____ _____ _____ _____ _____ one. How about this pyramid-shaped one? It's _____ _____ _____ _____ when you think of Egypt.
W Oh, my mom already has one. So, I _____ _____ _____ _____ _____.
M Then, you can buy one of these. They depict pharaohs.
W Great. I'll take the one _____ _____ _____ on it.
M I'm sure your mother will like it.

2 | 언급하지 않은 내용 고르기

다음을 듣고, 스마트 화분에 관해 언급되지 않은 것을 고르시오.
① 회사명 ② 제품명 ③ 기능
④ 가격 ⑤ 이용 방법

🎯 적중! Tip use your

[유즈 유얼]보다는 [유쥬얼]로 들린다. use는 동사로 쓰일 때는 [유즈]로, 명사로 쓰일 때는 [유스]로 발음되고, [z]로 끝나는 단어 뒤에 y-로 시작하는 단어가 이어지면 두 소리가 연결되어 [쥬]로 발음되기 때문이다.

W Green Thinking is _____ _____ _____ _____ for indoor plants on August 4th. This state-of-the-art pot uses technology to alert plant owners _____ _____ _____ _____ _____. It does this through technology that tracks sunlight in the area and _____ _____ _____ _____. Just use your phone to _____ _____ _____ _____ _____ through an app, and the pot will give instructions for caring for it. The pot is only 20 dollars and the app is five dollars per month. So, sign up today and _____ _____ _____ _____ in stores soon!

3 | 목적 고르기

대화를 듣고, 남자가 여자에게 전화한 목적으로 가장 적절한 것을 고르시오.
① 예약을 취소하려고
② 숙박 기간을 연장하려고
③ 위치를 물어보려고
④ 비용을 문의하려고
⑤ 방문 시간을 알리려고

[Telephone rings.]
W Wexler Resorts, this is Susie. How can I help you?
M Hi, this is Nathan Andrews. I'm _____ _____ _____ _____ next month. However, I won't be able to come.
W I'm _____ _____ _____ _____ _____. Let me see. [Typing sound] Mr. Andrews, I see you were scheduled _____ _____ _____, from the 5th through the 7th.
M Right. And I'd like to _____ _____ _____ _____.
W I'll do that for you. _____ _____ _____ there is a 50-dollar cancellation fee.
M That's fine. Thanks.

4 | 시간 정보 고르기

대화를 듣고, 여자가 강당을 사용하기로 한 요일을 고르시오.

① 월요일   ② 화요일   ③ 수요일
④ 목요일   ⑤ 금요일

W Hello, Mr. Hicks. I'd like to _____ _____ _____ for a
    Spanish club meeting after school next week.

M Okay. _____ _____ _____ _____ to use it
    on?

W Can we use it on Thursday?

M I'm sorry, but the art club _____ _____ _____ _____
    for that day. How about Friday?

W We can't meet on Fridays. Can we _____ _____ _____
    _____ ?

M Let me check. [Pause] Yes. It _____ _____ _____
    _____ .

W Great. Thank you.

5 | 심정 고르기

대화를 듣고, 여자의 심정으로 가장 적절한 것을 고르시오.

① scared   ② nervous   ③ relieved
④ satisfied   ⑤ frustrated

🎯 적중! Tip   **cre**d**it**
[크레딧]보다는 [크레릿]으로 들린다. [d]가 모음 사이에서 발음될 때는 약화되어 [r]에 가깝게 발음되기 때문이다.

M _____ _____ _____ your meal?

W Yes, I liked it.

M Good. Would _____ _____ _____ _____ _____ ?

W Okay. Thank you.

M _____ _____ _____ _____ credit card or with cash?

W Credit card. And I want to use this 20% discount coupon.

M Alright. [Pause] Sorry, but _____ _____ _____ _____
    _____ anymore. Last Friday was the last day to use it.

W Really? Let me check. Oh, you're right.

M Then, sign here, please.

W _____ _____ _____ I missed the date!

6 | 그림 상황에 적절한 대화 고르기

다음 그림의 상황에 가장 적절한 대화를 고르시오.

① W Why don't we _____ _____ _____ ?
   M Good idea. I don't want to cook.

② W That was _____ _____ _____ .
   M I'm glad you liked it.

③ W _____ _____ _____ your steak, sir?
   M Medium, please.

④ W Could you wash the dishes now?
   M Sure. I'm not busy.

⑤ W What are you _____ _____ _____ ?
   M It's chicken noodle soup.

대화를 듣고, 남자가 여자에게 부탁한 일로 가장 적절한 것을 고르시오.

① 현재 위치 확인하기　② 타이어 교체하기
③ 회사까지 태워주기　④ 주유소 들르기
⑤ 정비사 부르기

🎯 **적중! Tip** bu**s s**top

[버스 스탑]보다는 [버스탑]으로 들린다. 발음이 같은 자음이 나란히 나오면 앞 단어의 끝 자음이 탈락되기 때문이다.
· thi**s S**unday [디선데이]　· ban**k c**ard [뱅칼드]

[Cellphone rings.]

W Darling, how's your day going?
M Actually, it's _____ _____ _____ _____ .
W What's wrong? Are you at work?
M Not yet. _____ _____ _____ _____ on the way to work.
W Oh, no. Where are you?
M I'm pulled over downtown. I'm _____ _____ _____ to pick up my car.
W Do you need any help? I'm not busy at the moment.
M Yes. I'd love you to _____ _____ _____ _____ to work. There's no bus stop close to me.
W Sure. Just _____ _____ _____ _____ .

다음을 듣고, 주스에 관해 언급되지 않은 것을 고르시오.

① 출시일　② 제조사　③ 재료
④ 가격　⑤ 맛

M Hello, customers. Our team at Natural Juices is excited to _____ _____ _____ of two new and delicious flavors of fruit juices. _____ _____ _____ are Blackberry Mint and Strawberry Lime. These tasty juices _____ _____ _____ 100% natural fruits and contain lots of healthy vitamins and minerals. _____ _____ _____ _____ , one bottle is only eight dollars. We hope you enjoy our new flavors _____ _____ _____ _____ _____ . Cheers!

다음을 듣고, 무엇에 관한 설명인지 고르시오.

① 마스크　② 튜브　③ 낙하산
④ 보안경　⑤ 구명조끼

M This is something _____ _____ _____ _____ . You usually wear this on a boat. When people cannot swim well, they _____ _____ _____ _____ in the water at all times. It often _____ _____ _____ _____ and is made of plastic. To wear it correctly, you need to buckle all the straps tightly. It _____ _____ _____ in the water and saves your life.

다음을 듣고, 두 사람의 대화가 **어색한** 것을 고르시오.

①　②　③　④　⑤

🎯 **적중! Tip** I hope ~.

희망이나 기대감을 나타낼 때 사용되는 표현으로 '~하면 좋겠다, ~하기를 바란다'라는 의미이다.
· I hope you get better soon.
　네가 빨리 나으면 좋겠다.

① **W** Are you feeling okay? You look pale.
　M I have _____ _____ _____ .
② **W** Will you walk the dog?
　M Can I do that later? I need to _____ _____ _____ _____ first.
③ **W** Could you help me _____ _____ _____ in the garden?
　M Sure. Which flower bouquet do you want?
④ **W** I really hope I get a good grade for my presentation.
　M I think you will. _____ _____ _____ .

⑤ W _____ _____ _____ _____ _____ the air conditioner?

M No. It is getting a little cold in here.

11 | 할 일 고르기

대화를 듣고, 여자가 할 일로 가장 적절한 것을 고르시오.

① 영화 티켓 구매하기　② 버스 시간 확인하기
③ 포스터 구매하기　　④ 시사회 참석하기
⑤ 게임 레벨 올리기

W I can't believe Ryan Pitt's _____ _____ _____ tomorrow!

M I know. We waited two years for the premiere of *Level Up 2.*

W _____ _____ _____ book our tickets for?

M 5 p.m. But we should get there early.

W Okay. I'll check _____ _____ _____.

M Great. Let's _____ _____ _____ the theater at 4:30 then.

W Sounds like a plan.

12 | 위치 고르기

다음 숙소 내부 배치도를 보면서 대화를 듣고, 여자가 잠을 잘 곳을 고르시오.

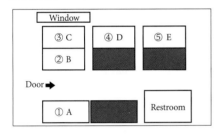

W Hi, I'd like to check in. My name is Georgia Brown.

M Welcome. _____ _____ _____ _____ in a woman's dormitory room, right?

W Yes. Are there _____ _____ _____?

M We have a few. You can choose either a bunk bed or a regular bed.

W I want to _____ _____ _____ _____. How about a top bunk?

M Sure. Do you _____ _____ _____?

W I don't want to be too close to the restroom.

M You can choose from these two.

W I'll take this one. It might be cold _____ _____ _____ _____.

M Here's your key.

13 | 시간 정보 고르기

대화를 듣고, 남자가 박물관을 방문할 날짜를 고르시오.

① 2월 1일　② 2월 8일　③ 2월 15일
④ 2월 16일　⑤ 2월 23일

[Telephone rings.]

W Hello, National Museum of Space.

M Hi. _____ _____ _____ when the reopening date of the museum will be.

W _____ _____ _____ _____ by February 1st, but reopening was delayed to the 8th.

M Oh, is that so? Are you open _____ _____ _____? The 16th of February.

W Sorry, but we don't open on that day.

M Hmm... Are you _____ _____ _____ _____ this month?

W _____ _____ _____ _____ _____ the reopening day? We'll have a ceremony for the reopening of the museum. It's _____.

M Okay, I'll do so. Thank you for the information.

14 | 한 일 고르기

대화를 듣고, 남자가 지난 연휴에 한 일로 가장 적절한 것을 고르시오.

① 호수 캠핑 가기　　② 도난 신고하기
③ 기차표 예매하기　　④ 가방 쇼핑하기
⑤ 신분증 신청하기

🎯 적중! Tip　**leave it at**

[리브 잇 앳]보다는 [리비랫]으로 들린다. 앞에 나온 단어의 끝 자음과 뒤에 나온 단어의 첫 모음이 연음되고, [t]가 모음 사이에서 발음될 때는 약화되어 [r]에 가깝게 발음되기 때문이다.

W Did you enjoy the long weekend, Jooho?
M No. ＿＿＿＿＿ ＿＿＿＿＿ ＿＿＿＿＿.
W But you said you were ＿＿＿＿＿ ＿＿＿＿＿ ＿＿＿＿＿ ＿＿＿＿＿ ＿＿＿＿＿.
M I couldn't go. When I got to the train station on Saturday, I realized ＿＿＿＿＿ ＿＿＿＿＿ ＿＿＿＿＿ ＿＿＿＿＿.
W Did you leave it at home?
M No. I think it was ＿＿＿＿＿ ＿＿＿＿＿ ＿＿＿＿＿ ＿＿＿＿＿. I immediately filed a report with the police.
W Well, maybe ＿＿＿＿＿ ＿＿＿＿＿ ＿＿＿＿＿ ＿＿＿＿＿ soon.
M I hope so. Otherwise, I will need to replace my ID cards.

15 | 목적 고르기

다음을 듣고, 방송의 목적으로 가장 적절한 것을 고르시오.

① 현장 학습 장소를 공지하려고
② 장기 자랑 우승자를 발표하려고
③ 수업 일정 변경을 알리려고
④ 안전 수칙을 설명하려고
⑤ 견학 준비 사항을 안내하려고

W Attention, students. This is your principal, Ms. Roberts. ＿＿＿＿＿ ＿＿＿＿＿ ＿＿＿＿＿, the 10th grade field trip is next month. However, you need ＿＿＿＿＿ ＿＿＿＿＿ ＿＿＿＿＿ before you can go. First of all, ＿＿＿＿＿ ＿＿＿＿＿ ＿＿＿＿＿ ＿＿＿＿＿ a permission slip. It must be signed by a parent or guardian. ＿＿＿＿＿ ＿＿＿＿＿ ＿＿＿＿＿ ＿＿＿＿＿ to your homeroom teacher by April 1st. Second, you must pay the trip fee. The 25-dollar trip fee can be ＿＿＿＿＿ ＿＿＿＿＿ ＿＿＿＿＿ ＿＿＿＿＿ ＿＿＿＿＿. It is due on the same date. Have a great day, everyone.

16 | 금액 정보 고르기

대화를 듣고, 남자가 지불할 금액을 고르시오.

① $ 10　　② $ 15　　③ $ 20
④ $ 25　　⑤ $ 30

🎯 적중! Tip　Got it.

상대방의 말을 듣고 이해했음을 나타낼 때 사용되는 표현이다.

W Welcome to Pet World. How may I help you?
M Hello. I'd like to buy some food for my cat. Do you ＿＿＿＿＿ ＿＿＿＿＿ ＿＿＿＿＿?
W The bags on the left shelf are 20 dollars each. However, the ones ＿＿＿＿＿ ＿＿＿＿＿ ＿＿＿＿＿ ＿＿＿＿＿ are for kittens, and they are 15 dollars each.
M I'll take ＿＿＿＿＿ ＿＿＿＿＿ ＿＿＿＿＿ ＿＿＿＿＿ for little cats.
W Got it. Is there anything else you need?
M What about this toy? Is it popular?
W It ＿＿＿＿＿ ＿＿＿＿＿ ＿＿＿＿＿ ＿＿＿＿＿, and it's only 10 dollars.
M Then, I'll also buy that.

17 | 적절한 응답 고르기

대화를 듣고, 여자의 마지막 말에 대한 남자의 응답으로 가장 적절한 것을 고르시오.

Man: ＿＿＿＿＿＿＿＿＿＿＿＿＿＿＿

① Yes. I want to hear your opinion on the topic.
② Let's take our cloth bags to the supermarket.
③ The trash can is over there.
④ Thanks. I can learn a lot about how to recycle.
⑤ The newspaper says we should reduce food waste.

W What are you working on, Ron?
M It's a paper ＿＿＿＿＿ ＿＿＿＿＿ ＿＿＿＿＿ ＿＿＿＿＿.
W What is it about?
M It ＿＿＿＿＿ ＿＿＿＿＿ ＿＿＿＿＿ ＿＿＿＿＿ appropriately.
W Why did you pick that topic?
M Well, a lot of people aren't recycling properly. I think we need to ＿＿＿＿＿ ＿＿＿＿＿ ＿＿＿＿＿ ＿＿＿＿＿.

W Yeah. It _____ _____ _____ _____ recycling.
M Yes. And I also _____ _____ _____ _____ .
W Can I read your paper? I'd love to learn more.

18 | 적절한 응답 고르기

대화를 듣고, 남자의 마지막 말에 대한 여자의 응답으로 가장 적절한 것을 고르시오.

Woman: _____

① Don't worry. We can rent them easily.
② Yeah. Riding a bike is good exercise.
③ I want to buy cherries for her.
④ No problem. The trail leads this way.
⑤ Alright. I'll lend you my transportation card.

[Cellphone rings.]
M What's up, Stella?
W Hey. _____ _____ _____ _____ today?
M I was going to play games with my brother, but he is too busy now.
W Then, _____ _____ _____ _____ with me?
M Sure. What do you want to do?
W The cherry blossoms in the park are _____ _____ _____ . Why don't we go see them?
M Alright. Do you want to take the subway?
W It's a fine day, so _____ _____ _____ _____ instead.
M But I _____ _____ _____ _____ .

19 | 적절한 응답 고르기

대화를 듣고, 남자의 마지막 말에 대한 여자의 응답으로 가장 적절한 것을 고르시오.

Woman: _____

① I think the summer vacation is too short.
② My family will go fishing or swimming.
③ I'm looking forward to seeing Big Ben in London.
④ We're on our way to the airport now.
⑤ I would rather take a plane.

W Time really _____ _____ _____ . It's almost the last day of school.
M Yeah. But I am excited for summer.
W What will you do _____ _____ _____ ?
M I will go to a summer camp in America.
W Wow! How long will you be there?
M _____ _____ _____ _____ . I can't wait. What are your plans?
W I will _____ _____ _____ _____ with my parents.
M That also sounds really fun. Where are you _____ _____ _____ _____ in Europe?

20 | 상황에 적절한 말 고르기

다음 상황 설명을 듣고, Mike가 접수원에게 할 말로 가장 적절한 것을 고르시오.

Mike: _____

① Please be careful not to fall.
② Can I please book an appointment for 5 p.m.?
③ Could you tell me when the hospital opens?
④ My ankle still hurts, so I want to get an X-ray this time.
⑤ Sorry, but the doctor is busy right now.

M Last weekend, Mike _____ _____ _____ with his friends. He fell _____ _____ _____ _____ and sprained his ankle. Mike thought _____ _____ _____ _____ , but it still hurts. He wants a doctor to _____ _____ _____ today. So, he decides to call the doctor's office and ask the receptionist if he can _____ _____ _____ _____ _____ . In this situation, what would Mike most likely say to the receptionist?

영어듣기 만점을 위한 **완벽한 실전 대비서**

해커스
중학영어듣기
모의고사 24회

LEVEL
3

초판 2쇄 발행 2023년 1월 2일
초판 1쇄 발행 2022년 9월 1일

지은이	해커스 어학연구소
펴낸곳	㈜해커스 어학연구소
펴낸이	해커스 어학연구소 출판팀

주소	서울특별시 서초구 강남대로61길 23 ㈜해커스 어학연구소
고객센터	02-537-5000
교재 관련 문의	publishing@hackers.com
	해커스북 사이트(HackersBook.com) 고객센터 Q&A 게시판
동영상강의	star.Hackers.com

ISBN	978-89-6542-491-8 (53740)
Serial Number	01-02-01

**중고등영어 1위,
해커스북 HackersBook.com**

· 수준별로 속도를 선택해서 듣는 **기본 속도 MP3, 1.2배속 MP3, 1.5배속 MP3**
· 복습이 간편해지는 **딕테이션 MP3 및 문항별 MP3**
· 학습한 단어의 암기 여부를 쉽게 점검할 수 있는 **어휘 리스트 및 어휘 테스트**

한경비즈니스 선정 2020 한국품질만족도 교육(온·오프라인 중·고등영어) 부문 1위

Smart, Useful, and Essential Grammar

HACKERS
GRAMMAR SMART

Smart, Skillful, and Fun Reading

HACKERS
READING SMART

해커스북 중·고등
HackersBook.com

영어듣기 만점을 위한 **완벽한 실전 대비서**

해커스
중학영어듣기
모의고사 24회

LEVEL
3

정답 및 해설

영어듣기 만점을 위한 **완벽한 실전 대비서**

해커스
중학영어듣기
모의고사 24회

LEVEL
3

정답 및 해설

ㅠ 해커스어학연구소

1 알맞은 그림 고르기
정답 ②

W Hello. May I help you?

M I'm looking for a rug for my living room.

W Okay. Which type do you like better, square or round ones?

M I prefer round ones.

W Great. Then, you can choose from these two styles, plain and floral.

M Oh, I like the ones with the floral patterns.

W All right. One of them has lace along the edge.

M Hmm... I think the one without lace is better. I'll get that one.

W Good choice.

여 안녕하세요. 도와드릴까요?

남 제 거실에 둘 러그를 찾고 있어요.

여 그러시군요. 네모난 것이나 둥근 것 중에 어떤 종류가 더 좋으신가요?

남 저는 둥근 것을 선호해요.

여 좋습니다. 그럼, 무늬가 없는 것과 꽃무늬 중에서 고르실 수 있습니다.

남 오, 저는 꽃무늬가 있는 것이 좋아요.

여 알겠어요. 그것들 중 하나는 테두리를 따라서 레이스가 달려있어요.

남 흠... 저는 레이스가 없는 것이 더 좋은 것 같아요. 그걸 살게요.

여 좋은 선택이에요.

해설 | 남자가 꽃무늬의 레이스가 없는 둥근 러그를 구입할 것이라고 했으므로 정답은 ②이다.

어휘 | look for ~을 찾다 prefer [prifə́:r] 동 선호하다 plain [plein] 형 무늬가 없는 floral [flɔ́:rəl] 형 꽃무늬의 edge [edʒ] 명 테두리, 가장자리

2 언급하지 않은 내용 고르기
정답 ⑤

M Excuse me. I need to buy a new bicycle. How much is that one over there?

W Do you mean the green one?

M No. The blue one near the window.

W Oh, that one is 225 dollars. It is made by Downing Bikes.

M Is it very heavy?

W No. It is only 10 kilograms. It is much lighter than our other models.

M That sounds perfect. Can I try riding it?

W Of course. Let's take it outside.

남 실례합니다. 저는 새 자전거를 사야 해요. 저기 있는 저것은 얼마인가요?

여 초록색 자전거 말씀이신가요?

남 아니요. 창가에 있는 파란 자전거요.

여 오, 그건 225달러예요. Downing Bikes사에서 만들었어요.

남 그건 아주 무거운가요?

여 아니요. 겨우 10kg이에요. 다른 모델들보다 훨씬 더 가볍죠.

남 완벽하네요. 한번 타볼 수 있나요?

여 물론이죠. 밖으로 가지고 갑시다.

해설 | ① 색상(파란색), ② 가격(225달러), ③ 제조사(Downing Bikes), ④ 무게(10kg)에 대해 언급했으므로 정답은 ⑤ '모델명'이다.

어휘 | heavy [hévi] 형 무거운 light [lait] 형 가벼운 명 빛 outside [àutsáid] 부 밖으로, ~의 바깥쪽에

3 목적 고르기
정답 ②

[Telephone rings.]

M Lucaria Audio. I'm Carl. What can I do for you today?

W Hi. This is Jenna Gomez. I placed an order online last night.

M Okay. Was there an issue?

W Yes. I ordered two pairs of headphones, but I only wanted to order one. Is it possible to change my order?

M Could I ask for the order number?

W It's AJ-4821.

M Let me check. [Typing sound] We can. It hasn't been shipped yet, so we'll provide you with a refund for the extra pair.

W Great. Thank you so much!

[전화기가 울린다.]

남 Lucaria Audio입니다. 저는 Carl입니다. 오늘 무엇을 도와 드릴까요?

여 안녕하세요. 저는 Jenna Gomez입니다. 지난밤에 온라인 주문을 했는데요.

남 그러시군요. 문제가 있으셨나요?

여 네. 제가 두 개의 헤드폰을 주문했는데, 저는 오직 한 개만 주문하고 싶었어요. 주문을 변경하는 것이 가능한가요?

남 주문 번호를 여쭤봐도 될까요?

여 AJ-4821입니다.

남 확인해 보겠습니다. [타자치는 소리] 할 수 있어요. 아직 발송되지 않았으니, 저희가 여분의 헤드폰에 대한 환불을 제공해 드리겠습니다.

여 좋네요. 정말 감사합니다!

해설 | 여자가 남자에게 주문을 변경하는 것이 가능한지 물었으므로 정답은 ② '주문 내역을 변경하려고'이다.

어휘 | place an order 주문하다 issue [íʃuː] 명 문제 ship [ʃip] 동 발송하다, 보내다 명 선박 provide [prəváid] 동 제공하다

---

4 시간 정보 고르기
정답 ⑤

W	James, do you have any plans for Sunday?	여	James, 일요일에 계획 있니?
M	Not yet. Why?	남	아직 없어. 왜?
W	I've wanted to see the movie *Lost Time* for a while. Do you want to watch it together?	여	내가 영화 <Lost Time>을 한동안 보고 싶었어. 같이 볼래?
M	Sure. When does it start?	남	물론이지. 언제 시작하는데?
W	Let me check the times. *[Pause]* We can see it at 4, 6, or 8 p.m.	여	시간 확인해 볼게. *[잠시 멈춤]* 우리는 오후 4시, 6시, 혹은 8시에 볼 수 있어.
M	The last showing would work best for me. I'm meeting my aunt for dinner at 5, and we probably won't finish until 7.	남	가장 마지막 상영이 나에게는 가장 좋아. 5시에 저녁 식사를 하러 이모를 만날 예정이고, 아마 7시는 되어야 마칠 거야.
W	That's fine with me. I'll buy the tickets online now.	여	나는 괜찮아. 내가 지금 온라인으로 표를 살게.

해설 | 여자가 오후 4시, 6시, 혹은 8시 영화를 볼 수 있다고 했고, 남자가 가장 마지막 상영이 좋다고 했으므로 정답은 ⑤ '8 p.m.'이다.

어휘 | showing [ʃóuiŋ] 명 (영화) 상영 aunt [ænt] 명 이모, 고모 probably [prábəbli] 부 아마도 not A until B B가 되어서야 A하다

---

5 심정 고르기
정답 ④

W	Frank, did you enter the speaking contest?	여	Frank, 너 말하기 대회에 참가 신청했니?
M	Not yet. I'll sign up for it this afternoon.	남	아직 안 했어. 오늘 오후에 등록할 거야.
W	Oh, no. You can't.	여	오, 안 돼. 넌 못 해.
M	Why not?	남	왜 못 해?
W	The deadline was yesterday.	여	마감일이 어제였어.
M	No way! I thought the deadline was today.	남	그럴 리 없어! 나는 마감일이 오늘이라고 생각했어.
W	Let me check again. *[Pause]* Look at this. It says the last day to register was yesterday.	여	내가 다시 확인해볼게. *[잠시 멈춤]* 이거 봐. 여기 등록할 수 있는 마지막 날이 어제라고 쓰여 있어.
M	I should have read the notice more thoroughly.	남	내가 공지를 더 철저히 읽었어야 했어.

해설 | 남자가 대회 신청 마감일을 놓친 것에 대해 공지를 더 철저히 읽었어야 했다고 했으므로 정답은 ④ 'regretful'이다.

선택지 해석
① 지루한 ② 무서운 ③ 안도한 ④ 후회하는 ⑤ 만족하는

어휘 | enter [éntər] 동 참가 신청하다, 등록하다; 들어가다 deadline [dédlàin] 명 마감일 register [rédʒistər] 동 등록하다 notice [nótis] 명 공지; 주의
thoroughly [θə́ːrouli] 부 철저히, 완벽하게

---

6 그림 상황에 적절한 대화 고르기
정답 ⑤

① M	Where do you work?	① 남	어디에서 일하시나요?
W	I work at a hair salon downtown.	여	저는 시내의 미용실에서 일해요.
② M	Let's ask for directions.	② 남	길을 물어보자.
W	I don't think that is necessary.	여	그럴 필요는 없을 것 같아.
③ M	Why was I pulled over?	③ 남	왜 제 차를 세우셨나요?
W	You were driving above the speed limit.	여	제한 속도보다 빠르게 달리고 계셨어요.
④ M	Where is your map?	④ 남	지도는 어디에 있어?
W	It's in my backpack.	여	그건 내 배낭 안에 있어.
⑤ M	How do I get to the National Museum?	⑤ 남	국립 박물관에 어떻게 가나요?
W	Go straight one block, and then turn right.	여	한 블록 직진한 후에 우회전하세요.

해설 | 남자가 박물관에 어떻게 가는지 묻고 있고, 경찰관인 여자가 길을 알려주는 상황이므로 정답은 ⑤이다.

어휘 | directions [dirékʃənz] 명 길, 안내 (direction [dirékʃən] 명 방향) pull over 차를 길가에 세우다, 대다 limit [límit] 명 제한

7 부탁·요청한 일 고르기
정답 ④

M	What are you looking for, Mom?
W	I can't find the flour in this cupboard.
M	Isn't it next to the salt and sugar?
W	I thought so, but it isn't here.
M	That's strange. *[Pause]* Oh, I forgot I put it by the cake mix last time I baked a cake.
W	I see. Now, could you get some frozen strawberries?
M	No problem.

남	뭘 찾고 계세요, 엄마?
여	이쪽 찬장에서 밀가루를 못 찾겠어.
남	소금과 설탕 옆에 있지 않아요?
여	그렇다고 생각했는데, 여기에 없어.
남	이상하네요. *[잠시 멈춤]* 오, 지난번에 제가 케이크를 구울 때 케이크 믹스 옆에 둔 것을 잊었어요.
여	그렇구나. 이제, 냉동 딸기를 좀 가져다줄 수 있니?
남	물론이죠.

해설 | 여자가 남자에게 냉동 딸기를 가져다 달라고 부탁했으므로 정답은 ④ '냉동 딸기 가져오기'이다.

어휘 | flour [fláuər] 몡 밀가루 cupboard [kʌ́bərd] 몡 찬장 strange [streinʒ] 혱 이상한 frozen [fróuzn] 혱 냉동의, 얼린

8 언급하지 않은 내용 고르기
정답 ⑤

W	Do you need to take a break from daily life? If so, you should visit Green Leaf Spa. We offer various services, such as massages and beauty treatments. All staff members are professionally trained. We are located at 128 Center Avenue. Our hours are Monday to Saturday from 8 a.m. to 9 p.m. Call us at 555-9282 to make an appointment. We hope to see you soon!

여	일상으로부터의 휴식이 필요하신가요? 만약 그렇다면 Green Leaf Spa를 방문하십시오. 저희는 마사지와 미용 관리 같은 다양한 서비스를 제공합니다. 모든 직원들은 전문적인 훈련을 받았습니다. 저희는 센터 가 128번지에 위치하고 있습니다. 운영 시간은 월요일에서 토요일 오전 8시에서 오후 9시까지입니다. 예약을 잡으시려면 555-9282로 전화 주십시오. 곧 만나 뵙길 기대하고 있겠습니다!

해설 | ① 제공 서비스(마사지와 미용 관리), ② 위치(센터 가 128번지), ③ 운영 시간(월요일에서 토요일 오전 8시에서 오후 9시), ④ 전화번호(555-9282)에 대해 언급했으므로 정답은 ⑤ '주차 가능 여부'이다.

어휘 | various [vέriəs] 혱 다양한 professionally [prəfέʃ(ə)nəli] 凰 전문적으로 train [trein] 됨 훈련하다 be located 위치하다

9 화제 고르기
정답 ④

W	This is a sport that doesn't require a player to use any special equipment. Players try to set a better record. They run fast and then try to leap over a very high bar. The bar is raised when players jump over it. When a player hits the bar three times, they lose the competition. To win, a player must leap the highest among all of the other players.

여	이것은 선수들에게 어떤 특별한 장비도 요구하지 않는 운동입니다. 선수들은 더 좋은 기록을 세우기 위해 노력합니다. 그들은 빨리 달려서 매우 높이 있는 막대를 뛰어넘으려고 시도합니다. 선수들이 그것을 뛰어넘으면 막대를 올립니다. 선수들이 막대에 세 번 부딪히면, 그들은 경기에서 집니다. 이기기 위해서는, 다른 모든 선수들 중 가장 높이 뛰어넘어야만 합니다.

해설 | 이것(This)을 하는 선수들은 빨리 달려서 매우 높이 있는 막대를 뛰어넘으려고 시도하고, 이기기 위해서는 다른 모든 선수들 중 가장 높이 뛰어넘어야 한다고 했으므로 정답은 ④ '높이뛰기'이다.

어휘 | require [rikwáiər] 됨 요구하다 equipment [ikwípmənt] 몡 장비 leap over 뛰어넘다 competition [kàmpətíʃən] 몡 경기 among [əmʌ́ŋ] 젠 ~중에

10 어색한 대화 고르기
정답 ①

① W	What time did you go to bed last night?
M	I usually eat breakfast at 8 a.m.
② W	Do you want to go to the hockey game next week?
M	Sure! Let me buy the tickets.
③ W	Can I use your smartphone?
M	Yes. Here it is.
④ W	Where did you find that scarf?
M	It was at the bottom of my closet.
⑤ W	Wow. That dance class was really exciting.
M	I know. I'm exhausted now.

① 여	어젯밤에 몇 시에 자러 갔니?
남	나는 보통 오전 8시에 아침 식사를 해.
② 여	다음 주 하키 경기에 갈래?
남	물론이지! 내가 티켓을 살게.
③ 여	네 스마트폰을 쓸 수 있을까?
남	응. 여기 있어.
④ 여	그 목도리 어디서 찾았니?
남	내 옷장 바닥에 있었어.
⑤ 여	우와. 그 댄스 수업은 정말 재미있었어.
남	맞아. 나 지금 기진맥진해.

해설 | 여자가 남자에게 몇 시에 자러 갔는지 물었으므로, 남자는 자러 간 시각을 답해야 한다. 그러나 남자가 오전 8시에 아침 식사를 한다는 어색한 대답을 했으므로 정답은 ①이다.

어휘 | bottom [bátəm] 명 바닥　exhausted [igzɔ́:stid] 형 기진맥진한

11 할 일 고르기　　　　　　　　　　　　　　　정답 ②

W　What are you doing, Sehun?	여　뭐 하고 있니, 세훈아?
M　I'm trying to use this library computer, but it's so slow.	남　이 도서관 컴퓨터를 쓰려고 시도하는 중인데, 너무 느려.
W　Why don't you use your laptop instead?	여　그 대신에 너의 노트북을 쓰는 게 어때?
M　It's broken right now. I need to get it fixed.	남　그건 지금 고장 났어. 수리를 받아야 해.
W　I understand. Do you have an urgent assignment to do?	여　그렇구나. 해야 할 급한 숙제가 있니?
M　Yes. I need to do some research for an essay.	남　응. 에세이를 쓰기 위해서 조사를 좀 해야 해.
W　Then, I'll lend you my laptop for today. You can use it for your research.	여　그럼, 오늘 내 노트북을 빌려줄게. 조사에 그걸 사용해도 돼.
M　That's so kind of you.	남　너 정말 친절하다.

해설 | 여자가 남자에게 노트북을 빌려주겠다고 했으므로 정답은 ② '노트북 빌려주기'이다.

어휘 | urgent [ə́:rdʒənt] 형 급한, 긴급한　assignment [əsáinmənt] 명 숙제, 과제　research [risə́:rtʃ] 명 조사

12 도표에서 알맞은 항목 고르기　　　　　　　　　정답 ②

M　Hi. What can I do for you today?	남　안녕하세요. 오늘은 무엇을 도와드릴까요?
W　Hello. I want to take a language class.	여　안녕하세요. 저는 언어 수업을 듣고 싶어요.
M　Okay. Here's our class schedule. Currently, we only have French and German classes.	남　그러시군요. 여기 저희 수업 일정이 있습니다. 현재는 프랑스어와 독일어 수업만 있어요.
W　I'd like to study French since I enjoy French movies.	여　저는 프랑스 영화를 즐겨봐서 프랑스어를 공부하고 싶어요.
M　Great. We have French on Mondays and Fridays.	남　좋습니다. 월요일과 금요일마다 프랑스어 수업이 있어요.
W　Hmm... I go to the gym every Monday morning, so I can't take one then.	여　흠... 저는 매주 월요일 아침엔 체육관에 가서 그때는 들을 수 없어요.
M　Then, you can choose from the other two classes.	남　그럼 다른 두 수업 중에 고르실 수 있어요.
W　I'll take the earlier one.	여　더 이른 것을 들을게요.

해설 | 여자가 금요일에 있는 프랑스어 수업 중 더 이른 것을 듣겠다고 했으므로 정답은 ②이다.

어휘 | language [lǽŋgwidʒ] 명 언어　schedule [skédʒu:l] 명 일정　currently [kə́:rəntli] 부 현재는　since [sins] 접 ~해서, ~ 때문에; ~한 이후

13 시간 정보 고르기　　　　　　　　　　　　　정답 ②

M　Hey, Katie. I'm going to the park tomorrow afternoon to take photographs of the flowers. Do you want to come?	남　안녕, Katie. 나는 내일 오후에 꽃 사진을 찍으러 공원에 갈 거야. 너도 갈래?
W　Sure. When do you want to go?	여　물론이지. 언제 가고 싶은데?
M　I want to get there by 3 p.m.	남　난 그곳에 오후 3시까지 도착하고 싶어.
W　Okay. Why don't we play badminton there together too? It'll be a lovely day for working out.	여　그래. 우리 거기서 배드민턴도 치는 게 어때? 운동하기에 딱 좋은 날일 거야.
M　I'd love to. Then, when should we meet?	남　나도 그러고 싶어. 그럼 우리 언제 만나야 할까?
W　Is 2 o'clock okay?	여　2시 괜찮아?
M　We will need more time to play. How about 1?	남　배드민턴 치려면 시간이 더 필요할 거야. 1시 어때?
W　That works for me.	여　난 좋아.

해설 | 남자가 1시는 어떤지 제안하자 여자가 좋다고 했으므로 정답은 ② '1 p.m.'이다.

어휘 | take a photograph of ~의 사진을 찍다　work out 운동하다

W　Why didn't you go to baseball practice yesterday, Brad?	여　어제 왜 야구 연습에 가지 않았어, Brad?
M　Unfortunately, I was too busy to go.	남　안타깝게도, 가기에는 너무 바빴어.
W　Really? What were you doing?	여　정말? 뭐 하고 있었는데?
M　Well, my parents visited my uncle in the hospital.	남　음, 우리 부모님께서 병원에 계신 삼촌을 방문하셨어.
W　I see. Did you go with them?	여　그렇구나. 너도 함께 갔니?
M　No. I had to watch my younger brother at home while they were at the hospital.	남　아니. 나는 부모님이 병원에 계시는 동안 집에서 남동생을 봐야 했어.
W　What did you do with him?	여　남동생이랑 뭐 했는데?
M　Nothing much, actually. He had lots of homework to do that day.	남　별것 안 했어, 사실. 그날 남동생이 숙제가 많았거든.

해설 | 남자가 어제 부모님이 병원에 계시는 동안 남동생을 봐야 했다고 했으므로 정답은 ③ '남동생 돌보기'이다.

어휘 | unfortunately [ʌnfɔ́rtʃənətli] 뿐 안타깝게도, 유감스럽게도; 불행하게도　actually [ǽktʃuəli] 뿐 사실

W　Hi, everyone. Welcome to the Moss Museum of Fine Art. I'd like to explain a few rules before our tour begins. First, no food or drink is allowed. I will have to ask you to leave if you bring any into the exhibit areas. Secondly, you may not take any photographs or videos. Just enjoy the experience while you are here. Lastly, do not touch any of the works on display. Now please follow me into the east wing.	여　안녕하세요, 여러분. 모스 미술 박물관에 오신 것을 환영합니다. 저희 투어를 시작하기 전에 몇 가지 규칙에 대해 설명하려고 합니다. 첫 번째로, 음식과 음료수는 허용되지 않습니다. 전시장에 가지고 들어오신다면 저희가 퇴장을 요청해야 할 것입니다. 두 번째로, 사진이나 동영상 촬영을 하실 수 없습니다. 여기에 있는 동안 그저 즐겁게 경험해주십시오. 마지막으로, 전시되어 있는 어떤 작품도 만지지 말아주십시오. 이제 동관으로 저를 따라 들어오십시오.

해설 | 여자가 미술 박물관 투어를 시작하기 전에 몇 가지 규칙에 대해 설명하고 있으므로 정답은 ⑤ '박물관 관람 시 주의 사항을 안내하려고'이다.

어휘 | allowed [əláud] 형 허용된　exhibit [igzíbit] 명 전시　experience [ikspíəriəns] 명 경험　display [displéi] 명 전시　wing [wiŋ] 명 관, 건물; 날개

W　Hello. Can I help you with anything?	여　안녕하세요. 무엇을 도와드릴까요?
M　Hi. I need some new notebooks for school. Do you have any recommendations?	남　안녕하세요. 저는 학교에서 쓸 새 공책이 좀 필요해요. 추천해 주실 만한 게 있나요?
W　This is one of our most popular notebooks, and it's just four dollars.	여　이게 가장 인기 있는 공책이고, 고작 4달러예요.
M　That's perfect. I'll buy three of them.	남　완벽하네요. 그걸 세 권 살게요.
W　If you want some pens too, these are three dollars each. Are you interested in buying any?	여　만약 펜도 원하신다면 이것들은 각각 3달러예요. 사고 싶으신가요?
M　That's okay. I'll just take the notebooks for now.	남　괜찮아요. 지금은 공책만 살게요.
W　Okay. You can pay over here.	여　네. 저쪽에서 계산하시면 돼요.

해설 | 공책이 4달러이고 남자가 공책만 세 권을 사겠다고 했으므로 정답은 ③ '$ 12'이다.

어휘 | notebook [nóutbuk] 명 공책　recommendation [rèkəməndéiʃən] 명 추천

17 적절한 응답 고르기 　　　　　　　　정답 ③

M	Your performance at the talent show was amazing, Sohee!
W	Thanks. I practiced a lot.
M	What kind of songs do you usually sing?
W	I prefer rock music. I want to be in a famous band one day.
M	Really? I'm actually in a band now.
W	Wow! I didn't know that. Who do you play with?
M	I play with Jaehong and Bohyun. You should practice with us sometime.
W	I would love to sing with you guys!

남	장기 자랑에서 한 네 공연은 놀라웠어, 소희야!
여	고마워. 나 연습 많이 했어.
남	너는 보통 어떤 종류의 노래를 부르니?
여	나는 록 음악을 선호해. 언젠가 유명한 밴드에 들어가고 싶어.
남	정말? 나 사실 지금 밴드하고 있어.
여	우와! 몰랐네. 누구랑 같이 연주하니?
남	나는 재홍이랑 보현이와 연주해. 우리랑 언제 같이 연습하자.
여	나도 너희들과 함께 노래 부르고 싶어!

해설 | 남자가 같이 밴드 연습할 것을 제안했으므로 정답은 제안을 수락하는 ③ 'I would love to sing with you guys!'이다.

　선택지 해석
① 나는 클래식 음악을 가장 좋아해.　② 우승자가 곧 발표될 거야.　③ 나도 너희들과 함께 노래 부르고 싶어!　④ 공연 중에는 조용히 해줘.
⑤ 내 친구들이 나중에 우리와 함께할 거야.

어휘 | performance [pərfɔ́ːrməns] 명 공연　amazing [əméiziŋ] 형 놀라운　announce [ənáuns] 동 발표하다

18 적절한 응답 고르기 　　　　　　　　정답 ⑤

	[Cellphone rings.]
W	Hello?
M	Hi. This is Global Technology Store. Is this Jiwon Kim?
W	Yes, that's me.
M	I'm calling about your new air conditioner. It was going to be delivered today at 3 p.m.
W	That's right. Is there a problem?
M	Well, a few of our employees are sick, so we can't make all of our deliveries. Is it okay if our team comes tomorrow instead?
W	Oh, sure. But I won't be home in the morning, so please come in the afternoon.
M	We will visit around 2 p.m. then.

	[휴대폰이 울린다.]
여	여보세요?
남	안녕하세요. Global Technology Store입니다. 김지원 씨이신가요?
여	네, 전데요.
남	고객님의 새 에어컨에 대해 전화 드렸습니다. 그건 오늘 오후 3시에 배송될 예정이었는데요.
여	맞아요. 문제가 있나요?
남	음, 저희 직원들 중 몇 명이 아파서, 모든 건을 배송할 수 없겠어요. 그 대신에 저희 팀이 내일 방문해도 괜찮을까요?
여	오, 물론이죠. 하지만 아침에는 제가 집에 없을 예정이니, 오후에 와주세요.
남	그럼 오후 2시쯤에 방문하겠습니다.

해설 | 여자가 아침에는 집에 없을 예정이니 오후에 와달라고 부탁했으므로 정답은 부탁을 수락하는 ⑤ 'We will visit around 2 p.m. then.'이다.

　선택지 해석
① 잠시 에어컨을 꺼주세요.　② 아프면 휴식을 취해야 해요.　③ 그녀는 지난주에 그 소포를 보냈어요.　④ 그들은 지금 컴퓨터를 고치고 있어요.
⑤ 그럼 오후 2시쯤에 방문하겠습니다.

어휘 | air conditioner 에어컨　deliver [dilívər] 동 배송하다, 배달하다 (delivery [dilívəri] 명 배송, 배달)　employee [implɔ́iːi] 명 직원

19 적절한 응답 고르기 　　　　　　　　정답 ①

M	Heather, what are you writing down?
W	Oh, I'm just making some notes for video ideas.
M	I didn't know you made videos.
W	I don't yet, but I want to start my own channel.
M	What will your videos be about?
W	I'm trying to decide between doing book reviews or recording my daily life.
M	I think the book idea is great. You know so much about books.
W	Really? Would you watch my videos?
M	Of course. I can't wait to see them.

남	Heather, 넌 뭘 적고 있니?
여	오, 그냥 영상 찍을 아이디어들을 기록하고 있었어.
남	네가 영상을 만드는지 몰랐어.
여	아직은 안 하지만, 나만의 채널을 시작하고 싶어.
남	어떤 것에 대한 영상을 만들 거야?
여	책 리뷰하는 것과 일상생활을 찍는 것 중에서 결정하려 하고 있어.
남	책에 대한 아이디어가 좋은 것 같아. 너 책에 대해 매우 많이 알고 있잖아.
여	정말? 내 영상 봐줄 거야?
남	물론이지. 빨리 보고 싶어.

해설 | 여자가 자신의 영상을 봐줄 것인지 물었으므로 정답은 그러겠다고 답하는 ① 'Of course. I can't wait to see them.'이다.

선택지 해석
① 물론이지. 빨리 보고 싶어.   ② 내 영상은 500뷰를 넘겼어.   ③ 보고서에 뭘 써야 할지 모르겠어.   ④ 그 쇼는 다른 채널에서 해.   ⑤ 그 책 가게에 막 풀렸어.

어휘 | write down 적다, 기록하다   make a note 기록하다   decide [disáid] 통 결정하다

20 상황에 적절한 말 고르기   정답 ②

W   David and Karen are in the same math class. David often forgets to bring an eraser to class. As he sits next to Karen, he asks to borrow hers. The first time this happened, Karen did not mind. But now it is starting to bother her. She wants to tell David to always bring an eraser to class. In this situation, what would Karen most likely say to David?

Karen   David, remember to bring an eraser each day.

여   David과 Karen은 같은 수학 수업을 듣습니다. David는 종종 수업에 지우개 가져오는 것을 잊어버립니다. 그는 Karen 옆에 앉기 때문에, 그는 그녀의 것을 빌려달라고 요청합니다. 처음 이런 일이 일어났을 때, Karen은 신경 쓰지 않았습니다. 하지만 이제 그것은 그녀를 성가시게 합니다. 그녀는 David에게 수업에 항상 지우개를 가져오라고 말하고 싶습니다. 이러한 상황에서, Karen이 David에게 가장 할 것 같은 말은 무엇입니까?

Karen   David, 잊지 말고 매일 지우개 가져와.

해설 | Karen이 David에게 수업에 항상 지우개를 가져오라고 말하고 싶다고 했으므로 정답은 ② 'remember to bring an eraser each day.'이다.

선택지 해석
① 다른 학생들을 성가시게 하지 마.   ② 잊지 말고 매일 지우개 가져와.   ③ 너 수학 숙제 다 했어?   ④ 넌 다른 책상에 앉아야 해.   ⑤ 네 지우개 빌려도 돼?

어휘 | borrow [bárou] 통 빌리다   mind [maind] 통 신경 쓰다 명 마음, 정신   bother [báðər] 통 성가시게 하다

(02회) 실전 모의고사

| 문제 pp.34-35

1	⑤	2	④	3	②	4	②	5	④	6	④	7	③	8	③	9	③	10	④
11	④	12	⑤	13	③	14	①	15	⑤	16	④	17	③	18	②	19	⑤	20	③

1 알맞은 그림 고르기   정답 ⑤

M   Hello, do you need help?

W   Yes. I'm looking for a suitcase for my trip to France.

M   All right. Would you like a suitcase with two wheels or four?

W   I'd prefer a four-wheeled suitcase. It would be more stable.

M   Okay. We have ones with prints and ones without them. They are all very trendy. You can choose any of these.

W   I like simple things, so the ones without a print would be better.

M   Good choice! Now, do you need one with a front pocket?

W   Yes. That would be more convenient. So, I'll take the one with a front pocket.

M   Okay. I hope you have a wonderful trip.

남   안녕하세요, 도와드릴까요?

여   네. 저는 프랑스로 여행 갈 때 쓸 여행 가방을 찾고 있어요.

남   알겠습니다. 바퀴 2개짜리를 원하시나요, 아니면 4개짜리를 원하시나요?

여   바퀴 4개짜리 여행 가방이 좋겠어요. 그게 더 안정적일 거예요.

남   네. 무늬가 있는 것과 없는 것이 있어요. 모두 최신 유행이랍니다. 이것들 중에서 고르시면 됩니다.

여   전 단순한 걸 좋아해서, 무늬가 없는 게 더 낫겠어요.

남   잘 고르셨어요! 그러면, 앞주머니가 달린 게 필요하세요?

여   네. 그게 더 편리할 것 같아요. 그러니, 앞주머니가 있는 이걸로 살게요.

남   알겠습니다. 멋진 여행 하시길 바랄게요.

해설 | 여자가 바퀴 4개의 무늬가 없으며 앞주머니가 있는 여행 가방을 사겠다고 했으므로 정답은 ⑤이다.

어휘 | suitcase [sútkeis] 명 여행 가방   stable [stéibl] 형 안정적인   trendy [tréndi] 형 최신 유행의   front [frʌnt] 명 앞   convenient [kənvíːnjənt] 형 편리한

2 언급하지 않은 내용 고르기
정답 ④

W	Do you use a music app, Ken?
M	I do. I listen to songs on CloudR.
W	What do you think of it?
M	First of all, CloudR has more songs than other apps. And it recommends songs that I would like by analyzing my song lists.
W	But isn't it a little expensive?
M	It is 15 dollars per month. But it offers a discount with certain types of credit cards.
W	I only pay five dollars for the app I use.
M	Well, that's much cheaper.
W	Maybe I don't need to use CloudR then.

여	너 음악 앱 사용하니, Ken?
남	사용하지. 난 CloudR로 노래를 들어.
여	그거 어떤 것 같아?
남	먼저, CloudR은 다른 앱보다 노래가 더 많아. 그리고 그건 내 선곡표를 분석해서 내가 좋아할 것 같은 노래들을 추천해줘.
여	그렇지만 그거 좀 비싸지 않아?
남	한 달에 15달러야. 그런데 특정 종류의 신용 카드에는 할인을 제공해.
여	난 내가 사용하는 앱에 겨우 5달러만 내고 있어.
남	음, 그게 훨씬 싸네.
여	그러면 난 CloudR을 사용할 필요가 없을지도 모르겠어.

해설 | ① 이름(CloudR), ② 구독료(한 달에 15달러), ③ 특징(노래가 더 많고 좋아할 것 같은 노래를 추천해 줌), ⑤ 할인 정보(특정 종류의 신용 카드에 할인을 제공함)에 대해 언급했으므로 정답은 ④ '음질'이다.

어휘 | recommend [rèkəménd] ⑧ 추천하다 analyze [ǽnəlàiz] ⑧ 분석하다 discount [dískaunt] ⑲ 할인 certain [sɔ́:rtn] ⑲ 특정한 credit card 신용 카드

3 목적 고르기
정답 ②

	[Cellphone rings.]
W	Hello, Brett.
M	Hi, Kyla. Are you busy right now?
W	No. What do you need?
M	I forgot my English textbook at school. I can't do my homework without it.
W	Oh, do you want to borrow my textbook?
M	That's why I called, actually.
W	Okay. Can you come pick it up now?
M	What about after dinner? I could drop by around 8.
W	That's fine. I'll see you then.

	[휴대폰이 울린다.]
여	안녕, Brett.
남	안녕, Kyla. 지금 바빠?
여	아니. 뭐 필요해?
남	학교에 내 영어 교과서를 깜빡하고 두고 왔어. 그게 없으면 숙제를 할 수가 없어.
여	오, 내 교과서를 빌리고 싶은 거야?
남	사실, 그래서 전화한 거야.
여	알겠어. 지금 가지러 올 수 있어?
남	저녁 이후엔 어때? 8시쯤에 들를 수 있어.
여	괜찮아. 그때 보자.

해설 | 여자가 자신의 교과서를 빌리고 싶은 건지 묻자 남자가 그래서 전화했다고 했으므로 정답은 ② '교과서를 빌리려고'이다.

어휘 | textbook [tékstbuk] ⑲ 교과서 drop by 들르다

4 시간 정보 고르기
정답 ②

W	Hello. I'd like to do some volunteer work here this Saturday.
M	We have a few programs. What time are you free?
W	I'd like to come in the morning.
M	We have a reading program at 9. Volunteers read to our patients during breakfast.
W	That's a little early. Are there any later programs?
M	We also have a game time that begins at 10:30.
W	What time does that end?
M	It lasts for an hour, so you'd be done by 11:30.
W	That's perfect. I'll come for that then.

여	안녕하세요. 전 이번 주 토요일에 여기에서 자원봉사를 좀 하고 싶은데요.
남	저희는 몇 가지 프로그램이 있어요. 몇 시가 괜찮으세요?
여	오전에 방문하고 싶어요.
남	9시에 독서 프로그램이 있어요. 봉사자들이 아침 식사 동안에 환자분들에게 읽어줘요.
여	그건 좀 이르네요. 더 이후의 프로그램이 있을까요?
남	10시 30분에 시작하는 게임 시간도 있어요.
여	그건 몇 시에 끝나나요?
남	한 시간 동안 이어지니까, 11시 30분에는 끝날 거예요.
여	아주 좋네요. 그러면 그걸 하러 갈게요.

해설 | 남자가 10시 30분에 시작하는 게임 시간을 얘기하자 여자가 그것을 하러 가겠다고 했으므로 정답은 ② '10:30 a.m.'이다.

어휘 | volunteer work 자원봉사 patient [péiʃənt] ⑲ 환자 end [end] ⑧ 끝나다 ⑲ 끝 last [læst] ⑧ 이어지다, 계속되다

5 심정 고르기

M	Is everyone enjoying my magic show so far?
W	Yes. It's fantastic!
M	For my next trick, I need a helper. Is anyone interested?
W	I'd love to!
M	Thank you. Please come up to the stage.
W	Alright. [Pause] What should I do for you?
M	Please look inside this magic hat.
W	There's nothing inside the hat.
M	It was empty. But now there's a rabbit inside it.
W	Wow, amazing! I can't believe it!

남	모두 지금까지 제 마술쇼를 즐기고 있으신가요?
여	네. 환상적이에요!
남	제 다음 트릭을 위해, 도와줄 분이 필요한데요. 관심 있는 분 있으세요?
여	제가 하고 싶어요!
남	감사합니다. 무대 위로 올라와 주세요.
여	알겠어요. [잠시 멈춤] 제가 뭘 해드리면 되나요?
남	이 마술 모자 안쪽을 봐주세요.
여	모자 안에는 아무것도 없어요.
남	아무것도 없었죠. 하지만 지금은 안에 토끼가 있답니다.
여	우와, 놀라워요! 믿을 수가 없네요!

해설 | 빈 모자에서 토끼가 나오는 마술 트릭을 보고 여자가 놀랍고 믿을 수 없다고 했으므로 정답은 ④ 'surprised'이다.

선택지 해석
① 수줍은 ② 짜증이 난 ③ 안도한 ④ 놀란 ⑤ 후회하는

어휘 | so far 지금까지 fantastic [fæntǽstik] 형 환상적인 amazing [əméiziŋ] 형 놀라운

6 그림 상황에 적절한 대화 고르기

① M	This magazine article is interesting.
W	What is it about?
② M	Can I see your library card?
W	I forgot to bring it.
③ M	How long can I borrow books for?
W	Two weeks.
④ M	What are you doing?
W	I'm studying for my history test.
⑤ M	What are you watching?
W	It's a documentary about gorillas.

① 남	이 잡지 기사 흥미롭다.
여	뭐에 관한 건데?
② 남	도서관 카드를 보여주시겠어요?
여	가져오는 걸 잊어버렸어요.
③ 남	책을 얼마 동안 빌릴 수 있나요?
여	2주요.
④ 남	뭐 하고 있어?
여	역사 시험공부 중이야.
⑤ 남	뭐 보고 있어?
여	고릴라에 관한 다큐멘터리야.

해설 | 여자가 책을 보며 시험공부를 하고 있고 남자가 그 옆에서 질문을 하고 있는 상황이므로 정답은 ④이다.

어휘 | magazine [mǽgəzìːn] 명 잡지 article [áːrtikl] 명 기사 documentary [dàkjuméntəri] 명 다큐멘터리

7 부탁·요청한 일 고르기

W	Why are you awake so early, Honey?
M	I have a big meeting at work today, so I want to prepare for it.
W	Do you want some breakfast? We have eggs and bacon.
M	Sure. And do we have any coffee left?
W	Let me check. [Pause] Oh, no. We don't.
M	I can go to the store for some quickly.
W	No. You stay here and prepare for your meeting. I will go. Could you just hand me the car keys on the table?
M	Of course.

여	왜 이렇게 일찍 깼어, 여보?
남	오늘 회사에서 중요한 회의가 있어서, 그걸 준비하려고.
여	아침 좀 먹을래? 달걀이랑 베이컨이 있는데.
남	그럼 좋지. 그리고 커피 좀 남아 있어?
여	확인해볼게. [잠시 멈춤] 오, 이런. 없네.
남	내가 빨리 커피를 사러 가게에 갈 수 있어.
여	아니야. 당신은 여기 남아서 회의를 준비해. 내가 갈게. 식탁 위에서 차 열쇠만 건네줄래?
남	당연하지.

해설 | 여자가 남자에게 식탁 위에 놓인 차 열쇠를 건네 달라고 부탁했으므로 정답은 ③ '차 열쇠 건네주기'이다.

어휘 | awake [əwéik] 형 깨어 있는 prepare [pripέər] 동 준비하다 hand [hænd] 동 건네주다 명 손

8 언급하지 않은 내용 고르기 　　　　　　　정답 ③

M	Welcome to the Morris Elementary School Talent Show. I am <mark>Principal Jim Williams</mark>, and I will <u>be the host</u> of the competition. Before we begin today, I want to explain the contest. Each student will have <u>five minutes</u> to perform. <mark>Four teachers</mark> will be the judges. The student <u>with the most points</u> from the judges will win. The prize for the winner is <u>a large trophy</u>. I hope all of you enjoy the show today.	남	모리스 초등학교의 장기 자랑 대회에 오신 걸 환영합니다. 저는 교장 Jim Williams이고, 제가 대회의 진행을 맡겠습니다. 오늘 시작하기 전에, 대회에 관해 설명해드리겠습니다. 각 학생이 공연할 5분의 시간을 가질 겁니다. 네 명의 선생님들이 심사위원을 맡아주실 겁니다. 심사위원들로부터 가장 많은 점수를 받은 학생이 우승합니다. 우승자가 받을 상품은 대형 트로피입니다. 오늘 여러분 모두가 이 행사를 즐기시길 바랍니다.

해설 | ① 진행자(Jim Williams 교장 선생님), ② 공연 길이(5분), ④ 상품 종류(대형 트로피), ⑤ 심사위원 수(4명)에 대해 언급했으므로 정답은 ③ '참가 자격'이다.

어휘 | host [houst] 명 진행자, 사회자; 주인　competition [kὰmpətíʃən] 명 대회, 경쟁　judge [dʒʌdʒ] 명 심사위원; 재판관　prize [praiz] 명 상품, 상

9 화제 고르기 　　　　　　　정답 ③

M	This is enjoyed in various ways by people all over the world. It can be a snack, <u>a side dish</u>, or a meal. It is especially popular in Asia. To make it, you take flour and make some dough. Next, <mark>you make small round pieces of dough</mark>. Then, <mark>you put some filling inside</mark>. Popular things <u>to put inside</u> are meat and vegetables. After you close the piece of dough, <mark>you boil it, fry it, or steam it</mark>.	남	이것은 전 세계의 사람들이 다양한 방식으로 즐기고 있습니다. 이건 간식이나, 반찬, 또는 식사가 될 수 있습니다. 이것은 특히 아시아에서 인기가 많습니다. 이걸 만들려면, 밀가루를 가지고 반죽을 만듭니다. 다음으로, 작고 둥근 반죽 조각을 만듭니다. 그러고 나면, 안에 속을 넣어줍니다. 속에 넣을 인기 있는 것들은 고기와 채소입니다. 반죽 조각을 오므린 후에, 그것을 끓이거나 튀기거나 찝니다.

해설 | 이것(This)은 작고 둥근 밀가루 반죽 안에 고기와 채소 같은 속을 채운 뒤 끓이거나 튀기거나 쪄서 만든다고 했으므로 정답은 ③ '만두'이다.

어휘 | side dish 반찬　dough [dou] 명 밀가루 반죽　filling [fíliŋ] 명 속, 소; 충전　fry [frai] 동 튀기다　steam [sti:m] 동 찌다 명 증기

10 어색한 대화 고르기 　　　　　　　정답 ④

① M	Do you want to have the lesson in the morning or the afternoon?	① 남	수업을 오전에 듣고 싶으세요 아니면 오후에 듣고 싶으세요?
W	<u>Either time</u> is okay with me.	여	어느 때든 괜찮아요.
② M	Excuse me. Where is the pool?	② 남	실례합니다. 수영장은 어디에 있나요?
W	It's <u>behind the building</u>. I'll show you where it is.	여	건물 뒤에 있어요. 제가 어디 있는지 알려드릴게요.
③ M	I saw that a new gardening store opened.	③ 남	나 새 원예용품 가게가 개업한 걸 봤어.
W	Oh, let's go there. We need some <u>seeds to plant</u>.	여	오, 거기에 가보자. 우리는 심을 씨앗이 필요해.
④ M	<mark>It's too cold in here. Let's turn on the heater.</mark>	④ 남	여기 너무 춥다. 난방기를 켜자.
W	<mark>I think I have a cold too.</mark>	여	나도 감기에 걸린 것 같아.
⑤ M	I'd like to speak with the manager.	⑤ 남	관리자와 얘기하고 싶습니다.
W	I'm the manager. How can I help you?	여	제가 관리자입니다. 무엇을 도와드릴까요?

해설 | 남자가 여자에게 난방기를 켜자고 제안했으므로, 여자는 제안에 대한 동의나 거절을 말해야 한다. 그러나 여자가 자신도 감기에 걸린 것 같다는 어색한 대답을 했으므로 정답은 ④이다.

어휘 | either [íːðər] 형 어느 쪽의　seed [si:d] 명 씨앗　plant [plænt] 동 심다 명 식물　turn on 켜다　have a cold 감기에 걸리다　manager [mǽnidʒər] 명 관리자, 경영자

11 할 일 고르기 　　　　　　　정답 ④

	[Cellphone rings.]		[휴대폰이 울린다.]
M	<u>What's up</u>, Wendy?	남	무슨 일이야, Wendy?
W	Hi, James. What are you doing right now?	여	안녕, James. 지금 뭐 하고 있어?
M	I'm shopping at the mall. Why?	남	쇼핑몰에서 쇼핑 중이야. 왜?
W	Really? I need to <u>buy school supplies</u>. Can I join you?	여	정말? 나 학용품을 사야 하는데. 합류해도 될까?
M	Sure. When can you come?	남	물론이지. 언제 올 수 있어?
W	I'll be there in 30 minutes.	여	30분 후면 거기에 도착할 거야.
M	Okay. <mark>I'll shop for clothes</mark> while I wait for you.	남	알겠어. 나는 널 기다리는 동안 옷을 사야겠어.
W	Alright. I'll <u>text</u> you when I arrive.	여	그래. 도착하면 문자 보낼게.

12 위치 고르기
정답 ⑤

W	Jack, should we get tickets for the movie tonight?
M	Yeah, let's check for seats. Where do you usually sit in a theater?
W	I always sit close to the exit. I usually go to the restroom in the middle of the movie.
M	One section is for the disabled, so we can't sit there. Also, I like sitting near the speakers.
W	It's okay to sit in the back this time.
M	Thanks. It seems like Section D's already full. We can choose between E and F.
W	How about the one closer to the speaker and the exit?
M	Great.

여 Jack, 오늘 밤 영화표를 사야 할까?
남 응, 좌석을 확인해보자. 보통 영화관에서 어디 앉아?
여 난 항상 출구 가까이에 앉아. 보통 영화 중간에 화장실에 가거든.
남 한 구역은 장애인석이니까, 거기 앉을 수는 없겠네. 그리고, 내가 스피커 근처에 앉는 걸 좋아하거든.
여 이번에는 뒤에 앉아도 괜찮아.
남 고마워. D 구역은 이미 다 찬 거 같네. E 구역과 F 구역 중에서 고르면 되겠다.
여 스피커와 출구에 더 가까운 곳은 어때?
남 좋지.

해설 | 여자가 E 구역과 F 구역 중에서 스피커와 출구에 더 가까운 곳을 제안하자 남자가 좋다고 했으므로 정답은 ⑤이다.

어휘 | seat [si:t] 圆 좌석   exit [ɛ́gzit] 圆 출구   restroom [rɛ́stru:m] 圆 화장실   disabled [diséibld] 圈 장애의, 신체장애가 있는

13 시간 정보 고르기
정답 ③

	[Cellphone rings.]
M	Hi, Jenny. What are you up to this Friday?
W	I'm going to an art exhibit at the Coleman Gallery on that evening. Do you want to come?
M	Well, I'm supposed to meet another friend at 9 p.m.
W	We could go before then. I was thinking of heading to the gallery around 5.
M	I don't finish work until 6.
W	Then, what about 7? We'll be done by 8 at the latest. So, you'll still have time to get to your other appointment.
M	Perfect. And how about coming with me after the exhibit? I'm sure my friend would love to meet you.
W	Sure. I'd love to hang out.

[휴대폰이 울린다.]
남 안녕, Jenny. 이번 주 금요일에 뭐 할 거야?
여 그날 저녁에 콜먼 미술관에서 열릴 미술 전시회에 갈 거야. 너도 갈래?
남 글쎄, 난 9시에 다른 친구를 만나야 해.
여 그 전에 갈 수도 있어. 미술관에 5시쯤에 갈까 생각 중이었거든.
남 난 6시는 되어야 일이 끝나.
여 그러면, 7시는 어때? 늦어도 8시에는 끝날 거야. 그러면 여전히 네 다른 약속에 갈 시간이 있겠지.
남 완벽해. 그리고 전시회 끝나고 나랑 같이 가는 건 어때? 내 친구가 널 만나고 싶어 할 거 같아.
여 물론이지. 나도 같이 놀고 싶어.

해설 | 여자가 7시에 만나서 전시회에 가는 것을 제안하자 남자가 완벽하다고 했으므로 정답은 ③ '7 p.m.'이다.

어휘 | be supposed to ~해야 하다, 하기로 되어 있다   head [hed] 图 가다, 향하다 圆 머리   at the latest 늦어도   hang out 놀다, 어울리다

14 한 일 고르기
정답 ①

M	Mia, are you okay? Your face is a little red.
W	Yeah. It's because I was in the sun all day.
M	What did you do?
W	My family went to the beach for a week.
M	Did you forget to wear sunscreen?
W	I was so careful all week. But then we went on a boat ride yesterday, and I forgot a hat and sunscreen.
M	Oh, no. I hope your sunburn gets better soon.
W	Thank you.

남 Mia, 너 괜찮아? 얼굴이 약간 빨개.
여 응. 그건 내가 온종일 햇볕을 쫴서 그래.
남 뭘 했길래?
여 우리 가족은 일주일 동안 바닷가에 가 있었거든.
남 자외선 차단제 바르는 걸 잊었던 거야?
여 난 한 주 내내 정말 조심했어. 그런데 어제 보트 타러 갔는데, 모자랑 자외선 차단제를 깜빡했어.
남 오, 이런. 햇볕에 탄 게 빨리 낫길 바랄게.
여 고마워.

해설 | 여자가 어제 가족들과 보트를 타러 갔다고 했으므로 정답은 ① '보트 타기'이다.

어휘 | sunscreen [sʌ́nskri:n] 圆 자외선 차단제, 선크림   careful [kɛ́ərfəl] 圈 조심하는   sunburn [sʌ́nbə̀rn] 圆 햇볕에 탐

15 목적 고르기　　　　　　　　　　　　　정답 ⑤

M　Good evening, customers. We hope you are finding everything you need at Nature's Market. Since it is the end of the day, we have some fresh items currently on sale. Our broccoli and cucumbers are up to 50% off right now. In addition, a few of our baked goods are also being sold at a reduced price. Please pick up these products before we close to take advantage of these discounts. Happy shopping!

남　안녕하세요, 고객님들. 여러분이 Nature's Market에서 필요로 하는 모든 걸 찾으시길 바랍니다. 오늘의 마감 시간이므로, 신선 품목들 몇 가지가 지금 할인에 들어갑니다. 브로콜리와 오이가 당장 최대 50%까지 할인됩니다. 게다가, 저희의 제과 제품들 역시 할인된 가격에 팔고 있습니다. 이 할인 혜택을 누리시려면 저희가 마감하기 전에 이 제품들을 구입해 주세요. 즐거운 쇼핑 되세요!

해설 | 남자가 마트의 신선 품목과 제과 제품이 할인된 가격에 팔리고 있음을 설명하고 있으므로 정답은 ⑤ '할인 정보를 안내하려고'이다.

어휘 | up to 최대 ~까지 off [ɔːf] ⊡ 할인하여; 떨어져 in addition 게다가 reduce [ridjúːs] ⑧ 할인하다; 줄이다
take advantage of ~의 혜택을 누리다, ~을 이용하다

16 금액 정보 고르기　　　　　　　　　　　정답 ④

W　Welcome to Johnson City Aquarium. What can I help you with?
M　Hi. I'd like to buy two tickets. How much are they?
W　A general ticket is 20 dollars, but a ticket for the guided experience is 30 dollars.
M　Two tickets for the guided experience, please.
W　Okay, then your total is 60 dollars.
M　Can I use this discount coupon?
W　Let me check. [Pause] Yes. You can get 10 dollars off.
M　Great. I'll pay with cash then.

여　존슨 시티 수족관에 오신 걸 환영합니다. 무엇을 도와드릴까요?
남　안녕하세요. 티켓 2장을 사고 싶어요. 얼마인가요?
여　일반 티켓은 20달러이지만, 안내 체험 티켓은 30달러입니다.
남　안내 체험으로 2장 주세요.
여　알겠습니다, 그러면 총 60달러입니다.
남　이 할인 쿠폰을 쓸 수 있을까요?
여　확인해보겠습니다. [잠시 멈춤] 네. 10달러 할인받으실 수 있으세요.
남　좋네요. 그러면 현금으로 지불할게요.

해설 | 남자가 30달러짜리 안내 체험 티켓을 2장 구매하겠다고 했고, 할인 쿠폰을 사용해서 10달러를 할인받았으므로 정답은 ④ '$ 50'이다.

어휘 | aquarium [əkwéəriəm] ⑨ 수족관 guided [gáidid] ⑧ 안내를 받는 experience [ikspíəriəns] ⑨ 체험, 경험 cash [kæʃ] ⑨ 현금

17 적절한 응답 고르기　　　　　　　　　　정답 ③

W　I'm sorry for being late. The bus took so long.
M　That's okay. It's a long drive here.
W　Yes. But it is beautiful here. It's so nice being outside of the city.
M　Right. It's so green here.
W　I'm also so excited for picking apples. How many apples can we pick?
M　As many as this basket can hold.
W　Great! We should give some to our teacher next week. She loves apples.
M　That's right! She'd love some of them.

여　늦어서 미안해. 버스가 너무 오래 걸렸어.
남　괜찮아. 여기까지 오래 걸리잖아.
여　응. 그런데 여기 진짜 아름답다. 도시 밖에 나와 있는 것도 참 좋고.
남　맞아. 여긴 참 푸릇푸릇해.
여　또 사과 따는 것도 너무 기대돼. 우리 사과를 몇 개까지 딸 수 있어?
남　이 바구니에 담을 수 있을 만큼.
여　좋았어! 다음 주에 우리 선생님께 좀 드려야겠어. 선생님이 사과를 좋아하시잖아.
남　맞아! 그것들을 좋아하실 거야.

해설 | 여자가 선생님에게 오늘 딴 사과 일부를 드리는 것을 제안하고 있으므로 정답은 제안에 동의하는 ③ 'That's right! She'd love some of them.'이다.

〖선택지 해석〗
① 알겠어. 다음에는 일찍 나올게.　② 선생님은 모든 종류의 과일을 키우셔.　③ 맞아! 그것들을 좋아하실 거야.　④ 농장에서 할 수 있는 활동들이 더 있어.
⑤ 이 바구니를 더 작은 걸로 바꾸자.

어휘 | outside [àutsáid] ⑧ 밖의 pick [pik] ⑧ 따다; 고르다 hold [hould] ⑧ 담다, 수용할 수 있다; 잡다 show up 나오다; 나타나다
activity [æktívəti] ⑨ 활동

18 적절한 응답 고르기 　　　　　　　　　　　　정답 ②

[Telephone rings.]	[전화기가 울린다.]
M　Home Décor Warehouse. How can I help you?	남　Home Décor Warehouse입니다. 무엇을 도와드릴까요?
W　Hi. I want to check on a refund for a purchase.	여　안녕하세요. 구매 건에 대해 환불을 확인하고 싶어요.
M　Alright. Can you tell me your order number?	남　그러시군요. 주문 번호를 말씀해 주시겠어요?
W　I'm looking at the email with the purchase details, but I can't find the order number.	여　구매 내역이 적힌 이메일을 보고 있는데요, 주문 번호를 못 찾겠어요.
M　It should be at the beginning of the email.	남　그건 이메일의 첫 부분에 있을 거예요.
W　Okay. Hold on. [Pause] It's G4BIWI.	여　네. 잠시만요. [잠시 멈춤] G4BIWI예요.
M　Got it. Thanks. So, what is your question about the refund?	남　알겠습니다. 감사합니다. 그러면, 환불 관련하여 무엇을 묻고 싶으세요?
W　When will I receive the money?	여　언제 돈을 받을 수 있나요?

해설ㅣ 남자가 환불에 관하여 무엇을 묻고 싶은지 물었으므로 정답은 환불과 관련된 구체적인 질문을 하는 ② 'When will I receive the money?'이다.

선택지 해석
① 그 상품은 막 동났습니다.　② 언제 돈을 받을 수 있나요?　③ 그녀는 어제 저에게 이메일을 보내줬어요.　④ 실수로 영수증을 잃어버렸어요.
⑤ 고객님의 소파는 내일 배송될 겁니다.

어휘ㅣ purchase [pə́ːrtʃəs] 명 구매 동 구매하다　detail [ditéil] 명 내역, 세부　accidentally [æksədéntəli] 부 실수로; 우연히　receipt [risíːt] 명 영수증
couch [kautʃ] 명 소파, 카우치

19 적절한 응답 고르기 　　　　　　　　　　　　정답 ⑤

W　Are you going to the dance club practice tonight, Jaemin?	여　오늘 밤 댄스 동아리 연습에 갈 거니, 재민아?
M　Yes. I'll be there. It's at 5 o'clock, isn't it?	남　응. 갈 거야. 5시잖아, 안 그래?
W　Actually, it starts two hours later today.	여　사실, 오늘 두 시간 늦게 시작할 거야.
M　Oh, that's pretty late. What about dinner?	남　오, 그건 꽤 늦는데. 저녁은 어쩌고?
W　It's okay because we will order pizza. We can eat and then practice.	여　피자 시킬 거라서 그건 괜찮아. 먹고 나서 연습하면 돼.
M　I need to tell my parents then. We usually have dinner together.	남　그러면 우리 부모님께 말씀드려야겠다. 우린 보통 저녁을 함께 먹거든.
W　You should call them now.	여　지금 전화 드려.
M　[Pause] I don't have my phone. I left it at home this morning. Can I borrow yours?	남　[잠시 멈춤] 내 휴대폰이 없네. 아침에 집에 두고 왔어. 네 걸 빌려도 될까?
W　Of course. Here you go.	여　물론이지. 여기 있어.

해설ㅣ 남자가 여자의 휴대폰을 빌려 달라고 부탁했으므로 정답은 부탁을 수락하는 ⑤ 'Of course. Here you go.'이다.

선택지 해석
① 네 휴대폰 번호를 알려줘.　② 응. 스테이크랑 채소를 먹을 거야.　③ 지연돼서 정말 미안해.　④ 이번 주엔 매일 춤 연습했어.　⑤ 물론이지. 여기 있어.

어휘ㅣ pretty [príti] 부 꽤 형 예쁜　delay [diléi] 명 지연 동 연기하다

20 상황에 적절한 말 고르기 　　　　　　　　　　　　정답 ③

M　Martin needs some new running shoes, so he visits the local mall to look at some. He tries on lots of shoes until he finally finds a pair that he likes. They are blue and very comfortable. However, they are a little too big. So, Martin wants to ask the store employee for a smaller size. In this situation, what would Martin most likely say to the store employee?	남　Martin은 새 운동화가 좀 필요해서, 몇몇 제품을 알아보러 지역 쇼핑몰을 방문합니다. 그는 많은 신발을 신어보고 나서야 마침내 그가 좋아하는 것을 찾아냅니다. 신발은 파란색이고 매우 편안합니다. 하지만, 그건 약간 많이 큽니다. 그래서, Martin은 가게 직원에게 더 작은 사이즈를 요청하고 싶습니다. 이러한 상황에서, Martin이 가게 직원에게 가장 할 것 같은 말은 무엇입니까?
Martin　Do you have these in a smaller size?	Martin　이거 더 작은 사이즈로 있나요?

해설ㅣ Martin이 가게 직원에게 더 작은 사이즈의 운동화를 요청하고 싶다고 했으므로 정답은 ③ 'Do you have these in a smaller size?'이다.

선택지 해석
① 이 신발 얼마인가요?　② 전 보통 5km 정도를 달려요.　③ 이거 더 작은 사이즈로 있나요?　④ 글쎄요, 이 신발은 저한테 너무 꽉 끼어요.
⑤ 이 파란색 신발이 제 스타일이에요.

어휘ㅣ local [lóukəl] 형 지역의, 지방의　try on 신어보다, 입어 보다　comfortable [kʌ́mfərtəbl] 형 편안한　employee [implɔ́ii:] 명 직원
tight [tait] 형 꽉 끼는; 단단히 맨

1	④	2	④	3	⑤	4	⑤	5	⑤	6	②	7	⑤	8	①	9	②	10	③
11	①	12	④	13	①	14	③	15	④	16	②	17	②	18	④	19	②	20	④

1 알맞은 그림 고르기

정답 ④

M Welcome to Women's Clothing. May I help you find something?

W Yes. I'm looking for a new skirt for this summer.

M I see. Do you want a specific style of skirt?

W I need a longer one that reaches my ankle.

M Okay. How about this jean skirt? We just got it.

W Hmm... No. The material doesn't look comfortable.

M Alright. Then, you can choose from these linen ones. They come in several colors and patterns.

W I like the one with palm trees on it. It makes me feel like I'm on vacation.

M Great choice! It is really comfortable and popular.

남 Women's Clothing에 오신 걸 환영합니다. 찾으시는 걸 도와드릴까요?

여 네. 전 이번 여름에 입을 새 치마를 찾고 있어요.

남 알겠습니다. 원하시는 특정한 치마 스타일이 있으신가요?

여 제 발목까지 닿는 긴 치마가 필요해요.

남 알겠습니다. 이 청치마는 어떠세요? 이건 막 들어온 겁니다.

여 흠... 아니요. 옷감이 편해 보이지 않네요.

남 그러시군요. 그러면 이 리넨 치마들 중에서 고르시면 됩니다. 색상과 무늬가 여러 가지로 나와 있죠.

여 야자나무 무늬가 있는 게 마음에 들어요. 휴가 온 것 같은 기분이 들게 하네요.

남 훌륭한 선택이세요! 그건 정말 편하고 인기가 많아요.

해설 | 여자가 발목까지 닿는 긴 리넨 치마에 야자나무 무늬가 있는 것이 좋다고 했으므로 정답은 ④이다.

어휘 | specific [spisífik] 혱 특정한　reach [ri:tʃ] 통 닿다　ankle [ǽŋkl] 명 발목　material [mətíəriəl] 명 옷감; 재료　palm tree 야자나무

2 언급하지 않은 내용 고르기

정답 ④

W Todd, thank you for coming.

M Sure, Ms. Sanchez. Do you want to talk about my essay on horses?

W Yes. You did a good job. But there were some problems.

M I see.

W First off, don't write too much. I asked for a four-page essay, but yours has seven pages.

M Okay. I'll be careful about the length next time.

W Good. You should also turn in your essay on time. It was due Thursday. But you handed it in a day late, didn't you?

M Yes. I'm sorry about that.

여 Todd, 와 줘서 고맙구나.

남 당연하죠, Sanchez 선생님. 말에 관한 제 작문에 대해 말씀하시고 싶으신가요?

여 그렇단다. 아주 잘했어. 하지만 몇 가지 문제가 있었지.

남 그렇군요.

여 우선, 너무 많이 쓰지 말거라. 내가 4쪽 분량의 작문을 요구했는데, 네 것은 7쪽이더구나.

남 알겠습니다. 다음에는 분량에 주의할게요.

여 좋아. 또한 제때 작문을 제출해야 한다. 그건 목요일까지였어. 그런데 넌 하루 늦게 제출했었지, 그렇지 않니?

남 맞아요. 죄송합니다.

해설 | ① 주제(말), ② 요구 분량(4쪽), ③ 실제 제출일(금요일), ⑤ 마감 기한(목요일)에 대해 언급했으므로 정답은 ④ '양식'이다.

어휘 | first off 우선　length [leŋkθ] 명 분량, 길이　turn in 제출하다　due [dju:] 혱 ~까지인, 예정인　hand in 제출하다

3 목적 고르기   정답 ⑤

[Telephone rings.]

W You've reached Anderson Grill. This is Amanda speaking.

M Hi, Amanda. I'm Jake from Vernon Food Supplies. I'm calling about your order.

W Oh, is there a problem?

M There is. Due to the poor road conditions, we can't deliver your items this afternoon.

W I see. When will our supplies arrive then?

M We will deliver everything by 10 a.m. tomorrow. We can't bring them any earlier. My apologies.

W Okay. Well, thanks for letting me know.

[전화기가 울린다.]

여 Anderson Grill에 전화 주셨습니다. Amanda입니다.

남 안녕하세요, Amanda. 저 Vernon Food Supplies의 Jake예요. 주문하신 것 관련해서 전화 드렸어요.

여 오, 문제가 있나요?

남 네. 도로 상황이 안 좋기 때문에, 오늘 오후에 물건을 배달할 수 없겠어요.

여 그렇군요. 그럼 언제 저희 물품이 도착할까요?

남 내일 오전 10시까지는 전부 배달할게요. 더 일찍은 못 가져다드려요. 사과드립니다.

여 괜찮아요. 음, 알려줘서 고마워요.

해설 | 남자가 여자의 주문과 관련하여 도로 상황 때문에 오늘 중으로 배달할 수 없겠다고 했으므로 정답은 ⑤ '배달 지연을 알리려고'이다.

어휘 | due to ~ 때문에 condition [kəndíʃən] 뗑 상황, 상태 supplies [səpláiz] 뗑 물품 (supply [səplái] 뗑 공급 통 공급하다) apology [əpɑ̀lədʒi] 뗑 사과

4 시간 정보 고르기   정답 ⑤

[Cellphone rings.]

M Hi, Mom. Can I ask you a favor?

W Of course. What is it?

M Could you pick me up from the department store this afternoon?

W Sure. When will your shopping be finished?

M By 2. But I want to play arcade games afterward. Can you come at 3?

W I'll be busy until 3:30. Would 4 be too late to pick you up?

M No. That's fine. I'll wait for you at the main entrance.

[휴대폰이 울린다.]

남 여보세요, 엄마. 부탁 하나 해도 될까요?

여 물론이지. 무엇이니?

남 오늘 오후에 백화점으로 데리러 와주실 수 있어요?

여 그럼. 언제 쇼핑이 끝나니?

남 2시에요. 그런데 이후에 오락실 게임을 하고 싶어요. 3시에 와주실 수 있어요?

여 내가 3시 30분까지는 바쁠 것 같구나. 4시에 데리러 가면 너무 늦겠니?

남 아니요. 괜찮아요. 정문에서 기다릴게요.

해설 | 여자가 4시에 데리러 가면 너무 늦을지 묻자 남자가 괜찮다고 했으므로 정답은 ⑤ '4:00 p.m.'이다.

어휘 | ask ~ a favor ~에게 부탁을 하다 department store 백화점 arcade game 오락실의 (비디오) 게임 afterward [ǽftərwərd] 閈 이후에, 뒤에
main entrance 정문

5 장소 고르기   정답 ⑤

W How can I help you?

M Can you clean these shirts? I spilled some ink on them.

W I think so. How many do you have in total?

M There are five here.

W Okay. Is there anything else you need?

M I also have this pair of pants. They need to be cleaned too.

W Alright. Your clothes will be ready in two days.

M Thank you.

여 무엇을 도와드릴까요?

남 이 셔츠를 세탁해주실 수 있나요? 위에 잉크를 흘렸어요.

여 가능할 것 같아요. 총 몇 장을 맡기실 건가요?

남 여기 5장이요.

여 네. 다른 필요하신 거 있으세요?

남 이 바지 한 벌도 있는데요. 이것도 세탁이 필요해요.

여 알겠습니다. 손님 옷은 이틀 후에 준비될 거예요.

남 감사합니다.

해설 | 남자가 셔츠와 바지를 세탁해 달라고 하자 여자가 이틀 후에 준비될 것이라고 대답하는 것으로 보아 정답은 ⑤ '세탁소'이다.

어휘 | spill [spil] 통 흘리다, 엎지르다 in total 총, 전체로 ready [rédi] 뒝 준비된

6 그림 상황에 적절한 대화 고르기   정답 ②

① W   Can I make an appointment on Saturday?
    M   I'm sorry. We're completely booked.
② W   How long will I have to wear this?
    M   Your arm is healing, but it will be two more weeks.
③ W   I'm here to see Dr. Robinson.
    M   Please write your name down here.
④ W   My arm is in pain.
    M   I think you should do some stretches.
⑤ W   You need to start eating healthier foods.
    M   Okay. I'll stop eating junk food.

① 여   토요일로 예약할 수 있나요?
    남   죄송합니다. 예약이 완전히 다 찼어요.
② 여   이걸 얼마 동안 차고 있어야 할까요?
    남   팔이 낫고는 있지만, 2주 더 걸릴 거예요.
③ 여   Robinson 박사님을 뵈러 왔어요.
    남   여기에 성함을 적어주세요.
④ 여   팔이 아파.
    남   스트레칭을 좀 해야 할 것 같아.
⑤ 여   넌 좀 더 건강에 좋은 음식을 먹기 시작해야 해.
    남   알겠어. 즉석식품 먹는 걸 그만둘게.

해설 | 여자가 팔에 한 붕대를 가리키고 있고 남자가 엑스레이를 보며 말하고 있는 상황이므로 정답은 ②이다.

어휘 | completely [kəmplíːtli] 囝 완전히   heal [hiːl] 图 낫다   write down 적다   in pain 아픈   healthy [hélθi] 囵 건강에 좋은; 건강한
junk food 즉석식품, 정크 푸드

7 부탁·요청한 일 고르기   정답 ⑤

[Cellphone rings.]
M   What's up, Mina?
W   Hey. I'm about five minutes away from your house.
M   Perfect. I'm almost finished packing my bag.
W   Did you pack bug spray and sunscreen for the hike?
M   Yes. I also packed some extra blankets. It might get cold in the tent.
W   Good idea. We have everything then.
M   Oh, what about music? Did you bring a speaker?
W   I totally forgot. Can you pack yours instead?
M   Yes. I'll get it now.

[휴대폰이 울린다.]
남   무슨 일이야, 미나야?
여   있지. 나 네 집에서 5분 정도 떨어진 곳에 있어.
남   완벽해. 나도 가방 거의 다 챙겼어.
여   등산할 때 쓸 방충제랑 자외선 차단제는 챙겼어?
남   응. 여분의 담요도 챙겼어. 텐트 안이 추워질 수도 있을 것 같아서.
여   좋은 생각이야. 그러면 전부 챙긴 거네.
남   오, 음악은? 스피커 가져왔어?
여   완전히 잊고 있었어. 네 걸 대신 챙겨줄래?
남   그래. 지금 그걸 가져갈게.

해설 | 여자가 남자에게 스피커를 대신 챙겨 달라고 부탁했으므로 정답은 ⑤ '스피커 챙기기'이다.

어휘 | bug spray 방충제, 방충 스프레이   extra [ékstrə] 囵 여분의   blanket [blǽŋkit] 囮 담요   totally [tóutəli] 囝 완전히

8 언급하지 않은 내용 고르기   정답 ①

W   Hi, class. There will be a school book fair next month. It'll be held for three days from February 20th. We will accept both cash and credit cards for book purchases at the fair. You can also order books before the event through the book fair website at bookfair20.com. Also, everyone will be given a bookmark as a gift.

여   안녕하세요, 학생 여러분. 다음 달에 학교 도서 박람회가 있을 예정입니다. 2월 20일부터 3일 동안 열릴 예정입니다. 박람회에서의 도서 구매에 대해 현금과 신용 카드 둘 다 받을 예정입니다. 도서 박람회 웹사이트인 bookfair20.com에서 행사 전에 도서를 주문하실 수도 있습니다. 또한, 모든 사람에게 책갈피가 선물로 증정될 것입니다.

해설 | ② 날짜(2월 20일부터 3일 동안), ③ 지불 방법(현금과 신용 카드 둘 다), ④ 웹사이트(bookfair20.com), ⑤ 기념품(책갈피)에 대해 언급했으므로 정답은 ① '장소'이다.

어휘 | fair [fɛər] 囮 박람회 囵 공정한   accept [æksépt] 图 받다, 받아들이다   both A and B A와 B 둘 다

9 화제 고르기   정답 ②

W   People who have this job work for an orchestra or a choir. When a group of musicians or singers perform, they direct the group. They move around their hands or a stick made of wood to help people play or sing at the correct speed. To have this job, you need to know a lot about music.

여   이 직업을 가진 사람들은 오케스트라나 합창단에서 일합니다. 연주자들이나 성악가들이 공연할 때, 그들은 그 집단을 지휘합니다. 그들은 사람들이 정확한 속도로 연주하거나 노래하도록 돕기 위해 손이나 나무로 만든 막대기를 움직입니다. 이 직업을 갖기 위해서는, 음악에 관해 많은 것을 알고 있어야 합니다.

해설 | 이 직업(this job)을 가진 사람들은 연주자들이나 성악가들이 공연할 때 그들을 지휘한다고 했으므로 정답은 ② '지휘자'이다.

어휘 | choir [kwaiər] 몡 합창단 direct [dirékt] 툉 지휘하다, 지도하다 stick [stik] 몡 막대기

---

10 어색한 대화 고르기 정답 ③

① M	I saw a great movie last night.	
W	Oh, yeah? What's the title of the movie?	
② M	The math test was so hard.	
W	Don't worry. You'll get a good score!	
③ M	How much did the concert tickets cost?	
W	They will play this song at the concert.	
④ M	Do you like drinking coffee?	
W	Yes. I drink two cups a day.	
⑤ M	What do you think about this novel?	
W	I think it's thrilling.	

① 남 어젯밤에 아주 좋은 영화를 봤어.
여 오, 그래? 영화 제목이 뭔데?
② 남 수학 시험이 너무 어려웠어.
여 걱정하지 마. 좋은 점수를 받을 거야!
③ 남 콘서트 티켓은 얼마였어?
여 그들은 콘서트에서 이 노래를 연주할 거야.
④ 남 너 커피 마시는 거 좋아해?
여 응. 하루에 두 잔씩 마셔.
⑤ 남 이 소설에 대해 어떻게 생각해?
여 스릴 만점인 것 같아.

해설 | 남자가 여자에게 콘서트 티켓이 얼마였는지 물었으므로, 여자는 구체적인 가격을 답해야 한다. 그러나 여자가 그들은 콘서트에서 이 노래를 연주할 것이라는 어색한 대답을 했으므로 정답은 ③이다.

어휘 | score [skɔːr] 몡 점수 novel [návəl] 몡 소설 thrilling [θríliŋ] 혱 스릴 만점의; 감격적인

---

11 할 일 고르기 정답 ①

M How are the plans for Aaron's surprise party going?
W Well, we still need food and some decorations.
M Balloons would look good for decorations.
W Yes. But I don't know where to buy them.
M I'll buy them at a store later. Can you prepare the food?
W Thank you. I ordered a cake, but I need to get food for dinner.
M Why don't you just order some pizza?
W Okay, I will. I can do that now.

남 Aaron의 깜짝 파티 계획은 어떻게 돼가고 있어?
여 글쎄, 우린 아직 음식과 몇 가지 장식들이 필요해.
남 풍선이 장식으로 좋아 보일 것 같은데.
여 그래. 그런데 그걸 어디에서 사야 할지 모르겠어.
남 내가 나중에 가게에서 살게. 넌 음식을 준비해 줄 수 있을까?
여 고마워. 내가 케이크를 주문했는데, 저녁 식사로 먹을 음식을 사야 해.
남 그냥 피자를 좀 주문하는 건 어때?
여 알겠어, 그렇게. 지금 할 수 있어.

해설 | 남자가 피자를 주문하는 것을 제안하자 여자가 알겠다며 지금 할 수 있다고 했으므로 정답은 ① '피자 주문하기'이다.

어휘 | decoration [dèkəréiʃən] 몡 장식 balloon [bəlúːn] 몡 풍선

---

12 위치 고르기 정답 ④

M Ms. Evans, should I book a booth for the coffee expo?
W Yes, please. Do you have the map?
M Yes. Where should we set up our booth?
W Somewhere far from the restroom. It smelled so bad last year.
M Okay. How about this one?
W Hmm... I think it's better to have our booth across from the contest stage. We can watch the other people compete too.
M Sure. Do we need a large booth this year?
W I don't think so. Let's get a smaller one.
M Okay. We have two choices left.
W Let's book the one closer to the Business Lounge.
M No problem.

남 Evans씨, 커피 엑스포 부스를 예약할까요?
여 네, 그래 주세요. 지도 있으세요?
남 네. 어디에 우리 부스를 설치해야 할까요?
여 화장실에서 멀리 떨어진 어딘가요. 작년에 냄새가 정말 안 좋았거든요.
남 네. 여기는 어떠세요?
여 흠... 대회 무대 맞은편에 우리 부스를 두는 게 나을 거 같아요. 다른 사람들이 경쟁하는 걸 볼 수도 있잖아요.
남 그럼요. 올해는 넓은 부스가 필요할까요?
여 그럴 것 같진 않아요. 작은 걸로 하죠.
남 알겠습니다. 두 가지 선택지가 남았네요.
여 비즈니스 라운지에 가까운 곳으로 예약하죠.
남 알겠습니다.

해설 | 여자가 대회 무대 맞은편에 위치한 작은 부스 중에서 비즈니스 라운지에 가까운 곳으로 예약하자고 했으므로 정답은 ④이다.

어휘 | set up 설치하다 far from ~에서 멀리 떨어진 smell [smel] 툉 냄새가 나다 across from ~의 맞은편에 book [buk] 툉 예약하다 몡 책

---

13 시간 정보 고르기   정답 ①

[Telephone rings.]	[전화기가 울린다.]
M This is the Express Air customer service center. What can I do for you?	남 Express Air 고객 센터입니다. 무엇을 도와드릴까요?
W I'd like to change my flight.	여 제 항공편을 변경하고 싶어요.
M Could you tell me your name and booking number?	남 성함과 예약 번호를 말씀해주시겠습니까?
W My name is Louis White, and my booking number is 94848.	여 이름은 Louis White고, 예약 번호는 94848이에요.
M Okay, Ms. White. I see you are booked on a flight to Oakland on June 14th. It leaves at 4 p.m.	남 알겠습니다, White씨. 제가 보니까 6월 14일에 오클랜드행 항공편을 예약하셨군요. 오후 4시에 출발하네요.
W That's right. I'd like to arrive before 12 p.m. on the same day.	여 맞아요. 전 같은 날 오후 12시 전에 도착하고 싶어요.
M Let me see. [Typing sound] Then, I suggest you take the flight that leaves at 7 a.m. and arrives at 11 a.m. Will that work?	남 어디 볼게요. [타자치는 소리] 그러면, 오전 7시에 출발해서 오전 11시에 도착하는 비행기를 타시는 걸 제안 드려요. 그거면 되실까요?
W Yes. Thanks.	여 네. 감사합니다.

해설 | 남자가 여자에게 오전 7시에 출발하는 비행기를 탈 것을 제안하자 여자가 그러겠다고 했으므로 정답은 ① '7 a.m.'이다.

어휘 | customer service center 고객 센터   flight [flait] 뗑 항공편, 비행기   suggest [səgdʒést] 뙤 제안하다

14 한일 고르기   정답 ③

M Emma, how was your weekend? Didn't you have a soccer game?	남 Emma, 주말 어땠어? 축구 경기하지 않았어?
W Actually, it was canceled, so we couldn't play.	여 사실, 그게 취소돼서, 경기할 수 없었어.
M That's a pity. Why was it canceled?	남 안 됐다. 왜 취소됐는데?
W The field was too wet because of the rain.	여 비 때문에 경기장이 너무 젖었거든.
M It did rain a lot. So, what did you do instead?	남 비가 정말 많이 왔지. 그래서, 대신 뭘 했어?
W I just watched a TV series at home yesterday.	여 그냥 어제 집에서 TV 시리즈를 시청했어.
M That sounds relaxing.	남 편안했겠네.
W Yes. I enjoyed not being so busy.	여 응. 그렇게 바쁘지 않은 걸 즐겼어.

해설 | 여자가 어제 집에서 TV 시리즈를 시청했다고 했으므로 정답은 ③ 'TV 시리즈 보기'이다.

어휘 | cancel [kǽnsəl] 뙤 취소하다   field [fiːld] 뗑 경기장; 들, 벌판   wet [wet] 휑 젖은   relaxing [rilǽksiŋ] 휑 편안한

15 목적 고르기   정답 ④

W Listeners, don't miss your chance to go to Adventure World! Throughout the next hour, we'll be giving away free tickets to the theme park. To get your tickets, call in to make a song request in the next hour. Seven callers will be picked to join DJ Max on air. And if you can answer a simple question about your favorite band, you'll win four all-day passes for Adventure World. So, stay tuned, and give us a call at 555-3257.	여 청취자 여러분, Adventure World에 가실 기회를 놓치지 마세요! 다음 시간 내내, 저희가 그 테마파크의 무료 티켓을 나눠드릴 겁니다. 티켓을 얻으시려면, 다음 한 시간 안에 전화로 신청 곡을 알려주십시오. 전화를 거신 일곱 분이 뽑혀서 DJ Max와 함께 방송에 참여할 예정입니다. 그리고 여러분이 좋아하는 밴드에 대한 간단한 질문에 답해주시면, Adventure World의 종일 이용권을 4장 얻으실 겁니다. 그러니 채널 고정하시고 555-3257로 전화 주세요.

해설 | 여자가 청취자들에게 테마파크의 무료 티켓을 얻을 수 있는 방법을 설명하고 있으므로 정답은 ④이다.

어휘 | throughout [θruːáut] 젠 ~ 내내; 도처에   give away 나눠주다   pass [pæs] 뗑 이용권, 입장권 뙤 지나가다   stay tuned 채널 고정하다, 계속 시청하다

16 금액 정보 고르기 정답 ②

W	Welcome to Quality Candles. How may I help you?
M	I'd like to <u>buy</u> a <u>candle</u> for my friend. Which one do you recommend?
W	Our most popular candle is the one that smells like lavender. A <u>medium-sized candle</u> is 15 dollars, and <u>a large one is 20 dollars</u>.
M	Okay. I'll take a medium-sized lavender candle.
W	If you buy a large one, you will get a set of small candles <u>for free</u>.
M	Really? Then, <u>I'll buy the large one</u> instead.
W	Excellent idea.

여	Quality Candles에 오신 것을 환영합니다. 무엇을 도와드 릴까요?
남	친구에게 줄 캔들을 사고 싶어요. 어떤 걸 추천하시나요?
여	저희의 가장 인기 있는 캔들은 라벤더 향이 나는 거예요. 중간 크기의 캔들이 15달러이고 대형은 20달러입니다.
남	알겠습니다. 중간 크기의 라벤더 캔들로 할게요.
여	만약 대형을 사시면, 소형 캔들 세트도 무료로 얻으실 수 있어요.
남	정말요? 그러면, 대신 대형 캔들을 살게요.
여	훌륭한 생각이에요.

해설 | 여자가 한 개에 20달러인 대형 캔들을 사면 소형 캔들 세트를 무료로 얻을 수 있다고 하자, 남자가 대형 캔들을 사겠다고 했으므로 정답은 ② '$ 20'이다.

어휘 | candle [kǽndl] 옝 캔들, 양초   recommend [rèkəménd] 동 추천하다   medium-sized 옝 중간 크기의   for free 무료로
excellent [éksələnt] 옝 훌륭한

17 적절한 응답 고르기 정답 ②

M	The holiday is coming up. Do you have any plans?
W	I might go to Jeonju, but <u>I'm worried about the traffic</u>.
M	Yeah. It can be pretty bad if you take a bus. Have you looked at train tickets?
W	Yes. But they're <u>all sold out</u>. I think a bus is my only option.
M	You can leave really early in the morning. The traffic might be better.
W	That's true. I hope it <u>will be worth it</u>.
M	I'm sure you'll have a lot of fun. <u>What do you want to do there</u>?
W	I'd love to look around the traditional village.

남	휴일이 다가오고 있어. 넌 무슨 계획 있니?
여	난 전주에 갈지도 모르겠는데, 교통이 걱정이야.
남	그러게. 버스를 탄다면 꽤 안 좋을 수 있겠어. 기차표는 알 아봤어?
여	응. 그런데 모두 매진이야. 버스가 내 유일한 선택지인 것 같아.
남	아침에 진짜 일찍 출발하면 돼. 교통이 아마 더 나을 거야.
여	그건 맞아. 그만한 가치가 있으면 좋겠다.
남	분명 넌 아주 재미있을 거야. 거기에서 뭘 하고 싶어?
여	전통 마을을 둘러보고 싶어.

해설 | 남자가 전주에서 무엇을 하고 싶은지 물었으므로 정답은 하고 싶은 일을 언급하는 ② 'I'd love to look around the traditional village.'이다.

> [선택지 해석]
> ① 길 아래편에서 자동차 사고가 났어.   ② 전통 마을을 둘러보고 싶어.   ③ 표를 구매하려면 웹사이트를 방문해야 해.
> ④ 지난번에 거기를 여행했을 때 한복을 입었어.   ⑤ 버스로 거기까지 가는 데 4시간 걸릴 거야.

어휘 | come up 다가오다, 도달하다   traffic [trǽfik] 옝 교통(량)   sold out 매진인   worth [wəːrθ] 옝 가치가 있는   traditional [trədíʃənəl] 옝 전통의

18 적절한 응답 고르기 정답 ④

W	Hey, Mingyu. Is this your dog? It's so cute.
M	Yes! I'm just <u>taking him on a walk</u> around the neighborhood.
W	How often do you walk him?
M	I take him outside twice a day, but he <u>still becomes bored</u>.
W	Does he have any toys?
M	Yes. But they're very old, so he doesn't like to play with them.
W	<u>You ought to buy</u> more toys. Then, he won't get bored easily.
M	You're right. I'll go by the pet store.

여	안녕, 민규야. 네 개니? 너무 귀엽다.
남	응! 막 이 녀석을 데리고 동네 주변을 산책하는 중이야.
여	얼마나 자주 산책시키니?
남	하루에 두 번 정도 밖에 데려가는데, 계속 지루해 해.
여	장난감은 있어?
남	응. 그런데 엄청 낡아서, 그걸 가지고 노는 걸 안 좋아해.
여	더 많은 장난감을 사야겠네. 그러면 얘도 쉽게 지루해하지 않을 거야.
남	네 말이 맞아. 반려동물용품점에 들러야겠어.

해설 | 여자가 남자의 반려견에게 더 많은 장난감을 사줘야겠다고 충고했으므로 정답은 충고에 동의하는 ④ 'You're right. I'll go by the pet store.'이다.

> [선택지 해석]
> ① 내 개에게 하루에 두 번 먹이를 주고 있어.   ② 내 친구들이 바빠서 지루해.   ③ 알겠어. 혼자서 재미있게 지낼 수 있도록 노력할게.
> ④ 네 말이 맞아. 반려동물용품점에 들러야겠어.   ⑤ 밖에 날이 너무 좋으니까 함께 산책하러 가자.

어휘 | neighborhood [néibərhùd] 옝 동네, 이웃   bored [bɔːrd] 옝 지루한   go by 들르다, 방문하다   feed [fiːd] 동 먹이를 주다   by oneself 혼자서, 홀로

19 적절한 응답 고르기　　　　　　　　　　　　　　　정답 ②

W	What time does the movie start, Jungwon?	여	영화가 몇 시에 시작하니, 정원아?
M	It starts at 2 p.m.	남	오후 2시에 시작해.
W	Really? It's only 11 a.m. now. We have a lot of time before it begins.	여	정말? 지금 겨우 오전 11시잖아. 시작하기 전까지 시간이 엄청 많네.
M	I know. What should we do?	남	맞아. 우리 뭘 해야 할까?
W	Well, we can spend some time in the park. It's a beautiful day.	여	글쎄, 공원에서 시간을 보내도 돼. 날씨가 좋잖아.
M	Why don't we get some drinks first? We can take our beverages to the park.	남	마실 것을 먼저 사는 건 어때? 우리 음료를 공원에 가져가면 되잖아.
W	Sure. What do you want to drink?	여	물론이지. 뭘 마시고 싶은데?
M	I'd like a smoothie or juice.	남	스무디나 주스를 마시고 싶어.
W	Let's try that new café down the street then.	여	그러면 길 아래 새로 생긴 카페에 가보자.
M	Great. I've wanted to go there for a while.	남	좋아. 한동안 거기에 가보고 싶었어.

해설 | 여자가 새로 생긴 카페에 가보자고 제안했으므로 정답은 제안에 동의하는 ② 'Great. I've wanted to go there for a while.'이다.

선택지 해석

① 난 공포물보다 로맨스물을 더 좋아해.　② 좋아. 한동안 거기에 가보고 싶었어.　③ 내가 지금 음료를 주문할게.
④ 그냥 이 길을 따라 아래로 간 다음, 좌회전해.　⑤ 고맙지만, 나 이미 배불러.

어휘 | spend [spend] 통 (시간을) 보내다　beverage [bévəridʒ] 명 음료　prefer A to B B보다 A를 더 좋아하다　full [ful] 형 배부른; 가득한

20 상황에 적절한 말 고르기　　　　　　　　　　　　　정답 ④

W	Peter is at a restaurant with some of his friends. They order lots of food and enjoy a delicious meal. However, Peter is still hungry and wants to order a dessert. He doesn't remember the dessert options, and there is no menu at his table. So, he decides to ask the server if he can see the menu again. In this situation, what would Peter most likely say to the server?	여	Peter는 그의 친구 몇몇과 식당에 있습니다. 그들은 많은 음식을 주문하고 맛있는 식사를 즐기고 있습니다. 하지만, Peter는 여전히 배가 고파서 디저트를 주문하고 싶습니다. 그는 디저트 옵션이 기억나지 않는데, 그의 자리에는 메뉴판이 없습니다. 그래서, 그는 종업원에게 메뉴판을 다시 볼 수 있을지 묻기로 결심합니다. 이러한 상황에서, Peter가 종업원에게 가장 할 것 같은 말은 무엇입니까?
Peter	Could you show me the dessert list, please?	Peter	디저트 목록을 보여주실 수 있나요?

해설 | Peter가 디저트를 주문하기 위해 종업원에게 메뉴판을 볼 수 있을지 묻기로 결심했다고 했으므로 정답은 ④ 'Could you show me the dessert list, please?'이다.

선택지 해석

① 치즈 케이크 한 조각으로 주세요.　② 어떤 요리를 추천하시나요?　③ 메뉴판을 지금 바로 가져다드리겠습니다.　④ 디저트 목록을 보여주실 수 있나요?
⑤ 네 명 자리가 필요해요.

어휘 | delicious [dilíʃəs] 형 맛있는　server [sə́ːrvər] 명 종업원　dish [diʃ] 명 요리; 접시

| 1 | ② | 2 | ② | 3 | ③ | 4 | ⑤ | 5 | ④ | 6 | ① | 7 | ③ | 8 | ⑤ | 9 | ④ | 10 | ② |
| 11 | ② | 12 | ② | 13 | ⑤ | 14 | ④ | 15 | ⑤ | 16 | ③ | 17 | ① | 18 | ③ | 19 | ④ | 20 | ⑤ |

---

1 알맞은 그림 고르기

정답 ②

M	Welcome. What can I do for you?
W	I lost my earphone case, so I need to buy one.
M	Alright. Our cases have many unique designs from animals to food. The dinosaur-shaped one is the most popular.
W	Oh, it reminds me of my old case. That had a dinosaur on it. But this time, I want to try something new.
M	Then, how about this cupcake-shaped one?
W	Wow, that is cute. The chocolate cupcake looks sweet.
M	Good. And we can add some lettering on it if you want.
W	Thanks, but that's okay.

남	어서 오세요. 무엇을 도와드릴까요?
여	제가 이어폰 케이스를 잃어버려서, 하나 사야 해요.
남	그러시군요. 저희 케이스들은 동물부터 음식까지 독특한 디자인을 많이 갖고 있어요. 공룡 모양이 가장 인기가 많죠.
여	오, 제 옛날 케이스를 떠오르게 하네요. 공룡이 그려져 있었거든요. 하지만 이번에는 뭔가 새로운 걸 해보고 싶어요.
남	그렇다면, 이 컵케이크 모양은 어떠세요?
여	우와, 그거 귀엽네요. 초콜릿 컵케이크가 달콤해 보여요.
남	좋아요. 그리고 원하신다면 위에 레터링을 추가해드릴 수 있어요.
여	감사하지만, 괜찮아요.

해설 | 여자가 초콜릿 컵케이크 모양의 이어폰 케이스가 귀엽다고 했고, 레터링은 추가하지 않아도 괜찮다고 했으므로 정답은 ②이다.

어휘 | unique [juːník] ⑱ 독특한   from A to B A부터 B까지   dinosaur [dáinəsɔːr] ⑲ 공룡   remind A of B A에게 B를 떠오르게 하다, 상기시키다

---

2 언급하지 않은 내용 고르기

정답 ②

W	What are you doing, Brad?
M	I'm playing a new video game. It was released on May 10th.
W	What's it called?
M	Its name is Space Attack. You fly a spaceship and fight aliens.
W	Which company made it?
M	Bright Star Media. It is that company's first game.
W	Is it difficult to play?
M	No. It's very easy, actually.
W	Maybe I will buy it then. It sounds fun.

여	뭐 하고 있어, Brad?
남	새로운 비디오 게임을 하는 중이야. 5월 10일에 발매됐어.
여	이름이 뭐야?
남	이름은 <Space Attack>이야. 우주선을 날려서 외계인과 싸우는 거지.
여	어떤 회사가 만든 거야?
남	Bright Star Media야. 그 회사의 첫 게임이야.
여	하기 어려워?
남	아니. 정말 쉬워, 사실은.
여	그럼 나도 그걸 사볼까 해. 재미있을 것 같아.

해설 | ① 이름(<Space Attack>), ③ 제조사(Bright Star Media), ④ 발매일(5월 10일), ⑤ 난이도(정말 쉬움)에 대해 언급했으므로 정답은 ② '가격'이다.

어휘 | release [rilíːs] ⑧ 발매하다; 해방하다   spaceship [spéisʃip] ⑲ 우주선   alien [éiljən] ⑲ 외계인   company [kʌ́mpəni] ⑲ 회사

3 목적 고르기 정답 ③

	[Cellphone rings.]
M	Hello, is this Jenny Barnes?
W	Yes, that's me.
M	This is Grant from Pampered Pets. I'm calling about your dog, Rex.
W	Is everything okay?
M	Of course. I am done washing and cutting his hair, so he is ready for pickup.
W	Oh, I see. But I'm at an appointment right now. Can I pick him up later?
M	Yes. What time can you get him?
W	I should be done around 3 p.m., so I can get there by 3:30.
M	That's fine. We close at 5 p.m.
W	Great. Thank you for letting me know.

	[휴대폰이 울린다.]
남	안녕하세요, Jenny Barnes씨 되시나요?
여	네, 접니다.
남	저는 Pampered Pets의 Grant예요. 고객님의 강아지 Rex 때문에 전화 드렸어요.
여	별일 없는 거죠?
남	그럼요. Rex의 털을 씻기고 자르는 걸 끝내서, 이제 데려가실 준비가 됐어요.
여	오, 그렇군요. 그런데 제가 지금은 약속 장소에 있어서요. 나중에 데려가도 될까요?
남	네. 몇 시에 데려가실 수 있나요?
여	오후 3시쯤에는 마치니까, 거기 3시 30분까지는 갈 수 있어요.
남	그럼 괜찮아요. 저희는 오후 5시에 마치거든요.
여	잘됐네요. 알려주셔서 감사합니다.

해설 | 남자가 여자의 반려견 미용 작업이 끝나서 데려갈 준비가 되었다고 했으므로 정답은 ③ '미용 작업이 완료되었음을 알리려고'이다.

어휘 | wash [waʃ] 통 씻기다, 씻다   cut [kʌt] 통 자르다, 베다   appointment [əpɔ́intmənt] 명 약속 장소; 약속, 예약

4 시간 정보 고르기 정답 ⑤

M	Mom, can I take a swimming lesson on Saturdays at the pool downtown?
W	Sure. What time does the lesson start?
M	I'd like to join the lesson my friend is in. It begins at 10 a.m. and lasts for one hour.
W	Oh, no. I have to take your sister to soccer practice at 9 a.m. on Saturdays.
M	What time does her practice end?
W	It doesn't end until 11 a.m.
M	In that case, there is another one that starts at 1 p.m.
W	Okay. Sign up for that one.

남	엄마, 저 시내에 있는 수영장에서 토요일마다 수영 수업을 들어도 될까요?
여	물론이지. 수업이 몇 시에 시작하니?
남	친구가 있는 수업을 함께 듣고 싶어요. 그건 오전 10시에 시작해서 1시간 동안 계속돼요.
여	오, 이런. 토요일마다 오전 9시에는 네 여동생을 축구 연습에 데려다줘야 한단다.
남	연습이 몇 시에 끝나는데요?
여	오전 11시 이후에야 끝나.
남	그 경우에는, 오후 1시에 시작하는 다른 수업이 있어요.
여	그래. 그걸 신청하렴.

해설 | 남자가 오후 1시에 시작하는 수영 수업이 있다고 하자, 여자가 그것을 신청하라고 했으므로 정답은 ⑤ '1 p.m.'이다.

어휘 | downtown [dáuntaun] 부 시내에   practice [prǽktis] 명 연습; 습관, 관행   case [keis] 명 경우   sign up for ~을 신청하다

5 심정 고르기 정답 ④

W	Brandon, are you okay?
M	I'm not feeling good.
W	Did you see a doctor?
M	Yes. The doctor suggested that I get a blood test. So, I'm waiting for the results.
W	When will you get the results?
M	Sometime next week. I'm afraid I have a serious illness.
W	Don't worry. I'm sure everything will be fine.
M	But I can't stop myself from imagining the worst.

여	Brandon, 너 괜찮니?
남	몸이 좋지 않아.
여	진찰은 받아 봤어?
남	응. 의사 선생님이 혈액 검사를 받으라고 제안하셨어. 그래서, 결과를 기다리는 중이야.
여	결과를 언제 받아볼 수 있는데?
남	다음 주 언젠가. 내게 심각한 병이 있을까 봐 걱정이야.
여	걱정하지 마. 분명 모든 게 괜찮을 거야.
남	하지만 난 최악을 상상하는 걸 멈출 수가 없어.

해설 | 남자가 혈액 검사 결과가 안 좋을까 봐 걱정되고 최악의 상상을 하게 된다고 했으므로 정답은 ④ 'concerned'이다.

선택지 해석

① 기쁜   ② 감사하는   ③ 편안한   ④ 걱정하는   ⑤ 놀란

어휘 | blood [blʌd] 명 혈액, 피   result [rizʌ́lt] 명 결과   illness [ílnis] 명 병, 질병   stop A from B A가 B하는 것을 멈추다   imagine [imǽdʒin] 통 상상하다

6 그림 상황에 적절한 대화 고르기   정답 ①

① W Do you want some popcorn?
   M No. I'm not very hungry.
② W Are you almost done with your homework?
   M It will take 30 more minutes.
③ W That will be 12 dollars and 50 cents, please.
   M Here you go.
④ W Why don't we take a taxi to the theater?
   M I'd prefer to walk.
⑤ W Where is the nearest bus stop?
   M There's one over there.

① 여 팝콘 좀 먹을래?
   남 아니. 난 그렇게 배고프지 않아.
② 여 숙제 거의 끝났어?
   남 30분 더 걸릴 거야.
③ 여 그건 12달러 50센트 되겠습니다.
   남 여기 있습니다.
④ 여 영화관으로 택시 타고 가는 게 어때?
   남 난 걷고 싶어.
⑤ 여 가장 가까운 버스 정류장이 어디에 있나요?
   남 저쪽에 하나 있어요.

해설 | 영화관의 매점 앞에서 남자와 여자가 팝콘 기계를 가리키며 대화를 하고 있는 상황이므로 정답은 ①이다.

어휘 | be done with ~을 끝내다, 마치다

7 부탁·요청한 일 고르기   정답 ③

M Your poem was fantastic, Erica.
W Thank you, Mr. Park.
M Do you write often?
W I try to write every day.
M That's great. You could be a poet one day.
W I hope so. Could you read some more of my poems? I'd love to hear your opinions.
M Bring them to me at any time.

남 네 시는 환상적이구나, Erica.
여 감사합니다, 박 선생님.
남 시를 자주 쓰니?
여 매일 쓰려고 노력하고 있어요.
남 훌륭하구나. 넌 언젠가 시인이 될 수 있겠어.
여 저도 그러길 바라고 있어요. 제 시를 좀 더 읽어보실 수 있을까요? 선생님의 의견을 꼭 듣고 싶어요.
남 언제든 내게 가져오렴.

해설 | 여자가 남자에게 자신의 시를 좀 더 읽어 달라고 부탁했으므로 정답은 ③ '작품 검토하기'이다.

어휘 | poem [póuəm] 몡 시 (poet [póuit] 몡 시인) opinion [əpínjən] 몡 의견 at any time 언제든, 언제라도

8 언급하지 않은 내용 고르기   정답 ⑤

W Good morning, students. I would like to remind you about the Drama Festival. Mr. Ferris, the club advisor, and his drama club have organized the event this year. There will be four short plays. They will be performed in our school's gym. The festival will last for two days, beginning on April 15th. I hope that all of you will attend. And please remember to invite your friends and family members!

여 좋은 아침입니다, 학생 여러분. 저는 Drama Festival을 여러분에게 상기시켜드리고 싶습니다. 동아리의 고문 선생님인 Ferris 선생님과 그의 연극 동아리가 올해 이 행사를 준비했습니다. 네 개의 짧은 연극이 있을 예정입니다. 연극은 우리 학교 체육관에서 공연될 것입니다. 축제는 4월 15일에 시작해서, 이틀 동안 진행될 것입니다. 여러분 모두가 참석하길 바랍니다. 그리고 여러분의 친구와 가족들을 초대하는 걸 꼭 기억해 주세요!

해설 | ① 주최자(Ferris 선생님과 그의 연극 동아리), ② 연극 개수(4개), ③ 개최 장소(학교 체육관), ④ 행사 기간(4월 15일부터 이틀 동안)에 대해 언급했으므로 정답은 ⑤ '배우 이름'이다.

어휘 | advisor [ædváizər] 몡 고문, 조언자 drama club 연극 동아리 organize [ɔ́ːrgənàiz] 통 준비하다; 조직하다 festival [féstəvəl] 몡 축제 invite [inváit] 통 초대하다

9 화제 고르기   정답 ④

M People can enjoy nature at this place. This place has many gardens with plants from all over the world. During the spring, many people visit this place to see beautiful flowers. The workers at this place can teach you about the different plants there. Sometimes this place hosts fun events, but its main purpose is to collect, grow, and study diverse plants.

남 사람들은 이 장소에서 자연을 즐길 수 있습니다. 이 장소에는 전 세계의 식물을 갖춘 정원이 많이 있습니다. 봄 동안에는, 많은 사람이 아름다운 꽃을 보기 위해 이곳을 방문합니다. 이곳의 직원들은 그곳의 여러 식물에 대해 가르쳐 줄 수 있습니다. 때때로 이 장소에서는 재미있는 행사가 열리지만, 그곳의 주된 목적은 다양한 식물을 수집하고, 재배하고, 연구하는 것입니다.

해설 | 이 장소(this place)에는 전 세계의 식물을 갖춘 정원이 있으며, 주된 목적은 다양한 식물을 수집, 재배, 연구하는 것이라고 했으므로 정답은 ④ '식물원'이다.

어휘 | nature [néitʃər] 몡 자연 purpose [pə́:rpəs] 몡 목적 collect [kəlékt] 동 수집하다 diverse [daivə́:rs] 혱 다양한

---

10 어색한 대화 고르기   정답 ②

① W My face really <u>got</u> <u>sunburned</u>.	① 여 얼굴이 햇볕에 매우 타버렸어.
M I told you to wear a hat.	남 모자를 쓰라고 말했잖아.
② W <u>Did you paint this beautiful picture?</u>	② 여 이 아름다운 그림을 당신이 그리신 건가요?
M <u>The paint brush is 10 dollars.</u>	남 그 페인트 붓은 10달러입니다.
③ W Does this bus go to the Bradford?	③ 여 이 버스 브래드퍼드로 가나요?
M It does. It takes about 15 minutes.	남 갑니다. 15분 정도 걸려요.
④ W <u>Do you want to eat</u> burgers for lunch?	④ 여 점심으로 햄버거 먹을래?
M Sure. I'm hungry.	남 물론이지. 나 배고파.
⑤ W I have a question to ask you.	⑤ 여 네게 물어볼 질문이 있어.
M <u>Go ahead.</u> What is it?	남 말해봐. 뭔데?

해설 | 여자가 남자에게 이 그림을 그린 것인지 물었으므로, 남자는 그림을 그렸는지를 답해야 한다. 그러나 남자가 페인트 붓이 10달러라는 어색한 대답을 했으므로 정답은 ②이다.

어휘 | sunburned [sʌ́nbə̀rnd] 혱 햇볕에 탄

---

11 할 일 고르기   정답 ②

M It's finally warm outside.	남 드디어 밖이 따뜻해졌어.
W I know! Last week was really cold.	여 그러니까 말이야! 지난주는 정말 추웠어.
M Let's eat at that <u>new sandwich place</u> by the river today. They have outside tables, so we can <u>enjoy the weather</u>.	남 오늘은 강가에 새로 생긴 샌드위치 가게에서 먹자. 야외 자리가 있어서, 날씨를 즐길 수 있잖아.
W Yes. Their food looks delicious, but isn't it always busy? Can we even get a table?	여 그래. 음식도 맛있어 보여. 그런데 거기 항상 바쁘지 않아? 우리 자리를 얻을 수나 있을까?
M I'll call them and <u>make a reservation</u> now.	남 내가 지금 전화해서 예약할게.
W That'll be great.	여 그러면 좋겠다.

해설 | 남자가 지금 샌드위치 가게에 전화해서 예약하겠다고 했으므로 정답은 ② '식당에 전화하기'이다.

어휘 | finally [fáinəli] 뮈 드디어, 마침내 reservation [rèzərvéiʃən] 몡 예약

---

12 도표에서 알맞은 항목 고르기   정답 ②

M Honey, I'm going to <u>order a laptop</u> now.	남 여보, 나 이제 노트북 주문하려고.
W Oh, okay. Are you going to get one with a 17-inch screen?	여 오, 알겠어. 17인치 화면이 있는 걸로 살 거야?
M No. It is <u>too expensive</u>.	남 아니. 그건 너무 비싸.
W I see. Well, <u>a 15-inch screen should be big enough</u>.	여 그렇구나. 음, 15인치 화면도 충분히 클 테니까.
M Do you think I should get a white or a black one?	남 내가 흰색으로 사야 할까, 아니면 검은색으로 사야 할까?
W Look. The black ones are more expensive than the white ones. I think you should get <u>the cheaper one</u>.	여 보자. 검은색 노트북이 흰색보다 더 비싸네. 더 싼 걸 사야 할 것 같아.
M <u>I agree.</u> I'll order it now.	남 동감이야. 그걸로 지금 주문해야겠다.

해설 | 여자가 15인치 화면도 충분히 크다고 했고, 검은색과 흰색 중에서 더 싼 것으로 사라고 하자 남자가 동의했으므로 정답은 ②이다.

어휘 | laptop [lǽptɑp] 몡 노트북 screen [skri:n] 몡 화면, 스크린 enough [inʌ́f] 뮈 충분히

13 시간 정보 고르기   정답 ⑤

[Telephone rings.]	**[전화기가 울린다.]**
W Hello?	여 여보세요?
M Hello, this is Grayson Electronics. I'm calling about the air conditioner you ordered last week.	남 안녕하세요, Grayson Electronics입니다. 지난주에 주문하셨던 에어컨 때문에 전화 드렸어요.
W Oh, is there <u>something</u> <u>wrong</u> <u>with</u> <u>the</u> <u>order</u>?	여 오, 주문에 무슨 문제가 있나요?
M No. It's just that orders are piled up, so the delivery and installation date <u>will</u> <u>be</u> <u>delayed</u> a bit.	남 아니요. 그저 주문이 쌓여 있어서, 배송과 설치 날짜가 다소 지연될 것 같아요.
W That's fine. When can I get it installed then?	여 그건 괜찮아요. 그러면 언제 설치 받을 수 있나요?
M <u>The</u> <u>earliest</u> <u>day</u> would be June 19th.	남 가장 빠른 날은 6월 19일이에요.
W Let me see. *[Pause]* I'll be on a holiday during that week. What about <u>the</u> <u>week</u> <u>after</u> <u>that</u>?	여 어디 볼게요. *[잠시 멈춤]* 그 주 동안 휴가를 갈 거라서요. 그다음 주는 어때세요?
M You can choose between the 22nd and 24th.	남 22일과 24일 중에 고르실 수 있어요.
W The 24th sounds okay.	여 24일이 좋겠어요.
M Perfect.	남 아주 좋습니다.

해설ㅣ 여자가 6월 22일과 24일 중에서 24일이 좋겠다고 했으므로 정답은 ⑤ '6월 24일'이다.

어휘ㅣ pile up 쌓다   installation [instɔ́ːleiʃn] 몡 설치 (install [instɔ́ːl] 통 설치하다)   delay [diléi] 통 지연시키다, 연기하다

---

14 한일 고르기   정답 ④

M Did you finish your music project, Nora?	남 음악 과제 끝냈어, Nora?
W No, <u>not</u> <u>yet</u>. I'm doing it now.	여 아니, 아직. 지금 하는 중이야.
M Oh, you usually finish your projects so early. What happened?	남 오, 넌 보통 과제를 엄청 일찍 끝내놓잖아. 무슨 일 있었어?
W My family decided to <u>visit</u> <u>my</u> <u>grandparents</u> in the countryside last Sunday. We were there all day.	여 우리 가족이 지난주 일요일에 조부모님을 뵈러 시골에 가기로 했었거든. 우린 거기에서 온종일 있었어.
M What did you do there?	남 거기에서 뭐 했어?
W We helped them <u>with</u> <u>their</u> <u>farm</u>. It was hard work, but we enjoyed <u>spending</u> <u>time</u> <u>together</u>.	여 농장 일을 도와드렸어. 힘든 일이었지만, 함께 시간을 보내는 게 즐거웠어.
M That sounds like a nice day.	남 좋은 하루였던 것 같네.

해설ㅣ 여자가 지난 일요일에 조부모님 댁을 방문하여 그들의 농장 일을 도와드렸다고 했으므로 정답은 ④ '농장 일 돕기'이다.

어휘ㅣ project [prɑ́dʒekt] 몡 과제; 계획   countryside [kʌ́ntrisaid] 몡 시골

---

15 목적 고르기   정답 ⑤

M Good afternoon, everyone. We hope you all are enjoying your time at Riverside Park. <u>Here</u> <u>are</u> <u>some</u> <u>reminders</u> <u>for</u> <u>using</u> the park. Please <u>make</u> <u>sure</u> <u>that</u> you throw all of your trash away before leaving the area. Also, you must <u>clean</u> <u>up</u> <u>after</u> your pets if you bring them. Lastly, be careful not to walk on the flowers in the park, and <u>use</u> <u>our</u> <u>trails</u> instead. Thank you for your time.	남 안녕하십니까, 여러분. 모두 리버사이드 공원에서의 시간을 즐기고 계시길 바랍니다. 여기 공원 이용에 관한 몇 가지 주의 사항이 있습니다. 공원을 떠나시기 전에 여러분의 모든 쓰레기를 꼭 버려주십시오. 또한, 반려동물을 데려오셨다면 반드시 뒷정리를 해야 합니다. 마지막으로, 공원의 꽃을 밟지 않도록 주의해주시고, 대신 저희의 산책로를 이용해 주십시오. 시간 내주셔서 감사합니다.

해설ㅣ 남자가 공원 이용객들에게 공원 이용에 관한 주의 사항 몇 가지를 전달하고 있으므로 정답은 ⑤이다.

어휘ㅣ reminder [rimáindər] 몡 (상기시키는) 주의, 생각나게 하는 것   make sure 꼭 ~하다, 확실하게 하다   throw away 버리다   trail [treil] 몡 산책로, 둘레길

16 금액 정보 고르기   정답 ③

W	Welcome to Travel Car Rentals. How may I help you?
M	Hello. I need to <u>rent a car</u>. How much is it?
W	<u>A car rental</u> is 30 dollars per day. How long will you use the car?
M	I will use it for three days.
W	Then, <u>your total is 90 dollars.</u>
M	Okay. And how much is this booklet about <u>local tourist attractions</u>? It looks very interesting.
W	<u>That's actually free.</u> You can take it.
M	Great. I'll <u>pay for the car</u> then.

여	Travel Car Rentals에 오신 것을 환영합니다. 무엇을 도와 드릴까요?
남	안녕하세요. 차를 빌려야 하는데요. 얼마죠?
여	차 임대료는 하루에 30달러입니다. 얼마 동안 차를 이용하실 건가요?
남	3일 동안 이용할 거예요.
여	그럼, 총 90달러입니다.
남	알겠습니다. 그리고 지역 관광 명소에 관한 이 소책자는 얼마인가요? 매우 흥미로워 보이네요.
여	그건 사실 무료예요. 가져가셔도 돼요.
남	잘됐네요. 그러면 자동차에 대한 비용을 지불하겠습니다.

해설 | 차 임대료는 하루에 30달러이고 남자가 3일 동안 이용하겠다고 했으며, 소책자는 무료라고 했으므로 정답은 ③ '$ 90'이다.

어휘 | rent [rent] ⑧ 빌리다 ⑲ 세, 임대료 (rental [réntl] ⑲ 임대료) booklet [búklit] ⑲ 소책자, 팸플릿 tourist attraction 관광 명소

17 적절한 응답 고르기   정답 ①

W	David, have you bought your present for Maria?
M	No, I haven't. I think I <u>need help in choosing</u> one. I can't decide on a gift.
W	I went to Arts and Crafts Central in the mall. There are <u>lots of journals and pens</u>. It's a good place to look.
M	Arts and Crafts Central?
W	Yes. I think Maria wants a new pencil case, and the store has many.
M	That sounds perfect then. <u>Where can I find the store</u>?
W	It's on the second floor of the mall.

여	David, 너 Maria에게 줄 선물 샀어?
남	아니, 안 샀어. 그걸 고르는 데 도움이 필요한 거 같아. 선물을 못 고르겠거든.
여	내가 쇼핑몰에 있는 Arts and Crafts Central에 갔었거든. 그곳에는 일기장과 펜이 많아. 거기 둘러보기 좋은 장소야.
남	Arts and Crafts Central이라고?
여	응. Maria가 새 필통을 원하는 것 같은데, 그 가게엔 많더라고.
남	그러면 딱 좋은 것 같네. 그 가게를 어디에서 찾을 수 있어?
여	쇼핑몰 2층에 있어.

해설 | 남자가 쇼핑몰 어디에서 그 가게를 찾을 수 있을지 물었으므로 정답은 가게의 위치를 설명하는 ① 'It's on the second floor of the mall.'이다.

선택지 해석
① 쇼핑몰 2층에 있어. ② 그녀는 내일 15살이 돼. ③ 내 일기장은 서랍 안에 잠가서 보관해. ④ 연필 빌릴 수 있을까? ⑤ 아직 선물을 열어보지 마.

어휘 | present [préznt] ⑲ 선물 ⑱ 출석해 있는 journal [dʒə́:rnl] ⑲ 일기장; 일지 lock [lak] ⑧ 잠그다 ⑲ 자물쇠 drawer [drɔ:r] ⑲ 서랍

18 적절한 응답 고르기   정답 ③

M	Sunhee, are you <u>interested in volunteering</u>?
W	I would love to volunteer. I used to help out at the children's hospital.
M	Well, a local orchard will <u>donate some of their fruit</u> to people who need food.
W	<u>What a great idea!</u>
M	But the orchard needs help with picking them. Do you want to go with me?
W	Sure. Where can I get the sign-up form?
M	I'm <u>on my way</u> to get one now.
W	Oh, I have to change clothes for P.E. class. <u>Can you get one</u> for me?
M	Sure. I'll give it to you later.

남	선희야, 너 자원봉사에 관심 있어?
여	자원봉사 하고 싶어. 어린이 병동 일을 거들기도 했었어.
남	음, 지역 과수원에서 과일 일부를 음식이 필요한 사람들에게 기부할 거야.
여	아주 멋진 생각이야!
남	그런데 과수원에서 그걸 따는 일에 도움을 요해. 나랑 같이 갈래?
여	물론이지. 참가 신청서는 어디에서 받을 수 있어?
남	내가 지금 받으러 가는 길이야.
여	오, 난 체육 수업 들으려면 옷을 갈아입어야 해. 네가 내 것도 받아와 줄래?
남	물론이지. 이따가 줄게.

해설 | 여자가 자신의 참가 신청서도 받아와 달라고 부탁했으므로 정답은 부탁을 수락하는 ③ 'Sure. I'll give it to you later.'이다.

선택지 해석
① 그게 마지막 복숭아야. ② 미안, 네게는 허용되지 않아. ③ 물론이지. 이따가 줄게. ④ 우리 직원을 도와줘서 고마워. ⑤ 목록에서 네 이름이 안 보이는걸.

어휘 | help out 거들다 orchard [ɔ́:rtʃərd] ⑲ 과수원 donate [dóuneit] ⑧ 기부하다 form [fɔ:rm] ⑲ 신청서; 모양 P.E. class 체육 수업

19 적절한 응답 고르기   정답 ④

[Cellphone rings.]	[휴대폰이 울린다.]
M Hi, Tabby.	남 안녕, Tabby.
W Hey. Did Justin <u>complete the race</u>?	여 안녕. Justin은 경주 마쳤어?
M No. But he should finish soon.	남 아니. 그런데 곧 끝마칠 거야.
W Okay. Where are you now? I will <u>come and stand with you</u>.	여 알겠어. 지금 어디야? 내가 가서 너랑 같이 서 있을게.
M I'm at the finish line. I have a big sign with his name on it.	남 난 결승선에 있어. Justin의 이름이 적힌 큰 팻말을 갖고 있어.
W That's great! I'm so <u>proud of him</u> for doing this race.	여 좋다! 난 Justin이 이 경주를 하는 게 너무 자랑스러워.
M Yeah. I think he'll be happy to see us <u>cheering for him</u>.	남 응. 그 녀석도 우리가 응원해주는 걸 보면 기뻐할 것 같아.
W Should I <u>buy any snacks</u> or water for him? I can go to the store quickly.	여 내가 Justin에게 줄 간식이나 물을 사 갈까? 빨리 가게에 갈 수 있어.
M Don't worry. <u>I already got some.</u>	남 걱정하지 마. 내가 이미 좀 샀거든.

해설 | 여자가 가게에 들러 간식이나 물을 사 갈지 물었으므로 정답은 사지 않아도 된다고 대답하는 ④ 'Don't worry. I already got some.'이다.

> **선택지 해석**
> ① 그는 6개월이 넘도록 훈련했어.   ② 물론이지. 내가 음료를 좀 사 올게.   ③ 응. 그는 여기 곧 올 거야.   ④ 걱정하지 마. 내가 이미 좀 샀거든.
> ⑤ 나는 매일 아침 달리러 나가.

어휘 | complete [kəmplíːt] ⑧ 마치다 ⑧ 완전한   finish line 결승선   sign [sain] ⑨ 팻말; 기호   cheer for 응원하다   train [trein] ⑧ 훈련하다

20 상황에 적절한 말 고르기   정답 ⑤

M Angela is visiting New York for a holiday. She <u>plans to visit</u> the Museum of Modern Art. She wants to take the subway there, but she cannot <u>find a station</u>. Luckily, she sees a police officer standing in front of a store. <u>She decides to ask him for directions to the nearest subway station.</u> In this situation, what would Angela most likely say to the police officer?	남 Angela는 연휴를 맞아 뉴욕을 방문 중입니다. 그녀는 현대 미술 박물관에 방문할 계획입니다. 그녀는 그곳에서 지하철을 타고 싶지만, 지하철역을 찾을 수 없습니다. 다행히도, 그녀는 가게 앞에 경찰관이 서 있는 걸 봅니다. 그녀는 경찰관에게 가장 가까운 지하철역으로 가는 길을 묻기로 결심합니다. 이러한 상황에서, Angela가 경찰관에게 가장 할 것 같은 말은 무엇입니까?
Angela Excuse me, <u>where is the closest subway station</u>?	Angela 실례합니다, 가장 가까운 지하철역이 어디인가요?

해설 | Angela가 경찰관에게 가장 가까운 지하철역으로 가는 길을 묻기로 결심했다고 했으므로 정답은 ⑤ 'where is the closest subway station?'이다.

> **선택지 해석**
> ① 지하철이 얼마나 늦게까지 운행하나요?   ② 이 가게는 몇 시에 문을 여나요?   ③ 전시회 티켓을 한 장 사고 싶은데요.
> ④ 여기에서 박물관으로 어떻게 가나요?   ⑤ 가장 가까운 지하철역이 어디인가요?

어휘 | luckily [lʌ́kili] ⑨ 다행히도   directions to ~로 가는 길 (안내)   run [rʌn] ⑧ 운행하다; 달리다   exhibition [èksəbíʃən] ⑨ 전시회; 전시

1	⑤	2	③	3	⑤	4	④	5	③	6	②	7	①	8	③	9	①	10	③
11	①	12	③	13	④	14	⑤	15	③	16	④	17	②	18	④	19	⑤	20	⑤

1 알맞은 그림 고르기
정답 ⑤

M Hey, Mijin. How about buying one of <u>these</u> <u>traditional</u> <u>folding</u> <u>fans</u> for your friend Emily?

W I like that idea! The paintings on them all look beautiful.

M Oh, I like this fan with a picture of two birds.

W Well, Emily <u>prefers</u> <u>plants</u> <u>to</u> <u>animals</u>.

M Then, this one has a picture of <u>bamboos</u> <u>under</u> <u>the</u> <u>moon</u>. Emily will like it.

W Perfect. And I also like that it has the word "KOREA" on it. I'll take this one.

남 저기, 미진아. 여기 접이식 전통 부채 중에서 하나를 네 친구 Emily에게 사주는 게 어때?

여 그 생각 마음에 든다! 이것들에 그려진 그림들 모두 아름다워 보여.

남 오, 난 두 마리의 새 그림이 있는 이 부채가 좋아.

여 글쎄, Emily는 동물보다 식물을 더 좋아해.

남 그러면, 이건 달 아래 대나무 그림이 있어. Emily가 이걸 좋아할 거야.

여 완벽해. 그리고 난 거기에 'KOREA'라는 글자가 쓰여 있는 것도 마음에 들어. 이걸 사야겠어.

해설 | 여자가 달 아래 대나무 그림이 있는 접이식 부채가 완벽하다고 했고, 거기에 'KOREA'라는 글자가 쓰여 있는 것도 마음에 든다고 했으므로 정답은 ⑤이다.

어휘 | folding fan 접이식 부채, 쥘부채 bamboo [bæmbúː] 명 대나무

2 언급하지 않은 내용 고르기
정답 ③

W I finally got the jeans I ordered on the Internet.

M What color are they?

W They're <u>light gray</u>.

M Oh, they look a bit big for you.

W Let me check. *[Pause]* Oh, no! They sent me <u>the wrong size</u>.

M You need to exchange them for the correct size.

W And these also <u>have</u> <u>no</u> <u>pockets</u>. This isn't the design I ordered.

M Look here. You can call 555-3251 to <u>reach</u> <u>the</u> <u>manufacturer</u>.

W I think I should call.

여 드디어 인터넷으로 주문했던 청바지를 받았어.

남 무슨 색이야?

여 연회색이야.

남 오, 너한테 약간 커 보이는걸.

여 확인해볼게. [잠시 멈춤] 오, 이런! 내게 잘못된 사이즈를 보내줬네.

남 맞는 사이즈로 교환해야겠어.

여 그리고 이건 주머니도 없어. 내가 주문했던 디자인이 아냐.

남 여기 봐. 제조사와 연락하려면 555-3251로 전화하면 돼.

여 전화해봐야 할 것 같아.

해설 | ① 색상(연회색), ② 사이즈(큰 사이즈로 잘못 보내줌), ④ 디자인(주머니 없음), ⑤ 제조사 번호(555-3251)에 대해 언급했으므로 정답은 ③ '가격'이다.

어휘 | light [lait] 형 연한 명 빛 exchange [ikstʃéindʒ] 동 교환하다 reach [riːtʃ] 동 연락하다; 닿다 manufacturer [mænjufǽktʃərər] 명 제조사, 제조업자

3 목적 고르기
정답 ⑤

[Cellphone rings.]

W Hi, Terry. How are you?

M Hey, Jane. <u>My</u> <u>flight</u> <u>was</u> <u>delayed</u> by four hours.

W Oh, I'm sorry to hear it.

M Yeah. Now I <u>won't</u> <u>arrive</u> <u>in</u> Chicago until 2 a.m.

W That's so late!

M I know. I'm really sorry, but could you <u>pick</u> <u>me</u> <u>up</u> at the airport then?

W Of course. I'll come and get you.

M Thank you so much. I <u>owe</u> <u>you</u> <u>one</u>.

[휴대폰이 울린다.]

여 안녕, Terry. 무슨 일이야?

남 안녕, Jane. 내 항공편이 네 시간 정도 지연됐어.

여 오, 유감이야.

남 응. 이제 난 새벽 2시가 되어서야 시카고에 도착할 거야.

여 너무 늦다!

남 맞아. 정말 미안한데, 그때 날 공항에 데리러 와줄 수 있어?

여 당연하지. 데리러 갈게.

남 정말 고마워. 신세 졌네.

해설 | 남자가 여자에게 새벽 2시에 공항으로 데리러 와 달라고 부탁했으므로 정답은 ⑤ '데리러 올 것을 부탁하려고'이다.

어휘 | by [bai] 전 ~ 정도로, ~ 차이로; ~ 옆에 not A until B B가 되어서야 A하다 owe [ou] 동 신세지다; 빚지다

4 시간 정보 고르기   정답 ④

[Cellphone rings.]	[휴대폰이 울린다.]
M Hi, Anne.	남 안녕, Anne.
W Hello, Samuel. What's up?	여 안녕, Samuel. 무슨 일이야?
M I just saw that the Brentwood Community Center is offering free art lectures on Saturday. I was wondering if you'd like to attend one with me.	남 내가 방금 브렌트우드 주민센터에서 토요일에 무료 미술 강좌를 제공한다는 걸 봤어. 네가 나랑 같이 다니고 싶은지 궁금해서 말이야.
W That sounds interesting. Umm... What time do you want to go?	여 재미있겠는걸. 음... 몇 시로 가고 싶은데?
M I was thinking of going to the one that begins at 10 a.m. It lasts for two hours.	남 오전 10시에 시작하는 걸 갈까 생각 중이었어. 그건 2시간 짜리야.
W I don't know. I usually work out at the gym on Saturday mornings. I don't finish until 11.	여 모르겠네. 난 보통 토요일 아침마다 체육관에서 운동하거든. 11시는 돼야 끝나.
M Then, what about in the afternoon? There is one that runs from 2 to 4 p.m.	남 그러면 오후는 어때? 오후 2시부터 4시까지 운영하는 강좌가 있어.
W Great. Let's attend that one.	여 좋아. 거기에 다니자.

해설 | 남자가 오후 2시부터 4시까지 운영되는 미술 강좌를 제안하자 여자가 다니겠다고 했으므로 정답은 ④ '2 p.m.'이다.

어휘 | offer [ɔ́:fər] 图 제공하다   lecture [léktʃər] 圐 강좌, 강의   wonder [wʌ́ndər] 图 궁금하다   attend [əténd] 图 다니다, 참석하다   work out 운동하다

---

5 심정 고르기   정답 ③

M Rachel, are you studying?	남 Rachel, 공부 중이니?
W Yes. I'm busy working on my math homework, Andy.	여 응. 수학 숙제하느라 바빠, Andy.
M Mom made apple juice for you. How about taking a break?	남 엄마가 네게 줄 사과주스를 만드셨어. 잠시 쉬는 게 어때?
W Sounds great. But I got stuck on this problem. I don't know how to solve it.	여 좋아. 그런데 이 문제에서 막혔어. 어떻게 푸는지 모르겠네.
M Then, I can help you. I'm quite good at math.	남 그러면, 내가 도와줄게. 내가 수학을 꽤 잘하잖아.
W Really? But do you have time? I don't want to bother you.	여 정말? 그런데 시간 괜찮아? 귀찮게 하고 싶지 않아.
M It's no problem. I can always make time for you.	남 문제없어. 널 위해서라면 언제든 시간을 내줄 수 있어.
W You're so kind. I really appreciate it.	여 참 친절하네. 진짜 고마워.

해설 | 남자가 여자의 수학 숙제를 도와준다고 하자 여자가 정말 고맙다고 했으므로 정답은 ③ 'grateful'이다.

> 선택지 해석
> ① 두려운   ② 화난   ③ 고마운   ④ 느긋한   ⑤ 낙담한

어휘 | take a break 잠시 쉬다, 휴식을 취하다   stuck [stʌk] 圐 막힌, 갇힌   solve [sɑlv] 图 풀다, 해결하다   be good at ~을 잘하다   quite [kwait] 凰 꽤   bother [bɑ́ðər] 图 귀찮게 하다, 괴롭히다   appreciate [əprí:ʃieit] 图 고마워하다; 평가하다

---

6 그림 상황에 적절한 대화 고르기   정답 ②

① M Did you remember to lock the door?	① 남 문 잠그는 거 기억했지?
W Of course I did.	여 당연히 잠갔지.
② M Don't forget your umbrella!	② 남 우산 챙기는 거 잊지 말렴!
W I have it right here.	여 바로 여기 있어요.
③ M I'm glad the rain finally stopped.	③ 남 비가 마침내 그쳐서 다행이야.
W Me too. I didn't want to get wet.	여 나도. 젖고 싶지 않았거든.
④ M Is this your house? It's very nice.	④ 남 여기가 네 집이야? 정말 근사하다.
W Actually, I live in the one across the street.	여 사실, 난 길 건너편 집에 살고 있어.
⑤ M Why did you come home so early?	⑤ 남 왜 이렇게 일찍 집에 왔어?
W I wasn't feeling well.	여 몸이 안 좋았어.

해설 | 비가 오는 날 집을 나서는 여자에게 남자가 베란다에서 말을 건네자 여자가 우산을 보여주고 있는 상황이므로 정답은 ②이다.

어휘 | lock [lak] 图 잠그다 圐 자물쇠   wet [wet] 圐 젖은

7 **부탁·요청한 일 고르기**

정답 ①

M	What's wrong with your arm, Hyomin?
W	I hurt it <u>during volleyball practice</u> yesterday.
M	Oh, no. When will your arm be better?
W	I have to <u>wear</u> these <u>bandages</u> for two weeks.
M	Can you write during class?
W	I tried, but it is difficult. Could you help me take notes today?
M	Sure. Don't worry about it.

남	팔이 왜 그래, 효민아?
여	어제 배구 연습 중에 다쳤어.
남	오, 이런. 팔이 언제 좋아지니?
여	이 붕대를 2주 동안 차고 있어야 해.
남	수업 중에 글씨는 쓸 수 있어?
여	해봤는데, 어려워. 오늘 필기하는 걸 도와줄 수 있어?
남	물론이지. 그건 걱정하지 마.

해설 | 여자가 남자에게 필기하는 걸 도와 달라고 부탁했으므로 정답은 ① '필기 도와주기'이다.

어휘 | volleyball [válibɔ̀ːl] 몡 배구　bandage [bǽndidʒ] 몡 붕대　take a note 필기하다

8 **언급하지 않은 내용 고르기**

정답 ③

M	Hi, students. This is Henry Mann, the German teacher. The school is holding <u>an optional field trip</u> next month on Saturday, <u>November 5th</u>. We will be visiting the annual Pumpkin Festival. Anyone from <u>the first and second grades</u> can attend if interested. You'll <u>need a permission form</u> signed by your parents. Also, don't forget to <u>wear warm clothes</u> since it will be a little cold in the pumpkin field. I hope you can come join us.

남 안녕하세요, 학생 여러분. 독일어 선생님인 Henry Mann입니다. 학교에서 다음 달 토요일인 11월 5일에 선택적 현장학습을 갈 것입니다. 저희는 매년 열리는 Pumpkin Festival을 방문할 것입니다. 1, 2학년 중 누구나 관심이 있다면 참석할 수 있습니다. 부모님의 서명을 받은 동의서가 필요할 것입니다. 또한, 호박밭에서는 약간 추울 테니 따뜻한 옷을 입는 걸 잊지 마십시오. 여러분이 저희와 함께하러 오길 바랍니다.

해설 | ① 날짜(11월 5일), ② 참가 대상(1, 2학년 학생), ④ 복장(따뜻한 옷), ⑤ 필요 서류(부모님의 서명을 받은 동의서)에 대해 언급했으므로 정답은 ③ '목적'이다.

어휘 | optional [ápʃənəl] 혱 선택적인, 임의의　annual [ǽnjuəl] 혱 매년 열리는, 연례의　grade [greid] 몡 학년, 등급　permission form 동의서

9 **화제 고르기**

정답 ①

M	People who have this job help the sick. They ask customers <u>about their symptoms</u> and recommend different medications to help them feel better. <u>They also prepare and give out medicine to patients</u> after they see a doctor. You need to give them a doctor's note to get certain medicine. To do this job, you must <u>get a license</u>.

남 이 직업을 가진 사람들은 아픈 사람들을 돕습니다. 그들은 손님들에게 증상에 관해 묻고 낫도록 돕기 위해 여러 가지 약을 추천합니다. 그들은 또한 환자들이 진찰받은 후에는 약을 준비해서 지급합니다. 특정한 약을 받으려면 의사의 진단서를 그들에게 줘야 합니다. 이 일을 하기 위해서는, 면허증을 얻어야 합니다.

해설 | 이 직업(this job)을 가진 사람들은 의사의 진찰을 받은 환자들에게 약을 준비해서 지급한다고 했으므로 정답은 ① '약사'이다.

어휘 | symptom [símptəm] 몡 증상　medication [mèdəkéiʃən] 몡 약, 약물; 투약　give out 지급하다, 나눠주다　license [láisəns] 몡 면허증; 면허

10 **어색한 대화 고르기**

정답 ③

① W	Are you going to the school play tonight?
M	Yes. I think it's going to be interesting.
② W	Is it okay to drink coffee here?
M	No. Not <u>inside the library</u>.
③ W	I love the red painting in the living room.
M	Oh, I <u>spilled tomato sauce</u> everywhere.
④ W	How's the weather outside?
M	It's perfect right now.
⑤ W	What did you do today? You look happy.
M	I <u>made a new friend</u> at school.

① 여 오늘 밤 학교 연극에 갈 거야?
　남 응. 흥미로울 것 같아.
② 여 여기에서 커피를 마셔도 되나요?
　남 아니요. 도서관 안에서는 안 됩니다.
③ 여 거실에 있는 붉은색 그림이 아주 마음에 드네요.
　남 오, 제가 토마토소스를 사방에 흘렸어요.
④ 여 밖에 날씨는 어때?
　남 지금은 완벽해.
⑤ 여 오늘 뭐 했니? 행복해 보이는구나.
　남 학교에서 새로운 친구를 사귀었어요.

해설 | 여자가 남자에게 붉은색 그림이 마음에 든다고 했으므로, 남자는 그 그림에 관해 말해야 한다. 그러나 남자가 토마토소스를 사방에 흘렸다는 어색한 대답을 했으므로 정답은 ③이다.

어휘 | spill [spil] 동 흘리다, 엎지르다

11 할 일 고르기　　　　　　　　　　　　　　　　정답 ①

W	Where are you going, Richard?
M	Hey, Katie. I'm going to see Mr. Brown.
W	I'll walk with you. Why are you seeing Mr. Brown?
M	I need to talk to him about an assignment. Do you need to see him too?
W	No. But the sign-up sheet for the art club is next to his room.
M	Are you going to sign up for the club?
W	Yes. I'm looking forward to it.

여	어디 가는 중이야, Richard?
남	안녕, Katie. 난 Brown 선생님을 뵈러 가는 중이야.
여	나도 너랑 같이 갈게. 너는 왜 선생님을 뵈러 가니?
남	과제에 관해 말씀드릴 게 있어서. 너도 선생님을 봬야 해?
여	아니. 그런데 미술 동아리 가입 신청서가 선생님 교실 옆에 있거든.
남	미술 동아리에 가입할 거니?
여	응. 난 기대 중이야.

해설 | 남자가 미술 동아리에 가입할 것인지 묻자 여자가 그렇다고 했으므로 정답은 ① '동아리 가입하기'이다.

어휘 | assignment [əsáinmənt] 몡 과제; 할당　sign-up sheet 가입 신청서, 참가 신청서　look forward to ~을 기대하다

12 위치 고르기　　　　　　　　　　　　　　　　정답 ③

W	Honey, let's make a reservation for a campsite for the weekend.
M	Are we camping at the same campground as last time?
W	Yeah. But I want to stay at a different site. There were too many bugs.
M	I think it was because of the forest. Let's stay at one close to the beach this time.
W	Okay. How about Site A?
M	But I want to watch people playing beach volleyball. It looked so fun.
W	Then, we have two options.
M	Why don't we choose the one closer to the showers? It'll be much more convenient.
W	Sure. I'll book that site.

여	여보, 주말에 갈 야영장을 예약하자.
남	지난번과 같은 야영장에서 캠핑하는 거지?
여	응. 그런데 다른 위치에서 머무르고 싶어. 벌레가 너무 많았거든.
남	그건 숲 때문이었던 것 같아. 이번엔 바닷가 가까운 곳에서 지내자.
여	알겠어. A 위치는 어때?
남	그런데 난 사람들이 비치발리볼 하는 걸 보고 싶어. 정말 재미있어 보였거든.
여	그럼, 두 가지 선택지가 있어.
남	샤워장에 더 가까운 곳을 고르는 건 어때? 거기가 훨씬 더 편할 거야.
여	그래. 그 위치로 예약할게.

해설 | 남자가 바닷가 가까운 곳의 비치발리볼 하는 것을 볼 수 있고 샤워장에 더 가까운 위치를 제안하자 여자가 동의했으므로 정답은 ③이다.

어휘 | campsite [kǽmpsàit] 몡 야영장, 야영지　campground [kǽmpgraund] 몡 야영장, 캠프장　site [sait] 몡 위치, 장소　bug [bʌg] 몡 벌레
shower [ʃáuər] 몡 샤워장, 샤워실　convenient [kənvíːnjənt] 혱 편한, 편리한

13 시간 정보 고르기　　　　　　　　　　　　　　정답 ④

	[Cellphone rings.]
M	Hello. This is Ben Nicholas at Spring Gym.
W	Hi, this is Kelly Johnson. I'd like to change my appointment for personal training this week.
M	Okay. The original date was April 5th, right?
W	No. It was April 7th. But I won't be able to come because of a family trip.
M	When do you want to change the date to?
W	Can I change it to the 6th?
M	Sorry, but our gym will be closed that day. How about the 8th?
W	Yeah. I think I can make it that day.
M	Alright. I'll put it in my schedule.
W	Thank you.

	[휴대폰이 울린다.]
남	여보세요. Spring Gym의 Ben Nicholas입니다.
여	안녕하세요, 저는 Kelly Johnson이에요. 이번 주 개인 운동 강습 예약 시간을 바꾸고 싶어서요.
남	알겠습니다. 원래 날짜는 4월 5일이었죠, 맞나요?
여	아니요. 4월 7일이었어요. 그런데 가족 여행 때문에 못 갈 거 같아요.
남	언제로 날짜를 바꾸고 싶으세요?
여	6일로 바꿀 수 있을까요?
남	죄송하지만, 저희 체육관이 그날은 휴관이에요. 8일은 어떠세요?
여	네. 그날은 갈 수 있을 것 같아요.
남	알겠습니다. 제 일정에 넣어둘게요.
여	감사합니다.

해설 | 4월 7일로 예약된 개인 운동 강습 날짜를 바꾸는 과정에서, 남자가 8일을 제안하자 여자가 그날 갈 수 있겠다고 했으므로 정답은 ④ '4월 8일'이다.

어휘 | personal [pə́rsənəl] 혱 개인의　original [ərídʒənəl] 혱 원래의, 본래의　change A to B A를 B로 바꾸다　make it 가다, 시간에 대다; 성공하다

14 한 일 고르기

정답 ⑤

M Do you like pasta, Chloe?

W Yes. It's <u>my favorite food</u>. Why?

M There's a new pasta restaurant that opened around the corner. The food <u>looks delicious</u>.

W I saw it. It does look nice.

M Do you want to eat there this afternoon? I'd like to try it.

W Actually, <u>I cooked pasta yesterday</u>, so I already have some at home.

M I see. We can go another time then.

남 너 파스타 좋아해, Chloe?

여 응. 그건 내가 가장 좋아하는 음식이야. 왜?

남 근처에 문을 연 새 파스타 식당이 있어. 음식이 맛있어 보이더라.

여 나도 봤어. 정말 근사해 보이더라.

남 오늘 오후에 그곳에서 식사할래? 먹어보고 싶거든.

여 사실, 내가 어제 파스타를 요리해서, 집에 이미 좀 있어.

남 그렇구나. 그러면 다음번에 가면 되겠다.

해설 | 여자가 어제 파스타를 요리했다고 했으므로 정답은 ⑤ '파스타 요리하기'이다.

어휘 | around the corner 근처에, 바로 가까이에 **cook** [kuk] 통 요리하다

15 목적 고르기

정답 ③

M Thanks for coming everyone. <u>Before the St. Louis Orchestra takes the stage, I want to</u> <u>discuss some rules</u> for audience members. Firstly, we ask that everyone <u>remain quiet</u> during the performance. <u>Don't</u> <u>disturb others</u> by loudly talking. Second, eating and drinking is <u>strictly forbidden</u>. Lastly, you are not allowed to make any recordings for the concert. Anyone recording a video will be <u>asked to leave</u>. Thanks for listening.

남 모두 와주셔서 감사합니다. St. Louis Orchestra가 무대에 오르기 전에, 청중 여러분에게 몇 가지 규칙을 이야기하고 싶습니다. 첫째로, 공연 중에는 모두 조용히 있으시길 부탁드립니다. 시끄럽게 떠들어서 다른 사람들을 방해하지 말아 주십시오. 둘째로, 먹는 것과 마시는 것은 엄격히 금지되어 있습니다. 마지막으로, 연주회를 조금이라도 녹화하는 것은 허용되지 않습니다. 동영상을 촬영하는 누구든 퇴장하라는 요청을 받을 겁니다. 들어주셔서 감사합니다.

해설 | 남자가 공연에 앞서 청중에게 공연장에서 지켜야 할 규칙들을 설명하고 있으므로 정답은 ③ '공연장 예절을 안내하려고'이다.

어휘 | discuss [diskΛs] 통 이야기하다; 논의하다 **audience** [ɔ́:diəns] 명 청중, 관중 **disturb** [distə́:rb] 통 방해하다 **strictly** [stríktli] 부 엄격히 **forbid** [fərbíd] 통 금지하다

16 금액 정보 고르기

정답 ④

W Hello. How may I help you?

M I'd like to <u>send a package</u> to Finland. How much would it be?

W It's five dollars per kilogram. Please put the package <u>on the scale</u>.

M Sure. *[Beeping sound]* It's seven kilograms.

W Then, <u>it's 35 dollars in total</u>.

M Okay. I need some more tape for my package. Do I need to <u>pay extra</u> for some?

W No. <u>It's free</u>. You can find it over there.

M Thank you.

여 안녕하세요. 무엇을 도와드릴까요?

남 핀란드로 이 택배를 보내고 싶어요. 얼마가 될까요?

여 1kg당 5달러입니다. 택배를 저울 위에 올려놓아 주세요.

남 물론이죠. [삑 하는 소리] 7kg이네요.

여 그러면, 총 35달러입니다.

남 알겠습니다. 택배에 쓸 테이프가 좀 더 필요한데요. 추가 요금을 내야 하나요?

여 아니요. 공짜입니다. 저쪽에서 찾으실 수 있어요.

남 감사합니다.

해설 | 택배 요금은 1kg당 5달러이고 남자의 택배는 7kg이라고 했으며, 택배에 쓸 테이프는 무료라고 했으므로 정답은 ④ '$ 35'이다.

어휘 | package [pǽkidʒ] 명 택배, 소포 **scale** [skeil] 명 저울; 저울눈, 눈금 **extra** [ékstrə] 명 추가 요금 형 추가의

M   How was your day, Grace?

W   It was a long day, Dad.

M   What happened?

W   I lost one of my earphones, and I also forgot my lunch.

M   Oh, no. I'm sorry you had a bad day. Why don't we do something fun tonight to cheer you up?

W   Okay. What should we do?

M   Let's get some ice cream. We can bring it home and watch your favorite drama.

W   That's a great plan. Thanks!

남	오늘 하루는 어땠니, Grace?
여	긴 하루였어요, 아빠.
남	무슨 일이 있었는데?
여	제 이어폰 한 짝을 잃어버리고, 제 점심도 깜빡했어요.
남	오, 이런. 안 좋은 하루를 보냈다니 유감이구나. 널 격려해 주기 위해 오늘 밤 뭔가 재미있는 걸 해보는 게 어떠니?
여	알겠어요. 뭘 하면 될까요?
남	아이스크림을 좀 사러 가자. 그걸 집에 가져와서 네가 가장 좋아하는 드라마를 보는 거지.
여	훌륭한 계획이에요. 고마워요!

해설 | 남자가 아이스크림을 사 와서 드라마를 보며 먹자고 제안했으므로 정답은 제안에 동의하는 ② 'That's a great plan. Thanks!'이다.

선택지 해석

① 네. 좋은 시간을 보냈네요.   ② 훌륭한 계획이에요. 고마워요!   ③ 어제 그걸 찾았어요.   ④ 오늘은 아이스크림을 주는 날이에요.

⑤ 죄송해요, 회의가 오래 걸렸어요.

어휘 | cheer up 격려하다   serve [səːrv] 통 주다, 제공하다; 복무하다   meeting [míːtiŋ] 명 회의; 만남

M   Honey, I'm so happy to be on vacation. What should we do at the lake today?

W   Let's go swimming or water skiing. Then, we can enjoy the nice view of the hills around the lake.

M   That sounds fun, but the water is a little cold right now.

W   Oh, you're probably right.

M   Why don't we go for a hike around the lake? We can stop at a café somewhere too.

W   Is the trail difficult? I didn't bring any hiking shoes.

M   No. The ones you're wearing are fine.

남	여보, 난 휴가를 오게 돼서 너무 행복해. 오늘 호수에서 뭘 하면 될까?
여	수영하러 가거나 수상 스키를 타러 가자. 그러면, 호수 근처 언덕의 멋진 풍경을 즐길 수 있을 거야.
남	재미있을 것 같긴 한데, 지금은 물이 좀 차가워.
여	오, 어쩌면 당신 말이 맞을지도 몰라.
남	호수 주변을 하이킹하러 가는 건 어때? 거기 어딘가의 카페에 들를 수도 있어.
여	둘레길이 험해? 하이킹용 신발은 안 가져왔는데.
남	아니. 당신이 신고 있는 걸로도 괜찮아.

해설 | 여자가 둘레길이 험한지 물었으므로 정답은 험하지 않다고 대답하는 ④ 'No. The ones you're wearing are fine.'이다.

선택지 해석

① 응. 우린 빠르게 올라왔네.   ② 난 내일 휴가를 떠나.   ③ 우리 호텔은 바로 저기 언덕 위에 있어.   ④ 아니. 당신이 신고 있는 걸로도 괜찮아.

⑤ 수영복 가져오는 거 잊었어?

어휘 | water ski 수상 스키를 하다; 수상 스키   view [vjuː] 명 풍경; 견해   probably [prábəbli] 부 어쩌면, 아마   swimsuit [swímsuːt] 명 수영복

[Cellphone rings.]

M   What's up, Jessica?

W   Hi, Edward. Did you ever finish that new book, *Endless Smile*?

M   I finished it last week. Why?

W   Can I borrow it? I want to read it on the subway. After my move, it takes longer to get to school.

M   Sure. But please return it as soon as possible. My sister wants to read it too.

W   No problem. Can I come and pick it up today?

M   Yes. You can come any time after 6.

W   Alright. I'll drop by at 6:30 then.

	[휴대폰이 울린다.]
남	무슨 일이야, Jessica?
여	안녕, Edward. 새로 나온 책 <Endless Smile> 다 읽었어?
남	지난주에 다 읽었지. 왜?
여	내가 빌려도 될까? 지하철에서 읽고 싶거든. 이사한 이후로, 학교 가는 데 더 오래 걸려.
남	물론이지. 그렇지만 되도록 빨리 돌려줘. 내 여동생도 그걸 읽고 싶어하거든.
여	문제없어. 오늘 내가 가지러 가도 될까?
남	응. 6시 이후엔 언제든 와도 돼.
여	알겠어. 그러면 6시 30분에 들를게.

해설 | 남자가 6시 이후에는 언제든지 와도 된다고 했으므로 정답은 방문 시각을 알려주는 ⑤ 'Alright. I'll drop by at 6:30 then.'이다.

선택지 해석
① 우리 통학 시간은 대략 2시간이야. ② 내 여동생에게 널 소개해 줄게. ③ 독후감을 끝마쳐서 행복해. ④ 그들은 버스 대신에 지하철을 탔어.
⑤ 알겠어. 그러면 6시 30분에 들를게.

어휘 | as soon as possible 되도록 빨리 drop by 들르다 commute [kəmjúːt] 圈 통학 시간 圄 통근하다 instead of ~ 대신에

20 상황에 적절한 말 고르기

정답 ⑤

M The other day, Phil made plans with his friend Olivia. They were going to watch a new action movie together on Saturday. However, Phil woke up that morning with a headache. Phil would like to ask Olivia if they can see the movie another day instead. In this situation, what would Phil most likely say to Olivia?

Phil Olivia, can we see the movie another time?

남 며칠 전에, Phil은 그의 친구 Olivia와 계획을 짰습니다. 그들은 토요일에 함께 신작 액션 영화를 보러 갈 예정이었습니다. 하지만, Phil은 그날 아침에 일어나자 두통이 있었습니다. Phil은 Olivia에게 그들이 영화를 다른 날에 대신 봐도 되는지 묻고 싶습니다. 이러한 상황에서, Phil이 Olivia에게 가장 할 것 같은 말은 무엇입니까?

Phil Olivia, 우리 다음번에 영화 봐도 될까?

해설 | Phil이 Olivia에게 다른 날에 영화를 봐도 되는지 묻고 싶다고 했으므로 정답은 ⑤ 'can we see the movie another time?'이다.

선택지 해석
① 난 곧 병원에 가야 해. ② 영화 끝나고 뭐 하고 싶어? ③ 영화관에서 11시에 만나자. ④ 유감인데 티켓을 못 구하겠어. ⑤ 우리 다음번에 영화 봐도 될까?

어휘 | the other day 며칠 전에, 일전에 headache [hédeik] 圈 두통

06회 실전 모의고사

| 문제 pp.66~67

1	③	2	④	3	③	4	④	5	②	6	④	7	③	8	②	9	④	10	②
11	④	12	⑤	13	⑤	14	⑤	15	①	16	④	17	①	18	③	19	④	20	①

1 알맞은 그림 고르기

정답 ③

W Mark, are you ready? It's time to leave for the studio.
M Wait, Mom. I need to get my light-up cheer stick.
W Oh, what's that?
M I made this to cheer on Jane. I want her to win the quiz show.
W Your sister will love it! How did you make it?
M It was simple. First, I wrote the words "GO JANE" on a piece of black paper, and then cut it into a star shape.
W Then, you attached it to a yellow LED stick.
M Yes.

여 Mark, 준비됐니? 방송국으로 출발할 시간이야.
남 잠시만요, 엄마. 빛이 나오는 제 응원봉을 가져와야 해요.
여 오, 그게 뭐니?
남 Jane을 응원하려고 만들었어요. Jane이 퀴즈쇼에서 우승하면 좋겠거든요.
여 네 여동생이 무척 좋아하겠구나! 어떻게 만들었니?
남 간단했어요. 먼저, 검은색 종이 위에 'GO JANE'이라는 글자를 쓰고, 그러고 나서 그걸 별 모양으로 오렸어요.
여 그리고, 그걸 노란색 LED 봉에 붙였구나.
남 맞아요.

해설 | 남자가 검은색 종이 위에 'GO JANE'이라는 글자를 쓴 후 별 모양으로 오렸다고 했고, 여자가 그 후 그것을 노란색 LED 봉에 붙였다고 했으므로 정답은 ③이다.

어휘 | studio [stjúːdiòu] 圈 방송국; 작업장 cheer stick 응원봉 attach [ətǽtʃ] 圄 붙이다

2   언급하지 않은 내용 고르기   정답 ④

M	Welcome to the Trek Store. How can I help you?
W	I need to buy a new backpack. I enjoy climbing on the weekends.
M	This brown one is popular with climbers.
W	What is it made of?
M	Leather and nylon.
W	How much does it cost?
M	It is on sale for 65 dollars.
W	That is a little expensive.
M	Well, it comes with a rain cover and a water bottle.
W	Hmm... In that case, I'll take it.

남 Trek Store에 오신 걸 환영합니다. 무엇을 도와드릴까요?
여 전 새 배낭을 사야 해요. 주말마다 등산하는 걸 즐기거든요.
남 이 갈색 배낭이 등산객들에게 인기가 많아요.
여 그건 뭐로 만들어진 거죠?
남 가죽과 나일론입니다.
여 얼마인가요?
남 할인해서 65달러입니다.
여 약간 비싸네요.
남 그래도, 우천 시 방수 덮개와 물병이 딸려 있어요.
여 흠... 그렇다면, 그걸 살게요.

해설 | ① 소재(가죽과 나일론), ② 색상(갈색), ③ 가격(65달러), ⑤ 추가 구성품(우천 시 방수 덮개와 물병)에 대해 언급했으므로 정답은 ④ '크기'이다.

어휘 | leather [léðər] 평 가죽 on sale 할인 중인, 세일 중인; 판매 중인 come with ~이 딸려 있다 in that case 그렇다면, 그런 경우에는

3   목적 고르기   정답 ③

	[Cellphone rings.]
M	Hello?
W	Hi, could I speak with Jacob Simmons?
M	That's me.
W	This is Carol from Dr. Kim's office. I'm calling about your dental appointment.
M	Sure. What is it?
W	Dr. Kim is going to be out of the office on Saturday, so we have to reschedule your appointment.
M	Okay. When can I come in?
W	You can see him on Thursday at 4 p.m. or Friday at 2 p.m.
M	I'll come on Thursday.

[휴대폰이 울린다.]
남 여보세요?
여 안녕하세요, Jacob Simmons씨와 통화할 수 있을까요?
남 전데요.
여 저는 김 박사님 사무실의 Carol이에요. 치과 진료 예약 때문에 전화 드렸습니다.
남 그렇군요. 무슨 일이시죠?
여 김 박사님이 토요일에 사무실에 안 계실 예정이라서, 일정을 변경해야 해요.
남 알겠습니다. 언제 가면 될까요?
여 목요일 오후 4시나 금요일 오후 2시에 진료 가능하세요.
남 목요일에 가겠습니다.

해설 | 여자가 남자의 치과 진료 예약 일정을 변경해야 한다고 했으므로 정답은 ③ '예약 시간을 변경하려고'이다.

어휘 | dental appointment 치과 진료 예약 reschedule [rìːskéʒuːl] 통 일정을 변경하다, 예정을 다시 세우다

4   시간 정보 고르기   정답 ④

	[Telephone rings.]
W	World Connections Airlines. How may I help you?
M	Hello. My flight from London to Boston was just canceled, so I need to book a different flight.
W	Alright. Let me see. [Typing sound] Do you want business or economy class?
M	My last ticket was for business class.
W	Well, there's a flight that leaves at 2 p.m. with business-class seats.
M	I won't have enough time to make that flight.
W	What about 4? There is only economy class left for that flight.
M	That will be fine.
W	Okay. I'll book your ticket now then.

[전화기가 울린다.]
여 World Connections Airlines입니다. 무엇을 도와드릴까요?
남 안녕하세요. 런던에서 출발하는 보스턴행 비행기가 방금 취소돼서, 다른 비행기를 예약해야 해요.
여 알겠습니다. 확인해 볼게요. [타자치는 소리] 비즈니스석을 원하세요, 아니면 이코노미석을 원하세요?
남 제 이전 표는 비즈니스석이었어요.
여 음, 비즈니스석으로는 오후 2시에 출발하는 비행기가 있네요.
남 그걸 탈 시간이 충분하지 않겠어요.
여 4시는 어떠세요? 이때는 남은 게 이코노미석뿐이에요.
남 그건 괜찮을 거예요.
여 네. 그러면 바로 표를 예약해드릴게요.

해설 | 여자가 4시에 출발하는 비행기가 어떤지 묻자 남자가 괜찮을 것 같다고 했으므로 정답은 ④ '4 p.m.'이다.

어휘 | cancel [kǽnsəl] 통 취소하다 book [buk] 통 예약하다 명 책 business class (비행기의) 비즈니스석

5 그림 상황에 적절한 대화 고르기   정답 ②

① M Could you fold this box for me?
   W Sure. I'll do it in a minute.
② M Where should I put this?
   W In the bedroom, please.
③ M Did you order some new bedding?
   W Yes. It should be delivered this week.
④ M Did we get any mail today?
   W I got a letter from Mr. Dave.
⑤ M Why are you washing your sneakers?
   W I stepped in a puddle earlier.

① 남 저 대신 이 상자를 접어줄래요?
   여 물론이죠. 당장 할게요.
② 남 이건 어디에 둬야 하나요?
   여 침실로 부탁해요.
③ 남 새로운 침구류를 좀 주문했니?
   여 응. 그건 이번 주에 배송될 거야.
④ 남 오늘 우편물 받은 게 있나요?
   여 Dave씨에게서 편지를 받았어요.
⑤ 남 왜 운동화를 빨고 있어?
   여 아까 물웅덩이를 밟았거든.

해설 | 이삿짐을 나르고 있는 남자에게 여자가 집 안을 가리키며 침실을 말하고 있는 상황이므로 정답은 ②이다.
어휘 | in a minute 당장, 금방   bedding [bédiŋ] 뗑 침구류   puddle [pʎdl] 뗑 물웅덩이

6 장소 고르기   정답 ④

M Do you like this painting, Bora?
W Yes. The beach in it is beautiful with the sunset.
M I love this painting of the mountains too. The artist is very talented.
W Do you prefer paintings of nature?
M Yes. I like them because I like being in nature.
W Right. But I prefer the portraits of historical people.
M Oh, really? Do you like history?
W Yes. It's my favorite subject. I find the stories behind the paintings so interesting.

남 이 그림이 마음에 드니, 보라야?
여 응. 그림 속 해변과 저녁노을이 아름다워.
남 난 여기 산을 그린 그림도 너무 좋아. 화가가 아주 재능이 뛰어나.
여 자연을 그린 그림을 좋아하니?
남 응. 자연 속에 있는 걸 좋아해서 그런 걸 좋아해.
여 그렇구나. 근데 난 역사적 인물을 그린 초상화를 더 선호해.
남 오, 정말? 너 역사를 좋아하니?
여 응. 그건 내가 가장 좋아하는 주제야. 그림의 뒷이야기가 아주 흥미롭다고 생각하거든.

해설 | 남자와 여자가 자연을 그린 그림을 보면서 화가가 재능이 뛰어나고 그림이 마음에 든다고 대화를 하는 것으로 보아 정답은 ④ '미술관'이다.
어휘 | sunset [sʎnsèt] 뗑 저녁노을; 일몰   portrait [pɔ́ːrtrit] 뗑 초상화   historical [histɔ́ːrikəl] 혱 역사적인, 역사상 실재한   subject [sʎbdʒikt] 뗑 주제

7 부탁·요청한 일 고르기   정답 ③

W Honey, where are the kids?
M They're playing games on the computer.
W Are they ready to go? The movie starts at 6 p.m.
M Yes, they are ready. So, I don't think we have to hurry.
W Actually, the traffic looks bad. We should leave early.
M Okay. Should I tell the kids that we are leaving now?
W I'll do it. Can you just call a cab?
M Yes. I'll do that now.

여 여보, 애들은 어디 있어?
남 애들은 컴퓨터 게임을 하는 중이야.
여 갈 준비는 된 거야? 영화는 오후 6시에 시작해.
남 응, 준비됐지. 그러니까, 우리 서두를 필요가 없는 거 같아.
여 사실, 교통이 안 좋아 보여. 일찍 출발해야겠어.
남 알겠어. 내가 애들한테 우리 지금 출발한다고 말할까?
여 내가 할게. 당신은 그냥 택시를 불러줄래?
남 응. 지금 할게.

해설 | 여자가 남자에게 택시를 불러 달라고 부탁했으므로 정답은 ③ '택시 부르기'이다.
어휘 | hurry [hʎːri] 통 서두르다   cab [kæb] 뗑 택시

W　This is an announcement for members of Health First Gym. We want to give you the best experience, so we've decided to remodel our facility. The construction process will take three months, and it will begin on September 1st. We understand that this will cause some inconvenience, so we will give all members a 30% discount on their fees during this time. When the construction is finished, we will have new fitness rooms for classes and upgraded machines. We apologize again, and thank you for your support.

여　Health First Gym 회원분들에게 알리는 공지입니다. 저희는 여러분에게 최상의 경험을 제공하고 싶어, 저희 시설을 리모델링하기로 결정했습니다. 공사 과정은 세 달이 걸릴 예정이고, 공사는 9월 1일부터 시작될 것입니다. 저희는 이것이 몇몇 불편을 일으킬 수 있음을 알고 있으므로, 이 기간 동안 모든 회원분에게 30% 요금 할인을 제공할 것입니다. 공사가 끝나면, 새로운 수업용 체력 단련실과 최신식의 기계들이 있을 것입니다. 다시 한번 사과드리며, 성원에 감사드립니다.

해설 | ① 목적(회원들에게 최상의 경험을 제공하기 위해), ③ 소요 기간(3달), ④ 시작 일자(9월 1일), ⑤ 보상 방법(30% 요금 할인 제공)에 대해 언급했으므로 정답은 ② '담당자'이다.

어휘 | announcement [ənáunsmənt] 몡 공지, 발표　facility [fəsíləti] 몡 시설　construction [kənstrʌ́kʃən] 몡 공사, 건설
inconvenience [ìnkənvíːnjəns] 몡 불편

W　This is something you wear on your hands. You need this when you cook or bake in the kitchen. It's usually made of thick cloth and comes in various colors and patterns. You simply put your hand inside of it to use it. Then, you can pick up and move hot dishes with your covered hand. Without this, you can burn your skin badly.

여　이것은 손에 착용하는 것입니다. 부엌에서 요리하거나 빵을 구울 때 이것이 필요합니다. 이것은 보통 두꺼운 천으로 만들어지고 다양한 색상과 무늬로 나옵니다. 이것을 사용하려면 간단하게 안쪽으로 손을 넣으면 됩니다. 그러고 나서, 이것으로 덮은 손으로 뜨거운 접시를 집어서 옮길 수 있습니다. 이것이 없다면, 피부에 심하게 화상을 입을 수 있습니다.

해설 | 이것(This)은 부엌에서 요리하거나 빵을 구울 때 필요하며, 이것으로 덮은 손으로 뜨거운 접시를 집어서 옮길 수 있다고 했으므로 정답은 ④ '오븐 장갑'이다.

어휘 | thick [θik] 헹 두꺼운　various [vɛ́riəs] 헹 다양한　burn [bəːrn] 동 화상을 입히다; 타다　skin [skin] 몡 피부　badly [bǽdli] 분 심하게; 틀리게

① M　Did you do anything fun last weekend?
　 W　Yes. I went skiing with some friends.
② M　Do you want to order a pizza or some chicken?
　 W　Dinner isn't ready.
③ M　Where do you usually get your hair cut?
　 W　I go to Sally's Salon.
④ M　How can I help you?
　 W　Where is the frozen foods section?
⑤ M　Here is the tool I borrowed.
　 W　Thank you for returning it so quickly!

① 남　지난 주말에 뭔가 재미있는 걸 했니?
　 여　응. 친구들이랑 스키 타러 갔어.
② 남　피자를 주문할까 아니면 치킨을 주문할까?
　 여　저녁 준비가 안 됐어.
③ 남　보통 넌 어디에서 머리를 잘라?
　 여　난 Sally's Salon에 가.
④ 남　무엇을 도와드릴까요?
　 여　냉동식품 코너는 어디에 있나요?
⑤ 남　여기 제가 빌린 도구입니다.
　 여　이렇게나 빠르게 돌려주셔서 고마워요!

해설 | 남자가 여자에게 피자를 주문할지 아니면 치킨을 주문할지 물었으므로, 여자는 둘 중 무엇을 주문할지 답해야 한다. 그러나 여자가 저녁 준비가 안 됐다는 어색한 대답을 했으므로 정답은 ②이다.

어휘 | frozen [fróuzn] 헹 냉동의, 언　tool [tuːl] 몡 도구　return [ritə́ːrn] 동 돌려주다; 돌아오다

M　That bicycle ride was hard, Honey.
W　I agree. I'm so tired.
M　Do you want to sit on the couch and relax?
W　Yes. But it's a little hot in here.
M　I just showered, but I'm still sweating from the workout.
W　I'll turn on the fan then.
M　Good. I'll get us two cups of iced water.

남　자전거 타는 거 힘들었어, 여보.
여　동감이야. 정말 피곤하다.
남　소파에 앉아서 쉴까?
여　그래. 그런데 안이 좀 덥네.
남　나 방금 샤워했는데, 여전히 운동 후 흘린 땀이 계속 나.
여　그럼 선풍기를 켤게.
남　좋아. 난 얼음물을 두 잔 가져올게.

해설 | 여자가 안이 더워서 선풍기를 켜겠다고 했으므로 정답은 ④ '선풍기 틀기'이다.

어휘 | tired [taiərd] 휑 피곤한   relax [riláeks] 통 쉬다; 긴장을 늦추다   sweat [swet] 통 땀이 나다, 땀을 흘리다   fan [fæn] 명 선풍기; 부채

12 시간 정보 고르기

정답 ⑤

W	Jake, do you want to have lunch this Friday?
M	Okay. <u>What time do you want</u> to meet?
W	How about 12? We can go to that Chinese restaurant downtown.
M	Actually, I have <u>a doctor's appointment</u> at 11 a.m., and it will take longer than an hour. What about meeting at 2?
W	That's <u>a little late</u> for me. I'll need to eat before then.
M	Then, why don't we just <u>meet for dinner</u>?
W	Yeah. That's a good idea. <u>Is 6 okay?</u>
M	<u>That works for me.</u> See you then.

여 Jake, 이번 주 금요일에 점심 먹을래?
남 그래. 몇 시에 만나고 싶어?
여 12시는 어때? 시내에 있는 중식당에 가면 돼.
남 사실, 내가 오전 11시에 진료 예약이 있는데, 한 시간보다 더 오래 걸릴 거야. 2시에 만나는 건 어때?
여 그건 좀 늦어. 그전에 먹어야 할 것 같아.
남 그러면, 그냥 저녁 먹으러 만나지 않을래?
여 응. 그게 좋겠어. 6시 괜찮아?
남 난 괜찮아. 그때 보자.

해설 | 여자가 6시는 괜찮은지 묻자 남자가 괜찮다고 했으므로 정답은 ⑤ '6 p.m.'이다.

어휘 | downtown [dáuntaun] 위 시내에, 상업지구로

13 위치 고르기

정답 ⑤

M	Sarah, did you book a study room for our group project?
W	Not yet. I just found this new study café. It looks quiet.
M	Oh, that's nice. Let's <u>reserve one</u> there.
W	How about Room C? <u>It looks spacious.</u>
M	There are only four of us, so <u>we don't need a room that big.</u>
W	Okay. How about Room A or Room D?
M	<u>I don't want to book those rooms because they are close to the elevator and the restroom.</u>
W	I agree with you. Then, we have two options left.
M	<u>I think the one in the corner</u> would be quiet.
W	Let's choose that one then.

남 Sarah, 너 우리 그룹 과제를 할 스터디룸 예약했어?
여 아직. 내가 방금 이 새로운 스터디 카페를 발견했거든. 조용해 보여.
남 오, 좋은데. 거기로 예약하자.
여 C 룸은 어때? 넓어 보이는데.
남 우리는 겨우 4명뿐이니까, 그렇게 큰 방은 필요하지 않아.
여 그래. A 룸이나 D 룸은 어때?
남 그 방들은 엘리베이터와 화장실에 가까워서 예약하고 싶지 않아.
여 네 말에 동의해. 그러면, 두 가지 선택지가 남아 있어.
남 구석에 있는 게 조용할 것 같아.
여 그러면 그걸로 고르자.

해설 | 남자가 그렇게 크지 않으며, 엘리베이터와 화장실에 가깝지 않고, 구석에 있는 스터디룸이 조용할 것 같다고 했으므로 정답은 ⑤이다.

어휘 | spacious [spéiʃəs] 휑 넓은   elevator [éləvèitər] 명 엘리베이터, 승강기

14 한일 고르기

정답 ⑤

M	That's a cool jacket, Zoe.
W	Thank you. It was made by a local designer.
M	Where did you find it?
W	<u>I went to the market</u> on Friday and saw it. There are so many nice clothes there.
M	Are they expensive?
W	<u>Not at all.</u> But this jacket is a little big for me, so I will <u>get the sleeves shortened</u> later today.
M	Maybe I will go to the market too. I need <u>some new clothes.</u>
W	You should.

남 그거 멋진 재킷이다, Zoe.
여 고마워. 이건 현지 디자이너가 만든 거야.
남 어디에서 찾았어?
여 금요일에 시장에 갔다가 이걸 봤어. 거기엔 정말 멋진 옷들이 많아.
남 비싸니?
여 전혀 아니야. 그런데 이 재킷은 나한텐 약간 커서, 오늘 이따가 소매를 줄일 거야.
남 나도 그 시장에 가볼까 해. 새 옷이 좀 필요하거든.
여 꼭 가봐.

해설 | 여자가 금요일에 시장에 가서 옷을 봤다고 했으므로 정답은 ⑤ '시장 방문하기'이다.

어휘 | local [lóukəl] 휑 현지의; 지방의   sleeve [sliːv] 명 소매   shorten [ʃɔ́ːrtn] 통 줄이다, 짧게 하다

15 목적 고르기
정답 ①

W　This is Vanessa Watkins at *BBS News*. This morning, the city marathon was held. It was a hot day, but thousands of people ran in the race. In the men's competition, Benson Turner won for the third year in a row with a time of two hours and four minutes. Gina Jenkins won the women's race. She finished in two hours and 30 minutes. We congratulate both winners and everyone else who participated today.

여　저는 <BBS News>의 Vanessa Watkins입니다. 오늘 아침, 시의 마라톤 경기가 열렸습니다. 더운 날이었지만, 수천 명의 사람이 경기를 뛰었습니다. 남자 경기에서는, Benson Turner가 2시간 4분의 기록으로 삼 년 연속 우승했습니다. 여자 경기에서는 Gina Jenkins가 우승했습니다. 그녀는 2시간 30분 만에 경기를 마쳤습니다. 우승자들과 오늘 참여해주신 다른 모든 분에게 축하를 보냅니다.

해설 | 여자가 오늘 열린 마라톤 경기에서 누가 우승했는지를 알려주고 있으므로 정답은 ① '경기 결과를 보도하려고'이다.

어휘 | marathon [mǽrəθɑ̀n] 圐 마라톤 (경기, 경주)　in a row 연속적으로; 일렬로　congratulate [kəngrǽtʃuleit] 圐 축하하다

16 금액 정보 고르기
정답 ④

M　Hi. How may I help you?
W　I'm interested in taking a German class for beginners. How much is it?
M　If you take the class twice a week, it's 35 dollars. But you can also take the class three times a week if you pay more.
W　How much is the extra class?
M　You have to pay 10 dollars more.
W　That's a great deal. Can I sign up for three classes per week then, please?
M　Of course. If you enjoy it, you can sign up for more classes afterward.
W　Thank you.

남　안녕하세요. 무엇을 도와드릴까요?
여　제가 초급자용 독일어 수업을 듣는 것에 관심이 있는데요. 얼마인가요?
남　일주일에 두 번 수업을 들으신다면, 35달러입니다. 하지만 돈을 좀 더 내시면 일주일에 세 번도 들으실 수 있습니다.
여　추가 수업은 얼마인가요?
남　10달러만 더 내시면 됩니다.
여　정말 좋은 조건이네요. 지금 일주일에 세 번 수업으로 신청할 수 있나요?
남　당연하죠. 거기서 재미를 느끼시면, 나중에는 더 많은 수업을 신청하셔도 돼요.
여　감사합니다.

해설 | 일주일에 두 번 수업을 들으면 35달러이고, 10달러를 더 내면 일주일에 세 번 들을 수 있다고 하자 여자가 세 번짜리 수업을 신청했으므로 정답은 ④ '$ 45'이다.

어휘 | twice [twais] 凹 두 번　afterward [ǽftərwərd] 凹 나중에

17 적절한 응답 고르기
정답 ①

M　We need to finish our article for the school newspaper, Hanna.
W　I agree. We should work on it this weekend.
M　We have so much to do, so let's meet before then.
W　I'm sorry, but I'm taking care of my sister every night this week. My parents will work late.
M　Oh, so you can't go anywhere?
W　No. She's too young to stay home alone.
M　That's fine. If you want, I can come to your house and we can work there.
W　That's so helpful. I appreciate it.

남　우리는 학교 신문에 낼 기사를 끝내야 해, 한나야.
여　맞아. 이번 주말에 그걸 해야겠지.
남　우린 할 일이 아주 많아, 그러니까 그전에 만나자.
여　미안하지만, 내가 이번 주에는 매일 밤 여동생을 돌봐주고 있어. 우리 부모님이 늦게까지 일하셔서.
남　오, 그러면 어디도 못 가?
여　응. 동생이 집에 혼자 있기에는 너무 어리거든.
남　그럼 괜찮아. 네가 원한다면, 내가 너희 집으로 가서 거기서 같이 작업하면 돼.
여　정말 도움이 될 거야. 고마워.

해설 | 남자가 여자의 집으로 가서 그곳에서 작업해도 된다고 제안했으므로 정답은 제안을 고마워하는 ① 'That's so helpful. I appreciate it.'이다.

　선택지 해석
　① 정말 도움이 될 거야. 고마워.　② 다음 기사로 넘어가자.　③ 정말? 벌써 끝났다고?　④ 미안. 답을 모르겠어.　⑤ 내 여동생의 이름은 Rachel이야.

어휘 | article [ɑ́ːrtikl] 圐 기사　take care of ~를 돌보다　helpful [hélpfəl] 훵 도움이 되는

18 적절한 응답 고르기　　　　　　　　정답 ③

[Cellphone rings.]	[휴대폰이 울린다.]
W Hello?	여 여보세요?
M Mom, can you bring my science notebook to David's house?	남 엄마, David네 집으로 제 과학 공책 가져다주실 수 있어요?
W Oh, did you forget it?	여 오, 그걸 챙기는 걸 잊었니?
M Yes. I left it at home and brought my math homework instead. But we are working on science today.	남 네. 그건 집에 두고 오고 대신 제 수학 숙제를 가져왔어요. 그런데 오늘은 과학 공부를 할 거라서요.
W I see. I'll bring it over now then. Do you need anything else?	여 알겠구나. 그러면 지금 갖다주도록 하마. 다른 건 필요한 거 없니?
M Actually, can you also bring my highlighters? I want them for studying.	남 저, 제 형광펜도 가져다주실 수 있어요? 공부할 때 쓰고 싶어요.
W Sure. Do you want the ones on your desk?	여 물론이란다. 네 책상 위에 있는 거면 되니?
M Yeah. The blue and the pink one.	남 네. 파란색이랑 분홍색이요.

해설 | 여자가 책상 위에 놓인 형광펜을 가져다주길 원하는지 물었으므로 정답은 원하는 형광펜 색을 말하는 ③ 'Yeah. The blue and the pink one.'이다.

선택지 해석

① 아니요. 공책은 서랍 안에 있어요.　② 오늘 수업에서는 실험을 할 거예요.　③ 네. 파란색이랑 분홍색이요.　④ 과학 숙제 가져가는 걸 잊었어요.
⑤ 저쪽 책상에 앉으시면 돼요.

어휘 | highlighter [háilaitər] 명 형광펜　drawer [drɔːr] 명 서랍　experiment [ikspérəmənt] 명 실험

19 적절한 응답 고르기　　　　　　　　정답 ④

M Are you ready for the concert tonight, Minji?	남 오늘 밤 콘서트 갈 준비 됐지, 민지야?
W I'm so excited. Are we meeting outside of the stadium at 6?	여 나 너무 기대돼. 우리 6시에 경기장 밖에서 만나는 거지?
M Maybe we should grab a bite to eat before the show. What do you think?	남 어쩌면 우린 공연 전에 간단히 먹어야 할지도 모르겠어. 어떻게 생각해?
W That's a great idea. Where should we eat?	여 좋은 생각이야. 어디에서 먹을까?
M There aren't a lot of places by the stadium, so we can go somewhere at the next subway stop.	남 경기장 옆에는 가게들이 많지 않으니까, 그다음 지하철역 어딘가로 가면 되겠어.
W Yeah. That area has lots of restaurants.	여 그래. 그곳에는 식당이 많지.
M And I know a nice salad place around there.	남 그리고 내가 거기 주변에 괜찮은 샐러드 가게를 알고 있어.
W That's perfect! Let's go there then.	여 아주 훌륭해! 그러면 거기로 가자.

해설 | 남자가 지하철역 주변의 괜찮은 샐러드 가게를 알고 있다고 제안했으므로 정답은 제안을 수락하는 ④ 'That's perfect! Let's go there then.'이다.

선택지 해석

① 난 이미 식사해서, 배가 고프지 않아.　② 이건 안으로 들어가는 줄이야.　③ 2호선을 타고 나서 1호선을 타.　④ 아주 훌륭해! 그러면 거기로 가자.
⑤ 우리 예약은 오후 7시야.

어휘 | stadium [stéidiəm] 명 경기장　grab a bite to eat 간단히 먹다

20 상황에 적절한 말 고르기　　　　　　　　정답 ①

W Kelly is at her high school graduation. She is happy because her entire family came to the event to congratulate her. Kelly wants a photograph to remember this day. So, she decides to ask a man standing next to her family to take a picture. In this situation, what would Kelly most likely say to the man?	여 Kelly는 그녀의 고등학교 졸업식에 와 있습니다. 그녀는 가족 전부가 그녀를 축하해주려 이 행사에 왔기 때문에 기쁩니다. Kelly는 이날을 기억하기 위해 사진을 찍고 싶습니다. 그래서, 그녀의 가족 옆에 서 있는 남자에게 사진을 찍어달라고 부탁하기로 결심합니다. 이러한 상황에서, Kelly가 남자에게 가장 할 것 같은 말은 무엇입니까?
Kelly Would you take a picture of us, please?	Kelly 저희 사진을 찍어주시겠어요?

해설 | Kelly가 남자에게 사진을 찍어달라고 부탁하기로 결심했다고 했으므로 정답은 ① 'Would you take a picture of us, please?'이다.

선택지 해석

① 저희 사진을 찍어주시겠어요?　② 카메라를 향해 웃어주세요!　③ 끝나고 점심 먹으러 가지 않을래요?　④ 와주셔서 정말 감사합니다.　⑤ 졸업 축하드려요.

어휘 | graduation [grædʒuéiʃən] 명 졸업식; 졸업　entire [intáiər] 형 전부의　photograph [fóutəgræf] 명 사진

1	④	2	⑤	3	④	4	②	5	④	6	⑤	7	①	8	⑤	9	③	10	②
11	④	12	③	13	③	14	①	15	⑤	16	③	17	③	18	①	19	④	20	④

---

1 알맞은 그림 고르기

정답 ④

W Good afternoon. How can I help you?

M I'm looking for sleep masks for my son.

W How about this one with closed eyes on it?

M It's not bad, but it's not his style.

W Alright. Then, how about these animal ones? You can choose from a chick, raccoon, or fox face.

M My son will like the raccoon the most. I'll take that one.

W Good choice.

여 안녕하세요. 무엇을 도와드릴까요?

남 제 아들이 쓸 수면 안대를 찾고 있어요.

여 감은 눈이 그려진 이건 어떠세요?

남 나쁘진 않지만, 아들의 스타일은 아니네요.

여 알겠습니다. 그렇다면, 이 동물 안대들은 어떠세요? 병아리, 너구리, 또는 여우 얼굴 중에서 고르실 수 있어요.

남 제 아들은 너구리를 가장 좋아할 거예요. 그걸로 살게요.

여 좋은 선택이세요.

해설 | 남자가 자신의 아들이 너구리 얼굴 안대를 가장 좋아할 것이라고 했으므로 정답은 ④이다.

어휘 | sleep mask 수면 안대, 수면 마스크 chick [tʃik] 몡 병아리 raccoon [rækúːn] 몡 너구리

---

2 언급하지 않은 내용 고르기

정답 ⑤

W Dirk, did you see *The Latest Show* last night?

M You mean the show hosted by Jeremy Wilson, right? I missed it.

W Oh, why?

M I don't know when the show comes on.

W It's on TV at 9 o'clock every Saturday. I'm sorry that you missed it. They had a special guest yesterday.

M I know! Wasn't Hojun Shin on it to promote his new movie?

W Yeah. He was so funny that I laughed through the whole 60 minutes.

M I guess I'll have to watch it on the Internet later.

여 Dirk, 너 어젯밤에 <The Latest Show> 봤어?

남 Jeremy Wilson이 진행하는 쇼 말하는 거, 맞지? 못 봤어.

여 오, 왜?

남 쇼가 언제 방송되는지 모르거든.

여 매주 토요일 9시에 방송돼. 네가 못 봤다니 유감이야. 어제는 특별한 게스트가 나왔거든.

남 그러니까! 신호준이 그의 새 영화를 홍보하기 위해 출연하지 않았어?

여 맞아. 그는 정말 웃겨서 난 전체 60분 내내 웃었어.

남 나도 나중에 인터넷으로 봐야 할 것 같네.

해설 | ① 진행자(Jeremy Wilson), ② 방영 시간(매주 토요일 9시), ③ 초대 손님(신호준), ④ 길이(60분)에 대해 언급했으므로 정답은 ⑤ '수상 기록'이다.

어휘 | miss [mis] 통 보지 못하다, 놓치다 come on 방송되다 promote [prəmóut] 통 홍보하다; 승진시키다 whole [houl] 혱 전체의, 전부의

---

3 목적 고르기

정답 ④

[Telephone rings.]

W Good morning. Four-Star Electronics customer service.

M Hi. I'd like to know about your company's return policy.

W Are you having a problem with one of our products?

M I'm not happy with my new headphones. Their sound quality isn't that great.

W Well, if you've had them for less than 15 days, you can return them with no penalty.

M I've only had them for four days.

W Then, you'll just need to mail them to us in the original packaging. If there is any damage, however, we cannot accept them.

M Got it. Thanks for the explanation.

[전화기가 울린다.]

여 좋은 아침입니다. Four-Star Electronics 고객센터입니다.

남 안녕하세요. 회사의 환불 정책에 대해 알고 싶은데요.

여 저희 제품으로 문제를 겪고 있으신가요?

남 제 새 헤드폰이 마음에 들지 않아요. 음질이 그렇게 훌륭하지는 않네요.

여 음, 받으신 지 15일 이내라면, 아무 불이익 없이 환불받으실 수 있어요.

남 받은 지 겨우 나흘 됐어요.

여 그러면, 그걸 원래의 포장 상자에 넣어서 우편으로 보내주시기만 하면 됩니다. 하지만, 만약 어떤 파손이 있다면, 그걸 받아줄 수 없어요.

남 알겠습니다. 설명해주셔서 감사합니다.

해설 | 남자가 구매한 헤드폰이 마음에 들지 않아 환불 정책을 알고 싶다고 했으므로 정답은 ④ '환불 규정을 확인하려고'이다.

어휘 | policy [pάləsi] 몡 정책, 규정 quality [kwάləti] 몡 질, 품질 penalty [pénəlti] 몡 불이익; 형벌 explanation [èksplənéiʃən] 몡 설명

4 시간 정보 고르기　　　　　　　　　　　　　　　정답 ②

M	Excuse me. I'd like to make an appointment to get my hair cut.	남	실례합니다. 머리 자르는 걸 예약하고 싶어요.
W	Okay. When do you want to come in?	여	알겠습니다. 언제 오시고 싶으세요?
M	Tomorrow morning would work best for me.	남	내일 아침이 제일 좋아요.
W	Of course. We usually open at 11 in the morning.	여	그렇군요. 저희는 보통 아침 11시에 문을 열어요.
M	Hmm... I'm supposed to do an interview at 10. I want to look nice in the interview.	남	흠... 제가 10시에 면접을 보기로 되어 있어서요. 면접에서 멋지게 보이고 싶어요.
W	Then, I can open earlier than usual. How about 9?	여	그럼, 평소보다 일찍 열도록 할게요. 9시는 어떠세요?
M	Thank you so much. That would be best.	남	정말 감사합니다. 아주 좋을 것 같네요.

해설 | 여자가 9시는 어떤지 묻자 남자가 아주 좋을 것 같다고 했으므로 정답은 ② '9 a.m.'이다.

어휘 | be supposed to ~하기로 되어 있다, ~해야만 하다 interview [íntərvjuː] 몡 면접

5 장소 고르기　　　　　　　　　　　　　　　　정답 ④

W	I'm so excited for this play.	여	이 연극 너무 기대돼.
M	Me too. And I can't believe we got such good seats!	남	나도. 그리고 우리가 이렇게 좋은 자리를 구했다니 믿기지 않아!
W	Yes. There are some very famous actors in this play, so I was afraid I wouldn't get any tickets.	여	그러게. 이 연극에는 엄청 유명한 배우들이 나오잖아, 그래서 표를 아예 못 구할까 봐 걱정했거든.
M	The story also sounds very exciting.	남	줄거리도 정말 흥미진진한 것 같아.
W	Yeah. I read some good reviews of this play in a magazine.	여	응. 이 연극에 대한 좋은 평을 잡지에서 읽었어.
M	I'm really thrilled to see it. By the way, did you silence your phone? It starts soon!	남	이걸 보게 돼서 아주 기뻐. 그런데, 너 휴대폰은 무음으로 했니? 곧 시작할 거야!
W	I think so, but I'll check again.	여	그런 것 같은데, 다시 확인해볼게.

해설 | 여자가 연극이 기대된다고 했고 남자가 연극이 곧 시작할 것이라고 하는 것으로 보아 정답은 ④ '극장'이다.

어휘 | review [rivjúː] 몡 평, 평론 thrilled [θrild] 형 아주 기쁜, 황홀한 by the way 그런데 silence [sáiləns] 동 무음으로 하다, 침묵시키다 몡 침묵

6 그림 상황에 적절한 대화 고르기　　　　　　　　정답 ⑤

①	W	How did you hurt yourself?	① 여	어쩌다가 다치셨나요?
	M	I tripped on the stairs.	남	계단에서 넘어졌어요.
②	W	I'd like to buy some flowers, please.	② 여	꽃을 좀 사고 싶어요.
	M	What kind do you want?	남	어떤 종류를 원하세요?
③	W	Can I ride my bike in this park?	③ 여	공원에서 자전거 타도 되나요?
	M	No. It's not permitted.	남	아니요. 그건 허용되지 않습니다.
④	W	You should wear a cap in the pool.	④ 여	수영장에서는 수영모를 착용해야 해.
	M	You're right. I'll put it on now.	남	네 말이 맞아. 지금 쓸게.
⑤	W	Is that a new bike?	⑤ 여	그거 새 자전거야?
	M	Yes. I bought it yesterday.	남	응. 어제 샀어.

해설 | 여자가 남자의 자전거를 가리키고 있으며 남자가 그 옆에서 뿌듯해하는 모습을 보이고 있는 상황이므로 정답은 ⑤이다.

어휘 | trip [trip] 동 넘어지다 몡 여행 permit [pərmít] 동 허용하다, 허락하다 put on 쓰다, 입다

7 부탁·요청한 일 고르기　　　　　　　　정답 ①

[Cellphone rings.]
M　What's up, Hayley?
W　Hey. I'm a little worried about my history project.
M　Did you finish it?
W　I did, but I don't feel confident about it.
M　How can I help?
W　You're just so good at history. Do you mind looking it over?
M　Of course. Just email it to me.

[휴대폰이 울린다.]
남　무슨 일이야, Hayley?
여　있잖아. 나 역사 과제 때문에 좀 걱정이 돼.
남　그거 끝냈어?
여　끝냈지, 근데 자신이 없어.
남　내가 어떻게 도와줄 수 있을까?
여　너 역사를 진짜 잘하잖아. 한번 훑어봐 줄래?
남　당연하지. 내 이메일로 보내줘.

해설 | 여자가 남자에게 자신의 역사 과제를 훑어봐 달라고 부탁했으므로 정답은 ① '과제 검토하기'이다.

어휘 | confident [kánfədənt] 형 자신 있는; 확신하는　look over 훑어보다, 검토하다

8 언급하지 않은 내용 고르기　　　　　　　정답 ⑤

W　Welcome to the Oakhill Art Gallery. Before the tour begins, I will tell you about our gallery, which is owned by Peter Williams. He opened this gallery in 1983 to support local artists. Many of the exhibits include photographs and paintings. The gallery is open from 10 a.m. to 11 p.m., Monday to Saturday. However, we sometimes admit visitors on Sundays for special events. Now, let's start the tour.

여　오크힐 미술관에 오신 걸 환영합니다. 투어를 시작하기에 앞서, Peter Williams의 소유인 저희 미술관에 대해 말씀드리려 합니다. 그는 1983년에 지역 예술가들을 지원하기 위해 이 미술관을 개관했습니다. 많은 전시품들은 사진과 그림을 포함합니다. 미술관은 월요일부터 토요일, 오전 10시에서 오후 11시까지 문을 엽니다. 하지만, 저희는 때때로 특별한 행사가 있으면 일요일에도 방문객의 입장을 허락합니다. 이제, 투어를 시작하겠습니다.

해설 | ① 소유자(Peter Williams), ② 개관 연도(1983년), ③ 전시품 종류(사진과 그림), ④ 운영 시간(월요일부터 토요일 오전 10시부터 오후 11시까지)에 대해 언급했으므로 정답은 ⑤ '입장료'이다.

어휘 | own [oun] 동 소유하다 형 자기 자신의　include [inklú:d] 동 포함하다　admit [ædmít] 동 입장을 허락하다, 들어가게 하다

9 화제 고르기　　　　　　　　　　　　정답 ③

M　This is a very useful experiment tool for scientists. People use this device to observe tiny objects by looking through the lens. It makes objects appear bigger, so it is easy to study them. Many people learn to use this device in school, and it is used everyday in labs around the world.

남　이것은 과학자들에게 매우 유용한 실험 도구입니다. 사람들은 아주 작은 물체를 관찰하기 위해 렌즈를 통해 바라보며 이 기구를 사용합니다. 이것은 물체가 더욱 커 보이도록 해서, 물체를 살펴보기 쉽습니다. 많은 사람들이 학교에서 이 기구를 사용하는 것을 배우고, 전 세계 연구실에서 매일같이 사용되고 있습니다.

해설 | 이것(This)은 물체가 커 보이도록 만들어서 사람들이 작은 물체를 관찰하는 데 사용된다고 했으므로 정답은 ③ '현미경'이다.

어휘 | device [diváis] 명 기구, 장치　observe [əbzé:rv] 동 관찰하다　tiny [táini] 형 아주 작은　object [ábdʒikt] 명 물체, 물건
appear [əpíər] 동 ~하게 보이다; 나타나다　study [stʌ́di] 동 살펴보다 명 공부　lab [læb] 명 연구실

10 어색한 대화 고르기　　　　　　　　　정답 ②

① W　Do you think you can fix my computer?
　 M　I bet I can. Let me try.
② W　Is it snowing outside?
　 M　No. I wore my snow boots.
③ W　Can you sign an autograph for me?
　 M　Of course. I'd be happy to.
④ W　Is it for here or to go?
　 M　Here, please. I'm too hungry to wait until I get home.
⑤ W　Let's go for a hike this afternoon.
　 M　I have a doctor's appointment at 2 p.m.

① 여　내 컴퓨터를 고칠 수 있을 것 같아?
　 남　틀림없이 할 수 있을 거야. 시도해 볼게.
② 여　밖에 눈이 오고 있니?
　 남　아니. 난 스노우 부츠를 신었어.
③ 여　제게 사인을 해주실래요?
　 남　당연하죠. 기꺼이 해 드릴게요.
④ 여　여기서 드실 건가요, 아니면 가져가실 건가요?
　 남　여기서요. 배가 너무 고파서 집에 갈 때까지 기다릴 수 없어요.
⑤ 여　오늘 오후에 하이킹하러 가자.
　 남　난 오후 2시에 진료 예약이 있어.

해설 | 여자가 남자에게 밖에 눈이 오는지 물었으므로, 남자는 눈이 오는지 아닌지 말해야 한다. 그러나 남자가 아니라고 하면서 스노우 부츠를 신었다는 어색한 대답을 했으므로 정답은 ②이다.

어휘 | fix [fiks] 동 고치다; 고정시키다 autograph [ɔ́ːtəɡræf] 명 사인, 자필 서명

11 할 일 고르기   정답 ④

M	Hi. Do you need help?	남	안녕하세요. 도움이 필요하신가요?
W	Yes. I'm looking for <u>a new phone case</u>.	여	네. 새 휴대폰 케이스를 찾고 있어요.
M	What kind of design do you want?	남	어떤 종류의 디자인을 원하시나요?
W	I don't want <u>a design on it</u>. I just want it to be one color.	여	케이스에 무늬가 있는 건 원하지 않아요. 그냥 단색이면 좋겠어요.
M	Here are some phone cases in <u>many different colors</u>.	남	여기 여러 가지 많은 색상의 휴대폰 케이스들이 있어요.
W	I like the purple one. Can I buy it, please?	여	보라색이 좋네요. 그걸로 살 수 있을까요?
M	Sure. I'll get you a bag for it.	남	물론이죠. 케이스를 담을 가방을 갖다 드릴게요.
W	No need. I'll <u>just put it</u> on my phone now.	여	그러실 필요 없어요. 그냥 지금 그걸 제 휴대폰에 끼울게요.

해설 | 여자가 새 휴대폰 케이스를 바로 끼우겠다고 했으므로 정답은 ④ '케이스 교체하기'이다.

어휘 | design [dizáin] 명 디자인, 무늬 동 설계하다 purple [pə́ːrpl] 형 보라색의, 자주색의

12 도표에서 알맞은 항목 고르기   정답 ③

M	What can I do for you?	남	무엇을 도와드릴까요?
W	Hi. I'd like to reserve a ticket to New York on May 14th, please.	여	안녕하세요. 5월 14일에 뉴욕행 표를 예매하고 싶어요.
M	Would you like a one-way ticket or <u>a round-trip ticket</u>?	남	편도로 드릴까요, 아니면 왕복으로 드릴까요?
W	One-way, please.	여	편도로 주세요.
M	Let's see. There are <u>seats</u> <u>available</u> on the 8 a.m. flight. However, the business-class section is full.	남	어디 볼게요. 오전 8시 비행기에 이용할 수 있는 자리가 있네요. 하지만, 비즈니스석은 다 찼어요.
W	I'm <u>fine with economy class</u>.	여	이코노미석도 괜찮아요.
M	Which do you prefer, a window seat or <u>an aisle seat</u>?	남	창가 자리가 좋으세요, 아니면 통로 쪽이 좋으세요?
W	A window seat please. I like <u>looking out the window</u> while flying.	여	창가 자리로 주세요. 비행하는 동안 창밖을 바라보는 걸 좋아해서요.

해설 | 여자가 편도를 원한다고 했고, 이코노미석도 괜찮다고 했으며, 창가 자리로 달라고 했으므로 정답은 ③이다.

어휘 | one-way 형 편도의, 일방통행의 round-trip 형 왕복의 available [əvéiləbl] 형 이용할 수 있는 aisle [ail] 명 통로, 측면 복도

13 시간 정보 고르기   정답 ③

W	Honey, have you looked in <u>our backyard recently</u>?	여	여보, 최근에 우리 뒤뜰 들여다본 적 있어?
M	No. Why?	남	아니. 왜?
W	I think some of the trees are withering.	여	나무 몇 그루가 시들고 있는 것 같아.
M	Oh, I thought they <u>were growing well</u>.	남	오, 난 잘 자라고 있는 줄 알았는데.
W	No. So, I think we should <u>get some fertilizer</u>. Are you free on Thursday?	여	아니야. 그래서 우리 비료를 좀 사야 할 것 같아. 목요일에 시간 괜찮아?
M	Isn't that April 19th? Did you forget about Jenny's school concert? I don't think we'll have time to <u>go to the gardening store</u> that day.	남	그날 4월 19일 아니야? Jenny의 학교 콘서트 잊은 거야? 우리 그날은 원예용품점에 갈 시간이 없을 것 같아.
W	You're right. I completely forgot. What about the 22nd?	여	당신 말이 맞아. 완전히 잊고 있었네. 22일은 어때?
M	But that's Sunday. The store will be closed then. Let's <u>go on Saturday</u>.	남	하지만 그날은 일요일이잖아. 가게는 그때 문을 닫아. 토요일에 가자.
W	That sounds perfect. We can spread the fertilizer on Sunday.	여	완벽한 것 같아. 일요일에는 비료를 뿌리면 되겠어.

해설 | 남자가 4월 19일에는 학교 콘서트 때문에 안 된다고 했고, 여자가 22일은 어떤지 묻자 일요일에는 가게가 문을 닫으니 토요일에 가자고 했으므로 정답은 ③ 'April 21st'이다.

어휘 | backyard [bǽkjɑ̀rd] 명 뒤뜰 wither [wíðər] 동 시들다 grow [grou] 동 자라다 fertilizer [fə́ːrtəlàizər] 명 비료 completely [kəmplíːtli] 부 완전히 spread [spred] 동 뿌리다; 펴다

W	I have some good news, Daejun.
M	What is it?
W	I just finished reading *The Secret Crime*, so you can finally borrow the book.
M	Oh, thank you. But I don't need it anymore.
W	Really? You said you were excited to read it.
M	I am, but I ordered the book online yesterday.
W	But why?
M	It's a long book, and I didn't want to wait for you to finish it. But you read it so quickly.
W	Yes. I couldn't put the book down.

여	좋은 소식이 있어, 대준아.
남	그게 뭔데?
여	내가 막 <The Secret Crime>을 다 읽었으니까, 드디어 네가 그 책을 빌려 갈 수 있어.
남	오, 고마워. 그런데 난 더 이상 필요 없어.
여	정말? 너 그걸 읽길 기대한다고 말했었잖아.
남	지금도 기대되지만, 어제 온라인으로 책을 주문했거든.
여	그렇지만 왜?
남	두꺼운 책이라서, 네가 다 읽기를 기다리고 싶지 않았어. 그런데 넌 정말 빨리 읽었구나.
여	응. 책을 내려놓을 수가 없더라고.

해설 | 남자가 어제 책을 온라인으로 주문했다고 했으므로 정답은 ① '책 주문하기'이다.

어휘 | anymore [ènimɔ́ːr] 閉 더 이상, 이제는   wait for ~를 기다리다   quickly [kwíkli] 閉 빨리, 서둘러

W	Hello, students. This is your principal, Ms. Greer. I hope exam season is going well. I know this can be a stressful time of year, so I want to share some ways to stay healthy and happy during this time. First, please remember to get enough sleep. Your body and brain both need rest to work hard. Everyone should also take a 20-minute break every hour or so while studying. Lastly, eat lots of nutritious food such as fruit and vegetables. Good luck!

여	안녕하세요, 학생 여러분. 전 여러분의 교장 Greer 선생님입니다. 시험 기간이 잘 되어가길 바라고 있습니다. 이 시기가 일 년 중 스트레스가 많을 때라는 걸 알기에, 이 기간 동안 건강하고 행복하게 지낼 수 있는 몇 가지 방법을 공유하고 싶습니다. 먼저, 충분한 수면을 취하는 걸 기억해 두십시오. 열심히 공부하려면 여러분의 몸도 뇌 모두 휴식이 필요합니다. 모두 공부하는 동안 한 시간 정도마다 20분의 휴식 또한 취해야 합니다. 마지막으로, 과일과 채소 같은 영양분이 풍부한 음식을 많이 드십시오. 행운을 빕니다!

해설 | 여자가 학생들이 시험 기간 동안 건강하고 행복하게 지낼 수 있는 방법을 공유해주고 있으므로 정답은 ⑤ '시험 기간에 건강하게 지낼 방법을 알려주려고'이다.

어휘 | principal [prínsəpəl] 명 교장 형 주요한   season [síːzn] 명 기간, 시기   or so ~정도, ~쯤   nutritious [njuːtríʃəs] 형 영양분이 풍부한

M	Hello. Are you ready to order?
W	Yes. I'd like a chocolate donut, please.
M	That will be four dollars. But if you pay two dollars more, you can get a coffee as well.
W	Oh, that's great. I'll pay two dollars more then.
M	Okay. Would you like any other donuts? We have some new flavors.
W	Thanks, but I'm okay.
M	Alright. Will you eat this here?
W	Yes, I'll have it here.

남	안녕하세요. 주문하시겠어요?
여	네. 초콜릿 도넛 하나 주세요.
남	그건 4달러 되겠습니다. 하지만 2달러를 더 내시면, 커피도 드실 수 있어요.
여	오, 좋네요. 그러면 2달러를 더 낼게요.
남	알겠습니다. 다른 도넛은 안 드시겠습니까? 몇 가지 새로운 맛이 있어요.
여	감사하지만, 괜찮아요.
남	그러시군요. 여기에서 드시겠습니까?
여	네, 여기서 먹을게요.

해설 | 여자가 4달러짜리 초콜릿 도넛 한 개를 주문했고, 추가로 2달러를 더 내고 커피를 주문했으므로 정답은 ③ '$ 6'이다.

어휘 | as well ~도, 또한   flavor [fléivər] 명 맛, 풍미

17 적절한 응답 고르기
정답 ③

W How was the beach last weekend, Woobin?

M It was beautiful! The sky was clear, and it was very warm.

W Did you take some pictures?

M Sure. I have some here on my phone.

W Wow! These are incredible. You're so good at photography.

M Thanks. I love to take photographs of nature.

W Can you send me some of these? I want to make one of them the background image on my phone.

M Sure. Make sure to tell me which one you picked.

여 지난 주말 바닷가는 어땠어, 우빈아?

남 아름다웠어! 하늘은 맑았고 날씨는 정말 따뜻했어.

여 사진 좀 찍었어?

남 당연하지. 여기 내 휴대폰에 좀 있어.

여 우와! 정말 놀랍다. 너 사진 진짜 잘 찍는다.

남 고마워. 난 자연 사진 찍는 걸 좋아해.

여 내게 이것 중 몇 개 보내줄 수 있어? 이 중 하나를 내 휴대폰 배경 화면으로 하고 싶어.

남 물론이지. 어떤 걸 골랐는지 확실히 말해줘.

해설 | 여자가 휴대폰 배경 화면으로 하게 사진을 보내달라고 부탁했으므로 정답은 부탁을 수락하는 ③ 'Sure. Make sure to tell me which one you picked.'이다.

선택지 해석

① 자외선 차단제 가져오는 걸 잊었어. ② 이 사진으로 너 진짜 멋져 보여. ③ 물론이지. 어떤 걸 골랐는지 확실히 말해줘.
④ 이 아름다운 사진들을 공유해줘서 고마워. ⑤ 카메라에 뭔가 문제가 있어.

어휘 | incredible [inkrédəbl] 형 놀라운, 믿어지지 않는 background [bǽkgraund] 명 배경 make sure to 확실히 ~하다 share [ʃɛər] 동 공유하다

18 적절한 응답 고르기
정답 ①

[Cellphone rings.]

M Hi, Molly. I don't see you. Are you aware we leave for our field trip soon?

W I know, Mr. Jones. But I just missed the bus. I will be late.

M Can you ask your parents for a ride?

W They are both at work now.

M I see. Well, some other students will also be late. So, Ms. Baker will drive you all to the zoo later.

W That's a relief. And I'm sorry for being late.

M That's okay, but please hurry up.

W I'll try to arrive as soon as possible.

[휴대폰이 울린다.]

남 안녕, Molly. 네가 안 보이는구나. 우리 곧 현장 학습을 떠난다는 걸 알고 있는 거지?

여 알고 있어요, Jones 선생님. 그런데 제가 방금 버스를 놓쳐서요. 늦을 것 같아요.

남 부모님께 태워달라고 부탁할 수 있니?

여 두 분 다 지금 일하고 있으세요.

남 그렇구나. 음, 다른 몇몇 학생들도 늦을 것 같구나. 그래서, Baker 선생님이 너희들 모두를 나중에 동물원으로 태워주실 거란다.

여 정말 다행이네요. 그리고 지각해서 죄송해요.

남 괜찮단다, 그렇지만 서두르렴.

여 가능한 빨리 도착하게끔 노력할게요.

해설 | 남자가 서두르라고 했으므로 정답은 그러겠다고 말하는 ① 'I'll try to arrive as soon as possible.'이다.

선택지 해석

① 가능한 빨리 도착하게끔 노력할게요. ② 버스가 동물원으로 가는지 모르겠어요. ③ 저를 비난하지 마세요. 제 잘못이 아니에요.
④ 제가 지각한 걸 용서해주시다니 그분은 너그러우시네요. ⑤ 행운을 빌어 드릴게요!

어휘 | aware [əwɛ́ər] 형 알고 있는 blame [bleim] 동 비난하다 generous [dʒénərəs] 형 너그러운 forgive [fərgív] 동 용서하다
keep one's fingers crossed 행운을 빌다

19 적절한 응답 고르기
정답 ④

W Do you want to study together tonight, Daniel?

M I'm sorry, but I can't. I have to go to a tennis lesson.

W I didn't know you played tennis. When did you start playing?

M I started lessons when I was nine. I play at least twice a week.

W You must be good then. I want to play tennis too.

M Do you want my instructor's phone number? He really helped me get better.

W Sure. But I am only at a beginner level.

M That's okay. He teaches all levels.

여 오늘 밤에 함께 공부할래, Daniel?

남 미안하지만, 안 되겠어. 테니스 수업에 가야 하거든.

여 네가 테니스 치는 줄 몰랐네. 언제부터 시작한 거야?

남 9살 때부터 시작했어. 적어도 매주 두 번은 쳐.

여 그러면 넌 잘 치겠구나. 나도 테니스 치고 싶다.

남 내 강사님 휴대폰 번호를 알려줄까? 그분은 내 실력이 나아지는 데 정말로 도움을 주셨어.

여 물론이지. 그런데 난 겨우 초보자 수준이야.

남 괜찮아. 그분은 모든 수준을 가르치셔.

해설 | 여자가 자신은 겨우 초보자 수준이라고 염려했으므로 정답은 괜찮다고 말하는 ④ 'That's okay. He teaches all levels.'이다.

<u>선택지 해석</u>
① 내가 숙제를 도와줄 수 있어. ② 그분이 전화를 안 받으셨어. ③ 나는 내일이면 15살이 돼. ④ 괜찮아. 그분은 모든 수준을 가르치셔.
⑤ 넌 그 경기에서 잘할 거야.

어휘 | at least 적어도, 최소한   instructor [instrʌ́ktər] 명 강사, 교사, 지도자   assignment [əsáinmənt] 명 숙제, 과제; 할당   match [mætʃ] 명 경기

---

20 상황에 적절한 말 고르기   정답 ④

W   Jane is riding on the train. She is on the way to <u>visit her grandparents</u> in the countryside. She is trying to read her book, but the man next to her is <u>playing</u> <u>his</u> <u>music</u> <u>loudly</u>. Jane is not enjoying her ride because of this. So, <mark>she wants to ask the man to lower the volume</mark> of his music. In this situation, what would Jane most likely say to the man?

Jane   Excuse me, <u>can you turn your music down?</u>

여   Jane은 기차를 타고 있습니다. 그녀는 시골에 계신 그녀의 조부모님은 방문하러 가는 길입니다. 그녀는 책을 읽으려고 노력하지만, 그녀 옆자리의 남자가 음악을 크게 틀고 있습니다. Jane은 이것 때문에 그녀의 여정을 즐기지 못하고 있습니다. 그래서, 그녀는 남자에게 음악 소리를 줄여달라고 부탁하고 싶습니다. 이러한 상황에서, Jane이 남자에게 가장 할 것 같은 말은 무엇입니까?

Jane   실례합니다, 음악 소리를 줄여주시겠어요?

해설 | Jane이 남자에게 음악 소리를 줄여달라고 부탁하고 싶다고 했으므로 정답은 ④ 'can you turn your music down?'이다.

<u>선택지 해석</u>
① 커튼을 쳐주시겠어요? ② 이 기차 여행은 얼마나 오래 걸리나요? ③ 여기가 제가 내릴 정류장이라 내려야 해요. ④ 음악 소리를 줄여주시겠어요?
⑤ 이 노래는 케이팝 가수의 노래군요, 맞죠?

어휘 | ride [raid] 통 타다 명 여정, 여행   countryside [kʌ́ntrisaid] 명 시골   loudly [láudli] 부 크게   lower [lóuər] 통 줄이다; 낮추다   turn down 줄이다
get off 내리다

(08회) 실전 모의고사 | 문제 pp.82-83

1	⑤	2	①	3	④	4	③	5	④	6	⑤	7	④	8	③	9	⑤	10	④
11	②	12	⑤	13	①	14	③	15	④	16	①	17	⑤	18	④	19	④	20	⑤

---

1 알맞은 그림 고르기   정답 ⑤

M   Hello, I'm here to buy a helmet.
W   You're in the right place. Do you want ones <u>with goggles</u>?
M   No. I don't need them.
W   Then, <u>what do you think of this one with four holes on the top</u>? It's light but strong.
M   Sorry, but I don't like the word "FAST" on it. <mark>Do you have the same model <u>without any words</u>?</mark>
W   Sure. It comes in black or blue.
M   That's good. I'll take <u>the blue one</u>.
W   Okay.

남   안녕하세요, 헬멧을 사러 왔는데요.
여   제대로 찾아오셨네요. 고글이 달린 걸 원하시나요?
남   아니요. 그건 필요 없어요.
여   그러면, 맨 위에 구멍이 4개 뚫려 있는 이건 어떻게 생각하세요? 가볍지만 튼튼해요.
남   죄송하지만, 'FAST'라는 글자가 마음에 들지 않아요. 아무런 글자가 없는 같은 모델도 있나요?
여   물론이죠. 검은색이나 파란색으로 나와 있답니다.
남   잘됐네요. 파란색으로 할게요.
여   알겠습니다.

해설 | 남자가 고글이 달려 있지 않고 맨 위에 구멍이 4개 뚫려 있는 디자인에, 아무런 글자가 없는 파란색 헬멧을 사겠다고 했으므로 정답은 ⑤이다.

어휘 | goggles [gáglz] 명 고글, 보호안경 (goggle [gágl] 통 눈을 부릅뜨다)   hole [houl] 명 구멍

2 부탁·요청한 일 고르기   정답 ①

W I'd like to start a knitting club, Mike. Would you like to help me?
M That's a good idea. But how do we start one?
W Well, we can make posters and put them around the school. If people want to join, they can tell us.
M Okay. Should we make posters this weekend?
W Yes. We can meet at my house.
M What should I bring?
W Can you bring some crayons? I will buy the poster paper.
M Sounds good.

여 나 뜨개질 동아리를 시작하고 싶어, Mike. 네가 날 도와줄래?
남 좋은 생각이야. 그런데 어떻게 시작하지?
여 글쎄, 포스터를 만들어서 학교 곳곳에 붙여놓을 수 있겠어. 가입하고 싶으면, 우리에게 말해줄 수 있잖아.
남 알겠어. 이번 주말에 포스터를 만들까?
여 그래. 우리 집에서 만나면 되겠다.
남 내가 뭘 가져갈까?
여 크레파스 좀 가져올 수 있어? 내가 포스터 종이를 살게.
남 좋아.

해설 | 여자가 남자에게 크레파스를 가져와 달라고 부탁했으므로 정답은 ① '크레파스 가져오기'이다.

어휘 | knitting [nítiŋ] 몡 뜨개질   crayon [kréiən] 몡 크레파스, 크레용

3 그림 상황에 적절한 대화 고르기   정답 ④

① W Could you turn down the TV?
   M Sorry. I didn't realize it was too loud.
② W I don't see any empty tables.
   M Let's go to another restaurant.
③ W How much were the concert tickets?
   M They were 50 dollars each.
④ W Have you played the piano long?
   M I just started taking lessons.
⑤ W The song on the radio is my favorite.
   M It's very nice.

① 여 TV 소리 좀 줄여줄래?
   남 미안. 이게 그렇게 시끄러운지 몰랐어.
② 여 빈자리가 안 보이네.
   남 다른 식당으로 가자.
③ 여 콘서트 티켓은 얼마였어?
   남 한 장에 50달러였어.
④ 여 피아노를 오래 쳤니?
   남 이제 막 수업을 듣기 시작했어.
⑤ 여 라디오에서 나오는 노래는 내가 가장 좋아하는 거야.
   남 정말 좋다.

해설 | 남자가 피아노를 치고 있고 여자가 옆에서 질문을 하고 있는 상황이므로 정답은 ④이다.

어휘 | turn down 줄이다   realize [ríːəlàiz] 동 알다, 깨닫다   empty [émpti] 형 빈, 비어 있는

4 시간 정보 고르기   정답 ③

M What's the matter, Suyeon?
W I'm enjoying our family trip, but my feet hurt, Dad. I walked too much.
M Then, we'd better take a city tour bus tomorrow. I got this pamphlet for a city tour.
W That sounds fun. Why don't we leave at 10 a.m.?
M The earliest tour bus leaves at 11. But your mom wants to try the hotel buffet for lunch. I think we should leave at 2.
W What time will we get back?
M The tour lasts for a couple of hours, so we should return to our hotel by 5.
W That sounds great. Book the tickets on the 2 p.m. bus then.

남 무슨 일이니, 수연아?
여 가족 여행은 즐거운데, 다리가 아파요, 아빠. 너무 많이 걸었어요.
남 그러면, 내일은 시티투어버스를 타는 게 좋겠구나. 내가 시티투어에 대한 이 소책자를 챙겼단다.
여 재미있을 것 같네요. 오전 10시에 출발하는 게 어때요?
남 가장 이른 투어버스가 11시에 출발하는구나. 그런데 네 엄마가 점심에 호텔 뷔페를 먹어보고 싶어 한단다. 2시에 출발해야 할 것 같구나.
여 몇 시에 돌아오나요?
남 투어는 몇 시간 동안 이어지니까, 5시까지는 호텔로 돌아올 거야.
여 좋은 거 같아요. 그러면 오후 2시 버스로 표를 예매하세요.

해설 | 남자가 2시에 출발할 것을 제안했고, 여자가 오후 2시의 시티투어버스 표를 예매하라고 했으므로 정답은 ③ '2 p.m.'이다.

어휘 | pamphlet [pǽmflət] 몡 소책자, 팸플릿   buffet [bəféi] 몡 뷔페; 찬장   a couple of 몇 개의; 둘의

5 언급하지 않은 내용 고르기　　　　　　　　　정답 ④

M	Hyojoo, what is that painting you're looking at?
W	This is a painting by Claude Monet. It's called *Houses of Parliament, Sunset*.
M	Oh, I've heard about Monet. He is a French painter, right?
W	That's right. This is one of my favorite pieces by him.
M	The orange and purple colors in the sky are beautiful.
W	I know, right? It's part of a series. He painted the same place at different times of day.
M	How old is the painting?
W	Monet painted this one in 1903.

남	효주야, 지금 보고 있는 그림은 어떤 거야?
여	이건 클로드 모네의 그림이야. <국회의사당, 해질녁>이라고 불려.
남	오, 모네에 관해 들어본 적 있어. 그는 프랑스 화가잖아, 맞지?
여	맞아. 이건 내가 가장 좋아하는 그의 작품 중 하나야.
남	하늘 속 주황색과 보라색이 아름답다.
여	그렇지? 이건 연작 중 일부야. 그는 같은 장소를 각기 다른 시간대에 그렸어.
남	이 그림은 그려진 지 몇 년이나 된 거야?
여	모네는 1903년에 이걸 그렸어.

해설 | ① 작품명(<국회의사당, 해질녁>), ② 사용된 색(주황색과 보라색), ③ 작가의 출신 국가(프랑스), ⑤ 작품 제작 연도(1903년)에 대해 언급했으므로 정답은 ④ '작품 시리즈 수'이다.

어휘 | house of parliament 국회의사당　sunset [sʌ́nsèt] 몡 해질녁, 일몰　piece [piːs] 몡 작품; 한 조각　series [síəriːz] 몡 연작, 연속물, 시리즈; 일련

6 장소 고르기　　　　　　　　　정답 ⑤

W	Josh, they just made an announcement. Our flight leaves at 5 p.m. now.
M	Oh, I really didn't expect the delay.
W	Yeah. Me neither. We were supposed to get on the plane an hour ago.
M	We have so much time before the flight. What will we do?
W	Why don't we get some coffee and snacks while we wait?
M	But we have all of our luggage here. It will be hard to carry around.
W	Then, one of us can wait here with the luggage.
M	Okay. I'll go get the drinks and snacks then.

여	Josh, 방금 공지가 나왔어. 우리 비행기는 이제 오후 5시에 출발할 거야.
남	오, 난 진짜 이런 지연은 예상 못했어.
여	그러게. 나도 예상 못했어. 우린 한 시간 전에 비행기를 타기로 되어 있었잖아.
남	비행 전까지 시간이 많이 있는데. 뭘 하지?
여	기다리는 동안 커피랑 간식을 먹는 게 어때?
남	그런데 짐이 여기 다 있잖아. 그걸 들고 다니기는 어려울 거야.
여	그러면, 우리 중 한 명이 짐과 함께 여기에서 기다리면 되겠다.
남	알겠어. 그러면 내가 음료랑 간식을 사러 갈게.

해설 | 여자가 한 시간 전에 타기로 되어 있던 비행기의 출발 시간 공지가 나왔다고 했고, 짐과 함께 이곳에서 기다리면 되겠다고 하는 것으로 보아 정답은 ⑤ '공항'이다.

어휘 | expect [ikspékt] 동 예상하다, 기대하다　delay [diléi] 몡 지연 동 연기하다　luggage [lʌ́gidʒ] 몡 짐, 수화물

7 어색한 대화 고르기　　　　　　　　　정답 ④

① W	Aren't you late for your violin lesson?
M	I still have an hour left.
② W	Jerry's not here. Would you like to leave a message?
M	No. I'll call him back later.
③ W	When did you take this amazing picture of a rainbow?
M	I took it while I was walking in the park.
④ W	How often do you watch a movie?
M	I finished reading it a few hours ago.
⑤ W	That will be 10 dollars and 92 cents.
M	Here's my credit card.

① 여	너 바이올린 수업에 늦은 거 아니니?
남	아직 한 시간 남았어.
② 여	Jerry는 자리에 없어요. 메시지를 남기시겠어요?
남	아니요. 나중에 다시 전화할게요.
③ 여	이 놀라운 무지개 사진은 언제 찍은 거야?
남	공원을 걷는 중에 찍었어.
④ 여	영화를 얼마나 자주 봐?
남	몇 시간 전에 다 읽었어.
⑤ 여	10달러 92센트 되겠습니다.
남	여기 제 신용카드요.

해설 | 여자가 남자에게 영화를 얼마나 자주 보는지 물었으므로, 남자는 영화를 보는 횟수를 답해야 한다. 그러나 남자가 몇 시간 전에 다 읽었다는 어색한 대답을 했으므로 정답은 ④이다.

어휘 | rainbow [réinbou] 몡 무지개　credit card 신용카드

8 부탁·요청한 일 고르기

정답 ③

[Cellphone rings.]

W Could you do me a favor, Justin?

M Sure, Alice. What's up?

W You are at the post office, right?

M Yes. I'm waiting in line to send my package.

W Then, can you buy me some of the newly released stamps? They're sold only during this week.

M Sure. But there are a lot of different ones here. Which ones do you want?

W Can you get me the Lunar New Year ones? They have a tiger on them. I just want one pack.

M No problem. I'll get some now.

[휴대폰이 울린다.]

여 부탁 하나만 들어줄래, Justin?

남 물론이지, Alice. 무슨 일인데?

여 너 우체국에 있잖아, 맞지?

남 응. 택배 보내려고 줄 서서 기다리는 중이야.

여 그러면, 새로 발행된 우표를 좀 사다 줄래? 이번 주 동안에만 판매되거든.

남 물론이지. 그런데 여기엔 다양한 우표가 많이 있어. 어떤 걸 원하는 거야?

여 음력 설 우표를 사다 줄래? 호랑이가 그려져 있어. 한 묶음이면 돼.

남 문제없어. 지금 살게.

해설 | 여자가 남자에게 새로 발행된 음력 설 우표를 사다 달라고 부탁했으므로 정답은 ③ '우표 사 오기'이다.

어휘 | wait in line 줄을 서서 기다리다   stamp [stæmp] 몡 우표   lunar [lúːnər] 혱 음력의; 달의

9 주제 고르기

정답 ⑤

W Attention, please. I'm Maria, your museum tour guide. Let me tell you some guidelines to follow for your visit to the museum today. First, please do not take photographs of the artworks in the exhibits. Second, do not touch any of the items on display, and keep a safe distance from them. Third, running is not allowed in the museum at any time. We thank you for your cooperation and hope you enjoy your time here.

여 주목해주세요. 저는 박물관의 관람 안내원 Maria입니다. 오늘 여러분의 박물관 관람 시 따라야 할 몇 가지 지침을 알려 드리겠습니다. 먼저, 전시회에 있는 예술작품들은 사진을 찍지 말아 주세요. 둘째로, 전시된 물건은 어떤 것에도 손대지 마시고 안전거리를 유지해 주세요. 셋째로, 박물관 내에서 뛰는 것은 언제라도 허용되지 않습니다. 협조해주셔서 감사드리고 이곳에서 즐거운 시간 보내시길 바라겠습니다.

해설 | 여자가 박물관 관람 시 따라야 할 지침을 알려주고 있으므로 정답은 ⑤ '박물관 주의 사항'이다.

어휘 | guideline [gáidlain] 몡 지침   artwork [ártwərk] 몡 예술작품   on display 전시된   safe distance 안전거리   cooperation [kouὰpəréiʃən] 몡 협조

10 금액 정보 고르기

정답 ④

M Can I help you find something?

W Yes. I'm looking for a scarf.

M Our best-selling scarves are the brown and gray ones. They are 10 dollars each.

W I'll take a brown one, please.

M Okay. Do you need anything else?

W Well, I'd also like a winter hat. Do you have any that match this scarf?

M We do. The hat is 15 dollars.

W Then, I'll take one of those too.

M Great. Here you are.

남 찾으시는 걸 도와드릴까요?

여 네. 목도리를 찾고 있어요.

남 가장 잘 팔리는 건 갈색과 회색 목도리예요. 각각 10달러입니다.

여 갈색 목도리로 할게요.

남 알겠습니다. 또 필요한 게 있으신가요?

여 음, 겨울용 모자도 하나 주세요. 이 목도리와 어울리는 모자가 있나요?

남 있어요. 이 모자는 15달러입니다.

여 그러면, 그것도 하나 주세요.

남 좋습니다. 여기 있습니다.

해설 | 여자가 10달러짜리 목도리 하나와 15달러짜리 모자 하나를 달라고 했으므로 정답은 ④ '$ 25'이다.

어휘 | scarf [skɑːrf] 몡 목도리, 스카프   match [mætʃ] 툉 어울리다 몡 대등한 것

정답 ②

M	Hello. Do you need help with anything?	남	안녕하세요. 도와드릴 게 있을까요?
W	I'm looking for a rubber tree for my office.	여	제 사무실에 둘 고무나무를 찾고 있어요.
M	We have many options here. How big do you want it to be?	남	여기 여러 선택지가 있습니다. 얼마나 크기를 원하세요?
W	I have a small office, so it can't be huge.	여	작은 사무실이라서, 거대하면 안 돼요.
M	What about this one? It's a good size.	남	이건 어떠세요? 적당한 크기랍니다.
W	That's perfect! I'll take that one.	여	완벽해요! 그걸로 할게요.
M	Okay. You can pay now, and then I'll carry it to your car for you.	남	알겠습니다. 지금 결제하시면, 제가 차까지 운반해 드리겠습니다.
W	Thank you for your help.	여	도와주셔서 감사해요.

해설 | 남자가 나무를 여자의 차까지 운반해 주겠다고 했으므로 정답은 ② '나무 운반하기'이다.

어휘 | rubber tree 고무나무   huge [hjuːdʒ] 혱 거대한, 큰

정답 ⑤

| M | Hello, residents in Ashton Apartments. This is George Hallow from the Ashton Apartments Committee. I'm proud to announce that we'll be holding our annual food donation event on July 17th. It'll be held at our community center on the second floor. You can donate canned or dry food at this event. It will be donated to the local senior home to help the elderly. Please call 555-3251 if you have any questions. | 남 | 안녕하세요, 애슈턴 아파트 입주민 여러분. 저는 애슈턴 아파트 위원회의 George Hallow입니다. 저희가 7월 17일에 연례 음식 기부 행사를 열게 됐음을 알리게 되어 영광입니다. 그 행사는 저희 주민센터 2층에서 열릴 예정입니다. 여러분은 통조림 식품이나 건조식품을 기부하실 수 있습니다. 그것은 노인 분들을 돕기 위해 지역 양로원에 기부될 것입니다. 질문이 있으시다면 555-3251로 전화 주십시오. |

해설 | ① 행사 날짜(7월 17일), ② 행사 장소(주민센터 2층), ③ 기부 품목(통조림 식품이나 건조식품), ④ 기부 목적(노인 분들을 돕기 위해)에 대해 언급했으므로 정답은 ⑤ '신청 방법'이다.

어휘 | resident [rézidənt] 명 입주민, 거주자   committee [kəmíti] 명 위원회   donation [dounéiʃən] 명 기부 (donate [dóuneit] 동 기부하다)
canned food 통조림 식품   senior home 양로원   the elderly 노인들, 노인층

정답 ①

W	Dad, they rent bikes here. Can we rent one?	여	아빠, 여기서 자전거를 빌려주고 있어요. 우리도 하나 빌릴 수 있을까요?
M	You don't know how to ride a bike.	남	넌 자전거 타는 법을 모르잖니.
W	Yeah. But they have bikes for two people.	여	맞아요. 그렇지만 2인용 자전거도 있는걸요.
M	Why don't I teach you instead? Let's get one with one seat.	남	그보다는 내가 가르쳐주는 건 어떻겠니? 안장이 1개인 걸로 하자.
W	Okay. I think the pink one is for little children. It is too small.	여	알겠어요. 분홍색 자전거는 어린 아이용인 것 같아요. 너무 작아요.
M	There are still two other options.	남	그래도 여전히 두 가지 선택지가 있구나.
W	The more expensive one looks too big for me though.	여	그렇지만 더 비싼 건 저한테 너무 커 보여요.
M	I think so. You won't need that.	남	그런 것 같구나. 그건 필요 없겠어.
W	I agree. I'll rent the cheaper one. I'm so excited!	여	동의해요. 더 싼 걸로 빌릴게요. 너무 신나요!

해설 | 남자가 안장이 1개인 자전거를 빌리자고 했고, 여자가 분홍색 자전거는 너무 작으며 남은 선택지 중 더 싼 것으로 빌리겠다고 했으므로 정답은 ①이다.

어휘 | rent [rent] 동 빌리다 명 방세   though [ðou] 부 그렇지만 접 ~이지만

정답 ③

| M | Many people think this animal is an insect, but it is not, actually. This animal is found all over the world. It has eight legs. It can bite you, but it is not always dangerous. This animal is famous for its webs. It makes them with silk and uses them to catch bugs. Many people are scared of this animal, but some have one as a pet. | 남 | 많은 사람이 이 동물을 곤충이라고 생각하지만, 사실은 아닙니다. 이 동물은 전 세계에서 발견됩니다. 그것은 다리가 여덟 개입니다. 그것은 물 수도 있지만, 늘 위험한 건 아닙니다. 이 동물은 거미줄로 유명합니다. 그것은 실크로 거미줄을 만들어 벌레를 잡는 데 사용합니다. 많은 사람이 이 동물을 두려워하지만, 일부는 그것을 반려동물로 키웁니다. |

해설 | 이 동물(this animal)은 벌레를 잡는 데 사용하는 거미줄로 유명하다고 했으므로 정답은 ③ '거미'이다.

어휘 | insect [ínsekt] 명 곤충 bite [bait] 통 물다 dangerous [déindʒərəs] 형 위험한 be famous for ~으로 유명하다 web [web] 명 거미줄; 직물 catch [kætʃ] 통 잡다 be scared of ~을 두려워하다

---

15 할 일 고르기   정답 ④

M	Honey, what should we do today?
W	The house is very dirty. We should clean.
M	Yes. We are so busy during the week.
W	I know. But we can get it done quickly together now.
M	That's true. I will clean the kitchen first then.
W	I'll organize our closet first. Could you play some music?
M	Yes. I'll put some on.

남	여보, 오늘 우리 뭐 할까?
여	집이 너무 더러워. 청소를 해야겠어.
남	그래. 주중에는 너무 바빠.
여	그러게. 그렇지만 지금 같이 하면 빠르게 끝낼 수 있어.
남	맞는 말이야. 그러면 내가 부엌 먼저 청소할게.
여	난 옷장을 먼저 정리할게. 당신이 노래 좀 틀어줄래?
남	그래. 틀어둘게.

해설 | 여자가 옷장을 먼저 정리하겠다고 했으므로 정답은 ④ '옷장 정리하기'이다.

어휘 | organize [ɔ́:rgənaiz] 통 정리하다; 조직하다 closet [klázit] 명 옷장; 벽장

---

16 시간 정보 고르기   정답 ①

W	James, do you want to take a cooking class with me?
M	Sounds interesting! Where can we take it?
W	Our community center offers cooking classes on weekends.
M	Cool. I have free time on Saturdays.
W	What time can you go?
M	Is there a class that starts at 3 or 4 p.m.? I don't think I can take a morning class.
W	Let me check. [Pause] No. But there is one that starts at 1.
M	The 1 p.m. class is fine. I'm really looking forward to this. It will be a lot of fun.

여	James, 나랑 요리 수업 들을래?
남	재미있겠는걸! 어디에서 들을 수 있어?
여	우리 주민 센터에서 주말마다 요리 수업을 제공하고 있어.
남	멋지다. 난 토요일엔 한가해.
여	몇 시에 갈 수 있어?
남	오후 3시나 4시에 시작하는 수업이 있어? 아침 수업은 못 들을 것 같아.
여	확인해 볼게. [잠시 멈춤] 없어. 그런데 1시에 시작하는 건 있어.
남	오후 1시 수업도 괜찮아. 진짜 기대돼. 엄청 재미있을 거야.

해설 | 여자가 1시에 시작하는 수업이 있다고 하자, 남자가 괜찮다고 했으므로 정답은 ① '1 p.m.'이다.

어휘 | look forward to ~을 기대하다

---

17 적절한 응답 고르기   정답 ⑤

	[Telephone rings.]
M	This is Richard from Furniture World. How may I help you?
W	I just got home after buying a chair from your store.
M	Okay. Is there a problem with your purchase?
W	Yes. I opened the package with the chair parts, and one of the legs is broken.
M	I apologize for that. You can return the chair today if you want.
W	Do I need to bring anything else?
M	Just bring all of the parts and your receipt.
W	Okay. I will come back to the store this afternoon.

	[전화기가 울린다.]
남	Furniture World의 Richard입니다. 무엇을 도와드릴까요?
여	당신 가게에서 의자를 사서 지금 막 집에 왔는데요.
남	그러시군요. 구매하신 것에 무슨 문제가 있으신가요?
여	네. 의자 부품이 든 포장을 열었는데 다리 하나가 부러져 있었어요.
남	죄송합니다. 원하신다면 오늘 의자를 반품하실 수 있으세요.
여	제가 더 가져가야 할 게 있나요?
남	부품 전부와 영수증만 가지고 와주세요.
여	알겠습니다. 오늘 오후에 가게에 다시 들를게요.

해설 | 남자가 의자를 반품하려면 부품 전부와 영수증을 가지고 와 달라고 했으므로 정답은 가게에 방문하겠다는 ⑤ 'Okay. I will come back to the store this afternoon.'이다.

선택지 해석

① 제가 의자를 고쳐드릴 수 있어요. 그건 쉬워요. ② 점장님은 지금 여기 안 계세요. ③ 환불이나 교환을 받으실 수 있어요. ④ 못과 망치가 필요해요.
⑤ 알겠습니다. 오늘 오후에 가게에 다시 들를게요.

어휘 | purchase [pə́:rtʃəs] 명 구매한 것 통 구매하다 receipt [risí:t] 명 영수증 nail [neil] 명 못 hammer [hǽmər] 명 망치

W	What are you laughing at, Hajun?	여	뭘 보고 웃고 있는 거야, 하준아?
M	It's a video of a cat that makes a funny sound.	남	이건 웃긴 소리를 내는 고양이 영상이야.
W	Oh, can I see?	여	오, 나도 봐도 돼?
M	Sure. Let me restart it.	남	물론이지. 내가 다시 시작시킬게.
W	[Pause] That's so funny! Do you know any other good animal videos?	여	[잠시 멈춤] 이거 너무 웃기다! 너 다른 재미있는 동물 영상 아는 거 있어?
M	Yes. I like to watch them in my free time.	남	응. 난 쉴 때 그런 거 보는 거 좋아하거든.
W	Are there any videos with hamsters in them? They're my favorite animal.	여	햄스터가 나오는 영상도 있어? 햄스터는 내가 제일 좋아하는 동물이거든.
M	Yes, I know a great one with a hamster eating seeds.	남	응, 씨앗을 먹는 햄스터가 나오는 좋은 영상을 알고 있지.
W	Please send it to me. I'd love to watch it.	여	그걸 나한테 보내줘. 너무 보고 싶다.
M	I'll give you the link instead.	남	링크를 대신 보내줄게.

해설 | 여자가 영상을 보내달라고 부탁했으므로 정답은 부탁을 수락하는 ④ 'I'll give you the link instead.'이다.

선택지 해석
① 내 고양이는 가끔 웃긴 행동을 해. ② 어떤 영상도 찍지 말아 주세요. ③ 우리 햄스터에게 먹이 줘야 해. ④ 링크를 대신 보내줄게.
⑤ 물론이지. 나도 코미디 영화 보는 거 좋아해.

어휘 | restart [riːstáːrt] ⑧ 다시 시작하다, 재개시키다   seed [siːd] ⑲ 씨앗   act [ækt] ⑧ 행동하다 ⑲ 행동   feed [fiːd] ⑧ 먹이를 주다

M	Welcome to A Taste of Rome. How may I help you?	남	A Taste of Rome에 오신 걸 환영합니다. 무엇을 도와드릴까요?
W	Can you recommend a dish for me?	여	요리를 추천해주실 수 있나요?
M	Our spaghetti is very popular.	남	저희 스파게티가 아주 인기가 많아요.
W	I'll have an order of that then, please.	여	그러면 그걸로 하나 주문할게요.
M	Do you mind mushrooms and onions in the sauce?	남	소스에 버섯과 양파가 들어가도 괜찮으신가요?
W	That's fine. I just don't want any cheese with it.	여	괜찮아요. 전 치즈가 들어가는 것만은 원하지 않아요.
M	I will tell the chef. Also, please let me know what side dish you would like.	남	요리사에게 말해두겠습니다. 또, 곁들일 요리는 어떤 걸 원하시는지 알려주세요.
W	The tomato salad will be good.	여	토마토 샐러드가 좋겠어요.

해설 | 남자가 어떤 곁들일 요리를 원하는지 알려달라고 했으므로 정답은 원하는 요리를 언급하는 ④ 'The tomato salad will be good.'이다.

선택지 해석
① 저는 작년 여름에 이탈리아에 갔었어요. ② 네. 지금 계산할게요. ③ 그녀는 매운 음식을 못 먹어요. ④ 토마토 샐러드가 좋겠어요.
⑤ 저는 버섯에 알레르기가 있어요.

어휘 | mushroom [mʌ́ʃruːm] ⑲ 버섯   onion [ʌ́njən] ⑲ 양파   allergic [əlɔ́ːrdʒik] ⑲ 알레르기의

| M | Isaac and Rachel have to do a science project together. Because it is due next week, they need to work on the project soon. Isaac wants to meet Rachel on Saturday to work on it. They decide to meet in the afternoon, but they don't pick a location. Isaac wants to ask Rachel about where she'd like to meet. In this situation, what would Isaac most likely say to Rachel? | 남 | Isaac과 Rachel은 과학 과제를 함께 해야 합니다. 그건 다음 주까지이기 때문에, 그들은 곧바로 과제를 진행해야 합니다. Isaac은 토요일에 Rachel을 만나서 과제를 하고 싶습니다. 그들은 오후에 만나기로 하지만, 장소는 고르지 않았습니다. Isaac은 Rachel에게 어디에서 만나고 싶은지 묻고 싶습니다. 이러한 상황에서, Isaac이 Rachel에게 가장 할 것 같은 말은 무엇입니까? |
| Isaac | Rachel, where do you want to meet on Saturday? | Isaac | Rachel, 토요일에 어디에서 만나고 싶어? |

해설 | Isaac이 Rachel에게 토요일 오후 어디에서 만나고 싶은지 묻고 싶다고 했으므로 정답은 ⑤ 'where do you want to meet on Saturday?'이다.

선택지 해석
① 나 오늘 이미 계획이 있어. ② 3시에 만나는 게 어때? ③ 어떤 부분을 맡고 싶어? ④ 과학 교과서를 가져와 줄 수 있어? ⑤ 토요일에 어디에서 만나고 싶어?

어휘 | due [djuː] ⑲ ~까지인, ~ 예정인   location [loukéiʃən] ⑲ 장소, 위치

1	③	2	②	3	⑤	4	⑤	5	④	6	②	7	④	8	④	9	②	10	③
11	①	12	②	13	③	14	②	15	③	16	③	17	②	18	④	19	⑤	20	③

1 알맞은 그림 고르기

정답 ③

M Yeri, did you make the tablecloth in the kitchen? It looks handmade.

W Yes, Dad. I made it in an after-school program.

M Great! You used two different kinds of fabric. They go well together.

W Thanks. At first, I thought of making it with the checkered fabric only, but it would look plain.

M I see. That's why you sewed the apple-patterned cloth in the middle.

W That's right. The apple pattern makes our kitchen look brighter.

M You're right.

남 예리야, 네가 부엌의 식탁보를 만들었니? 손수 만든 것 같아 보이는구나.

여 네, 아빠. 방과 후 프로그램에서 만들었어요.

남 훌륭하구나! 두 가지 다른 종류의 천을 썼네. 서로 잘 어울리는구나.

여 고마워요. 처음에는 체크무늬 천으로만 만들려고 생각했는데, 그러면 단순해 보일 거 같았어요.

남 그렇구나. 그래서 네가 사과 무늬의 천을 가운데에 꿰맨 거구나.

여 맞아요. 사과 무늬가 부엌을 더 밝아 보이도록 해줘요.

남 네 말이 맞구나.

해설 | 여자가 처음에 체크무늬 천으로만 만들려고 했다고 한 후, 남자가 가운데에 사과 무늬의 천을 꿰맸다고 했으므로 정답은 ③이다.

어휘 | fabric [fǽbrik] 몡 천, 직물 checkered [tʃékərd] 혱 체크무늬인 plain [plein] 혱 단순한, 꾸미지 않은; 명백한 sew [sou] 동 꿰매다

2 부탁·요청한 일 고르기

정답 ②

[Cellphone rings.]

W Are you at the park, Darling?

M Yes. I'm sitting outside on a bench.

W Okay. I'm almost there.

M What do you want to do after you arrive? We can go to dinner.

W It's a little early. Let's do an activity before dinner.

M There are some new paintings at a gallery next to the park. We could go look at them.

W That sounds fun. Can you go ahead and buy tickets?

M Okay. See you at the gallery then.

[휴대폰이 울린다.]

여 공원에 있는 거야, 여보?

남 응. 밖에 벤치에 앉아 있어.

여 알았어. 난 거의 다 왔어.

남 도착하면 당신은 뭘 하고 싶어? 저녁을 먹으러 갈 수도 있어.

여 약간 이른걸. 저녁 먹기 전에 뭔가 하자.

남 공원 옆 미술관에 새로운 그림들이 몇 점 들어왔어. 그걸 보러 가도 돼.

여 재미있을 것 같아. 당신이 먼저 가서 티켓을 사 줄래?

남 알겠어. 그러면 미술관에서 봐.

해설 | 여자가 남자에게 미술관에 먼저 가서 티켓을 사다 달라고 부탁했으므로 정답은 ② '입장권 구매하기'이다.

어휘 | almost [ɔ́ːlmoust] 뫼 거의 ahead [əhéd] 뫼 먼저, 앞서

3 그림 상황에 적절한 대화 고르기

정답 ⑤

① M Where are the T-shirts?

  W They are in that drawer.

② M Which tie is better?

  W The green one looks better on you.

③ M When does the store open?

  W In about an hour.

④ M I'd like to return these shorts.

  W Do you have the receipt?

⑤ M I don't think it is the right size.

  W I agree. Try on a larger one.

① 남 티셔츠는 어디에 있어?

  여 저 서랍 안에 있어.

② 남 어떤 넥타이가 더 괜찮아?

  여 초록색 넥타이가 너한테 더 잘 어울려.

③ 남 가게 문은 언제 여시나요?

  여 한 시간쯤 후에요.

④ 남 이 반바지를 반품하고 싶어요.

  여 영수증 있으세요?

⑤ 남 이게 맞는 사이즈인지 모르겠어.

  여 동의해. 더 큰 걸 입어 봐.

해설 | 남자가 작아 보이는 재킷을 입은 채 여자와 대화하고 있는 상황이므로 정답은 ⑤이다.

어휘 | drawer [drɔːr] 몡 서랍 shorts [ʃɔːrts] 몡 반바지 try on 입어 보다

4　시간 정보 고르기　　　　　　정답 ⑤

[Telephone rings.]	*[전화기가 울린다.]*
W　Hello, Global Language School. What can I do for you?	여　안녕하세요, 글로벌 어학원입니다. 무엇을 도와드릴까요?
M　Hi, I'd like to <u>sign up</u> for <u>French</u> classes.	남　안녕하세요, 프랑스어 수업을 신청하고 싶어요.
W　We have a popular French class on Wednesday mornings. Would that <u>work</u> <u>for</u> <u>you</u>?	여　수요일 아침에 인기가 좋은 프랑스어 수업이 있어요. 그걸로 괜찮으실까요?
M　I can't come on Wednesdays. I have <u>many</u> <u>meetings</u> <u>at</u> <u>work</u> on that day. Do you have classes on Saturdays too?	남　수요일엔 못 가요. 그날은 직장에서 회의가 많거든요. 토요일 수업도 있나요?
W　We do, but they are all full right now. What about Sunday?	여　있는데, 지금은 모두 꽉 찼어요. 일요일은 어떠세요?
M　I could do Sunday.	남　일요일은 할 수 있어요.
W　Great. I'll take your information and sign you up.	여　좋아요. 회원님의 정보를 가지고 등록해 드릴게요.
M　Thank you for the help.	남　도와주셔서 감사합니다.

해설 | 여자가 일요일에 프랑스어 수업을 듣는 것은 어떤지 묻자 남자가 할 수 있다고 했으므로 정답은 ⑤ '일요일'이다.

어휘 | information [ìnfərméiʃən] 몡 정보

5　언급하지 않은 내용 고르기　　　　정답 ④

M　Can I help you find anything?	남　찾으시는 걸 도와드릴까요?
W　Yes. I want to buy a new suitcase.	여　네. 새 여행 가방을 사고 싶어요.
M　This red one is popular.	남　이 붉은색 여행 가방이 인기가 많아요.
W　I saw that on your website. It is made by Glide Luggage, right?	여　이건 웹사이트에서 봤어요. Glide Luggage사에서 만든 거죠, 맞죠?
M　Yes. It is on sale right now for 125 dollars.	남　네. 지금은 할인해서 125달러예요.
W　Is it <u>made</u> of <u>plastic</u>?	여　플라스틱으로 만들어진 건가요?
M　That's right. So, it is very light. In fact, it only weighs three kilograms.	남　맞아요. 그래서, 아주 가벼워요. 실제로, 무게가 겨우 3kg이에요.
W　It seems perfect. I'll take it.	여　완벽한 것 같네요. 그걸로 할게요.
M　Okay. I'll carry it <u>to</u> the <u>checkout</u> <u>counter</u> for you.	남　알겠습니다. 계산대까지 옮겨 드릴게요.

해설 | ① 소재(플라스틱), ② 제조사(Glide Luggage), ③ 가격(125달러), ⑤ 색상(붉은색)에 대해 언급했으므로 정답은 ④ '크기'이다.

어휘 | suitcase [súːtkeis] 몡 여행 가방　light [lait] 휑 가벼운　weigh [wei] 동 무게가 ~이다　checkout counter 계산대

6　장소 고르기　　　　　　정답 ②

W　Oh, no. There are <u>no</u> <u>more</u> <u>good</u> <u>seats</u> left for *The Police Officer*.	여　오, 이런. <The Police Officer>에 좋은 자리가 더 이상 남아 있지 않아.
M　Really?	남　정말?
W　Yes. The 7 p.m. show only has seats <u>in</u> the <u>front</u> <u>row</u>.	여　응. 오후 7시 영화는 앞줄에만 자리가 있어.
M　What about the 7:30 p.m. show?	남　오후 7시 30분 영화는 어때?
W　Let me check. *[Pause]* There are still some good seats.	여　확인해 볼게. *[잠시 멈춤]* 좋은 자리가 아직 몇 개 있네.
M　Alright, then let's get two seats in the middle row. We can buy some popcorn and wait a little longer for the movie.	남　그래, 그러면 가운뎃줄로 두 자리를 사자. 팝콘을 사서 영화를 약간 더 오래 기다리면 돼.
W　Good idea. I'll buy the tickets while you get the popcorn.	여　좋은 생각이야. 네가 팝콘 사 오는 동안 내가 티켓을 살게.
M　Sure. I'll go to <u>the</u> <u>snack</u> <u>bar</u> now.	남　좋아. 내가 지금 스낵바로 갈게.

해설 | 남자가 팝콘을 사서 영화 보기까지 좀 더 기다리자고 하는 것으로 보아 정답은 ② '영화관'이다.

어휘 | show [ʃou] 몡 영화, 상연 작품 동 보여주다　row [rou] 몡 줄　middle [mídl] 휑 가운데의

7 어색한 대화 고르기   정답 ④

① W	What did you eat for lunch?
M	I ate some noodles with Fred.
② W	Did you bring an umbrella?
M	No. But it's not going to rain today.
③ W	Where did you get these muffins?
M	I bought them at the bakery on Main Street.
④ W	How many mangoes do you want?
M	It smells really fresh.
⑤ W	Do you need a plastic bag?
M	No, thank you. I brought my bag.

① 여 점심으로 뭐 먹었어?
　남 Fred랑 국수를 먹었어.
② 여 우산 가져왔어?
　남 아니. 그런데 오늘 비 안 올 거야.
③ 여 이 머핀 어디서 났어?
　남 메인 가에 있는 제과점에서 샀어.
④ 여 망고 몇 개 드릴까요?
　남 정말 신선한 향이 나네요.
⑤ 여 비닐봉지가 필요하신가요?
　남 아니요, 괜찮습니다. 봉지를 갖고 왔어요.

해설 | 여자가 남자에게 망고를 몇 개 줄지 물었으므로, 남자는 망고의 개수를 답해야 한다. 그러나 남자가 망고에서 신선한 향이 난다는 어색한 대답을 했으므로 정답은 ④이다.

어휘 | noodle [núːdl] 몡 국수   plastic bag 비닐봉지

8 부탁·요청한 일 고르기   정답 ④

W	Let's go to the amusement park today, Dad.
M	I don't know. The house is very messy, and you have homework.
W	We can do everything after we come back home.
M	No. We will be too tired afterward.
W	Then, why don't we do our chores now? After we finish them, we can visit the park.
M	That could work. But what about your homework?
W	I promise I will do it tomorrow morning.
M	Alright. Then, can you begin by mopping the kitchen floor?
W	Of course!

여 오늘 놀이공원에 가요, 아빠.
남 잘 모르겠네. 집은 매우 지저분하고, 넌 숙제가 있잖니.
여 집에 돌아온 후에 전부 할 수 있어요.
남 아니. 나중엔 너무 피곤할 거야.
여 그러면, 지금 집안일을 하는 게 어때요? 끝내고 나서, 놀이공원에 가도 되잖아요.
남 그러면 되겠구나. 그런데 네 숙제는 어떻게 할 거니?
여 내일 아침에 하겠다고 약속할게요.
남 알겠다. 그러면, 부엌 바닥을 대걸레로 닦는 것부터 시작해 줄래?
여 물론이죠!

해설 | 남자가 여자에게 부엌 바닥을 대걸레로 닦는 것부터 시작해 달라고 부탁했으므로 정답은 ④ '부엌 청소하기'이다.

어휘 | messy [mési] 혱 지저분한   chores [tʃɔːrz] 집안일, 농장일 (chore [tʃɔːr] 몡 잡일)   mop [map] 동 대걸레로 닦다 몡 대걸레

9 주제 고르기   정답 ②

W	Can I have your attention? I'm Ms. Andrews, principal of the Clay Middle School. Before we begin the semester, I want to go over a couple of guidelines at our school. First, all students must wear their school uniform. Second, cellphones cannot be used during class unless there are special instructions from the teacher. Lastly, any kind of violent behavior will not be tolerated. Thank you for listening, and have a great day.

여 주목해주시겠습니까? 클레이 중학교 교장 Andrews 선생님입니다. 학기를 시작하기 전에, 학교 지침 몇 가지를 다시 말해드리고 싶습니다. 먼저, 모든 학생은 반드시 교복을 착용해야 합니다. 둘째로, 선생님께서 특별한 지시가 있는 것이 아니라면 수업 중에 휴대폰은 쓸 수 없습니다. 마지막으로, 어떤 종류의 폭력적인 행동도 허용되지 않을 것입니다. 들어주셔서 감사하고, 좋은 하루 보내세요.

해설 | 여자가 학기가 시작되기 전 학교 지침 몇 가지를 설명해주고 있으므로 정답은 ② '학교생활 규칙'이다.

어휘 | go over 다시 말하다   instructions [instrʌ́kʃənz] 몡 지시 (instruction [instrʌ́kʃən] 몡 교육)   violent [váiələnt] 혱 폭력적인
tolerate [táləreit] 동 허용하다

10 금액 정보 고르기   정답 ③

M	Welcome to Neighborhood Flower Shop. Can I help you?
W	Hello. I'd like to buy some flowers for my friend. <u>Can you recommend any</u>?
M	Our yellow roses are gorgeous today. <u>Five of them cost 10 dollars.</u>
W	<u>I'll take 10 yellow roses then.</u>
M	Great choice. <u>Would you like anything else</u>?
W	Umm... A vase for the flowers would also be nice.
M	<u>This one here is 10 dollars.</u> It would look beautiful with the flowers.
W	Okay. <u>I'll buy that vase</u> too.

남	Neighborhood Flower Shop에 오신 걸 환영합니다. 도와드릴까요?
여	안녕하세요. 제 친구에게 줄 꽃을 좀 사고 싶어요. 추천해 주시겠어요?
남	오늘 노란색 장미가 아주 좋아요. 다섯 송이에 10달러예요.
여	그러면 노란색 장미 열 송이를 살게요.
남	훌륭한 선택이에요. 다른 것도 드릴까요?
여	음... 꽃을 꽂을 꽃병도 있으면 좋겠네요.
남	여기 이건 10달러예요. 꽃이 있으면 아름다워 보일 거예요.
여	네. 그 꽃병도 살게요.

해설ㅣ 여자가 다섯 송이에 10달러인 노란색 장미 열 송이와 10달러짜리 꽃병 하나를 사겠다고 했으므로 정답은 ③ '$ 30'이다.

어휘ㅣ gorgeous [ɡɔ́ːrʒəs] 혱 아주 좋은, 호화로운   vase [veis] 몡 꽃병

11 할 일 고르기   정답 ①

W	Minjun, I will run in <u>the big race</u> next month.
M	That's amazing!
W	Thanks. Now I need to start preparing for it.
M	What are you going to do?
W	I <u>plan to run</u> six kilometers every day.
M	Wow. I'm sure you'll <u>do well</u> in the race.
W	I hope so. My parents are coming to watch. You should too.
M	Of course. <u>I'll make a sign to wave</u> while I cheer.
W	That's so nice of you.

여	민준아, 난 다음 달에 큰 경기에서 뛸 거야.
남	대단한걸!
여	고마워. 이제 난 준비를 시작해야 해.
남	뭘 할 건데?
여	매일 6km를 달릴 계획이야.
남	우와. 넌 틀림없이 경기를 잘할 거야.
여	나도 그러면 좋겠어. 우리 부모님이 경기 보러 오시거든. 너도 와.
남	당연하지. 내가 응원할 때 흔들 팻말도 만들게.
여	정말 친절하다.

해설ㅣ 남자가 여자를 응원할 때 흔들 팻말을 만들겠다고 했으므로 정답은 ① '응원 팻말 만들기'이다.

어휘ㅣ sign [sain] 몡 팻말; 기호   wave [weiv] 동 흔들다 몡 파도

12 언급하지 않은 내용 고르기   정답 ②

M	Good afternoon, everyone. We offer <u>many fun activities</u> during <u>our five-day cruise</u>. Throughout the day, we offer several <u>free fitness classes</u>. Every night after dinner, there will be <u>live music from our band</u>. So, come join us on the dance floor. Also, our ship features three pools, a roller-skating rink, and <u>a movie theater</u>. The ship <u>will stop in</u> San Juan, Puerto Rico and in Cozumel, Mexico. Welcome aboard, everyone!

남	안녕하세요, 여러분. 저희는 5일간의 크루즈 여행 동안 많은 재미있는 활동들을 제공합니다. 온종일, 여러 개의 무료 체력 단련 수업을 제공합니다. 매일 밤 저녁 식사 후에, 저희 밴드의 라이브 음악이 있을 것입니다. 그러니, 무도장에서 저희와 함께 해 주십시오. 또한, 저희의 선박은 세 개의 수영장과 롤러스케이트장, 그리고 영화관을 특별히 포함하고 있습니다. 선박은 푸에르토리코의 산후안과 멕시코의 코즈멜에 정박할 예정입니다. 탑승을 환영합니다, 여러분!

해설ㅣ ① 여행 기간(5일), ③ 활동(무료 체력 단련 수업, 밴드의 라이브 음악), ④ 부대시설(세 개의 수영장, 롤러스케이트장, 영화관), ⑤ 정박 장소(푸에르토리코의 산후안, 멕시코의 코즈멜)에 대해 언급했으므로 정답은 ② '관광 비용'이다.

어휘ㅣ feature [fíːtʃər] 동 특별히 포함하다 몡 특징   aboard [əbɔ́ːrd] 閉 탑승하여, 타고

13 위치 고르기
정답 ③

W	Where do you want to sit, Chris?
M	How about the table near the entrance?
W	Wouldn't it be too noisy? And the restroom is a bit close.
M	You're right. I think it's better to sit next to the window.
W	Yeah. I like watching people passing by.
M	I want to sit far away from the counter. People will be walking around.
W	I agree. Let's take the table in the corner then.
M	Great. Why don't you go sit down? I'll order the coffee.

여	어디에 앉고 싶어, Chris?
남	입구 근처 자리는 어때?
여	거기 너무 시끄럽지 않겠어? 그리고 화장실도 좀 가깝잖아.
남	네 말이 맞아. 창가 옆에 앉는 게 더 나을 것 같네.
여	응. 난 사람들이 지나다니는 걸 보는 걸 좋아해.
남	난 계산대에서 멀리 떨어져서 앉고 싶어. 사람들이 돌아다닐 테니까.
여	동감이야. 그러면 구석에 있는 자리로 하자.
남	좋아. 가서 앉지 않을래? 내가 커피를 주문할게.

해설 | 남자가 창가 옆자리 중 계산대에서 멀리 떨어진 곳에 앉는 것이 더 낫겠다고 했고, 여자가 구석에 있는 자리에 앉자고 했으므로 정답은 ③이다.
어휘 | entrance [éntrəns] 명 입구 noisy [nɔ́izi] 형 시끄러운 pass by 지나다니다

14 화제 고르기
정답 ②

M	This is a team sport. There are two teams and they stand in a big square. The square has a line in the middle. One team stands on one side and the other team stands on the other. Players throw a ball at each other. If the ball hits a player, the player is out. But if a player catches the ball, the player can keep playing. The goal is to eliminate all players.

남	이것은 단체 운동입니다. 두 팀이 있고 그들은 큰 사각형 안에 섭니다. 그 사각형 가운데에는 선이 그어져 있습니다. 한 팀이 한쪽에 서고 다른 한 팀은 나머지 한쪽에 섭니다. 선수들은 서로를 향해 공을 던집니다. 만약 공이 선수를 맞추면, 그 선수는 아웃입니다. 그러나 만약 선수가 공을 잡으면, 계속 경기할 수 있습니다. 목표는 모든 선수를 탈락시키는 것입니다.

해설 | 이것은(This)을 하는 선수들은 던져진 공에 맞으면 아웃이고, 공을 잡으면 계속 경기할 수 있다고 했으므로 정답은 ② '피구'이다.
어휘 | throw [θrou] 동 던지다 catch [kætʃ] 동 잡다 eliminate [ilímǝneit] 동 탈락시키다; 제거하다

15 할 일 고르기
정답 ③

M	Mom, I made this bowl for Grandma.
W	Oh, Doyoon, it's so beautiful! I love the color.
M	Thank you. I want to give it to her soon.
W	Well, we'll visit her next month.
M	How about sending it to her in a package? Then, she can get it sooner.
W	Okay. I'll mail the package this week.

남	엄마, 제가 할머니께 드리려고 이 그릇을 만들었어요.
여	오, 도윤아, 정말 아름답구나! 색이 참 마음에 드네.
남	감사해요. 이걸 할머니께 빨리 드리고 싶어요.
여	글쎄, 우린 다음 달에나 할머니를 찾아뵐 거란다.
남	택배로 이걸 보내는 건 어떨까요? 그러면, 할머니께서 더 빨리 받으실 수 있을 거예요.
여	알겠어. 내가 이번 주에 택배를 부치마.

해설 | 여자가 이번 주에 택배를 부치겠다고 했으므로 정답은 ③ '택배 보내기'이다.
어휘 | bowl [boul] 명 그릇 package [pǽkidʒ] 명 택배, 소포

16 시간 정보 고르기
정답 ③

W	Brian, do you know when the Apple Festival starts this year?
M	I think it starts around September 20th.
W	Let's check the calendar.
M	Oh, it starts on September 15th this year. That's early.
W	I want to see the parade this year. I missed it last year.
M	The festival's held for three days, and the parade runs every day.
W	Why don't we go on the 17th then? They always have fireworks on the last day of the festival.
M	That's a good idea.

여	Brian, 올해는 언제 Apple Festival이 시작되는지 알아?
남	9월 20일 정도에 시작하는 거 같아.
여	달력을 확인해 보자.
남	오, 올해는 9월 15일에 시작하네. 이르다.
여	올해는 퍼레이드를 보고 싶어. 작년엔 놓쳤거든.
남	축제는 삼 일 동안 열리는데, 퍼레이드는 매일 진행돼.
여	그러면 17일에 가는 건 어때? 축제 마지막 날에는 항상 불꽃놀이를 하잖아.
남	좋은 생각이야.

해설 | 여자가 9월 15일부터 삼 일 중에서 17일에 가자고 제안하자 남자가 좋은 생각이라고 했으므로 정답은 ③ '9월 17일'이다.
어휘 | calendar [kǽlǝndǝr] 명 달력 firework [faiǝrwǝːrk] 명 불꽃놀이

[Cellphone rings.]		[휴대폰이 울린다.]	
M	Hello?	남	여보세요?
W	Hi, Jin. I'm in your neighborhood. I will be at your house soon.	여	안녕, Jin. 난 네 동네에 와 있어. 너희 집에 곧 도착할 거야.
M	Great! Do you know where it is?	남	아주 좋아! 우리 집 어디인지 알지?
W	It's on Park Street, right?	여	파크 가에 있잖아, 맞지?
M	Yes. It's the white house close to the police station.	남	응. 경찰서 근처의 하얀색 집이야.
W	Got it. Do you want me to bring anything to your house?	여	알겠어. 내가 너희 집에 뭐 좀 가져갈까?
M	Actually, can you buy some juice? I ran out of orange juice.	남	사실은 말이야, 주스 좀 사다 줄 수 있을까? 오렌지 주스가 다 떨어졌어.
W	Yes. I'll stop by the store before I come.	여	응. 가기 전에 가게 들를게.
M	Thank you. I'll see you soon.	남	고마워. 곧 보자.

해설 | 여자가 남자의 부탁을 수락하여 가게에 들르겠다고 했으므로 정답은 감사를 표시하는 ② 'Thank you. I'll see you soon.'이다.

선택지 해석

① 분실물을 신고해야 해.   ② 고마워. 곧 보자.   ③ 거실은 복도 아래에 있어.   ④ 우리 집으로 오는 길을 알려줄게.   ⑤ 좋아. 네가 주스 만드는 걸 돕고 싶어.

어휘 | neighborhood [néibərhùd] 몡 동네, 이웃   run out of ~이 다 떨어지다, 동나다   stop by 들르다   report [ripɔ́ːrt] 통 신고하다, 보고하다 몡 보고서

M	Have you finished your story for English class, Haneul?	남	영어 수업 때 낼 이야기 다 썼어, 하늘아?
W	Not yet. I don't know what to write about.	여	아직. 뭐에 관해 써야 할지 모르겠어.
M	Well, the assignment is due soon. You should think of something fast.	남	이런, 숙제 곧 제출해야 하잖아. 뭔가 빨리 생각해내야 해.
W	I know. What did you write about?	여	알아. 넌 뭐에 관해 썼어?
M	My story is about a person who goes back in time.	남	내 이야기는 시간을 거슬러 올라간 사람에 관한 거야.
W	That's so interesting! How did you come up with that?	여	정말 흥미로운걸! 어떻게 그런 걸 생각해냈어?
M	I write lots of stories in my free time. I picked my favorite one.	남	난 여가 시간에 이야기를 많이 쓰거든. 내가 제일 좋아하는 걸 골랐을 뿐이야.
W	I wish I were more creative.	여	내가 좀 더 창의적이면 좋을 텐데.
M	I can help you think of some topics.	남	내가 소재들을 떠올리는 걸 도와줄 수 있어.
W	That'll help. I need ideas.	여	도움이 될 거야. 난 아이디어가 필요하거든.

해설 | 남자가 이야기 소재를 떠올리는 걸 도와주겠다고 제안했으므로 정답은 제안을 수락하는 ④ 'That'll help. I need ideas.'이다.

선택지 해석

① 응. 어제 제출했어.   ② 사람들은 그의 이야기를 믿어주지 않았어.   ③ 좋았는데, 결말이 마음에 들지 않았어.   ④ 도움이 될 거야. 난 아이디어가 필요하거든. ⑤ 난 영어를 유창하게 구사할 수 있어.

어휘 | come up with 생각해내다, 떠올리다   creative [kriéitiv] 혱 창의적인, 창조적인   turn in 제출하다   fluently [flúːəntli] 믐 유창하게

M	I can't believe that Cindy is moving.	남	Cindy가 이사 간다는 게 믿기지 않아.
W	Yeah. She's a great friend.	여	그러게. 참 좋은 친구인데.
M	We should give her something to show her that we will miss her.	남	우리가 Cindy를 그리워할 거라는 걸 보여줄 뭔가를 줘야겠어.
W	Okay. What about making her a memory book? We can add some of our photographs together.	여	알겠어. 메모리 북을 만들어주는 건 어때? 우리가 함께 찍은 사진 몇 장을 추가하면 되잖아.
M	She'd love that. I have lots of pictures of us.	남	Cindy가 아주 좋아하겠는걸. 내겐 우리 사진이 많이 있어.
W	Great! Can you print them? I will buy a notebook.	여	좋아! 네가 그걸 인화해줄래? 난 공책을 살게.
M	Yeah. We can meet this weekend to put it all together.	남	응. 이번 주말에 만나서 전부 모아 메모리 북을 만들자.
W	Okay. I'll go to the store today then.	여	알겠어. 그러면 내가 오늘 가게에 갈게.

해설 | 남자가 사진 인화와 공책 구매의 역할 분담에 동의하며 주말에 만나자고 했으므로 정답은 만나기 전 할 일을 언급하는 ⑤ 'Okay. I'll go to the store today then.'이다.

선택지 해석
① 내가 짐 챙기는 걸 도와줘서 고마워.   ② 곧 널 보러 갈게.   ③ 여기에선 사진 찍으시면 안 됩니다.   ④ 선물은 영수증이 있으면 반품하실 수 있습니다.
⑤ 알겠어. 그러면 내가 오늘 가게에 갈게.

어휘 | miss [mis] 통 그리워하다; 놓치다   memory book 메모리 북(추억담, 편지, 사진 등을 담은 책)   add [æd] 통 추가하다; 덧붙이다

20 상황에 적절한 말 고르기

정답 ③

W	George is a tourist in Spain. After a long day of exploring the city, George returns to his hotel for some rest. Eventually, he becomes hungry. He wants to eat at a nice traditional restaurant. So, he would like to ask the hotel employee if she knows a good place for Spanish food. In this situation, what would George most likely say to the hotel employee?
George	Could you recommend a traditional restaurant for me?

여	George는 스페인을 방문한 여행객입니다. 도시를 탐방하며 긴 하루를 보낸 후, George는 휴식을 취하러 호텔로 돌아옵니다. 마침내, 그는 배가 고파집니다. 그는 근사한 전통 음식점에서 식사하고 싶습니다. 그래서, 그는 호텔 직원에게 스페인 음식을 먹을 좋은 장소를 알고 있는지 묻고 싶습니다. 이러한 상황에서, George가 호텔 직원에게 가장 할 것은 말은 무엇입니까?
George	저에게 전통 음식점을 추천해 주시겠습니까?

해설 | George가 호텔 직원에게 스페인 음식을 먹을 좋은 장소를 알고 있는지 묻고 싶다고 했으므로 정답은 ③ 'Could you recommend a traditional restaurant for me?'이다.

선택지 해석
① 가장 가까운 지하철역이 어디인가요?   ② 내일 관광을 예약하고 싶습니다.   ③ 저에게 전통 음식점을 추천해 주시겠습니까?
④ 호텔에서는 어떤 종류의 음식 서비스를 제공하고 있습니까?   ⑤ 고객님의 수화물은 곧 배송될 겁니다.

어휘 | tourist [túərist] 명 관광객   explore [ikspló:r] 통 탐방하다, 탐험하다   traditional [trədíʃənəl] 형 전통의   shortly [ʃɔ́:rtli] 부 곧

(10회) 실전 모의고사

| 문제 pp.98-99

1	②	2	⑤	3	③	4	①	5	⑤	6	②	7	①	8	④	9	③	10	④
11	⑤	12	③	13	④	14	④	15	②	16	①	17	⑤	18	④	19	⑤	20	③

1 알맞은 그림 고르기

정답 ②

W	Do you need any help?
M	Yes. I'm looking for a kitchen scale.
W	We have digital and mechanical ones. Which do you prefer?
M	I want a digital one.
W	Alright. How about this square one? It can measure up to five kilograms.
M	That's good. But it doesn't have a power button.
W	Yeah. When you put things on it, it automatically turns on.
M	Wow, amazing! I'll take that one.

여	도움이 필요하신가요?
남	네. 주방 저울을 찾고 있어요.
여	전자식과 기계식 저울이 있어요. 어떤 걸 선호하세요?
남	전자식 저울로 주세요.
여	알겠습니다. 이 네모난 건 어떠세요? 5kg까지 측정할 수 있어요.
남	좋아요. 그런데 전원 버튼이 없네요.
여	네. 물건을 위에 올려두시면, 자동으로 켜진답니다.
남	우와, 놀랍네요! 그걸로 할게요.

해설 | 남자가 전원 버튼이 없는 네모난 전자식 주방 저울을 사겠다고 했으므로 정답은 ②이다.
어휘 | mechanical [məkǽnikəl] 형 기계식의; 기계의   measure [méʒər] 통 측정하다 명 치수   up to ~까지   automatically [ɔ̀:təmǽtikəli] 부 자동으로

2 목적 고르기   정답 ⑤

[Cellphone rings.] M Hello. W Hey, Greg. This is Amanda from the drama club. M Hi, Amanda. What's going on? W It's about the rehearsal for the play we are going to perform next week. M Has it been canceled? W No, that's not it. We are going to start an hour later than planned. So, be there at 4 p.m. M Okay. Why was the schedule changed? W Another club is using the room until 3:30.	[휴대폰이 울린다.] 남 여보세요. 여 안녕, Greg. 나 연극 동아리의 Amanda야. 남 안녕, Amanda. 무슨 일이야? 여 다음 주에 공연할 연극 예행연습에 관한 거야. 남 그거 취소됐어? 여 아니, 그건 아니야. 우리는 계획했던 것보다 한 시간 늦게 시작할 거야. 그러니까, 오후 4시에 와. 남 알겠어. 일정이 왜 변경된 거야? 여 다른 동아리가 3시 30분까지 그 장소를 쓸 거야.

해설 | 여자가 연극 예행연습이 계획보다 한 시간 늦게 시작될 것이라고 말했으므로 정답은 ⑤ '연습 시간이 변경됐음을 알려주려고'이다.

어휘 | drama [drɑ́:mə] 명 연극; 희곡   rehearsal [rihɔ́:rsəl] 명 예행연습, 리허설   schedule [skédʒuːl] 명 일정, 예정

3 그림 상황에 적절한 대화 고르기   정답 ③

① W Excuse me, this seat is for the disabled.
   M Oh, sorry. I didn't notice it.
② W When does the bus arrive?
   M In about 20 minutes.
③ W Would you like me to close the window?
   M Yes, please. I feel a little cold.
④ W How long have you lived here?
   M For about nine years now.
⑤ W There are many people in the station.
   M That's because it's the weekend.
	① 여 실례합니다, 이 자리는 장애인석이에요.
	   남 오, 죄송해요. 몰랐어요.
	② 여 버스가 언제 도착하나요?
	   남 20분쯤 후에요.
	③ 여 제가 창문을 닫아 드릴까요?
	   남 네, 그래 주세요. 약간 춥네요.
	④ 여 여기에서 얼마나 오래 살았어?
	   남 지금까지 9년 정도 됐어.
	⑤ 여 역에 사람들이 정말 많네.
	   남 주말이라서 그래.

해설 | 버스에 앉아 있는 여자가 열려 있는 창문을 가리키며 남자에게 말을 걸고 있는 상황이므로 정답은 ③이다.

어휘 | disabled [diséibld] 형 장애의, 신체장애가 있는   notice [nóutis] 동 알다, 알아차리다 명 주의   station [stéiʃən] 명 역, 정거장

4 시간 정보 고르기   정답 ①

[Phone rings.] W Hello, this is the university library help desk. M Hi, I'd like to reserve a study room. W You can use the study rooms from Monday to Saturday. M How long can I reserve a room for? W You can make a reservation for up to five hours. M Are computers available to rent too? W Yes. But computers are unavailable on the weekends. M Okay. I'll make a reservation for a room with a computer for Tuesday then. W Sure.	여 안녕하세요, 대학 도서관 안내 데스크입니다. 남 안녕하세요, 스터디룸을 예약하고 싶은데요. 여 스터디룸은 월요일부터 토요일까지 이용하실 수 있어요. 남 얼마 동안 예약할 수 있나요? 여 최대 다섯 시간까지 예약하실 수 있어요. 남 컴퓨터도 빌리는 게 가능한가요? 여 네. 하지만 컴퓨터는 주말에는 이용하실 수 없어요. 남 알겠습니다. 그러면 화요일에 컴퓨터와 스터디룸을 예약할게요. 여 그럼요.

해설 | 남자가 스터디룸과 컴퓨터를 화요일에 빌리는 것으로 예약하겠다고 했으므로 정답은 ① '화요일'이다.

어휘 | reserve [rizɔ́:rv] 동 예약하다; 남겨 두다 (reservation [rèzərvéiʃən] 명 예약)
available [əvéiləbl] 형 이용 가능한, 이용할 수 있는 (unavailable [ènəvéiləbl] 형 이용할 수 없는)

5 언급하지 않은 내용 고르기　　　　　　　　　　　　　　　　　　정답 ⑤

M	Are you looking to have fun with your family? Visit the Grandview Amusement Park. Our park is located in Central City Plaza. The entrance fee is 15 dollars for children and 25 dollars for adults. This includes 10 ride tickets. Be sure to try our famous roller coaster or our amazing Ferris wheel. If you get hungry, there are many food stands and restaurants on our grounds. So, visit us soon to enjoy all of the fun experiences.	남 가족과 즐겁게 보내기를 기대하고 계십니까? 그랜드뷰 놀이공원을 방문하십시오. 저희 놀이공원은 센트럴 시티 플라자에 위치해 있습니다. 입장료는 어린이가 15달러이고 어른은 25달러입니다. 여기엔 10가지 기구 탑승권이 포함되어 있습니다. 저희의 유명한 롤러코스터나 멋진 관람차를 꼭 타보십시오. 만약 배가 고파지시면, 저희 부지에 음식 가판대와 식당이 많이 있습니다. 그러니, 모든 재미있는 경험을 즐기시려면 저희 놀이공원을 바로 방문하십시오.

해설 | ① 위치(센트럴 시티 플라자), ② 입장료(어린이 15달러, 어른 25달러), ③ 기구 종류(롤러코스터, 관람차), ④ 식당 유무(음식 가판대와 식당 있음)에 대해 언급했으므로 정답은 ⑤ '특별 공연'이다.

어휘 | look to 기대하다, 바라다　entrance fee 입장료　Ferris wheel 관람차　stand [stænd] 몡 가판대 통 서다
grounds [graunz] 몡 부지, 구내 (ground [graund] 몡 땅)

6 관계 고르기　　　　　　　　　　　　　　　　　　　　　　　　　정답 ②

M	Excuse me, but you should use your headphones while watching movies on the train.	남 실례지만, 기차에서 영화를 보실 때는 헤드폰을 사용하셔야 해요.
W	Oh, really?	여 오, 그런가요?
M	Yes. The noise can make the other passengers uncomfortable.	남 네. 소음이 다른 승객들을 불편하게 만들 수 있어요.
W	Got it. Just to check, can I drink my coffee on the train?	여 알겠습니다. 그냥 확인차 묻는 건데, 기차 내에서 커피를 마셔도 되나요?
M	That's fine. Drinks are allowed during the trip.	남 그건 괜찮습니다. 이동 중에 음료는 허용됩니다.
W	Good. Also, I want to change seats. Is that okay?	여 좋아요. 또, 자리를 바꾸고 싶은데요. 괜찮나요?
M	Yes. But if a person gets on the train with a ticket for that seat, you have to move.	남 네. 하지만 그 자리의 표를 가진 사람이 기차에 타면, 이동하셔야 합니다.

해설 | 남자가 기차에서 영화를 볼 때는 헤드폰을 사용해야 하고 이동 중에 음료는 허용된다고 하는 것으로 보아 정답은 ② '승무원 — 승객'이다.

어휘 | noise [nɔiz] 몡 소음　passenger [pǽsəndʒər] 몡 승객　trip [trip] 몡 이동; 여행　get on 타다

7 어색한 대화 고르기　　　　　　　　　　　　　　　　　　　　　정답 ①

① W Did you go to the mall yesterday?　M Of course, I'll make some now.	① 여 어제 쇼핑몰 갔어?　남 당연하지, 지금 만들어줄게.
② W Do you need me to give you a ride?　M No. I'll take the subway.	② 여 내가 널 태워다 줘야 하니?　남 아니. 난 지하철 탈 거야.
③ W Do you like this sculpture?　M I think it's the best one in the museum.	③ 여 이 조각품이 마음에 드니?　남 박물관에서 이게 가장 좋은 것 같아.
④ W What would you recommend at this bakery?　M Well, the garlic bread is the most popular thing here.	④ 여 이 제과점에서 뭘 추천하세요?　남 음, 마늘빵이 여기에서 가장 인기가 많은 거예요.
⑤ W Why did you miss school yesterday?　M I had a high fever.	⑤ 여 어제 왜 학교 빠졌어?　남 열이 높았어.

해설 | 여자가 남자에게 어제 쇼핑몰에 갔는지 물었으므로, 남자는 방문 여부를 답해야 한다. 그러나 남자가 지금 만들어주겠다는 어색한 대답을 했으므로 정답은 ①이다.

어휘 | sculpture [skʌ́lptʃər] 몡 조각품, 조각　garlic [gɑ́:rlik] 몡 마늘　fever [fí:vər] 몡 열

8 부탁·요청한 일 고르기   정답 ④

[Cellphone rings.]	[휴대폰이 울린다.]
W Where are you, Dad?	여 어디세요, 아빠?
M I'm on my way home. I just left work.	남 집에 가는 길이란다. 막 퇴근했어.
W Do you want me to start cooking dinner?	여 제가 저녁 준비 시작할까요?
M We don't have any food. I'll go by the supermarket now.	남 음식이 전혀 없단다. 내가 지금 슈퍼마켓에 들를게.
W What will you get?	여 뭘 사실 거예요?
M We can eat fish or chicken. Which sounds better?	남 생선이나 닭고기를 먹어도 돼. 어떤 게 더 좋은 것 같니?
W Chicken sounds delicious. But can you also buy some milk? We just ran out.	여 닭고기가 맛있을 것 같아요. 그런데 우유도 사 오실래요? 다 떨어졌어요.
M Yes, I'll get some.	남 그래, 사 가마.

해설 | 여자가 남자에게 우유를 사다 달라고 부탁했으므로 정답은 ④ '우유 사 오기'이다.

어휘 | go by 들르다, 방문하다   run out 다 떨어지다, 다하다

9 의도 고르기   정답 ③

M Are you okay? You seem nervous.	남 너 괜찮아? 불안해 보여.
W Yeah. I'm worried about my final exam for biology class.	여 그래. 난 생물학 수업의 기말고사가 걱정돼.
M Is that tomorrow?	남 그거 내일이야?
W Yeah. And the exam is worth 50% of my grade.	여 응. 그 시험은 내 성적의 50%를 차지해.
M There's nothing to worry about. We can review the material together tonight.	남 걱정할 거 없어. 오늘 밤에 같이 시험 자료를 복습하면 돼.
W Thanks. But I'm not sure if that will be enough.	여 고마워. 그런데 그걸로 충분할지 모르겠어.
M You're a great student. And you studied hard all semester. You'll be fine.	남 넌 훌륭한 학생이야. 그리고 학기 내내 열심히 공부했잖아. 괜찮을 거야.

해설 | 남자가 시험을 앞둔 여자에게 학기 내내 열심히 공부했으니 괜찮을 것이라고 했으므로 정답은 ③ '격려'이다.

어휘 | biology [baiάlədʒi] 閔 생물학   review [rivjú:] 통 복습하다 閔 평론   material [mətíəriəl] 閔 (조사 등의) 자료; 재료   semester [siméstər] 閔 학기

10 금액 정보 고르기   정답 ④

W Welcome to Best Haircuts. How may I help you?	여 Best Haircuts에 오신 걸 환영합니다. 무엇을 도와드릴까요?
M Hello. How much is a haircut?	남 안녕하세요. 이발하는 데 얼마인가요?
W It is 15 dollars.	여 15달러예요.
M Okay. I'd like a haircut then, please.	남 알겠습니다. 그러면 이발해주세요.
W Great. Do you want me to wash and dry your hair too?	여 좋아요. 제가 머리를 감기고 말려드리기도 할까요?
M How much is the washing service?	남 머리 감겨주는 데는 얼마인가요?
W It is another five dollars.	여 별개로 5달러입니다.
M Sure. I'll do that as well.	남 그렇군요. 그것도 할게요.
W Okay. Then, please follow me.	여 네. 그러면 저를 따라오세요.

해설 | 이발은 15달러이고 머리를 감겨주는 건 따로 5달러가 더 든다고 했고, 남자가 둘 다 하겠다고 했으므로 정답은 ④ '$ 20'이다.

어휘 | haircut [héərkʌt] 閔 이발   dry [drai] 통 말리다 閔 건조한   as well ~도, 또한

11 할 일 고르기   정답 ⑤

W	What's wrong, Nick?
M	I fell off of my skateboard, and now my leg hurts.
W	Let me see. [Pause] Oh, you have a big cut.
M	Yeah. It's bleeding a lot. I should clean it.
W	You'll also need some bandages.
M	Is there a pharmacy near here?
W	Yes. I'll go now. You stay here and rest.
M	Thank you so much.

여	무슨 일이야, Nick?
남	스케이트보드에서 넘어져서, 다리를 다쳤어.
여	어디 봐. [잠시 멈춤] 오, 상처가 크게 났어.
남	그러게. 피가 많이 난다. 상처를 깨끗이 해야겠어.
여	붕대도 좀 필요할 거야.
남	근처에 약국이 있나?
여	응. 내가 지금 갈게. 넌 여기서 쉬고 있어.
남	정말 고마워.

해설ㅣ 여자가 근처 약국에 지금 가겠다고 했으므로 정답은 ⑤ '약국 방문하기'이다.
어휘ㅣ fall off 넘어지다, 떨어지다 bleed [bliːd] 图 피가 나다, 출혈하다 bandage [bǽndidʒ] 圕 붕대 pharmacy [fɑ́ːrməsi] 圕 약국

12 언급하지 않은 내용 고르기   정답 ③

W	Good afternoon, class. Tomorrow is career day. You will learn about different types of jobs. Then, we will have three special guest speakers. They are a doctor, an astronaut, and an author. They are all parents of students here at Parker Middle School. They will visit our classroom and explain their work for us. For homework, I want you to write three questions for each speaker.

여	안녕하세요, 학생 여러분. 내일은 직업의 날입니다. 여러분은 다양한 종류의 직업에 관해 배울 것입니다. 그러고 나면, 특별한 초빙 연사를 세 분 모실 예정입니다. 그분들은 의사, 우주 비행사, 그리고 작가입니다. 그분들은 모두 여기 파커 중학교 학생 여러분의 부모님들입니다. 그분들이 저희 교실에 방문하셔서 직업에 관해 설명해주실 것입니다. 숙제로, 각 연사님에게 물어볼 질문 세 가지를 써 오세요.

해설ㅣ ① 행사 진행 순서(다양한 종류의 직업을 배운 후 초빙 연사의 직업 설명 듣기), ② 초빙 연사 수(3명), ④ 행사 장소(파커 중학교의 교실), ⑤ 준비 사항(질문 3가지 써오기)에 대해 언급했으므로 정답은 ③ '행사 목적'이다.
어휘ㅣ astronaut [ǽstrənɔːt] 圕 우주 비행사 author [ɔ́ːθər] 圕 작가 explain [ikspléin] 图 설명하다

13 도표에서 알맞은 항목 고르기   정답 ④

W	Sam, what have you got there?
M	It's a schedule for taekwondo classes. I'm going to take one this summer.
W	Can I take it with you?
M	Why not? I haven't decided which one to take though.
W	I go swimming on Tuesdays and Thursdays.
M	There are three options we can choose then.
W	Do you know which taekwondo instructor is the best?
M	My friend recommended Mr. Jones.
W	Then, let's take this class.
M	Isn't it too early?
W	There isn't any class later than that.

여	Sam, 거기 뭘 들고 있는 거야?
남	태권도 수업 일정표야. 이번 여름에 하나 들으려고.
여	나도 너랑 같이 들어도 돼?
남	왜 안 되겠어? 그런데 난 어떤 걸 들을지 못 정했어.
여	난 화요일과 목요일에는 수영하러 가.
남	그러면 우리가 선택할 수 있는 선택지가 세 개네.
여	어떤 태권도 사범님이 가장 좋은지 알아?
남	내 친구가 Jones 사범님을 추천했어.
여	그러면 이 수업을 듣자.
남	너무 이르지 않아?
여	그 이후에는 수업이 없어.

해설ㅣ 여자가 화요일과 목요일에는 수영을 하러 가서 수업을 들을 수 없다고 했고, 남자가 Jones 사범의 수업을 추천했으며, 여자가 고른 수업 이후에는 다른 수업이 없다고 했으므로 정답은 ④이다.
어휘ㅣ instructor [instrʌ́ktər] 圕 사범, 교사, 지도자

14 화제 고르기   정답 ④

W	This vehicle moves passengers or things up to higher places. It carries people in cabins that hang from thick wires. The wires move with a motor, so the cabins go up and down high places like mountains. Usually, a small group of passengers can board this and enjoy beautiful views on their way to the top.

여	이 운송 수단은 승객이나 운반물을 높은 곳으로 옮겨줍니다. 그것은 두꺼운 전선에 매달려 있는 객실 안에 사람들을 실어 나릅니다. 전선은 모터로 움직이므로, 객실은 산과 같은 높은 곳을 오르내립니다. 보통, 소규모의 승객들이 이것에 탑승하여 꼭대기로 가는 중에 아름다운 경치를 즐길 수 있습니다.

해설ㅣ 이 운송 수단(This vehicle)은 두꺼운 전선에 매달려 있는 객실 안에 사람들을 태워 실어 나른다고 했으므로 정답은 ④ '케이블카'이다.
어휘ㅣ vehicle [víːikl] 圕 운송 수단, 탈것 cabin [kǽbin] 圕 객실; 오두막집 hang [hæŋ] 图 매달려 있다; 걸다 wire [waiər] 圕 전선

15 할일 고르기   정답 ②

W	Here is your steak with a side of mashed potatoes, sir.
M	Thank you.
W	How was your salad?
M	It was very fresh. I am enjoying my meal so far.
W	Great. Do you need anything else?
M	Can I have some salt, please?
W	Of course. I'll get that right away. Would you also like some more water?
M	That would be great.

여	여기 주문하신 으깬 감자를 곁들인 스테이크입니다, 손님.
남	감사합니다.
여	샐러드는 어떠셨나요?
남	매우 신선했어요. 지금까진 맛있게 식사하고 있습니다.
여	아주 좋습니다. 다른 필요하신 게 있으신가요?
남	소금을 좀 주시겠어요?
여	물론이죠. 지금 바로 가져다드리겠습니다. 물도 좀 더 드릴까요?
남	그러면 좋겠군요.

해설 | 남자가 소금을 달라고 부탁하자 여자가 지금 바로 가져다주겠다고 했으므로 정답은 ② '소금 가져다주기'이다.

어휘 | mash [mæʃ] 통 으깨다, 짓이기다 meal [mi:l] 명 식사 salt [sɔːlt] 명 소금

16 특정 정보 고르기   정답 ①

M	Do we need to buy anything for Yuna's housewarming party tonight?
W	Maybe we should get her a small gift for her new house.
M	What about some coffee mugs or new plates?
W	She already has so many of those. We could get her some cushions for her couch instead?
M	Hmm... But they might not match the room decorations.
W	That's true. I'll just buy her a candle then. I can go to the store quickly now.
M	That's a good idea.

남	오늘 밤 유나의 집들이를 위해 우리가 뭔가 사야 할까?
여	유나의 새집에 어울릴 작은 선물을 사줘야 할까 봐.
남	커피 머그잔이나 새 접시는 어때?
여	이미 그건 많이 갖고 있는걸. 우리 그보다는 소파에 둘 쿠션을 사줄 수 있겠는데?
남	흠... 그렇지만 그건 방의 장식과 어울리지 않을 수 있어.
여	그건 맞아. 그러면 그냥 캔들을 사줄래. 내가 지금 빨리 가게에 가면 되겠어.
남	좋은 생각이야.

해설 | 여자가 집들이 선물로 캔들을 사주겠다고 했으므로 정답은 ① 'candle'이다.

> 선택지 해석
> ① 캔들 ② 접시 ③ 쿠션 ④ 머그잔 ⑤ 포크

어휘 | housewarming party 집들이 plate [pleit] 명 접시 decoration [dèkəréiʃən] 명 장식

17 적절한 응답 고르기   정답 ⑤

W	I'm excited to be partners with you for this project, Alex.
M	Yes. I think we will work well together.
W	I agree. How should we divide the work between us?
M	Well, we have to make a slide show and give a presentation.
W	I get nervous in front of crowds. Can you give the presentation?
M	That's fine. You can make the slide show.
W	Cool. I brought my laptop, so we can begin our research now.
M	Excellent. Let's get started.

여	이 수행평가를 너랑 짝이 되어 하게 돼서 신나, Alex.
남	맞아. 우린 서로 잘 해낼 거 같아.
여	동감이야. 우리 일은 어떻게 분담해야 할까?
남	글쎄, 우린 슬라이드 쇼를 만들어서 발표해야 하잖아.
여	난 많은 사람 앞에서는 긴장을 하거든. 네가 발표를 해줄 수 있을까?
남	괜찮아. 넌 슬라이드 쇼를 만들면 되겠다.
여	좋아. 내가 노트북을 가져왔으니, 지금 조사를 시작할 수 있겠어.
남	훌륭해. 시작하자.

해설 | 여자가 노트북을 가져왔으므로 지금 조사를 시작할 수 있겠다고 제안했으므로 정답은 제안에 동의하는 ⑤ 'Excellent. Let's get started.'이다.

> 선택지 해석
> ① 사람이 너무 많다. 나중에 다시 와야겠어. ② 이제 끝나서 정말 다행이야. ③ 오늘 들어주셔서 감사했습니다. ④ 아니. 우린 아직 안 끝났어.
> ⑤ 훌륭해. 시작하자.

어휘 | divide [diváid] 통 분담하다, 나누다 crowd [kraud] 명 많은 사람들, 군중 (crowded [kráudid] 형 사람이 많은, 붐비는) get started 시작하다

18 적절한 응답 고르기 　　　　　정답 ④

M	How was your weekend, Wendy?
W	I met my favorite celebrity, so it was amazing!
M	Who is your favorite celebrity?
W	His name is Robert Stan. He was so nice, and he gave me his autograph.
M	I don't know him. What is he famous for?
W	He's the main character in that television show, *After Dark*.
M	Is that a fantasy series about vampires?
W	Yes. I highly recommend it.
M	I usually prefer crime shows, but I will watch it later.
W	I bet you'll like it.

남	주말 어땠어, Wendy?
여	내가 제일 좋아하는 연예인을 만나서 너무 좋았어!
남	네가 제일 좋아하는 연예인이 누군데?
여	이름은 Robert Stan이야. 그는 참 친절했고 사인도 해줬어.
남	나는 그를 모르겠어. 뭐로 유명해?
여	<After Dark>라는 TV쇼의 주인공이야.
남	그거 뱀파이어에 관한 판타지물이지?
여	맞아. 난 그걸 아주 추천해.
남	난 보통 범죄물을 선호하지만, 나중에 볼게.
여	분명 네 마음에 들 거야.

해설 | 여자가 판타지물을 추천하자, 남자가 범죄물을 선호하지만 보겠다고 말했으므로 정답은 추천한 작품에 대한 확신을 나타내는 ④ 'I bet you'll like it.'이다.

선택지 해석
① 인터뷰는 잘 진행됐어. ② 그가 내게 연기를 가르쳐줬어. ③ 알겠어. 채널을 바꾸자. ④ 분명 네 마음에 들 거야. ⑤ 네가 판타지물을 좋아하는지 몰랐네.

어휘 | celebrity [səlébrəti] 연예인; 유명 인사　autograph [ɔ́ːtəgræf] 사인, 자필 서명　highly [háili] 아주, 대단히　crime [kraim] 범죄

19 적절한 응답 고르기 　　　　　정답 ⑤

W	What are you reading, Dad?
M	I just got a message. Our zip line experience was canceled. The company needs to do some repairs on it today.
W	Oh, no. What should we do instead?
M	Why don't we look around the city today? There are plenty of places to visit here.
W	Where would you like to go?
M	The traditional market looks interesting, and there's a palace. We have enough time to see both of them.
W	Should we take the bus?
M	A cab is easier. Let's find a taxi stand.
W	The sign says it's over there.

여	뭘 읽는 중이에요, 아빠?
남	방금 문자를 받았단다. 우리 집라인 체험이 취소됐구나. 업체에서 오늘 그걸 좀 수리해야 한다네.
여	오, 이런. 우리 대신 뭐 할까요?
남	오늘은 도시를 둘러보는 게 어떻겠니? 여기는 방문할 곳이 많아.
여	어디를 가고 싶으세요?
남	전통 시장이 흥미로워 보이고, 궁전도 있단다. 우린 둘 다 구경할 시간이 충분해.
여	버스를 탈까요?
남	택시가 더 편하겠어. 택시 승차장을 찾아보자.
여	그건 저쪽에 있다고 안내판에 쓰여 있어요.

해설 | 남자가 택시 승차장을 찾아보자고 했으므로 정답은 승차장의 위치를 언급하는 ⑤ 'The sign says it's over there.'이다.

선택지 해석
① 알겠어요. 저기에서 버스를 기다리면 되겠어요. ② 입장료가 없네요. ③ 집라인은 너무 높이 있어요. 전 무서워요. ④ 좀 더 빨리 운전해 주세요. 전 급해요. ⑤ 그건 저쪽에 있다고 안내판에 쓰여 있어요.

어휘 | repair [ripɛ́ər] 수리 수리하다　plenty of 많은　palace [pǽlis] 궁전　taxi stand 택시 승차장　terrified [térəfàid] 무서운

20 상황에 적절한 말 고르기 　　　　　정답 ③

M	Lisa went shopping for some new clothes at a store. Then, she left to meet her friend for a coffee. She realized at the café her phone was missing, so she returned to the store. Lisa wants to tell the store's clerk that she left her phone there. In this situation, what would Lisa most likely say to the store's clerk?
Lisa	I'm sorry, but I think I left my phone here.

남	Lisa는 새 옷을 사러 가게에 갔습니다. 그리고 나서, 그녀는 친구와 만나 커피를 마시기 위해 떠났습니다. 그녀는 카페에서 그녀의 휴대폰이 없어졌음을 깨달아서, 가게로 돌아갔습니다. Lisa는 가게 점원에게 그녀가 그곳에 휴대폰을 두고 갔다고 말하고 싶습니다. 이러한 상황에서, Lisa가 가게 점원에게 가장 할 것 같은 말은 무엇입니까?
Lisa	죄송하지만, 여기에 휴대폰을 두고 간 것 같아요.

해설 | Lisa가 가게 점원에게 휴대폰을 가게에 두고 갔다고 말하고 싶다고 했으므로 정답은 ③ 'I'm sorry, but I think I left my phone here.'이다.

선택지 해석
① 제가 원피스를 입어보다가 그걸 떨어뜨렸어요. ② 잠시 당신의 휴대폰을 쓸 수 있을까요? ③ 죄송하지만, 여기에 휴대폰을 두고 간 것 같아요. ④ 카푸치노 한 잔 주세요. ⑤ 이건 더 작은 사이즈로도 나오나요?

어휘 | missing [mísiŋ] 없어진, 실종된　clerk [kləːrk] 점원, 직원, 사무원　drop [drap] 떨어뜨리다 방울

1	③	2	③	3	③	4	④	5	②	6	⑤	7	④	8	③	9	②	10	⑤
11	⑤	12	④	13	③	14	③	15	①	16	③	17	①	18	②	19	④	20	③

---

1 알맞은 그림 고르기   정답 ③

M	Welcome to Modern Furniture. Can I help you with something?
W	Hello. I want a cabinet for my office.
M	Alright. How many drawers do you want in the cabinet? We have cabinets with either three or five drawers.
W	I don't need to store many items in the cabinet. So, I'd like a three-drawer one.
M	Okay. Then, how about this one with wheels?
W	Yeah. That looks good. The wheels would be convenient when I need to move it.
M	Right. Now, do you need one with or without handles?
W	Hmm... The one without handles looks more stylish. I'll take it.
M	Great choice! Please let me know the delivery address.

남	Modern Furniture에 오신 걸 환영합니다. 무엇을 도와드릴까요?
여	안녕하세요. 제 사무실에 둘 서랍장을 사고 싶어요.
남	그러시군요. 서랍장에 서랍은 몇 개이길 바라세요? 서랍이 3개이거나 5개인 서랍장이 있답니다.
여	서랍장에 많은 물건을 보관할 필요는 없어요. 그러니까, 3단 서랍장으로 주세요.
남	알겠습니다. 그러면, 바퀴가 달린 이건 어떠세요?
여	네, 좋아 보이네요. 서랍장을 옮겨야 할 때 바퀴가 편리할 거예요.
남	맞습니다. 이제, 손잡이가 있는 게 필요하신가요, 아니면 없는 게 필요하신가요?
여	흠... 손잡이가 없는 게 더 멋져 보이네요. 그걸로 할게요.
남	훌륭한 선택이에요! 배송 주소를 제게 알려주세요.

해설 | 여자가 바퀴가 달려 있고 손잡이는 없는 3단 서랍장을 사겠다고 했으므로 정답은 ③이다.

어휘 | cabinet [kǽbənit] 몡 서랍장, 진열장; 내각 store [stɔːr] 통 보관하다 몡 가게 address [ədrés] 몡 주소

---

2 언급하지 않은 내용 고르기   정답 ③

M	What are you reading, Amy?
W	It's an article about a new cleaning robot.
M	Oh, that sounds interesting. How is it different from older ones?
W	It can wipe the floor with a mop.
M	Oh, really? It's not a vacuum cleaner?
W	No. And it goes back to the charger when the battery's low.
M	Cool! But isn't it expensive?
W	No. It's only 160 dollars. It's cheaper than I expected.
M	Maybe I should get one.
W	Make sure to buy it soon. You can get an early bird discount until March 13th.

남	뭘 읽고 있어, Amy?
여	이건 새로운 청소 로봇에 관한 기사야.
남	오, 흥미롭게 들리는데. 옛날 거랑 어떻게 다른 거야?
여	이건 바닥을 걸레로 닦을 수 있어.
남	오, 정말? 그게 진공청소기는 아니지?
여	아니야. 그리고 배터리가 낮아지면 충전기로 돌아가.
남	멋지다! 그런데 비싸지 않아?
여	아니. 겨우 160달러야. 내가 예상했던 것보다 더 싸.
남	나도 하나 사야 할지도 모르겠는걸.
여	꼭 빨리 사. 3월 13일까지는 얼리버드 할인을 받을 수 있어.

해설 | ① 기능(바닥을 걸레로 닦음), ② 충전 방식(배터리가 낮아지면 충전기로 돌아감), ④ 가격(160달러), ⑤ 할인 정보(3월 13일까지 얼리버드 할인)에 대해 언급했으므로 정답은 ③ '출시일'이다.

어휘 | wipe [waip] 통 닦다 vacuum cleaner 진공청소기 charger [tʃɑ́ːrdʒər] 몡 충전기 early bird discount 얼리버드 할인(조기 구매 시 제공되는 할인)

3 목적 고르기

정답 ③

[Telephone rings.]

M Hello. Erikson Flower Shop.

W Hi. I bought a cactus from your shop a few days ago, and I wanted to ask a question about it.

M Oh, hi. You bought the one with little flowers, didn't you?

W Yeah, that's right. How often do I have to water it again?

M Once a month. But do not soak the soil. A cactus can easily die because of too much water.

W Okay. Thank you.

M No problem.

[전화기가 울린다.]

남 안녕하세요. Erikson Flower Shop입니다.

여 안녕하세요. 며칠 전에 당신의 가게에서 선인장을 샀는데, 그것에 관해 질문을 드리고 싶어요.

남 오, 안녕하세요. 작은 꽃이 핀 걸로 사 가셨죠, 그렇지 않나요?

여 네, 맞아요. 제가 물을 얼마나 자주 다시 줘야 하나요?

남 한 달에 한 번이요. 하지만 흙을 흠뻑 적시지 마세요. 선인장은 물을 너무 많이 주면 쉽게 죽어요.

여 알겠습니다. 고마워요.

남 천만에요.

해설 | 여자가 선인장에 관해 질문을 하고 싶다고 한 후 물을 얼마나 자주 줘야 하는지 물었으므로 정답은 ③ '물 주는 법을 문의하려고'이다.

어휘 | cactus [kǽktəs] 명 선인장 water [wɔ́:tər] 통 물을 주다 명 물 soak [souk] 통 (흠뻑) 적시다

4 시간 정보 고르기

정답 ④

M Sally, did you finish decorating your house for Christmas?

W Not yet. Can you give me a hand?

M No problem. I'll be free this Sunday.

W Great. Could you come to my house at 11 a.m.?

M I have to go to church. I should be finished by 1 p.m.

W Why don't you come at 3? We'll be done around 5, and then I'll treat you to dinner.

M Okay. See you then.

남 Sally, 너 크리스마스 맞이 집 꾸미기는 끝냈니?

여 아직. 네가 날 도와줄 수 있을까?

남 문제없지. 난 이번 주 일요일에 한가할 거야.

여 잘됐다. 우리 집에 오전 11시에 올 수 있어?

남 난 교회에 가야 해. 오후 1시에는 끝날 거야.

여 3시에 오는 건 어때? 5시에 정도에 마치면, 저녁 대접할게.

남 알겠어. 그때 보자.

해설 | 여자가 3시에 집으로 오라고 제안하자 남자가 알겠다고 했으므로 정답은 ④ '3 p.m.'이다.

어휘 | decorate [dékərèit] 통 꾸미다, 장식하다 give ~ a hand ~를 도와주다 church [tʃəːrtʃ] 명 교회 treat A to B A에게 B를 대접하다

5 심정 고르기

정답 ②

M Hi, Cathy. How are you doing?

W I'm fine, thanks. Did you see the ice hockey game last night?

M Of course. It was the big match between the United States and Canada.

W Then, you saw the moment the player scored the winning goal, right?

M Sure. David Wood did it! He's an amazing player.

W Actually, that's my brother.

M Wow! Now I understand why you are all smiles.

W Yeah. I'm so happy that he did well in the game.

남 안녕, Cathy. 잘 지내고 있니?

여 잘 지내지, 고마워. 너 어젯밤에 아이스하키 경기 봤어?

남 당연하지. 미국과 캐나다 간의 큰 경기였잖아.

여 그러면, 선수가 우승골을 득점한 순간도 봤겠네, 맞지?

남 물론이지. David Wood가 득점했잖아! 그는 정말 대단한 선수야.

여 사실, 그 선수가 내 오빠야.

남 우와! 난 이제야 네가 왜 아주 행복해 보이는지 이해가 된다.

여 응. 난 오빠가 경기에서 잘해서 너무 기뻐.

해설 | 여자가 자신의 오빠가 아이스하키 경기에서 활약한 것을 두고 기쁘다고 했으므로 정답은 ② 'proud'이다.

선택지 해석

① 속상한 ② 자랑스러운 ③ 평화로운 ④ 부끄러운 ⑤ 우울한

어휘 | score [skɔːr] 통 득점하다 명 득점 be all smiles 아주 행복해 보이다, 희색이 만면하다 ashamed [əʃéimd] 형 부끄러운 depressed [diprést] 형 우울한

① M   I don't see any empty parking spaces.

W   There is one over there!

② M   Thank you for buying me tea.

W   It was my pleasure.

③ M   Do you need a receipt?

W   No. That won't be necessary.

④ M   How is your food?

W   It's a little salty, actually.

⑤ M   Are you ready to order?

W   Yes. I'll have a hamburger, please.

① 남   빈 주차 공간이 하나도 안 보이네.

여   저쪽에 하나 있어!

② 남   차 사줘서 고마워.

여   천만에.

③ 남   영수증 필요하세요?

여   아니요. 필요 없을 것 같아요.

④ 남   음식은 어떠세요?

여   실은, 약간 짜요.

⑤ 남   주문하시겠어요?

여   네. 햄버거 하나 주세요.

해설 | 메뉴판을 들고 있는 여자에게 식당의 직원으로 보이는 남자가 말을 걸고 있는 상황이므로 정답은 ⑤이다.

어휘 | parking space 주차 공간   salty [sɔ́ːlti] 형 짠

W   What did you do for your birthday, Max?

M   I stayed in a nice hotel with my parents.

W   That sounds lovely.

M   Yeah. We had fun at the pool and ate lots of steak.

W   Did you get any presents?

M   Actually, my parents got me this smartphone.

W   Wow! I really want that phone. Can you tell me what its best features are?

M   Sure. It takes great photographs. I recommend buying it.

여   생일에 뭐 했어, Max?

남   부모님이랑 근사한 호텔에 묵었어.

여   즐거웠겠다.

남   응. 수영장에서 재미있게 놀았고 스테이크를 많이 먹었어.

여   선물은 받았니?

남   사실, 우리 부모님이 이 스마트폰을 사 주셨어.

여   우와! 나 진짜 이 휴대폰을 갖고 싶었는데. 가장 좋은 특징이 뭔지 말해줄래?

남   물론이지. 그건 사진이 엄청 잘 찍혀. 사는 걸 추천할게.

해설 | 여자가 남자에게 스마트폰의 가장 좋은 특징이 무엇인지 말해 달라고 부탁했으므로 정답은 ④ '휴대폰 장점 설명하기'이다.

어휘 | lovely [lʌ́vli] 형 즐거운; 사랑스러운   feature [fíːtʃər] 명 특징

M   This is an announcement for supporters of The Friendly Dog Shelter. From this Tuesday, we will start a new program called Walk and Play. Every Tuesday and Thursday from 12 to 5 p.m., people will have the chance to walk and interact with our shelter dogs. Our goal is to socialize our dogs and introduce them to potential new owners. Everyone must apply to take part beforehand on our website, www.friendlydog.com. Children under 12 are not allowed to participate. As always, thank you for your help.

남   The Friendly Dog Shelter의 후원자 여러분들에게 드리는 공지입니다. 이번 주 화요일부터, 저희는 Walk and Play라고 불리는 새로운 프로그램을 시작할 것입니다. 매주 화요일과 목요일 오후 12시부터 5시까지, 여러분은 저희 보호소의 유기견들과 산책하고 교류할 기회를 가질 것입니다. 저희의 목표는 유기견을 사회화해서 잠재적 새 주인에게 소개하는 것입니다. 참여하기 위해서는 반드시 저희 웹사이트 www.friendlydog.com에서 미리 신청하셔야 합니다. 12살 이하의 어린이들은 참여할 수 없습니다. 늘 그랬듯이, 도와주셔서 감사합니다.

해설 | ① 이름(Walk and Play), ② 진행 시간(화요일과 목요일 오후 12시부터 5시까지), ④ 목적(유기견을 사회화해서 잠재적 새 주인에게 소개하기), ⑤ 제한 사항(12살 이하 어린이는 참여 불가)에 대해 언급했으므로 정답은 ③ '진행 절차'이다.

어휘 | interact [íntərækt] 동 교류하다   socialize [sóuʃəlaiz] 동 사회화하다   potential [pəténʃəl] 형 잠재적인   take part 참여하다
beforehand [bifɔ́ːrhænd] 부 미리

9 화제 고르기   정답 ②

M This is a device used in places like concert halls and auditoriums. It usually has a long handle with a circular part at the top of it. People speak into the circular part to make their voices louder. For example, people speak into this so that a large audience can hear them. They just press a button to turn it on. With this, people can also record their voices.

남 이것은 콘서트홀과 강당 같은 곳에서 사용되는 장치입니다. 이것은 보통 긴 손잡이가 있고 그 위에 둥근 부분이 있습니다. 사람들은 목소리를 더 크게 내기 위해 그 둥근 부분에 대고 말을 합니다. 예를 들어, 사람들은 많은 청중이 들을 수 있도록 이것에 대고 말을 합니다. 이것을 켜기 위해서는 단순히 버튼을 누르기만 하면 됩니다. 이것을 가지고, 사람들은 또한 목소리를 녹음할 수도 있습니다.

해설 | 이것은 긴 손잡이와 그 위에 둥근 부분이 있으며, 사람들은 둥근 부분에 말을 해서 목소리를 더 크게 낼 수 있다고 했으므로 정답은 ② '마이크'이다.

어휘 | device [diváis] 명 장치   auditorium [ɔ̀ːditɔ́ːriəm] 명 강당; 관객석   circular [sə́ːrkjulər] 형 둥근, 원형의   audience [ɔ́ːdiəns] 명 청중

10 어색한 대화 고르기   정답 ⑤

① W What did you do in art class today?
　 M Our teacher showed us how to draw birds.
② W Hi. Can I return this shirt I bought last week?
　 M Yes. Just give me the receipt, please.
③ W How long will you stay at the hotel?
　 M I will be there for two nights.
④ W Hi. Can you send someone to fix my sink?
　 M Sure. Please describe the details.
⑤ W What time will you arrive home after school?
　 M We met in the morning.

① 여 오늘 미술 시간에 뭐 했니?
　 남 저희 선생님께서 새를 그리는 방법을 알려주셨어요.
② 여 안녕하세요. 지난주에 산 이 셔츠를 반품할 수 있을까요?
　 남 네. 영수증만 저에게 주세요.
③ 여 호텔에서 며칠이나 묵으실 거예요?
　 남 이틀 밤을 지낼 거예요.
④ 여 안녕하세요. 싱크대를 고쳐줄 사람을 보내주실래요?
　 남 물론이죠. 자세한 내용을 설명해주세요.
⑤ 여 학교 끝나고 집에 몇 시에 도착할 것 같니?
　 남 저희는 아침에 만났어요.

해설 | 여자가 남자에게 집에 몇 시에 도착할지를 물었으므로 남자는 귀가 시간을 말해야 한다. 그러나 남자가 아침에 만났다는 어색한 대답을 했으므로 정답은 ⑤이다.

어휘 | sink [siŋk] 명 싱크대, 개수대   describe [diskráib] 동 설명하다, 묘사하다   detail [ditéil] 명 자세한 내용, 세부 사항

11 할 일 고르기   정답 ⑤

M Are you going to Anna's costume party?
W Yes, I am.
M I'm very excited. There's a prize for the person with the best costume.
W I still don't know which costume to wear.
M Did you look at costumes online?
W Yes. But I want to just make one at home. What will you dress up as?
M I'll wear a pirate costume. I have a fake bird and an eye patch.
W That will look great.
M Yes. I hope to win the costume contest.

남 Anna의 코스튬 파티에 갈 거니?
여 응, 갈 거야.
남 너무 기대돼. 최고의 의상을 입은 사람에게는 상품도 있어.
여 난 아직 어떤 의상을 입어야 할지 모르겠어.
남 온라인으로 의상을 살펴봤어?
여 응. 그런데 그냥 집에서 하나 만들고 싶어. 넌 뭐로 분장할 거야?
남 난 해적 의상을 입을 거야. 가짜 새랑 안대도 있어.
여 그거 멋있어 보이겠다.
남 응. 난 코스튬 대회에서 우승하고 싶어.

해설 | 남자가 코스튬 파티에서 해적 의상을 입을 것이라고 했으므로 정답은 ⑤ '해적 옷 입기'이다.

어휘 | dress up as ~으로 분장하다, ~의 복장을 하다   pirate [páiərət] 명 해적   fake [feik] 형 가짜의 동 날조하다   eye patch 안대

12 위치 고르기
정답 ④

M	Welcome to Tote's Bookstore. How can I help you?
W	I'm looking for a novel. Could you tell me where the mystery section is?
M	It's between the science fiction and children's sections.
W	Thank you. [Pause] Could you help me find the book? I don't see it at the mystery's section.
M	What's the title of the book?
W	It's *Into the Shadows*.
M	Oh! You can find it at the best-seller section.
W	Where's that section?
M	It's between the new arrivals and the children's section.
W	Thanks again.

남	Tote's Bookstore에 오신 걸 환영합니다. 무엇을 도와드릴까요?
여	소설을 찾고 있어요. 추리소설 코너가 어디인지 알려주시겠어요?
남	그건 공상과학소설 코너와 아동 코너 사이에 있어요.
여	감사합니다. [잠시 멈춤] 제가 책 찾는 걸 도와주시겠어요? 추리소설 코너에서 그게 안 보여요.
남	책 제목이 뭔가요?
여	<Into the Shadows>예요.
남	오! 그건 베스트셀러 코너에서 찾으실 수 있어요.
여	그건 어디에 있나요?
남	신간 코너와 아동 코너 사이에 있어요.
여	다시 한번 감사드려요.

해설 | 여자가 찾고 있는 책은 신간 코너와 아동 코너 사이에 있는 베스트셀러 코너에 있다고 했으므로 정답은 ④이다.

어휘 | novel [návəl] 몡 소설 mystery [místəri] 몡 추리소설; 미스터리, 불가사의 science fiction 공상과학소설 new arrival 신간, 신착품

13 시간 정보 고르기
정답 ③

W	Do you want to go with me to the shopping mall this weekend, Charlie?
M	Yeah. I need to buy a few things. When do you want to go?
W	Can you meet at 9 a.m. on Sunday?
M	Oh, I don't know. That's very early. How about 11 instead?
W	Well, my favorite store opens before that, and I want to get there early.
M	Then, is 10 o'clock alright?
W	That should be fine. I'll meet you there then.

여	나랑 같이 이번 주말에 쇼핑몰 갈래, Charlie?
남	그래. 나 사야 할 게 몇 개 있어. 언제 가고 싶어?
여	일요일 오전 9시에 만날 수 있어?
남	오, 잘 모르겠어. 너무 일러. 대신 11시는 어때?
여	글쎄, 내가 가장 좋아하는 가게가 그전에 문을 열어서, 난 거기에 일찍 가고 싶어.
남	그러면, 10시는 괜찮니?
여	괜찮을 거야. 그때 거기서 만나자.

해설 | 남자가 10시에 만나는 것이 괜찮을지 묻자 여자가 괜찮을 것이라고 했으므로 정답은 ③ '10 a.m.'이다.

어휘 | weekend [wíːkend] 몡 주말 a few 몇의, 몇몇의

14 한일 고르기
정답 ③

M	I didn't see you during the winter vacation, Caroline. Did you go skiing?
W	No, I didn't. I was abroad for the vacation.
M	Really? Where were you?
W	I was in Australia, so it was really hot outside. We stayed with my dad's family.
M	That's amazing. What did you do there?
W	I took surfing lessons. It was a great way to spend the vacation.
M	You must have had a lot of fun.
W	I did. I hope to go back.

남	겨울 방학 동안 너를 못 만났어, Caroline. 스키 타러 갔었니?
여	아니, 안 갔어. 난 방학 동안 해외에 있었어.
남	정말? 어디에 있었는데?
여	호주에 있어서, 밖이 정말 더웠어. 우린 친가 쪽 식구들이랑 지냈어.
남	정말 멋있다. 거기에서 뭐 했어?
여	서핑 수업을 들었어. 방학을 보내기에 좋은 방법이었어.
남	분명 엄청 재미있었겠다.
여	그랬지. 다시 가고 싶어.

해설 | 여자가 겨울 방학에 호주에서 서핑 수업을 들었다고 했으므로 정답은 ③ '서핑 수업 듣기'이다.

어휘 | abroad [əbrɔ́ːd] 뿐 해외로, 국외로 Australia [ɔːstréiljə] 몡 호주, 오스트레일리아

15 목적 고르기

정답 ①

W Good afternoon, listeners. This is Lora Willis with tips for dealing with modern technology. Today, I want to talk about protecting your personal data. Just follow a few simple rules, and you'll keep your information safe. You won't need any special software for this. First, make sure to change your passwords often. Once a month should be fine. Secondly, use different passwords for every site. Finally, don't ever share your login information with others. I hope you follow these tips to protect your personal data.

여 안녕하세요, 청취자 여러분. 저는 현대 기술을 다룰 방법을 가지고 온 Lora Willis입니다. 오늘, 저는 여러분의 개인 정보를 보호하는 것에 관해 이야기하고자 합니다. 단순히 몇 가지 간단한 수칙만 따르면, 여러분의 정보를 안전하게 지킬 수 있습니다. 이것엔 어떤 특별한 소프트웨어도 필요하지 않습니다. 먼저, 여러분의 비밀번호를 반드시 자주 바꾸세요. 한 달에 한 번이 좋겠습니다. 둘째로, 모든 사이트마다 다른 비밀번호를 사용하세요. 마지막으로, 여러분의 로그인 정보를 다른 사람들과 공유하지 마세요. 여러분이 이 방법을 지켜서 여러분의 개인 정보를 보호하시길 바랍니다.

해설 | 여자가 청취자들에게 개인 정보를 보호하는 방법을 설명해주고 있으므로 정답은 ①이다.

어휘 | deal with 다루다 technology [teknάlədʒi] 몡 기술 personal date 개인 정보 password [pǽswərd] 몡 비밀번호, 암호

16 금액 정보 고르기

정답 ③

M Hello, and welcome to The Travel Gift Shop. How may I help you?
W I'd like to buy some postcards for my friends. How much are they?
M These hand-painted postcards are seven dollars each, and the photograph postcards are five dollars each.
W I love the hand-painted ones.
M Okay. If you buy two, then we will give you a third one for free.
W That's amazing! I'll take two hand-painted postcards.
M Great. I'll help you pay at the counter.

남 안녕하세요, The Travel Gift Shop에 오신 걸 환영합니다. 무엇을 도와드릴까요?
여 친구들에게 줄 엽서를 몇 장 사고 싶어요. 얼마죠?
남 이 손으로 그린 그림이 있는 엽서는 한 장에 7달러이고, 사진엽서는 한 장에 5달러예요.
여 전 손으로 그린 그림이 있는 게 마음에 들어요.
남 알겠습니다. 손님이 두 장을 사시면, 한 장을 더 무료로 드릴게요.
여 굉장해요! 손으로 그린 그림이 있는 엽서를 두 장 살게요.
남 좋습니다. 계산대에서 계산을 도와드릴게요.

해설 | 여자가 한 장에 7달러인 손으로 그린 그림이 있는 엽서를 두 장 사겠다고 했으므로 정답은 ③ '$ 14'이다.

어휘 | postcard [póustkard] 몡 엽서 hand-painted 혱 손으로 그린 counter [káuntər] 몡 계산대, 카운터

17 적절한 응답 고르기

정답 ①

W Your dad is almost done with lunch, Tom.
M Great! I'm so hungry. What did he make?
W He made noodles with vegetables.
M That sounds delicious. But can I eat it in my room?
W Why? Are you busy?
M I need to do some homework. It's taking a long time.
W Alright. You can eat your lunch in your room then.
M Also, can I borrow Dad's laptop? Mine is so slow.
W Yes. But be careful with it.
M No problem. I promise I will.

여 네 아빠가 점심을 거의 다 차리셨단다, Tom.
남 잘됐네요! 저 정말 배고파요. 아빠가 뭘 만드셨어요?
여 야채 국수를 만들었단다.
남 맛있을 거 같아요. 그런데 저 제 방에서 먹어도 될까요?
여 왜? 바쁘니?
남 숙제를 좀 해야 해서요. 시간이 오래 걸리고 있거든요.
여 알겠다. 그러면 방에서 점심을 먹으렴.
남 그리고, 아빠 노트북을 빌려도 될까요? 제 것은 너무 느려요.
여 그래. 그렇지만 조심히 다루렴.
남 당연하죠. 그러겠다고 약속할게요.

해설 | 여자가 노트북을 빌려 달라는 남자의 부탁을 수락하면서도 조심히 다룰 것을 당부했으므로 정답은 당부를 지키겠다고 약속하는 ① 'No problem. I promise I will.'이다.

선택지 해석
① 당연하죠. 그러겠다고 약속할게요. ② 아니요. 저는 당근을 좋아하지 않아요. ③ 죄송하지만, 점심 준비가 아직 안 됐어요.
④ 물론이죠. 제가 노트북을 수리점에 가져갈게요. ⑤ 네. 숙제는 내일까지예요.

어휘 | careful [kéərfəl] 혱 조심하는 promise [prάmis] 동 약속하다

18 적절한 응답 고르기 정답 ②

W	What are you looking at, Dahoon?
M	I found some nice headphones over here. Do you like them?
W	Wow, those are the ones I want too.
M	I think these are the only ones left.
W	You should buy them then. I'll get them later.
M	But didn't your headphones break?
W	Yes. They broke at school last week.
M	Then, you should have them. I will order the same ones online.
W	You're so nice. I'll return the favor.

여	뭘 보고 있니, 다훈아?
남	이쪽에서 근사한 헤드폰을 발견했어. 마음에 드니?
여	우와, 이건 나도 갖고 싶은 거야.
남	이것만 남아 있는 것 같아.
여	그러면 넌 이걸 사도록 해. 난 나중에 살게.
남	그런데 네 헤드폰 고장 나지 않았어?
여	맞아. 지난주에 학교에서 고장 났어.
남	그러면, 네가 이걸 갖도록 해. 난 같은 걸 온라인으로 주문할게.
여	정말 친절하구나. 내가 보답할게.

해설 | 남자가 하나 남은 헤드폰을 양보하겠다고 했으므로 정답은 양보에 감사하는 ② 'You're so nice. I'll return the favor.'이다.

선택지 해석
① 죄송합니다. 이 헤드폰을 못 고치겠어요. ② 정말 친절하구나. 내가 보답할게. ③ 더 많은 정보를 원하신다면 저희 웹사이트를 방문해 주세요. ④ 어디에서도 내 지갑을 못 찾겠어. ⑤ 아니, 괜찮아. 난 이미 새 걸 주문했어.

어휘 | headphones [hǽdfounz] 몡 헤드폰 break [breik] 동 고장 나다; 깨다, 부수다 return a favor 보답하다, 은혜를 갚다 wallet [wálit] 몡 지갑

19 적절한 응답 고르기 정답 ④

W	I don't think we can swim tomorrow, Richard.
M	Oh, why not?
W	The weather report says that it will rain a lot.
M	Really? That's a shame. I was excited to go to the outdoor pool.
W	Me too. But we can do something else.
M	Do you have any ideas?
W	There's a new exhibit at the history museum. It just opened.
M	That might be interesting. What's the exhibit about?
W	Its main theme is the Second World War.

여	내일 수영 못 할 것 같아, Richard.
남	오, 왜 못 하는데?
여	일기예보에서 비가 많이 올 거래.
남	진짜? 아쉽다. 난 야외 수영장 가는 걸 기대했었거든.
여	나도 그래. 하지만 우린 다른 걸 할 수도 있어.
남	무슨 아이디어 있어?
여	역사박물관에 새 전시회가 있어. 막 열린 거야.
남	재미있을지도 모르겠네. 뭐에 관한 전시야?
여	주요 주제는 2차 세계대전이야.

해설 | 남자가 역사박물관의 새 전시회가 무엇에 관한 것인지 물었으므로 정답은 전시회의 주제를 언급하는 ④ 'Its main theme is the Second World War.'이다.

선택지 해석
① 편의점에서 우산 사면 돼. ② 수영장에서는 수영모를 착용해 주십시오. ③ 많은 예술가가 그 전시회에 참여했어. ④ 주요 주제는 2차 세계대전이야. ⑤ 역사 수업에서 이제 그것에 대해 배울 거야.

어휘 | weather report 일기예보 outdoor [áutdɔ̀:r] 혱 야외의 theme [θi:m] 몡 주제 convenience store 편의점

20 상황에 적절한 말 고르기 정답 ③

M	Aria is leaving for her trip to Mexico. When it is time for her to board the plane, she notices that a man is sitting in her seat. Aria booked the window seat so that she could enjoy the view during the flight. So, she wants to tell the man that he is sitting in her seat. In this situation, what would Aria most likely say to the man?
Aria	Excuse me, I think you are in my seat.

남	Aria는 멕시코로 여행을 떠나려 합니다. 그녀가 비행기에 탑승할 시간이 되었을 때, 그녀는 한 남자가 그녀의 자리에 앉아 있는 것을 알아차립니다. Aria는 비행 중 경치를 즐길 수 있도록 창가 자리를 예약했습니다. 그래서, 그녀는 남자에게 그가 그녀의 자리에 앉아 있다고 말하고 싶습니다. 이러한 상황에서, Aria가 남자에게 가장 할 것 같은 말은 무엇입니까?
Aria	실례합니다, 제 자리에 앉아 계신 것 같아요.

해설 | Aria가 남자에게 그가 그녀의 자리에 앉아 있다고 말하고 싶다고 했으므로 정답은 ③ 'I think you are in my seat.'이다.

선택지 해석
① 저랑 자리 바꿔실래요? ② 비행기가 왜 지연됐는지 아세요? ③ 제 자리에 앉아 계신 것 같아요. ④ 택시 타고 공항에 가야 해요. ⑤ 창문 좀 열어도 괜찮을까요?

어휘 | notice [nótis] 동 알아차리다 몡 주의 change seats with ~와 자리를 바꾸다

| 1 | ③ | 2 | ④ | 3 | ④ | 4 | ③ | 5 | ① | 6 | ④ | 7 | ⑤ | 8 | ④ | 9 | ① | 10 | ③ |
| 11 | ① | 12 | ③ | 13 | ③ | 14 | ③ | 15 | ② | 16 | ④ | 17 | ④ | 18 | ② | 19 | ② | 20 | ① |

---

1 알맞은 그림 고르기

정답 ③

W Hi. I heard your store has lots of fashionable bed covers.

M It was nice of you to come here. What size bed cover do you need?

W I need one for a queen-size bed.

M Then, you can choose from these. How about this one with a leaf pattern?

W It looks cozy, but could you show me some other designs?

M No problem. We also have these designs with a sea theme. The whale, turtle, and starfish are all popular.

W Oh, I like the one with the whale on it. I'll take it.

여 안녕하세요. 이 가게에 최신 유행하는 침대 커버가 많다고 들었어요.

남 여기 와주시다니 감사합니다. 어떤 사이즈의 침대 커버가 필요하세요?

여 퀸사이즈 침대에 맞는 것이 필요해요.

남 그럼, 이것들 중에서 고르실 수 있어요. 잎사귀 무늬가 있는 이것은 어떠세요?

여 포근해 보이긴 한데, 다른 디자인도 보여주실 수 있나요?

남 그럼요. 저희는 바다를 주제로 한 디자인도 있어요. 고래, 거북이, 불가사리가 모두 인기 있어요.

여 오, 고래가 있는 것이 맘에 드네요. 그걸로 할게요.

해설 | 여자가 고래가 있는 이불이 마음에 든다고 했으므로 정답은 ③이다.

어휘 | fashionable [fǽʃənəbl] 혱 최신 유행의   cozy [kóuzi] 혱 포근한, 아늑한   starfish [stάːrfiʃ] 몡 불가사리

---

2 언급하지 않은 내용 고르기

정답 ④

W Brian, do you need any more art supplies for your school art project?

M Yeah. I need some green and brown paint. Also, I need another paint brush.

W What is the assignment?

M I have to make a painting with only four colors. I'm going to paint a forest.

W Oh, that's interesting. And when is it due?

M Next Friday.

W Then, let's go to the art supply store now.

M Sure!

여 Brian, 학교 미술 숙제를 하는 데 필요한 미술용품이 더 있니?

남 응. 초록색과 갈색 물감이 좀 필요해. 그리고, 붓도 하나 더 필요해.

여 과제가 뭔데?

남 네 개의 색깔만 사용해서 그림을 그려야 해. 나는 숲을 그릴 거야.

여 오, 흥미롭다. 그럼 언제까지 해야 하니?

남 다음 주 금요일.

여 그럼, 지금 미술용품점에 가자.

남 그래!

해설 | ① 추가 재료(초록색과 갈색 물감, 붓), ② 색상 개수(4개), ③ 그림 대상(숲), ⑤ 마감일(다음 주 금요일)에 대해 언급했으므로 정답은 ④ '크기'이다.

어휘 | art supplies 미술용품   assignment [əsáinmənt] 몡 과제   forest [fɔ́ːrist] 몡 숲

3 목적 고르기   정답 ④

[Telephone rings.]

W   Hello, Best Fit Clothing Store. How can I help you?

M   Hi. I just received some shirts from your shop in the mail, but they are not the ones I ordered.

W   I apologize for that. Would you like a refund?

M   No. I still want the other shirts.

W   Okay. You can ship them back to us for free. Then, we will send you the new shirts.

M   How long will that process take?

W   It should only take a week.

M   That's fine then.

[전화기가 울린다.]

여   안녕하세요, Best Fit Clothing Store입니다. 무엇을 도와드릴까요?

남   안녕하세요. 방금 당신의 가게에서 셔츠 몇 장을 택배로 받아보았는데, 제가 주문했던 것들이 아니네요.

여   그건 사과드리겠습니다. 환불을 원하시나요?

남   아니요. 저는 여전히 다른 셔츠가 필요해요.

여   알겠습니다. 저희에게 무료로 되돌려 보내실 수 있어요. 그러면, 저희가 새 셔츠를 보내드리겠습니다.

남   이 과정이 얼마나 걸릴까요?

여   겨우 일주일 걸릴 거예요.

남   그럼 괜찮아요.

해설 | 남자가 택배로 받은 셔츠가 자신이 주문했던 것이 아니라고 한 후 다른 셔츠가 필요하다고 했으므로 정답은 ④ '오배송 문제를 해결하려고'이다.

어휘 | receive [risíːv] 图 받다   ship [ʃip] 图 보내다 圑 선박   process [práses] 圑 과정, 절차

4 시간 정보 고르기   정답 ③

M   Has the bus for Preston left already?

W   Yes. It departed at 1 p.m. You missed it by 30 minutes.

M   I see. Is there another one at 2?

W   Unfortunately, no. But there is one at 3 p.m.

M   I have an appointment in Preston at 5. Will I get there in time?

W   I think so. You will arrive there at 4 p.m.

M   I'll get the ticket for the 3 p.m. bus then.

W   Okay. That will be 15 dollars.

남   프레스턴으로 가는 버스는 이미 떠났나요?

여   네. 오후 1시에 출발했어요. 30분 차이로 놓치셨네요.

남   그렇군요. 2시에 또 한 대 있나요?

여   안타깝게도, 없어요. 그렇지만 오후 3시에는 있습니다.

남   제가 프레스턴에서 5시에 약속이 있어요. 제시간에 도착할 수 있을까요?

여   그럴 것 같아요. 오후 4시에 도착하실 거예요.

남   그럼 오후 3시 버스표를 살게요.

여   네. 15달러 되겠습니다.

해설 | 남자가 오후 3시 버스표를 사겠다고 했으므로 정답은 ③ '3 p.m.'이다.

어휘 | depart [dipáːrt] 图 출발하다, 떠나다   unfortunately [ənfɔ́rtʃənətli] 图 안타깝게도, 불행하게도   in time 제시간에

5 심정 고르기   정답 ①

W   Jake, you're in a good mood today.

M   Yeah. You know I sent my song to my favorite singer.

W   Did you get an answer from him?

M   Yes. He said he wants to include my song on his next album.

W   Congratulations! I'm happy to hear that.

M   It's like I'm walking on air.

W   You must feel great.

M   Yeah. I couldn't be better.

여   Jake, 오늘 기분이 좋네.

남   맞아. 내가 가장 좋아하는 가수에게 내 노래를 보냈었잖아.

여   그에게 답장받았어?

남   응. 자기의 다음 앨범에 내 노래를 넣고 싶대.

여   축하해! 너무 잘 됐다.

남   마치 하늘을 나는 기분이야.

여   정말 기분 좋겠다.

남   응. 이보다 더 좋을 순 없을 거야.

해설 | 남자가 자신의 노래가 좋아하는 가수의 앨범에 들어가게 되어 기분이 이보다 더 좋을 수는 없을 것이라고 했으므로 정답은 ① 'excited'이다.

> 선택지 해석
>
> ① 신난   ② 편안한   ③ 질투하는   ④ 슬픈   ⑤ 실망스러운

어휘 | mood [muːd] 圑 기분   include [inklúːd] 图 넣다, 포함하다   sorrowful [sárəfəl] 톙 슬픈

6 그림 상황에 적절한 대화 고르기 　정답 ④

① W Did you make a reservation?

　M Yeah. I booked a table for two.

② W How far is the beach from here?

　M It's about a 10-minute drive.

③ W What's the weather like?

　M It's starting to rain.

④ W Do you want to go for a swim?

　M No. I want to finish reading this chapter.

⑤ W Is there a problem?

　M Yeah. The umbrella's broken.

① 여 예약했어?

　남 응. 2인 자리를 예약했어.

② 여 여기서 해변이 얼마나 멀어?

　남 차로 약 10분 거리야.

③ 여 날씨가 어때?

　남 비가 오기 시작했어.

④ 여 수영하러 갈래?

　남 아니. 이 챕터까지 다 읽을래.

⑤ 여 문제가 있어?

　남 응. 우산이 고장 났어.

해설 | 바닷가에서 책을 읽고 있는 남자에게 여자가 수영하러 갈지 묻고 있는 상황이므로 정답은 ④이다.

어휘 | broken [bróukən] 형 고장 난

7 부탁·요청한 일 고르기 　정답 ⑤

M Alright. We're going to Paris, Honey! I just booked the flights.

W I'm so excited! What are the exact dates for the trip?

M We leave on March 13th and return home on March 27th.

W Excellent. We have a lot to do before then.

M Yes. I'll start looking at tours and activities.

W Good thinking. There will be so many options to choose from.

M Can you look at hotels? We should reserve a room soon.

W I'll start looking now.

남 좋아. 우리 파리에 가는 거야, 여보! 방금 비행기 예약했어.

여 너무 신난다! 정확한 여행 날짜가 어떻게 돼?

남 우리는 3월 13일에 떠나서 3월 27일에 집에 돌아와.

여 훌륭해. 그 전에 우리 해야 할 일이 많네.

남 맞아. 나는 투어 프로그램과 활동들을 찾아보기 시작할게.

여 좋은 생각이야. 고를 수 있는 선택지가 너무 많을 거야.

남 당신은 호텔을 찾아봐 줄 수 있어? 빨리 객실을 예약해야 해.

여 지금 찾아보기 시작할게.

해설 | 남자가 여자에게 호텔을 찾아봐 달라고 부탁했으므로 정답은 ⑤ '머무를 호텔 찾아보기'이다.

어휘 | exact [igzǽkt] 형 정확한　return [ritə́:rn] 통 돌아오다　reserve [rizə́:rv] 통 예약하다

8 언급하지 않은 내용 고르기 　정답 ④

M Good afternoon. We are here to celebrate the completion of the new library. At this location, we started building the Fairview Library 12 months ago. It will open next week, at the beginning of the new year. The new five-story building will have new study spaces and thousands of books. There will also be electronic versions of textbooks and a children's literature collection. The library will also have a café with a beautiful garden where visitors can take a break from time to time. Thank you for making this possible, everyone.

남 안녕하세요. 우리는 새 도서관의 완공을 축하하기 위해 여기 모였습니다. 이곳에서, 우리는 12개월 전에 페어뷰 도서관을 짓기 시작했습니다. 도서관은 새해의 시작인 다음 주에 개관합니다. 5층짜리 새 건물에는 새로운 학습 공간과 수천 권의 장서가 있을 예정입니다. 또한 전자판 교과서와 아동 문학 모음집도 있을 것입니다. 이 도서관에는 방문객들이 때때로 휴식을 취할 수 있는 아름다운 정원이 딸린 카페도 있겠습니다. 이것을 가능하게 만들어주셔서 감사합니다, 여러분.

해설 | ① 공사 기간(12개월), ② 개관 시기(다음 주), ③ 층수(5층), ⑤ 시설(새로운 학습 공간과 정원이 딸린 카페)에 대해 언급했으므로 정답은 ④ '이용 자격'이다.

어휘 | celebrate [séləbrèit] 통 축하하다　completion [kəmplíːʃən] 명 완공; 완성　story [stɔ́ːri] 명 (건물의) 층; 이야기　electronic [ilektránik] 형 전자의　literature [lítərətʃər] 명 문학　from time to time 때때로, 가끔

9 화제 고르기 　정답 ①

W This is a public place of government. Many kinds of decisions based on laws are made in this place. Judges and lawyers work here. People go to this place to settle their disputes with other people in trials. When a person commits a crime, they visit this place to learn about their punishment.

여 이곳은 정부에 속한 공공장소입니다. 법에 기반한 많은 종류의 결정들이 이 장소에서 내려집니다. 판사들과 변호사들이 여기에서 일합니다. 사람들은 재판에서 다른 사람과의 분쟁을 해결하기 위해 이 장소에 갑니다. 어떤 사람이 범죄를 저지르면, 그들은 처벌을 알기 위해 이 장소를 방문합니다.

해설 | 법에 기반한 많은 종류의 결정들이 이 장소에서 내려지고, 판사들과 변호사들이 여기에서 일한다고 했으므로 정답은 ① '법원'이다.

어휘 | public place 공공장소　government [gʌ́vərnmənt] 명 정부　based on ~에 기반한　settle [sétl] 통 해결하다　dispute [dispjúːt] 명 분쟁　trial [tráiəl] 명 재판　commit a crime 범죄를 저지르다　punishment [pʌ́niʃmənt] 명 처벌

10 어색한 대화 고르기
정답 ③

① M Is Monday a national holiday?
　 W No. That's next Tuesday.
② M Will you try this and <u>tell me if it tastes</u> okay?
　 W Wow, this sauce is delicious!
③ M <u>We agreed to meet</u> at 11 a.m. What happened?
　 W <u>My train leaves at 2 in the afternoon.</u>
④ M That blue hat looks really <u>nice on you</u>!
　 W Thanks. My brother gave it to me as a birthday present.
⑤ M Can I help you find something?
　 W I <u>am looking for</u> the *Harry Potter* series.

① 남 월요일이 공휴일이야?
　 여 아니. 그건 다음 주 화요일이야.
② 남 이거 한 번 먹어보고 맛이 괜찮은지 말해줄래?
　 여 우와, 이 소스 맛있다!
③ 남 우리 오전 11시에 만나기로 약속했잖아. 무슨 일 있었어?
　 여 기차가 오후 2시에 출발해.
④ 남 그 파란 모자 너한테 정말 잘 어울린다!
　 여 고마워. 남동생이 나한테 생일 선물로 줬어.
⑤ 남 찾으시는 걸 도와드릴까요?
　 여 저는 <해리 포터> 시리즈를 찾고 있어요.

해설 | 남자가 여자에게 오전 11시에 만나기로 했었다며 무슨 일이 있었는지 물었으므로, 여자는 일어난 일에 대해 답해야 한다. 그러나 여자가 기차가 오후 2시에 출발한다는 어색한 대답을 했으므로 정답은 ③이다.
어휘 | national holiday 공휴일, 국경일　taste [teist] 图 맛이 ~하다 명 맛　agree [əgríː] 图 약속하다; 동의하다

11 할 일 고르기
정답 ①

W Do you see my volleyball uniform anywhere, Dad?
M No. Did you look <u>in your room</u>?
W Yes. I looked everywhere in my room. It's not there.
M Let me <u>look in the laundry basket</u>. *[Pause]* Oh, it's in here, but it's dirty.
W Oh, no. I have a game tomorrow.
M <u>I'll wash it now</u>, and it might have time to dry.
W Can we <u>hang it outside</u> after it's washed? It will dry faster in the sun.
M Good idea.

여 제 배구 유니폼 어딘가에서 보셨어요, 아빠?
남 아니. 네 방 안은 찾아봤니?
여 네. 제 방의 모든 곳을 찾아봤어요. 거기엔 없어요.
남 빨래 바구니를 볼게. *[잠시 멈춤]* 오, 여기 있긴 한데, 더러운 상태네.
여 오, 이런. 저 내일 경기가 있어요.
남 지금 빨아둘게, 그러면 마를 시간이 있을 수도 있겠구나.
여 빨고 나서 바깥에 걸어두면 될까요? 햇빛에서 더 빨리 마를 거예요.
남 좋은 생각이구나.

해설 | 남자가 지금 배구 유니폼을 빨겠다고 했으므로 정답은 ① '유니폼 빨기'이다.
어휘 | dry [drai] 图 마르다, 건조되다　hang [hæŋ] 图 걸다, 매달다　outside [àutsáid] 분 바깥에

12 도표에서 알맞은 항목 고르기
정답 ③

W May I <u>take your order</u>?
M Yes, please. I'd like a latte.
W Sorry, sir. We're <u>out of milk</u> right now, so you can order a black coffee or green tea.
M Then, <u>I'll have a black coffee</u>.
W Do you want a small or large one?
M <u>Make it a large</u>, please.
W Sure. <u>Do you want syrup in your coffee</u>?
M <u>No, thanks.</u>
W The total is four dollars.

여 주문하시겠어요?
남 네, 그럴게요. 라테 주세요.
여 죄송합니다, 손님. 지금 우유가 다 떨어져서, 블랙커피나 녹차를 주문하실 수 있어요.
남 그럼, 블랙커피로 할게요.
여 스몰과 라지 사이즈 중 어떤 것을 원하세요?
남 라지로 해주세요.
여 네. 커피에 시럽 넣어드릴까요?
남 아니요, 괜찮아요.
여 총 4달러입니다.

해설 | 남자가 라지 사이즈의 블랙커피를 주문했으며, 시럽은 넣지 않겠다고 했으므로 정답은 ③이다.
어휘 | be out of ~이 다 떨어지다, (다 써서) 없다

13 시간 정보 고르기
정답 ③

[Telephone rings.]	[전화기가 울린다.]
W Hello?	여 여보세요?
M Hello. This is Brandon Miller from Apex Repair Shop.	남 안녕하세요. 저는 Apex Repair Shop의 Brandon Miller입니다.
W Oh, I've been waiting for you to call.	여 오, 전화해주시기를 기다렸어요.
M Yes. I called to schedule the visit to fix your air conditioner.	남 네. 고객님의 에어컨을 수리하기 위해 방문 일정을 잡으려고 전화 드렸어요.
W When is the earliest you can come?	여 가장 빨리 오실 수 있는 게 언제죠?
M It would be July 4th. Next Tuesday.	남 7월 4일이 되겠습니다. 다음 주 화요일이요.
W I won't be in town that day. How about July 6th?	여 제가 그날 이 동네에 없어요. 7월 6일은 어때요?
M Yeah. That works for me.	남 네. 저는 괜찮아요.
W Good. What time will you visit?	여 좋네요. 몇 시에 방문하실 건가요?
M Does 10 a.m. sound okay to you?	남 오전 10시 괜찮으시겠어요?
W Sure. I'll see you then!	여 좋아요. 그때 뵐게요!

해설 | 여자가 7월 6일은 어떤지 묻자 남자가 그 날짜가 괜찮다고 했으므로 정답은 ③ '7월 6일'이다.

어휘 | wait for ~를 기다리다   schedule [skédʒuːl] ⑧ 일정을 잡다

14 한일 고르기
정답 ③

M What are you doing after school today, Sofia?	남 오늘 학교 끝나고 뭐 할 거야, Sofia?
W I will go to the post office to send a package.	여 택배를 보내기 위해 우체국에 갈 거야.
M What package?	남 무슨 택배?
W It's a gift for my friend in Thailand. It's for her birthday.	여 태국에 있는 내 친구에게 줄 선물이야. 그녀의 생일을 위한 거지.
M That's nice of you.	남 너 정말 친절하다.
W Yes. She loves the snacks from here, so I bought some for her yesterday. I will send them to her in the package.	여 응. 그녀는 이곳의 과자들을 정말 좋아해서, 어제 그녀에게 줄 과자를 좀 샀어. 그걸 택배로 그녀에게 보낼 거야.
M Will they get there on her birthday?	남 생일에 맞춰 도착할까?
W I hope so. Her birthday is next week.	여 그러길 바라고 있어. 그녀의 생일은 다음 주거든.

해설 | 여자가 어제 친구에게 줄 과자를 샀다고 했으므로 정답은 ③ '과자 구입하기'이다.

어휘 | Thailand [táilænd] ⑲ 태국

15 목적 고르기
정답 ②

W Hello, loyal customers. This is Hannah Godwin, the founder of Bada Bank. Are you tired of waiting on the phone for help with banking? Well, now you don't have to. Bada Bank will now offer live chat options for people online. Simply enter your name in the chat, and you will be connected to a representative online. We hope you find this more convenient. Thank you.	여 안녕하세요, 단골 고객님들. 바다 은행의 창립자인 Hannah Godwin입니다. 은행 업무에 대해 도움을 받기 위해 통화를 기다리는 것이 지겨우시죠? 음, 이제 여러분은 그러실 필요가 없습니다. 바다 은행은 이제 온라인 고객분들을 위한 실시간 채팅 옵션을 제공합니다. 간단히 채팅창에 여러분의 성함을 입력하시면, 온라인으로 담당자와 연결될 것입니다. 여러분이 이걸 더 편리하게 여겨주시길 바랍니다. 감사합니다.

해설 | 여자가 은행에서 온라인 고객을 위한 실시간 채팅 기능을 새로 제공하는 것에 대해 설명하고 있으므로 정답은 ② '새로운 온라인 기능을 소개하려고'이다.

어휘 | loyal customer 단골 고객, 충성 고객   connect [kənékt] ⑧ 연결하다   representative [rèprizéntətiv] ⑲ 담당자, 대리인, 대표자

16 금액 정보 고르기
정답 ④

M	Hello. How may I help you?
W	Hi. I'd like to buy <u>tickets</u> <u>for</u> <u>the</u> <u>play</u> at 6 p.m. How much are they?
M	An <u>adult</u> ticket is 15 dollars, and a ticket for a child <u>under</u> <u>10</u> <u>years</u> <u>old</u> is 10 dollars.
W	One adult and one child, please.
M	Okay. Your total is 25 dollars.
W	I have a five-dollar discount coupon. Can I use it?
M	I'm sorry, but you <u>can't</u> <u>use</u> <u>it</u> for this performance.
W	That's okay. Here's my credit card.

남	안녕하세요. 무엇을 도와드릴까요?
여	안녕하세요. 오후 6시 연극 티켓을 사고 싶어요. 얼마인가요?
남	성인 티켓은 15달러이고, 10살 이하의 어린이 티켓은 10달러입니다.
여	성인 1명과 어린이 1명이요.
남	네. 총 25달러입니다.
여	저 5달러짜리 할인 쿠폰이 있어요. 이거 쓸 수 있나요?
남	죄송하지만, 이 공연에는 쓰실 수 없습니다.
여	괜찮아요. 여기 제 신용카드요.

해설 | 남자가 총 25달러라고 했고, 5달러짜리 할인 쿠폰은 이 공연에 쓸 수 없다고 했으므로 정답은 ④ '$ 25'이다.

어휘 | play [plei] 몡 연극 adult [ədʌ́lt] 몡 성인, 어른 performance [pərfɔ́ːrməns] 몡 공연; 수행

17 적절한 응답 고르기
정답 ④

W	Did you see Namjun at the soccer game yesterday?
M	No. He couldn't <u>play</u> <u>in</u> <u>the</u> <u>game</u>.
W	Why not?
M	He was <u>in</u> <u>a</u> <u>car</u> <u>accident</u> the other day.
W	Oh, no! Is he okay?
M	He <u>hurt</u> <u>his</u> <u>arm</u>, but it wasn't serious.
W	That's a relief. We should go see him soon.
M	Yes. He's resting at home right now. I <u>plan</u> <u>to</u> <u>go</u> <u>there</u> after school today.
W	I will come with you then.

여	어제 축구 경기에서 남준이 봤니?
남	아니. 남준이는 경기를 뛰지 못했어.
여	왜 못 뛰었어?
남	며칠 전에 차 사고를 당했어.
여	오, 이런! 괜찮은 거야?
남	팔을 다쳤는데, 심각한 건 아니었어.
여	다행이다. 빨리 보러 가야겠다.
남	응. 남준이는 지금 집에서 쉬고 있어. 오늘 방과 후에 거기에 갈 계획이야.
여	그럼 나도 너와 함께 갈래.

해설 | 남자가 방과 후에 친구의 집에 병문안을 갈 계획이라고 했으므로 정답은 동행할 의사를 밝히는 ④ 'I will come with you then.'이다.

> **선택지 해석**
> ① 수고했어! 경기 정말 잘했어. ② 다치지 않게 조심해. ③ 길을 건너기 전에는 항상 살펴봐. ④ 그럼 나도 너와 함께 갈래. ⑤ 증상을 설명해 드릴게요.

어휘 | serious [síəriəs] 휑 심각한 relief [rilíːf] 몡 다행, 안도; 경감 cross [krɔːs] 똥 건너다 몡 십자가 symptom [símptəm] 몡 증상

18 적절한 응답 고르기
정답 ②

M	You <u>look</u> <u>lost</u>. Can I help you find something?
W	Oh, yes. I want to go to the city hall.
M	It's just <u>down</u> <u>this</u> <u>street</u> on the right.
W	Thank you for your help. I just moved here, so I don't know the area well.
M	Don't mention it. Do you need <u>any</u> <u>more</u> <u>directions</u>?
W	Actually, I also need to go to a supermarket. Do you know <u>the</u> <u>closest</u> <u>one</u>?
M	There are two near here. There is a big one and a small one.
W	I just need to buy one ingredient. Can you tell me where the small one is?
M	It's around the corner over there.

남	길을 잃으신 것으로 보여요. 길 찾는 것 도와드릴까요?
여	오, 네. 저는 시청에 가고 싶어요.
남	그건 오른쪽 이 길의 아래에 있어요.
여	도와주셔서 감사합니다. 제가 막 여기로 이사 와서, 이 지역을 잘 몰라요.
남	별말씀을요. 길 안내가 더 필요하세요?
여	사실은, 슈퍼마켓도 가야 해요. 가장 가까운 곳을 아세요?
남	여기 근처에 두 곳이 있어요. 큰 곳과 작은 곳이요.
여	재료 하나만 사면 돼요. 작은 곳이 어딘지 말해주실래요?
남	저쪽 길모퉁이를 끼고 돌면 있어요.

해설 | 여자가 작은 슈퍼마켓이 어딘지 말해줄 수 있는지 물었으므로 정답은 위치를 설명하는 ② 'It's around the corner over there.'이다.

> **선택지 해석**
> ① 이사 업체 서비스를 이용했어요. ② 저쪽 길모퉁이를 끼고 돌면 있어요. ③ 오늘 밤 감자수프를 만들 거예요. ④ 그러면, 그 대신에 시청으로 데려다줄게요. ⑤ 큰 슈퍼마켓에서 많은 품목들을 팔아요.

어휘 | city hall 시청 ingredient [ingríːdiənt] 몡 재료

19 적절한 응답 고르기

정답 ②

W	Welcome to Finest Jewelry. How can I help you?
M	I want to buy my wife a necklace for our wedding anniversary.
W	All of our most popular necklaces are over here. Do you like any of these?
M	These are all very big. She usually wears simple jewelry.
W	I have this one here too. It's new to the store.
M	That's perfect. Can I buy that one, please?
W	Yes. I'll prepare it for you now.
M	Can you wrap it too? I want the package to look nice.
W	Of course. Just give me a few minutes.

여 Finest Jewelry에 오신 것을 환영합니다. 무엇을 도와드릴까요?
남 결혼기념일을 맞아서 제 아내에게 목걸이를 사주고 싶어요.
여 저희의 가장 인기 있는 목걸이들은 여기에 있어요. 이 중에 맘에 드는 것 있으세요?
남 이것들은 다 매우 크네요. 아내는 보통 간단한 장신구를 착용해요.
여 여기 이것도 있어요. 저희 가게에 새로 들어왔답니다.
남 완벽해요. 이걸 살 수 있을까요?
여 네. 지금 준비해드릴게요.
남 포장도 해주실 수 있나요? 포장이 멋져 보였으면 해요.
여 당연하죠. 잠시만 기다려주세요.

해설 | 남자가 목걸이를 포장해 달라고 요청했으므로 정답은 요청을 수락하는 ② 'Of course. Just give me a few minutes.'이다.

[선택지 해석]
① 드레스에 이 목걸이를 할 거예요.   ② 당연하죠. 잠시만 기다려주세요.   ③ 사실, 저희는 벌써 선물을 열어보기 시작했어요.   ④ 예쁜 꽃 고마워요.
⑤ 네. 저희의 다섯 번째 기념일이에요.

어휘 | anniversary [ænəvə́ːrsəri] 몡 기념일 wrap [ræp] 동 포장하다, 싸다

20 상황에 적절한 말 고르기

정답 ①

| W | Mollie sits next to Ben in history class. Ben often falls asleep while the teacher is talking. He doesn't take notes when this happens, and he asks Mollie for hers. Ben sometimes tells Mollie that he is tired because he stays up late playing games. Mollie thinks that Ben should take his own notes. So, she wants to tell him that he should get more sleep so that he can pay attention in class. In this situation, what would Mollie most likely say to Ben? |
| Mollie | Ben, you'd better go to bed early and focus in class. |

여 Mollie는 역사 수업 시간에 Ben 옆에 앉습니다. Ben은 선생님이 말씀하고 계시는 동안 자주 잡니다. 이런 일이 일어날 때 그는 필기하지 않고, Mollie에게 그녀의 것을 달라고 합니다. Ben은 종종 Mollie에게 그가 게임을 하느라 늦게까지 깨어 있기 때문에 피곤하다고 말합니다. Mollie는 Ben이 스스로 필기해야 한다고 생각합니다. 그래서, 그녀는 그가 수업에 집중할 수 있도록 더 많이 자야 한다고 그에게 말하고 싶습니다. 이러한 상황에서, Mollie가 Ben에게 가장 할 것 같은 말은 무엇입니까?
Mollie Ben, 너 일찍 자고 수업 시간에 집중하는 것이 좋겠어.

해설 | Mollie가 Ben에게 수업에 집중할 수 있도록 더 많이 자야 한다고 말하고 싶다고 했으므로 정답은 ① 'you'd better go to bed early and focus in class.'이다.

[선택지 해석]
① 너 일찍 자고 수업 시간에 집중하는 것이 좋겠어.   ② 보통 어떤 게임을 해?   ③ 네 필기를 또 복사해도 괜찮을까?   ④ 역사 수업이 시작하기 전에 깨워줘.
⑤ 네 글씨를 못 알아보겠어.

어휘 | fall asleep 잠들다 take a note 필기하다, 기록하다 stay up 깨어 있다, 안 자다 pay attention 집중하다 focus [fóukəs] 동 집중하다
copy [kápi] 동 복사하다 handwriting [hǽndraitiŋ] 몡 글씨; 필체

1	⑤	2	④	3	④	4	⑤	5	③	6	②	7	②	8	①	9	②	10	②
11	③	12	②	13	②	14	①	15	④	16	⑤	17	②	18	③	19	②	20	③

1 알맞은 그림 고르기   정답 ⑤

M How may I help you?

W I'd like to buy a padded vest.

M Okay. Do you have any design in mind?

W I want one that comes down to the waist.

M Then, would you like a vest with buttons or a zipper?

W I guess one with a zipper would be easier to fasten.

M Got it. You can choose from these two. One has a hood, and the other doesn't.

W I like the one with a hood. It will keep me warmer than the one without a hood.

M That's true. Covering the head is good for staying warm.

남 무엇을 도와드릴까요?

여 패딩 조끼를 사고 싶어요.

남 그러시군요. 염두에 둔 디자인이 있으신가요?

여 허리까지 내려오는 걸 원해요.

남 그럼 버튼이 있는 조끼와 지퍼가 있는 조끼 중 어느 것이 좋으신가요?

여 지퍼가 있는 게 더 잠그기 쉬울 것 같아요.

남 알겠습니다. 이 두 개 중에서 고르실 수 있어요. 하나는 후드가 있고, 나머지 하나는 없어요.

여 저는 후드가 있는 것이 좋아요. 그건 후드가 없는 것보다 더 따뜻하게 해줄 거예요.

남 맞아요. 머리를 덮는 것이 온기를 유지하는 데 좋죠.

해설 | 여자가 지퍼와 후드가 있고 허리까지 내려오는 패딩 조끼를 사고 싶다고 했으므로 정답은 ⑤이다.

어휘 | padded [pǽdid] 휑 패딩의, 속을 채워 넣은   vest [vest] 뎽 조끼   come down to ~까지 내려오다, 길이가 ~이다   waist [weist] 뎽 허리
fasten [fǽsn] 됭 잠그다   cover [kʌ́vər] 됭 덮다

2 언급하지 않은 내용 고르기   정답 ④

W Do you want to see a movie tonight?

M Which one?

W What about *Ocean Adventure*?

M I haven't heard about that film.

W Yeah, that's because it's an independent documentary movie.

M That sounds interesting. Who stars in it?

W Brett Williams has the leading role.

M What time does it start?

W We can watch it at 7 tonight.

M Is it playing at the Odeon Theater?

W Yeah. That's the only place.

M Okay. Let's go watch it.

여 오늘 밤에 영화 볼래?

남 어떤 거?

여 <Ocean Adventure>는 어때?

남 그 영화에 대해 들어본 적이 없어.

여 맞아, 왜냐하면 그건 독립 다큐멘터리 영화거든.

남 흥미롭게 들리네. 누가 출연하니?

여 Brett Williams가 주연이야.

남 몇 시에 시작해?

여 오늘 밤 7시에 볼 수 있어.

남 그거 오데온 극장에서 상영하고 있니?

여 응. 거기가 유일한 곳이야.

남 그래. 보러 가자.

해설 | ① 장르(독립 다큐멘터리 영화), ② 주연 배우(Brett Williams), ③ 상영 시각(7시), ⑤ 상영 장소(오데온 극장)에 대해 언급했으므로 정답은 ④ '길이'이다.

어휘 | independent [ìndipéndənt] 휑 독립적인   star in 출연하다, 주연을 맡다   leading role 주연

3 목적 고르기　　　　　　　　　　　정답 ④

[Cellphone rings.]	[휴대폰이 울린다.]

W Hello?
M Hi. This is Tom from Taste of Home Restaurant.
W Oh, is this about my reservation?
M That's right. Do you still plan to come at 7 p.m.?
W Yes, I do.
M I called to double-check your reservation since you made it over a month ago.
W I see. I made it so early because it's my anniversary dinner with my husband.
M Thank you for letting us know. We will prepare a free dessert for you then.

여 여보세요?
남 안녕하세요. Taste of Home Restaurant의 Tom입니다.
여 오, 제 예약에 관한 건가요?
남 맞습니다. 여전히 오후 7시에 오실 계획이신가요?
여 네, 맞아요.
남 손님께서 예약을 한 달여 전에 하셔서 재확인하려고 연락드렸습니다.
여 그렇군요. 남편과의 기념일 저녁 식사라서 그렇게 일찍 예약한 거였어요.
남 알려주셔서 감사합니다. 그렇다면 무료 디저트를 준비해드릴게요.

해설 | 남자가 여자에게 식당 예약을 한 달여 전에 해서 재확인하려고 연락했다고 했으므로 정답은 ④ '예약을 확인하려고'이다.
어휘 | reservation [rèzərvéiʃən] 圆 예약　prepare [pripέər] 图 준비하다

4 시간 정보 고르기　　　　　　　　　　정답 ⑤

W Do you have a minute, Mr. Davidson?
M Sure, Wendy. What do you need?
W It's about the class field trip on Thursday. I'm worried because I have band practice that day.
M We'll leave for the museum at 10 in the morning. Is that a problem for you?
W No. I was just wondering what time we would come back.
M Well, our bus will leave at 1:30, so we will arrive back at the school around 2:30.
W Oh, great. My band practice starts at 3:30. I don't have to be worried about missing it.

여 잠시 시간 있으세요, Davidson 선생님?
남 물론이지, Wendy. 뭐가 필요하니?
여 목요일에 있을 학급 체험학습에 대한 거예요. 그날 밴드 연습이 있어서 걱정돼요.
남 우리는 아침 10시에 박물관으로 떠날 거야. 그게 문제가 될까?
여 아니요. 그냥 언제 돌아올지 궁금했어요.
남 음, 버스가 1시 30분에 출발할 거니까, 학교에 2시 30분쯤 돌아올 거야.
여 오, 잘됐네요. 밴드 연습이 3시 30분에 시작하거든요. 빠질까 봐 걱정할 필요가 없겠어요.

해설 | 여자가 밴드 연습이 3시 30분에 시작한다고 했으므로 정답은 ⑤ '3:30 p.m.'이다.
어휘 | practice [prǽktis] 圆 연습; 관습　wonder [wʌ́ndər] 图 궁금해하다　miss [mis] 图 빠지다, 빼먹다; 놓치다

5 장소 고르기　　　　　　　　　　　정답 ③

M Hello. Would you like to try a chocolate chip cookie?
W No, thank you. I am here to order a cake for my friend's birthday.
M Okay. What kind of cake do you want?
W I want a chocolate cake with vanilla icing.
M What size do you want, a small, medium, or large?
W I want a large cake, please. Also, can you add basketball decorations to the cake? My friend loves basketball.
M Of course. Your cake should be ready on Thursday.

남 안녕하세요. 초코칩 쿠키 드셔보시겠어요?
여 아니요, 괜찮습니다. 친구 생일 케이크를 주문하러 왔어요.
남 알겠습니다. 어떤 종류의 케이크를 원하시나요?
여 저는 바닐라 아이싱이 있는 초콜릿케이크를 원해요.
남 작은 것, 중간 것, 큰 것 중에 어떤 크기를 원하세요?
여 큰 케이크로 주세요. 그리고, 케이크에 농구공 장식을 추가해 주실 수 있으신가요? 제 친구가 농구를 매우 좋아해요.
남 물론이죠. 케이크는 목요일에 준비될 거예요.

해설 | 여자가 친구의 생일 케이크를 주문하러 왔다고 하는 것으로 보아 정답은 ③ '제과점'이다.
어휘 | icing [áisiŋ] 圆 아이싱(케이크 등의 표면에 바르거나 장식하는 설탕 크림)　decoration [dèkəréiʃən] 圆 장식

① M What would you like to drink?

    W Coffee, please.

② M Oh, no! I spilled my drink.

    W It's okay. Let me get you some tissue.

③ M Who broke that glass?

    W I did. I'm so sorry.

④ M Would you like to have some orange juice?

    W Yes, please. It's so hot today.

⑤ M Whose notebook is that?

    W I think it is Brent's.

① 남 뭐 마시고 싶어?

  여 커피 부탁할게.

② 남 오, 이런! 음료를 쏟았어.

  여 괜찮아. 휴지 가져다줄게.

③ 남 누가 저 유리를 깼니?

  여 내가 그랬어. 정말 미안해.

④ 남 오렌지 주스 좀 마실래?

  여 응, 부탁할게. 오늘 정말 덥다.

⑤ 남 저건 누구의 공책이니?

  여 Brent의 것 같아.

해설 | 남자가 음료수를 쏟아서 당황스러워하고 있고 여자가 진정시키려고 하는 상황이므로 정답은 ②이다.

어휘 | spill [spil] ⑧ 쏟다, 흘리다   tissue [tíʃuː] ⑲ 휴지; 조직

W Yoonsu, hurry up! You'll be late for school.

M I'm sorry, Mom. I woke up late this morning.

W Why? Didn't you hear your alarm clock?

M I slept through my alarm because I was tired. I studied for a quiz all night.

W Well, you will miss the bus. I will just drive you to school.

M Okay. Can you grab my scarf from the closet? I will pack my book bag.

W Sure. But we need to leave in five minutes.

여 윤수야, 서둘러! 학교에 늦겠어.

남 죄송해요, 엄마. 오늘 아침에 늦게 일어났어요.

여 왜? 알람 시계 못 들었니?

남 피곤해서 알람에도 깨지 않고 잤어요. 밤새 시험공부를 했거든요.

여 이런, 버스를 놓치겠구나. 그냥 내가 학교에 데려다줄게.

남 네. 옷장에서 제 목도리를 빨리 챙겨주실 수 있으세요? 저는 책가방을 챙길게요.

여 물론이지. 그렇지만 5분 내로 출발해야 한단다.

해설 | 남자가 여자에게 옷장에서 목도리를 챙겨 달라고 부탁했으므로 정답은 ② '목도리 가져다주기'이다.

어휘 | sleep through ~에도 깨지 않고 자다   grab [græb] ⑧ 급히 하다, 잡다; 붙잡다

M The Voyager electric bicycle will change the way you ride. Its electric motor will help you get up hills or carry heavy loads. Plus, it is not only useful but also very stylish. It is available in many different colors. And, compared to other electric bikes, it's light. It only weighs 15 kilograms. The Voyager electric bike will be available on our website and in stores around the country. What are you waiting for? Start your voyage today.

남 Voyager 전기 자전거는 자전거 타는 방식을 바꿀 것입니다. 이것의 전기 모터는 언덕을 오르거나 무거운 짐을 옮기는 데 도움이 될 것입니다. 게다가, 이것은 유용할 뿐만 아니라 매우 멋있기도 합니다. 이것은 여러 가지 많은 색상으로 구매가 가능합니다. 그리고 다른 전기 자전거와 비교하여 이것은 가볍습니다. 이것은 무게가 겨우 15kg만 나갑니다. Voyager 전기 자전거는 저희 웹사이트와 전국의 매장에서 구매가 가능합니다. 무엇을 기다리시나요? 오늘 여행을 시작하세요.

해설 | ② 성능(언덕을 오르거나 무거운 짐을 옮길 수 있음), ③ 색상(여러 가지 많은 색상), ④ 무게(15kg), ⑤ 판매 장소(웹사이트와 전국 매장)에 대해 언급했으므로 정답은 ① '발매일'이다.

어휘 | electric [iléktrik] ⑱ 전기의   load [loud] ⑲ 짐   not only A but also B A뿐만 아니라 B도   compared to ~과 비교하여   voyage [vɔ́iidʒ] ⑲ 여행; 항해

W People who have this job work with wood and lots of tools. When a person needs a new piece of furniture for their home, they can make it. They can also help build wooden bridges or buildings. To have this job, you need to learn about different types of wood and the tools to cut and shape wood.

여 이 직업을 가진 사람들은 목재와 많은 도구를 가지고 일합니다. 사람들이 집에 둘 새로운 가구를 필요로 할 때, 그들은 그것을 만들 수 있습니다. 그들은 또 나무로 된 다리나 건물을 짓는 것을 도울 수 있습니다. 이 직업을 갖기 위해서는, 여러 종류의 목재와 그것을 자르고 다듬는 도구에 대해 배울 필요가 있습니다.

해설 | 이 직업(this job)을 가진 사람들은 목재와 많은 도구를 가지고 일하고, 가구를 만들 수 있다고 했으므로 정답은 ② '목수'이다.

어휘 | tool [tuːl] ⑲ 도구   furniture [fɔ́ːrnitʃər] ⑲ 가구   bridge [bridʒ] ⑲ 다리   shape [ʃeip] ⑧ 다듬다

10 어색한 대화 고르기   정답 ②

① W	Are you almost ready to go? We have to leave soon.
M	Give me five minutes.
② W	Is there anything I can help you with?
M	Of course. Help yourself to a snack.
③ W	Aren't you feeling a little cold?
M	I am. I think I'll put on a sweater.
④ W	Is this your new cat? She's so cute.
M	Thank you. Her name is Shadow.
⑤ W	I don't like this drama. Let's watch something else.
M	But I want to finish watching it.

① 여 갈 준비 거의 다 됐어? 우리 곧 떠나야 해.
　남 5분만 줘.
② 여 제가 도와드릴 것이 있나요?
　남 물론이죠. 간식 좀 드세요.
③ 여 약간 춥지 않니?
　남 추워. 스웨터를 입어야 할 것 같아.
④ 여 이건 네 새 고양이니? 너무 귀엽다.
　남 고마워. 이름은 Shadow야.
⑤ 여 난 이 드라마가 마음에 들지 않아. 다른 걸 보자.
　남 하지만 나는 끝까지 보고 싶어.

해설 | 여자가 남자에게 도와줄 것이 있는지 물었으므로, 남자는 도움이 필요한지 아닌지 말해야 한다. 그러나 남자가 물론이라며 간식을 좀 먹으라는 어색한 대답을 했으므로 정답은 ②이다.

어휘 | almost [ɔ́:lmoust] ⑤ 거의　help oneself to (자유로이) 먹다　put on 입다, 착용하다

11 할 일 고르기   정답 ③

W	Do you know any other languages, Edward?
M	Yes. I know some Chinese.
W	Really? I want to speak Chinese.
M	You have to study a lot, but the work is worth it.
W	I want to learn it because I want to be a diplomat one day.
M	I can give you some of my old books for studying it. But the best way to learn is with a teacher.
W	Yeah. I'll contact one soon. Do you have any recommendations?
M	Yes. I have a few.

여 너 다른 언어를 아는 것이 있니, Edward?
남 응. 나는 중국어를 약간 알아.
여 정말? 나는 중국어를 구사하고 싶어.
남 공부를 많이 해야 하지만, 그럴 가치가 있어.
여 나는 언젠가 외교관이 되고 싶어서 그걸 배우고 싶어.
남 내 예전 중국어 공부용 책 몇 권을 줄 수 있어. 하지만 제일 좋은 공부법은 선생님과 하는 거야.
여 응. 곧 연락해 볼 거야. 추천해 줄 사람 있니?
남 응. 몇 명 있어.

해설 | 남자가 중국어를 공부하는 가장 좋은 방법은 선생님과 하는 것이라고 하자, 여자가 곧 연락해 볼 것이라고 했으므로 정답은 ③ '선생님께 연락하기'이다.

어휘 | worth [wə:rθ] ⑱ 가치가 있는　diplomat [dípləmæt] ⑲ 외교관　contact [kántækt] ⑧ 연락하다　recommendation [rèkəməndéiʃən] ⑲ 추천

12 위치 고르기   정답 ②

M	Honey, where are the kids?
W	They are on the slide at the playground.
M	I see. Do you want to go to the café?
W	I brought a picnic mat. Why don't we sit on the grass?
M	Sure. How about over there?
W	I think we should sit where we can keep our eyes on the kids.
M	Yeah, I agree. How about near the entrance?
W	It's a bit crowded. Why don't we go over there?
M	Oh, nice. And it's right next to the ice cream shop. I'll go get some if you set up our spot.

남 여보, 아이들 어디 있어?
여 놀이터에서 미끄럼틀을 타고 있어.
남 그렇구나. 카페에 갈래?
여 돗자리를 가져왔어. 잔디에 앉는 게 어때?
남 그래. 저기 어때?
여 아이들을 계속 지켜볼 수 있는 곳에 앉아야 할 것 같아.
남 응, 동의해. 입구 근처는 어때?
여 거기는 약간 붐비는 것 같아. 우리 저기로 가는 게 어때?
남 오, 좋아. 그리고 아이스크림 가게 바로 옆이잖아. 당신이 자리를 잡고 있으면 내가 가서 사 올게.

해설 | 여자가 놀이터에 있는 아이들을 지켜볼 수 있는 곳에 앉자고 제안했고, 남자가 동의한 곳이 아이스크림 가게 옆이라고 했으므로 정답은 ②이다.

어휘 | slide [slaid] ⑲ 미끄럼틀　picnic mat 돗자리　keep an eye on ~을 계속 지켜보다, ~에서 눈을 떼지 않다　spot [spat] ⑲ 자리, 장소

13 시간 정보 고르기   정답 ②

M	Beth, let's study for the history test together in the library on Sunday.
W	Okay. What time do you want to meet?
M	Is 9 a.m. too early?
W	Yeah. I like to sleep late on the weekends. How about at 2 p.m. instead?
M	Actually, I have to take care of my sister between 3 and 5 on that day. My parents will go out.
W	Oh, I am going to my grandparent's house for dinner that evening. Maybe we should meet in the morning after all.
M	How about 11 a.m.?
W	That's fine. I will see you then.

남	Beth, 일요일에 도서관에서 같이 역사 시험공부 하자.
여	그래. 몇 시에 만나고 싶어?
남	오전 9시는 너무 이르니?
여	응. 주말에는 늦게까지 자는 게 좋아. 대신 오후 2시는 어때?
남	사실, 그날 3시에서 5시 사이에 여동생을 돌봐야 해. 부모님이 외출할 예정이셔.
여	오, 나는 그날 저녁에 조부모님 댁에 저녁 식사를 하러 갈 거야. 결국 아침에 만나야 할지도 모르겠다.
남	오전 11시는 어때?
여	괜찮아. 그때 보자.

해설 | 남자가 오전 11시는 어떤지 물었고 여자가 괜찮다고 했으므로 정답은 ② '11 a.m.'이다.

어휘 | take care of 돌보다   go out 외출하다   after all 결국

14 한일 고르기   정답 ①

M	How was summer camp, Sojin?
W	It was great! I didn't want to go home at the end of it.
M	Don't you usually ride horses there?
W	Yes. But this year I wanted to do a different activity, so I chose hiking. I hiked up many mountains over the summer.
M	Will you continue to hike in the future?
W	Yes. It's my new hobby. I'll go on the weekends now.
M	I hope I can join you on a hike sometime.

남	여름 캠프는 어땠니, 소진아?
여	굉장했어! 끝날 무렵에는 집에 가고 싶지 않았어.
남	거기서는 보통 승마를 하지 않니?
여	맞아. 하지만 올해는 다른 활동을 해보고 싶어서 등산을 선택했어. 여름 동안 많은 산에 올랐어.
남	앞으로도 계속 등산을 할 예정이니?
여	응. 이건 내 새로운 취미야. 이제 주말마다 갈 거야.
남	나도 언젠가 너와 함께 등산을 가면 좋겠다.

해설 | 여자가 여름 캠프 활동으로 등산을 했다고 했으므로 정답은 ① '등산하기'이다.

어휘 | activity [æktívəti] 명 활동   continue [kəntínjuː] 동 계속하다

15 목적 고르기   정답 ④

M	Good morning, everyone. I want to remind you about the school essay contest. The deadline to submit a personal essay is May 1st. Your essay should be about your favorite novel. You should explain why it is your favorite and why others should read it. The essay should be 500 to 1,000 words long. The judges will not read your essay if it is too long or too short. The top three essay writers will win prizes. Thank you for listening.

남	안녕하세요, 여러분. 저는 학교 작문 대회에 대해 다시 한번 알려드리려고 합니다. 직접 쓴 글을 제출할 마감일은 5월 1일입니다. 그것은 여러분이 가장 좋아하는 소설에 관한 것이어야 합니다. 왜 그것을 가장 좋아하는지와 왜 다른 사람들이 그것을 읽어야 하는지를 설명해야 합니다. 글은 500자에서 1,000자 내외여야 합니다. 심사위원들은 글이 너무 길거나 짧으면 읽지 않을 것입니다. 상위 세 명의 저자가 상을 탈 것입니다. 들어주셔서 감사합니다.

해설 | 남자가 학교 작문 대회에 대한 세부 사항을 안내하고 있으므로 정답은 ④ '작문 대회 참가를 안내하려고'이다.

어휘 | remind [rimáind] 동 다시 한번 알리다, 상기시키다   deadline [dédlàin] 명 마감일   submit [səbmít] 동 제출하다
personal [pə́rsənəl] 형 자신이 직접 하는; 개인의   judge [dʒʌdʒ] 명 심사위원

16 금액 정보 고르기　　　　　　　　　　　정답 ⑤

M　Hello. Are you interested in a boat tour?

W　Yes. I'd like two tickets for the Midday Boat Tour. How much is it?

M　The tickets are 15 dollars each, but you can enjoy lunch on the boat if you pay more.

W　How much is the lunch?

M　It's 10 dollars per person. Would you like to add it?

W　Hmm... Okay. Please add the meal for two people.

M　Great. I'll book your tour now then.

남　안녕하세요. 보트 투어에 관심이 있으신가요?

여　네. Midday Boat Tour 표 두 장 주세요. 얼마인가요?

남　장당 15달러이지만, 더 지불하시면 보트 위에서 점심 식사를 즐기실 수 있어요.

여　점심 식사는 얼마인데요?

남　인당 10달러입니다. 추가하고 싶으신가요?

여　흠... 네. 두 명의 식사를 추가해 주세요.

남　좋습니다. 그럼 지금 투어를 예약해 드리겠습니다.

해설 | 여자가 장당 15달러인 보트 투어 표를 두 장 샀고, 인당 10달러인 점심 식사를 두 명 추가했으므로 정답은 ⑤ '$ 50'이다.

어휘 | be interested in ~에 관심이 있다　per [pər:] 젠 ~당, ~마다　meal [mi:l] 몡 식사

17 적절한 응답 고르기　　　　　　　　　　정답 ②

M　Excuse me. You dropped your phone.

W　Oh, thank you. Where was it?

M　It was on the floor over there. It fell out of your bag.

W　Thank you for bringing it to me.

M　Don't mention it.

W　[Pause] Oh, no. The screen cracked.

M　It probably broke during the fall. Can you still use it?

W　I don't think so. It's pretty damaged. But I need to call my friend.

M　Here. You can use mine.

남　실례합니다. 휴대폰을 떨어뜨리셨어요.

여　오, 감사합니다. 어디에 있었나요?

남　저쪽 바닥에 있었어요. 당신 가방에서 떨어졌어요.

여　가져다주셔서 감사합니다.

남　천만에요.

여　[잠시 멈춤] 오, 이런. 화면이 깨졌네요.

남　아마 떨어질 때 깨졌나 봐요. 아직 쓸 수 있나요?

여　못 쓸 것 같아요. 꽤 파손됐네요. 그런데 친구에게 전화해야 하는데요.

남　여기요. 제 것을 쓰세요.

해설 | 여자가 파손된 휴대폰을 두고 친구에게 전화해야 한다고 말하고 있으므로 정답은 대안을 제시하는 ② 'Here. You can use mine.'이다.

선택지 해석
① 당신 탓이에요. 당신이 제 휴대폰을 떨어뜨렸어요.　② 여기요. 제 것을 쓰세요.　③ 이 충전기는 작동하지 않아요.　④ 그가 다시 전화했나요?
⑤ 제 가방 좀 살펴볼게요.

어휘 | crack [kræk] 동 깨지다, 금이 가다　pretty [príti] 부 꽤 형 귀여운　damaged [dǽmidʒd] 형 파손된, 손상된　blame [bleim] 동 탓하다, 비난하다

18 적절한 응답 고르기　　　　　　　　　　정답 ③

W　Did you just move in to a new house, Chris?

M　Yes. My parents wanted more space.

W　Do you like it?

M　I do. It has a nice yard. Plus, my room is really big.

W　Did you already decorate it?

M　No. I have some posters and pictures, but I didn't put them on the wall yet.

W　I can help you. I love to decorate.

M　Sure. You can come over on Saturday. I'll treat you to pizza after doing it.

W　Okay. I'll be there then.

여　너 새집으로 막 이사 들어갔니, Chris?

남　응. 부모님이 더 많은 공간을 원하셨거든.

여　마음에 드니?

남　마음에 들어. 근사한 마당이 있거든. 게다가, 내 방이 정말 커.

여　벌써 방을 장식했니?

남　아니. 포스터 몇 장과 그림들이 있는데, 아직 벽에 붙이지 않았어.

여　내가 도와줄 수 있어. 난 꾸미는 걸 좋아하거든.

남　그래. 토요일에 와도 돼. 하고 나서 피자 사줄게.

여　응. 그때 갈게.

해설 | 남자가 토요일에 집으로 와서 방을 꾸미고 나면 피자를 사주겠다고 제안했으므로 정답은 제안에 동의하는 ③ 'Okay. I'll be there then.'이다.

선택지 해석
① 난 이 방을 초록색으로 칠하고 싶어.　② 고객님의 피자는 지금 배달 중입니다.　③ 응. 그때 갈게.　④ 너는 새집을 장식하려면 디자이너가 필요해.
⑤ 포스터 가게는 2층에 있어.

어휘 | space [speis] 몡 공간　yard [ja:rd] 몡 마당　treat A to B A에게 B를 사주다, 대접하다

19 적절한 응답 고르기

정답 ②

W Who are you writing a letter to, Carl?

M This is a letter for my friend in Spain. His name is Lucas.

W Wow! How did you meet him?

M We started to write letters to each other through school.

W Through school?

M Yes. Everyone in my school has to write a letter to a student in another country.

W That's so cool! But why did you pick someone from Spain?

M I want to travel there in the future. It's my dream.

W I hope you can go there one day.

여 누구에게 편지를 쓰고 있니, Carl?

남 이건 스페인에 있는 친구에게 보낼 편지야. 그의 이름은 Lucas야.

여 우와! 그를 어떻게 알게 됐니?

남 우리는 학교를 통해서 서로에게 편지를 쓰기 시작했어.

여 학교를 통해서?

남 응. 우리 학교 학생은 모두 다른 나라에 있는 학생에게 편지를 써야 해.

여 그거 정말 멋지다! 근데 왜 스페인에 있는 사람을 고른 거야?

남 장래에 그곳을 여행하고 싶거든. 내 꿈이야.

여 언젠가 네가 그곳에 갈 수 있길 바랄게.

해설 | 남자가 장래에 스페인을 여행하는 것이 자신의 꿈이라고 했으므로 정답은 남자의 꿈을 응원하는 ② 'I hope you can go there one day.'이다.

선택지 해석

① 뭐라고 하셨나요? 이해하지 못했어요. ② 언젠가 네가 그곳에 갈 수 있길 바랄게. ③ 그 편지는 오늘 오후에 발송될 거야.

④ 우리는 전에 서로를 만난 적이 없어. ⑤ 여행 잘 다녀와!

어휘 | meet [miːt] 통 아는 사이가 되다; 만나다 through [θruː] 전 ~을 통해서 Pardon me? 뭐라고 하셨나요?

20 상황에 적절한 말 고르기

정답 ③

W Mr. Bryant is a high school soccer coach. One day after school, he is helping his team practice. A girl on the team named Sarah refuses to pass the ball to her teammates because she wants to score a goal. Mr. Bryant decides to tell Sarah to apologize to her teammates after practice. In this situation, what would Mr. Bryant most likely say to Sarah?

Mr. Bryant   Sarah, you need to say sorry to your teammates.

여 Bryant 선생님은 고등학교 축구 코치입니다. 방과 후 어느 날, 그는 팀 연습을 돕고 있습니다. 팀에 있는 Sarah라는 이름의 한 여자아이가 골을 넣고 싶어서, 그녀의 팀원들에게 공을 패스하는 것을 거부합니다. Bryant 선생님은 Sarah에게 연습 후에 그녀의 팀원들에게 사과하라고 말하기로 결심합니다. 이러한 상황에서, Bryant 선생님이 Sarah에게 가장 할 것 같은 말은 무엇입니까?

Bryant 선생님   Sarah, 네 팀원들에게 미안하다고 해야 해.

해설 | Bryant 선생님이 Sarah에게 그녀의 팀원들에게 사과하라고 말하기로 결심했다고 했으므로 정답은 ③ 'you need to say sorry to your teammates.'이다.

선택지 해석

① 기분을 상하게 해서 미안하구나. ② 다음 경기는 이번 주말이야. ③ 네 팀원들에게 미안하다고 해야 해. ④ 팀에 온 것을 환영한다.

⑤ 다시는 연습에 늦지 말렴.

어휘 | refuse [rifjúːz] 통 거부하다, 거절하다 apologize [əpálədʒaiz] 통 사과하다, 미안해하다

14회 실전 모의고사

1	①	2	①	3	③	4	④	5	②	6	①	7	③	8	④	9	⑤	10	②
11	⑤	12	⑤	13	④	14	②	15	①	16	③	17	④	18	②	19	⑤	20	④

1 알맞은 그림 고르기   정답 ①

M Hello. May I help you?

W Yes. I'm looking for a souvenir postcard to remember my trip to Italy.

M How about this one with an image of Venice?

W Well, I only visited Rome and Pisa during this trip.

M I see. Then, I guess you would like this one with a picture of the Leaning Tower of Pisa.

W Oh, that's perfect. The tower was really impressive. I also like the postcard has the word "PISA" on it.

남 안녕하세요. 도와드릴까요?

여 네. 이탈리아 여행을 기억하기 위해 기념품 엽서를 찾고 있어요.

남 베니스 그림이 있는 이건 어떠세요?

여 글쎄요, 저는 이번 여행 동안 로마와 피사만 방문했어요.

남 그렇군요. 그럼, 피사의 사탑 사진이 있는 이것을 좋아하실 것 같아요.

여 오, 딱 좋아요. 그 탑은 정말로 인상 깊었어요. 이 엽서에 'PISA'라는 글자가 있는 것도 맘에 드네요.

해설 | 남자가 피사의 사탑 사진이 있는 엽서를 권하자 여자가 좋다면서 'PISA'라는 글자도 마음에 든다고 했으므로 정답은 ①이다.

어휘 | souvenir [sùːvəníər] 몡 기념품 image [ímidʒ] 몡 그림; 이미지, 인상 impressive [imprésiv] 혱 인상 깊은

2 언급하지 않은 내용 고르기   정답 ①

M What are you writing, Jisun?

W This is my story for English class.

M Oh, I didn't start mine yet. What is yours about?

W It's a science fiction story. It's set in space.

M That sounds interesting. What are the main characters like?

W The main character is a woman named Johanna. She's very brave. And there's a really evil villain.

M You wrote a lot. How long is your story?

W Right now, it's eight pages, but I will add two more.

M That's great! I should start mine soon.

남 뭘 쓰고 있니, 지선아?

여 영어 수업에 가져갈 이야기야.

남 오, 난 아직 내 것을 시작하지 않았어. 네 것은 뭐에 대한 거야?

여 공상과학 이야기야. 우주를 배경으로 하고 있어.

남 흥미로운걸. 주인공들은 어때?

여 주인공은 Johanna라는 이름의 여성이야. 그녀는 매우 용감해. 그리고 아주 사악한 악당이 나와.

남 많이 썼구나. 이야기가 얼마나 길어?

여 지금은 8장인데, 2장 더 추가할 거야.

남 멋지다! 나도 빨리 내 것을 시작해야겠어.

해설 | ② 장르(공상과학), ③ 배경(우주), ④ 등장인물(주인공 Johanna와 악당), ⑤ 예상 분량(10장)에 대해 언급했으므로 정답은 ① '제목'이다.

어휘 | be set in ~를 배경으로 하다 main character 주인공 evil [íːvəl] 혱 사악한 villain [vílən] 몡 악당

3 목적 고르기   정답 ③

[Cellphone rings.]

W Hi, Dave.

M Hi, Mindy. What are you doing this afternoon?

W I don't have any plans yet. Why?

M Are you ready for the math test on Monday?

W Not really. I was planning to study for it today or tomorrow.

M Why don't we do that together? We could go to the library at 2 p.m.

W That sounds like a good plan. I will see if Jenna wants to join us as well.

M Great! I'll meet you by the main entrance.

[휴대폰이 울린다.]

여 안녕, Dave.

남 안녕, Mindy. 오늘 오후에 뭐 할 거니?

여 아직 아무 계획 없어. 왜?

남 월요일에 있을 수학 시험 준비됐어?

여 별로. 오늘이나 내일 시험공부를 하려고 계획 중이었어.

남 우리 같이 하는 게 어때? 오후 2시에 도서관에 갈 수 있어.

여 좋은 계획인 것 같아. Jenna도 같이 가고 싶은지 알아볼게.

남 좋아! 정문에서 만나.

해설 | 남자가 여자에게 같이 수학 시험공부를 하는 것이 어떤지 물었으므로 정답은 ③ '같이 공부할 것을 제안하려고'이다.

어휘 | as well ~도, 또한 main entrance 정문

4 시간 정보 고르기 정답 ④

W	Hi. Do you need a ticket?
M	Yes. I'd like to buy a ticket for a ferry to Devon Island.
W	When would you like to go?
M	I'd like to leave this morning.
W	There's a ferry at 10 a.m. But there are no more seats available on that boat, so you would have to stand.
M	How long is the ferry ride?
W	It is about two hours long.
M	That's too long to stand. What about the ferry after that?
W	There's one that leaves at 11 a.m., and there are seats open.
M	Okay. I'll buy a ticket for that ferry then.

여	안녕하세요. 표가 필요하신가요?
남	네. 데번섬으로 가는 여객선표를 사고 싶어요.
여	언제 가시고 싶으세요?
남	오늘 오전에 출발하고 싶어요.
여	오전 10시에 여객선이 있어요. 그런데 이용하실 수 있는 좌석이 더 이상 없어서, 손님은 서서 가셔야 해요.
남	여객선을 얼마나 오래 타야 하나요?
여	약 2시간 정도요.
남	서서 가기에는 너무 기네요. 그다음 여객선은 어떤가요?
여	오전 11시에 떠나는 것이 하나 있고, 빈 좌석이 있어요.
남	네. 그럼 그 여객선표를 살게요.

해설 | 여자가 오전 11시에 떠나는 여객선에 빈 좌석이 있다고 하자 남자가 그 여객선표를 사겠다고 했으므로 정답은 ④ '11 a.m.'이다.

어휘 | ferry [féri] 명 여객선   available [əvéiləbl] 형 이용할 수 있는   open [óupən] 형 빈, 공석의; 열린

5 심정 고르기 정답 ②

W	Henry, what's the problem?
M	I had a fight with my sister.
W	Oh, what happened?
M	I get mad when I think about it.
W	Don't get worked up, and tell me the story.
M	She spilled a drink on my favorite T-shirt! I can't stand her anymore.
W	Calm down. I guess she didn't do it on purpose.
M	I think she did. My sister enjoys bothering me.

여	Henry, 뭐가 문제야?
남	여동생과 싸웠어.
여	오, 무슨 일이었는데?
남	그 일을 생각하니 화가 나.
여	속상해하지 말고 이야기해봐.
남	내가 가장 좋아하는 티셔츠에 동생이 음료수를 쏟았어! 난 더 이상 참아줄 수 없어.
여	진정해. 동생이 일부러 그러진 않았을 거야.
남	난 그랬다고 생각해. 내 여동생은 날 괴롭히는 것을 즐겨.

해설 | 남자가 여동생과 싸운 일을 생각하면 화가 난다고 했고 동생을 더 이상 참아줄 수 없다고 했으므로 정답은 ② 'annoyed'이다.

선택지 해석

① 외로운 ② 짜증이 난 ③ 기쁜 ④ 고마운 ⑤ 걱정하는

어휘 | have a fight 싸우다   get worked up 속상해하다   stand [stænd] 동 참다, 견디다; 서다   on purpose 일부러, 고의로
bother [báðər] 동 괴롭히다, 신경 쓰이게 하다

6 그림 상황에 적절한 대화 고르기 정답 ①

① W I thought you opened at 8?
   M At 9, actually.
② W This is my favorite exhibit.
   M It is quite impressive.
③ W The line is very long.
   M Many people want to buy tickets.
④ W Did you enjoy the guided tour?
   M I found it a little boring.
⑤ W Which museum should we visit?
   M The science one.

① 여 저는 8시에 문을 여시는 줄 알았는데요?
   남 사실은, 9시에 열어요.
② 여 이건 내가 가장 좋아하는 전시회야.
   남 꽤 인상 깊다.
③ 여 줄이 엄청 길다.
   남 많은 사람들이 티켓을 사고 싶어 해.
④ 여 가이드 투어는 즐거우셨나요?
   남 저는 조금 지루했어요.
⑤ 여 어떤 박물관을 방문해야 할까요?
   남 과학 박물관이요.

해설 | 닫힌 전시회장 문 앞에서 여자가 남자에게 개장 시간에 대해 물어보고 있는 상황이므로 정답은 ①이다.

어휘 | exhibit [igzíbit] 명 전시회 동 전시하다   boring [bɔ́:riŋ] 형 지루한

7 부탁·요청한 일 고르기   정답 ③

[Cellphone rings.]

M   What's up, Daphne?
W   Hey, Chulho. Did you buy everything for tomorrow?
M   What's tomorrow?
W   It's Ms. Kang's last day of teaching!
M   Oh, no! I forgot about that.
W   You still have time to buy a card.
M   I'll go to the shop now. Do I need to do anything else?
W   Can you pick up the cake I ordered? The bakery is on your way.
M   Okay, I will.

[휴대폰이 울린다.]

남   무슨 일이야, Daphne?
여   안녕, 철호야. 내일 필요한 걸 모두 샀니?
남   내일 무슨 날이야?
여   강 선생님께서 수업하시는 마지막 날이잖아!
남   오, 이런! 잊어버렸었어.
여   아직 카드를 살 시간은 남아 있어.
남   지금 가게에 가야겠다. 내가 해야 할 다른 일이 있을까?
여   내가 주문한 케이크를 찾아와줄 수 있어? 그 제과점은 가는 길에 있어.
남   응, 그럴게.

해설 | 여자가 남자에게 자신이 주문한 케이크를 찾아와 달라고 부탁했으므로 정답은 ③ '케이크 찾아오기'이다.

어휘 | pick up ~을 찾아오다

8 언급하지 않은 내용 고르기   정답 ④

M   Good afternoon, community members. I am Jack Richards from the city council. This is an announcement about our city's newest event, Music in the Park. We will hold a concert on the first Sunday of every month in Central Park to showcase different types of musicians and bands. The event will take place from 3 to 6 p.m. There will be food and activities such as face painting for kids. All families are welcome and are encouraged to bring picnic blankets and chairs. Please come and enjoy some live music with us!

남   안녕하세요, 주민 여러분. 저는 시의회의 Jack Richards입니다. 우리 시의 최신 행사인 Music in the Park에 대한 안내입니다. 저희는 다양한 타입의 음악가와 밴드를 소개하기 위해서 센트럴 공원에서 매달 주 첫째 주 일요일에 콘서트를 개최할 예정입니다. 이 행사는 오후 3시부터 6시까지 열립니다. 음식과 아이들을 위한 페이스 페인팅 같은 활동들도 있을 것입니다. 모든 가족들을 환영하며 돗자리와 의자를 가져오시는 것을 권합니다. 부디 오셔서 저희와 함께 라이브 음악을 즐겨주세요!

해설 | ① 제목(Music in the Park), ② 요일(매달 첫째 주 일요일), ③ 장소(센트럴 공원), ⑤ 활동(아이들을 위한 페이스 페인팅)에 대해 언급했으므로 정답은 ④ '참가비'이다.

어휘 | city council 시의회   showcase [ʃóukeis] 통 소개하다; 전시하다   take place 열리다   encourage [inkə́:ridʒ] 통 권하다; 격려하다
picnic blanket 돗자리

9 화제 고르기   정답 ⑤

M   People who have this job try to make products sell well. They choose the words to describe items and make short texts for advertisements. They also check the sentences on a company's website for errors. When there is a mistake in an advertisement, they correct it. To do this job, you need to be creative and good at writing.

남   이 직업을 가진 사람들은 상품이 잘 팔리게 하려고 노력합니다. 그들은 물건을 묘사할 수 있는 단어를 선택하고 광고에 들어갈 짧은 글을 씁니다. 그들은 또한 기업의 웹사이트에 오류가 있는지 글을 확인합니다. 광고에 실수가 있을 때는, 그것을 고칩니다. 이 일을 하기 위해서는, 창의적이어야 하고 글쓰기를 잘해야 합니다.

해설 | 이 직업(this job)을 가진 사람들은 물건을 묘사할 수 있는 단어를 선택하고 광고에 들어갈 짧은 글을 쓴다고 했으므로 정답은 ⑤ '카피라이터'이다.

어휘 | describe [diskráib] 통 묘사하다   advertisement [ædvərtáizmənt] 명 광고   correct [kərékt] 통 고치다   creative [kriéitiv] 형 창의적인

① W   I think you are a great singer.

    M   Thank you. I practiced a lot.

② W   I'd like to mail a package to New Zealand.

    M   I'm sorry, but all the flights are fully booked.

③ W   What time will you get home tonight?

    M   I will be home late because I have a swimming lesson.

④ W   Do you want to get some popcorn before the movie?

    M   Yeah. Let's get soda too.

⑤ W   Have you ever been to Brazil?

    M   No. I've never been to South America.

① 여   당신은 훌륭한 가수인 것 같아요.
    남   고마워요. 저 연습 많이 했어요.

② 여   뉴질랜드로 택배를 보내고 싶어요.
    남   죄송하지만, 모든 비행기가 매진되었어요.

③ 여   오늘 밤 몇 시에 집에 들어갈 거니?
    남   수영 강습이 있어서 집에 늦게 갈 예정이야.

④ 여   영화 시작 전에 팝콘을 좀 살래?
    남   응. 탄산음료도 사자.

⑤ 여   브라질에 가본 적 있니?
    남   아니. 남미에는 가본 적이 없어.

해설 | 여자가 남자에게 뉴질랜드로 택배를 보내고 싶다고 했으므로, 남자는 택배에 대한 내용을 답해야 한다. 그러나 남자가 모든 비행기가 매진되었다는 어색한 대답을 했으므로 정답은 ②이다.

어휘 | get home 집에 들어가다, 귀가하다

[Cellphone rings.]

W   Jinsu, where are you?

M   I'm walking to the café now.

W   Did you miss the bus?

M   No. I got lost, but I can see the café sign now.

W   There are many people waiting to order coffee, so I'll get in line now.

M   Thank you. I'll be there in a few minutes.

W   See you soon.

[휴대폰이 울린다.]

여   진수야, 너 어디야?

남   지금 카페로 걸어가는 중이야.

여   버스를 놓쳤니?

남   아니. 길을 잃었는데, 이제 카페 간판이 보여.

여   커피를 주문하려고 기다리는 사람들이 많으니, 내가 지금 줄을 설게.

남   고마워. 나 몇 분 뒤면 거기 도착해.

여   곧 보자.

해설 | 여자가 커피를 주문하려고 기다리는 사람들이 많아서 지금 줄을 서겠다고 했으므로 정답은 ⑤ '주문 줄 서기'이다.

어휘 | lost [lɔːst] 휑 길을 잃은; 분실한   sign [sain] 뗑 간판 图 서명하다

M   Kate, which room are we going to use for the meeting on Thursday?

W   I was thinking about the room next to the lounge. It's spacious and has a large window.

M   But isn't it always noisy because of the lounge? People chat a lot there.

W   You're right. Hmm... What about Room A?

M   Mr. Jenkins already booked A and C for interviews.

W   We have two options left. Oh! Aren't they done remodeling the one near the elevator?

M   I think so. And I think that one would be a perfect size.

W   Let's have our meeting there.

남   Kate, 어떤 회의실을 우리가 목요일에 있을 회의에 사용할 거야?

여   난 라운지 옆에 있는 회의실을 생각하고 있었어. 거긴 널찍하고 큰 창문이 있어.

남   그렇지만 라운지 때문에 항상 시끄럽지 않아? 사람들이 그곳에서 수다를 많이 떨잖아.

여   맞아. 흠... A 회의실은 어때?

남   Jenkins씨가 면접을 위해 A와 C 회의실을 이미 예약했어.

여   남은 선택지가 2개네. 오! 엘리베이터 근처에 있는 회의실이 리모델링 끝나지 않았어?

남   그런 것 같아. 그리고 그곳이 딱 좋은 크기인 것 같아.

여   거기서 회의를 하자.

해설 | 여자가 B와 E 회의실 중 엘리베이터 근처에 있는 곳에서 회의를 하자고 했으므로 정답은 ⑤이다.

어휘 | spacious [spéiʃəs] 휑 널찍한   chat [tʃæt] 图 수다를 떨다   interview [íntərvjuː] 뗑 면접, 면담

13 시간 정보 고르기

정답 ④

[Telephone rings.]	*[전화기가 울린다.]*
M Hello, Susie's Grill. How may I help you?	남 안녕하세요, Susie's Grill입니다. 무엇을 도와드릴까요?
W Hi, I'd like to make a reservation for July 6th.	여 안녕하세요, 7월 6일에 예약하고 싶은데요.
M I'm sorry, but we don't take reservations on Saturdays.	남 죄송하지만, 저희는 토요일에는 예약을 받지 않아요.
W Can I make a reservation for Friday then?	여 그럼 금요일에는 예약할 수 있나요?
M How many guests will there be?	남 몇 분이 오실 예정이세요?
W It'll be a group of eight.	여 8명 모임이에요.
M We're currently fully booked for tables of more than six on the 5th.	남 현재 5일에 6인 이상의 자리는 예약이 다 찼어요.
W Is it possible on the 12th, a week after that?	여 그다음 주인 12일에는 가능한가요?
M Yes. Would you like a table for eight on that day?	남 네. 그날 8인용 자리로 하시겠어요?
W That would be great.	여 그래 주시면 좋겠어요.

해설 | 여자가 7월 12일에 예약이 가능한지 묻자 남자가 가능하다며 그날로 예약하겠냐고 되물었고, 여자가 좋다고 했으므로 정답은 ④ 'July 12th'이다.

어휘 | currently [kə́ːrəntli] 부 현재, 지금   possible [pásəbl] 형 가능한

14 한일 고르기

정답 ②

M Did you make it to the amusement park's grand opening last Saturday, Eva?	남 지난 토요일 놀이공원 개장일에 갔었어, Eva?
W No, I didn't. I felt sick that day.	여 아니, 못 갔어. 그날 내가 아팠거든.
M Oh, no. What were you sick with?	남 오, 이런. 뭐 때문에 아팠어?
W I had a fever, so I stayed home over the weekend.	여 열이 좀 나서, 주말 내내 집에 있었어.
M I'm sorry you missed it.	남 그날 네가 놓쳤다니 아쉽다.
W It's okay. I booked tickets online yesterday so that I can go this weekend instead.	여 괜찮아. 대신 이번 주에 갈 수 있도록 어제 온라인으로 티켓을 예매해놨거든.
M That's great! Can I join you?	남 잘됐다! 나도 가도 돼?
W Of course.	여 당연하지.

해설 | 여자가 어제 온라인으로 놀이공원 티켓을 예매해놨다고 했으므로 정답은 ② '티켓 예매하기'이다.

어휘 | make it 가다; 성공하다   grand opening 개장, 개시; 개업식

15 목적 고르기

정답 ①

M Good morning, residents of Ocean Shores Apartments. This is an announcement about some electrical repairs in the building. From 3 p.m. to 6 p.m. today, the building will have no power while a problem is fixed. We apologize for this inconvenience and hope that it does not affect your day too seriously. Thank you.	남 좋은 아침입니다, 오션 쇼어스 아파트 입주민 여러분. 건물 전기 보수에 대한 안내입니다. 오늘 오후 3시부터 6시까지, 문제가 고쳐지는 동안 전력이 공급되지 않겠습니다. 불편을 드려 죄송하고 이것이 여러분의 하루에 아주 심각하게 영향을 끼치지 않기를 바랍니다. 감사합니다.

해설 | 남자가 건물 전기 보수에 대해 안내를 하며, 문제가 고쳐지는 동안 전력이 공급되지 않는다고 했으므로 정답은 ① '수리로 인한 정전을 공지하려고'이다.

어휘 | resident [rézidənt] 명 입주민, 거주자   repair [ripɛ́ər] 명 보수, 수리   power [páuər] 명 전력; 힘   fix [fiks] 동 고치다; 고정시키다
affect [əfékt] 동 영향을 끼치다

16 금액 정보 고르기 정답 ③

M	Hello. How may I help you?
W	Hi. My friend and I want to <u>rent a tennis court</u>. How much would that be?
M	It's five dollars per hour. How long will you play tennis?
W	Around three hours.
M	Then, <u>it's 15 dollars in total</u>.
W	We also <u>need some balls</u>. Do we need to pay for those?
M	<u>The balls are free to use</u>. There are baskets of them here.
W	Thank you. I'll <u>pay with cash</u>.

남	안녕하세요. 무엇을 도와드릴까요?
여	안녕하세요. 제 친구와 제가 테니스 코트를 대여하고 싶은데요. 얼마인가요?
남	한 시간에 5달러예요. 얼마나 오랫동안 테니스를 치실 건가요?
여	약 3시간 정도요.
남	그럼, 총 15달러예요.
여	저희는 공도 필요해요. 이것도 돈을 지불해야 하나요?
남	공은 무료로 사용하실 수 있어요. 여기 공 바구니가 있어요.
여	감사합니다. 현금으로 지불할게요.

해설 | 여자가 한 시간 대여료가 5달러인 테니스 코트를 3시간 동안 대여하겠다고 했고, 공은 무료로 사용할 수 있다고 했으므로 정답은 ③ '$ 15'이다.

어휘 | around [əráund] ⊞ 약, 대략 free [fri:] 휑 무료의; 자유의

17 적절한 응답 고르기 정답 ④

M	This is a beautiful campsite.
W	I know! Thank you for <u>planning this trip</u>, Honey.
M	Of course. I'm excited to sit by the fire tonight.
W	Me too. Are there <u>any rules for using</u> the campsite?
M	We need to <u>keep the area clean</u>.
W	Alright. Anything else?
M	We should not make a lot of noise after 9 p.m.
W	That's fine. I will probably <u>go to sleep early</u> tonight.
M	Me too. I'm tired after the long drive here.

남	여기는 아름다운 캠프장이네.
여	내 말이! 이 여행을 계획해줘서 고마워, 여보.
남	천만에. 난 오늘 밤에 모닥불 옆에 앉을 것이 기대돼.
여	나도. 캠프장을 이용하는 데 규칙이 있어?
남	우리는 구역을 깨끗하게 유지해야 해.
여	알았어. 또 다른 것은?
남	밤 9시 이후에는 소음을 많이 내지 말아야 해.
여	좋아. 난 아마 오늘 밤 일찍 잠을 잘 것 같아.
남	나도. 여기까지 장거리 운전을 하고 나니 피곤하네.

해설 | 여자가 오늘 밤 일찍 잠을 잘 것 같다고 했으므로 정답은 이에 동의하는 ④ 'Me too. I'm tired after the long drive here.'이다.

선택지 해석

① 내가 꼭 깨워줄게. ② 10분 후에 캠프장에 도착할 거야. ③ 자기 전에 라디오를 켜는 게 어때? ④ 나도. 여기까지 장거리 운전을 하고 나니 피곤하네.
⑤ 나는 낮 동안 낮잠 자는 것을 안 좋아해.

어휘 | campsite [kǽmpsàit] 휑 캠프장, 야영장 area [ɛ́əriə] 휑 구역, 지역 make a noise 소음을 내다, 시끄럽게 하다 probably [prάbəbli] ⊞ 아마
take a nap 낮잠 자다

18 적절한 응답 고르기 정답 ②

M	Can I go to Steven's house, Mom?
W	I don't know... You need to <u>wake up early tomorrow</u> for school.
M	But I won't stay late, and I have already finished all of my homework.
W	What will you do there?
M	We want to <u>read the new comic books</u> he bought.
W	I guess that's fine. But be home before 9.
M	Okay. <u>Can I take some of the grapes</u> to share with him?
W	Yes. They are in the refrigerator.

남	저 Steven네 집에 가도 돼요, 엄마?
여	글쎄다... 너 학교 가려면 내일 일찍 일어나야 하잖아.
남	하지만 늦게까지 있지는 않을 거예요, 그리고 전 모든 숙제를 이미 끝냈어요.
여	거기서 뭘 할 거니?
남	Steven이 산 신간 만화책을 읽고 싶어요.
여	그럼 괜찮을 것 같네. 하지만 9시 전에 집에 오렴.
남	네. Steven과 나눠 먹게 포도를 좀 가져가도 돼요?
여	그래. 냉장고에 있단다.

해설 | 남자가 친구와 나눠 먹게 포도를 가져가도 되는지 물었으므로 정답은 이를 허락하는 ② 'Yes. They are in the refrigerator.'이다.

선택지 해석

① 오전 6시로 알람을 설정하렴. ② 그래. 냉장고에 있단다. ③ 알겠어. 그를 잘 보살펴주렴. ④ 아니. 남은 설탕이 없구나.
⑤ 왜 안 되겠니? 너희 아빠를 위해 포도를 좀 사자.

어휘 | refrigerator [rifrídʒəreitər] 휑 냉장고

19 적절한 응답 고르기
정답 ⑤

M	What's wrong, Sumi?
W	I can't find my scarf anywhere.
M	It's not in your bag?
W	No. It might be at the restaurant.
M	Maybe you left it on your chair.
W	I think I did. Should I go back for it tomorrow?
M	We aren't too far away from there now. We can get off at the next stop and go back to find it.
W	Okay. But let's call the restaurant first. Maybe they found it already.
M	I'll do that while you check your bag again.

남	무슨 일 있니, 수미야?
여	나 어디에서도 내 스카프를 못 찾겠어.
남	네 가방에 없어?
여	없어. 식당에 있을지도 모르겠어.
남	아마 의자에 두고 왔나 봐.
여	그랬던 것 같아. 내일 다시 가봐야 할까?
남	우리 지금 거기에서 아주 먼 곳에 있는 게 아니잖아. 다음 정거장에서 내려서 스카프 찾으러 돌아갈 수 있어.
여	그래. 하지만 먼저 식당에 전화해보자. 이미 찾아놨을지도 몰라.
남	네가 가방을 다시 확인하는 동안 내가 할게.

해설 | 여자가 식당에 전화를 해보자고 제안했으므로 정답은 제안에 동의하는 ⑤ 'I'll do that while you check your bag again.'이다.

선택지 해석
① 손잡이에 스카프가 둘러진 이 가방을 사고 싶어. ② 분실물 센터가 어디야? ③ 따뜻한 옷을 챙겨야 해. ④ 죄송하지만, 이 자리는 예약석입니다.
⑤ 네가 가방을 다시 확인하는 동안 내가 할게.

어휘 | get off 내리다, 하차하다 handle [hǽndl] 명 손잡이 lost and found center 분실물 센터

20 상황에 적절한 말 고르기
정답 ④

W	Dean is at a Spanish lesson. His teacher is Ms. Garcia. She is teaching grammar today. Dean is doing very well in the lesson, but suddenly he gets a text from his mom. His grandfather is sick, so Dean needs to go home. Dean would like to tell Ms. Garcia that he needs to end the lesson early. In this situation, what would Dean most likely say to Ms. Garcia?
Dean	Ms. Garcia, I'm afraid I need to stop the lesson now.

여	Dean은 스페인어 수업을 듣고 있습니다. 그의 선생님은 Garcia 선생님입니다. 그녀는 오늘 문법을 가르치는 중입니다. Dean은 수업을 잘 듣고 있는데, 갑자기 엄마로부터 문자메시지를 받습니다. 그의 할아버지께서 편찮으셔서, Dean은 집에 가야 합니다. Dean은 Garcia 선생님께 그가 수업을 일찍 마쳐야 한다고 말씀드리고 싶습니다. 이러한 상황에서, Dean이 Garcia 선생님께 가장 할 것 같은 말은 무엇입니까?
Dean	Garcia 선생님, 죄송하지만 지금 수업을 중단해야 해요.

해설 | Dean이 Garcia 선생님께 수업을 일찍 마쳐야 한다고 말씀드리고 싶다고 했으므로 정답은 ④ 'I'm afraid I need to stop the lesson now.'이다.

선택지 해석
① 병원에 가시는 길이세요? ② 이 단어의 뜻이 무엇인가요? ③ 수업 시간에는 휴대폰을 꺼주세요. ④ 죄송하지만 지금 수업을 중단해야 해요.
⑤ 수업 일정을 변경할 수 있을까요?

어휘 | grammar [grǽmər] 명 문법 suddenly [sʌ́dnli] 부 갑자기 turn off 끄다 reschedule [rìːskédʒuːl] 동 일정을 변경하다

1	③	2	①	3	②	4	③	5	①	6	②	7	③	8	③	9	⑤	10	④
11	⑤	12	④	13	⑤	14	①	15	①	16	③	17	②	18	④	19	③	20	①

1 알맞은 그림 고르기 정답 ③

W Tim, something smells good in this kitchen. What is it?
M I baked some cookies, Sally. Now, they're finished.
W Wow, you made these to celebrate Halloween!
M Yeah. I'll take them to school tomorrow.
W Pumpkin-shaped cookies are perfect for Halloween. You even made faces on them! Great job!
M Thanks. I think I'll make ghost-shaped cookies next year.
W Good idea.

여 Tim, 주방에서 뭔가 좋은 냄새가 나. 뭐야?
남 내가 쿠키를 좀 구웠어, Sally. 이제, 다 만들어졌어.
여 우와, 핼러윈을 기념하기 위해 이것들을 만들었구나!
남 맞아. 내일 학교에 가져갈 거야.
여 호박 모양 쿠키가 핼러윈에는 딱 좋지. 심지어 그 위에 표정도 넣었구나! 잘했다!
남 고마워. 내년에는 유령 모양 쿠키를 만들 것 같아.
여 좋은 생각이야.

해설 | 남자가 구운 쿠키를 보고 여자가 호박 모양 쿠키가 핼러윈에는 딱 좋다고 했으므로 정답은 ③이다.

어휘 | smell [smel] 图 냄새가 나다 celebrate [séləbrèit] 图 기념하다, 축하하다

2 언급하지 않은 내용 고르기 정답 ①

W Scott, do you remember how much the delivery fee is from Billy's Restaurant?
M Yeah. It's five dollars. Why?
W I was thinking of ordering from there. Would you recommend it for lunch?
M Yes. They have many delicious healthy options.
W Great. I wanted to get a salad.
M The sandwiches are good too. One of them is on sale every day for six dollars.
W That's nice. Do they open on weekends too?
M Sadly, no. They're closed on weekends.

여 Scott, 너 Billy's Restaurant의 배달 요금이 얼마인지 기억나?
남 응. 5달러야. 왜?
여 거기서 주문할지 생각 중이었어. 점심 식사로 추천하니?
남 응. 거기는 맛있고 건강한 선택지가 많아.
여 좋네. 난 샐러드를 먹고 싶었거든.
남 샌드위치도 괜찮아. 그중에 하나는 매일 6달러로 할인을 해.
여 그거 좋은데. 주말에도 문을 여니?
남 슬프게도, 아니야. 주말에는 문을 닫아.

해설 | ② 배달료(5달러), ③ 메뉴(샐러드, 샌드위치), ④ 할인 여부(샌드위치 중 하나가 매일 할인), ⑤ 휴무일(주말)에 대해 언급했으므로 정답은 ① '식당 규모'이다.

어휘 | fee [fi:] 명 요금 recommend [rèkəménd] 图 추천하다 sadly [sædli] 图 슬프게도

3 목적 고르기   정답 ②

[Cellphone rings.]

W Hi. This is Morales Electronics. We received your message about a broken appliance.

M Yes. I left a message.

W We wanted to check a few details. Can you describe the problem you're experiencing?

M My washing machine won't turn on. I don't know why.

W I can send someone to check your washing machine.

M That would be great.

W Okay. Our technician can stop by tomorrow morning. Will you be home around 10?

M Yes. That's perfect.

W All right. I'll schedule a visit for then.

[휴대폰이 울린다.]

여 안녕하세요. Morales Electronics입니다. 고장 난 가전제품에 대한 고객님의 메시지를 받았습니다.

남 네. 제가 메시지를 남겼어요.

여 몇 가지 세부 사항들을 확인하고 싶어요. 겪고 계신 문제를 설명해주실 수 있나요?

남 세탁기가 켜지지 않아요. 왜 그런지 모르겠어요.

여 세탁기를 점검할 사람을 보내드릴 수 있어요.

남 그럼 좋죠.

여 네. 저희 기술자가 내일 아침에 들를 수 있어요. 10시쯤에 집에 계실 건가요?

남 네. 딱 좋네요.

여 알겠습니다. 그때로 방문 일정을 잡겠습니다.

해설 | 여자가 남자의 고장 난 가전제품에 대한 몇 가지 세부 사항들을 확인하고 싶다고 했으므로 정답은 ② '문제 사항을 확인하려고'이다.

어휘 | appliance [əpláiəns] 뗑 가전제품   detail [ditéil] 뗑 세부 사항   washing machine 세탁기   technician [tekníʃən] 뗑 기술자   stop by 들르다

4 시간 정보 고르기   정답 ③

M Pardon me, but I can't find the new sneakers from Gonza anywhere in the store.

W They are sold out. But we already ordered more, and they will arrive tomorrow.

M What time will they arrive exactly?

W They will get here at 10 a.m. But the shoes probably won't be on the shelves until 11.

M I was thinking of dropping by around 6 p.m. Is that too late?

W Hmm... You might need to come earlier. Those sneakers are very popular.

M I see. Well, I have a lunch break from 11:30 to 1:00, so I will come at noon. Thanks.

남 실례지만, Gonza에서 나온 운동화 신상품을 가게 어디에서도 찾을 수 없어요.

여 품절됐어요. 하지만 저희가 이미 더 주문해두어서, 내일 도착할 예정이에요.

남 정확히 몇 시쯤 도착하나요?

여 오전 10시에 여기 올 거예요. 하지만 아마 그 신발은 11시는 되어야 진열대에 올라올 거예요.

남 오후 6시쯤에 들르려고 생각 중이었는데요. 너무 늦나요?

여 흠... 더 일찍 오실 필요가 있을 것 같아요. 그 운동화는 인기가 정말 많아서요.

남 알겠습니다. 음, 제가 11시 30분부터 1시까지 점심시간이니, 정오에 올게요. 감사합니다.

해설 | 남자가 정오에 온다고 했으므로 정답은 ③ '12 p.m.'이다.

어휘 | exactly [igzǽktli] 틧 정확히   drop by 들르다   lunch break 점심시간

5 그림 상황에 적절한 대화 고르기   정답 ①

① W Could you please take my picture?
   M Sure. I'd be happy to.

② W How much is this camera?
   M It's on sale for 145 dollars.

③ W Which poster should I get?
   M Why don't you get the one with a statue on it?

④ W Where should we hang this family picture?
   M How about in the living room?

⑤ W I like your hat.
   M Thanks. I got it as a gift.

① 여 사진 좀 찍어주실 수 있으세요?
   남 그럼요. 기꺼이 찍어드릴게요.

② 여 이 카메라 얼마예요?
   남 세일해서 145달러예요.

③ 여 어떤 포스터를 사야 할까?
   남 동상이 그려진 것을 사는 게 어때?

④ 여 이 가족사진을 어디에 걸어야 할까?
   남 거실은 어때?

⑤ 여 네 모자 마음에 든다.
   남 고마워. 선물로 받았어.

해설 | 여자가 동상 앞에 서서 남자에게 카메라를 건네주고 있는 상황이므로 정답은 ①이다.

어휘 | statue [stǽtʃuː] 뗑 동상   hang [hæŋ] 동 걸다, 매달다

6 장소 고르기 정답 ②

W	What did Mom tell us to buy, Rick?	여	엄마가 뭘 사 오라고 하셨지, Rick?
M	She said that we need some carrots, onions, and beef.	남	당근, 양파, 그리고 소고기가 좀 필요하다고 하셨어.
W	Alright. I'll go find the vegetables, and you go get the meat.	여	알았어. 내가 가서 채소를 찾아볼 테니 넌 가서 고기를 가져와.
M	Where is the meat? I don't see it in this section.	남	고기가 어디 있어? 이 구역에는 안 보이네.
W	I think it's next to the fish. We can look for it together after I get the vegetables.	여	내 생각엔 생선 옆에 있을 것 같아. 내가 채소를 가져온 후에 같이 찾아볼 수 있어.
M	Okay. Do you think we will need a basket?	남	그래. 우리 바구니가 필요할 것 같아?
W	Yeah. I'll grab one now.	여	응. 지금 하나 가져올게.

해설 | 여자가 남자에게 자신이 채소를 찾아볼 테니 고기를 가져오라고 하는 것으로 보아 정답은 ② '식료품점'이다.

어휘 | vegetable [védʒətəbl] 몡 채소 section [sékʃən] 몡 구역, 부분

7 부탁·요청한 일 고르기 정답 ③

	[Cellphone rings.]		[휴대폰이 울린다.]
M	Where are you, Nara? I'm already at the basketball court.	남	어디니, 나라야? 나 벌써 농구장이야.
W	I'm so sorry, but I arrived home from school late.	여	미안한데, 나 학교에서 집에 늦게 도착했어.
M	Then, when will you arrive here?	남	그러면, 여기에는 언제 도착할 예정이야?
W	I will change my clothes and ride my bicycle there. I should arrive in 20 minutes.	여	옷 갈아입고 거기에 자전거를 타고 갈 거야. 20분 후에는 도착할 거야.
M	That's fine. I'll buy a bottle of water and wait.	남	그 정도는 괜찮아. 생수 한 병 사서 기다릴게.
W	Is it crowded there? If so, I'd like to play with other people.	여	거기 붐비니? 그렇다면, 다른 사람들과 시합하고 싶어.
M	Sure. Oh, can you bring another basketball? Mine is really old.	남	좋지. 오, 농구공 하나 가져올 수 있어? 내 것은 정말 낡았거든.
W	Yes. I will bring mine.	여	응. 내 것을 가져갈게.

해설 | 남자가 여자에게 농구공 하나를 가져와 달라고 부탁했으므로 정답은 ③ '농구공 가져오기'이다.

어휘 | basketball [bǽsbkitbɔːl] 몡 농구; 농구공 crowded [kráudid] 혱 (사람들이) 붐비는 bring [briŋ] 동 가져오다

8 언급하지 않은 내용 고르기 정답 ③

W	Greetings, fellow students. This is Amy Logan, editor of the school's literary magazine, *Creative Flow*. I'd like to announce that our team finally released the 2022 edition of our magazine. You can order one on our school's website www.DublinSchool.com, or you can purchase one from our club guidance teacher, Ms. Green. The magazine costs five dollars, and all the profits will be donated to replacing our library computers. Thank you for your support.	여	안녕하십니까, 학우 여러분. 학교의 문학잡지인 <Creative Flow>의 편집장 Amy Logan입니다. 저희 팀이 드디어 잡지의 2022년 판을 발간했다는 것을 알리고자 합니다. 학교 웹사이트 www.DublinSchool.com에서 주문하거나, 동아리 지도 교사이신 Green 선생님에게서 구매할 수 있습니다. 잡지는 5달러이며, 수익금 전액이 도서관 컴퓨터를 교체하는 데 기부될 것입니다. 성원에 감사합니다.

해설 | ① 이름(<Creative Flow>), ② 가격(5달러), ④ 구매 방법(학교 웹사이트나 Green 선생님에게 주문), ⑤ 수익금 용도(도서관 컴퓨터 교체)에 대해 언급했으므로 정답은 ③ '발매일'이다.

어휘 | Greetings. 안녕하십니까 (greeting [gríːtiŋ] 몡 인사) fellow students 학우 editor [édətər] 몡 편집장, 편집자 profit [práfit] 몡 수익금, 이익 donate [dóuneit] 동 기부하다 replace [ripléis] 동 교체하다

9 화제 고르기 정답 ⑤

W	This is a martial sport. Two people compete against each other in a fight. To score points, a player needs to kick and punch the other player on the body or head. The players all wear white uniforms with colored belts. These belts show the rank of the player. The players must also wear a lot of protective equipment for safety. It was started in Korea, but now it's enjoyed all over the world.	여	이것은 무예 운동입니다. 두 사람이 싸움에서 서로 겨룹니다. 점수를 얻기 위해서, 한 선수는 다른 선수의 몸이나 머리를 발로 차고 주먹으로 때려야 합니다. 선수들은 모두 흰색 유니폼을 입고 색깔 있는 벨트를 착용합니다. 이 벨트는 선수의 급수를 나타냅니다. 선수들은 안전을 위해 많은 보호 장비도 착용해야 합니다. 이것은 한국에서 시작되었지만, 지금은 전 세계에서 즐기고 있습니다.

해설 | 이것(This)은 무예 운동이며 선수들은 모두 흰색 유니폼을 입고 색깔 있는 벨트를 착용한다고 했으므로 정답은 ⑤ '태권도'이다.

어휘 | martial sport 무예 운동, 무술 운동   rank [ræŋk] 圀 급수, 계급   protective [prətéktiv] 쥉 보호용의   equipment [ikwípmənt] 圀 장비, 용품

10   어색한 대화 고르기   정답 ④

① W   Which sticker do you like best?

   M   I like the one with the bear.

② W   What's wrong? You are walking strangely.

   M   I exercised a lot yesterday, and now my body's sore.

③ W   Did you cook this soup? It's delicious!

   M   Actually, I bought it at the restaurant down the street.

④ W   Would you like to drink some lemonade?

   M   That café sells different kinds of tea and coffee.

⑤ W   That was a long run!

   M   Yeah. I think we ran 10 kilometers.

① 여   어떤 스티커가 가장 좋아?

   남   난 곰이 있는 게 좋아.

② 여   무슨 일이야? 너 이상하게 걷고 있어.

   남   어제 운동을 많이 해서, 지금 몸이 쑤셔.

③ 여   이 수프 네가 요리한 거야? 맛있다!

   남   사실, 이 길 따라 내려가면 있는 식당에서 사 왔어.

④ 여   레모네이드 좀 마실래?

   남   저 카페는 여러 종류의 차와 커피를 팔아.

⑤ 여   긴 달리기였어!

   남   응. 우리 10km는 뛴 것 같아.

해설 | 여자가 남자에게 레모네이드를 마시겠는지 물었으므로, 남자는 마실 것인지 여부를 답해야 한다. 그러나 남자가 저 카페는 여러 종류의 차와 커피를 판다는 어색한 대답을 했으므로 정답은 ④이다.

어휘 | strangely [stréindʒli] 囝 이상하게   sore [sɔːr] 쥉 쑤시는, 아픈

11   할 일 고르기   정답 ⑤

[Cellphone rings.]

W   What's up, Joonwoo?

M   Hey. What are you doing this Saturday?

W   I might go to the park and play badminton. Why?

M   Do you want to take a day trip to the beach?

W   Oh, that would be lovely. But how will we get there?

M   We can take a bus there. I'll book the tickets.

W   Great. I can't wait.

[휴대폰이 울린다.]

여   무슨 일이야, 준우야?

남   안녕. 이번 주 토요일에 뭐해?

여   공원에 가서 배드민턴 칠 것 같아. 왜?

남   해변으로 당일치기 여행 갈래?

여   오, 좋을 것 같아. 하지만 그곳에 어떻게 가?

남   버스를 타고 갈 수 있어. 내가 표를 예매할게.

여   좋아. 너무 기대된다.

해설 | 남자가 자신이 버스표를 예매하겠다고 했으므로 정답은 ⑤ '버스표 예매하기'이다.

어휘 | day trip 당일치기 여행

12   시간 정보 고르기   정답 ④

M   Excuse me. Can I ask you something?

W   Sure. What is it?

M   I heard Janice Walker will sign copies of her new novel at this bookstore tomorrow.

W   That's right. She will be here at 5 p.m.

M   I'd love to meet her. But I have to work until 6. Would I be too late if I came here at 6:30?

W   That will be fine. Ms. Walker will stay until 7:30.

M   Wonderful. Thank you.

남   실례합니다. 뭐 좀 여쭤봐도 될까요?

여   그럼요. 뭔가요?

남   Janice Walker가 이 서점에서 내일 그녀의 신간 소설책에 사인을 할 예정이라고 들었어요.

여   맞아요. 그녀는 여기에 오후 5시에 올 거예요.

남   저는 그녀를 정말 만나고 싶어요. 하지만 6시까지 일을 해야 해서요. 6시 30분에 여기에 오면 너무 늦을까요?

여   괜찮을 거예요. Walker씨는 7시 30분까지 계실 거예요.

남   정말 좋네요. 감사합니다.

해설 | 남자가 6시 30분에 오면 너무 늦을지 묻자 여자가 괜찮을 것이라고 했으므로 정답은 ④ '6:30 p.m.'이다.

어휘 | sign [sain] 통 사인하다, 서명하다

13 위치 고르기

정답 ⑤

M	Erica, let's get tickets for the musical.
W	Where do you want to sit?
M	I want to <u>sit in the front</u>. But I think those seats are a bit expensive.
W	Yeah. They are 200 dollars. How about in the middle?
M	I think that section <u>is already full</u>. There are only three sections left then.
W	Is there <u>a price difference</u> among the three?
M	Let me see. *[Pause]* No. They are all 100 dollars.
W	Well, then I'd like to sit <u>near the exit</u>.
M	Okay.

남	Erica, 뮤지컬 티켓을 사자.
여	어디에 앉고 싶어?
남	앞쪽에 앉고 싶어. 하지만 그 좌석들은 조금 비쌀 것 같아.
여	응. 거기는 200달러야. 중간은 어때?
남	그 구역은 벌써 만석인 것 같아. 그럼 세 개 구역만 남았네.
여	그 세 구역에 가격 차이가 있어?
남	어디 보자. *[잠시 멈춤]* 아니. 모두 100달러야.
여	음, 그럼 출구 근처에 앉고 싶어.
남	그래.

해설 | 여자가 뒤쪽 세 구역 중 출구 근처에 앉고 싶다고 했으므로 정답은 ⑤이다.

어휘 | difference [dífərəns] 몡 차이   exit [égzit] 몡 출구

14 한일 고르기

정답 ①

M	What are you doing this Friday, Subin?
W	I don't have any plans. Why?
M	I will <u>host a party</u> at my house, and I'd love for you to come.
W	That sounds nice. What are we celebrating?
M	I finally finished redecorating my house. I painted the last room yesterday, and the new furniture will be delivered tomorrow.
W	That's great news. I know <u>you worked on your house</u> for a long time.
M	Yes. I can't wait for you to see it.

남	이번 주 금요일에 뭐해, 수빈아?
여	아무 계획 없어. 왜?
남	우리 집에서 파티를 열 건데, 네가 와주면 좋겠어.
여	좋을 것 같아. 뭘 축하하려는 거야?
남	드디어 우리 집 실내 장식을 새로 하는 것을 끝냈거든. 어제 마지막 남은 방을 페인트칠했고, 새 가구는 내일 배송될 거야.
여	좋은 소식이네. 내가 알기로 넌 오랫동안 집에 공을 들였잖아.
남	응. 네가 그걸 보는 게 기대돼.

해설 | 남자가 어제 마지막 남은 방을 페인트칠했다고 했으므로 정답은 ① '방 페인트칠하기'이다.

어휘 | host [houst] 동 (파티를) 열다, 주최하다   redecorate [riːdèkəréit] 동 실내 장식을 새로 하다   work on ~에 공을 들이다

15 목적 고르기

정답 ①

M	Good morning! This is Peter from the student council. Next Wednesday, our school will be holding Eco Day. I'd like to encourage you to join this event. There will be information booths about various environmental issues. For example, you can learn <u>how to save electricity</u> and recycle properly. Anyone who wants to set up a booth should visit the student council's website. You <u>will find more details</u> about the event there. I hope many of you participate. Thanks!

남 좋은 아침입니다! 학생회의 Peter입니다. 다음 주 수요일에, 우리 학교에서 Eco Day를 개최할 예정입니다. 여러분이 이 행사에 참여하기를 권장하고 싶습니다. 다양한 환경 문제에 대한 안내 부스가 열릴 것입니다. 예를 들어, 여러분은 전기를 절약하는 법과 올바르게 재활용하는 법을 배울 수 있습니다. 부스를 설치하고 싶은 학생은 누구든 학생회 웹사이트를 방문하십시오. 행사에 대한 자세한 내용은 그곳에서 확인할 수 있습니다. 많은 분이 참여해주시길 바랍니다. 감사합니다!

해설 | 남자가 다음 주에 있을 Eco Day 행사에 참여하기를 권장하고 싶다고 했으므로 정답은 ① '행사 참여를 독려하려고'이다.

어휘 | student council 학생회   encourage [inkə́ːridʒ] 동 권장하다   environmental [invàiərənméntl] 형 환경의   electricity [ilektrísəti] 몡 전기   recycle [riːsáikəl] 동 재활용하다   properly [prápərli] 부 올바르게

16 금액 정보 고르기　　　　　　　　　　　　　　정답 ③

W	Hi. How may I help you?
M	I'm checking out of my room, and I'd like to <u>pay my bill</u> for room service.
W	Alright, let me see. *[Typing sound]* Were you in Room 402?
M	That's correct.
W	Your dinner was 35 dollars last night. Did you have <u>anything from the refrigerator</u>?
M	Yes. I had a bottle of soda.
W	Okay. It's three dollars for the soda and 35 dollars <u>for the meal then</u>.
M	Thanks. Here's my credit card.

여	안녕하세요. 무엇을 도와드릴까요?
남	객실 체크아웃을 할 건데, 룸서비스에 대한 요금도 지불하고 싶어요.
여	알겠습니다, 어디 봅시다. *[타자치는 소리]* 402호실에 계셨나요?
남	맞아요.
여	어젯밤 저녁 식사는 35달러였습니다. 냉장고에서 드신 것 있으세요?
남	네. 탄산음료 한 병을 마셨어요.
여	알겠습니다. 그럼 탄산음료는 3달러이고 식사는 35달러입니다.
남	감사합니다. 여기 제 신용카드요.

해설 | 남자가 먹었던 탄산음료는 3달러이고 식사는 35달러라고 했으므로 정답은 ③ '$ 38'이다.

어휘 | pay one's bill (돈을) 지불하다

17 적절한 응답 고르기　　　　　　　　　　　　　정답 ②

M	Who was on the phone, Jaemin?
W	It was my friend, Andy. I'm sorry <u>you had to pause</u> the movie.
M	I don't mind. Is everything okay?
W	Oh, yes. We just made plans to go to the aquarium next week.
M	Remember that <u>we are visiting</u> Aunt Mijung on Thursday for the holiday.
W	Oh, <u>I completely forgot</u>. What time are we leaving?
M	We're leaving the house around 7 a.m. <u>Write it down</u> in your calendar so you don't forget.
W	Yes. I'll do that right now.

남	누구랑 전화했어, 재민아?
여	내 친구 Andy였어. 영화를 잠시 멈추게 해서 미안해.
남	난 상관없어. 괜찮은 거지?
여	오, 응. 그냥 다음 주에 수족관에 갈 계획을 짠 거야.
남	우리 휴일을 맞아서 목요일에 미정 이모 댁에 방문할 예정이잖아.
여	오, 나 완전히 잊었어. 우리 몇 시에 떠날 예정이야?
남	오전 7시쯤에 집에서 출발할 거야. 잊지 않도록 달력에 적어놔.
여	응. 지금 바로 할게.

해설 | 남자가 여자에게 일정을 달력에 적어놓으라고 충고하고 있으므로 정답은 충고에 동의하는 ② 'Yes. I'll do that right now.'이다.

　選택지 해석
① 좋아. 팝콘과 음료수를 좀 가져다줄게.　② 응. 지금 바로 할게.　③ 해파리 구역 먼저 가는 걸 추천해.　④ 응. 차에 휘발유 채우는 걸 잊지 않을게.
⑤ 내 일정은 오늘 다 찼어, 미안.

어휘 | pause [pɔːz] ⑧ 잠시 멈추다　aquarium [əkwɛ́əriəm] ⑨ 수족관　completely [kəmplíːtli] ⑨ 완전히　jellyfish [dʒélifiʃ] ⑨ 해파리　fill up 채우다
gas [gæs] ⑨ 휘발유; 가스

18 적절한 응답 고르기　　　　　　　　　　　　　정답 ④

W	I love your shirt, Tom.
M	Thanks. It's my first time <u>wearing it</u>.
W	The color is so unique. Where did you get it?
M	I actually <u>bought it at a store</u> in New York.
W	Oh, that's a shame. I want to buy one too.
M	They <u>might have a website</u>. It's a big store.
W	Can you tell me the name of the store? I'll <u>look it up</u>.
M	Of course. The store is called Unique Style.

여	네 셔츠 정말 마음에 들어, Tom.
남	고마워. 처음 입은 거야.
여	색깔이 정말 독특하다. 어디서 샀어?
남	사실 뉴욕에 있는 어떤 가게에서 샀어.
여	오, 아깝다. 나도 하나 사고 싶어.
남	웹사이트가 있을지도 몰라. 큰 가게거든.
여	가게 이름을 말해줄 수 있어? 내가 찾아볼게.
남	당연하지. 그 가게는 Unique Style이라고 불러.

해설 | 여자가 가게 이름을 말해줄 수 있는지 물었으므로 정답은 가게 이름을 언급하는 ④ 'Of course. The store is called Unique Style.'이다.

　選택지 해석
① 그 가게는 오전 8시에 열어.　② 이 셔츠는 품절됐어. 안됐다.　③ 직원이 곧 도와줄 거야.　④ 당연하지. 그 가게는 Unique Style이라고 불러.
⑤ 그 단어를 온라인에서 찾아보는 게 어때?

어휘 | unique [juːníːk] ⑧ 독특한　look up (정보를) 찾아보다　shortly [ʃɔ́ːrtli] ⑨ 곧, 이내

19 적절한 응답 고르기 　　　　　　　　　　　정답 ③

W	Are you okay, Woomin?
M	No. I feel dizzy.
W	Did you drink some water?
M	Actually, I finished all of my water earlier in the hike.
W	Have some of mine then. And let's sit down for a while.
M	How far is the top of the mountain?
W	We are really close, but you need to take a break before we hike again.
M	Oh, I feel like eating something too.
W	You can have one of my snacks.

여	괜찮니, 우민아?
남	아니. 어지러워.
여	물 좀 마셨니?
남	실은, 등산 초반에 내 물을 다 마셔버렸어.
여	그럼 내 것을 좀 마셔. 그리고 잠시 앉아있자.
남	산 정상은 얼마나 멀었어?
여	정말 가까워져 있지만, 다시 등반을 시작하기 전에 넌 휴식을 취해야겠어.
남	오, 뭘 좀 먹고 싶기도 해.
여	내 간식 중 하나를 먹어도 돼.

해설 | 남자가 등산 중 휴식을 취하면서 뭘 먹고 싶다고 했으므로 정답은 먹을 것을 주겠다고 제안하는 ③ 'You can have one of my snacks.'이다.

　선택지 해석
① 여기 위에서 보는 경치가 아름답다.　② 의사 선생님께서 내가 집에 있기를 원하셔.　③ 내 간식 중 하나를 먹어도 돼.　④ 감자튀김을 좀 시켰어.
⑤ 가게에서 물 한 병을 사다 줘.

어휘 | dizzy [dízi] 휑 어지러운　top [tap] 뎽 정상, 꼭대기　take a break 휴식을 취하다　feel like ~하고 싶다

20 상황에 적절한 말 고르기 　　　　　　　　　정답 ①

M	Emma and her friend Max are in the library. They are both doing homework on their laptops. Emma still needs to do some research online, but her laptop is almost out of battery. Unfortunately, she forgot to bring a charger. So, she wants to ask Max if she can borrow his charger. In this situation, what would Emma most likely say to Max?
Emma	Max, can you lend me your laptop charger?

남	Emma와 그녀의 친구 Max는 도서관에 있습니다. 둘 다 노트북으로 숙제를 하고 있습니다. Emma는 아직도 온라인으로 조사를 더 해야 하지만, 그녀의 노트북은 배터리가 거의 다 닳았습니다. 공교롭게도, 그녀는 충전기를 가져오는 것을 잊어버렸습니다. 그래서, 그녀는 Max에게 그의 충전기를 빌릴 수 있을지 물어보고 싶습니다. 이러한 상황에서, Emma가 Max에게 가장 할 것 같은 말은 무엇입니까?
Emma	Max, 네 노트북 충전기를 빌려줄 수 있을까?

해설 | Emma가 Max에게 그의 충전기를 빌릴 수 있을지 물어보고 싶다고 했으므로 정답은 ① 'can you lend me your laptop charger?'이다.

　선택지 해석
① 네 노트북 충전기를 빌려줄 수 있을까?　② 우리 숙제를 빨리 끝내야 해.　③ 우리가 타자를 칠 때 너무 시끄러운 것 같아.　④ 그 웹사이트는 뭐라고 불러?
⑤ 내가 정보를 찾는 것을 도와줄 수 있어?

어휘 | be out of ~이 다 닳다, 다 떨어지다　charger [tʃɑ́ːrdʒər] 뎽 충전기　lend [lend] 뚱 빌려주다　search for ~을 찾다

16회 실전 모의고사

1	①	2	②	3	②	4	④	5	①	6	③	7	①	8	④	9	③	10	④
11	②	12	④	13	④	14	⑤	15	⑤	16	④	17	④	18	①	19	②	20	②

1 알맞은 그림 고르기

정답 ①

W Hello. What can I do for you?

M I'd like to buy a picture frame for my family photo.

W Is there any particular type you would like?

M I'd like to have one that my five-year-old daughter would like.

W All right. We have these animal-shaped ones. You can choose from an elephant, rabbit, or hedgehog.

M They all look good. But my daughter would prefer the elephant. I'll take it.

W Great choice. I'm sure she'll be glad to get it.

여 안녕하세요. 무엇을 도와드릴까요?

남 저는 가족사진을 넣을 액자를 사고 싶어요.

여 원하시는 특정한 유형이 있으신가요?

남 제 다섯 살 난 딸이 좋아할 만한 것을 갖고 싶어요.

여 그러시군요. 이 동물 모양의 액자들이 있습니다. 코끼리, 토끼, 고슴도치 중에서 고르실 수 있어요.

남 다 좋아 보이네요. 하지만 제 딸은 코끼리를 좋아할 거예요. 그걸로 할게요.

여 훌륭한 선택이세요. 그걸 받으면 따님이 틀림없이 좋아할 거예요.

해설 | 남자가 자신의 딸은 코끼리를 좋아할 것이라며 그걸로 하겠다고 했으므로 정답은 ①이다.

어휘 | picture frame 액자 hedgehog [hédʒhɑːg] 몡 고슴도치

2 언급하지 않은 내용 고르기

정답 ②

M Hey, Amy. Have you ever tried a Happy Pillow before?

W Yes. I use one every night. Why?

M I'm thinking of buying one for my mom.

W Great idea. They're famous for their relaxing effects.

M Then, it'll be perfect for my mom because she doesn't sleep well nowadays.

W Yeah, she'll love it. You can choose from many different patterns online. All the designs look nice, but the one with flowers is my favorite.

M Good to know. Can you tell me how much it is?

W Of course. It's only nine dollars.

M I see. Does it come in a large size?

W Yes. There are many different sizes you can choose from.

M Okay, thanks a lot.

남 안녕, Amy. 너 전에 Happy Pillow 써봤니?

여 응. 매일 밤 쓰고 있어. 왜?

남 엄마에게 하나 사드릴까 생각 중이야.

여 좋은 생각이야. 그것들은 마음을 편하게 해주는 효과로 유명해.

남 그럼, 엄마가 요즘 잠을 잘 못 주무시니까 꼭 맞겠다.

여 그래, 좋아하실 거야. 온라인에서는 많은 다양한 무늬들 중에서 고를 수 있어. 모든 디자인이 좋아 보이지만, 꽃이 있는 게 내가 가장 좋아하는 거야.

남 좋은 정보네! 얼마인지 알려줄 수 있니?

여 물론이지. 그건 겨우 9달러야.

남 그렇구나. 큰 사이즈도 나오니?

여 응. 네가 고를 수 있는 많은 다양한 사이즈들이 있어.

남 알겠어, 정말 고마워.

해설 | ① 기능(마음을 편하게 해주는 효과), ③ 무늬(꽃무늬를 포함하여 많이 다양함), ④ 가격(9달러), ⑤ 크기(큰 사이즈를 포함하여 많이 다양함)에 대해 언급했으므로 정답은 ② '색상'이다.

어휘 | relaxing [rilǽksiŋ] 혱 마음을 편하게 해주는 effect [ifékt] 몡 효과 nowadays [náuədeiz] 囝 요즘에, 오늘날에는

3 목적 고르기
정답 ②

[Telephone rings.]

M Good afternoon. You've reached the Danton Language School.

W Hi. A friend told me that you have a beginner Russian course.

M That's right. Classes are held on Tuesday and Thursday evenings, and they last for one hour.

W Great. I'd like to sign up for it. How do I do that?

M Just go to our website. You will see an option to register for courses on the main page.

W Got it. Can I pay for it online as well?

M Of course. And if you have any problems, feel free to call me back.

W I appreciate your help.

[전화기가 울린다.]

남 안녕하세요. 단톤 어학원으로 전화주셨습니다.

여 안녕하세요. 친구가 여기에 초급 러시아어 강좌가 있다고 알려줬어요.

남 맞습니다. 수업은 화요일과 목요일 저녁에 열리고, 한 시간 동안 진행됩니다.

여 좋네요. 등록하고 싶어요. 어떻게 하면 되나요?

남 저희 웹사이트로 가세요. 메인 화면에서 강좌 등록을 위한 선택지가 보일 거예요.

여 이해했어요. 온라인으로 지불도 가능한가요?

남 물론이죠. 그리고 만약 문제가 생기면, 얼마든지 저에게 다시 전화해 주세요.

여 도와주셔서 감사해요.

해설 | 여자가 남자에게 러시아어 강좌를 등록하고 싶다면서 어떻게 하면 되는지 물었으므로 정답은 ② '수업 등록 방법을 문의하려고'이다.

어휘 | course [kɔːrs] 圐 강좌; 과정 register [rédʒistər] 图 등록하다 feel free to 얼마든지 ~하다, 부담 없이 ~하다 appreciate [əpríːʃieit] 图 감사하다

4 시간 정보 고르기
정답 ④

W Dad, do you want to play tennis this afternoon?

M Sure. I have to go to the supermarket right now, but I should be back by 1 p.m.

W Why don't we go to the tennis court at 4?

M What about playing earlier? We could start at 2.

W My favorite TV show is on from 2 to 3. I really want to see it.

M Oh, then 4 is fine. But we'll just have to make sure we are done by 5.

W No problem! I think an hour will be enough time to play tennis.

여 아빠, 오늘 오후에 테니스 치실래요?

남 물론이지. 지금은 슈퍼마켓에 가야 하지만 오후 1시까지는 돌아올 거야.

여 4시에 테니스 코트에 가지 않을래요?

남 더 일찍 치는 게 어떠니? 2시에 시작할 수 있단다.

여 제가 가장 좋아하는 TV 프로가 2시부터 3시까지 해요. 그걸 정말 보고 싶어요.

남 오, 그럼 4시도 괜찮아. 그렇지만 5시까지는 반드시 끝내야 해.

여 물론이죠! 한 시간은 테니스를 치기에 충분한 시간 같아요.

해설 | 여자가 2시부터 3시까지는 가장 좋아하는 TV 프로를 보고 싶다고 하자, 남자가 그럼 4시도 괜찮다고 했으므로 정답은 ④ '4 p.m.'이다.

어휘 | make sure 반드시 ~하다 enough [inʌ́f] 뒝 충분한

5 장소 고르기
정답 ①

M Good morning. Are you feeling okay today?

W I think so, but my head hurts a little.

M That's normal for now. How are your eyes?

W They are fine. Did the surgery go well?

M Yes, it did. Your eyesight should recover soon.

W So, when can I leave?

M You need to stay here for another day for some tests. After that, we will give you some medicine, and you can go home.

남 좋은 아침입니다. 오늘은 좀 나으시나요?

여 그런 것 같은데, 머리가 약간 아파요.

남 지금은 그게 정상이에요. 눈은 어떠신가요?

여 괜찮아요. 수술이 잘 됐나요?

남 네, 잘 됐어요. 시력이 곧 회복될 거예요.

여 그럼, 언제 떠날 수 있나요?

남 몇 가지 검사를 해야 하니 여기 하루 더 계셔야 합니다. 그 이후에는 약을 드릴 거고, 그러면 집에 가셔도 돼요.

해설 | 여자가 눈은 괜찮다고 하며 수술이 잘 됐는지 묻자 남자가 시력이 곧 회복될 것이라고 했으므로 정답은 ① '안과'이다.

어휘 | surgery [sə́ːrdʒəri] 圐 수술 eyesight [áisait] 圐 시력 recover [rikʌ́vər] 图 회복하다 medicine [médisən] 圐 약

6 그림 상황에 적절한 대화 고르기　　　　정답 ③

① W	Let's go home.
M	Good idea. I'm a little tired.
② W	This is a great fitness center.
M	Maybe you should get a membership.
③ W	Why don't we play some badminton?
M	I'd rather watch this soccer game on TV.
④ W	What's the score?
M	I'm ahead by three points.
⑤ W	Is the pharmacy open today?
M	No. It is closed on Sundays.

① 여 집에 가자.
　 남 좋은 생각이야. 나 약간 피곤해.
② 여 여긴 정말 좋은 체육관이야.
　 남 어쩌면 회원권을 사는 게 좋겠어.
③ 여 배드민턴 치지 않을래?
　 남 난 차라리 TV로 이 축구 경기를 볼래.
④ 여 몇 점이야?
　 남 내가 3점 차로 앞서 있어.
⑤ 여 약국 오늘 열었니?
　 남 아니. 일요일엔 닫아.

해설 | 배드민턴을 치자고 제안하는 여자에게 남자가 TV로 축구를 보겠다고 말하고 있는 상황이므로 정답은 ③이다.

어휘 | membership [mémbərʃip] 몡 회원권　would rather 차라리 ~하겠다　ahead [əhéd] 뮈 앞서　by [bai] 젠 ~ 차이로; ~ 옆에
pharmacy [fáːrməsi] 몡 약국

7 부탁·요청한 일 고르기　　　　정답 ①

W	Can I talk to you, Jake?
M	Sure, Ms. Reed. What's going on?
W	You didn't do well on your last test. Is there something wrong?
M	No. I'm just so busy lately. Swimming practice takes up a lot of time.
W	Well, remember that school is important too.
M	I know. Can you give me any materials to study more?
W	Sure. Stop by after class to pick them up.

여 이야기 좀 할 수 있을까, Jake?
남 물론이죠, Reed 선생님. 무슨 일인가요?
여 지난 시험을 잘 못 봤는데. 무슨 문제라도 있니?
남 아니요. 단지 최근에 매우 바빴어요. 수영 연습에 시간이 많이 들거든요.
여 음, 학업도 중요하다는 걸 기억하렴.
남 알아요. 공부를 더 할 수 있는 자료를 주실 수 있으신가요?
여 물론이지. 방과 후에 가지러 오렴.

해설 | 남자가 여자에게 공부를 더 할 수 있는 자료를 달라고 부탁했으므로 정답은 ① '보충 자료 주기'이다.

어휘 | lately [léitli] 뮈 최근에　take up (시간이) 들다, 걸리다　material [mətíəriəl] 몡 자료; 재료

8 언급하지 않은 내용 고르기　　　　정답 ④

W	Good evening, everyone. Thank you for coming to our play tonight. I'm the drama club director, Kendra Young. This is the 14th play by our drama club since 2002. I want to thank the student-actors. All 10 of our actors worked so hard on this play. After the performance, don't leave right away. We will serve snacks outside the auditorium. Also, you'll be able to take pictures with our cast members.

여 안녕하십니까, 여러분. 오늘 밤 저희 연극에 와주셔서 감사합니다. 저는 연극 동아리 감독 Kendra Young입니다. 이번이 2002년 이후로 저희 연극 동아리의 14번째 연극입니다. 학생 배우들에게 감사를 표하고 싶습니다. 저희 배우 열 명 모두 이 연극을 열심히 준비했습니다. 공연이 끝난 후, 바로 떠나지 마십시오. 강당 바깥에서 간식을 제공할 예정입니다. 그리고, 우리 출연진들과 함께 사진 촬영을 하실 수 있습니다.

해설 | ① 공연 회차(14번째), ② 감독 이름(Kendra Young), ③ 출연진 수(10명), ⑤ 다과 제공 여부(간식 제공 예정)에 대해 언급했으므로 정답은 ④ '연극의 길이'이다.

어휘 | director [diréktər] 몡 감독　auditorium [ɔ̀ːditɔ́ːriəm] 몡 강당　cast [kæst] 몡 출연진, 배역

9 화제 고르기　　　　정답 ③

W	This is one of the most popular tropical fruits. This is a very common fruit, so you can buy it in most stores. You can eat this for breakfast or as a healthy snack between meals. It is long and has a bright yellow peel. To eat it, you must remove its peel and eat the white part inside. Then, you can enjoy its sweet taste. When this fruit becomes too old to eat, it begins to turn brown.

여 이것은 가장 인기 있는 열대 과일 중 하나입니다. 이것은 매우 흔한 과일로, 대부분의 가게에서 살 수 있습니다. 이것을 아침이나 식사 사이의 건강한 간식으로 먹을 수 있습니다. 이것은 길고 껍질이 밝은 노란색입니다. 이것을 먹기 위해서는 껍질을 벗기고 속에 있는 하얀 부분을 먹어야 합니다. 그럼, 이것의 달콤한 맛을 즐길 수 있습니다. 이 과일은 먹기에 너무 오래되면, 갈변하기 시작합니다.

해설 | 이것(This)은 길고 껍질이 밝은 노란색이라고 했고, 속에 있는 하얀 부분을 먹는다고 했으므로 정답은 ③ '바나나'이다.

어휘 | tropical [trápikəl] 혱 열대의　common [kámən] 혱 흔한　peel [piːl] 몡 껍질　remove [rimúːv] 동 벗기다, 제거하다　turn brown 갈변하다

10 어색한 대화 고르기 정답 ④

① W What do you think of your new phone?
   M I like it because it's <u>much faster than</u> my old one.
② W Which one is your house?
   M That one <u>with the little rose garden</u> is mine.
③ W Can you help me? I can't open this bottle.
   M <u>Let me open it</u> for you.
④ W <u>What size shirt do you usually wear?</u>
   M <u>I like the ones with the blue collars.</u>
⑤ W How was your presentation about polar bears?
   M I was <u>so nervous at first</u>, but I think I did well.

① 여 네 새 휴대폰에 대해 어떻게 생각해?
   남 이전 것보다 훨씬 더 빨라서 좋아.
② 여 어느 집이 너희 집이니?
   남 작은 장미 정원이 있는 저 집이 내 집이야.
③ 여 도와줄 수 있니? 이 병을 못 열겠어.
   남 내가 열어 줄게.
④ 여 너는 보통 어떤 사이즈의 셔츠를 입니?
   남 나는 파란 옷깃이 있는 것이 좋아.
⑤ 여 북극곰에 대한 발표는 어땠니?
   남 처음에는 너무 긴장했는데, 잘한 것 같아.

해설 | 여자가 남자에게 어떤 사이즈의 셔츠를 입는지 물었으므로, 남자는 셔츠의 사이즈를 답해야 한다. 그러나 남자가 자신은 파란 옷깃이 있는 것이 좋다는 어색한 대답을 했으므로 정답은 ④이다.

어휘 | collar [kálər] 명 옷깃, 칼라 polar bear 북극곰

11 할 일 고르기 정답 ②

[Cellphone rings.]
W Hey, Carson.
M Hi. Are you <u>coming to my house</u> tonight?
W Yes. Did you <u>pick a movie yet?</u>
M Not yet. There are two new films that were just released. One is a comedy, and the other is a drama.
W <u>I prefer comedies.</u>
M Okay. And how about you pick up something to eat on your way here?
W Sure. I'll <u>buy some ice cream.</u>
M Perfect. I can't wait for our movie night!

[휴대폰이 울린다.]
여 안녕, Carson.
남 안녕. 오늘 밤에 우리 집에 올 거니?
여 응. 영화 벌써 골랐니?
남 아직 아니야. 막 개봉한 신작 영화가 두 편 있어. 하나는 코미디이고 나머지 하나는 드라마야.
여 나는 코미디를 더 좋아해.
남 그래. 그리고 여기 오는 길에 먹을 것을 사 오는 게 어때?
여 물론이지. 내가 아이스크림을 좀 살게.
남 완벽해. 오늘 밤 영화를 빨리 보고 싶어!

해설 | 여자가 남자의 집에 가는 길에 아이스크림을 사겠다고 했으므로 정답은 ② '아이스크림 사기'이다.

어휘 | yet [jet] 부 벌써; 아직 release [rilíːs] 동 개봉하다; 해방하다

12 도표에서 알맞은 항목 고르기 정답 ④

W Larry, you need to choose which exhibition you want to go to tomorrow.
M Okay. <u>What types of exhibitions</u> are there?
W You can choose between <u>a history or an art</u> exhibition.
M History sounds boring. <u>Let's go to an art exhibition.</u>
W Sure. <u>I want to go to the one at the Lake Plaza</u> so that we can <u>go shopping</u> afterward.
M Is there an audio tour for the exhibit? Those are <u>always so interesting.</u>
W <u>Sadly, there isn't.</u> But we can get a brochure.
M That will do.

여 Larry, 내일 어떤 전시회에 가고 싶은지 골라야 해.
남 알겠어. 어떤 종류의 전시회가 있니?
여 역사나 미술 전시회 중에서 고를 수 있어.
남 역사는 지루할 것 같아. 미술 전시회에 가자.
여 그래. 나는 나중에 우리가 쇼핑하러 갈 수 있게 Lake Plaza 에서 하는 걸 가고 싶어.
남 전시회에 오디오 투어가 있니? 그건 언제나 매우 흥미로운데.
여 슬프게도, 없어. 하지만 소책자는 얻을 수 있어.
남 그거면 될 거야.

해설 | 남자가 미술 전시회에 가자고 하자 여자는 Lake Plaza로 가고 싶다고 했고, 오디오 투어는 없다고 했으므로 정답은 ④이다.

어휘 | exhibition [èksəbíʃən] 명 전시회 afterward [ǽftərwərd] 부 나중에 brochure [brouʃúər] 명 소책자, 팸플릿

13 시간 정보 고르기   정답 ④

M Did you say you <u>want</u> <u>to</u> <u>go</u> camping, Jamie?
W Yeah. I already borrowed the equipment from my brother.
M Oh, really? Well, let's choose a campground. This one <u>in</u> <u>front</u> <u>of</u> <u>the</u> <u>lake</u> looks nice.
W I've seen that place before. <u>Are</u> <u>there</u> <u>sites</u> <u>available</u> on May 5th? It's a national holiday.
M No, I don't think so. But it seems that we can reserve a site on the 4th or 7th.
W Isn't May 4th a Wednesday? I have a yoga class that day.
M <u>Can't</u> <u>you</u> <u>skip</u> <u>it</u>?
W I can, but I don't want to. <u>Let's</u> <u>go</u> <u>on</u> <u>the</u> <u>7th.</u>
M <u>Sure.</u> I'll <u>make</u> <u>a</u> <u>reservation</u> now.

남 너 캠핑 가고 싶다고 했었니, Jamie?
여 응. 나 이미 내 남동생에게 장비를 빌렸어.
남 오, 정말? 그렇다면, 캠프장을 고르자. 호수 앞에 이곳이 좋아 보이네.
여 나 전에 거기 봤어. 5월 5일에 이용 가능한 곳이 있니? 공휴일이잖아.
남 아니, 안될 것 같아. 하지만 4일이나 7일에는 한 곳을 예약할 수 있는 것처럼 보여.
여 5월 4일은 수요일 아니야? 나는 그날 요가 수업이 있어.
남 빠질 수 없니?
여 그럴 수 있지만 그러고 싶지 않아. 7일에 가자.
남 물론이지. 내가 지금 예약 할게.

해설 | 여자가 5월 4일에는 요가 수업이 있으니 7일에 가자고 했고 남자도 동의했으므로 정답은 ④ '5월 7일'이다.
어휘 | equipment [ikwípmənt] 명 장비 available [əvéiləbl] 형 이용 가능한 reserve [rizə́:rv] 동 예약하다 (reservation [rèzərvéiʃən] 명 예약)

14 한일 고르기   정답 ⑤

W Tim, I messaged you on Tuesday but <u>got</u> <u>no</u> <u>reply</u>.
M I'm sorry. What was your message about?
W Don't worry about it. I just wanted to <u>have</u> <u>a</u> <u>chat</u> with you. By the way, why didn't you see my message?
M I <u>dropped</u> <u>my</u> <u>phone</u> in the sink, so it stopped working.
W Oh, no. Did you take it to the repair shop?
M Yes. <u>I just</u> <u>got it</u> <u>fixed</u> yesterday.
W I'm glad it's fixed now.

여 Tim, 화요일에 너에게 메시지를 보냈는데 답장을 못 받았어.
남 미안해. 메시지가 뭐에 관한 거였니?
여 신경 쓰지 마. 그냥 너랑 수다 떨고 싶었어. 그런데, 내 메시지를 왜 못 봤던 거야?
남 싱크대에 휴대폰을 떨어뜨렸더니, 작동을 멈췄어.
여 오, 이런. 수리점에 가져갔니?
남 응. 어제 막 수리받았어.
여 지금은 수리되었다니 다행이다.

해설 | 남자가 어제 막 휴대폰의 수리를 받았다고 했으므로 정답은 ⑤ '휴대폰 수리 맡기기'이다.
어휘 | reply [riplái] 명 답장, 대답 동 답장하다 chat [tʃæt] 명 수다, 잡담 동 수다를 떨다 by the way 그런데

15 목적 고르기   정답 ⑤

W Good morning, passengers. Please note the following information. As the weather gets warmer, we will be <u>running the air conditioning</u> on the subway more often. If you <u>find the temperature uncomfortable</u>, please text us at 8877. Make sure the message includes your subway car number and whether it is too hot or too cold. In addition, passengers who are <u>sensitive to the cold</u> should ride in the first six cars of the train. It will be <u>warmer in those cars</u> than in the others. Thank you for listening, and I hope you enjoy your ride today!

여 좋은 아침입니다, 승객 여러분. 다음 안내를 참고하시기 바랍니다. 날씨가 따뜻해짐에 따라, 저희는 지하철 에어컨을 더 자주 가동할 예정입니다. 만약 온도가 불편하시다면, 8877로 문자를 보내주십시오. 메시지에 지하철 차량 번호와 너무 더운지 또는 추운지를 반드시 포함해 주시기 바랍니다. 추가적으로, 추위에 민감한 승객 여러분께서는 앞의 열차 여섯 량에 탑승하십시오. 다른 차량에 비해 이 차량들이 더 따뜻할 것입니다. 청취해 주셔서 감사하며, 오늘 탑승도 즐거우시길 바랍니다!

해설 | 여자가 지하철 에어컨을 더 자주 가동할 예정임을 설명하면서 온도가 불편할 경우 취할 수 있는 방법들을 안내하고 있으므로 정답은 ⑤ '지하철 냉방 운영 지침을 안내하려고'이다.
어휘 | temperature [témpərətʃər] 명 온도 uncomfortable [ʌnkʌ́mfərtəbəl] 형 불편한 include [inklú:d] 동 포함하다 sensitive to ~에 민감한

M	How may I help you?
W	I'd like to order a cake for a birthday party. How much will it be?
M	It'll be 20 dollars, but you can get candles and decorations with it for an extra fee.
W	How much will that be?
M	It'll be 10 dollars. Do you want the additions?
W	Okay. But can I use this discount coupon?
M	Yes, you can. That will take five dollars off.
W	Great. I'll go ahead and pay then.

남 무엇을 도와드릴까요?
여 생일 파티용 케이크를 주문하고 싶어요. 얼마일까요?
남 20달러 되겠습니다만, 추가 비용으로 양초와 장식을 받으실 수 있습니다.
여 그건 얼마일까요?
남 10달러 되겠습니다. 추가를 원하시나요?
여 네. 그런데 이 할인 쿠폰을 사용할 수 있나요?
남 네, 사용하실 수 있습니다. 5달러 할인되겠습니다.
여 좋네요. 그럼 돈을 지불할게요.

해설 | 케이크가 20달러이며 여자가 10달러를 더 지불하여 양초와 장식을 추가한 후 5달러 할인 쿠폰을 사용했으므로 정답은 ④ '$ 25'이다.

어휘 | extra fee 추가 비용, 추가 요금   addition [ədíʃən] 명 추가   discount [dískaunt] 명 할인   take off (값을) 할인하다

W	What are you doing tonight, Minjae?
M	I don't have any plans. Why?
W	There's a lecture on stars. Do you want to come with me?
M	A lecture on stars?
W	Yes. Experts will point out different stars to us, and they will teach us about them.
M	I'd be delighted to go. I'm very interested in space. What time does it start?
W	It begins at 7 in the park downtown.
M	I'll meet you there then.

여 오늘 밤에 뭐 하니, 민재야?
남 아무 계획 없어. 왜?
여 별에 관한 강연이 있어. 나와 같이 갈래?
남 별에 관한 강연이라고?
여 응. 전문가들이 여러 가지 별들을 짚어줄 예정이고, 우리에게 그것들에 대해 가르쳐 줄 거야.
남 기꺼이 갈래. 난 우주에 매우 관심이 많아. 그건 언제 시작하니?
여 시내에 있는 공원에서 7시에 시작해.
남 그때 거기서 만나자.

해설 | 여자가 별에 관한 강연에 가자고 했고, 시내에 있는 공원에서 7시에 시작한다고 알리고 있으므로 정답은 약속 장소와 시간을 정하는 ④ 'I'll meet you there then.'이다.

선택지 해석
① 나는 그 행성의 이름을 몰라. ② 그 쇼는 <Space Travels>라고 불려. ③ 너무 어두워서 아무것도 볼 수가 없어. ④ 그때 거기서 만나자.
⑤ 그건 별을 관찰할 좋은 기회였어.

어휘 | lecture [léktʃər] 명 강연, 강의   expert [ékspəːrt] 명 전문가   be delighted to 기꺼이 ~하다   planet [plǽnit] 명 행성   observe [əbzéːrv] 동 관찰하다

M	You're glued to your phone. What are you playing with?
W	A new picture app was just released. Do you want to see it?
M	What does it do?
W	You can edit the photographs you take on your phone. See? There are lots of stickers and effects.
M	That's really cool. What photographs did you change with it?
W	I added heart and flower stickers to this one of me and my friends. And I changed the colors in this one.
M	It looks so different now. Can I try changing one?
W	Sure. Let's take a photograph that you can use.

남 휴대폰에 열중하고 있네. 뭐 하고 노는 거야?
여 새로운 사진 앱이 막 출시됐거든. 볼래?
남 뭘 하는 건데?
여 네가 휴대폰으로 찍은 사진들을 편집할 수 있어. 보여? 스티커와 특수 효과가 많아.
남 정말 멋지다. 그걸로 어떤 사진을 바꿨니?
여 나는 나와 내 친구들이 있는 이 사진에 하트와 꽃 스티커를 붙였어. 그리고 이것의 색을 바꿨어.
남 그건 이제 엄청 달라 보여. 나도 하나 바꿔봐도 되니?
여 물론이지. 네가 쓸 수 있는 사진을 찍자.

해설 | 남자가 앱을 이용하여 사진을 바꿔봐도 되는지 부탁했으므로 정답은 부탁을 수락하는 ① 'Sure. Let's take a photograph that you can use.'이다.

선택지 해석
① 물론이지. 네가 쓸 수 있는 사진을 찍자. ② 고마워. 네 메시지 방금 받았어. ③ 네 얼굴을 오른쪽으로 돌려 봐. ④ 이 케이스는 내 휴대폰에 맞지 않아.
⑤ 그다음, 여기에서 이 앱에 별점을 줄 수 있어.

어휘 | be glued to ~에 열중하다   edit [édit] 동 편집하다   effects [ifékts] 명 특수 효과 (effect [ifékt] 명 영향, 효과, 결과)   fit [fit] 동 (꼭) 맞다 형 알맞은

19 적절한 응답 고르기

M	What are you doing, Jude?
W	I'm planning my next dance video.
M	I didn't know you made dance videos.
W	I pick my favorite songs, and then I dance to them. I like to post the videos online so other people can see them.
M	Do you have lots of followers?
W	Yes. But I don't care about followers. Dancing makes me happy.
M	Good for you. I'm jealous of your hobby.
W	I'm sure you'll find one too.
M	Maybe. I'd love to watch some of your videos. Please tell me the name of your channel.
W	I'll write it down for you so you can look it up later.

남	뭐 하고 있니, Jude?
여	다음 댄스 영상을 구상하고 있어.
남	네가 댄스 영상을 만드는지 몰랐어.
여	나는 내가 가장 좋아하는 노래를 골라서 그것들에 맞춰 춤을 춰. 다른 사람들이 볼 수 있도록 그 영상들을 온라인에 올리는 걸 좋아하거든.
남	팔로워가 많니?
여	응. 하지만 나는 팔로워를 신경 쓰지 않아. 춤추는 것은 나를 행복하게 만들어.
남	잘됐다. 네 취미 부럽다.
여	너도 꼭 하나 찾을 수 있을 거라고 생각해.
남	아마도. 네 영상을 좀 보고 싶어. 네 채널의 이름을 알려줘.
여	나중에 찾아볼 수 있도록 적어줄게.

해설 | 남자가 여자의 채널 이름을 알려달라고 요청했으므로 정답은 요청을 수락하는 ② 'I'll write it down for you so you can look it up later.'이다.

선택지 해석

① 영상 제목은 <Sing Along>이야. ② 나중에 찾아볼 수 있도록 적어줄게. ③ 공연 중에는 어떤 촬영도 하지 말아 주세요. ④ 응. 당연히 너랑 같이 춤출 거야. ⑤ 네가 남긴 댓글은 정말 사려 깊었어.

어휘 | plan [plæn] 동 구상하다; 계획하다 jealous [dʒéləs] 형 부러운 thoughtful [θɔ́:tfəl] 형 사려 깊은

20 상황에 적절한 말 고르기

M	Elizabeth is at the hair salon to get a haircut. The hairdresser washes and cuts her hair. Then, he starts to dry it. Elizabeth likes her haircut, but she wants her hair to be shorter. So, she decides to ask the hairdresser if he can cut more of her hair off. In this situation, what would Elizabeth most likely say to the hairdresser?
Elizabeth	Can you cut my hair shorter, please?

남	Elizabeth는 머리를 자르기 위해 미용실에 있습니다. 미용사가 그녀의 머리를 감기고 자릅니다. 그리고 그는 머리를 말리기 시작합니다. Elizabeth는 그녀의 머리 모양이 마음에 들지만, 머리가 더 짧기를 바랍니다. 그래서 그녀는 미용사에게 그녀의 머리를 좀 더 잘라줄 수 있는지 묻기로 결심합니다. 이러한 상황에서, Elizabeth가 미용사에게 가장 할 것 같은 말은 무엇입니까?
Elizabeth	제 머리를 좀 더 짧게 잘라 주시겠어요?

해설 | Elizabeth가 미용사에게 머리를 좀 더 잘라줄 수 있는지 묻기로 결심했다고 했으므로 정답은 ② 'Can you cut my hair shorter, please?'이다.

선택지 해석

① 물이 너무 뜨거워요. ② 제 머리를 좀 더 짧게 잘라 주시겠어요? ③ 죄송한데, 색이 마음에 들지 않아요. ④ 빗 있으세요? ⑤ 머리가 아름다워 보여요.

어휘 | haircut [héərkʌt] 명 머리 자르기; (머리를 잘라서 만든) 머리 모양 comb [koum] 명 빗

1	②	**2**	④	**3**	⑤	**4**	②	**5**	③	**6**	⑤	**7**	④	**8**	④	**9**	④	**10**	②
11	⑤	**12**	②	**13**	②	**14**	③	**15**	⑤	**16**	⑤	**17**	①	**18**	③	**19**	⑤	**20**	②

1 알맞은 그림 고르기

정답 ②

M Excuse me. Do you have <u>any eco-friendly wrapping paper</u>?
W Of course. These are the ones we have. They are all <u>made from recycled paper</u>.
M I think a patterned paper would <u>go better with</u> my gift.
W I see. How about this one with hearts on it?
M It's pretty, but I'm worried it would <u>look a bit childish</u>.
W Okay. Then, <u>how about this one with snowflakes on it?</u>
M Oh, <u>it looks nice. I'll buy it.</u>

남 실례합니다. 친환경 포장지가 있나요?
여 물론이죠. 이것들이 저희가 가지고 있는 것들이에요. 모두 재활용 종이로 만들어졌어요.
남 무늬가 있는 포장지가 제 선물과 더 잘 어울릴 것 같네요.
여 그렇군요. 하트가 있는 이것은 어떠세요?
남 예쁘긴 한데 약간 유치하게 보일 것 같아 걱정돼요.
여 알겠습니다. 그럼, 눈송이가 있는 이것은 어떠신가요?
남 오, 좋아 보이네요. 그걸 살게요.

해설 | 남자가 눈송이가 무늬가 있는 친환경 포장지가 좋아 보여서 사겠다고 했으므로 정답은 ②이다.

어휘 | eco-friendly 휑 친환경의 wrapping paper 포장지 recycled [riːsáikld] 휑 재활용된 childish [tʃáildiʃ] 휑 유치한 snowflake [snóufleik] 휑 눈송이

2 부탁·요청한 일 고르기

정답 ④

W Are you <u>having a fun time</u> at the beach, Danny?
M Yes, Mom! The water is <u>perfect for swimming</u>.
W I'm glad. Where is your sister?
M She's <u>building a sandcastle</u> down the beach.
W Okay. We'll stay here for another two hours and then go back to the hotel.
M <u>Can you put some more sunscreen</u> on my back then? I feel like it is burning a bit.
W Sure. We don't want you to get burned badly.

여 해변에서 즐거운 시간 보내고 있니, Danny?
남 네, 엄마! 물이 수영하는 데 딱 좋아요.
여 다행이구나. 네 여동생은 어디 있니?
남 해변 아래쪽에서 모래성을 쌓고 있어요.
여 알겠어. 우리는 여기 두 시간 더 있다가 호텔로 돌아갈 거란다.
남 그럼 제 등에 선크림 좀 더 발라주시겠어요? 등이 약간 탄 것 같아요.
여 물론이지. 우리는 네가 심한 화상을 입길 바라지 않는단다.

해설 | 남자가 여자에게 등에 선크림을 좀 더 발라달라고 부탁했으므로 정답은 ④ '선크림 발라주기'이다.

어휘 | sandcastle [sǽndkæsl] 휑 모래성 sunscreen [sʌ́nskriːn] 휑 선크림, 자외선 차단제 back [bæk] 휑 등 get burned 화상을 입다

3 그림 상황에 적절한 대화 고르기

정답 ⑤

① M Do you have the key?
　 W You just need to <u>enter a code</u>.
② M Your garden looks beautiful.
　 W <u>It's kind of</u> you to say that.
③ M Can I help you with something?
　 W Yes. I can't <u>reach the jar</u> on this shelf.
④ M Do you want me to mail this letter for you?
　 W No. I'll go to the post office later.
⑤ M <u>Let me open the door</u> for you.
　 W <u>Thanks for your help.</u>

① 남 열쇠를 가지고 있니?
　 여 그냥 번호를 입력하면 돼.
② 남 정원이 정말 아름답군요.
　 여 그렇게 말해주셔서 고맙습니다.
③ 남 제가 뭔가 도와드릴 것이 있나요?
　 여 네. 이 선반에 있는 병이 닿지 않아요.
④ 남 이 편지 내가 너 대신에 부쳐줄까?
　 여 아니야. 내가 나중에 우체국에 갈게.
⑤ 남 제가 문을 열어드리겠습니다.
　 여 도와주셔서 감사합니다.

해설 | 남자가 여자를 대신하여 출입문을 열어 주고 있는 상황이므로 정답은 ⑤이다.

어휘 | code [koud] 휑 번호; 암호 reach [riːtʃ] 튕 닿다 jar [dʒɑːr] 휑 병, 항아리

4 시간 정보 고르기   정답 ②

	[Telephone rings.]
M	Thank you for calling Western Rail. How can I help you?
W	I need to get to Seattle by 4 p.m. Could I reserve a seat on the 3 p.m. train?
M	Unfortunately, that one is fully booked. But there are still tickets available for the 12 p.m. train.
W	That would get me to Seattle too early.
M	Then, how about a 1 p.m. departure? You would arrive at 2.
W	I guess that will do.
M	Okay. Could I get your name, please?
W	It is Sarah Warren.

[전화기가 울린다.]
남   Western Rail에 전화 주셔서 감사합니다. 무엇을 도와드릴까요?
여   저는 시애틀에 오후 4시까지 도착해야 해요. 3시 기차의 좌석을 예약할 수 있을까요?
남   유감스럽게도, 그 기차는 예약이 꽉 찼습니다. 하지만 오후 12시 기차의 표는 여전히 구매가 가능합니다.
여   그건 시애틀에 너무 일찍 도착할 거예요.
남   그렇다면, 오후 1시 출발은 어떠신가요? 2시에 도착하실 거예요.
여   그러면 될 것 같네요.
남   알겠습니다. 성함을 알 수 있을까요?
여   Sarah Warren이에요.

해설 | 남자가 오후 1시에 출발하는 기차가 어떤지 묻자 여자가 그러면 될 것 같다고 했으므로 정답은 ② '1 p.m.'이다.

어휘 | reserve [rizə́ːrv] 동 예약하다   departure [dipá:rtʃər] 명 출발

5 언급하지 않은 내용 고르기   정답 ③

M	Mary, did you see the posters about the talent show?
W	I did. Every student in the school can join, right?
M	Yeah! Do you want to sing a song together?
W	Sure, that sounds fun. When is the show happening?
M	On April 7th.
W	How do we sign up?
M	We can register online. The deadline is Thursday.
W	Let's sign up this afternoon.

남   Mary, 장기 자랑에 관한 포스터 봤니?
여   봤어. 학교의 모든 학생이 참가할 수 있잖아, 그렇지?
남   응! 우리 같이 노래 부를래?
여   물론이지, 재미있겠다. 장기 자랑은 언제 열리는데?
남   4월 7일이야.
여   어떻게 신청해?
남   온라인으로 등록할 수 있어. 목요일이 마감일이야.
여   오늘 오후에 신청하자.

해설 | ① 참가 자격(학교의 모든 학생), ② 공연 날짜(4월 7일), ④ 신청 방법(온라인 등록), ⑤ 신청 마감일(목요일)에 대해 언급했으므로 정답은 ③ '공연 장소'이다.

어휘 | sign up 신청하다   register [rédʒistər] 동 등록하다   deadline [dédlàin] 명 마감일

6 장소 고르기   정답 ⑤

W	Excuse me. I'd like to borrow this book, please.
M	Alright. Can I see your student ID?
W	Yes. Here you go.
M	Let me check your account. [Pause] Well, you have another book that you did not return yet.
W	Really? Which one?
M	It's *Flowers of Europe*. It was due last Wednesday.
W	Oh, no. I left that in class yesterday. I'll bring it back tomorrow.

여   실례합니다. 이 책을 빌리고 싶은데요.
남   알겠습니다. 학생증을 볼 수 있을까요?
여   네. 여기 있어요.
남   계정을 확인할게요. [잠시 멈춤] 음, 아직 반납하지 않은 책이 한 권 있네요.
여   정말요? 어떤 거죠?
남   <Flowers of Europe>이에요. 지난 수요일까지였네요.
여   오, 이런. 어제 그걸 교실에 놓고 왔어요. 내일 반납할게요.

해설 | 여자가 책을 빌리고 싶다고 했고, 남자가 여자에게 반납하지 않은 책이 있다고 하는 것으로 보아 정답은 ⑤ '도서관'이다.

어휘 | account [əkáunt] 명 계정; 계좌   return [ritə́ːrn] 동 반납하다   bring back 반납하다, 돌려주다

7 어색한 대화 고르기 정답 ④

① M Did you see the soccer game last night?
  W Yeah. It was a close game.
② M Can you water the flowers on the balcony this afternoon?
  W Sure. I'll water them before dinner.
③ M What time does the bank close today?
  W It closes at 5 o'clock.
④ M May I use your phone please?
  W I'm here to buy a new phone.
⑤ M The bus will leave in three minutes.
  W Let's run since I don't want to miss it.

① 남 어젯밤에 축구 경기 봤니?
  여 응. 아슬아슬한 경기였어.
② 남 오늘 오후에 발코니의 꽃에 물을 줄 수 있니?
  여 물론이지. 저녁 식사 전에 줄게.
③ 남 오늘 은행이 몇 시에 닫나요?
  여 5시에 닫습니다.
④ 남 당신의 휴대폰을 써도 될까요?
  여 저는 새 휴대폰을 사러 왔어요.
⑤ 남 버스가 3분 후에 떠날 거야.
  여 그걸 놓치고 싶지 않으니 뛰자.

해설 | 남자가 여자에게 휴대폰을 써도 되는지 물었으므로, 여자는 허락 여부를 말해야 한다. 하지만 여자가 새 휴대폰을 사러 왔다는 어색한 대답을 했으므로 정답은 ④ 이다.

어휘 | close game 아슬아슬한 경기, 접전 balcony [bǽlkəni] 뗑 발코니 miss [mis] 통 놓치다

8 부탁·요청한 일 고르기 정답 ④

M When is the election for school president, Ms. Lewis?
W It will be next month. Why?
M I'm thinking about running in the election.
W Oh, you would do a good job.
M Really? What kinds of responsibilities would I have as school president?
W You would work with school council members to make the changes students want.
M Then, I want to sign up to run. Can you give me the form?
W Of course. Please fill out this form.

남 학생회장 선거는 언제인가요, Lewis 선생님?
여 다음 달에 있을 거란다. 왜?
남 선거에 출마할지 생각 중이거든요.
여 오, 넌 잘 할 수 있을 거야.
남 정말인가요? 학생회장으로서 제가 어떤 책임을 지게 되나 요?
여 학생들이 원하는 변화를 만들기 위해 학생회 위원들과 일 하게 된단다.
남 그럼, 출마하기 위해 등록하고 싶어요. 양식을 주실 수 있으 신가요?
여 물론이지. 이 양식을 채워주렴.

해설 | 남자가 학생회장 선거에 출마하기 위해 등록하겠다고 했고, 여자에게 양식을 달라고 부탁했으므로 정답은 ④ '입후보 신청서 건네주기'이다.

어휘 | run in the election 선거에 출마하다 responsibility [rispὰnsəbíləti] 뗑 책임 school council 학생회 form [fɔːrm] 뗑 양식 fill out 채우다, 기입하다

9 주제 고르기 정답 ④

W Can I have your attention, please? This is an announcement from North Ridge National Park. I'm excited to announce the dates for our annual children's camp this summer. The camp will take place from June 1st to 8th at the park. Children aged 10 to 15 are welcome to join us for activities such as swimming, hiking, and archery at the camp. Parents can sign their children up online from today. Thank you for listening, and enjoy the rest of your day.

여 주목해 주시겠습니까? 노스 리지 국립공원의 안내 방송입 니다. 올여름 연간 아동 캠프의 날짜를 발표하게 되어 기쁩 니다. 캠프는 6월 1일부터 8일까지 국립공원에서 열릴 것 입니다. 10세에서 15세까지의 아이들은 캠프에서의 수영, 등산, 양궁 같은 활동들을 위해 자유롭게 참가해도 좋습니 다. 부모님들은 오늘부터 온라인으로 아이들을 등록할 수 있습니다. 들어주셔서 감사하며, 남은 하루도 즐겁게 보내 십시오.

해설 | 여자가 노스 리지 국립공원에서 올여름에 열릴 아동 캠프 등록 안내를 하고 있으므로 정답은 ④ '여름 캠프 등록'이다.

어휘 | annual [ǽnjuəl] 뗑 연간의 take place 열리다 welcome [wélkəm] 뗑 자유롭게 ~해도 좋은 통 환영하다 archery [ɑ́ːrtʃəri] 뗑 양궁

10 금액 정보 고르기

정답 ②

M	Hi. Can I get you anything?
W	Yes. I'd like a peanut butter sandwich, please.
M	That will be five dollars. Do you need anything else?
W	How much are French fries and a drink?
M	If you pay three dollars more, you can get French fries and a drink too.
W	I'll take the sandwich, fries, and drink then.
M	Great choice. For here or to go?
W	To go, thank you.

남	안녕하세요. 뭐로 드릴까요?
여	네. 저는 땅콩버터 샌드위치를 먹고 싶어요.
남	5달러 되겠습니다. 다른 것도 필요하신가요?
여	감자튀김과 음료는 얼마인가요?
남	3달러 더 지불하시면, 감자튀김과 음료도 드실 수 있어요.
여	그럼 샌드위치, 감자튀김, 그리고 음료를 마실게요.
남	훌륭한 선택이세요. 여기서 드시나요, 포장이신가요?
여	포장해 주세요, 감사합니다.

해설 | 땅콩버터 샌드위치가 5달러이고, 여자가 3달러를 더 내고 감자튀김과 음료를 추가하겠다고 했으므로 정답은 ② '$ 8'이다.

어휘 | peanut [píːnʌt] 圕 땅콩 choice [tʃɔis] 圕 선택

11 할 일 고르기

정답 ⑤

M	How do you like our new house, Lily?
W	It has so much space, Dad!
M	I know. This room here will be the living room. And then our bedrooms are down that hall. Did you see them?
W	Not yet!
M	Well, you need to pick your room. There are two choices.
W	I'll look at both of them now.
M	Okay. When you are finished, come and help carry boxes.
W	Of course.

남	우리 새집 어떠니, Lily?
여	정말 공간이 많아요, 아빠!
남	맞아. 여기 이 방은 거실이 될 거야. 그리고 우리 침실 방들은 저 복도 끝에 있단다. 봤니?
여	아직이요!
남	음, 네 방을 골라야 한단다. 두 개의 선택지가 있어.
여	지금 둘 다 볼게요.
남	그래. 다 끝나면, 와서 상자들 나르는 것을 도와주렴.
여	물론이죠.

해설 | 남자가 두 개의 방 중 하나를 고르라고 하자 여자가 지금 둘 다 보겠다고 했으므로 정답은 ⑤ '방 살펴보기'이다.

어휘 | space [speis] 圕 공간 hall [hɔːl] 圕 복도, 현관; 홀

12 언급하지 않은 내용 고르기

정답 ②

W	Attention passengers, Ohio Airways Flight 221 to Daytona, Florida will be delayed. It will now take off at 11:05 p.m. The flight will still leave from the same departure gate: Gate 4C. Passengers with small children and any passengers requiring special assistance will board first. Have your passport and ticket ready when you get in line. Our team will try to check them as quickly as possible. We apologize for the inconvenience.

여	승객 여러분께 안내 말씀드립니다. 플로리다 데이토나행 Ohio Airways 221편은 지연될 예정입니다. 해당 항공기는 오후 11시 5분에 이륙할 예정입니다. 항공편은 여전히 동일한 탑승구인 4C 게이트에서 출발할 예정입니다. 어린아이가 있는 탑승객과 특별한 도움이 필요한 탑승객부터 탑승하겠습니다. 줄을 서실 때는 여권과 표를 준비해 주시기 바랍니다. 저희 팀이 가능한 한 빠르게 확인할 수 있도록 노력하겠습니다. 불편을 끼쳐 죄송합니다.

해설 | ① 목적지(플로리다 데이토나), ③ 출발 시각(오후 11시 5분), ④ 탑승 순서(어린아이가 있는 탑승객과 특별한 도움이 필요한 탑승객 먼저), ⑤ 탑승구(4C 게이트)에 대해 언급했으므로 정답은 ② '지연 사유'이다.

어휘 | require [rikwáiər] 圄 필요하다, 요구하다 assistance [əsístəns] 圕 도움 passport [pǽspɔːrt] 圕 여권 inconvenience [ìnkənvíːnjəns] 圕 불편

13 도표에서 알맞은 항목 고르기   정답 ②

M	Hello. Are you looking for something?
W	I need a new suitcase for my business trip tomorrow.
M	We have various colors and designs here. How about this red one?
W	It looks nice. Do you have a red one with four wheels?
M	I'm sorry, but it's out of stock right now. We only have gray and white ones with four wheels.
W	Can I see the gray ones then?
M	Here you go.
W	Hmm... How much are they?
M	This one is on sale, so it's 130 dollars. The other one is 150 dollars.
W	I'll get the one on sale.

남 안녕하세요. 뭘 찾고 있으신가요?
여 저는 내일 출장 때 쓸 새 여행 가방이 필요해요.
남 저희는 다양한 색상과 디자인이 있습니다. 이 빨간 것은 어떠신가요?
여 좋아 보이네요. 빨간 가방에 바퀴가 네 개 달린 것이 있나요?
남 죄송하지만, 현재 품절입니다. 바퀴가 네 개 달린 것은 회색과 흰색만 있어요.
여 그럼 회색을 볼 수 있을까요?
남 여기 있습니다.
여 흠... 얼마인가요?
남 이것은 할인 중이라서, 130달러입니다. 다른 것은 150달러예요.
여 할인 중인 걸로 살게요.

해설 | 여자는 바퀴가 4개 달린 것을 원한다고 했고, 130달러로 할인 중인 회색 여행 가방을 사겠다고 했으므로 정답은 ②이다.

어휘 | business trip 출장   wheel [hwiːl] 圆 바퀴   out of stock 품절인, 재고가 떨어진

14 화제 고르기   정답 ③

M	This is a very helpful device when you do housework. It is usually large and square-shaped. With this, we can clean our clothes and towels after we use them. We simply put them inside of the device and add some liquid soap. Then, we press some buttons and wait for the device to clean our clothes. It usually makes a beeping sound when it is finished with this.

남 이것은 집안일을 할 때 매우 유용한 기기입니다. 이것은 보통 크고 네모난 모양입니다. 이것을 가지고 옷과 수건을 사용한 후에 세탁할 수 있습니다. 단순히 기기 안에 넣고 액체비누를 추가하면 됩니다. 그리고 나서 몇 개의 버튼을 누르고 기기가 옷을 세탁하기를 기다립니다. 이것은 보통 끝나면 삑 하는 소리를 냅니다.

해설 | 이것(This)을 가지고 옷과 수건을 사용한 후에 세탁할 수 있다고 했으므로 정답은 ③ '세탁기'이다.

어휘 | device [diváis] 圆 기기, 장치   liquid [líkwid] 圆 액체의   press [pres] 图 누르다

15 할 일 고르기   정답 ⑤

W	It's so cold out here with the snow.
M	Why don't you zip up your coat? You must be freezing.
W	The zipper is broken on my coat.
M	Can you fix it?
W	I'm not sure. It's a really old coat.
M	Why don't you buy a new one? The Westwood Department Store is having a sale.
W	Yeah. I'll buy one this weekend.

여 여기 밖은 눈 때문에 너무 춥네.
남 코트 지퍼를 잠그는 것이 어때? 너 몹시 춥겠어.
여 내 코트는 지퍼가 고장 났어.
남 고칠 수 있니?
여 확실하지 않아. 이건 정말 오래된 코트거든.
남 새 걸 사는 게 어때? Westwood Department Store에서 할인을 하고 있어.
여 응. 이번 주말에 하나 살 거야.

해설 | 여자가 이번 주말에 코트를 하나 사겠다고 했으므로 정답은 ⑤ '코트 구매하기'이다.

어휘 | zip up 지퍼로 잠그다   freezing [fríːziŋ] 圆 몹시 추운; 영하의   fix [fiks] 图 고치다; 고정시키다

16 시간 정보 고르기 정답 ⑤

	[Telephone rings.]
M	Eastgate Service Center. How can I help you today?
W	Hi. My car is making a strange noise. I'd like to get it checked.
M	Okay. Which day is convenient for you to bring it in?
W	Saturday at 10 or 11 a.m. would be best.
M	Unfortunately, all our mechanics are busy then. Could you come in at 1 in the afternoon?
W	I have a doctor's appointment at that time. What about later that day? I'm free any time after 2.
M	One of our mechanics is available at 3.
W	That's fine.

[전화기가 울린다.]
남 Eastgate Service Center입니다. 오늘은 무엇을 도와드릴까요?
여 안녕하세요. 제 차에서 이상한 소리가 나서요. 정비를 받고 싶어요.
남 알겠습니다. 언제가 차를 가져오시기 편하실까요?
여 토요일 오전 10나 11시가 제일 좋을 것 같아요.
남 유감스럽게도, 저희 정비사들이 그때 모두 바빠서요. 오후 1시에 오실 수 있으신가요?
여 그때는 병원 진료가 있어요. 그날 더 늦게는 어떤가요? 2시 이후에는 아무 때나 한가해요.
남 저희 정비사 중 한 명이 3시에 가능합니다.
여 좋아요.

해설 | 여자가 2시 이후에는 아무 때나 한가하다고 했고, 남자가 정비사 중 한 명이 3시에 가능하다고 했으므로 정답은 ⑤ '3 p.m.'이다.

어휘 | strange [streinჳ] 혱 이상한 convenient [kənví:njənt] 혱 편한, 편리한 mechanic [məkǽnik] 몡 정비사

17 적절한 응답 고르기 정답 ①

M	Who are you drawing, Jisun?
W	I'm drawing my grandmother. This is a gift for her birthday.
M	It's really good with lots of details. She'll love it.
W	I hope so. I want to show her my respect and love.
M	Do you see her often?
W	Yes. She lives very close to me, so I visit her at least once a week.
M	You are lucky. My grandmother lives in the countryside, so I don't see her often.
W	When do you get to visit her?
M	I only see her during long holidays.

남 누구를 그리고 있니, 지선아?
여 우리 할머니를 그리고 있어. 이건 할머니 생신 선물이야.
남 세밀한 부분이 많고 정말 좋다. 할머니가 아주 좋아하실 거야.
여 그러셨으면 좋겠다. 내 존경과 사랑을 보여드리고 싶어.
남 할머니를 자주 뵙니?
여 응. 나와 매우 가까이 사셔서, 적어도 일주일에 한 번은 방문해.
남 넌 정말 운이 좋다. 우리 할머니는 시골에 사셔서, 자주 뵙지 못해.
여 언제 할머니를 방문하러 가는데?
남 긴 휴일 동안에만 뵐 수 있어.

해설 | 여자가 언제 할머니를 방문하러 가는지 물었으므로 정답은 방문 시기를 언급하는 ① 'I only see her during long holidays.'이다.

선택지 해석
① 긴 휴일 동안에만 뵐 수 있어. ② 응. 두 블록 떨어져 있어. ③ 그녀는 정선에 살고 계셔. ④ 나는 이 그림이 정말 마음에 들어.
⑤ 고마워! 네가 이걸 좋아하니 기쁘다.

어휘 | respect [rispékt] 몡 존경 countryside [kʌ́ntrisaid] 몡 시골

18 적절한 응답 고르기 정답 ③

M	You were so great in the play today, Subin.
W	Thank you! I practiced my part a lot.
M	I can tell. Did you always love acting?
W	Yes. I started acting at seven years old.
M	That's impressive.
W	Well, I hope to become a famous actress one day.
M	Do you want to be in movies or in plays?
W	I prefer plays. I love being on the stage.
M	But don't you get scared?
W	No. I like having a big audience.

남 오늘 연극에서 너 정말 대단했어, 수빈아.
여 고마워! 내 배역을 많이 연습했거든.
남 그런 것 같았어. 넌 항상 연기하는 것을 좋아했니?
여 응. 난 7살 때 연기를 시작했어.
남 그거 놀랍네.
여 음, 나는 언젠가 유명한 배우가 되고 싶어.
남 너는 영화계와 연극계 중 어디에 있고 싶니?
여 난 연극이 더 좋아. 내가 무대에 서는 걸 정말 좋아하거든.
남 그래도 무섭지 않니?
여 아니. 나는 관중이 많은 걸 좋아해.

해설 | 남자가 무대에 서는 것이 무섭지 않은지 물었으므로 정답은 무섭지 않다고 대답하는 ③ 'No. I like having a big audience.'이다.

선택지 해석
① 그 영화는 올해 후반에 나와. ② 그 연극 중간에는 휴식 시간이 있어. ③ 아니. 나는 관중이 많은 걸 좋아해. ④ 오디션은 화요일에 시작해.
⑤ 응. 나는 거미를 무서워해.

어휘 | be on the stage 무대에 서다 audience [ɔ́:diəns] 몡 관중

19 적절한 응답 고르기 정답 ⑤

[Cellphone rings.]

W Honey, what's up?

M Are you at home right now?

W No. I'm at the shop. We need some more shampoo.

M Can you also buy some toothpaste? We just ran out of that too.

W Of course. There are also some bathrobes for sale at a reduced price. Should I get a few?

M No. We don't need them. But could you drop by the bakery to get some bread?

W Sure. I'll be home after I buy everything.

M Oh, and remember to pick up Tommy from piano class today. I have a late meeting.

W Alright. I'll see you at home later then.

[휴대폰이 울린다.]

여 여보, 무슨 일이야?

남 지금 집에 있어?

여 아니. 지금 가게에 있어. 샴푸 몇 개가 더 필요해서.

남 치약도 좀 살 수 있어? 그것도 막 다 썼어.

여 당연하지. 할인가로 팔고 있는 목욕 가운이 있네. 몇 개 살까?

남 아니. 그건 필요하지 않아. 그렇지만 제과점에 들러서 빵 좀 사 올 수 있어?

여 물론이지. 다 산 다음에 집에 갈게.

남 오, 오늘 피아노 수업에서 Tommy를 꼭 데려와야 해. 난 회의가 늦게 있어.

여 알겠어. 그럼 나중에 집에서 봐.

해설 | 남자가 회의가 늦게 있어서 Tommy를 피아노 수업에서 데려와 달라고 부탁했으므로 정답은 부탁을 수락하는 ⑤ 'Alright. I'll see you at home later then.'이다.

선택지 해석
① Tommy는 괜찮아. 치과 진료 중이야. ② 우리 나가기 전에 난 샤워할 거야. ③ 선반에 있는 물건은 할인 중이야. ④ 수업은 오후 6시에 시작해. 늦지 마.
⑤ 알겠어. 그럼 나중에 집에서 봐.

어휘 | toothpaste [túθpèist] 圆 치약 run out of ~을 다 써버리다 bathrobe [bǽθroub] 圆 목욕 가운 drop by 들르다

---

20 상황에 적절한 말 고르기 정답 ②

M Veronica is a fan of art. She goes to the art gallery for a new exhibit. But it is closed when she arrives. Veronica is confused because the gallery usually opens at 9 a.m. She sees a security guard and decides to ask him why the gallery is still closed. In this situation, what would Veronica most likely say to the security guard?

Veronica Excuse me, why isn't it open yet?

남 Veronica는 미술을 아주 좋아합니다. 그녀는 새로운 전시회를 보러 미술관에 갑니다. 하지만 그녀가 도착했을 때 미술관은 닫혀 있습니다. 미술관은 보통 오전 9시에 열기 때문에 Veronica는 당황합니다. 그녀는 경비원을 보고 왜 미술관이 여전히 닫혀 있는지 묻기로 결심합니다. 이러한 상황에서, Veronica가 경비원에게 가장 할 것 같은 말은 무엇입니까?

Veronica 실례합니다, 왜 아직도 문을 열지 않았나요?

해설 | Veronica가 경비원에게 왜 미술관이 여전히 닫혀 있는지를 묻기로 결심했다고 했으므로 정답은 ② 'why isn't it open yet?'이다.

선택지 해석
① 티켓은 어디서 사나요? ② 왜 아직도 문을 열지 않았나요? ③ 저희 미술관은 오후 9시 이후에 닫아요. ④ 줄을 서서 기다리셔야 해요.
⑤ 이 그림은 언제 그려졌나요?

어휘 | confused [kənfjúːzd] 圆 당황한, 혼란한 security guard 경비원 wait in line 줄 서서 기다리다

1	④	2	④	3	②	4	④	5	④	6	②	7	⑤	8	③	9	①	10	⑤
11	③	12	③	13	⑤	14	②	15	④	16	③	17	①	18	⑤	19	③	20	②

---

1 알맞은 그림 고르기

정답 ④

M	Mom, what's in the box?
W	Handmade soap. As you know, I took soap-making classes.
M	Oh, please show me what you made.
W	Okay. Here it is.
M	It has an ordinary round shape. *[Pause]* Wow, you made watermelon soap! I didn't notice until I turned the soap over.
W	Yeah. I wanted the soap to be fun. Putting on the black seeds was the hardest part.
M	You're skillful with your hands.

남 엄마, 상자 안에 뭐가 있나요?
여 수제 비누란다. 너도 알다시피, 내가 비누 만들기 수업을 들었잖아.
남 오, 만드신 걸 보여주세요.
여 그래. 여기 있다.
남 이건 평범한 원형이네요. *[잠시 멈춤]* 우와, 수박 모양 비누를 만드셨네요! 비누를 뒤집고 나서야 알아차렸어요.
여 그래. 나는 비누가 재미있기를 원했거든. 까만 씨앗을 올리는 것이 가장 어려운 부분이었지.
남 엄마는 정말 손재주가 있으시네요.

해설 | 여자가 만든 비누를 보고 남자가 평범한 원형이라고 한 후 수박 모양 비누임을 알아차렸다고 했으므로 정답은 ④이다.

어휘 | ordinary [ɔ́ːrdəneri] 휑 평범한 turn over ~을 뒤집다 seed [siːd] 뎽 씨앗 skillful with one's hands 손재주가 있는

---

2 부탁·요청한 일 고르기

정답 ④

W	Are you okay, Darling? You don't look well.
M	My throat hurts badly.
W	Do you have a fever?
M	Hold on, I'll take my temperature. *[Pause]* Oh, yes. My temperature is high.
W	Well, you should rest then. Why don't you lay down?
M	But I have to take the kids to school soon.
W	Don't worry about that. I can do it. Do you need anything while I'm out?
M	Can you get some medicine? I think it would help.
W	Sure. Now, go rest.

여 괜찮아, 여보? 안 좋아 보여.
남 목이 심하게 아파.
여 열이 있어?
남 기다려봐, 체온을 재 볼게. *[잠시 멈춤]* 오, 그러네. 내 체온이 높아.
여 음, 그럼 휴식을 취해야겠다. 눕는 게 어때?
남 하지만 아이들을 곧 학교에 데려다줘야 해.
여 그건 걱정하지 마. 내가 할 수 있어. 내가 나가 있는 동안 필요한 게 있을까?
남 약을 좀 사다 줄 수 있어? 도움이 될 것 같아.
여 물론이지. 이제 가서 쉬어.

해설 | 남자가 목이 아프고 열이 나서 여자에게 약을 사다 달라고 부탁했으므로 정답은 ④ '감기약 사 오기'이다.

어휘 | throat [θrout] 뎽 목 temperature [témpərətʃər] 뎽 체온, 온도 lay down 눕다

---

3 그림 상황에 적절한 대화 고르기

정답 ②

① M Should we call a taxi?
   W Let's walk, instead.
② M Where do you need to go?
   W The Coleman Bank on Freedman street, please.
③ M Thanks for driving me to work.
   W Don't mention it.
④ M I like your new car.
   W I bought it last month.
⑤ M My order number is 8373.
   W Just a minute, please.

① 남 우리 택시를 부를까?
   여 그 대신에, 걷자.
② 남 어디로 가셔야 하나요?
   여 프리드먼 가의 콜먼 은행으로 가주세요.
③ 남 회사로 태워다줘서 고마워.
   여 천만에.
④ 남 네 새 차 마음에 든다.
   여 지난달에 샀어.
⑤ 남 제 주문 번호는 8373입니다.
   여 잠시만 기다려주세요.

해설 | 택시 운전수인 남자에게 여자가 은행으로 가달라고 하고 있는 상황이므로 정답은 ②이다.

어휘 | instead [instéd] 🔒 대신에

4 시간 정보 고르기   정답 ④

[Cellphone rings.]	[휴대폰이 울린다.]
M Hi, Lisa. Do you remember that new restaurant next to the park? It finally opened.	남 안녕, Lisa. 공원 옆에 있는 그 새 식당 기억나? 거기 드디어 열었어.
W Oh, really? We should go try it!	여 오, 정말? 우리 가서 먹어보자!
M I think so too. Are you free for dinner on Thursday?	남 나도 그렇게 생각해. 너 목요일 저녁에 시간 있니?
W Actually, I'm not. My book club meets on Thursday nights. How about Saturday?	여 실은, 없어. 독서회가 목요일 밤마다 열리거든. 토요일은 어때?
M On Saturday I will go on a camping trip out of town. Is Friday good?	남 토요일에는 내가 캠핑하러 가서 마을에 없을 거야. 금요일은 괜찮니?
W I can meet on Friday. Let's try to go around 7.	여 금요일에는 만날 수 있어. 7시쯤 가도록 하자.
M Alright. I'll make the reservation then.	남 알겠어. 내가 예약할게 그럼.

해설 | 남자가 금요일은 괜찮은지 묻자 여자가 금요일에는 만날 수 있다고 했으므로 정답은 ④ '금요일'이다.

어휘 | finally [fáinəli] 🔒 드디어, 마침내   meet [mi:t] 🔒 (모임 등이) 열리다; 만나다

5 언급하지 않은 내용 고르기   정답 ④

M Zoey, did you do anything fun last weekend?	남 Zoey, 지난 주말에 재미있는 거 했니?
W Yeah. I went to a special café with some friends. It's called Café Mer.	여 응. 나는 몇몇 친구들과 특별한 카페에 갔어. 그곳은 Café Mer라고 불려.
M Café Mer? Is that the one next to the beach?	남 Café Mer? 그거 바닷가 옆에 있는 거니?
W That's right. It's famous for its strawberry latte.	여 맞아. 거긴 딸기 라테로 유명해.
M Oh, that sounds delicious.	남 오, 맛있겠다.
W The shop won a big award recently too. It was named best café in the city. You should really try it!	여 최근에 그 가게는 큰 상을 받기도 했어. 그곳은 도시에서 가장 좋은 카페로 지명됐어. 넌 정말 가봐야 해!
M I will.	남 그럴게.

해설 | ① 이름(Café Mer), ② 위치(바닷가 옆), ③ 인기 음료(딸기 라테), ⑤ 수상 이력(큰 상을 받았음)에 대해 언급했으므로 정답은 ④ '영업시간'이다.

어휘 | be famous for ~으로 유명하다   award [əwɔ́:rd] 🔒 상   recently [rí:sntli] 🔒 최근에   name [neim] 🔒 지명하다; 이름을 지어주다

6 장소 고르기   정답 ②

M Christine, that Ferris wheel was so fun!	남 Christine, 저 관람차는 정말 재미있었어!
W I know. The view from the top was amazing.	여 내 말이. 꼭대기에서 보는 경치는 굉장했어.
M What do you want to ride next?	남 다음으로 뭘 타고 싶니?
W Well, I'm actually a little thirsty. Can we get some drinks?	여 음, 난 사실 약간 목이 말라. 마실 것 좀 사도 될까?
M Sure. But after that, I really want to ride the roller coaster.	남 물론이지. 하지만 그 후에 롤러코스터를 정말 타고 싶어.
W Isn't there a long line for it?	여 그거 줄이 길지 않니?
M The line isn't too long right now because it is still early in the day.	남 지금은 아직 이른 시간이라 줄이 그렇게 길지 않아.
W Alright, let's buy drinks and go wait in line.	여 그래, 음료수를 사고 줄을 서러 가자.

해설 | 남자가 관람차가 재미있었다고 했고 롤러코스터를 정말 타고 싶다고 했으므로 정답은 ② '놀이공원'이다.

어휘 | Ferris wheel 관람차   view [vju:] 🔒 경치   thirsty [θə́:rsti] 🔒 목마른

7 어색한 대화 고르기   정답 ⑤

① M Why don't we take a break?
   W Sure. Let's drink some water.
② M Do you want to come play soccer with us this weekend?
   W Yeah. I'd like to join you.
③ M Can I get you anything else?
   W I'm fine, thank you.
④ M It's so hot in the classroom!
   W I don't think so. It's just a little warm.
⑤ M Which color do you prefer, white or black?
   W I have this tie in blue.

① 남 우리 휴식을 취하는 게 어때?
   여 물론이지. 물을 좀 마시자.
② 남 이번 주말에 우리와 함께 축구 하러 올래?
   여 응. 같이 하고 싶어.
③ 남 다른 필요하신 것을 가져다드릴까요?
   여 괜찮아요, 감사합니다.
④ 남 교실이 너무 더워!
   여 난 그렇게 생각하지 않아. 그냥 조금 따뜻해.
⑤ 남 하얀색과 검은색 중에 어떤 색을 더 좋아하니?
   여 난 이 넥타이 파란색으로 있어.

해설ㅣ 남자가 하얀색과 검은색 중에 어떤 색을 더 좋아하는지 물었으므로 여자는 선호하는 색상을 말해야 한다. 그러나 여자가 이 넥타이 파란색으로 있다는 어색한 대답을 했으므로 정답은 ⑤이다.

어휘ㅣ take a break 휴식을 취하다   prefer [prifə́ːr] 통 더 좋아하다, 선호하다

8 부탁·요청한 일 고르기   정답 ③

W Honey, how should we decorate this room?
M Why don't we put the couch by the window?
W Okay. Then, we can put the yellow rug in the middle of the room.
M What about our paintings and pictures?
W I'll hold up this first painting on the wall. Tell me how it looks.
M Hmm... It doesn't look nice with the room. Can you hold up our family photograph instead?
W Sure. Let me get it.

여 여보, 우리 이 방을 어떻게 꾸며야 할까?
남 창문 옆에 소파를 두는 게 어때?
여 그래. 그럼 방 가운데에 노란 러그를 놓으면 되겠다.
남 우리 그림과 사진들은 어떻게 하지?
여 내가 첫 번째 그림을 벽에 대고 들고 있을게. 어떻게 보이는지 말해줘.
남 흠... 방이랑 잘 어울리지 않는 것 같아. 대신 가족사진을 들어볼래?
여 그래. 내가 받을게.

해설ㅣ 남자가 여자에게 그림 대신 가족사진을 들어봐 달라고 부탁했으므로 정답은 ③ '가족사진 들고 있기'이다.

어휘ㅣ decorate [dékərèit] 통 꾸미다, 장식하다   couch [kautʃ] 명 소파, 카우치   rug [rʌg] 명 러그, 깔개

9 주제 고르기   정답 ①

M Attention, students. I'm Dave, the school's sports director. I'm sorry to announce that the school's gym will be closed for a month from this Monday. The gym will be renovated. We are adding new floors and seating. School basketball and volleyball games will be held at other locations, and sports practices will take place at the local community center. We are sorry for the inconvenience, and thank you for all your patience.

남 주목해주십시오, 학생 여러분. 교내 운동 감독인 Dave입니다. 이번 주 월요일부터 한 달 동안 학교 체육관이 폐쇄될 것이라는 소식을 전하게 되어 유감입니다. 체육관은 개조될 것입니다. 새로운 바닥과 좌석을 추가할 것입니다. 학교 농구와 배구 경기는 다른 장소에서 열릴 것이며, 운동 연습은 지역 주민센터에서 진행될 것입니다. 불편을 끼쳐 죄송하며, 모두 기다려 주셔서 감사합니다.

해설ㅣ 남자가 이번 주 월요일부터 한 달 동안 학교 체육관이 폐쇄될 것이라고 했으므로 정답은 ① '학교 체육관 폐관'이다.

어휘ㅣ director [diréktər] 명 감독   renovate [rénəvèit] 통 개조하다, 수리하다   floor [flɔːr] 명 바닥   location [loukéiʃən] 명 장소, 위치

10 금액 정보 고르기   정답 ⑤

M Welcome to Every Song Music Store. How may I help you?
W I'd like to pay for these records.
M Let me see. [Beeping sound] Okay. It will be 25 dollars for the records. Did you want to buy anything else?
W How much is this pair of earphones?
M It is 30 dollars.
W Great. I'll take it and the records.

남 Every Song Music Store에 오신 것을 환영합니다. 무엇을 도와드릴까요?
여 이 음반들 계산하고 싶어요.
남 어디 볼게요. [삑 하는 소리] 좋습니다. 음반은 25달러 되겠습니다. 다른 것도 살 것이 있으셨을까요?
여 이 이어폰 한 쌍은 얼마인가요?
남 30달러입니다.
여 좋네요. 그거랑 음반들을 살게요.

해설ㅣ 음반은 25달러이고 여자가 30달러짜리 이어폰도 사겠다고 했으므로 정답은 ⑤ '$ 55'이다.

어휘ㅣ record [rékərd] 명 음반; 기록 [rikɔ́ːrd] 통 기록하다   pair [pɛər] 명 한 쌍

11 할 일 고르기

정답 ③

[Cellphone rings.]

W Hi, Jake. Is everything okay?

M Yes. I'm just packing for our trip now.

W Oh, great. What time is our train again?

M It leaves at 6 p.m.

W I'll go to the station right after work then.

M It'll be a long train ride.

W Why don't you bring your laptop? We can watch a movie together.

M Okay. I will. That will be fun.

[휴대폰이 울린다.]

여 안녕, Jake. 모두 괜찮은 거지?

남 응. 지금 막 우리 여행을 위해 짐을 챙기는 중이야.

여 오, 잘됐다. 우리 기차가 몇 시였지?

남 오후 6시에 출발해.

여 그럼 일이 끝나고 바로 역으로 갈게.

남 긴 기차 여행이 될 거야.

여 노트북을 가져오는 게 어때? 같이 영화를 볼 수 있잖아.

남 응. 그럴게. 재미있겠다.

해설 | 여자가 노트북을 가져오는 것이 어떤지 물었고, 남자가 그러겠다고 했으므로 정답은 ③ '노트북 가져오기'이다.

어휘 | pack [pæk] 통 짐을 챙기다 ride [raid] 명 여행 통 타다

12 언급하지 않은 내용 고르기

정답 ③

W Thank you for coming to this event. I'm Nora Burton, the CEO of Auden Technology. I'm pleased to announce our new VR headset. We are making it at our factory here in Canada. The headset will be available to buy on June 11th. This product is special for a three main reasons. First, the headset is lightweight and comfortable. Second, it is completely wireless. Finally, it works for five hours with a single charge. This means it has the best battery life on the market. Would you like to try it out?

여 이 행사에 와주셔서 감사합니다. 저는 Auden Technology의 최고 경영자 Nora Burton입니다. 저희의 새 VR 헤드셋을 발표하게 되어 기쁩니다. 저희는 이것을 여기 캐나다의 공장에서 만들고 있습니다. 헤드셋은 6월 11일부터 구매가 가능할 예정입니다. 이 제품은 세 가지의 주요 요인으로 특별합니다. 먼저, 이 헤드셋은 가볍고 편안합니다. 두 번째로, 이것은 완벽한 무선입니다. 마지막으로, 이것은 한 번의 충전으로 5시간 동안 사용이 가능합니다. 이는 저희 제품이 시장에서 가장 성능이 좋은 배터리 수명을 가지고 있다는 것을 의미합니다. 시험해 보시겠습니까?

해설 | ① 제조 공장 위치(캐나다), ② 제품 판매 시작일(6월 11일), ④ 제품 무게(가벼움), ⑤ 배터리 지속 시간(5시간)에 대해 언급했으므로 정답은 ③ '제품 가격'이다.

어휘 | lightweight [láitweit] 형 가벼운 wireless [wáiərlis] 형 무선의 try out (성능 등을 알아보기 위해) 시험해 보다

13 위치 고르기

정답 ⑤

W Excuse me, sir. I lost the bag I bought at the gift shop.

M When did you lose it?

W About an hour ago.

M No one brought anything to our desk. Why don't you check the lost and found?

W Could you tell me where that is?

M Do you know where the restroom is?

W Yeah. Is it in the office between the restroom and the gift shop?

M No. It's in the office between the restroom and the locker room.

W Oh, I see. Thanks for the help.

M You're welcome. I hope you find your bag.

여 실례합니다, 선생님. 제가 선물 가게에서 구입한 가방을 잃어버렸어요.

남 언제 잃어버리셨나요?

여 한 시간쯤 전에요.

남 아무도 저희 데스크에 뭘 가져오지 않았어요. 분실물 센터를 확인해 보시는 건 어떤가요?

여 그게 어디에 있는지 알려주시겠어요?

남 화장실이 어디 있는지 아세요?

여 네. 화장실과 선물 가게 사이의 사무실 안에 있는 건가요?

남 아니요. 그건 화장실과 탈의실 사이의 사무실 안에 있어요.

여 오, 그렇군요. 도와주셔서 감사합니다.

남 천만에요. 가방 찾으시길 바랄게요.

해설 | 남자가 여자에게 안내해 준 분실물 센터는 화장실과 탈의실 사이의 사무실 안에 있다고 했으므로 정답은 ⑤이다.

어휘 | lost and found 분실물 센터 locker room 탈의실

14 화제 고르기

정답 ②

W This is a land animal, but it spends lots of time in water. This animal lives in African rivers and lakes. It has a huge head and weighs a lot. It is usually a brown and pink color. This is the third largest land animal on the planet. It has big teeth, but it usually eats grass.

여 이것은 육지 동물이지만, 물속에서 많은 시간을 보냅니다. 이 동물은 아프리카의 강과 호수에 삽니다. 이것은 머리가 크고 무게가 많이 나갑니다. 이것은 보통 갈색과 분홍색입니다. 이것은 지구에서 세 번째로 큰 육지 동물입니다. 이것은 큰 이빨을 가지고 있지만, 보통 풀을 먹습니다.

해설 | 이것(This)는 육지 동물이지만 물속에서 많은 시간을 보낸다고 했으며, 큰 이빨을 가지고 있지만 보통 풀을 먹는다고 했으므로 정답은 ② '하마'이다.

어휘 | huge [hjuːdʒ] 휑 큰, 거대한　weigh [wei] 동 무게가 나가다　planet [plǽnit] 명 지구; 행성　grass [græs] 명 풀

15 할 일 고르기 　　　　　　　　　　　　　정답 ④

W	Are you ready for the concert, Charlie?
M	Not yet, Mom. How much time do we have until we leave?
W	We have about 30 minutes. Why?
M	I'm trying to finish these math problems now, but they're so hard.
W	Do you have many left to do?
M	Yes. And they are due tomorrow.
W	Well, you'd better finish them quickly. While you do that, I will make a snack for us.
M	Okay. I'll do my best.

여	콘서트 갈 준비 됐니, Charlie?
남	아직이요, 엄마. 출발할 때까지 시간이 얼마나 있나요?
여	30분 정도 있어. 왜?
남	이 수학 문제들을 지금 끝내려고 하는데, 너무 어려워요.
여	할 게 많이 남았니?
남	네. 그리고 내일까지예요.
여	음, 그걸 빨리 끝내는 게 좋겠다. 네가 그걸 하는 동안, 나는 우리 간식을 만드마.
남	좋아요. 최선을 다할게요.

해설 | 남자가 수학 문제를 푸는 동안 여자가 간식을 만들겠다고 했으므로 정답은 ④ '간식 준비하기'이다.

어휘 | hard [hɑːrd] 휑 어려운; 단단한　do one's best 최선을 다하다

16 시간 정보 고르기 　　　　　　　　　　　정답 ③

[Telephone rings.]

M	Hi, Phantom Airline. How can I help you?
W	Hi, I'd like to book a ticket to London. I want to go during the second week of August. The 8th, maybe?
M	Let me check. *[Pause]* I'm sorry, but we're fully booked that week.
W	Oh, no. What about the week after that?
M	We have seats on the 15th and 18th.
W	I need to attend a conference on the 17th.
M	Okay. You can either choose a flight that leaves in the morning or the afternoon on the 15th.
W	I'll take the earlier flight.

[전화기가 울린다.]

남	안녕하세요, Phantom Airline입니다. 무엇을 도와드릴까요?
여	안녕하세요, 런던행 표를 예약하고 싶어요. 8월 둘째 주 중에 가고 싶어요. 아마 8일 정도요?
남	확인해 보겠습니다. *[잠시 멈춤]* 죄송합니다만, 저희는 그 주 예약이 모두 완료되었습니다.
여	오, 이런. 그다음 주는 어떤가요?
남	15일과 18일에 좌석이 있습니다.
여	17일에는 회의에 참석해야 해요.
남	그러시군요. 15일 오전이나 오후에 출발하는 항공편 중에 고르실 수 있으세요.
여	더 일찍 출발하는 것으로 할게요.

해설 | 여자가 17일에는 회의에 참석해야 한다고 하자, 남자가 15일 오전이나 오후에 출발하는 항공편 중에 고르라고 했으므로 정답은 ③ '8월 15일'이다.

어휘 | attend [əténd] 동 참석하다, 참여하다　conference [kánfərəns] 명 회의

17 적절한 응답 고르기 　　　　　　　　　　정답 ①

M	I like your new hair style, Sua.
W	Thanks. I just got my hair cut and colored.
M	What made you want blue hair?
W	Well, it's my favorite color. And I was tired of my red hair.
M	I'm jealous of your overall style. It's so unique.
W	Don't you like your style, too?
M	I do, but I'm afraid to wear some things. People might not like them.
W	You should always wear clothes that you love. Don't worry about other people.
M	You're right. I shouldn't be afraid.

남	난 너의 새로운 머리 스타일이 마음에 들어, 수아야.
여	고마워. 그냥 자르고 염색해봤어.
남	왜 파란 머리를 하고 싶었니?
여	음, 그건 내가 가장 좋아하는 색이야. 그리고 내 빨간 머리에 싫증이 났거든.
남	네 전반적인 스타일이 부러워. 정말 독특해.
여	네 스타일도 좋아하지 않니?
남	좋아해, 하지만 어떤 것들은 입기가 무서워. 사람들이 좋아하지 않을 수 있잖아.
여	넌 항상 네가 좋아하는 옷을 입어야 해. 다른 사람에 대해 걱정하지 마.
남	네 말이 맞아. 무서워하면 안 되겠지.

해설 | 여자가 다른 사람에 대해 걱정하지 말고 남자가 좋아하는 옷을 입으라고 조언했으므로 정답은 조언에 동의하는 ① 'You're right. I shouldn't be afraid.'이다.

선택지 해석

① 네 말이 맞아. 무서워하면 안 되겠지.　② 그게 더 짧으면 좋겠어.　③ 아니. 그건 내 신발과 잘 어울리지 않아.　④ 이건 내가 가장 좋아하는 패션 잡지야.
⑤ 응. 나는 빨간색보다 파란색을 더 좋아하기도 해.

어휘 | be tired of 싫증이 나다　overall [óuvərɔ̀ːl] 휑 전반적인

18 적절한 응답 고르기　　　　　　　　정답 ⑤

W	What are you holding, Nick?	여	뭘 들고 있니, Nick?
M	I got a gift for you.	남	널 위한 선물이 있어.
W	Really? That's so nice!	여	진짜? 정말 친절하다!
M	It's a small plant. I bought it at the flower shop yesterday.	남	이건 작은 식물이야. 어제 꽃집에서 샀어.
W	Wow, I love it! I will put it next to my window.	여	우와, 정말 마음에 든다! 창문 옆에 놓을게.
M	That's good because it needs lots of sunlight.	남	햇빛을 많이 필요로 하니까 그게 좋아.
W	This type of plant doesn't require a lot of water, right?	여	이런 종류의 식물은 물을 많이 필요로 하지 않잖아, 그렇지?
M	Yes. You should only water it twice a month.	남	응. 한 달에 두 번만 물을 주면 돼.
W	Okay. I'll take a good care of it.	여	알겠어. 잘 돌볼게.

해설 | 남자가 식물을 선물하며 한 달에 두 번만 물을 주면 된다고 조언했으므로 정답은 조언을 따르겠다는 ⑤ 'Okay. I'll take a good care of it.'이다.

선택지 해석
① 이건 선인장의 일종이야.　② 좋은 생각이야. 여기에 꽃을 심자.　③ 가방 들어줘서 고마워.　④ 맞아. 양지에 둘게.　⑤ 알겠어. 잘 돌볼게.

어휘 | require [rikwáiər] ⑧ 필요로 하다　water [wɔ́ːtər] ⑲ 물 ⑧ 물을 주다　cactus [kǽktəs] ⑲ 선인장

19 적절한 응답 고르기　　　　　　　　정답 ③

W	Are you having another soda, Rob?	여	너 또 탄산음료 마시니, Rob?
M	Yes. This is my favorite beverage.	남	응. 이건 내가 제일 좋아하는 음료야.
W	But you already drank two today.	여	하지만 오늘 벌써 두 개 마셨잖아.
M	What's wrong with that?	남	그게 뭐가 잘못됐어?
W	There's a lot of sugar in soda. It's not good for your health if you drink too many.	여	탄산음료에는 설탕이 많이 들어있어. 너무 많이 마시면 건강에 좋지 않아.
M	I'm aware of that, but they're delicious.	남	알고 있지만, 맛있는걸.
W	Even so, you should avoid drinking them.	여	그렇다고 해도, 마시지 않도록 해야 해.
M	It's hard to quit so quickly. But I'll drink some sugarless soda instead for now.	남	그렇게 빨리 끊는 건 어려워. 그래도 당분간 무설탕 탄산음료를 대신 마실게.
W	That seems like a good idea.	여	그거 좋은 생각 같다.

해설 | 남자가 당분간 무설탕 탄산음료를 대신 마시겠다고 했으므로 정답은 남자의 의견에 동의하는 ③ 'That seems like a good idea.'이다.

선택지 해석
① 병원에 가는 게 어때?　② 그것들은 먹기엔 너무 달아. 날 아프게 해.　③ 그거 좋은 생각 같아.　④ 응. 그는 나이에 비해 아주 건강해.
⑤ 운동으로 걷는 걸 추천해.

어휘 | beverage [bévəridʒ] ⑲ 음료　be aware of 알다, 인지하다　even so 그렇다고 해도, 그렇기는 하나　quit [kwit] ⑧ 끊다, 그만두다
sugarless [ʃúgərlis] ⑱ 무설탕의, 설탕이 없는　for now 당분간

20 상황에 적절한 말 고르기　　　　　　정답 ②

W	Yuri is a lifeguard. She works at a neighborhood pool. One day, she is watching some kids play in the water. A boy gets out and starts running along the side of the pool. This is against the safety rules. He could fall because it's slippery. So, Yuri would like to tell him to stop running next to the pool. In this situation, what would Yuri most likely say to the boy?	여	유리는 인명구조 요원입니다. 그녀는 인근 수영장에서 근무합니다. 어느 날, 그녀는 아이들 몇 명이 물에서 노는 것을 지켜보고 있습니다. 한 소년이 밖으로 나와서 수영장 가장자리를 따라 뛰기 시작합니다. 그것은 안전 수칙에 어긋납니다. 미끄럽기 때문에 그는 넘어질 수도 있습니다. 그래서, 유리는 그에게 수영장 옆에서 뛰는 것을 그만두라고 말하고 싶습니다. 이러한 상황에서, 유리가 소년에게 가장 할 것 같은 말은 무엇입니까?
Yuri	Please stop running next to the pool.	유리	수영장 옆에서 그만 뛰세요.

해설 | 유리가 소년에게 수영장 옆에서 뛰는 것을 그만두라고 하고 싶다고 했으므로 정답은 ② 'Please stop runnig next to the pool.'이다.

선택지 해석
① 수영장은 30분 후에 닫습니다.　② 수영장 옆에서 그만 뛰세요.　③ 구명조끼를 착용해 주시겠어요?　④ 부모님 중 한 분과 같이 왔나요?
⑤ 안전 수칙을 설명해 주셔서 고맙습니다.

어휘 | lifeguard [láifgɑːrd] ⑲ 인명구조 요원　neighborhood [néibərhùd] ⑲ 인근; 이웃　slippery [slípəri] ⑱ 미끄러운　life jacket 구명조끼

| 문제 pp.170~171

1	⑤	2	①	3	①	4	③	5	⑤	6	①	7	②	8	③	9	③	10	②
11	①	12	⑤	13	④	14	④	15	③	16	⑤	17	②	18	④	19	③	20	③

1 알맞은 그림 고르기

정답 ⑤

W Welcome to Best Electronics. May I help you?

M Yes. I need a wireless speaker.

W Then, I recommend this square one. It even has a clock function.

M Well, I don't need that function. Do you have any others?

W How about this triangle one? It has a strap, so you can easily carry it anywhere.

M Sorry, but I don't like the brand logo on it. I see the round one also has a strap.

W Right. Do you want to buy this one?

M Yes. I'll take it.

여 Best Electronics에 오신 것을 환영합니다. 도와드릴까요?

남 네. 무선 스피커가 필요해요.

여 그럼, 이 네모난 것을 추천해요. 이건 시계 기능도 있어요.

남 음, 저는 그 기능은 필요하지 않아요. 다른 것이 있나요?

여 이 세모난 것은 어떠신가요? 이건 끈이 있어서, 어디든 쉽게 들고 다니실 수 있어요.

남 죄송하지만, 브랜드 로고가 있는 게 마음에 들지 않아요. 둥근 것도 끈이 있는 것 같은데요.

여 맞습니다. 이것을 사고 싶으신가요?

남 네. 그걸로 할게요.

해설 | 남자가 시계 기능은 필요하지 않다고 했고, 둥근 무선 스피커도 끈이 있다고 한 후 그걸로 하겠다고 했으므로 정답은 ⑤이다.

어휘 | wireless [wáiərlis] 휑 무선의   function [fʌ́ŋkʃən] 몡 기능   strap [stræp] 몡 끈

2 목적 고르기

정답 ①

[Cellphone rings.]

M Hello, Nancy. Is everything okay?

W Hi, David. I'm so sorry, but we have to change our lunch plans for today.

M What happened?

W I forgot about an important doctor's appointment. I have to be there at 12 o'clock.

M What time will it finish?

W It will be over around 1:30.

M That's no problem. We can just meet later then.

W Thanks for understanding.

[휴대폰이 울린다.]

남 안녕, Nancy. 무슨 일이니?

여 안녕, David. 정말 미안하지만, 오늘 우리 점심 계획을 변경해야 할 것 같아.

남 무슨 일이야?

여 중요한 병원 진료 예약을 잊어버렸어. 12시까지 거기에 가야 해.

남 언제 끝나는데?

여 1시 30분쯤 끝날 거야.

남 문제없어. 그럼 그냥 더 늦게 만나면 돼.

여 이해해줘서 고마워.

해설 | 여자가 오늘 점심 계획을 변경해야 할 것 같다고 한 후 약속 시간을 늦췄으므로 정답은 ① '약속 시간을 바꾸려고'이다.

어휘 | doctor's appointment (병원) 진료 예약   understand [ʌndərstǽnd] 용 이해하다

3 그림 상황에 적절한 대화 고르기

정답 ①

① W Is there another bathroom?

  M There's one on the second floor. I'll show you.

② W What time does the museum tour start?

  M It begins in about 20 minutes.

③ W How much does a gym membership cost?

  M It's 100 dollars per month.

④ W I'm looking for the Elderberry Library.

  M It's right down the block.

⑤ W I need a new television for the living room.

  M What about this model?

① 여 다른 화장실이 있나요?

  남 2층에 하나 있어요. 보여드릴게요.

② 여 박물관 투어는 언제 시작하나요?

  남 대략 20분 후에 시작해요.

③ 여 체육관 회원권이 얼마인가요?

  남 한 달에 100달러예요.

④ 여 엘더베리 도서관을 찾고 있어요.

  남 저 블록 바로 아래에 있어요.

⑤ 여 거실에 둘 새 텔레비전이 필요해요.

  남 이 모델은 어떠세요?

해설 | 빈집을 둘러보면서 여자가 남자에게 화장실에 관해 묻고 있는 상황이므로 정답은 ①이다.

어휘 | floor [flɔːr] 몡 층; 바닥   membership [mémbərʃip] 몡 회원권   per [pər] 젠 ~에 대해, ~마다

4 시간 정보 고르기   정답 ③

[Cellphone rings.]

W Hello, Mr. Richardson. I'm calling about your car. I am repairing it here at the Auto Repair Center.

M Is everything alright?

W Yes. Your car will be ready for pickup next week. What day would you like to come and get it?

M Can I come on Monday?

W I'm afraid we are closed on Mondays. How about Tuesday?

M I'm too busy on Tuesday. Does Wednesday work?

W That's fine.

[휴대폰이 울린다.]

여 안녕하세요, Richardson씨. 차 때문에 전화 드렸어요. 여기 Auto Repair Center에서 제가 수리 중이에요.

남 다 괜찮은가요?

여 네. 다음 주에는 차를 찾아가실 준비가 될 거예요. 언제 와서 가져가시겠어요?

남 월요일에 가도 될까요?

여 죄송하지만 월요일에는 저희가 쉬어요. 화요일은 어떠세요?

남 화요일에는 제가 너무 바빠요. 수요일은 되나요?

여 그날 괜찮아요.

해설 | 남자가 수요일은 되는지 묻자 여자가 그날은 괜찮다고 했으므로 정답은 ③ '수요일'이다.

어휘 | repair [ripέər] 통 수리하다

5 언급하지 않은 내용 고르기   정답 ⑤

W Hi, students. This is your music teacher, Ms. Torrance. I'm happy to tell you that a concert will be held by our school orchestra. They will perform beautiful songs they've practiced for a year, including some from the famous *Pirates of Caribbean* soundtrack. The concert will be at Danvers Auditorium on November 19th. Everyone is invited, so please come and join us. Thank you.

여 안녕하세요, 학생 여러분. 저는 여러분들의 음악 선생님인 Torrance입니다. 우리 학교 관현악단이 연주회를 열게 되었다는 것을 알리게 되어 기쁩니다. 그들은 유명한 <캐리비안의 해적>의 영화 음악 일부를 포함하여 일 년 동안 연습해 온 아름다운 곡들을 연주할 예정입니다. 연주회는 11월 19일에 댄버스 강당에서 있을 예정입니다. 모두 초대되셨으니, 와서 참석해 주십시오. 감사합니다.

해설 | ① 주최자(학교 관현악단), ② 연주곡(<캐리비안의 해적>의 영화 음악이 포함됨), ③ 장소(댄버스 강당), ④ 날짜(11월 19일)에 대해 언급했으므로 정답은 ⑤ '입장료'이다.

어휘 | perform [pərfɔ́:rm] 통 연주하다, 공연하다; 수행하다 including [inklú:diŋ] 전 ~을 포함하여

6 관계 고르기   정답 ①

W This is Jessica Smith reporting for *Morning News*. I'm honored to be here with David Kim.

M Thank you for inviting me.

W So, how do you feel about winning the election?

M I'm very excited and so thankful to all of the voters.

W What will you do first as a new leader of the city?

M I will work hard to reduce our city's pollution.

W And what is your opinion on the plan to increase public transportation?

M I support it. I hope to see more buses and trains in the future.

여 <Morning News>의 Jessica Smith가 보도 전해드립니다. 저는 영광스럽게도 여기 David Kim과 함께 있습니다.

남 초대해 주셔서 감사합니다.

여 자, 선거에 이긴 기분이 어떠신가요?

남 저는 매우 기대되고 모든 유권자 여러분에게 감사합니다.

여 도시의 새로운 지도자로서 먼저 무엇을 하실 건가요?

남 저는 저희 도시의 오염을 줄이기 위해 노력할 것입니다.

여 그리고 대중교통을 늘리려는 계획에 대한 의견은 어떠신가요?

남 저는 그 계획을 지지합니다. 미래에 더 많은 버스와 기차를 볼 수 있길 바랍니다.

해설 | 여자가 뉴스 보도에서 남자에게 선거에 이긴 기분과 도시의 새로운 지도자로서의 포부에 대해 묻고 있는 것으로 보아 정답은 ① '시장 — 기자'이다.

어휘 | be honored 영광으로 생각하다 election [ilékʃən] 명 선거 voter [vóutər] 명 유권자, 투표자 reduce [ridjú:s] 통 줄이다 pollution [pəlú:ʃən] 명 오염 public transportation 대중교통

7 어색한 대화 고르기   정답 ②

① M You like that board game *Wizards and Wheels*, don't you?

  W Yes. It's really fun. Let's play it now.

② M Something is wrong with the computer.

  W I got that question wrong too.

③ M How often do you exercise?

  W I do yoga once a week.

④ M Do you want me to throw out this newspaper?

  W No. I want to read it now.

⑤ M May I take your order, ma'am?

  W Yes, please. I'd like a steak with French fries.

---

① 남 너 <Wizard and Wheels>라는 보드게임을 좋아하지, 그렇지 않니?

  여 응. 그건 정말 재미있어. 지금 하자.

② 남 컴퓨터가 뭔가 잘못됐어.

  여 나도 그 문제 틀렸어.

③ 남 너는 얼마나 자주 운동하니?

  여 나는 일주일에 한 번 요가를 해.

④ 남 이 신문 버려줄까?

  여 아니. 나 지금 읽고 싶어.

⑤ 남 주문하시겠습니까, 손님?

  여 네, 할게요. 스테이크와 감자튀김으로 주세요.

해설 | 남자가 컴퓨터가 뭔가 잘못됐다고 했으므로, 여자는 컴퓨터의 문제에 대해 답해야 한다. 그러나 여자는 자신도 그 문제를 틀렸다는 어색한 대답을 했으므로 정답은 ②이다.

어휘 | throw out 버리다

8 부탁·요청한 일 고르기   정답 ③

[Cellphone rings.]

W Hi. What's going on, Honey?

M Did you see my gloves this morning?

W Hmm... No. Did you check the closet?

M Yes. But they aren't there.

W When did you wear them last?

M A few days ago. I built a snowman with the kids.

W Oh, they must be in the laundry room.

M Okay. Also, could you remember to pick up the dry cleaning tonight? We'll need our jackets tomorrow.

W I will.

[휴대폰이 울린다.]

여 여보세요. 무슨 일이야, 여보?

남 오늘 아침에 내 장갑 봤어?

여 흠... 아니. 옷장 확인해 봤어?

남 응. 그렇지만 거기엔 없어.

여 언제 마지막으로 썼어?

남 며칠 전에. 아이들과 눈사람을 만들었거든.

여 오, 세탁실에 있는 게 틀림없어.

남 알겠어. 그리고, 오늘 밤에 드라이 클리닝한 것을 잊지 말고 가져와 줄래? 우리 내일 재킷이 필요해.

여 그럴게.

해설 | 남자가 여자에게 오늘 밤에 드라이 클리닝한 것을 잊지 말고 가져와 달라고 부탁했으므로 정답은 ③ '세탁물 찾아오기'이다.

어휘 | closet [klázit] 옝 옷장 laundry room 세탁실

9 의도 고르기   정답 ③

M How are you doing, Liz?

W I'm busy. I have a lot of homework to finish by Friday.

M Yeah? What are you working on?

W I have to write two essays. One for my English class and another one for history.

M Let me know if you need help. I could proofread your writing.

W Thanks. That would really help.

남 어떻게 지내고 있니, Liz?

여 난 바빠. 금요일까지 끝내야 할 숙제가 많아.

남 그래? 뭐 하고 있어?

여 에세이를 두 개 써야 해. 하나는 영어 수업을 위한 거고 또 하나는 역사 수업 거야.

남 도움이 필요하면 나에게 알려줘. 내가 네 글을 교정봐 줄 수 있어.

여 고마워. 정말 도움이 될 거야.

해설 | 여자가 고맙다며 정말 도움이 될 것이라고 했으므로 정답은 ③ '감사'이다.

어휘 | proofread [prúːfríːd] 图 교정을 보다

10 금액 정보 고르기 　　　　　　　　　　　　　정답 ②

W	Hi. Did you find everything you need?
M	Yes. I'd like to buy these running shorts.
W	Okay. Those are 15 dollars.
M	Oh, and what about these socks? I didn't see those before.
W	These socks are on sale, so it's only two dollars for three pairs.
M	Can I get two packs of those too?
W	Of course. The total comes to 19 dollars.
M	I have a three-dollar discount coupon. Is it okay to use it with this purchase?
W	Yes. That will work.

여	안녕하세요. 필요하신 건 모두 찾으셨나요?
남	네. 이 달리기용 반바지를 사고 싶어요.
여	알겠습니다. 15달러입니다.
남	오, 그리고 이 양말은요? 전에는 못 봤던 거네요.
여	이 양말은 할인 중이라서 세 켤레에 겨우 2달러예요.
남	저것도 2묶음 주시겠어요?
여	물론이죠. 총 19달러 되겠습니다.
남	3달러 할인 쿠폰이 있어요. 이번 구매에 사용해도 되나요?
여	네. 돼요.

해설Ⅰ 여자가 총 19달러라고 했고, 남자가 3달러 할인 쿠폰을 사용하겠다고 했으므로 정답은 ② '$ 16'이다.

어휘Ⅰ shorts [ʃɔːrts] 圓 반바지　come to (총액이) ~이 되다　purchase [pə́ːrtʃəs] 圓 구매

11 할 일 고르기 　　　　　　　　　　　　　　　정답 ①

W	These cookies look delicious, Alan.
M	Thank you. I made them yesterday.
W	Do you bake often?
M	Yes. It's my passion. I love to bake, and I really want to open a bakery one day.
W	Well, you always bake amazing things. These cookies are so great.
M	Next week, I'll bake a raspberry and lemon cake. It's a new recipe.
W	Can I try it after it's finished?
M	Of course!

여	이 쿠키 맛있어 보여, Alan.
남	고마워. 어제 만들었어.
여	너 빵을 자주 굽니?
남	응. 그건 내가 아주 좋아하는 일이야. 나는 빵 굽는 것을 정말 좋아하고, 언젠가 빵집을 열고 싶어.
여	음, 넌 항상 놀라운 것들을 굽잖아. 이 쿠키도 정말 멋져.
남	다음 주에는, 라즈베리와 레몬 케이크를 구울 예정이야. 새로운 요리법이야.
여	완성되면 먹어봐도 되니?
남	당연하지!

해설Ⅰ 남자가 라즈베리와 레몬 케이크를 구울 예정이라고 했으므로 정답은 ① '케이크 만들기'이다.

어휘Ⅰ passion [pǽʃən] 圓 아주 좋아하는 것; 열정　recipe [résəpi] 圓 요리법, 조리법

12 언급하지 않은 내용 고르기 　　　　　　　　　정답 ⑤

W	Good morning, visitors. I'm Martha. I'll be your guide today on our bus tour. I will give you information about famous sites here in Madrid. Our first stop in the city will be the Prado Museum. Then, we'll head to Royal Palace of Madrid, among many other destinations. Remember, you can get off and spend time at every stop. If you want to, just hop off. You can get on the next bus for no extra charge.

여	안녕하세요, 방문객 여러분. 저는 Martha입니다. 제가 오늘 여러분의 버스 투어 가이드가 될 예정입니다. 저는 여기 마드리드의 유명한 장소들에 대한 정보를 드릴 것입니다. 저희의 첫 번째 정거장은 프라도 박물관입니다. 그다음에, 저희는 다른 많은 행선지들 중, 마드리드 왕궁으로 향할 것입니다. 기억하십시오, 모든 정거장에 내려서 시간을 보내실 수 있습니다. 만약 원하신다면, 그냥 내리십시오. 추가 비용 없이 다음 버스에 타실 수 있습니다.

해설Ⅰ ① 투어 장소(프라도 박물관, 마드리드 왕궁), ② 가이드 이름(Martha), ③ 하차 장소(모든 정거장), ④ 환승 비용(추가 비용 없음)에 대해 언급했으므로 정답은 ⑤ '운영 시간'이다.

어휘Ⅰ site [sait] 圓 장소　head [hed] 圄 향하다　destination [dèstənéiʃən] 圓 행선지, 목적지　hop off 내리다

13 도표에서 알맞은 항목 고르기   정답 ④

M	Hi. I'd like to get some flowers for my wife.
W	Okay. What does she like?
M	I'm not sure, but I know she doesn't like tulips.
W	How about these roses?
M	They are beautiful. What are those yellow ones?
W	They are roses too, but they are for a special order.
M	Oh. Then, can I have 10 red ones?
W	Would you like me to wrap them with a ribbon?
M	Yes, please. How much is it?

남	안녕하세요. 제 아내에게 줄 꽃을 좀 사고 싶어요.
여	알겠습니다. 아내 분은 무엇을 좋아하시나요?
남	잘 모르겠어요, 그런데 튤립은 좋아하지 않아요.
여	이 장미들은 어떤가요?
남	아름답네요. 저 노란 것은 뭔가요?
여	그것들도 장미들인데, 특별 주문용이에요.
남	오. 그럼 빨간 장미 열 송이를 살 수 있을까요?
여	리본으로 포장해 드릴까요?
남	네, 그렇게 해주세요. 얼마인가요?

해설 | 남자가 빨간 장미 열 송이를 리본으로 포장해 달라고 했으므로 정답은 ④이다.

어휘 | wrap [ræp] 图 포장하다

14 화제 고르기   정답 ④

W This is very helpful when you read books. It is usually long, flat, and has a rectangular shape. But it also comes in many different designs. It is inserted into a book between two pages. People use it to save their place in a book. With this, people don't have to fold the pages of their books.

여 이것은 책을 읽을 때 매우 유용합니다. 이것은 보통 길고 납작하며 직사각형의 모양입니다. 하지만 이것은 많은 다양한 디자인으로도 나옵니다. 이것은 책의 두 페이지 사이에 끼워 넣어집니다. 사람들은 책 속에 그들이 읽던 페이지를 저장하기 위해 이것을 사용합니다. 이것이 있다면 사람들은 책의 페이지를 접지 않아도 됩니다.

해설 | 이것은 책의 두 페이지 사이에 끼워 넣어지며, 사람들이 읽던 페이지를 저장하기 위해 사용한다고 했으므로 정답은 ④ '책갈피'이다.

어휘 | flat [flæt] 图 납작한   insert [insə́:rt] 图 끼워 넣다   place [pleis] 图 읽던 페이지, 읽던 대목; 장소   fold [fould] 图 접다

15 할 일 고르기   정답 ③

W	How was the water slide, Geonu?
M	It was fun! I went down the slide really fast.
W	What will you ride next?
M	There's another water ride, but I need a partner to ride it.
W	Well, your dad went to get a new life vest.
M	Then, why don't you ride it with me, Mom?
W	Sure. I'll ride it with you now.
M	Thanks, Mom.

여	워터슬라이드는 어땠니, 건우야?
남	재미있었어요! 미끄럼틀을 정말 빨리 내려갔어요.
여	다음엔 뭘 탈래?
남	저기 또 다른 물놀이 기구가 있는데, 그걸 타려면 파트너가 필요해요.
여	음, 네 아빠는 새 구명조끼를 가지러 갔단다.
남	그럼, 저랑 같이 타는 게 어때요, 엄마?
여	물론이지. 지금 너와 함께 타마.
남	고마워요, 엄마.

해설 | 남자가 다른 물놀이 기구를 타려면 파트너가 필요하다며 여자에게 같이 탈 것을 제안하자, 여자가 지금 함께 타겠다고 했으므로 정답은 ③ '물놀이 기구 타기'이다.

어휘 | ride [raid] 图 타다 图 놀이 기구   life vest 구명조끼

16 특정 정보 고르기   정답 ⑤

M	What are your plans tonight, Lily?
W	I'll go to my piano lesson. I have a class every Thursday evening.
M	When did you start taking those lessons?
W	I started to play the piano about two years ago.
M	You must be good then.
W	It helps me relax. But what about you? Do you play any instruments?
M	I used to play the drums, but now I want to play the guitar. I will start lessons soon.
W	I hope you enjoy it.

남	오늘 밤 네 계획이 뭐니, Lily?
여	난 피아노 수업에 갈 거야. 목요일 저녁마다 수업이 있어.
남	언제 수업을 받기 시작했니?
여	난 2년 전쯤부터 피아노를 치기 시작했어.
남	그럼 잘 치겠다.
여	그건 내가 쉬는 데 도움이 돼. 근데 넌 어때? 연주하는 악기가 있니?
남	난 드럼을 쳤었는데, 이제 기타를 치고 싶어. 곧 수업을 시작할 거야.
여	네가 즐겼으면 좋겠다.

해설 | 남자가 기타를 치고 싶다고 하면서, 곧 수업을 시작할 것이라고 했으므로 정답은 ⑤ 'guitar'이다.

  선택지 해석
  ① 피아노 ② 드럼 ③ 플루트 ④ 바이올린 ⑤ 기타

어휘 | instrument [ínstrəmənt] 图 악기

W	Excuse me. Is this seat taken?
M	No, it isn't. You can sit here.
W	Thank you. The other seats are full, and I don't want to stand during the ride.
M	I understand. Where are you traveling to?
W	I will go to Smithville to visit my family.
M	How many stops away is that?
W	It's at the end of the train line.
M	Oh, wow. It must be a long journey then.
W	Yes. It takes over four hours to get there.

여	실례합니다. 이 자리에 주인이 있나요?
남	아니요, 없어요. 앉으셔도 돼요.
여	감사합니다. 다른 자리가 다 찼는데, 타는 동안 서 있고 싶지 않았거든요.
남	이해해요. 어디로 여행가시나요?
여	가족을 방문하러 스미스빌에 갈 예정이에요.
남	몇 정거장이나 가야 하나요?
여	기차 노선 끝에 있어요.
남	오, 우와. 정말 긴 여행이겠군요 그럼.
여	네. 거기 가는 데 4시간 넘게 걸려요.

해설 | 남자가 정말 긴 여행이겠다고 했으므로 정답은 여행에 걸리는 시간을 언급하는 ② 'Yes. It takes over four hours to get there.'이다.

선택지 해석
① 폭설로 인해 버스가 취소됐어요.　② 네. 거기 가는 데 4시간 넘게 걸려요.　③ 아니요. 여동생이나 남동생은 없어요.　④ 당신은 잘못된 정거장에 와 있어요.
⑤ 저는 기차로 하는 짧은 여행을 좋아해요.

어휘 | journey [dʒə́ːrni] 명 여행, 여정　cancel [kǽnsəl] 동 취소하다

M	What is that, Laura?
W	It's my journal.
M	Do you write in it every day?
W	I try to keep a journal every day, but sometimes I forget.
M	What subjects do you write about?
W	I write about school, relationships with friends, and my goals. It organizes my thoughts and feelings.
M	That sounds like a great idea. Maybe I will buy a journal so I can keep one like you do.
W	Then, why don't we write in our journals together sometime?
M	I would love to do that.

남	그게 뭐니, Laura?
여	내 일기장이야.
남	너 매일 일기를 쓰니?
여	매일 쓰려고 노력하는데, 가끔 잊어버려.
남	어떤 주제에 대해 쓰니?
여	학교, 친구 관계, 그리고 내 목표에 대해서 써. 내 생각과 느낌을 정리해 주거든.
남	좋은 생각인 것 같아. 네가 하는 것처럼 나도 일기를 쓸 수 있게 일기장을 하나 사야 할까 봐.
여	그럼, 우리 언제 같이 일기를 쓰는 게 어때?
남	정말 그러고 싶다.

해설 | 여자가 일기를 같이 쓰자고 제안했으므로 정답은 제안에 동의하는 ④ 'I would love to do that.'이다.

선택지 해석
① 물론이지. 일기 쓰는 것은 너무 어려워 보여.　② 주제는 너의 꿈의 직업이야.　③ 맞아. 메모하는 건 좋은 습관이야.　④ 정말 그러고 싶다.
⑤ 내 가장 친한 친구의 이름은 Tim이야.

어휘 | keep a journal 일기를 쓰다　relationship [riléiʃənʃip] 명 관계　organize [ɔ́ːrgənáiz] 동 정리하다; 조직하다

M	What are those, Mom?
W	They're packages from your cousins in Switzerland.
M	Wow, what did they send?
W	I'm not sure. But they're probably presents for Christmas.
M	That's nice of them. Can I open the packages now?
W	Sure. Just be careful.
M	[Rustling sound] They sent us watches! I think this one is for me. It's so sophisticated.
W	Oh, yes. It seems like it's very high quality.
M	I will send pictures of it to my friends. I can't wait to wear it.
W	First, call your cousins. You need to say thank you.
M	I'll try to video call them now.

남	이것들은 뭔가요, 엄마?
여	그건 스위스에 있는 사촌들로부터 온 소포야.
남	우와, 뭘 보냈어요?
여	잘 모르겠어. 하지만 아마 크리스마스 선물일 거야.
남	사촌들이 친절하네요. 지금 소포를 열어봐도 돼요?
여	물론이지. 조심하렴.
남	[바스락거리는 소리] 우리에게 시계를 보냈어요! 이게 제 것 같아요. 정말 정교하네요.
여	오, 그렇구나. 품질이 정말 좋아 보이는구나.
남	시계 사진을 친구들에게 보낼래요. 이걸 찰 것이 기대돼요.
여	먼저, 사촌에게 전화하렴. 고맙다고 말해야 해.
남	지금 영상 통화를 해 볼게요.

해설 | 여자가 사촌들에게 전화해서 고맙다고 말해야 한다고 조언했으므로 정답은 그러겠다고 답하는 ③ 'I'll try to video call them now.'이다.

선택지 해석

① 스위스는 지금 오전 11시예요. ② 그들에게 감사 편지를 써주세요. ③ 지금 영상 통화를 해 볼게요. ④ 이 시계를 상자에 포장할게요.

⑤ 우리는 할 수 없어요. 오늘은 모두 문을 닫을 거예요.

어휘 | sophisticated [səfístəkèitid] 휑 정교한 quality [kwáləti] 몡 품질

20 상황에 적절한 말 고르기   정답 ③

W	Lucy loves to ride her bike to work. However, it's very old, so she needs a new one. She goes to the bike store and sees one that she likes. But it is black, and Lucy likes the color green. So, she would like to ask an employee if the bike comes in green. In this situation, what would Lucy most likely say to the employee?	여	Lucy는 자전거를 타고 출근하는 것을 좋아합니다. 하지만, 그것은 매우 낡아서, 그녀는 새것이 필요합니다. 그녀는 자전거 가게에 가서 마음에 드는 것을 봅니다. 하지만 그것은 검은색이고, Lucy는 초록색을 좋아합니다. 그래서, 그녀는 직원에게 그 자전거가 초록색으로도 나오는지 묻고 싶습니다. 이러한 상황에서, Lucy가 직원에게 가장 할 것 같은 말은 무엇입니까?
Lucy	Do you have this one in green?	Lucy	이거 초록색으로 있나요?

해설 | Lucy가 직원에게 자전거가 초록색으로도 나오는지 묻고 싶다고 했으므로 정답은 ③ 'Do you have this one in green?'이다.

선택지 해석

① 제 자전거를 수리해 주실 수 있나요? ② 자전거용 헬멧도 필요하지 않나요? ③ 이거 초록색으로 있나요? ④ 죄송하지만, 오늘 아침에 늦을 것 같아요.

⑤ 다행히, 이 모델은 많은 다양한 색깔로 나와요.

어휘 | employee [implɔ́iː] 몡 직원 luckily [lʌ́kili] 튄 다행히, 운 좋게

(20회) 실전 모의고사 | 문제 pp.178-179

1	③	2	②	3	④	4	④	5	③	6	④	7	②	8	⑤	9	①	10	④
11	②	12	⑤	13	②	14	①	15	④	16	②	17	②	18	④	19	⑤	20	①

1 알맞은 그림 고르기   정답 ③

M	Honey, what are we going to buy for our son this Children's Day?	남	여보, 이번 어린이날에는 우리 아들에게 뭘 사줄까?
W	He is into playing with building blocks. I suggest we buy one of these sets of toy blocks.	여	그는 블록 쌓기 놀이에 빠져 있어. 내 생각에는 이 놀이 블록 세트들 중 하나를 사는 게 좋을 것 같아.
M	Good! How about this clock tower?	남	좋아! 이 시계 탑은 어때?
W	Well, I think he'd prefer the castle toy.	여	음, 내 생각에는 성 장난감을 더 좋아할 것 같아.
M	Do you mean the one with the bridges?	남	다리가 있는 것 말하는 거야?
W	No. That one is too big. That one with flags on the top is a good size, though.	여	아니. 그건 너무 커. 꼭대기에 깃발들이 있는 것은 괜찮은 크기인 것 같지만.
M	Oh, I see. Let's buy it.	남	오, 그렇네. 그걸로 사자.

해설 | 여자가 아들에게 꼭대기에 깃발들이 있는 성 장난감을 사주자고 했으므로 정답은 ③이다.

어휘 | be into ~에 빠져 있다 flag [flæg] 몡 깃발 though [ðou] 튄 ~이지만, 그렇지만 쩝 ~임에도 불구하고

2 목적 고르기   정답 ②

[Telephone rings.]	[전화기가 울린다.]
W Thank you for calling the National Art Museum. How can I help you?	여 국립 미술 박물관에 전화해 주셔서 감사합니다. 무엇을 도와드릴까요?
M Hi. I'm interested in viewing the special exhibit of Egyptian art.	남 안녕하세요. 저는 이집트 미술 특별전을 보는 데 관심이 있어요.
W Okay. We will be holding it until June 15th.	여 그러시군요. 6월 15일까지 개최할 예정입니다.
M I saw that on your website. But I couldn't find any information about admission prices.	남 그건 웹사이트에서 봤어요. 그런데 입장료에 대한 정보를 전혀 찾을 수 없었어요.
W Oh, it is eight dollars for students, and 10 dollars for the general public.	여 오, 학생은 8달러이고, 일반 대중은 10달러예요.
M Great. Do I need to show my student ID card to get the discount?	남 좋네요. 할인을 받으려면 학생증을 보여드려야 하나요?
W That's right.	여 그렇습니다.
M Thank you.	남 감사합니다.

해설 | 남자가 이집트 미술 특별전을 보고 싶은데 입장료에 대한 정보를 전혀 찾을 수 없었다고 했으므로 정답은 ② '박물관 입장료를 문의하려고'이다.

어휘 | view [vju:] 통 보다   hold [hould] 통 개최하다   admission price 입장료   general public 일반 대중

---

3 그림 상황에 적절한 대화 고르기   정답 ④

① W We should give the dog a bath.	① 여 우리 개를 목욕시켜야겠어.
M Yeah. He played in the mud all day.	남 맞아. 온종일 진흙에서 놀았잖아.
② W Who left these clothes on the floor?	② 여 누가 바닥에 이 옷들을 뒀니?
M Sorry. I'll pick them up now.	남 미안해. 내가 지금 주울게.
③ W I fixed your printer.	③ 여 내가 네 프린터를 고쳤어.
M Thank you so much!	남 정말 고마워!
④ W Why are you so dirty?	④ 여 너 왜 그렇게 더럽니?
M I was working in the garden all morning.	남 아침 내내 정원에서 일하고 있었어.
⑤ W When will lunch be ready?	⑤ 여 점심 식사는 언제 준비가 되니?
M I'm almost done preparing it.	남 거의 다 준비했어.

해설 | 흙이 묻어 더러워진 옷을 입고 있는 남자에게 여자가 말을 걸고 있는 상황이므로 정답은 ④이다.

어휘 | give a bath 목욕시키다   mud [mʌd] 명 진흙   prepare [pripέər] 통 준비하다

---

4 시간 정보 고르기   정답 ④

W Hi, David. Do you want to go to the Spring Music Festival this year?	여 안녕, David. 올해 Spring Music Festival에 갈래?
M Of course! When is it?	남 당연하지! 언제인데?
W It starts on May 5th, and it continues until Sunday.	여 5월 5일에 시작해서, 일요일까지 계속돼.
M Okay. Do you want to go on the Friday?	남 그래. 금요일에 갈래?
W I'll be at work until late that day. What about Sunday?	여 그날 늦게까지 일하고 있을 거야. 일요일은 어때?
M I usually eat lunch with my parents.	남 난 보통 부모님과 점심을 먹어.
W Can you skip it that week?	여 그 주는 건너뛸 수 있을까?
M I don't think so. Are you free on Saturday?	남 안될 것 같아. 토요일에 시간 되니?
W Fine. Let's go on that day.	여 괜찮아. 그날 가자.

해설 | 남자가 토요일에 시간이 되는지 묻자 여자가 괜찮다고 하며 그날 가자고 했으므로 정답은 ④ '토요일'이다.

어휘 | continue [kəntínju:] 통 계속되다   skip [skip] 통 건너뛰다, 거르다

5 언급하지 않은 내용 고르기   정답 ③

M	Hello, students. This is your student president, Andy Thomas. As some of you already know, we are starting a new daily event called Snack Hour to allow students to take a break. Every day in the library's presentation room from 2 to 3 p.m., we will provide free snacks and iced tea for students. Please come, meet, and talk to your peers for a good break from studying. Maybe this is the perfect chance to meet a new friend or study partner. We hope to see you soon!	남	안녕하세요, 학생 여러분. 학생회장 Andy Thomas입니다. 여러분 중 일부는 이미 아시다시피, 저희는 학생들이 휴식을 취할 수 있게 하기 위해 Snack Hour라고 불리는 새로운 일일 행사를 시작할 것입니다. 매일 오후 2시에서 3시 사이에 도서관 발표실에서 학생들을 위해 무료 간식과 아이스티를 제공할 예정입니다. 공부로부터의 충분한 휴식을 위해, 와서 여러분의 친구들과 만나고, 이야기하세요. 아마 이것이 새로운 친구나 공부 파트너를 만날 완벽할 기회일지도 모릅니다. 곧 만나길 바랍니다!

해설 | ① 목적(학생들이 휴식을 취할 수 있게 하기 위함), ② 시간(오후 2시에서 3시 사이), ④ 장소(도서관 발표실), ⑤ 제공 물품(무료 간식과 아이스티)에 대해 언급했으므로 정답은 ③ '종료 일자'이다.

어휘 | daily [déili] 웹 일일의, 매일의 allow [əláu] 图 ~할 수 있게 하다; 허락하다 provide [prəváid] 图 제공하다 peer [piər] 圀 친구, 동료

6 관계 고르기   정답 ④

M	Ms. Johns, I'm finished checking your dog.	남	Johns씨, 강아지의 검사가 끝났어요.
W	So, what's wrong with him?	여	그래서, 뭐가 문제인가요?
M	He hurt his front right leg. That's why his behavior isn't normal.	남	오른쪽 앞다리를 다쳤어요. 그래서 행동이 정상적이지 않았던 거예요.
W	Maybe he got hurt at the park. He was running through thick bushes.	여	아마 공원에서 다쳤나 봐요. 빽빽한 덤불 사이로 뛰어다녔거든요.
M	Well, he needs to rest for a while. He shouldn't run for about a week.	남	음, 당분간 휴식을 취해야 해요. 한 주 정도는 뛰면 안 돼요.
W	Okay. Is there anything else I should do?	여	알겠습니다. 더 해야 할 것이 있나요?
M	I will give you some medicine for him.	남	강아지에게 먹일 약을 좀 드릴게요.

해설 | 남자가 검사 결과 여자의 강아지는 오른쪽 앞다리를 다쳤다고 했으므로 정답은 ④ '수의사 — 견주'이다.

어휘 | behavior [bihéivjər] 圀 행동 normal [nɔ́ːrməl] 웹 정상적인, 표준의 thick [θik] 웹 빽빽한, 두꺼운 bush [buʃ] 圀 덤불, 관목

7 어색한 대화 고르기   정답 ②

① W	Excuse me. Can you give me directions to the post office?	① 여	실례합니다. 우체국으로 가는 길을 알려주실 수 있나요?
M	No problem. Just walk straight that way.	남	물론이죠. 저쪽으로 쭉 걸어가세요.
② W	This book is so long and boring.	② 여	이 책은 너무 길고 지루해.
M	Don't worry. The train should be here in 30 minutes.	남	걱정하지 마. 기차는 30분 후에 도착할 거야.
③ W	What size shoes do you wear?	③ 여	신발 몇 사이즈 신니?
M	My shoe size is 250 millimeters.	남	내 신발 사이즈는 250mm야.
④ W	Would you mind passing me the salt?	④ 여	소금 좀 건네주시겠어요?
M	Here you go.	남	여기 있어요.
⑤ W	I heard that a new café opened on Anderson Street.	⑤ 여	앤더슨 가에 새 카페가 열렸다고 들었어.
M	Let's go there this Friday.	남	이번 주 금요일에 거기 가자.

해설 | 여자가 책이 너무 길고 지루하다고 했으므로, 남자는 책에 대해 말해야 한다. 하지만 남자가 걱정하지 말라면서 기차는 30분 후에 도착할 것이라는 어색한 대답을 했으므로 정답은 ②이다.

어휘 | pass [pæs] 图 건네주다; 지나가다

8 부탁·요청한 일 고르기 정답 ⑤

M	That was a nice movie.
W	Yes, it was. <u>What should we do</u> now?
M	Why don't we watch the sunset somewhere?
W	Okay. There's <u>a nice spot to watch</u> the sunset near the river.
M	Well, the sun is <u>going down fast</u>. How far is it?
W	It's a little far. We can rent some of those electric scooters.
M	Okay. But I don't know <u>how to rent one</u>. Can you show me how to do it?
W	Sure. It's easy.

남	좋은 영화였어.
여	맞아, 그랬어. 이제 우리 뭐할까?
남	어딘가에서 일몰을 보는 게 어때?
여	그래. 강 근처에 일몰을 보기 좋은 장소가 있어.
남	음, 해가 빠르게 지고 있어. 거기 얼마나 멀어?
여	약간 멀어. 우리 저 전동 스쿠터를 좀 빌려도 돼.
남	그래. 근데 나 어떻게 빌리는지 몰라. 어떻게 하는지 보여줄 수 있니?
여	물론이지. 쉬워.

해설 | 남자가 전동 스쿠터를 어떻게 빌리는지 모른다고 하며 어떻게 하는지 보여 달라고 부탁했으므로 정답은 ⑤ '전동 스쿠터 대여 방법 보여주기'이다.

어휘 | sunset [sə̀nsét] 몡 일몰   electric [iléktrik] 혱 전동의, 전기의

9 의도 고르기 정답 ①

W	Are you looking for something?
M	Yeah. I can't find <u>my laptop charger</u> anywhere.
W	I see. Does your laptop <u>have any battery</u> left?
M	No. It's completely out of power. And I need it to do some research.
W	<u>What laptop model</u> do you have?
M	It's an Orange Book 7.
W	I have the same one. How about <u>using my power cord</u>?

여	뭔가 찾고 있니?
남	응. 어디에서도 내 노트북 충전기를 못 찾겠어.
여	그렇구나. 노트북에 남은 배터리는 있니?
남	아니. 완전히 전원이 나갔어. 그리고 난 조사를 좀 하기 위해서 그게 필요해.
여	어떤 노트북 모델을 가지고 있는데?
남	Orange Book 7이야.
여	나 같은 걸 가지고 있어. 내 전원 코드를 쓰는 게 어때?

해설 | 여자가 같은 노트북을 가지고 있다고 하며 자신의 전원 코드를 쓰는 게 어떤지 물었으므로 정답은 ① '제안'이다.

어휘 | completely [kəmplíːtli] 뮈 완전히   power [páuər] 몡 전원; 힘   research [risə́ːrtʃ] 몡 조사   cord [kɔːrd] 몡 코드, 선

10 금액 정보 고르기 정답 ④

M	Are you <u>ready to pay</u>?
W	Yes. I'd like to buy these two cups.
M	Alright. <u>Each of those is</u> 10 dollars. Do you also want to buy some of these plates? They're discounted right now.
W	No, thank you. But can you <u>recommend some bowls</u>?
M	These over here are <u>our most popular ones</u>. They're 12 dollars each.
W	<u>Those are beautiful</u>. I'll take two.
M	Okay, so <u>it's 20 dollars for the cups and 24 dollars for the bowls</u>.
W	Thank you. Here is my card.

남	계산하시겠어요?
여	네. 저는 이 두 개의 컵을 사고 싶어요.
남	알겠습니다. 각각 10달러입니다. 이 접시도 몇 개 사시겠어요? 지금 할인 중이거든요.
여	아니요, 괜찮아요. 하지만 그릇 몇 개 추천해 주시겠어요?
남	여기 이것들이 가장 인기 있는 것들이에요. 하나에 12달러예요.
여	아름다워요. 두 개 살게요.
남	네, 그럼 컵은 20달러이고 그릇은 24달러입니다.
여	감사합니다. 여기 제 카드가 있어요.

해설 | 남자가 컵은 20달러이고 그릇은 24달러라고 했으므로 정답은 ④ '$ 44'이다.

어휘 | plate [pleit] 몡 접시   bowl [boul] 몡 그릇

11 할 일 고르기 　　　　　　　　　　　　　　　정답 ②

[Cellphone rings.]

M　Hey, Charlotte. What are you doing?
W　I'm with my friend Helen, Dad.
M　Do you need anything?
W　Helen asked me to go ski with her family tomorrow. Can I go?
M　Oh, I'm so sorry, but you have a gymnastics lesson tomorrow.
W　I forgot about that. We can ski another weekend then.
M　Okay. I'll see you at home soon.

[휴대폰이 울린다.]

남　안녕, Charlotte. 뭐 하고 있니?
여　제 친구 Helen과 있어요, 아빠.
남　필요한 게 있니?
여　Helen이 저에게 내일 그녀의 가족과 함께 스키를 타러 가자고 했어요. 가도 돼요?
남　오, 미안하지만, 내일 체조 수업이 있잖니.
여　잊어버렸어요. 그럼 다른 주말에 스키를 타러 가면 돼요.
남　그래. 집에서 곧 보자.

해설 | 남자가 여자는 내일 체조 수업이 있다고 했으므로 정답은 ② '체조 수업 듣기'이다.

어휘 | gymnastics [dʒimnǽstiks] 圐 체조

12 언급하지 않은 내용 고르기 　　　　　　　　　정답 ⑤

W　Hello, students. My name is Sumin Lee, and I'm in charge of the online information sessions for the National Art School. As you know, one will be held next Tuesday at 10 a.m. If you want to participate, please visit our website. We will discuss admission requirements, curriculum guidelines, and more. I'll contact you if there are any changes. Thank you.

여　안녕하세요, 학생 여러분. 제 이름은 이수민이고, 저는 국립 예술 학교의 온라인 설명회 담당자입니다. 다들 아시다시피, 다음 주 화요일 오전 10시에 설명회가 하나 열릴 예정입니다. 참가하고 싶으시다면, 저희 웹사이트를 방문해 주십시오. 입학 자격 요건, 교육 과정 지침, 그리고 더 많은 것들에 대해 논의할 것입니다. 변경 사항이 있다면 연락드리겠습니다. 감사합니다.

해설 | ① 일시(다음 주 화요일 오전 10시), ② 담당자(이수민), ③ 참가 방법(웹사이트 방문), ④ 설명 내용(입학 자격 요건, 교육 과정 지침 등)에 대해 언급했으므로 정답은 ⑤ '준비물'이다.

어휘 | in charge of ~을 담당하는, 관리하는　information session 설명회　requirement [rikwáiərmənt] 圐 자격 요건　curriculum [kəríkjuləm] 圐 교육 과정

13 도표에서 알맞은 항목 고르기 　　　　　　　　정답 ②

M　Hi. I'd like to book a study room for tomorrow morning.
W　How long will you use it?
M　I need it for at least an hour and a half. Maybe even longer.
W　How many people will be using it?
M　There will be four.
W　In that case, you have two options.
M　How much is the bigger one?
W　It's 12 dollars an hour.
M　That's too expensive. I'll get the smaller one.
W　Okay. Please write down your name and number here.

남　안녕하세요. 내일 아침에 쓸 스터디룸을 예약하고 싶은데요.
여　얼마나 오래 사용하실 건가요?
남　적어도 한 시간 반은 필요해요. 더 길 수도 있어요.
여　몇 명이 사용할 예정이신가요?
남　네 명이요.
여　그 경우에는, 두 가지 선택권이 있어요.
남　더 큰 것은 얼마인가요?
여　한 시간에 12달러예요.
남　그건 너무 비싸네요. 더 작은 걸로 할게요.
여　알겠습니다. 성함과 번호를 여기 적어주세요.

해설 | 남자가 내일 아침에 네 명이 적어도 한 시간 반 이상 사용할 것이라고 했고, 12달러보다 더 저렴한 작은 스터디룸으로 하겠다고 했으므로 정답은 ②이다.

어휘 | at least 적어도　half [hæf] 圐 반, 절반

14 화제 고르기 　　　　　　　　　　　　　　　정답 ①

M　This is an indoor sport. People of all ages can enjoy this sport. To play this game, people roll a heavy ball down a long track. There are 10 pins set up in a triangle at the end of the track. A player must knock down these pins to score points. Players can play this sport on teams or they can play alone.

남　이것은 실내 운동입니다. 모든 연령의 사람들이 이 운동을 즐길 수 있습니다. 경기를 하기 위해서 사람들은 무거운 공을 긴 트랙 아래로 굴립니다. 트랙의 끝에는 삼각형 모양으로 세워진 열 개의 핀이 있습니다. 점수를 얻기 위해 선수는 이 핀들을 넘어뜨려야 합니다. 선수들은 이 운동을 팀으로 하거나 혼자 할 수 있습니다.

해설 | 이것(This)은 무거운 공을 긴 트랙 아래로 굴려서 트랙의 끝에 있는 열 개의 핀을 넘어뜨려야 점수를 얻을 수 있다고 했으므로 정답은 ① '볼링'이다.

어휘 | indoor [índɔːr] 圐 실내의　age [eidʒ] 圐 연령, 나이　set up 세우다, 설치하다　knock down 넘어뜨리다

15 할 일 고르기
정답 ④

W	How was your time in Mexico, Junseo?	여	멕시코에서의 시간은 어땠니, 준서야?
M	It was fantastic. I didn't want to come home.	남	굉장했어. 난 집에 오고 싶지 않았어.
W	What did you do?	여	뭘 했는데?
M	I went hiking, swimming, and scuba diving.	남	난 등산, 수영, 그리고 스쿠버 다이빙을 했어.
W	Wow! Did you see any cool fish while scuba diving?	여	우와! 스쿠버 다이빙하는 동안에 멋진 물고기도 봤니?
M	Of course. I took some photographs with my camera.	남	당연하지. 내 카메라로 사진도 찍었어.
W	You can take your camera underwater?	여	물속에 카메라를 들고 갈 수 있어?
M	Yeah. I'll show you the pictures now.	남	응. 내가 지금 사진을 보여줄게.

해설 | 남자가 지금 사진을 보여주겠다고 했으므로 정답은 ④ '사진 보여주기'이다.

어휘 | fantastic [fæntǽstik] 휑 굉장한, 환상적인   underwater [ʌ̀ndərwɔ́tər] 븟 물속에 휑 물속의

16 시간 정보 고르기
정답 ②

W	Jiho, can you help me book my flight to Jeju?	여	지호야, 제주행행 비행기를 예약하는 것 좀 도와주겠니?
M	Sure, Mom. Let me just get my laptop. [Pause] What time do you want to leave tomorrow?	남	물론이죠, 엄마. 제 노트북만 가지고 올게요. [잠시 멈춤] 내일 몇 시에 떠나고 싶으신가요?
W	The conference starts at 2 p.m. Is there a flight that gets me there at 12 p.m.?	여	회의가 오후 2시에 시작해. 내가 거기 오후 12시에 도착하게 하는 비행기가 있니?
M	Hold on. [Typing sound] No. But there are seats on a flight that leaves at 10 a.m. and arrives at 11.	남	잠시만요. [타자치는 소리] 아니요. 하지만 오전 10시에 떠나서 11시에 도착하는 비행기에는 자리가 있어요.
W	That means I would have to be at the airport by 9. It's a little earlier than I planned, but I guess it's my only option.	여	내가 9시까지 공항에 도착해야 한다는 거네. 내가 계획한 것보다는 약간 이르지만, 그게 유일한 선택지인 것 같구나.
M	Okay. I'll book a seat on the 10 a.m. flight.	남	네. 오전 10시 비행기에 좌석을 예약할게요.
W	Thanks.	여	고마워.

해설 | 남자가 오전 10시 비행기의 좌석을 예약하겠다고 했으므로 정답은 ② '10 a.m.'이다.

어휘 | book [buk] 통 예약하다   conference [kɑ́nfərəns] 명 회의

17 적절한 응답 고르기
정답 ②

M	What are you looking for, Kelly?	남	뭘 찾고 있니, Kelly?
W	I'm picking out a hand lotion. I can't decide on one.	여	난 핸드 로션을 고르고 있어. 하나로 못 정하겠어.
M	What do they smell like?	남	무슨 향이 나는데?
W	This one smells like apple, and this one smells like vanilla.	여	이건 사과 향이 나고, 이건 바닐라 향이 나.
M	I like vanilla more, but it's your choice.	남	나는 바닐라가 더 좋지만, 네 선택이야.
W	I'll buy the vanilla one. Do you need anything from this store?	여	바닐라 향으로 사야겠어. 이 가게에서 필요한 것 있니?
M	No. But do you want to get some macarons after this? The shop is just around the corner.	남	아니. 하지만 그거 사고 나서 마카롱 사러 갈래? 가게가 바로 근처에 있어.
W	Okay. Just wait for me to pay for this.	여	그래. 이거 계산하는 것만 기다려줘.

해설 | 남자가 핸드 로션을 사고 나서 마카롱을 사러 가자고 제안했으므로 정답은 제안을 수락하는 ② 'Okay. Just wait for me to pay for this.'이다.

선택지 해석
① 이 과일들은 딸 준비가 됐어.   ② 그래. 이거 계산하는 것만 기다려줘.   ③ 아니. 내가 가장 좋아하는 맛은 바닐라야.   ④ 네가 켠 캔들은 향이 정말 좋다.
⑤ 여기서 먹으면 안 돼.

어휘 | pick out 고르다   decide on ~으로 정하다   light [lait] 통 켜다 명 빛

18 적절한 응답 고르기　　　　　　　　　　정답 ④

W	Are you <u>ready</u> <u>for</u> <u>our</u> <u>trip</u>, Logan?
M	Not yet, Mom. I want to check the weather before I pack.
W	It will <u>be</u> <u>rainy</u> <u>and</u> <u>cold</u>, so pack lots of pants and long sleeves.
M	Do I have <u>time</u> <u>to</u> <u>wash</u> some of my clothes?
W	Yes. But do it <u>as</u> <u>soon</u> <u>as</u> <u>possible</u>. We leave early on Wednesday, and they'll need time to dry.
M	Okay. I'll do that right now.
W	Oh, and <u>will you</u> <u>help</u> <u>your</u> <u>little</u> <u>brother</u> pack? He might <u>have some trouble</u> with it.
M	Yes. But I'll do the laundry first.

여　여행 준비 됐니, Logan?
남　아직이요, 엄마. 짐을 챙기기 전에 날씨를 확인하려고요.
여　비가 오고 추울 예정이니까, 긴 바지와 긴소매 옷을 많이 챙기렴.
남　제 옷을 몇 벌 빨 시간이 있을까요?
여　응. 하지만 가능한 한 빨리하렴. 우리는 수요일에 일찍 떠날 예정이고, 옷이 마를 시간이 필요하잖아.
남　알겠어요. 지금 바로 할게요.
여　오, 그리고 네 남동생이 짐 챙기는 걸 도와줄래? 짐 챙기는 데 어려움을 겪을지도 몰라.
남　네. 하지만 빨래 먼저 할게요.

해설 | 여자가 남동생의 짐을 챙기는 것을 도울 수 있는지 물었으므로 정답은 수락과 먼저 할 일을 언급하는 ④ 'Yes. But I'll do the laundry first.'이다.

선택지 해석
① 길은 이미 젖었어요.　② 그 셔츠는 너무 더러워요.　③ 오늘 아침에 우산을 깜빡했어요.　④ 네. 하지만 빨래 먼저 할게요.
⑤ 오, 이런. 우리 가방 하나가 없어요.

어휘 | long sleeves 긴소매 옷　have trouble ~하는 데 어려움을 겪다

19 적절한 응답 고르기　　　　　　　　　　정답 ⑤

M	Beth, are you <u>planning</u> <u>the</u> <u>class</u> <u>party</u> for the end of the year?
W	Yes! I'm <u>preparing</u> <u>the</u> <u>activities</u> and food.
M	Are you almost finished?
W	Yes. I came up with lots of fun games. But I think <u>we</u> <u>will</u> <u>need</u> <u>more</u> <u>food</u>.
M	What food will there be?
W	We will have hot dogs, but I need to find a dessert too.
M	Well, I'm really <u>good</u> <u>at</u> <u>baking</u> and love to make cookies. <u>I could make some for the party.</u>
W	Really? I think <u>everyone</u> <u>would</u> <u>love</u> <u>that</u>.
M	Sure. I'll make some almond cookies.

남　Beth, 연말 학급 파티를 계획 중이니?
여　응! 나는 활동들과 음식을 준비하고 있어.
남　거의 끝났니?
여　응. 재미있는 게임들을 많이 생각해냈어. 그런데 우리 음식이 더 필요할 것 같아.
남　무슨 음식이 있을 건데?
여　핫도그가 있을 건데, 후식도 찾아야 해.
남　음, 내가 정말 제빵을 잘하고 쿠키 만드는 것을 좋아하거든. 내가 파티용으로 좀 만들 수 있어.
여　정말? 모두 좋아할 것 같아.
남　물론이지. 내가 아몬드 쿠키를 좀 만들게.

해설 | 여자가 정말 쿠키를 만들어 올 수 있는지 되물었으므로 정답은 만들 쿠키의 종류를 언급하는 ⑤ 'Sure. I'll make some almond cookies.'이다.

선택지 해석
① 나는 초대장을 받지 못했어.　② 내가 게임의 규칙을 설명할게.　③ 나는 머스터드가 있는 핫도그를 주문했어.　④ 제과점에 치즈 케이크가 다 팔렸어.
⑤ 물론이지. 내가 아몬드 쿠키를 좀 만들게.

어휘 | come up with 생각해내다　invitation [ìnvitéiʃən] 圑 초대장

20 상황에 적절한 말 고르기　　　　　　　　　정답 ①

M　Chanho is going to a concert with Linda. It starts at 7 p.m. Linda <u>suggests</u> <u>taking</u> <u>the</u> <u>bus</u> there. However, Chanho is worried that they would be late <u>because</u> <u>of</u> <u>the</u> <u>heavy</u> <u>traffic</u>. He is very excited about the concert, so he doesn't want to be late. Therefore, <u>he wants to ask Linda</u> <u>about</u> <u>taking</u> <u>the subway</u> instead. In this situation, what would Chanho most likely say to Linda?

Chanho　Linda, why don't we take the subway instead?

남　찬호는 Linda와 연주회에 갈 예정입니다. 그것은 오후 7시에 시작합니다. Linda는 그곳에 버스를 타고 가는 것을 제안합니다. 하지만 찬호는 교통체증 때문에 늦을까 걱정됩니다. 그는 연주회를 매우 기대하고 있어서, 늦고 싶지 않습니다. 따라서, 그는 Linda에게 대신 지하철을 타는 것에 대해 묻고 싶습니다. 이러한 상황에서, 찬호가 Linda에게 가장 할 것 같은 말은 무엇입니까?

찬호　Linda, 우리 대신 지하철을 타는 게 어때?

해설 | 찬호가 Linda에게 버스 대신 지하철을 타는 것에 대해 묻고 싶다고 했으므로 정답은 ① 'why don't we take the subway instead?'이다.

선택지 해석
① 우리 대신 지하철을 타는 게 어때?　② 연주회 후에 음반을 좀 사도 될까?　③ 공연에 일찍 도착해줘.　④ 우리는 지하철을 탔어야 했어.
⑤ 자리가 여전히 있는지 확인해 보자.

어휘 | suggest [səgdʒést] 圐 제안하다　therefore [ðɛ́ərfɔ̀:r] 閉 따라서

1	②	2	④	3	⑤	4	⑤	5	④	6	①	7	③	8	④	9	③	10	②
11	①	12	②	13	②	14	③	15	④	16	③	17	②	18	②	19	①	20	②

1 알맞은 그림 고르기   정답 ②

W Hello. Do you need help?

M Yes. I'm looking for a lock.

W We have key locks and number locks. Which would you prefer?

M I think I would lose a key. So, I'd better get a number lock.

W Okay. The number locks have either a three-digit or a four-digit combination.

M I'd like a three-digit combination lock.

W Got it. Now, please pick the shape. You can choose between these two. We have square and heart ones.

M The heart-shaped one is perfect. I'll take it.

W Good choice.

여 안녕하세요. 도와드릴까요?

남 네. 자물쇠를 찾고 있어요.

여 열쇠 자물쇠와 번호 자물쇠가 있어요. 어떤 걸 선호하세요?

남 저는 열쇠를 잃어버릴 것 같아요. 그래서, 번호 자물쇠를 사는 게 좋겠어요.

여 그렇군요. 번호 자물쇠는 3단이나 4단 숫자 조합이 있어요.

남 3단 자물쇠로 할게요.

여 알겠습니다. 이제, 모양을 골라주세요. 이 두 가지 중에서 고르실 수 있어요. 네모난 것과 하트 모양이 있어요.

남 하트 모양이 아주 좋네요. 그걸로 할게요.

여 탁월한 선택이세요.

해설 | 남자가 3단 숫자 조합이 있는 하트 모양 번호 자물쇠를 사겠다고 했으므로 정답은 ②이다.

어휘 | lock [lak] 명 자물쇠   digit [dídʒit] 명 숫자, 자릿수   combination [kàmbənéiʃən] 명 조합, 결합

2 언급하지 않은 내용 고르기   정답 ④

W Good job with your presentation, Carl! I learned so much about turtles.

M Thanks, Linda.

W The pictures you showed were really helpful. I want to do something like that for my next speech.

M You should. Pictures make it easy to explain things.

W Did it take you a long time to prepare?

M Yes. I also practiced the whole presentation several times a day for a week.

W I see. Well, you definitely deserve that A+.

M Thanks for the compliment!

여 발표 잘했어, Carl! 거북이에 대해 많은 걸 배웠어.

남 고마워, Linda.

여 네가 보여준 사진들이 정말 도움이 됐어. 내 다음 발표 때 그런 걸 하고 싶어.

남 그렇게 해. 사진은 설명하는 것을 쉽게 만들어 줘.

여 준비하는 데 오래 걸렸니?

남 응. 일주일 동안 발표 전체를 하루에도 여러 번 연습하기도 했어.

여 그렇구나. 그래, 넌 분명히 A+를 받을 만했어.

남 칭찬해줘서 고마워!

해설 | ① 주제(거북이), ② 시각 자료(사진들), ③ 준비 기간(일주일), ⑤ 점수(A+)에 대해 언급했으므로 정답은 ④ '길이'이다.

어휘 | presentation [prèzəntéiʃən] 명 발표; 증정   definitely [défənitli] 부 분명히, 명확하게   deserve [dizé:rv] 동 받을 만하다
compliment [kámpləmənt] 명 칭찬

3 목적 고르기   정답 ⑤

[Cellphone rings.]

M The Garden Restaurant. How may I help you?

W Hello. I'd like a table for two tonight at 8.

M I'm sorry, but we can't accept any more reservations. The restaurant is fully booked tonight.

W Oh, that's too bad.

M The holiday is very busy for us. We do have tables left tomorrow, though.

W No, thanks. I'm just looking for a place for dinner tonight.

M I understand. Have a good day.

W You too.

[휴대폰이 울린다.]

남 The Garden Restaurant입니다. 무엇을 도와드릴까요?

여 안녕하세요. 오늘 밤 8시에 두 사람 자리를 원하는데요.

남 죄송합니다만, 더 이상의 예약을 받을 수가 없어요. 오늘 밤 예약이 다 찼습니다.

여 오, 안타깝네요.

남 연휴에는 저희가 매우 바빠서요. 그래도, 내일은 꼭 남는 자리가 있어요.

여 아니요, 괜찮아요. 오늘 밤 저녁 장소를 찾고 있는 거라서요.

남 알겠습니다. 즐거운 하루 보내세요.

여 당신도요.

해설 | 여자가 오늘 밤 8시에 두 사람 자리를 원하며, 저녁 장소를 찾고 있다고 했으므로 정답은 ⑤ '저녁 식사를 예약하려고'이다.

어휘 | accept [æksépt] 图 받다, 받아들이다 reservation [rèzərvéiʃən] 명 예약

4 시간 정보 고르기   정답 ⑤

W Good morning, Mr. Wilkins. Do you have a few minutes?

M Sorry, but I'm just going to give a lecture now.

W I wanted to ask about the school choir.

M Then, could you come back to the music room at 4 today?

W My last class will end at 5. Would 5:30 be okay?

M Sure. I'll be free after 5, so that will give us plenty of time to talk.

W Great. I'll see you then.

여 좋은 아침이에요, Wilkins 선생님. 잠시 시간 괜찮으세요?

남 미안하지만, 내가 지금 막 수업하러 가는 중이란다.

여 학교 합창단에 대해 여쭙고 싶었는데요.

남 그러면, 오늘 4시에 음악실로 다시 와주겠니?

여 제 마지막 수업이 5시에 끝나요. 5시 30분도 괜찮을까요?

남 물론이지. 5시 이후에는 한가하니, 그때는 우리에게 얘기할 시간이 많겠구나.

여 좋아요. 그때 뵐게요.

해설 | 여자가 5시 30분도 괜찮을지 묻자 남자가 물론이라고 했으므로 정답은 ⑤ '5:30 p.m.'이다.

어휘 | lecture [léktʃər] 명 수업, 강의 choir [kwaiər] 명 합창단 plenty of 많은

5 심정 고르기   정답 ④

W Martin, you're looking good today.

M Thanks. I have a job interview this afternoon.

W Oh, you must be anxious.

M Actually, I'm not that nervous.

W That's a bit surprising. How come?

M I had a part-time job at the company last summer.

W Wow. Lucky you! Then, the interview will likely go smoothly.

M Yeah. Unless there's an unexpected problem, I'm sure I'll get the job.

여 Martin, 너 오늘 멋있어 보인다.

남 고마워. 오늘 오후에 취업 면접이 있거든.

여 오, 걱정되겠다.

남 사실, 난 그렇게 긴장되지는 않아.

여 좀 놀랍네. 어째서?

남 지난여름에 그 회사에서 시간제 근무했었거든.

여 우와. 운이 좋았네! 그러면, 면접도 아마 순조롭게 진행되겠어.

남 응. 예기치 않은 문제가 생기지 않는다면, 내가 그 일자리를 얻을 거라 확신해.

해설 | 남자가 취업 면접을 앞두고 그렇게 긴장되지 않는다고 했고, 그 일자리를 얻을 것이라 확신한다고 했으므로 정답은 ④ 'confident'이다.

선택지 해석

① 기쁜 ② 무서운 ③ 긴장되는 ④ 확신하는 ⑤ 놀란

어휘 | anxious [ǽŋkʃəs] 혱 걱정하는 part-time job 시간제 근무, 아르바이트 likely [láikli] 閏 아마 혱 ~할 것 같은 smoothly [smúːðli] 閏 순조롭게, 매끄럽게 unless [ənlés] 젭 ~하지 않는다면 unexpected [ʌ̀nikspektid] 혱 예기치 않은

6 그림 상황에 적절한 대화 고르기   정답 ①

① W Do you think you can fix it?
   M No. We need to call a mechanic.
② W Would you please fasten your seatbelt?
   M Oh, okay. I almost forgot to do that.
③ W Take me to Main Street, please.
   M Sure. It'll take 20 minutes to get there.
④ W Where is the bus stop?
   M It's on the corner of this street.
⑤ W Traffic is heavier than usual today.
   M Maybe there was an accident.

① 여 그거 고칠 수 있겠어?
   남 아니. 정비사를 불러야겠어.
② 여 안전벨트를 매주시겠습니까?
   남 오, 알겠어요. 매는 걸 거의 잊고 있었어요.
③ 여 메인 가로 가 주세요.
   남 알겠습니다. 거기까지 20분 걸릴 거예요.
④ 여 버스 정류장이 어디에 있나요?
   남 이 길의 모퉁이에 있어요.
⑤ 여 오늘은 평소보다 차가 많이 막히네.
   남 아마도 사고가 있었나 봐.

해설 | 고장 난 차량을 두고 남자가 고칠 수 없겠다고 하는 상황이므로 정답은 ①이다.

어휘 | mechanic [məkǽnik] 몡 정비사, 수리공   fasten [fǽsn] 통 매다, 단단히 고정시키다   seatbelt [síːtbelt] 몡 안전벨트   accident [ǽksidənt] 몡 사고

7 부탁·요청한 일 고르기   정답 ③

W Henry, are you going on the club trip to Centerville this weekend?
M Yes. I'm so excited. Are you also going?
W No, I can't. My family is moving to a new apartment on Saturday.
M That's a pity. I wanted to explore the city with you.
W Actually, I went there last summer.
M Really? Can you recommend any good places?
W One of the most well-known foods there is peanut cookies. How about trying some?
M Sounds good! Where can I get them?
W There are stores by City Hall. If you go, could you buy me a few?
M Of course.

여 Henry, 너 이번 주말에 센터빌로 동아리 여행 갈 거야?
남 응. 너무 기대돼. 너도 가?
여 아니, 난 못 가. 우리 가족이 토요일에 새 아파트로 이사하거든.
남 안타깝다. 너와 함께 그 도시를 탐방하고 싶었거든.
여 실은, 나 거기 지난여름에 갔었어.
남 정말? 괜찮은 장소 좀 추천해줄 수 있어?
여 그곳의 유명한 음식 중 하나가 땅콩 쿠키야. 그걸 좀 사는 게 어때?
남 좋은 것 같아! 그걸 어디에서 살 수 있어?
여 시청 옆에 가게들이 있어. 만약 간다면, 내게도 조금 사다 줄래?
남 당연하지.

해설 | 여자가 남자에게 땅콩 쿠키를 파는 가게에 간다면 자신에게도 조금 사다 달라고 부탁했으므로 정답은 ③ '쿠키 사다 주기'이다.

어휘 | explore [ikspl*ɔ́*ːr] 통 탐방하다, 탐험하다   well-known 혱 유명한, 잘 알려진

8 언급하지 않은 내용 고르기   정답 ④

W Hello, customers. This is Lola from Blue Rhythm Dance School. I'm so happy to share that we will soon offer ballet classes at our school in addition to the tap, jazz, and ballroom dancing classes we already hold. The class's teacher is Emily Blake, a professional dancer at the local ballet company. She will teach a ballet class for beginners on Mondays at 7 p.m. and for higher levels on Tuesdays at 6 p.m. Please call us soon to sign up. We look forward to seeing you there!

여 안녕하세요, 고객님들. 저는 블루 리듬 댄스 학교의 Lola입니다. 우리 학교에서 이미 열고 있던 탭 댄스, 재즈 댄스, 그리고 사교댄스 수업에 더해 발레 수업을 곧 제공할 것이라는 소식을 전해드리게 되어 정말 기쁩니다. 수업의 선생님은 지역 발레단의 전문 무용수인 Emily Blake입니다. 그녀는 매주 월요일 오후 7시에는 초보자용, 매주 화요일 오후 6시에는 더 높은 수준을 위한 발레 수업을 가르쳐주실 겁니다. 등록하시려면 저희에게 일찍 전화 주세요. 여러분들을 그곳에서 뵙길 기대하고 있겠습니다!

해설 | ① 수업 종류(발레, 탭 댄스, 재즈 댄스, 사교댄스), ② 교사 이름(Emily Blake), ③ 수업 시간(매주 월요일 오후 7시, 매주 화요일 오후 6시), ⑤ 등록 방법(일찍 전화 주기)에 대해 언급했으므로 정답은 ④ '수업 비용'이다.

어휘 | in addition to ~에 더해   ballroom dance 사교댄스   professional [prəfé*ʃ*ənəl] 혱 전문의; 직업의   look forward to ~을 기대하다

9 화제 고르기　정답 ③

| W | People who have this job have careers of dealing with numbers. They help companies and people record the amounts of money they make and spend. They also help people when they need to pay taxes to the government. To do this job, you must pass a difficult exam and have good math skills. | 여 | 이 직업을 가진 사람들은 숫자를 다루는 일을 합니다. 그들은 기업이나 사람들이 벌거나 쓴 돈의 액수를 기록하는 것을 도와줍니다. 그들은 또한 사람들이 정부에 세금을 내야 할 때도 돕습니다. 이 일을 하기 위해서는, 반드시 어려운 시험을 통과해야 하고 훌륭한 수학 실력을 지녀야 합니다. |

해설 | 이 직업(this job)을 가진 사람들은 기업이나 사람들이 벌거나 쓴 돈의 액수를 기록하는 것을 돕는다고 했으므로 정답은 ③ '회계사'이다.

어휘 | career [kəríər] 명 일, 경력　deal with ~을 다루다　amount [əmáunt] 명 액수, 양　tax [tæks] 명 세금　government [ɡʌ́vərnmənt] 명 정부

10 어색한 대화 고르기　정답 ②

① M	We should get some ice cream, right?	① 남	우리 아이스크림을 사 먹어야겠어, 그럴래?
W	That sounds great.	여	좋은 생각이야.
② M	How often do you go to the gym?	② 남	체육관에 얼마나 자주 가?
W	I work out for an hour.	여	난 한 시간 동안 운동해.
③ M	Did you hear that the Joan's Furniture Store is closing?	③ 남	Joan's Furniture Store가 폐점한다는 거 들었어?
W	I didn't. That's too bad.	여	못 들었어. 안 됐다.
④ M	Do you want to go for a walk with me?	④ 남	나랑 산책하러 갈래?
W	No. I really need to finish this homework.	여	아니. 나 이 숙제 진짜 끝내야 해.
⑤ M	Wow. You have so many books in your room.	⑤ 남	우와. 네 방엔 책이 아주 많구나.
W	Well, I love reading books.	여	음, 내가 책 읽는 걸 좋아하거든.

해설 | 남자가 여자에게 얼마나 자주 체육관에 가는지 물었으므로, 여자는 구체적인 방문 횟수를 답해야 한다. 그러나 여자가 한 시간 동안 운동한다는 어색한 대답을 했으므로 정답은 ②이다.

어휘 | work out 운동하다; (일이) 잘 되어가다　go for a walk 산책하러 가다

11 할 일 고르기　정답 ①

M	What video are you watching, Haeun?	남	무슨 영상을 보고 있는 중이야, 하은아?
W	Oh, this is a virtual tour.	여	오, 이건 가상 투어야.
M	What's that?	남	그게 뭔데?
W	A tour guide in another part of the world shows you around a place online.	여	세계 다른 지역의 여행 가이드가 너에게 온라인으로 한 장소를 둘러보도록 구경시켜 주는 거야.
M	That's cool. So, you can see a famous place without actually being there?	남	그거 멋지다. 그래서, 넌 실제로는 그곳에 가지 않아도 유명한 장소를 볼 수 있는 거야?
W	Exactly. I'll send you the link for the website. I'm taking a tour of an Italian museum right now.	여	정확해. 내가 그 웹사이트 링크를 보내줄게. 난 지금 이탈리아 박물관을 둘러보고 있어.
M	Thank you. I'd love to try it.	남	고마워. 나도 체험해보고 싶다.

해설 | 여자가 가상 투어 웹사이트 링크를 보내주겠다고 했으므로 정답은 ① '링크 전달하기'이다.

어휘 | virtual [və́ːrtʃuəl] 형 가상의; 사실상의　show A around B A에게 B를 둘러보도록 구경시켜 주다

12 도표에서 알맞은 항목 고르기   정답 ②

M	May I help you?
W	Yes, please. I'd like a ticket to Busan.
M	There's a train at 9 p.m.
W	Is it an express train?
M	No, ma'am. It'll take more than four hours to reach Busan.
W	Oh, no. I have to get there as soon as I can.
M	Why don't you take the express train to Daegu and transfer there?
W	When does the train for Daegu leave?
M	There's one at 7 p.m. and another at 9 p.m.
W	I'll take the earlier one.

남	도와드릴까요?
여	네, 부탁드려요. 부산행 표를 사고 싶어요.
남	오후 9시 기차가 있어요.
여	급행인가요?
남	아니요, 손님. 부산에 도착하는 데 네 시간 넘게 걸릴 거예요.
여	오, 이런. 전 되도록 빨리 거기 도착해야 해요.
남	대구행 급행열차를 타고 가서 거기에서 갈아타시는 건 어때요?
여	대구행 기차는 언제 출발하는데요?
남	오후 7시 기차와 9시 기차가 한 대 있어요.
여	이른 걸로 할게요.

해설ㅣ 남자가 대구행 급행열차를 탄 뒤 갈아타는 것을 추천해주었고, 여자가 7시 기차와 9시 기차 중 이른 것으로 하겠다고 했으므로 정답은 ②이다.

어휘ㅣ express [iksprés] 휑 급행의 동 표현하다   as soon as one can 되도록 빨리   transfer [trænsféːr] 동 갈아타다; 옮기다

13 시간 정보 고르기   정답 ②

W	Greg, would you like to go to the amusement park on Saturday?
M	That sounds like fun. Should we meet at 3 p.m.?
W	I'd prefer to go a bit earlier. Can you come to the amusement park at 10:30 a.m.?
M	I have a dentist appointment at 10.
W	Oh, I see. Then, how about 1 p.m.?
M	Do you want to eat something first? We could meet for lunch at 12:30 and then enter the amusement park at around 1:30.
W	Good idea.

여	Greg, 토요일에 놀이공원 갈래?
남	재미있을 것 같아. 오후 3시에 만날까?
여	난 조금 더 일찍 가고 싶어. 놀이공원으로 오전 10시 30분에 올 수 있어?
남	난 10시에 치과 예약이 있어.
여	오, 그렇구나. 그러면, 오후 1시는 어때?
남	먼저 뭐 먹을래? 12시 30분에 점심을 먹으러 만나서 그다음 1시 30분 정도에 놀이공원에 입장하는 거야.
여	좋은 생각이야.

해설ㅣ 남자가 점심을 먹으러 12시 30분에 만나자고 하자 여자가 좋은 생각이라고 했으므로 정답은 ② '12:30 p.m.'이다.

어휘ㅣ amusement park 놀이공원, 유원지   a bit 조금, 약간   appointment [əpɔ́intmənt] 명 예약, 약속; 임명

14 한일 고르기   정답 ③

W	Are you excited for Rose's wedding, Michael?
M	Of course. Are you?
W	Yes. But I still need to buy a dress for it. I'm a little worried because the wedding is so soon.
M	I bought a suit last Wednesday, but I should buy some new shoes.
W	We can go to the mall together if you want.
M	Sure. When do you want to go?
W	Maybe we should go tonight. I don't want to be unprepared for the wedding.
M	All right.

여	Rose의 결혼식을 기대하고 있니, Michael?
남	당연하지. 너는?
여	나도. 그런데 난 아직 결혼식용 원피스를 사야 해. 결혼식이 너무 금방이라서 좀 걱정되네.
남	난 지난 수요일에 정장을 샀는데, 새 신발도 좀 사야겠어.
여	네가 원한다면 쇼핑몰에 같이 가도 되겠다.
남	물론이지. 언제 가고 싶어?
여	오늘 밤 가면 어떨까 싶어. 난 결혼식에 갈 준비가 안 된 채로 있고 싶지 않아.
남	알겠어.

해설ㅣ 남자가 지난 수요일에 정장을 샀다고 했으므로 정답은 ③ '정장 구매하기'이다.

어휘ㅣ suit [suːt] 명 정장, 슈트   unprepared [ʌ̀npripérd] 휑 준비가 안 된

15 목적 고르기 　　　　　　　　　　　　　　　　　　　정답 ④

M	Good evening, everyone. This is your captain speaking. I've turned on the seatbelt sign. This is because we are flying into a storm. We expect some turbulence in a few minutes. It will be a little bumpy, so please stay in your seats. Also, the meal service will be a little delayed. Dinner will only be served when we get out of the storm. Thanks in advance for your cooperation.	남	안녕하십니까, 여러분. 저는 여러분의 기장입니다. 안전벨트 표시등을 켰습니다. 저희가 폭풍 속으로 날아가고 있기 때문입니다. 몇 분 후면 난기류가 발생할 것으로 예상합니다. 비행기가 조금 덜컹거릴 테니, 부디 자리에 앉아 계십시오. 또한, 기내식이 약간 지연될 것입니다. 저녁은 폭풍을 벗어나면 제공될 예정입니다. 여러분의 협조에 미리 감사드립니다.

해설 | 비행기가 폭풍 속으로 날아가고 있어서 난기류가 발생할 것이라고 설명하면서 남자가 주의 사항을 전달하고 있으므로 정답은 ④ '난기류 대비 사항을 전달하려고'이다.

어휘 | turbulence [tə́ːrbjuləns] 몡 난기류, 폭풍 상태　bumpy [bʌ́mpi] 혱 덜컹거리는; 울퉁불퉁한　in advance 미리　cooperation [kouὰpəréiʃən] 몡 협조, 협력

16 금액 정보 고르기 　　　　　　　　　　　　　　　　　정답 ③

M	Welcome to Delicious Chicken. How may I help you?	남	Delicious Chicken에 오신 걸 환영합니다. 무엇을 도와드릴까요?
W	I'd like to order the original fried chicken.	여	오리지널 프라이드 치킨으로 주문할게요.
M	That will be 15 dollars. Would you like soda and fries as well?	남	15달러 되겠습니다. 음료와 감자튀김도 드시겠습니까?
W	Sure. How much are those?	여	좋아요. 그것들은 얼마예요?
M	Those are an extra five dollars. Your total is 20 dollars.	남	추가로 5달러입니다. 총 20달러입니다.
W	Okay. Do you have any dessert options?	여	알겠어요. 디저트 옵션도 있나요?
M	We have cookies for three dollars.	남	3달러짜리 쿠키가 있습니다.
W	I'll have one of those as well. Can I use this discount coupon?	여	그것도 하나 주세요. 이 할인 쿠폰을 쓸 수 있을까요?
M	Yes. It will take three dollars off of your total.	남	네. 그럼 총액에서 3달러가 할인될 겁니다.
W	Great.	여	좋네요.

해설 | 치킨과 음료, 감자튀김은 20달러, 쿠키는 3달러로 총 23달러에서 3달러 할인을 받았으므로 정답은 ③ '$ 20'이다.

어휘 | extra [ékstrə] 혱 추가의　take off (값을) 할인하다

17 적절한 응답 고르기 　　　　　　　　　　　　　　　　정답 ②

M	What's wrong, Soyoung?	남	뭐가 문제야, 소영아?
W	I don't understand my math notes. They're so confusing.	여	내 수학 필기 내용을 이해 못 하겠어. 너무 헷갈려.
M	Let me see. [Pause] Oh, you didn't write everything down.	남	어디 볼게. [잠시 멈춤] 오, 너 전부 적어 두진 않았구나.
W	I had to sit in the back of the class, so I couldn't see the board well.	여	반에서 뒷자리에 앉아야 해서, 칠판이 잘 안 보였어.
M	You had better wear glasses. They can help you see the board from far away.	남	안경을 끼는 게 낫겠어. 그건 네가 멀리 떨어진 칠판도 볼 수 있도록 도와줄 거야.
W	I know, but I heard they can be uncomfortable. So, I don't want to wear them.	여	나도 알아, 그렇지만 그게 불편할 수도 있다고 들었어. 그래서 안경을 끼고 싶지 않아.
M	But glasses will help you in class. I suggest that you get an eye test first.	남	그래도 안경이 수업 시간엔 도움이 될 거야. 우선 시력 검사부터 받는 걸 추천할게.
W	All right. I'll go to an eye clinic then.	여	알겠어. 그러면 안과에 가야겠다.

해설 | 남자가 시력 검사를 받는 것을 제안했으므로 정답은 제안을 수락하는 ② 'All right. I'll go to an eye clinic then.'이다.

　선택지 해석
① 그녀는 수업에 펜을 가져오지 않았어.　② 알겠어. 그러면 안과에 가야겠다.　③ 이걸 적어 둬.　④ 아니. 난 어디서도 표지판을 못 봤어.
⑤ 알았어. 자리를 바꿀게.

어휘 | confusing [kənfjúːziŋ] 혱 헷갈리는, 혼란시키는　write down 적어 두다　board [bɔːrd] 몡 칠판; 판자　eye clinic 안과

18 적절한 응답 고르기   정답 ②

W	Hey, what happened? You look so happy.
M	I just won tickets to a basketball game!
W	Wow, that's great! Which game are you going to?
M	I will watch the Eagles play the Dragons.
W	I'm so jealous. The Dragons are my favorite team.
M	You can come with me if you want. It should be a great game.
W	Really? That's so nice. When is it?
M	It's on Friday night at 7.
W	Oh, no! I have dinner with my grandparents then.
M	That's a shame. I wish you could come.

여	안녕, 무슨 일 있었어? 기분 엄청 좋아 보이네.
남	방금 농구 경기 표를 얻었거든!
여	우와, 잘 됐다! 어떤 경기에 갈 건데?
남	Eagles가 Dragons랑 경기하는 걸 볼 거야.
여	너무 부럽다. Dragons는 내가 가장 좋아하는 팀이야.
남	네가 원한다면 나랑 같이 가도 돼. 멋진 경기가 될 거야.
여	정말? 너무 좋다. 언제야?
남	금요일 밤 7시야.
여	오, 이런! 난 할머니 할아버지랑 그때 저녁 식사가 있어.
남	유감이야. 네가 오면 좋을 텐데.

해설 | 남자가 농구 경기를 같이 보러 가자고 제안했지만, 여자가 그때 조부모님과의 저녁 식사가 있다고 했으므로 정답은 유감을 나타내는 ② 'That's a shame. I wish you could come.'이다.

선택지 해석

① 그는 지난밤 경기에서 득점을 많이 했어. ② 유감이야. 네가 오면 좋을 텐데. ③ 그녀의 가족이 날 저녁 식사에 초대했어. ④ 여러분의 자리는 저 구역입니다.
⑤ 좋아. 경기장 앞에서 만나자.

어휘 | jealous [dʒéləs] 휑 부러운, 질투하는   stadium [stéidiəm] 뗑 경기장

19 적절한 응답 고르기   정답 ①

W	Are you doing anything this Sunday, Ben?
M	It's Annie's birthday on Sunday, so I want to celebrate with her.
W	Oh, I forgot about her birthday! Did she make any plans yet?
M	No. But I plan to have a surprise party for her.
W	Good idea. Can I help?
M	Sure. But first, we need to pick a place for the party.
W	Annie loves Vietnamese food. What about Tasty Pho?
M	Perfect! I'll call to make a reservation now.

여	이번 주 일요일에 뭐 할 거 있니, Ben?
남	일요일은 Annie의 생일이라서 축하해주고 싶어.
여	오, 나 Annie의 생일을 잊고 있었어! 벌써 계획을 세웠을까?
남	아니. 그런데 내가 깜짝 파티를 열어줄 계획이야.
여	좋은 생각이야. 내가 도울 수 있을까?
남	물론이지. 하지만 먼저, 파티 장소를 골라야 해.
여	Annie는 베트남 음식을 좋아하잖아. Tasty Pho는 어때?
남	완벽해! 내가 지금 예약하러 전화할게.

해설 | 남자가 파티 장소를 먼저 골라야 한다고 하자 여자가 베트남 음식점을 제안했으므로 정답은 제안을 수락하는 ① 'Perfect! I'll call to make a reservation now.'이다.

선택지 해석

① 완벽해! 내가 지금 예약하러 전화할게. ② 지난밤 파티에는 정말 사람들이 많았어. ③ 그러면, 내 계획을 취소해야겠다. ④ 그녀는 이미 초대장을 보냈어.
⑤ 여기 음식은 너무 매워.

어휘 | celebrate [séləbrèit] 통 축하하다   send out 보내다, 배부하다   spicy [spáisi] 휑 매운; 양념이 된

20 상황에 적절한 말 고르기   정답 ②

W	Lily is attending a piano competition. She is there to support her friend Tommy. When it is Tommy's turn to compete, he plays his song perfectly. Soon after, the judges announce that he won the competition. Lily goes to give Tommy flowers and a card when the award ceremony is finished. She wants to tell him that he did well in the performance. In this situation, what would Lily most likely say to Tommy?
Lily	Tommy, you played beautifully today.

여	Lily는 피아노 대회에 참석 중입니다. 그녀는 친구 Tommy를 응원하기 위해 그곳에 있습니다. Tommy가 경연할 차례가 되자, 그는 곡을 완벽하게 연주합니다. 곧이어, 심사위원들이 그가 대회에서 우승했다고 발표합니다. Lily는 시상식이 끝나자 Tommy에게 꽃다발과 카드를 주러 갑니다. 그녀는 Tommy에게 그가 연주를 잘했다고 말하고 싶습니다. 이러한 상황에서, Lily가 Tommy에게 가장 할 것 같은 말은 무엇입니까?
Lily	Tommy, 오늘 연주 정말 아름다웠어.

해설 | Lily가 Tommy에게 피아노 연주를 잘했다고 말하고 싶다고 했으므로 정답은 ② 'you played beautifully today.'이다.

선택지 해석

① 대회 잘 치러! ② 오늘 연주 정말 아름다웠어. ③ 다음번에는 더 잘할 거야. ④ 얼마나 자주 연습해? ⑤ 이 노래 제목이 뭐야?

어휘 | attend [əténd] 통 참석하다   support [səpɔ́ːrt] 통 응원하다; 받치다   judge [dʒʌdʒ] 뗑 심사위원; 재판관   award ceremony 시상식

22회 고난도 모의고사

| 문제 pp.196-197

| 1 | ② | 2 | ③ | 3 | ② | 4 | ④ | 5 | ⑤ | 6 | ② | 7 | ① | 8 | ③ | 9 | ④ | 10 | ⑤ |
| 11 | ② | 12 | ① | 13 | ③ | 14 | ② | 15 | ④ | 16 | ③ | 17 | ④ | 18 | ④ | 19 | ③ | 20 | ⑤ |

1 알맞은 그림 고르기   정답 ②

M Welcome. How may I help you?
W Hi, I'd like to buy my first skateboard.
M All right. We have lots of skateboards for beginners.
W Actually, I like the one with stripes on it. What do you think? Would it be good for a beginner?
M Well, it's too narrow. I suggest a wider one. It will be safer and easier to balance on.
W I see. Then, could you show me wider ones with a similar print?
M Sure. How about these ones with a lightning print?
W I prefer the one with the word "RUN" on it.
M Okay.

남 어서 오세요. 무엇을 도와드릴까요?
여 안녕하세요, 제 첫 스케이트보드를 사고 싶어요.
남 그러시군요. 저희는 초보자용 스케이트보드가 많답니다.
여 사실, 전 줄무늬가 그려진 게 마음에 들어요. 어떻게 생각하세요? 이게 초보자에게 괜찮을까요?
남 글쎄요, 그건 너무 좁네요. 더 넓적한 걸 제안해 드릴게요. 그 위에서 중심을 잡는 게 더 쉽고 안전할 거예요.
여 그렇군요. 그러면, 비슷한 무늬를 가진 것으로 더 넓적한 걸 보여주실래요?
남 물론이죠. 번개무늬가 있는 이것들은 어떠세요?
여 저는 'RUN'이라는 글자가 써진 게 마음에 드네요.
남 알겠습니다.

해설 | 남자가 번개무늬가 있는 더 넓적한 스케이트보드를 보여주자, 여자가 그중 'RUN'이라는 글자가 써진 것이 마음에 든다고 했으므로 정답은 ②이다.

어휘 | balance on ~ 위에서 중심을 잡다 similar [símələr] 혱 비슷한 lightning [láitniŋ] 혱 번개

2 언급하지 않은 내용 고르기   정답 ③

M Did you see the new *Wonder-Man* movie?
W Yeah. I watched it on the day it was released.
M Oh, yeah? I saw it on Wednesday too.
W What do you think of Thomas Moreland?
M He's great. I love the new villain, Dr. Perplexo too.
W I know. The atmosphere was terrifying. The end of the movie was weird, though.
M Yeah. I didn't understand the ending at all.
W Maybe the next *Wonder-Man* movie will explain what happened.
M I hope so.

남 새로 나온 <Wonder-Man> 영화 봤어?
여 응. 개봉한 날에 봤어.
남 오, 그래? 나도 수요일에 봤어.
여 Thomas Moreland에 대해 어떻게 생각해?
남 훌륭하다고 생각해. 난 새로운 악당인 Perplexo 박사도 마음에 들어.
여 맞아. 분위기가 무서웠어. 그런데, 영화의 결말이 이상했어.
남 응. 난 결말을 전혀 이해하지 못했어.
여 어쩌면 <Wonder-Man>의 다음 영화에서 무슨 일이 일어났는지 설명해줄지도 모르겠어.
남 그러면 좋겠다.

해설 | ① 개봉일(수요일), ② 등장인물(Thomas Moreland와 Perplexo 박사), ④ 결말(이상함), ⑤ 속편 여부(다음 편 나옴)에 대해 언급했으므로 정답은 ③ '배경'이다.
어휘 | villain [vílən] 몡 악당 atmosphere [ǽtməsfiər] 몡 분위기; 대기 weird [wiərd] 혱 이상한 not ~ at all 전혀 ~이 아닌

3 목적 고르기   정답 ②

[Cellphone rings.]
M Hello. You've reached Rob.
W Hi, this is Tina from QualNet Cable. You left us a message yesterday.
M Right. As I said in the message, I need a Wi-Fi connection installed in my new office.
W Yes. We can do the installation tomorrow.
M Great! What time will the technician be here?
W We'll send someone between the hours of 2 p.m. and 6 p.m.
M That will work. But please call me before they arrive.

[휴대폰이 울린다.]
남 안녕하세요. Rob입니다.
여 안녕하세요, 전 QualNet Cable의 Tina예요. 어제 저희에게 메시지를 남기셨더군요.
남 맞아요. 메시지에서 말씀드렸듯이, 저의 새 사무실에 와이파이 연결을 설치할 필요가 있어요.
여 네. 내일 설치해드릴 수 있어요.
남 잘됐네요! 기사님이 몇 시에 여기 오실까요?
여 오후 2시부터 오후 6시 사이에 사람을 보내드릴게요.
남 그럼 되겠네요. 그래도 도착 전에 전화 주세요.

해설 | 와이파이를 설치해 달라는 남자의 메시지를 듣고 전화한 여자가 내일 설치해줄 수 있다고 했으므로 정답은 ② '방문 일자를 정하려고'이다.

어휘 | connection [kənékʃən] 몡 연결; 결합　install [instɔ́:l] 통 설치하다 (installation [instɔ́:leiʃən] 몡 설치; 장치)　technician [tekníʃən] 몡 기사, 기술자

4　시간 정보 고르기　　　　　　　　　　　　　　　　　　정답 ④

W Welcome to the Power Fitness Center. How can I help you?	여 Power Fitness Center에 오신 걸 환영합니다. 무엇을 도와드릴까요?
M I'd like to take an aerobics class on Saturdays. Do you have one that starts at 3 p.m.?	남 토요일에 에어로빅 수업을 듣고 싶어요. 오후 3시에 시작하는 수업이 있나요?
W No, but there is one at 1. It ends at 2.	여 아니요, 하지만 1시에는 있어요. 그건 2시에 끝나요.
M I usually have lunch at 12, and I don't like to exercise right after a meal.	남 전 보통 12시에 점심을 먹어요, 식사 직후에 운동하고 싶지는 않네요.
W Then, what about 4? We have a class beginning then.	여 그러면, 4시는 어떠세요? 그때 시작하는 수업이 하나 있어요.
M So, it ends at 5?	남 그러면 5시에 끝나나요?
W That's right. It is one hour long.	여 맞아요. 1시간짜리에요.
M Okay. I'll sign up for that class.	남 좋아요. 그 수업으로 신청할게요.

해설 | 여자가 4시에 시작하는 에어로빅 수업이 어떤지 묻자 남자가 그 수업으로 신청하겠다고 했으므로 정답은 ④ '4 p.m.'이다.

어휘 | aerobics [ɛəróubiks] 몡 에어로빅; 유산소 운동　exercise [éksərsaiz] 통 운동하다 몡 운동　right after 직후, 바로 후

5　장소 고르기　　　　　　　　　　　　　　　　　　　　정답 ⑤

W Hello. What can I do for you?	여 안녕하세요. 무엇을 도와드릴까요?
M I need to send a package to Australia.	남 호주로 택배를 보내야 해요.
W Alright. What is in the package?	여 그러시군요. 택배 안에 뭐가 들었나요?
M I'd like to send some skin-care products like face masks to a friend.	남 친구에게 마스크팩 같은 피부관리 제품을 보내려고 해요.
W So, there's nothing fragile inside?	여 그러면, 안에 깨지기 쉬운 것은 없는 거죠?
M No. Those are the only items.	남 없어요. 그게 전부에요.
W Okay. Then, please fill out this form. You must write the address clearly so the package goes to the correct place.	여 알겠습니다. 그러면 이 양식을 작성해주세요. 택배가 올바른 장소로 가려면 주소를 분명하게 적으셔야 합니다.
M Got it. Also, I'd like to select the fastest shipping option.	남 알겠어요. 그리고, 가장 빠른 배송 방법을 고르고 싶은데요.
W Okay. Then, your package will arrive at its destination in three days.	여 네. 그러면 택배는 목적지에 3일 후에 도착할 거예요.

해설 | 남자가 호주로 택배를 보내야 한다고 하는 것으로 보아 정답은 ⑤ '우체국'이다.

어휘 | fragile [frǽdʒəl] 혱 깨지기 쉬운　shipping [ʃípiŋ] 몡 배송, 운송; 선적　destination [dèstənéiʃən] 몡 목적지

6　그림 상황에 적절한 대화 고르기　　　　　　　　　　정답 ②

① M How long does it take to get to Mirae University?	① 남 미래 대학교로 가는 데 얼마나 걸리나요?
W It takes 30 minutes on foot.	여 걸어서 30분 걸려요.
② M Could I see your ticket, please?	② 남 표를 보여주시겠습니까?
W Of course. Here you go.	여 물론이죠. 여기 있어요.
③ M I believe you are in the wrong seat.	③ 남 자리를 잘못 앉으신 것 같아요.
W Oh, sorry. I'll move.	여 오, 죄송해요. 제가 옮길게요.
④ M I hope you enjoyed your trip.	④ 남 즐거운 여행이 되셨길 바랍니다.
W It was a lot of fun.	여 정말 재미있었어요.
⑤ M Is the pool open today?	⑤ 남 오늘 수영장 문 여나요?
W It is closed on national holidays.	여 공휴일에는 문을 닫아요.

해설 | 여자가 버스에 타려 하고 있고 남자가 여자에게서 표를 건네받고 있는 상황이므로 정답은 ②이다.

어휘 | on foot 걸어서, 도보로　wrong [rɔ́:ŋ] 혱 잘못된; 나쁜　national holiday 공휴일, 국경일

7 부탁·요청한 일 고르기   정답 ①

W   I'm sorry, Mr. Evans. Are you busy?
M   Not at all. Do you need something?
W   I want to go to a special science camp this summer. I'm working on an application now.
M   That's great! You are excellent at science.
W   Well, I need two recommendations for the application. It's a very competitive program.
M   Who will you ask?
W   Can you write one for me? I'll get my science teacher from last year to write the other one.
M   I'd be happy to write one for you.

여   실례합니다, Evans 선생님. 바쁘세요?
남   전혀 아니야. 뭐 필요하니?
여   제가 올여름에 특별한 과학 캠프에 가고 싶은데요. 지금 신청서를 쓰는 중이에요.
남   잘됐네! 넌 과학을 정말 잘하잖니.
여   음, 신청서에 추천서 두 장이 필요해요. 정말 경쟁이 심한 프로그램이에요.
남   누구에게 부탁할 거니?
여   선생님께서 하나 써주실 수 있을까요? 나머지 하나는 작년 과학 선생님께 써달라고 부탁할 거예요.
남   기꺼이 써주도록 하마.

해설ㅣ 여자가 남자에게 여름 과학 캠프를 신청하는 데 필요한 추천서를 써달라고 부탁했으므로 정답은 ① '추천서 작성하기'이다.

어휘ㅣ application [æpləkéiʃən] 몡 신청서; 적용   recommendation [rèkəməndéiʃən] 몡 추천서; 추천   competitive [kəmpétətiv] 톙 경쟁이 심한; 경쟁의

8 언급하지 않은 내용 고르기   정답 ③

W   Hello, students. This is your principal, Ms. Foster. I'm excited to provide details about our school's annual culture festival. The event will take place on August 15th. It'll be held from 10 a.m. to 5 p.m. Each class will set up a booth and prepare food, games, and presentations representing a chosen country's culture. There will be over 10 countries represented at the event. Students will take turns running the booths and enjoying the rest of the festival. Parents and friends are also welcome to attend. We hope to see you there!

여   안녕하세요, 학생 여러분. 교장 Foster 선생님입니다. 우리 학교의 연례 문화 축제의 자세한 내용을 알려드리게 되어 기쁩니다. 행사는 8월 15일에 열릴 예정입니다. 그것은 오전 10시부터 오후 5시까지 진행될 것입니다. 각 학급은 부스를 설치하고 선택된 나라의 문화를 대표하는 음식, 게임, 그리고 발표를 준비할 겁니다. 그 행사에서 대표로 선보일 나라는 10개가 넘을 겁니다. 학생들은 교대로 부스를 운영하고 축제의 나머지를 즐길 겁니다. 부모님들과 친구들 또한 참석을 환영합니다. 그곳에서 여러분들을 뵙길 바랍니다!

해설ㅣ ① 날짜(8월 15일), ② 시간(오전 10시부터 오후 5시까지), ④ 활동(부스를 설치하고 나라의 문화를 대표하는 음식, 게임, 발표 준비하기), ⑤ 대표국 수(10개 이상)에 대해 언급했으므로 정답은 ③ '장소'이다.

어휘ㅣ represent [rèprizént] 동 대표하다   take turns 교대로 하다   rest [rest] 몡 나머지; 휴식

9 화제 고르기   정답 ④

W   This is one of the most useful school supplies. It is held in one hand. It is long and thin, and it comes in many different bright colors. With this, we can color words on a paper to help them stand out from other words. We can use it to emphasize important information. We simply remove its cap and press it down on words we want to color to use it.

여   이것은 가장 유용한 학용품 중 하나입니다. 이것은 한 손에 쥐어집니다. 이것은 길고 얇으며, 많은 다양한 밝은 색상으로 나옵니다. 이것으로, 종이에 쓰여 있는 글자가 다른 글자들 속에서 눈에 띄도록 색칠할 수 있습니다. 중요한 정보를 강조하기 위해 이것을 사용할 수 있습니다. 이것을 사용하려면 간단히 뚜껑을 제거하고 색칠하길 원하는 글자 위에 눌러서 쓰면 됩니다.

해설ㅣ 이것(This)은 글자를 다른 글자들 속에서 눈에 띄도록 색칠할 수 있고, 뚜껑을 제거한 후 글자 위에 눌러서 사용할 수 있다고 했으므로 정답은 ④ '형광펜'이다.

어휘ㅣ bright [brait] 톙 밝은   stand out 눈에 띄다, 두드러지다   emphasize [émfəsaiz] 동 강조하다   remove [rimúːv] 동 제거하다, 치우다

10 어색한 대화 고르기　　　　　　　정답 ⑤

① M Excuse me. Where is the restroom?
  W It's next to the exit.
② M I got a perfect score on my English test.
  W Nice. Congratulations!
③ M This soup is too spicy.
  W Really? It tastes fine to me.
④ M Is it okay if I use your calculator?
  W Sure. It's in my desk.
⑤ M Can you turn down the volume? The music is too loud.
  W Let me turn it on for you.

① 남 실례합니다. 화장실이 어디에 있나요?
  여 출입구 옆에 있어요.
② 남 나 영어 시험에서 만점 받았어.
  여 멋지다. 축하해!
③ 남 이 국은 너무 매워.
  여 정말? 나한테는 맛이 괜찮은데.
④ 남 네 계산기를 써도 괜찮을까?
  여 물론이지. 내 책상 안에 있어.
⑤ 남 소리 좀 줄여주시겠어요? 음악이 너무 시끄러워요.
  여 제가 그걸 켜 드릴게요.

해설 | 남자가 음악 소리가 시끄러워서 소리를 줄여달라고 했으므로 여자는 사과를 하거나 소리를 줄이겠다고 말해야 한다. 그러나 여자가 남자를 위해 켜 주겠다는 어색한 대답을 했으므로 정답은 ⑤이다.

어휘 | perfect score 만점　spicy [spáisi] 형 매운; 양념이 된　calculator [kǽlkjuleitər] 명 계산기

11 할 일 고르기　　　　　　　정답 ②

[Cellphone rings.]
M What's up, Mom?
W Hi, Joonwon. What are you doing?
M I'm playing some games. I just got home from school.
W Remember to complete all of your homework. I don't want you to stay up late.
M Sure. By the way, where are you?
W I'm taking your brother to his volunteer job now. Then, I'll stop by the supermarket.
M You won't be home for a while then. Should I take the dog for a walk?
W Yes. That would be great.
M Okay. I'll take her now.

[휴대폰이 울린다.]
남 무슨 일이세요, 엄마?
여 안녕, 준원아. 뭐 하고 있니?
남 게임을 좀 하고 있어요. 학교에서 방금 집에 왔어요.
여 숙제를 전부 끝내야 한다는 걸 기억하렴. 네가 늦은 시간까지 깨어있지 않으면 좋겠구나.
남 물론이죠. 그런데, 어디세요?
여 지금 네 남동생을 봉사활동 하는 곳에 데려다주고 있단다. 그러고 나면, 슈퍼마켓에 들를 거야.
남 그러면 한동안 집에 없으시겠네요. 제가 개를 산책시켜야 할까요?
여 그래. 그러면 좋겠구나.
남 알겠어요. 제가 지금 데리고 나갈게요.

해설 | 남자가 반려견을 산책시켜야 할지 물은 후 지금 데리고 나가겠다고 했으므로 정답은 ② '강아지 산책시키기'이다.

어휘 | complete [kəmplíːt] 동 끝내다, 완료하다 형 완전한　stay up late 늦은 시간까지 깨어있다

12 위치 고르기　　　　　　　정답 ①

M I'm so excited for our trip to LA!
W Me too. But we still have to make a reservation at a hotel.
M Originally, I wanted to stay at Hotel D. But it is too pricey.
W It's because they have a beautiful view of the lake and Central Park.
M I know. I want to avoid a view of the parking lot, though.
W Also, Hotel C is the worst because other hotels are blocking the view.
M In that case, we have two choices left.
W Let's stay at the hotel closer to the water park.
M Yeah. I agree with you.

남 우리의 LA 여행이 너무 기대돼!
여 나도. 그렇지만 우리 아직 호텔 예약을 해야 해.
남 원래, 나는 D 호텔에서 묵고 싶었어. 하지만 거긴 너무 비싸.
여 왜냐하면 그곳은 호수와 센트럴 공원의 아름다운 경치를 볼 수 있잖아.
남 그러게. 하지만 난 주차장이 보이는 것은 피하고 싶어.
여 또한, C 호텔은 다른 호텔들이 전망을 가려 최악이야.
남 그렇다면 두 가지 선택권이 남았네.
여 워터 파크에 더 가까운 호텔에 묵자.
남 좋아. 나도 동의해.

해설 | 여자가 워터 파크에 더 가까운 호텔에 묵자고 제안하자 남자가 좋다고 했으므로 정답은 ①이다.

어휘 | originally [ərìdʒənəli] 부 원래　pricey [práisi] 형 비싼　worst [wəːrst] 형 최악의, 가장 나쁜　block [blak] 동 가리다, 차단하다

13 시간 정보 고르기

정답 ③

[Cellphone rings.]	[휴대폰이 울린다.]
M Hello?	남 여보세요?
W Hi, James. I just <u>saw the advertisement</u> for *Welcome to the Nation*. Remember we talked about that musical last week?	여 안녕, James. 나 방금 <Welcome to the Nation>의 광고를 봤어. 지난주에 그 뮤지컬에 관해 이야기했던 거 기억해?
M Oh, yeah! I remember <u>how exciting it looked</u>. I'd love to see it soon. When does it premiere?	남 오, 그래! 그게 얼마나 흥미진진해 보였는지 기억나. 빨리 보고 싶다. 그거 언제 초연해?
W Next week. I think <u>the first performance</u> is on Wednesday.	여 다음 주에. 첫 공연이 수요일인 것 같아.
M That'd be the 19th, right?	남 그날이 19일이지, 맞지?
W Yeah. November 19th.	여 응. 11월 19일이야.
M I <u>can't go watch it</u> then. My grandmother's visiting our house on that day.	남 그러면 그건 보러 못 가겠다. 할머니가 그날 우리 집에 방문하실 거야.
W Then, <u>how about the next day?</u> I want to watch it before long.	여 그러면, 그다음 날은 어때? 난 그걸 빨리 보고 싶어.
M I'm <u>available</u> on that day. I'll book the tickets now.	남 그날은 시간이 있어. 내가 지금 표를 예매할게.

해설 | 여자가 11월 19일의 다음 날에 뮤지컬을 보러 갈 것을 제안하자 남자가 그날은 시간이 있다고 했으므로 정답은 ③ '11월 20일'이다.

어휘 | premiere [primíər] 图 초연하다, 첫 공연을 하다 圆 초연 available [əvéiləbl] 휑 시간이 있는; 이용할 수 있는

14 한 일 고르기

정답 ②

M Sally, I heard you <u>went to a play</u> with Greg yesterday. How was it?	남 Sally, 너 어제 Greg과 연극 보러 갔다고 들었어. 어땠어?
W Actually, we didn't go.	여 사실, 못 갔어.
M Oh, no. What happened?	남 오, 이런. 무슨 일이 있었던 거야?
W Greg was told his class <u>would have a quiz</u> today. So, we decided to go to a play this Sunday instead.	여 Greg이 오늘 반에서 쪽지 시험이 있을 거라는 얘기를 들었거든. 그래서, 우린 대신 이번 주 일요일에 보러 가기로 했어.
M What did you do yesterday then?	남 그러면 어제는 뭐 했어?
W I met another friend and <u>went bowling with her</u>.	여 다른 친구를 만나서 함께 볼링 치러 갔어.
M That sounds nice. Anyway, I hope you have fun this Sunday.	남 좋았겠다. 아무튼, 이번 주 일요일에 재미있게 보길 바랄게.
W Thanks. I'll <u>tell you about the performance</u> next week.	여 고마워. 내가 다음 주에 공연에 대해 말해줄게.

해설 | 남자가 여자에게 어제 무엇을 했는지 묻자 여자가 친구와 볼링을 치러 갔다고 했으므로 정답은 ② '볼링 치기'이다.

어휘 | bowling [bóuliŋ] 圆 볼링 anyway [éniwei] 閉 아무튼, 어쨌든

15 목적 고르기

정답 ④

M Hello. This is Samuel Reddy from the Riverside Fire Station. I want to talk to you about <u>how to prevent accidents</u> that cause fires. Fires can start in many ways. At home, they often start in the kitchen. When cooking, never <u>leave your food alone</u> for long. Stay near the oven or stove, or check it often. Also, unplug <u>all electronic devices</u> when they are not in use. Leaking electricity can easily cause a fire. Lastly, store flammable objects properly. <u>Keep these tips in mind</u>, and you'll be much safer.	남 안녕하세요. 리버사이드 소방서의 Samuel Reddy입니다. 화재를 일으키는 사고를 어떻게 예방할지에 관해 말씀드리려 합니다. 화재는 여러 방식으로 시작될 수 있습니다. 집에서, 화재는 대개 부엌에서 시작됩니다. 요리하실 때, 절대 음식을 오래 방치해두지 마십시오. 오븐이나 가스레인지 근처에 머무시거나, 자주 확인하십시오. 또한, 전자 기기는 사용하지 않으실 땐 코드를 뽑아두십시오. 누전은 쉽게 화재를 일으킬 수 있습니다. 마지막으로, 가연성 물질을 올바르게 보관하십시오. 이러한 조언을 명심하시면, 훨씬 더 안전해지실 겁니다.

해설 | 남자가 화재 사고를 어떻게 예방할지에 관해 설명해주고 있으므로 정답은 ④이다.

어휘 | leave alone 방치해두다, 내버려 두다 stove [stouv] 圆 가스레인지; 난로 unplug [ənplʌ́g] 图 코드를 뽑다 leak [liːk] 图 누출되다, 새다 flammable [flǽməbl] 휑 가연성의 keep in mind ~을 명심하다

W	Welcome to Home Goods Store. Do you need any help?
M	Hello, I'd like to buy this pillow. How much is it?
W	It's 13 dollars, but there's a special promotion today. If you buy two, you can get one for free.
M	Three for 26 dollars? That's a good deal. I'll take those three pillows then.
W	Great. Are you interested in anything else?
M	Actually, yes. I'd like a blanket too. How much is that one?
W	It's 20 dollars.
M	I'll buy that as well.

여	Home Goods Store에 오신 걸 환영합니다. 도움이 필요하신가요?
남	안녕하세요, 이 베개를 사고 싶은데요. 얼마죠?
여	그건 13달러이지만, 오늘은 특별한 판촉 행사가 있어요. 두 개를 사시면, 하나는 공짜로 받으실 수 있어요.
남	세 개에 26달러인 거죠? 엄청나게 싸네요. 그러면 이 베개 세 개를 살게요.
여	좋습니다. 달리 관심 있으신 게 있으실까요?
남	사실은, 네. 담요도 하나 사고 싶어요. 이건 얼마죠?
여	그건 20달러입니다.
남	그것도 살게요.

해설 | 남자가 사겠다고 한 베개 세 개는 26달러이고 담요는 하나에 20달러이므로 정답은 ③ '$ 46'이다.

어휘 | pillow [pílou] 뗑 베개   promotion [prəmóuʃən] 뗑 판촉; 승진   blanket [blǽŋkit] 뗑 담요

	[Cellphone rings.]
M	Hello?
W	Hi. This is Olivia from Amazing Boat Tours. I'm calling to confirm your reservation.
M	Oh, yes. The tour is tomorrow, right?
W	That's correct. You booked a tour for 11 a.m.
M	Excellent. How long is the tour?
W	It will be about two hours long. Please bring a hat and sunglasses because it will be very sunny.
M	What else do I need to do?
W	Safety instructions will be provided before boarding, so arrive at least 15 minutes early.
M	Got it. I'll get there by 10:45 a.m.

	[휴대폰이 울린다.]
남	여보세요?
여	안녕하세요. 전 Amazing Boat Tours의 Olivia입니다. 고객님의 예약을 확인하려고 전화 드렸어요.
남	오, 그러시군요. 투어가 내일이죠, 맞아요?
여	맞아요. 오전 11시에 투어를 예약하셨네요.
남	좋습니다. 투어가 몇 시간짜리죠?
여	2시간 정도 걸릴 거예요. 날이 몹시 화창할 것 같으니 모자와 선글라스를 가져와 주세요.
남	그밖에 해야 할 게 더 있나요?
여	안전 교육이 탑승 전에 제공될 예정이니, 최소한 15분 일찍 도착해주세요.
남	알겠습니다. 오전 10시 45분까지 거기로 갈게요.

해설 | 여자가 탑승 전 안전 교육 때문에 예약 시간보다 더 일찍 와 달라고 했으므로 정답은 일찍 가겠다고 대답하는 ④ 'Got it. I'll get there by 10:45 a.m.'이다.

<선택지 해석>
① 배는 30분마다 와요. ② 아니요. 아직 예약하지 않았어요. ③ 그러면, 안전을 위해 구명조끼를 착용해야겠네요.
④ 알겠습니다. 오전 10시 45분까지 거기로 갈게요. ⑤ 방문하기 가장 좋은 시기는 6월입니다.

어휘 | confirm [kənfə́:rm] 통 확인하다; 입증하다   instruction [instrʌ́kʃən] 뗑 교육   provide [prəváid] 통 제공하다   at least 최소한

W	Your lunch looks so healthy, Zach.
M	Yeah. I'm trying to eat better nowadays.
W	Why is that?
M	I watched a documentary about fast food. It's really bad for your health.
W	That's true. How has your diet changed then?
M	I eat more salads and fruit, and I have fast food only on the weekend.
W	Do you feel any difference?
M	Actually, I feel more energized now. Also, I find myself liking less salty food.
W	That's great. I ought to eat healthier too.

여	네 점심 식사 정말 건강해 보여, Zach.
남	응. 난 요즘에 더 잘 먹으려고 노력 중이야.
여	왜 그러는데?
남	즉석식품에 관한 다큐멘터리를 봤거든. 그건 건강에 정말 안 좋아.
여	맞는 말이야. 그럼 식단을 어떻게 바꿨어?
남	샐러드랑 과일을 더 많이 먹고, 즉석식품은 주말에만 먹어.
여	차이가 느껴져?
남	사실, 요즘 기운이 더 나는 기분이야. 그리고, 덜 짠 음식을 좋아하게 됐어.
여	잘됐다. 나도 더 건강하게 먹어야겠어.

해설 | 남자가 건강한 식단을 통해 기운이 더 나게 됐다는 좋은 변화를 말했으므로 정답은 건강한 식단에 동참하겠다는 ④ 'That's great. I ought to eat healthier too.' 이다.

선택지 해석
① 운동으로 더 많은 근육을 얻을 수 있어. ② 집에 가는 길에 음식을 좀 사 갈래. ③ 점심으로 이 샐러드를 가져가면 돼.
④ 잘됐다. 나도 더 건강하게 먹어야겠어. ⑤ 오, 그래서 네가 수프에 소금을 넣는 거구나.

어휘 | diet [dáiət] 몡 식단; 일상 음식 energize [énərdʒaiz] 통 기운을 북돋우다 salty [sɔ́ːlti] 혱 짠 gain [gein] 통 얻다 muscle [mʌ́sl] 몡 근육

19 적절한 응답 고르기   정답 ③

W	When will we arrive, Dad?	여	저희 언제 도착해요, 아빠?
M	We need to drive for another two hours.	남	두 시간 더 운전해야 한단다.
W	But I'm so bored. This drive is so long.	여	그런데 저 너무 지루해요. 운전이 너무 오래 걸리네요.
M	I know. But I must drive slowly in the snow.	남	그래. 그렇지만 눈길에서는 천천히 운전해야 해.
W	Can I charge my phone? It's almost out of battery.	여	제 휴대폰 충전할 수 있을까요? 배터리가 거의 다 됐어요.
M	Sure. Why don't you solve a crossword puzzle while it is charging?	남	물론이란다. 휴대폰이 충전되는 동안에 크로스 워드 퍼즐을 푸는 게 어떻겠니?
W	Okay. Can you also play some music?	여	좋아요. 아빠가 음악도 틀어주실래요?
M	My phone is connected to the speakers. Pick some songs.	남	내 휴대폰이 스피커에 연결되어 있단다. 노래 몇 곡을 골라 주렴.
W	Okay. I will create a playlist.	여	네. 제가 재생 목록을 만들게요.

해설 | 남자가 노래 몇 곡을 골라달라고 했으므로 정답은 재생 목록을 만들겠다는 ③ 'Okay. I will create a playlist.'이다.

선택지 해석
① 새 충전기를 사야 해요. ② 조심하세요. 너무 빠르게 운전하고 있어요. ③ 네. 제가 재생 목록을 만들게요. ④ 천만에요. 여기 제 휴대폰이요.
⑤ 그 퍼즐은 품절이에요.

어휘 | charge [tʃɑːrdʒ] 통 충전하다; 청구하다 (charger [tʃɑ́ːrdʒər] 몡 충전기) connect [kənékt] 통 연결하다

20 상황에 적절한 말 고르기   정답 ⑤

| W | Nathan wants to become a vet. So, he goes to the library to find a book about animals. While he is there, Nathan sees lots of interesting books on a variety of topics. However, he has difficulty finding books related to animals. He decides to ask the librarian where such publications are located. In this situation, what would Nathan most likely say to the librarian? | 여 | Nathan은 수의사가 되고 싶습니다. 그래서, 그는 동물에 관한 책을 찾기 위해 도서관에 갑니다. 그곳에 있는 동안, Nathan은 다양한 주제에 관한 흥미로운 책을 많이 봅니다. 하지만, 그는 동물에 관련된 책을 찾는 데 어려움을 겪습니다. 그는 사서 선생님에게 그러한 출판물이 어디에 있는지 묻기로 결심합니다. 이러한 상황에서, Nathan이 사서 선생님에게 가장 할 것 같은 말은 무엇입니까? |
| Nathan | Where is the animal section? | Nathan | 동물 서적 코너는 어디인가요? |

해설 | Nathan이 사서 선생님에게 동물에 관련된 출판물이 어디 있는지 묻기로 결심했다고 했으므로 정답은 ⑤ 'Where is the animal section?'이다.

선택지 해석
① 제 다음으로 읽으시면 돼요. ② 공상과학소설은 이쪽에 있어요. ③ 가장 좋아하는 동물이 뭔가요? ④ 동물 건강에 관한 책들은 지금 대출 중입니다.
⑤ 동물 서적 코너는 어디인가요?

어휘 | vet [vet] 몡 수의사 a variety of 다양한 related to ~에 관련된 publication [pʌ̀bləkéiʃən] 몡 출판물; 출판

1	③	2	①	3	③	4	②	5	⑤	6	①	7	④	8	⑤	9	④	10	④
11	⑤	12	⑤	13	④	14	⑤	15	③	16	②	17	⑤	18	②	19	③	20	②

1 알맞은 그림 고르기

정답 ③

M	Mom, do you know <u>how to add</u> a zipper to a bag?
W	Sorry, but <u>I don't know how.</u> Why do you ask?
M	I'm trying to make a shoe bag to <u>put my school slippers in.</u>
W	Wow! Did you make it all on your own?
M	Yes. I was thinking of drawing a horse on it, but I changed my mind. <u>I drew this unicorn</u> on it and added these two handles.
W	Awesome! But I don't think it needs a zipper. <u>How about just adding a button?</u>
M	<u>That's a good idea.</u> Thanks.

남 엄마, 가방에 지퍼 다는 법 아시나요?
여 미안하지만, 모르겠구나. 왜 묻는 거니?
남 제 학교 실내화를 담을 신발 가방을 만들려고 하고 있어요.
여 우와! 전부 너 혼자서 만든 거니?
남 네. 말을 그릴까 생각했었는데, 마음을 바꿨어요. 유니콘을 그리고 손잡이 두 개를 붙였어요.
여 훌륭하구나! 그런데 여기에 지퍼가 필요할 것 같진 않구나. 그냥 단추를 다는 게 어떻겠니?
남 좋은 생각이에요. 감사합니다.

해설 | 남자가 신발 가방에 유니콘을 그리고 손잡이 두 개를 붙였다고 했으며, 단추를 다는 것을 제안한 여자의 말에 좋은 생각이라고 했으므로 정답은 ③이다.

어휘 | on one's own 혼자서, 단독으로; 독립하여

2 부탁·요청한 일 고르기

정답 ①

W	Darling, do you want to go to the beach this weekend?
M	Well, we <u>have volunteer work</u> on Saturday.
W	That's right. I completely forgot. We'll be at <u>the senior center</u>, right?
M	Yes. We'll oversee the board games activity time.
W	Okay. I'll <u>select a few for us</u> to take.
M	Should we also <u>purchase some prizes</u> for the winners?
W	Sure. But <u>I need a favor. I won't be able to shop for</u> them on Friday.
M	No problem. I can visit the store before then.

여 여보, 이번 주말에 바닷가 갈래?
남 글쎄, 우리 토요일에 봉사활동 있잖아.
여 맞다. 완전히 잊고 있었어. 노인회관에 가 있어야지, 맞지?
남 응. 보드게임 활동 시간을 감독할 거야.
여 알겠어. 내가 가져갈 보드게임을 고를게.
남 우승자분들께 드릴 상품도 구매해야 할까?
여 물론이지. 그런데 부탁 하나만 할게. 내가 금요일에 상품을 사러 가지 못할 거 같아.
남 문제없어. 내가 그전에 가게에 방문하면 돼.

해설 | 여자가 남자에게 부탁이 있다고 하면서 금요일에 우승자에게 줄 상품을 사러 갈 수 없겠다고 했으므로 정답은 ① '우승 상품 준비하기'이다.

어휘 | senior center 노인회관, 노인 복지관 oversee [òvərsí] 동 감독하다 select [silékt] 동 고르다, 선택하다

3 그림 상황에 적절한 대화 고르기 　　　　　　　 정답 ③

① W　Would you like to go for a walk?
　 M　Let's do it tomorrow.
② W　Pets are not allowed in the store.
　 M　Oh, I didn't realize that.
③ W　Can I pet your dog?
　 M　Sure. He's very friendly.
④ W　Is it okay to park here?
　 M　I don't think it is allowed.
⑤ W　I can't find my wallet.
　 M　Did you check in the kitchen?

① 여　산책하러 갈래?
　 남　내일 하자.
② 여　반려동물은 가게에 입장할 수 없습니다.
　 남　오, 몰랐어요.
③ 여　제가 강아지를 쓰다듬어봐도 될까요?
　 남　물론이죠. 이 녀석은 엄청 순해요.
④ 여　여기에 주차해도 괜찮나요?
　 남　안 될 것 같아요.
⑤ 여　내 지갑을 못 찾겠어.
　 남　부엌 안은 확인해 봤어?

해설 | 개를 쓰다듬고 싶어 하는 여자가 개를 데리고 있는 남자에게 말을 걸고 있는 상황이므로 정답은 ③이다.

어휘 | pet [pet] 몡 반려동물 뭉 쓰다듬다 　friendly [fréndli] 혱 순한; 친절한 　park [pɑːrk] 뭉 주차하다 몡 공원 　wallet [wɑ́lit] 몡 지갑

4 시간 정보 고르기 　　　　　　　　　　　　 정답 ②

[Cellphone rings.]
W　Hi, Mike. I think you're interested in science, right?
M　Yes. Science is my favorite subject. Why?
W　The Museum of Science is offering several special programs during the holiday. Why don't we join one on Saturday?
M　That sounds interesting. But could we do it in the morning? I will play badminton with Dave from 2 to 4 that afternoon.
W　Sure. There are two programs in the morning. I like to join the program for observing insects. It starts at 9.
M　Well, do you mind attending the one about 3D printing that starts at 10 instead?
W　No. That seems interesting too. Let's go to it together.

[휴대폰이 울린다.]
여　안녕, Mike. 네가 과학에 흥미가 있는 것 같은데, 맞니?
남　응. 과학은 내가 제일 좋아하는 과목이야. 왜?
여　과학 박물관에서 연휴 동안에 몇몇 특별한 프로그램을 제공할 거야. 토요일에 하나 함께 듣지 않을래?
남　그거 재미있겠다. 그런데 오전에 들을 수 있을까? 난 오후 2시부터 4시까지 Dave랑 배드민턴 칠 거야.
여　물론이지. 오전에는 두 가지 프로그램이 있어. 난 곤충 관찰 프로그램에 참여하고 싶어. 그건 9시에 시작해.
남　음, 10시에 시작하는 3D 프린팅에 관한 프로그램에 나가도 될까?
여　그럼. 그것도 흥미로워 보여. 그걸 함께 듣자.

해설 | 남자가 10시에 시작하는 3D 프린팅에 관한 프로그램을 들어도 될지 묻자 여자가 좋다고 했으므로 정답은 ② '10 a.m.'이다.

어휘 | subject [sʌ́bdʒikt] 몡 과목; 주제 　observe [əbzə́ːrv] 뭉 관찰하다; 보다 　insect [ínsekt] 몡 곤충

5 언급하지 않은 내용 고르기 　　　　　　　　 정답 ⑤

[Telephone rings.]
M　Hero Gym. How can I help you?
W　Hello. I intend to register at your gym, so I want to ask some questions about the membership.
M　Okay. Please feel free to ask.
W　How long is a membership valid?
M　We have memberships for three months, six months, and a year. They cost 150 dollars, 240 dollars, and 360 dollars.
W　How about gym clothes? Are they provided?
M　For newly registered members, gym clothes are provided for free for three months.
W　Are you open around 10 p.m. today?
M　Yes. We're open 24 hours a day except on Sundays.
W　Okay. Thank you!

[전화기가 울린다.]
남　Hero Gym입니다. 무엇을 도와드릴까요?
여　안녕하세요. 거기 체육관에 등록할 생각이어서요. 회원권에 관해 몇 가지 질문을 드리고 싶어요.
남　알겠습니다. 부담 없이 물어보세요.
여　회원권 기간은 얼마 동안 유효한가요?
남　3개월, 6개월, 그리고 1년짜리 회원권이 있어요. 비용은 150달러, 240달러, 360달러입니다.
여　운동복은요? 제공되나요?
남　새로 등록하신 회원분들에게는, 운동복이 세 달 동안 무료로 제공됩니다.
여　오늘 밤 10시쯤에도 열려 있나요?
남　네. 저희는 일요일만 제외하고는 하루 24시간 동안 영업합니다.
여　알겠습니다. 감사합니다!

해설 | ① 회원권 종류(3개월, 6개월, 1년 회원권), ② 회원권 가격(150달러, 240달러, 360달러), ③ 운동복 제공 여부(신규 회원에게 세 달 동안 무료로 제공), ④ 운영 시간(일요일 제외하고 하루 24시간 동안 영업)에 대해 언급했으므로 정답은 ⑤ '샤워 시설'이다.

어휘 | intend [inténd] 뭉 (~하려고) 생각하다, ~할 작정이다 　feel free to 부담 없이 ~하다 　valid [vǽlid] 혱 유효한 　except [iksépt] 젠 ~을 제외하고

6 장소 고르기　　　　　　　　　　　　　정답 ①

W　I need to walk around after <u>sitting in the car</u> so long.

M　Well, we will be here for a few minutes because <mark>I need to go to the restroom.</mark>

W　How much longer will we drive after this?

M　Traffic is bad, so it will take another three hours to get to the hotel.

W　I will <u>get some snacks</u> on the way back to the car. Do you want anything?

M　I'd like some grilled potatoes and <u>a bottle of water</u>, please.

W　Alright.

여　차에 너무 오래 앉아 있었더니 좀 걸어 다녀야겠어.

남　음, 나도 화장실에 가야 하니까 몇 분 정도 여기 있자.

여　앞으로 얼마나 더 오래 운전해야 해?

남　교통 상황이 안 좋아서, 호텔로 가는 데 세 시간이 더 걸릴 거야.

여　차로 돌아오는 길에 간식을 좀 사 와야겠어. 너도 뭐 필요해?

남　통감자와 물 한 병 부탁할게.

여　알겠어.

해설 | 남자가 화장실에 들르겠다고 했고, 여자는 걷다가 차로 돌아오는 길에 간식을 사 오겠다고 하는 것으로 보아 정답은 ① '휴게소'이다.

어휘 | grilled potato 통감자, 감자구이

7 어색한 대화 고르기　　　　　　　　　　정답 ④

① W　I love your sunglasses.

　　M　Thanks. I <u>just bought them</u> yesterday.

② W　How do you like my new song?

　　M　It <u>is so moving</u>. I really like it.

③ W　Where did you <u>get this recipe</u> for bulgogi?

　　M　I found it online.

④ W　<mark>Have you ever read the book *Amy in Madrid*?</mark>

　　M　No. I've <u>never been there.</u>

⑤ W　Do you have any plans for this weekend?

　　M　I'm going <u>to surf with</u> my friends.

① 여　네 선글라스 너무 좋다.
　　남　고마워. 어제 막 산 거야.
② 여　내 신곡 어때?
　　남　아주 감동적이야. 정말 마음에 들어.
③ 여　이 불고기 요리법은 어디에서 났어?
　　남　온라인에서 발견했어.
④ 여　<Amy in Madrid>라는 책 읽어본 적 있어?
　　남　아니. 난 거기 가본 적 없어.
⑤ 여　이번 주말에 계획 있어?
　　남　친구들이랑 파도타기를 하러 갈 거야.

해설 | 여자가 남자에게 책을 읽어본 적 있는지 물었으므로 남자는 독서 여부를 말해야 한다. 그러나 남자가 그곳에 가본 적이 없다는 어색한 대답을 했으므로 정답은 ④이다.

어휘 | moving [múːviŋ] 휑 감동적인; 움직이는　recipe [résəpi] 몡 요리법　surf [səːrf] 동 파도타기를 하다, 서핑하다

8 부탁·요청한 일 고르기　　　　　　　　　정답 ⑤

M　Are you okay, Kelly? You <u>look stressed out</u>.

W　I'm not doing well in my math class, so I'm stressed <u>about my grade</u>.

M　Do you spend enough time on your homework?

W　I spend <u>a lot of time on it</u>, but it's always difficult for me to do.

M　Well, my math tutor is really helpful. I <u>improved my math skills</u> a lot with him.

W　<mark>Will you give me his phone number?</mark> I could use some help.

M　Sure. I'll text you his information.

남　괜찮니, Kelly? 스트레스로 지친 것 같아 보여.

여　난 수학 수업에서 잘하지 못해서, 성적에 대한 스트레스를 받고 있어.

남　숙제하는 데 충분한 시간은 쓰니?

여　숙제하는 데 많은 시간을 쓰는데도, 항상 하기 어려워.

남　음, 내 수학 과외 선생님이 진짜 도움을 많이 주시거든. 난 그 선생님이랑 함께 해서 수학 실력이 많이 나아졌어.

여　나한테 그분의 전화번호를 줄 수 있어? 도움이 필요해.

남　물론이지. 내가 선생님 연락처를 문자로 보내줄게.

해설 | 여자가 남자에게 수학 과외 선생님의 전화번호를 달라고 부탁했으므로 정답은 ⑤ '과외 선생님 연락처 알려주기'이다.

어휘 | stressed out 스트레스로 지친　tutor [tjúːtər] 몡 과외 선생님, 가정 교사　improve [imprúːv] 동 나아지다; 개선하다　skill [skil] 몡 실력; 솜씨

9 주제 고르기　　　　　　　　　　　　　　　　　　　　　정답 ④

M	Attention, please. This is <u>an announcement from</u> TSI Tours. I'm sorry to announce that today's glass-bottom boat tour <u>is canceled</u>. Strong winds are expected, and this <u>makes it hard to observe</u> the fish and other marine life. It is also dangerous because <u>there's a chance that</u> the boat may be overturned. You'll be able to <u>get a full refund</u> or exchange your ticket for another time with no charge. Again, I'd like to apologize for the inconvenience.	남 주목해 주십시오. TSI Tours에서 공지해 드립니다. 오늘 유리 바닥 선박 투어가 취소됨을 알려드리게 되어 유감스럽습니다. 강풍이 예상되어, 물고기와 다른 해양 생물을 관찰하는 것이 어려워졌습니다. 또한 선박이 뒤집힐 가능성이 있어서, 위험하기도 합니다. 여러분은 전액 환불받으시거나, 수수료 없이 티켓을 다른 시간대로 바꾸실 수 있습니다. 다시 한번, 불편을 끼쳐서 죄송합니다.

해설 | 남자가 오늘의 유리 바닥 선박 투어가 취소됨을 공지하고 있으므로 정답은 ④ '선박 관광 취소'이다.

어휘 | marine [məríːn] 혱 해양의　there's a chance that ~할 가능성이 있다　overturn [òuvərtə́rn] 동 뒤집히다, 전복하다

10 금액 정보 고르기　　　　　　　　　　　　　　　　　　　정답 ④

W	Hello. <u>Can I help you</u>?	여 안녕하세요. 도와드릴까요?
M	Yes. I'd like two tickets for the 5 p.m. train to New York.	남 네. 오후 5시 뉴욕행 기차표로 두 장 주세요.
W	<u>The tickets are 20 dollars each</u>. It's 40 dollars in total. Would you like to pay more for <u>some extra leg space</u>?	여 표는 한 장에 20달러입니다. 총 40달러입니다. 여분의 다리를 뻗을 공간을 위해 더 지불하시겠습니까?
M	<u>How much more</u> do I have to pay?	남 얼마를 더 내야 하는데요?
W	It would be an extra 10 dollars per person.	여 한 사람당 10달러씩 추가됩니다.
M	No, thank you. <u>I'll just get the two regular tickets</u>. But can I use this coupon too?	남 아니요, 괜찮습니다. 그냥 보통 표로 두 장 살게요. 그런데 이 쿠폰도 쓸 수 있나요?
W	Sure. With that coupon, <u>you can get a five-dollar discount on the total price</u>.	여 물론이죠. 그 쿠폰으로, 총액에서 5달러 할인받으실 수 있습니다.
M	Excellent.	남 좋네요.

해설 | 남자가 한 장에 20달러인 보통 기차표를 두 장 샀고, 쿠폰을 적용하여 총액에서 5달러를 할인받았으므로 정답은 ④ '$ 35'이다.

어휘 | leg space (비행기, 기차 등에서) 다리 뻗을 공간　regular [régjulər] 혱 보통의; 규칙적인

11 할 일 고르기　　　　　　　　　　　　　　　　　　　　　정답 ⑤

W	Hey, Siwoo. What are you doing?	여 안녕, 시우야. 뭐 하고 있어?
M	<u>I'm running errands</u> for my mom. What about you?	남 엄마 심부름 중이야. 너는?
W	I'm on my way to my modern dance class.	여 현대 무용 수업에 가는 길이야.
M	I <u>didn't know you danced</u>.	남 네가 무용을 하는지 몰랐어.
W	Yes. I take lessons three times a week.	여 응. 난 일주일에 세 번 수업을 들어.
M	Does the lesson start soon?	남 수업 곧 시작이야?
W	No. I <u>left my house early</u>. Do you want me to come to the store with you?	여 아니. 집에서 일찍 나왔어. 내가 너랑 같이 가게 가줄까?
M	Sure. <u>I'm just going to buy some ingredients for dinner tonight</u>. My mom is busy at home.	남 물론이지. 난 그냥 오늘 밤 저녁 식사 재료 몇 개만 살 거야. 엄마가 집에서 바쁘시거든.
W	Okay. <u>I'll help you find them</u>.	여 알겠어. 내가 찾는 걸 도와줄게.

해설 | 남자가 저녁 식사 재료를 살 것이라고 했으므로 정답은 ⑤ '식재료 구매하기'이다.

어휘 | run errands 심부름을 하다　ingredient [ingríːdiənt] 몡 재료, 성분

12 언급하지 않은 내용 고르기
정답 ⑤

W Hello, welcome to our showcase. I'll introduce you to our latest laptop model, the Air 20. This is the lightest laptop in existence at only 920 grams. Its slim design makes it easy to carry around. Moreover, after charging for 30 minutes, the battery will last for 20 hours. As for the safety features, you can log in using fingerprint recognition technology. Please try the sample products at the front of the room, and let me know if you have any questions.

여 안녕하세요, 저희 시연회에 오신 걸 환영합니다. 전 여러분에게 저희의 최신 노트북 모델인 Air 20을 소개해드리려 합니다. 이것은 현존하는 제품 중 가장 가벼운 것으로 겨우 920g입니다. 얇은 디자인은 그걸 들고 다니기 쉽게 만듭니다. 게다가, 30분 동안 충전한 후, 배터리는 20시간 동안 지속됩니다. 보안 기능으로는, 지문 인식 기술을 이용해 로그인하실 수 있습니다. 시연회장 앞쪽의 견본품을 체험해 보시고, 질문 있으시면 알려주세요.

해설 ┃ ① 모델명(Air 20), ② 무게(920g), ③ 보안 기능(지문 인식 기술로 로그인), ④ 충전 시간(30분)에 대해 언급했으므로 정답은 ⑤ '메모리 사양'이다.

어휘 ┃ showcase [ʃóukeis] 몡 시연회, 쇼케이스 in existence 현존하는 slim [slim] 혱 얇은 fingerprint [fíŋɡərprìnt] 몡 지문 recognition [rèkəɡníʃən] 몡 인식

13 도표에서 알맞은 항목 고르기
정답 ④

M Jess, which movie do you want to watch?
W How about that new horror movie? Adam Surley is my favorite actor.
M Sorry, but I really don't like horror movies.
W Oh, it's okay. Hmm... Why don't we watch the comedy? I'd like a good laugh.
M Sure. Does that star James Collins?
W Yeah. His movies are always hilarious.
M Great. It's 11:50 a.m. now. Should we eat something before the movie?
W I had a big breakfast, so I'm not that hungry.
M Me neither. Then, let's watch the earliest one.
W Sure.

남 Jess, 어떤 영화 보고 싶어?
여 새로 나온 공포 영화는 어때? Adam Surley는 내가 가장 좋아하는 배우야.
남 미안한데, 내가 진짜 공포 영화를 안 좋아해.
여 오, 괜찮아. 흠... 코미디 보는 건 어때? 실컷 웃고 싶어.
남 물론이지. 거기에 James Collins가 주연을 맡았니?
여 응. 그의 영화는 항상 유쾌해.
남 좋아. 지금 오전 11시 50분이네. 영화 전에 뭔가 먹을까?
여 난 아침을 많이 먹어서, 그렇게 배고프진 않아.
남 나도. 그럼, 가장 빠른 영화를 보자.
여 그래.

해설 ┃ 여자가 코미디 영화를 제안하자 남자가 동의했고, 그 영화에서 James Collins가 주연을 맡았다고 했으며, 남자가 그중 가장 빠른 영화를 보자고 했으므로 정답은 ④이다.

어휘 ┃ horror [hɔ́ːrər] 몡 공포 star [staːr] 동 주연을 맡다 몡 별 hilarious [hilέəriəs] 혱 유쾌한; 법석대는

14 화제 고르기
정답 ⑤

M This is a water sport. It is featured in the summer Olympics. Team members perform in the water to music. They move together, matching each other's motions. Once the performance is finished, the team is evaluated. The judge gives the team a score based on how well the members moved together. The judge also considers how the performance related to the music. The team that receives the highest score is the winner of the competition.

남 이것은 수상 운동입니다. 이것은 하계 올림픽에 포함되어 있습니다. 팀원들은 음악에 맞춰 물속에서 공연합니다. 그들은 서로의 동작을 일치시키며 함께 움직입니다. 일단 공연이 끝나면, 팀은 평가를 받습니다. 심사위원은 팀원들이 얼마나 잘 서로 맞춰서 움직였는지에 기반하여 점수를 줍니다. 심사위원은 공연이 어떻게 음악과 연관되었는지도 고려합니다. 가장 높은 점수를 받은 팀이 시합의 우승자입니다.

해설 ┃ 이것(This)을 하는 팀원들은 물속에서 음악에 맞춰 공연하고, 서로의 동작을 일치시키며 함께 움직인다고 했으므로 정답은 ⑤ '수중발레'이다.

어휘 ┃ feature [fíːtʃər] 동 (특별히) 포함하다 몡 특징 match [mætʃ] 동 일치시키다, 조화시키다 motion [móuʃən] 몡 동작; 움직임 once [wʌns] 접 일단 ~하면 튄 한 번 evaluate [ivǽljueit] 동 평가하다 based on ~에 기반하여 consider [kənsídər] 동 고려하다

15 할 일 고르기   정답 ③

W	Our poster on climate change looks perfect. This will be an amazing presentation.
M	I agree, but we aren't finished yet.
W	What else do we need to do?
M	We have to practice explaining the poster.
W	Well, you are better at speeches. How about I write the script, and then you present to the class?
M	That's fine with me. I'll add a remark on the future of the global climate at the end.

여	기후 변화에 관한 우리 포스터는 완벽해 보여. 이건 엄청난 발표가 될 거야.
남	나도 동의하지만 우린 아직 안 끝났어.
여	우리가 뭘 더 해야 해?
남	포스터 설명하는 걸 연습해야 해.
여	음, 네가 발표를 나보다 더 잘하잖아. 내가 대본을 쓰고, 네가 수업 때 발표하는 게 어때?
남	난 괜찮아. 마지막에는 지구 기후의 미래에 대한 의견을 덧붙일게.

해설 | 남자가 발표 마지막에 지구 기후의 미래에 대한 의견을 덧붙이겠다고 했으므로 정답은 ③ '기후 전망 발표하기'이다.

어휘 | climate [kláimit] 몡 기후 explain [ikspléin] 동 설명하다 script [skript] 몡 대본 remark [rimá:rk] 몡 의견, 발언 global [glóbəl] 혱 지구의; 세계적인

16 시간 정보 고르기   정답 ②

W	Excuse me. Does this hotel offer a free airport shuttle? I need to catch a flight tomorrow morning.
M	We do have one. What time does your flight depart?
W	It leaves at 11 a.m. But I need to be at the airport a couple of hours earlier.
M	Then, can I book you on the 6 a.m. shuttle? You will get to the airport at 8.
W	That's a little too early. Is there one that leaves at 7?
M	Yes. And it arrives at the airport at 9.
W	Perfect. Please reserve a seat on that shuttle.
M	No problem. I'll just need your name and room number, please.

여	실례합니다. 이 호텔에서 무료 공항 셔틀버스를 제공하나요? 전 내일 아침에 비행기에 탑승해야 해요.
남	제공합니다. 비행기가 몇 시에 출발하나요?
여	오전 11시에 출발해요. 그런데 공항에 몇 시간 일찍 도착해야 해요.
남	그러면, 오전 6시 셔틀버스에 예약해둘까요? 공항에는 8시에 도착할 거예요.
여	그건 좀 너무 이르네요. 7시에 출발하는 것도 있나요?
남	네. 그러면 공항에 9시에 도착해요.
여	딱 좋아요. 그 셔틀버스에 제 자리를 예약해주세요.
남	문제없습니다. 성함과 방 번호만 알려주시면 됩니다.

해설 | 여자가 7시에 출발하는 공항 셔틀버스를 예약해 달라고 했으므로 정답은 ② '7 a.m.'이다.

어휘 | catch a flight 비행기에 탑승하다 depart [dipá:rt] 동 출발하다

17 적절한 응답 고르기   정답 ⑤

M	What did you do last night, Jihyo?
W	I spent time with my parents and played that new phone game.
M	The one you downloaded yesterday?
W	Yes. I stayed up late to play it.
M	What level are you on?
W	I just got to level eight. But it took a long time.
M	Wow! That's really impressive. I also downloaded the game, but I'm only on level three.
W	Do you like it so far?
M	Yes. But I'm not doing so well on it right now. Can you help me get to the next level?
W	Sure. Get your phone out so I can show you.

남	어젯밤에 뭐 했어, 지효야?
여	부모님과 시간을 보냈고 새 휴대폰 게임을 했어.
남	네가 어제 다운받았던 거 말이야?
여	응. 그거 하느라고 밤을 새웠어.
남	지금 몇 단계야?
여	막 8단계가 됐어. 그런데 정말 오래 걸렸어.
남	우와! 그거 정말 놀랍다. 나도 그 게임을 다운받았는데, 난 겨우 3단계야.
여	지금까지는 게임이 마음에 드니?
남	응. 그런데 지금은 그걸 잘하지 못하겠어. 내가 다음 단계로 가도록 도와줄 수 있을까?
여	물론이지. 내가 알려줄 테니 휴대폰 꺼내 봐.

해설 | 남자가 여자에게 게임의 다음 단계로 가도록 도와 달라고 부탁했으므로 정답은 부탁을 수락하는 ⑤ 'Sure. Get your phone out so I can show you.'이다.

선택지 해석

① 네가 게임을 할 차례야.   ② 내가 시작 단계를 마치면 알려줄게.   ③ 우리 부모님은 두 분 다 서울 출신이셔.   ④ 그건 지루해. 난 환불받고 싶어.
⑤ 물론이지. 내가 알려줄 테니 휴대폰 꺼내 봐.

어휘 | impressive [imprésiv] 혱 놀라운; 인상적인 turn [tə:rn] 몡 차례 동 돌리다

[Telephone rings.]	[전화기가 울린다.]
W Hello?	여 여보세요?
M This is Cleaning Solutions. Could you put me through to Mr. Jones?	남 Cleaning Solutions입니다. Jones씨를 연결해 주시겠습니까?
W I'm sorry, but he's not in the office at the moment.	여 죄송하지만, 그는 지금 자리에 없어요.
M Can you give him a message then?	남 그러면 그에게 메시지를 전해주시겠어요?
W Sure. What is it?	여 물론이죠. 뭔가요?
M Please tell him that our team will be an hour late tomorrow. We will reduce the price for the cleaning because of this.	남 내일 저희 팀이 한 시간 늦을 거라고 말해 주세요. 저희는 이에 대해 청소 비용을 할인해 드릴 겁니다.
W Alright. I'll be sure to tell him later.	여 알겠습니다. 나중에 꼭 그에게 말해줄게요.
M I appreciate your help.	남 도와주셔서 감사합니다.

해설 | 메시지를 전해달라는 남자의 부탁에 여자가 그러겠다고 했으므로 정답은 부탁을 들어준 것에 감사하는 ② 'I appreciate your help.'이다.

선택지 해석
① 대걸레는 벽장 안에 있어요. ② 도와주셔서 감사합니다. ③ 이 기계는 지금은 다른 사람이 쓰고 있어요. ④ 제가 방금 돈을 부쳤습니다.
⑤ 로비를 먼저 청소해 주세요.

어휘 | put through (전화를) 연결하다 reduce [ridjúːs] 图 할인하다, 낮추다; 줄이다 mop [map] 圆 대걸레 closet [klɑ́zit] 圆 벽장

M Is this table okay, Mina?	남 이 자리 괜찮니, 미나야?
W Yes! The view is so nice. I really like the terrace of this café.	여 응! 경치가 아주 좋네. 난 이 카페의 테라스가 정말 마음에 들어.
M Me too. And sitting outside is always refreshing.	남 나도. 그리고 밖에 앉아 있는 건 늘 상쾌해.
W Yeah. I prefer sitting outside over sitting inside.	여 맞아. 난 안에 앉는 것보다 밖에 앉는 게 더 좋아.
M Do you want some tea? It looks like they have many kinds.	남 차 좀 마실래? 많은 종류가 있는 것 같아.
W Yeah. I will order some soon. But first I need to wash my hands. Do you need anything from inside?	여 그래. 내가 곧 주문할게. 그런데 손을 먼저 씻어야겠어. 안에서 뭔가 필요한 거 있니?
M Actually, can you tell someone to turn on this heater by our table? It's a little cold.	남 사실, 우리 자리 옆에 있는 난방기를 켜달라고 말해줄 수 있어? 약간 쌀쌀하네.
W Okay. I'll take care of that now.	여 알겠어. 내가 지금 처리할게.

해설 | 남자가 여자에게 안에 들어가서 직원에게 난방기를 켜달라고 말해줄 것을 부탁했으므로 정답은 부탁을 수락하는 ③ 'Okay. I'll take care of that now.'이다.

선택지 해석
① 테라스에서 산을 볼 수 있어. ② 이 나무 옆에서 내 사진을 찍어줘. ③ 알겠어. 내가 지금 처리할게. ④ 화장실이 어디 있는지 알려주시겠어요?
⑤ 죄송하게도 제가 음료를 흘렸어요.

어휘 | terrace [térəs] 圆 테라스; 단지 refreshing [rifréʃiŋ] 廖 상쾌한 take care of 처리하다; 돌보다 spill [spil] 图 흘리다, 엎지르다

M Ms. Brown is Mark's English teacher. She thinks that he is a very talented student. This is because he has written many imaginative and interesting stories for her class. In fact, she feels that he has the potential to be a professional author someday. So, she wants to suggest that he enter a national writing contest for students. In this situation, what would Ms. Brown most likely say to Mark?	남 Brown 선생님은 Mark의 영어 선생님입니다. 그녀는 Mark가 매우 재능 있는 학생이라고 생각합니다. 왜냐하면 그가 그녀의 수업 시간에 창의적이고 흥미로운 이야기들을 많이 썼기 때문입니다. 사실, 그녀는 그에게 언젠가 전문 작가가 될 가능성이 있다고 느낍니다. 그래서, 그녀는 그에게 전국 학생 글짓기 대회에 참가하라고 제안하고 싶습니다. 이러한 상황에서, Brown 선생님이 Mark에게 가장 할 것 같은 말은 무엇입니까?
Ms. Brown Mark, why don't you sign up for the competition?	Brown 선생님 Mark, 대회를 신청하는 게 어떻겠니?

해설 | Brown 선생님이 Mark에게 전국 학생 글짓기 대회에 참가하는 것을 제안하고 싶다고 했으므로 정답은 ② 'why don't you sign up for the competition?'이다.

선택지 해석
① 내가 쓴 이야기를 읽어주면 좋겠구나. ② 대회를 신청하는 게 어떻겠니? ③ 요즘 가장 좋아하는 작가는 누구니? ④ 영어 수업에 늦으면 안 된단다.
⑤ 네가 우승자였다니 멋지구나.

어휘 | talented [tǽləntid] 廖 재능 있는 imaginative [imǽdʒənətiv] 廖 창의적인, 상상력이 풍부한; 상상의 professional [prəféʃənəl] 廖 전문의; 직업의

24회 고난도 모의고사

| 문제 pp.212-213

1	②	2	②	3	①	4	②	5	⑤	6	⑤	7	③	8	①	9	⑤	10	③
11	②	12	④	13	②	14	②	15	⑤	16	④	17	①	18	①	19	③	20	②

1 알맞은 그림 고르기

정답 ②

M　What are you looking for, Emma?

W　Hey. I want a refrigerator magnet for my mom. She likes to collect them.

M　Then, let me help you pick one. How about this pyramid-shaped one? It's the first thing you imagine when you think of Egypt.

W　Oh, my mom already has one. So, I need to find something different.

M　Then, you can buy one of these. They depict pharaohs.

W　Great. I'll take the one without any words on it.

M　I'm sure your mother will like it.

남　뭘 찾고 있니, Emma?

여　안녕. 난 엄마에게 드릴 냉장고 자석을 원해. 그걸 모으는 것을 좋아하시거든.

남　그럼 내가 고르는 걸 도와줄게. 이 피라미드 모양은 어때? 이집트를 생각하면 가장 먼저 상상하는 거야.

여　오, 그건 이미 하나 가지고 있으셔. 그래서, 뭔가 다른 걸 찾아야 해.

남　그럼, 이것들 중 하나를 사면 되겠다. 이것들은 파라오를 묘사하고 있어.

여　좋아. 아무 글자도 없는 걸로 살게.

남　너희 엄마가 분명 좋아하실 거야.

해설 | 여자가 아무 글자도 없는 파라오 자석을 사겠다고 했으므로 정답은 ②이다.

어휘 | magnet [mǽgnit] 명 자석　collect [kəlékt] 동 모으다, 수집하다　imagine [imǽdʒin] 동 상상하다　depict [dipíkt] 동 묘사하다

2 언급하지 않은 내용 고르기

정답 ②

W　Green Thinking is releasing the newest smart pot for indoor plants on August 4th. This state-of-the-art pot uses technology to alert plant owners when to water their plants. It does this through technology that tracks sunlight in the area and water in the soil. Just use your phone to enter the type of plant through an app, and the pot will give instructions for caring for it. The pot is only 20 dollars and the app is five dollars per month. So, sign up today and look for the product in stores soon!

여　Green Thinking은 8월 4일에 실내 식물을 위한 최신형 스마트 화분을 발매합니다. 이 최첨단 기술을 사용한 화분은 소유자가 언제 그들의 식물에 물을 줘야 하는지 알리는 기술을 사용합니다. 스마트 화분은 그 장소의 햇빛과 토양 속의 수분을 추적하는 기술을 통해 그렇게 합니다. 휴대폰을 사용하여 앱에 식물의 종류를 입력만 하면, 화분이 그것을 보살피기 위한 안내를 할 것입니다. 이 화분은 단 20달러이며 앱은 한 달에 5달러입니다. 그러니, 오늘 등록하시고 매장에서 조만간 이 제품을 찾아보십시오!

해설 | ① 회사명(Green Thinking), ③ 기능(언제 식물에 물을 줘야 하는지 알림), ④ 가격(화분 20달러, 앱 매달 5달러), ⑤ 이용 방법(앱에 식물의 종류를 입력함)에 대해 언급했으므로 정답은 ② '제품명'이다.

어휘 | state-of-the-art 형 최첨단 기술을 사용한　alert [ələ́:rt] 동 알리다 형 기민한　track [træk] 동 추적하다　soil [sɔil] 명 토양　care for 보살피다, 돌보다

3 목적 고르기　　　　　　　　　　　　　　　　　　　정답 ①

[Telephone rings.]	*[전화기가 울린다.]*

W Wexler Resorts, this is Susie. How can I help you?

M Hi, this is Nathan Andrews. I'm scheduled to stay there next month. However, I won't be able to come.

W I'm sorry to hear that. Let me see. *[Typing sound]* Mr. Andrews, I see you were scheduled for three nights, from the 5th through the 7th.

M Right. And I'd like to cancel the whole stay.

W I'll do that for you. Please note that there is a 50-dollar cancellation fee.

M That's fine. Thanks.

여 Wexler Resorts의 Susie입니다. 무엇을 도와드릴까요?

남 안녕하세요, 저는 Nathan Andrews입니다. 다음 달에 거기에서 머물기로 예정되어 있어요. 그런데, 갈 수 없을 것 같아요.

여 그러시다니 유감입니다. 확인해 보겠습니다. *[타자치는 소리]* Andrews씨, 5일부터 7일까지 3일 동안 예약이 되어 있으셨네요.

남 맞아요. 그리고 전체 방문 일정을 취소하고 싶어요.

여 그렇게 해드리겠습니다. 취소 요금 50달러가 있다는 것을 유의해 주세요.

남 괜찮아요. 감사합니다.

해설 | 남자가 다음 달로 예약된 전체 방문 일정을 취소하고 싶다고 했으므로 정답은 ① '예약을 취소하려고'이다.

어휘 | be scheduled to ~할 예정이다　whole [houl] 혱 전체의　cancellation fee 취소 요금, 위약금

---

4 시간 정보 고르기　　　　　　　　　　　　　　　　　정답 ②

W Hello, Mr. Hicks. I'd like to use the auditorium for a Spanish club meeting after school next week.

M Okay. What day do you want to use it on?

W Can we use it on Thursday?

M I'm sorry, but the art club has already reserved it for that day. How about Friday?

W We can't meet on Fridays. Can we use it on Tuesday?

M Let me check. *[Pause]* Yes. It is available that day.

W Great. Thank you.

여 안녕하세요, Hicks 선생님. 다음 주 방과 후에 스페인어 동아리 모임을 위해 강당을 사용하고 싶은데요.

남 그래. 무슨 요일에 사용하고 싶니?

여 목요일에 사용할 수 있을까요?

남 미안하지만, 그날은 미술 동아리가 이미 예약해놨단다. 금요일은 어떠니?

여 금요일에는 모일 수가 없어요. 화요일에 쓸 수 있을까요?

남 확인해 보마. *[잠시 멈춤]* 그래. 그날은 사용이 가능하네.

여 좋아요. 감사합니다.

해설 | 여자가 화요일에 강당을 쓸 수 있는지 묻자 남자가 그날은 사용이 가능하다고 했으므로 정답은 ② '화요일'이다.

어휘 | auditorium [ɔ̀:ditɔ́:riəm] 혱 강당　reserve [rizə́:rv] 동 예약하다

---

5 심정 고르기　　　　　　　　　　　　　　　　　　　정답 ⑤

M Did you enjoy your meal?

W Yes, I liked it.

M Good. Would you like your bill?

W Okay. Thank you.

M Will you pay by credit card or with cash?

W Credit card. And I want to use this 20% discount coupon.

M Alright. *[Pause]* Sorry, but this coupon is not valid anymore. Last Friday was the last day to use it.

W Really? Let me check. Oh, you're right.

M Then, sign here, please.

W I can't believe I missed the date!

남 식사 즐거우셨습니까?

여 네, 좋았어요.

남 다행이네요. 계산서 드릴까요?

여 네. 감사합니다.

남 신용카드로 하시겠습니까, 현금으로 하시겠습니까?

여 신용카드요. 그리고 이 20% 할인 쿠폰을 쓰고 싶어요.

남 알겠습니다. *[잠시 멈춤]* 죄송합니다만 이 쿠폰은 더 이상 유효하지 않습니다. 지난 금요일이 사용할 수 있는 마지막 날이었네요.

여 정말요? 확인해 볼게요. 오, 맞네요.

남 그럼, 여기 서명해 주십시오.

여 제가 날짜를 놓쳤다니 믿을 수가 없네요!

해설 | 여자가 할인 쿠폰의 유효 기간 날짜를 놓친 것을 믿을 수 없다고 했으므로 정답은 ⑤ 'frustrated'이다.

> 선택지 해석
> ① 무서운　② 긴장한　③ 안도한　④ 만족한　⑤ 실망한

어휘 | bill [bil] 혱 계산서　valid [vǽlid] 혱 유효한　frustrated [frʌ́streitid] 혱 실망한, 낙담한

6 그림 상황에 적절한 대화 고르기 · 정답 ⑤

① W Why don't we order a pizza?
  M Good idea. I don't want to cook.
② W That was an excellent lunch.
  M I'm glad you liked it.
③ W How would you like your steak, sir?
  M Medium, please.
④ W Could you wash the dishes now?
  M Sure. I'm not busy.
⑤ W What are you making for dinner?
  M It's chicken noodle soup.

① 여 우리 피자를 시키는 게 어때?
  남 좋은 생각이야. 요리하고 싶지 않거든.
② 여 훌륭한 점심이었어.
  남 마음에 들었다니 기쁘다.
③ 여 스테이크를 어떻게 요리해드릴까요?
  남 중간 정도로요.
④ 여 지금 접시를 닦아 줄래?
  남 물론이지. 난 바쁘지 않아.
⑤ 여 저녁으로 뭘 요리하고 있니?
  남 치킨 누들 수프야.

해설 │ 남자가 요리를 하고 있고 여자가 옆에서 냄비를 보며 궁금해하고 있는 상황이므로 정답은 ⑤이다.

어휘 │ medium [míːdiəm] 혱 (굽는 방법이) 중간 정도의

7 부탁·요청한 일 고르기 · 정답 ③

[Cellphone rings.]
W Darling, how's your day going?
M Actually, it's not going so well.
W What's wrong? Are you at work?
M Not yet. My car broke down on the way to work.
W Oh, no. Where are you?
M I'm pulled over downtown. I'm waiting for the repairperson to pick up my car.
W Do you need any help? I'm not busy at the moment.
M Yes. I'd love you to give me a ride to work. There's no bus stop close to me.
W Sure. Just send me your location.

[휴대폰이 울린다.]
여 여보, 오늘 하루 어떻게 보내고 있어?
남 사실, 별로 좋지 않아.
여 뭐가 문제야? 회사에 있어?
남 아직. 회사 가는 중에 차가 고장 났어.
여 오, 이런. 어디야?
남 시내에서 차를 길가에 세웠어. 수리공이 내 차를 가지러 오길 기다리고 있어.
여 도움이 필요해? 지금은 바쁘지 않은데.
남 응. 회사로 태워다 주면 좋겠어. 근처에 버스 정류장이 없어.
여 물론이지. 위치 보내줘.

해설 │ 남자가 여자에게 회사로 태워다 주면 좋겠다고 했으므로 정답은 ③ '회사까지 태워주기'이다.

어휘 │ break down 고장 나다 pull over 길가에 세우다 at the moment 지금 location [loukéiʃən] 혱 위치

8 언급하지 않은 내용 고르기 · 정답 ①

M Hello, customers. Our team at Natural Juices is excited to announce the release of two new and delicious flavors of fruit juices. The newest additions are Blackberry Mint and Strawberry Lime. These tasty juices are made from 100% natural fruits and contain lots of healthy vitamins and minerals. Like our other flavors, one bottle is only eight dollars. We hope you enjoy our new flavors as much as we do. Cheers!

남 안녕하세요, 고객 여러분. Natural Juices사의 저희 팀은 두 가지 새롭고 맛있는 과일 주스 맛의 출시를 알리게 되어 기쁩니다. 가장 최근에 추가되는 것은 블랙베리 민트와 딸기 라임입니다. 이 맛있는 주스는 100% 천연 과일로 만들어졌으며, 건강한 비타민과 미네랄을 많이 함유하고 있습니다. 다른 맛들과 동일하게 한 병에 단 8달러입니다. 저희는 여러분이 새로운 맛을 저희만큼 즐기시길 바랍니다. 건배!

해설 │ ② 제조사(Natural Juices), ③ 재료(100% 천연 과일), ④ 가격(8달러), ⑤ 맛(블랙베리 민트와 딸기 라임)에 대해 언급했으므로 정답은 ① '출시일'이다.

어휘 │ tasty [téisti] 혱 맛있는 be made from ~으로 만들어지다 contain [kəntéin] 동 함유하다 Cheers! 건배!

9 화제 고르기 　　　　　　　　　　　　　　　　　정답 ⑤

M This is something you wear for protection. You usually wear this on a boat. When people cannot swim well, they need to wear this in the water at all times. It often comes in bright colors and is made of plastic. To wear it correctly, you need to buckle all the straps tightly. It helps you float in the water and saves your life.

남 이것은 보호를 위해 입는 것입니다. 이것은 보통 배 위에서 입습니다. 사람들이 수영을 잘하지 못할 때, 이것을 물속에서 항상 입고 있어야 합니다. 이것은 흔히 밝은색으로 나오며 플라스틱으로 만들어졌습니다. 이것을 올바르게 입기 위해서는, 모든 끈을 꽉 잠가야 합니다. 이것은 물에 뜰 수 있도록 도우며 생명을 구합니다.

해설 | 이것(This)은 사람들이 수영을 잘하지 못할 때 물속에서 항상 입고 있어야 한다고 했으며, 올바르게 입으려면 모든 끈을 꽉 잠가야 한다고 했으므로 정답은 ⑤ '구명조끼'이다.

어휘 | protection [prətékʃən] 뎽 보호　buckle [bʌ́kl] 뎽 잠그다　float [flout] 뎽 뜨다

10 어색한 대화 고르기 　　　　　　　　　　　　　　정답 ③

① W Are you feeling okay? You look pale.
　 M I have an upset stomach.
② W Will you walk the dog?
　 M Can I do that later? I need to finish doing the laundry first.
③ W Could you help me plant the flowers in the garden?
　 M Sure. Which flower bouquet do you want?
④ W I really hope I get a good grade for my presentation.
　 M I think you will. It was impressive.
⑤ W Do you mind turning off the air conditioner?
　 M No. It is getting a little cold in here.

① 여 너 괜찮니? 창백해 보여.
　 남 배탈이 났어.
② 여 개를 산책시켜줄래?
　 남 나중에 해도 될까? 먼저 빨래를 끝내야 하거든.
③ 여 정원에 꽃 심는 것을 도와줄 수 있어?
　 남 물론이지. 어떤 꽃다발을 원하니?
④ 여 내 발표로 좋은 점수를 받으면 정말 좋겠어.
　 남 그럴 거라고 생각해. 인상 깊었거든.
⑤ 여 에어컨 꺼도 되니?
　 남 그럼. 여기 약간 추워지고 있어.

해설 | 여자가 정원에 꽃 심는 것을 도와줄 수 있는지 물었으므로, 남자는 도울 수 있는지 여부를 답해야 한다. 그러나 남자가 어떤 꽃다발을 원하냐는 어색한 대답을 했으므로 정답은 ③이다.

어휘 | pale [peil] 뎽 창백한　upset stomach 배탈　bouquet [boukéi] 뎽 꽃다발, 부케

11 할 일 고르기 　　　　　　　　　　　　　　　　　정답 ②

W I can't believe Ryan Pitt's new movie comes out tomorrow!
M I know. We waited two years for the premiere of *Level Up 2*.
W What time did you book our tickets for?
M 5 p.m. But we should get there early.
W Okay. I'll check when my bus comes.
M Great. Let's meet in front of the theater at 4:30 then.
W Sounds like a plan.

여 Ryan Pitt의 새 영화가 내일 나온다니 믿을 수 없어!
남 맞아. 우리 <Level Up 2>의 개봉을 2년이나 기다렸잖아.
여 몇 시 티켓으로 예매했어?
남 오후 5시에. 그런데 우리 거기에 일찍 도착해야 해.
여 응. 내가 탈 버스가 언제 오는지 확인할게.
남 좋아. 극장 앞에서 4시 30분에 보자 그럼.
여 좋은 생각 같네.

해설 | 여자가 자신이 탈 버스가 언제 오는지 확인하겠다고 했으므로 정답은 ② '버스 시간 확인하기'이다.

어휘 | premiere [primíər] 뎽 개봉, 초연

12 위치 고르기
정답 ④

W	Hi, I'd like to check in. My name is Georgia Brown.
M	Welcome. You booked two nights in a woman's dormitory room, right?
W	Yes. Are there any beds left?
M	We have a few. You can choose either a bunk bed or a regular bed.
W	I want to try the bunk bed. How about a top bunk?
M	Sure. Do you have any preferences?
W	I don't want to be too close to the restroom.
M	You can choose from these two.
W	I'll take this one. It might be cold next to the window.
M	Here's your key.

여	안녕하세요, 체크인하려고요. 제 이름은 Georgia Brown이에요.
남	어서 오세요. 여성 숙소 방을 이틀 밤 예약하셨네요, 그렇죠?
여	네. 남은 침대가 있나요?
남	몇 개 있어요. 2층 침대나 일반 침대 둘 중 하나를 고르실 수 있어요.
여	2층 침대를 써보고 싶어요. 위쪽 침대 어때요?
남	그러세요. 선호하는 것이 있으신가요?
여	화장실과 너무 가깝지 않으면 좋겠어요.
남	이 두 개 중에서 고르실 수 있어요.
여	이걸로 할게요. 창문 옆은 추울 수도 있겠네요.
남	여기 열쇠 있습니다.

해설 | 여자가 2층 침대의 위쪽 침대를 원한다고 했고, 화장실과 너무 가깝지 않으면 좋겠다고 했으며, 창문 옆은 추울 수 있겠다고 했으므로 정답은 ④이다.

어휘 | either A or B A나 B 둘 중 하나 bunk bed 2층 침대 preference [préfərəns] 몡 선호(도)

13 시간 정보 고르기
정답 ②

	[Telephone rings.]
W	Hello, National Museum of Space.
M	Hi. I was wondering when the reopening date of the museum will be.
W	We'll be done remodeling by February 1st, but reopening was delayed to the 8th.
M	Oh, is that so? Are you open on the holiday? The 16th of February.
W	Sorry, but we don't open on that day.
M	Hmm... Are you holding any special events this month?
W	Why don't you visit on the reopening day? We'll have a ceremony for the reopening of the museum. It's open to the public.
M	Okay, I'll do so. Thank you for the information.

	[전화기가 울린다.]
여	안녕하세요, 국립 우주 박물관입니다.
남	안녕하세요. 박물관 재개장일이 언제일지 궁금해요.
여	2월 1일까지는 리모델링이 끝날 예정이지만, 재개장은 8일로 미뤄졌어요.
남	오, 그래요? 휴일에는 여나요? 2월 16일이요.
여	죄송하지만, 저희는 그날 열지 않아요.
남	흠... 이번 달에 주최되는 특별한 행사가 있나요?
여	재개장일에 방문하시는 건 어떠세요? 박물관의 재개장을 위한 행사가 있을 거예요. 대중에게 공개되는 거예요.
남	알겠습니다, 그렇게 할게요. 정보 감사합니다.

해설 | 여자가 재개장일은 2월 8일로 미뤄졌다고 했고, 남자가 재개장일에 방문하겠다고 했으므로 정답은 ② '2월 8일'이다.

어휘 | reopen [ríóupən] 동 재개장하다, 다시 열다 ceremony [sérəmouni] 몡 행사, 의식 public [pʌ́blik] 몡 대중

14 한 일 고르기
정답 ②

W	Did you enjoy the long weekend, Jooho?
M	No. It was terrible.
W	But you said you were going to visit the lake.
M	I couldn't go. When I got to the train station on Saturday, I realized my wallet was missing.
W	Did you leave it at home?
M	No. I think it was stolen from my backpack. I immediately filed a report with the police.
W	Well, maybe they will find it soon.
M	I hope so. Otherwise, I will need to replace my ID cards.

여	긴 주말 연휴 잘 보냈니, 주호야?
남	아니. 끔찍했어.
여	하지만 호수를 방문할 거라고 했잖아.
남	갈 수 없었어. 토요일에 기차역에 도착했을 때, 지갑이 없어진 걸 깨달았거든.
여	집에 두고 갔었니?
남	아니. 내 배낭에서 도둑맞은 것 같아. 난 경찰에 즉시 신고했어.
여	음, 경찰들이 곧 찾아줄 거야.
남	그러면 좋겠어. 그렇지 않으면 내 신분증을 바꿔야 해.

해설 | 남자가 지난 연휴 동안 지갑을 도둑맞아서 경찰에 신고했다고 했으므로 정답은 ② '도난 신고하기'이다.

어휘 | immediately [imíːdiətli] 묑 즉시 file a report 신고하다 otherwise [ʌ̀ðərwáiz] 묑 그렇지 않으면 replace [ripléis] 동 바꾸다, 교체하다

15 목적 고르기 정답 ⑤

W Attention, students. This is your principal, Ms. Roberts. As you know, the 10th grade field trip is next month. However, you need to do two things before you can go. First of all, you must turn in a permission slip. It must be signed by a parent or guardian. Give the signed form to your homeroom teacher by April 1st. Second, you must pay the trip fee. The 25-dollar trip fee can be paid on the school website. It is due on the same date. Have a great day, everyone.

여 주목해주세요, 학생 여러분. 여러분의 교장 Roberts 선생님입니다. 아시다시피, 10학년 견학이 다음 달입니다. 하지만, 가기 전에 두 가지를 해야 합니다. 우선, 허가서를 제출해야 합니다. 이것은 부모님이나 보호자에게 서명을 받아야 합니다. 서명받은 양식을 담임 선생님께 4월 1일까지 드리세요. 두 번째로, 견학 비용을 내야 합니다. 견학 비용 25달러는 학교 웹사이트에서 지불할 수 있습니다. 이것도 동일한 날짜까지입니다. 좋은 하루 보내세요, 여러분.

해설ㅣ 여자가 견학을 가기 전에 해야 할 일 두 가지를 안내하고 있으므로 정답은 ⑤ '견학 준비 사항을 안내하려고'이다.

어휘ㅣ turn in 제출하다 permission slip 허가서 guardian [gάːrdiən] 톙 보호자

16 금액 정보 고르기 정답 ④

W Welcome to Pet World. How may I help you?
M Hello. I'd like to buy some food for my cat. Do you have any recommendations?
W The bags on the left shelf are 20 dollars each. However, the ones on the right shelf are for kittens, and they are 15 dollars each.
M I'll take the bag of food for little cats.
W Got it. Is there anything else you need?
M What about this toy? Is it popular?
W It has very good reviews, and it's only 10 dollars.
M Then, I'll also buy that.

여 Pet World에 오신 것을 환영합니다. 무엇을 도와드릴까요?
남 안녕하세요. 제 고양이에게 먹일 사료를 사고 싶어요. 추천해 주실 만한 것이 있나요?
여 왼쪽 선반에 있는 포대는 각 20달러입니다. 하지만, 오른쪽 선반에 있는 것들은 새끼 고양이를 위한 것이고, 각 15달러예요.
남 새끼 고양이용 사료 포대를 살게요.
여 알겠습니다. 더 필요하신 것이 있으신가요?
남 이 장난감은 어떤가요? 인기가 있나요?
여 그건 후기가 매우 좋고, 단 10달러예요.
남 그럼 그것도 살게요.

해설ㅣ 남자가 사겠다고 한 새끼 고양이용 사료는 15달러이고 장난감은 10달러이므로 정답은 ④ '$ 25'이다.

어휘ㅣ recommendation [rèkəməndéiʃən] 톙 추천 kitten [kítn] 톙 새끼 고양이 review [rivjúː] 톙 후기

17 적절한 응답 고르기 정답 ①

W What are you working on, Ron?
M It's a paper for my science class.
W What is it about?
M It discusses ways to recycle appropriately.
W Why did you pick that topic?
M Well, a lot of people aren't recycling properly. I think we need to teach them to do it right.
W Yeah. It seems important to improve recycling.
M Yes. And I also talk about reducing waste.
W Can I read your paper? I'd love to learn more.
M Yes. I want to hear your opinion on the topic.

여 무슨 일을 하고 있니, Ron?
남 과학 수업에 낼 보고서야.
여 무엇에 대한 거니?
남 적절하게 재활용하는 방법을 이야기하고 있어.
여 왜 그 주제를 골랐니?
남 음, 많은 사람이 재활용을 제대로 하고 있지 않아. 우리가 옳게 하는 방법을 가르쳐야 한다고 생각해.
여 그래. 재활용을 개선하는 건 중요한 것 같아.
남 응. 그리고 나는 쓰레기를 줄이는 것에 대해서도 이야기해.
여 네 보고서 읽어도 되니? 더 배우고 싶어.
남 응. 이 주제에 대한 네 의견을 듣고 싶어.

해설ㅣ 여자가 남자의 보고서를 읽어도 되는지 물었으므로 정답은 된다고 허락하는 ① 'Yes. I want to hear your opinion on the topic.'이다.

선택지 해석
① 응. 이 주제에 대한 네 의견을 듣고 싶어. ② 우리 슈퍼마켓에 천 가방을 가지고 가자. ③ 쓰레기통은 저기 있어.
④ 고마워. 재활용을 어떻게 하는지에 대해 많이 배울 수 있겠다. ⑤ 신문에서는 우리가 음식물 쓰레기를 줄여야 한다고 해.

어휘ㅣ appropriately [əpróupriətli] 튀 적절하게 properly [prάpərli] 튀 제대로 improve [imprúːv] 통 개선하다, 향상하다
reduce [ridjúːs] 통 줄이다, 감소시키다

18 적절한 응답 고르기

정답 ①

[Cellphone rings.]	[휴대폰이 울린다.]
M What's up, Stella?	남 무슨 일이야, Stella?
W Hey. What are your plans today?	여 안녕. 오늘 네 계획이 뭐니?
M I was going to play games with my brother, but he is too busy now.	남 남동생과 게임을 하려고 했는데, 남동생이 지금 너무 바빠.
W Then, how about hanging out with me?	여 그럼, 나랑 노는 게 어때?
M Sure. What do you want to do?	남 그래. 뭘 하고 싶은데?
W The cherry blossoms in the park are in full bloom. Why don't we go see them?	여 공원의 벚꽃이 활짝 피어 있어. 보러 가지 않을래?
M Alright. Do you want to take the subway?	남 그래. 지하철 타고 갈래?
W It's a fine day, so let's ride bikes there instead.	여 날이 좋으니까, 대신 거기에 자전거를 타고 가자.
M But I don't have a bike.	남 하지만 난 자전거가 없어.
W Don't worry. We can rent them easily.	여 걱정하지 마. 쉽게 빌릴 수 있어.

해설 | 남자가 자전거가 없다고 우려를 표하고 있으므로 정답은 해결책을 제시하는 ① 'Don't worry. We can rent them easily.'이다.

선택지 해석

① 걱정하지 마. 쉽게 빌릴 수 있어.   ② 응. 자전거 타는 건 좋은 운동이야.   ③ 나는 그녀에게 체리를 사주고 싶어.   ④ 문제없어. 산책로는 이쪽으로 나 있어.
⑤ 좋아. 내 교통 카드를 빌려줄게.

어휘 | hang out 놀다, 어울리다   in full bloom 활짝 핀, 만개하여   trail [treil] 몡 산책로; 자국   lead [liːd] 통 (길이) 나 있다; 이끌다
transportation [trænspərtéiʃən] 몡 교통; 수송

19 적절한 응답 고르기

정답 ③

W Time really goes by fast. It's almost the last day of school.	여 시간이 정말 빨리 간다. 이제 거의 학기 마지막 날이야.
M Yeah. But I am excited for summer.	남 맞아. 하지만 난 여름이 기대돼.
W What will you do over the summer?	여 여름 동안 뭘 할 거니?
M I will go to a summer camp in America.	남 나는 미국에 여름 캠프를 갈 거야.
W Wow! How long will you be there?	여 우와! 거기 얼마나 오랫동안 있을 거니?
M Just over one month. I can't wait. What are your plans?	남 한 달 정도. 너무 기대돼. 네 계획은 뭐니?
W I will take a trip across Europe with my parents.	여 부모님과 유럽 횡단 여행을 할 거야.
M That also sounds really fun. Where are you most excited to go in Europe?	남 그것도 정말 재미있겠다. 유럽에서 어딜 가는 것이 제일 기대되니?
W I'm looking forward to seeing Big Ben in London.	여 런던의 빅벤을 보는 게 기대돼.

해설 | 남자가 여자에게 유럽의 어디에 가는 것이 제일 기대되는지 물었으므로 정답은 기대되는 장소를 언급하는 ③ 'I'm looking forward to seeing Big Ben in London.'이다.

선택지 해석

① 여름 방학은 너무 짧은 것 같아.   ② 우리 가족은 낚시나 수영을 갈 거야.   ③ 런던의 빅벤을 보는 게 기대돼.   ④ 우리는 지금 공항으로 가는 길이야.
⑤ 나는 차라리 비행기를 타겠어.

어휘 | on one's way to ~로 가는 길에   would rather 차라리 ~하겠다

M　Last weekend, Mike went on a hike with his friends. He fell while coming down the mountain and sprained his ankle. Mike thought his ankle would heal quickly, but it still hurts. He wants a doctor to look at it today. So, he decides to call the doctor's office and ask the receptionist if he can see a doctor after school. In this situation, what would Mike most likely say to the receptionist?

Mike　Can I please book an appointment for 5 p.m.?

남　지난 주말, Mike는 그의 친구들과 등산을 갔습니다. 그는 하산하면서 넘어졌고 발목을 삐었습니다. Mike는 그의 발목이 빠르게 나을 것이라고 생각했지만, 여전히 아픕니다. 그는 의사 선생님이 오늘 그의 발목을 살펴봐 주길 원합니다. 그래서, 그는 병원에 전화해서 접수원에게 방과 후에 의사 선생님을 뵐 수 있는지 물으려고 합니다. 이러한 상황에서, Mike가 접수원에게 가장 할 것 같은 말은 무엇입니까?

Mike　오후 5시에 진료 예약을 할 수 있을까요?

해설 ┃ Mike가 접수원에게 방과 후에 의사 선생님을 뵐 수 있는지 물으려 한다고 했으므로 정답은 ② 'Can I please book an appointment for 5 p.m.?'이다.

[선택지 해석]

① 넘어지지 않도록 조심하세요.　② 오후 5시에 진료 예약을 할 수 있을까요?　③ 병원이 언제 여는지 알려 주실래요?

④ 제 발목이 여전히 아파서, 이번에는 엑스레이를 찍고 싶어요.　⑤ 죄송하지만, 의사 선생님께서 지금은 바쁘세요.

어휘 ┃ sprain [sprein] 툉 삐다, 삐끗하다　ankle [ǽŋkl] 뗭 발목　heal [hiːl] 툉 낫다　receptionist [risépʃənist] 뗭 접수원

영어듣기 만점을 위한 **완벽한 실전 대비서**

해커스
중학영어듣기
모의고사 24회